The Divine Comedy
La Divina Commedia

By

Dante Alighieri

Translated by

Henry Wadsworth Longfellow

Incipit Comoedia Dantis Alagherii,
Florentini natione, non moribus.

Cover Artwork: Dante and the Three Kingdoms by Domenico di Michelino

ISBN: 978-1-78139-549-3

Contents

INFERNO

PURGATORIO

PARADISO

INFERNO

Inferno: Canto I

The Dark Forest. The Hill of Difficulty. The Panther, the Lion, and the Wolf. Virgil.

Nel mezzo del cammin di nostra vita
  mi ritrovai per una selva oscura
  che' la diritta via era smarrita.

Ahi quanto a dir qual era e` cosa dura
  esta selva selvaggia e aspra e forte
  che nel pensier rinova la paura!

Tant'e` amara che poco e` piu` morte;
  ma per trattar del ben ch'i' vi trovai,
  diro` de l'altre cose ch'i' v'ho scorte.

Io non so ben ridir com'i' v'intrai,
  tant'era pien di sonno a quel punto
  che la verace via abbandonai.

Ma poi ch'i' fui al pie` d'un colle giunto,
  la` dove terminava quella valle
  che m'avea di paura il cor compunto,

guardai in alto, e vidi le sue spalle
  vestite gia` de' raggi del pianeta
  che mena dritto altrui per ogne calle.

Allor fu la paura un poco queta
  che nel lago del cor m'era durata
  la notte ch'i' passai con tanta pieta.

E come quei che con lena affannata
  uscito fuor del pelago a la riva
  si volge a l'acqua perigliosa e guata,

cosi` l'animo mio, ch'ancor fuggiva,
  si volse a retro a rimirar lo passo
  che non lascio` gia` mai persona viva.

Midway upon the journey of our life
  I found myself within a forest dark,
  For the straightforward pathway had been lost.

Ah me! how hard a thing it is to say
  What was this forest savage, rough, and stern,
  Which in the very thought renews the fear.

So bitter is it, death is little more;
  But of the good to treat, which there I found,
  Speak will I of the other things I saw there.

I cannot well repeat how there I entered,
  So full was I of slumber at the moment
  In which I had abandoned the true way.

But after I had reached a mountain's foot,
  At that point where the valley terminated,
  Which had with consternation pierced my heart,

Upward I looked, and I beheld its shoulders,
  Vested already with that planet's rays
  Which leadeth others right by every road.

Then was the fear a little quieted
  That in my heart's lake had endured throughout
  The night, which I had passed so piteously.

And even as he, who, with distressful breath,
  Forth issued from the sea upon the shore,
  Turns to the water perilous and gazes;

So did my soul, that still was fleeing onward,
  Turn itself back to re-behold the pass
  Which never yet a living person left.

Poi ch'ei posato un poco il corpo lasso,
  ripresi via per la piaggia diserta,
  si` che 'l pie` fermo sempre era 'l piu` basso.

Ed ecco, quasi al cominciar de l'erta,
  una lonza leggera e presta molto,
  che di pel macolato era coverta;

e non mi si partia dinanzi al volto,
  anzi 'mpediva tanto il mio cammino,
  ch'i' fui per ritornar piu` volte volto.

Temp'era dal principio del mattino,
  e 'l sol montava 'n su` con quelle stelle
  ch'eran con lui quando l'amor divino

mosse di prima quelle cose belle;
  si` ch'a bene sperar m'era cagione
  di quella fiera a la gaetta pelle

l'ora del tempo e la dolce stagione;
  ma non si` che paura non mi desse
  la vista che m'apparve d'un leone.

Questi parea che contra me venisse
  con la test'alta e con rabbiosa fame,
  si` che parea che l'aere ne tremesse.

Ed una lupa, che di tutte brame
  sembiava carca ne la sua magrezza,
  e molte genti fe' gia` viver grame,

questa mi porse tanto di gravezza
  con la paura ch'uscia di sua vista,
  ch'io perdei la speranza de l'altezza.

E qual e` quei che volontieri acquista,
  e giugne 'l tempo che perder lo face,
  che 'n tutt'i suoi pensier piange e s'attrista;

tal mi fece la bestia sanza pace,
  che, venendomi 'ncontro, a poco a poco
  mi ripigneva la` dove 'l sol tace.

Mentre ch'i' rovinava in basso loco,
  dinanzi a li occhi mi si fu offerto
  chi per lungo silenzio parea fioco.

Quando vidi costui nel gran diserto,
  ""Miserere di me"", gridai a lui,
  ""qual che tu sii, od ombra od omo certo!"".

After my weary body I had rested,
  The way resumed I on the desert slope,
  So that the firm foot ever was the lower.

And lo! almost where the ascent began,
  A panther light and swift exceedingly,
  Which with a spotted skin was covered o'er!

And never moved she from before my face,
  Nay, rather did impede so much my way,
  That many times I to return had turned.

The time was the beginning of the morning,
  And up the sun was mounting with those stars
  That with him were, what time the Love Divine

At first in motion set those beauteous things;
  So were to me occasion of good hope,
  The variegated skin of that wild beast,

The hour of time, and the delicious season;
  But not so much, that did not give me fear
  A lion's aspect which appeared to me.

He seemed as if against me he were coming
  With head uplifted, and with ravenous hunger,
  So that it seemed the air was afraid of him;

And a she-wolf, that with all hungerings
  Seemed to be laden in her meagreness,
  And many folk has caused to live forlorn!

She brought upon me so much heaviness,
  With the affright that from her aspect came,
  That I the hope relinquished of the height.

And as he is who willingly acquires,
  And the time comes that causes him to lose,
  Who weeps in all his thoughts and is despondent,

E'en such made me that beast withouten peace,
  Which, coming on against me by degrees
  Thrust me back thither where the sun is silent.

While I was rushing downward to the lowland,
  Before mine eyes did one present himself,
  Who seemed from long-continued silence hoarse.

When I beheld him in the desert vast,
  "Have pity on me," unto him I cried,
  "Whiche'er thou art, or shade or real man!"

Rispuosemi: ""'Non omo, omo gia` fui,
   e li parenti miei furon lombardi,
   mantoani per patria ambedui.

Nacqui sub Iulio, ancor che fosse tardi,
   e vissi a Roma sotto 'l buono Augusto
   nel tempo de li dei falsi e bugiardi.

Poeta fui, e cantai di quel giusto
   figliuol d'Anchise che venne di Troia,
   poi che 'l superbo Ilion fu combusto.

Ma tu perche' ritorni a tanta noia?
   perche' non sali il dilettoso monte
   ch'e` principio e cagion di tutta gioia?""`.

""'Or se' tu quel Virgilio e quella fonte
   che spandi di parlar si` largo fiume?""`,
   rispuos'io lui con vergognosa fronte.

""'O de li altri poeti onore e lume
   vagliami 'l lungo studio e 'l grande amore
   che m'ha fatto cercar lo tuo volume.

Tu se' lo mio maestro e 'l mio autore;
   tu se' solo colui da cu' io tolsi
   lo bello stilo che m'ha fatto onore.

Vedi la bestia per cu' io mi volsi:
   aiutami da lei, famoso saggio,
   ch'ella mi fa tremar le vene e i polsi""`.

""'A te convien tenere altro viaggio""`,
   rispuose poi che lagrimar mi vide,
   ""'se vuo' campar d'esto loco selvaggio:

che' questa bestia, per la qual tu gride,
   non lascia altrui passar per la sua via,
   ma tanto lo 'mpedisce che l'uccide;

e ha natura si` malvagia e ria,
   che mai non empie la bramosa voglia,
   e dopo 'l pasto ha piu` fame che pria.

Molti son li animali a cui s'ammoglia,
   e piu` saranno ancora, infin che 'l veltro
   verra`, che la fara` morir con doglia.

Questi non cibera` terra ne' peltro,
   ma sapienza, amore e virtute,
   e sua nazion sara` tra feltro e feltro.

He answered me: "Not man; man once I was,
   And both my parents were of Lombardy,
   And Mantuans by country both of them.

'Sub Julio' was I born, though it was late,
   And lived at Rome under the good Augustus,
   During the time of false and lying gods.

A poet was I, and I sang that just
   Son of Anchises, who came forth from Troy,
   After that Ilion the superb was burned.

But thou, why goest thou back to such annoyance?
   Why climb'st thou not the Mount Delectable,
   Which is the source and cause of every joy?"

"Now, art thou that Virgilius and that fountain
   Which spreads abroad so wide a river of speech?"
   I made response to him with bashful forehead.

"O, of the other poets honour and light,
   Avail me the long study and great love
   That have impelled me to explore thy volume!

Thou art my master, and my author thou,
   Thou art alone the one from whom I took
   The beautiful style that has done honour to me.

Behold the beast, for which I have turned back;
   Do thou protect me from her, famous Sage,
   For she doth make my veins and pulses tremble."

"Thee it behoves to take another road,"
   Responded he, when he beheld me weeping,
   "If from this savage place thou wouldst escape;

Because this beast, at which thou criest out,
   Suffers not any one to pass her way,
   But so doth harass him, that she destroys him;

And has a nature so malign and ruthless,
   That never doth she glut her greedy will,
   And after food is hungrier than before.

Many the animals with whom she weds,
   And more they shall be still, until the Greyhound
   Comes, who shall make her perish in her pain.

He shall not feed on either earth or pelf,
   But upon wisdom, and on love and virtue;
   'Twixt Feltro and Feltro shall his nation be;

Di quella umile Italia fia salute
  per cui mori` la vergine Cammilla,
  Eurialo e Turno e Niso di ferute.

Questi la caccera` per ogne villa,
  fin che l'avra` rimessa ne lo 'nferno,
  la` onde 'nvidia prima dipartilla.

Ond'io per lo tuo me' penso e discerno
  che tu mi segui, e io saro` tua guida,
  e trarrotti di qui per loco etterno,

ove udirai le disperate strida,
  vedrai li antichi spiriti dolenti,
  ch'a la seconda morte ciascun grida;

e vederai color che son contenti
  nel foco, perche' speran di venire
  quando che sia a le beate genti.

A le quai poi se tu vorrai salire,
  anima fia a cio` piu` di me degna:
  con lei ti lascero` nel mio partire;

che' quello imperador che la` su` regna,
  perch'i' fu' ribellante a la sua legge,
  non vuol che 'n sua citta` per me si vegna.

In tutte parti impera e quivi regge;
  quivi e` la sua citta` e l'alto seggio:
  oh felice colui cu' ivi elegge!"".

E io a lui: ""Poeta, io ti richeggio
  per quello Dio che tu non conoscesti,
  accio` ch'io fugga questo male e peggio,

che tu mi meni la` dov'or dicesti,
  si` ch'io veggia la porta di san Pietro
  e color cui tu fai cotanto mesti""".

Allor si mosse, e io li tenni dietro.

Of that low Italy shall he be the saviour,
  On whose account the maid Camilla died,
  Euryalus, Turnus, Nisus, of their wounds;

Through every city shall he hunt her down,
  Until he shall have driven her back to Hell,
  There from whence envy first did let her loose.

Therefore I think and judge it for thy best
  Thou follow me, and I will be thy guide,
  And lead thee hence through the eternal place,

Where thou shalt hear the desperate lamentations,
  Shalt see the ancient spirits disconsolate,
  Who cry out each one for the second death;

And thou shalt see those who contented are
  Within the fire, because they hope to come,
  Whene'er it may be, to the blessed people;

To whom, then, if thou wishest to ascend,
  A soul shall be for that than I more worthy;
  With her at my departure I will leave thee;

Because that Emperor, who reigns above,
  In that I was rebellious to his law,
  Wills that through me none come into his city.

He governs everywhere, and there he reigns;
  There is his city and his lofty throne;
  O happy he whom thereto he elects!"

And I to him: "Poet, I thee entreat,
  By that same God whom thou didst never know,
  So that I may escape this woe and worse,

Thou wouldst conduct me there where thou hast said,
  That I may see the portal of Saint Peter,
  And those thou makest so disconsolate."

Then he moved on, and I behind him followed.

Inferno: Canto II

The Descent. Dante's Protest and Virgil's Appeal. The Intercession of the Three Ladies Benedight.

Lo giorno se n'andava, e l'aere bruno
 toglieva li animai che sono in terra
 da le fatiche loro; e io sol uno

m'apparecchiava a sostener la guerra
 si` del cammino e si` de la pietate,
 che ritrarra` la mente che non erra.

O muse, o alto ingegno, or m'aiutate;
 o mente che scrivesti cio` ch'io vidi,
 qui si parra` la tua nobilitate.

Io cominciai: ""Poeta che mi guidi,
 guarda la mia virtu` s'ell'e` possente,
 prima ch'a l'alto passo tu mi fidi.

Tu dici che di Silvio il parente,
 corruttibile ancora, ad immortale
 secolo ando`, e fu sensibilmente.

Pero`, se l'avversario d'ogne male
 cortese i fu, pensando l'alto effetto
 ch'uscir dovea di lui e 'l chi e 'l quale,

non pare indegno ad omo d'intelletto;
 ch'e' fu de l'alma Roma e di suo impero
 ne l'empireo ciel per padre eletto:

la quale e 'l quale, a voler dir lo vero,
 fu stabilita per lo loco santo
 u' siede il successor del maggior Piero.

Per quest'andata onde li dai tu vanto,
 intese cose che furon cagione
 di sua vittoria e del papale ammanto.

Day was departing, and the embrowned air
 Released the animals that are on earth
 From their fatigues; and I the only one

Made myself ready to sustain the war,
 Both of the way and likewise of the woe,
 Which memory that errs not shall retrace.

O Muses, O high genius, now assist me!
 O memory, that didst write down what I saw,
 Here thy nobility shall be manifest!

And I began: "Poet, who guidest me,
 Regard my manhood, if it be sufficient,
 Ere to the arduous pass thou dost confide me.

Thou sayest, that of Silvius the parent,
 While yet corruptible, unto the world
 Immortal went, and was there bodily.

But if the adversary of all evil
 Was courteous, thinking of the high effect
 That issue would from him, and who, and what,

To men of intellect unmeet it seems not;
 For he was of great Rome, and of her empire
 In the empyreal heaven as father chosen;

The which and what, wishing to speak the truth,
 Were stablished as the holy place, wherein
 Sits the successor of the greatest Peter.

Upon this journey, whence thou givest him vaunt,
 Things did he hear, which the occasion were
 Both of his victory and the papal mantle.

Andovvi poi lo Vas d'elezione,
 per recarne conforto a quella fede
 ch'e` principio a la via di salvazione.

Ma io perche' venirvi? o chi 'l concede?
 Io non Enea, io non Paulo sono:
 me degno a cio` ne' io ne' altri 'l crede.

Per che, se del venire io m'abbandono,
 temo che la venuta non sia folle.
 Se' savio; intendi me' ch'i' non ragiono"".

E qual e` quei che disvuol cio` che volle
 e per novi pensier cangia proposta,
 si` che dal cominciar tutto si tolle,

tal mi fec'io 'n quella oscura costa,
 perche', pensando, consumai la 'mpresa
 che fu nel cominciar cotanto tosta.

""S'i' ho ben la parola tua intesa"",
 rispuose del magnanimo quell'ombra;
 ""l'anima tua e` da viltade offesa;

la qual molte fiate l'omo ingombra
 si` che d'onrata impresa lo rivolve,
 come falso veder bestia quand'ombra.

Da questa tema accio` che tu ti solve,
 dirotti perch'io venni e quel ch'io 'ntesi
 nel primo punto che di te mi dolve.

Io era tra color che son sospesi,
 e donna mi chiamo` beata e bella,
 tal che di comandare io la richiesi.

Lucevan li occhi suoi piu` che la stella;
 e cominciommi a dir soave e piana,
 con angelica voce, in sua favella:

"O anima cortese mantoana,
 di cui la fama ancor nel mondo dura,
 e durera` quanto 'l mondo lontana,

l'amico mio, e non de la ventura,
 ne la diserta piaggia e` impedito
 si` nel cammin, che volt'e` per paura;

e temo che non sia gia` si` smarrito,
 ch'io mi sia tardi al soccorso levata,
 per quel ch'i' ho di lui nel cielo udito.

Thither went afterwards the Chosen Vessel,
 To bring back comfort thence unto that Faith,
 Which of salvation's way is the beginning.

But I, why thither come, or who concedes it?
 I not Aeneas am, I am not Paul,
 Nor I, nor others, think me worthy of it.

Therefore, if I resign myself to come,
 I fear the coming may be ill-advised;
 Thou'rt wise, and knowest better than I speak."

And as he is, who unwills what he willed,
 And by new thoughts doth his intention change,
 So that from his design he quite withdraws,

Such I became, upon that dark hillside,
 Because, in thinking, I consumed the emprise,
 Which was so very prompt in the beginning.

"If I have well thy language understood,"
 Replied that shade of the Magnanimous,
 "Thy soul attainted is with cowardice,

Which many times a man encumbers so,
 It turns him back from honoured enterprise,
 As false sight doth a beast, when he is shy.

That thou mayst free thee from this apprehension,
 I'll tell thee why I came, and what I heard
 At the first moment when I grieved for thee.

Among those was I who are in suspense,
 And a fair, saintly Lady called to me
 In such wise, I besought her to command me.

Her eyes where shining brighter than the Star;
 And she began to say, gentle and low,
 With voice angelical, in her own language:

'O spirit courteous of Mantua,
 Of whom the fame still in the world endures,
 And shall endure, long-lasting as the world;

A friend of mine, and not the friend of fortune,
 Upon the desert slope is so impeded
 Upon his way, that he has turned through terror,

And may, I fear, already be so lost,
 That I too late have risen to his succour,
 From that which I have heard of him in Heaven.

Or movi, e con la tua parola ornata
 e con cio` c'ha mestieri al suo campare
 l'aiuta, si` ch'i' ne sia consolata.

I' son Beatrice che ti faccio andare;
 vegno del loco ove tornar disio;
 amor mi mosse, che mi fa parlare.

Quando saro` dinanzi al segnor mio,
 di te mi lodero` sovente a lui".
 Tacette allora, e poi comincia' io:

"O donna di virtu`, sola per cui
 l'umana spezie eccede ogne contento
 di quel ciel c'ha minor li cerchi sui,

tanto m'aggrada il tuo comandamento,
 che l'ubidir, se gia` fosse, m'e` tardi;
 piu` non t'e` uo' ch'aprirmi il tuo talento.

Ma dimmi la cagion che non ti guardi
 de lo scender qua giuso in questo centro
 de l'ampio loco ove tornar tu ardi".

"Da che tu vuo' saver cotanto a dentro,
 dirotti brievemente", mi rispuose,
 "perch'io non temo di venir qua entro.

Temer si dee di sole quelle cose
 c'hanno potenza di fare altrui male;
 de l'altre no, che' non son paurose.

I' son fatta da Dio, sua merce', tale,
 che la vostra miseria non mi tange,
 ne' fiamma d'esto incendio non m'assale.

Donna e` gentil nel ciel che si compiange
 di questo 'mpedimento ov'io ti mando,
 si` che duro giudicio la` su` frange.

Questa chiese Lucia in suo dimando
 e disse: - Or ha bisogno il tuo fedele
 di te, e io a te lo raccomando -.

Lucia, nimica di ciascun crudele,
 si mosse, e venne al loco dov'i' era,
 che mi sedea con l'antica Rachele.

Disse: - Beatrice, loda di Dio vera,
 che' non soccorri quei che t'amo` tanto,
 ch'usci` per te de la volgare schiera?

Bestir thee now, and with thy speech ornate,
 And with what needful is for his release,
 Assist him so, that I may be consoled.

Beatrice am I, who do bid thee go;
 I come from there, where I would fain return;
 Love moved me, which compelleth me to speak.

When I shall be in presence of my Lord,
 Full often will I praise thee unto him.'
 Then paused she, and thereafter I began:

'O Lady of virtue, thou alone through whom
 The human race exceedeth all contained
 Within the heaven that has the lesser circles,

So grateful unto me is thy commandment,
 To obey, if 'twere already done, were late;
 No farther need'st thou ope to me thy wish.

But the cause tell me why thou dost not shun
 The here descending down into this centre,
 From the vast place thou burnest to return to.'

'Since thou wouldst fain so inwardly discern,
 Briefly will I relate,' she answered me,
 'Why I am not afraid to enter here.

Of those things only should one be afraid
 Which have the power of doing others harm;
 Of the rest, no; because they are not fearful.

God in his mercy such created me
 That misery of yours attains me not,
 Nor any flame assails me of this burning.

A gentle Lady is in Heaven, who grieves
 At this impediment, to which I send thee,
 So that stern judgment there above is broken.

In her entreaty she besought Lucia,
 And said, "Thy faithful one now stands in need
 Of thee, and unto thee I recommend him."

Lucia, foe of all that cruel is,
 Hastened away, and came unto the place
 Where I was sitting with the ancient Rachel.

"Beatrice" said she, "the true praise of God,
 Why succourest thou not him, who loved thee so,
 For thee he issued from the vulgar herd?

non odi tu la pieta del suo pianto?
  non vedi tu la morte che 'l combatte
  su la fiumana ove 'l mar non ha vanto? -.

Al mondo non fur mai persone ratte
  a far lor pro o a fuggir lor danno,
  com'io, dopo cotai parole fatte,

venni qua giu` del mio beato scanno,
  fidandomi del tuo parlare onesto,
  ch'onora te e quei ch'udito l'hanno".

Poscia che m'ebbe ragionato questo,
  li occhi lucenti lagrimando volse;
  per che mi fece del venir piu` presto;

e venni a te cosi` com'ella volse;
  d'inanzi a quella fiera ti levai
  che del bel monte il corto andar ti tolse.

Dunque: che e`? perche', perche' restai?
  perche' tanta vilta` nel core allette?
  perche' ardire e franchezza non hai,

poscia che tai tre donne benedette
  curan di te ne la corte del cielo,
  e 'l mio parlar tanto ben ti promette?"".

Quali fioretti dal notturno gelo
  chinati e chiusi, poi che 'l sol li 'mbianca
  si drizzan tutti aperti in loro stelo,

tal mi fec'io di mia virtude stanca,
  e tanto buono ardire al cor mi corse,
  ch'i' cominciai come persona franca:

""Oh pietosa colei che mi soccorse!
  e te cortese ch'ubidisti tosto
  a le vere parole che ti porse!

Tu m'hai con disiderio il cor disposto
  si` al venir con le parole tue,
  ch'i' son tornato nel primo proposto.

Or va, ch'un sol volere e` d'ambedue:
  tu duca, tu segnore, e tu maestro"".
  Cosi` li dissi; e poi che mosso fue,

intrai per lo cammino alto e silvestro.

Dost thou not hear the pity of his plaint?
  Dost thou not see the death that combats him
  Beside that flood, where ocean has no vaunt?"

Never were persons in the world so swift
  To work their weal and to escape their woe,
  As I, after such words as these were uttered,

Came hither downward from my blessed seat,
  Confiding in thy dignified discourse,
  Which honours thee, and those who've listened to
      it.'

After she thus had spoken unto me,
  Weeping, her shining eyes she turned away;
  Whereby she made me swifter in my coming;

And unto thee I came, as she desired;
  I have delivered thee from that wild beast,
  Which barred the beautiful mountain's short ascent.

What is it, then? Why, why dost thou delay?
  Why is such baseness bedded in thy heart?
  Daring and hardihood why hast thou not,

Seeing that three such Ladies benedight
  Are caring for thee in the court of Heaven,
  And so much good my speech doth promise thee?"

Even as the flowerets, by nocturnal chill,
  Bowed down and closed, when the sun whitens
      them,
  Uplift themselves all open on their stems;

Such I became with my exhausted strength,
  And such good courage to my heart there coursed,
  That I began, like an intrepid person:

"O she compassionate, who succoured me,
  And courteous thou, who hast obeyed so soon
  The words of truth which she addressed to thee!

Thou hast my heart so with desire disposed
  To the adventure, with these words of thine,
  That to my first intent I have returned.

Now go, for one sole will is in us both,
  Thou Leader, and thou Lord, and Master thou."
  Thus said I to him; and when he had moved,

I entered on the deep and savage way.

Inferno: Canto III

The Gate of Hell. The Inefficient or Indifferent. Pope Celestine V. The Shores of Acheron. Charon. The Earthquake and the Swoon.

Per me si va ne la citta` dolente,
  per me si va ne l'etterno dolore,
  per me si va tra la perduta gente.

Giustizia mosse il mio alto fattore:
  fecemi la divina podestate,
  la somma sapienza e 'l primo amore.

Dinanzi a me non fuor cose create
  se non etterne, e io etterno duro.
  Lasciate ogne speranza, voi ch'intrate".

Queste parole di colore oscuro
  vid'io scritte al sommo d'una porta;
  per ch'io: ""Maestro, il senso lor m'e` duro"".

Ed elli a me, come persona accorta:
  ""Qui si convien lasciare ogne sospetto;
  ogne vilta` convien che qui sia morta.

Noi siam venuti al loco ov'i' t'ho detto
  che tu vedrai le genti dolorose
  c'hanno perduto il ben de l'intelletto"".

E poi che la sua mano a la mia puose
  con lieto volto, ond'io mi confortai,
  mi mise dentro a le segrete cose.

Quivi sospiri, pianti e alti guai
  risonavan per l'aere sanza stelle,
  per ch'io al cominciar ne lagrimai.

Diverse lingue, orribili favelle,
  parole di dolore, accenti d'ira,
  voci alte e fioche, e suon di man con elle

"Through me the way is to the city dolent;
  Through me the way is to eternal dole;
  Through me the way among the people lost.

Justice incited my sublime Creator;
  Created me divine Omnipotence,
  The highest Wisdom and the primal Love.

Before me there were no created things,
  Only eterne, and I eternal last.
  All hope abandon, ye who enter in!"

These words in sombre colour I beheld
  Written upon the summit of a gate;
  Whence I: "Their sense is, Master, hard to me!"

And he to me, as one experienced:
  "Here all suspicion needs must be abandoned,
  All cowardice must needs be here extinct.

We to the place have come, where I have told thee
  Thou shalt behold the people dolorous
  Who have foregone the good of intellect."

And after he had laid his hand on mine
  With joyful mien, whence I was comforted,
  He led me in among the secret things.

There sighs, complaints, and ululations loud
  Resounded through the air without a star,
  Whence I, at the beginning, wept thereat.

Languages diverse, horrible dialects,
  Accents of anger, words of agony,
  And voices high and hoarse, with sound of hands,

facevano un tumulto, il qual s'aggira
  sempre in quell'aura sanza tempo tinta,
  come la rena quando turbo spira.

E io ch'avea d'error la testa cinta,
  dissi: ""Maestro, che e` quel ch'i' odo?
  e che gent'e` che par nel duol si` vinta?"".

Ed elli a me: ""Questo misero modo
  tegnon l'anime triste di coloro
  che visser sanza 'nfamia e sanza lodo.

Mischiate sono a quel cattivo coro
  de li angeli che non furon ribelli
  ne' fur fedeli a Dio, ma per se' fuoro.

Caccianli i ciel per non esser men belli,
  ne' lo profondo inferno li riceve,
  ch'alcuna gloria i rei avrebber d'elli"".

E io: ""Maestro, che e` tanto greve
  a lor, che lamentar li fa si` forte?"".
  Rispuose: ""Dicerolti molto breve.

Questi non hanno speranza di morte
  e la lor cieca vita e` tanto bassa,
  che 'nvidiosi son d'ogne altra sorte.

Fama di loro il mondo esser non lassa;
  misericordia e giustizia li sdegna:
  non ragioniam di lor, ma guarda e passa"".

E io, che riguardai, vidi una 'nsegna
  che girando correva tanto ratta,
  che d'ogne posa mi parea indegna;

e dietro le venia si` lunga tratta
  di gente, ch'i' non averei creduto
  che morte tanta n'avesse disfatta.

Poscia ch'io v'ebbi alcun riconosciuto,
  vidi e conobbi l'ombra di colui
  che fece per viltade il gran rifiuto.

Incontanente intesi e certo fui
  che questa era la setta d'i cattivi,
  a Dio spiacenti e a' nemici sui.

Made up a tumult that goes whirling on
  For ever in that air for ever black,
  Even as the sand doth, when the whirlwind
    breathes.

And I, who had my head with horror bound,
  Said: "Master, what is this which now I hear?
  What folk is this, which seems by pain so van-
    quished?"

And he to me: "This miserable mode
  Maintain the melancholy souls of those
  Who lived withouten infamy or praise.

Commingled are they with that caitiff choir
  Of Angels, who have not rebellious been,
  Nor faithful were to God, but were for self.

The heavens expelled them, not to be less fair;
  Nor them the nethermore abyss receives,
  For glory none the damned would have from them."

And I: "O Master, what so grievous is
  To these, that maketh them lament so sore?"
  He answered: "I will tell thee very briefly.

These have no longer any hope of death;
  And this blind life of theirs is so debased,
  They envious are of every other fate.

No fame of them the world permits to be;
  Misericord and Justice both disdain them.
  Let us not speak of them, but look, and pass."

And I, who looked again, beheld a banner,
  Which, whirling round, ran on so rapidly,
  That of all pause it seemed to me indignant;

And after it there came so long a train
  Of people, that I ne'er would have believed
  That ever Death so many had undone.

When some among them I had recognised,
  I looked, and I beheld the shade of him
  Who made through cowardice the great refusal.

Forthwith I comprehended, and was certain,
  That this the sect was of the caitiff wretches
  Hateful to God and to his enemies.

Questi sciaurati, che mai non fur vivi,
  erano ignudi e stimolati molto
  da mosconi e da vespe ch'eran ivi.

Elle rigavan lor di sangue il volto,
  che, mischiato di lagrime, a' lor piedi
  da fastidiosi vermi era ricolto.

E poi ch'a riguardar oltre mi diedi,
  vidi genti a la riva d'un gran fiume;
  per ch'io dissi: ""Maestro, or mi concedi

ch'i' sappia quali sono, e qual costume
  le fa di trapassar parer si` pronte,
  com'io discerno per lo fioco lume"".

Ed elli a me: ""Le cose ti fier conte
  quando noi fermerem li nostri passi
  su la trista riviera d'Acheronte"".

Allor con li occhi vergognosi e bassi,
  temendo no 'l mio dir li fosse grave,
  infino al fiume del parlar mi trassi.

Ed ecco verso noi venir per nave
  un vecchio, bianco per antico pelo,
  gridando: ""Guai a voi, anime prave!

Non isperate mai veder lo cielo:
  i' vegno per menarvi a l'altra riva
  ne le tenebre etterne, in caldo e 'n gelo.

E tu che se' costi`, anima viva,
  partiti da cotesti che son morti"".
  Ma poi che vide ch'io non mi partiva,

disse: ""Per altra via, per altri porti
  verrai a piaggia, non qui, per passare:
  piu` lieve legno convien che ti porti"".

E 'l duca lui: ""Caron, non ti crucciare:
  vuolsi cosi` cola` dove si puote
  cio` che si vuole, e piu` non dimandare"".

Quinci fuor quete le lanose gote
  al nocchier de la livida palude,
  che 'ntorno a li occhi avea di fiamme rote.

These miscreants, who never were alive,
  Were naked, and were stung exceedingly
  By gadflies and by hornets that were there.

These did their faces irrigate with blood,
  Which, with their tears commingled, at their feet
  By the disgusting worms was gathered up.

And when to gazing farther I betook me.
  People I saw on a great river's bank;
  Whence said I: "Master, now vouchsafe to me,

That I may know who these are, and what law
  Makes them appear so ready to pass over,
  As I discern athwart the dusky light."

And he to me: "These things shall all be known
  To thee, as soon as we our footsteps stay
  Upon the dismal shore of Acheron."

Then with mine eyes ashamed and downward cast,
  Fearing my words might irksome be to him,
  From speech refrained I till we reached the river.

And lo! towards us coming in a boat
  An old man, hoary with the hair of eld,
  Crying: "Woe unto you, ye souls depraved!

Hope nevermore to look upon the heavens;
  I come to lead you to the other shore,
  To the eternal shades in heat and frost.

And thou, that yonder standest, living soul,
  Withdraw thee from these people, who are dead!"
  But when he saw that I did not withdraw,

He said: "By other ways, by other ports
  Thou to the shore shalt come, not here, for passage;
  A lighter vessel needs must carry thee."

And unto him the Guide: "Vex thee not, Charon;
  It is so willed there where is power to do
  That which is willed; and farther question not."

Thereat were quieted the fleecy cheeks
  Of him the ferryman of the livid fen,
  Who round about his eyes had wheels of flame.

Ma quell'anime, ch'eran lasse e nude,	But all those souls who weary were and naked
cangiar colore e dibattero i denti,	Their colour changed and gnashed their teeth to-
ratto che 'nteser le parole crude.	gether,
	As soon as they had heard those cruel words.
Bestemmiavano Dio e lor parenti,	God they blasphemed and their progenitors,
l'umana spezie e 'l loco e 'l tempo e 'l seme	The human race, the place, the time, the seed
di lor semenza e di lor nascimenti.	Of their engendering and of their birth!
Poi si ritrasser tutte quante insieme,	Thereafter all together they drew back,
forte piangendo, a la riva malvagia	Bitterly weeping, to the accursed shore,
ch'attende ciascun uom che Dio non teme.	Which waiteth every man who fears not God.
Caron dimonio, con occhi di bragia,	Charon the demon, with the eyes of glede,
loro accennando, tutte le raccoglie;	Beckoning to them, collects them all together,
batte col remo qualunque s'adagia.	Beats with his oar whoever lags behind.
Come d'autunno si levan le foglie	As in the autumn-time the leaves fall off,
l'una appresso de l'altra, fin che 'l ramo	First one and then another, till the branch
vede a la terra tutte le sue spoglie,	Unto the earth surrenders all its spoils;
similemente il mal seme d'Adamo	In similar wise the evil seed of Adam
gittansi di quel lito ad una ad una,	Throw themselves from that margin one by one,
per cenni come augel per suo richiamo.	At signals, as a bird unto its lure.
Cosi` sen vanno su per l'onda bruna,	So they depart across the dusky wave,
e avanti che sien di la` discese,	And ere upon the other side they land,
anche di qua nuova schiera s'auna.	Again on this side a new troop assembles.
""Figliuol mio""", disse 'l maestro cortese,	"My son," the courteous Master said to me,
""quelli che muoion ne l'ira di Dio	"All those who perish in the wrath of God
tutti convegnon qui d'ogne paese:	Here meet together out of every land;
e pronti sono a trapassar lo rio,	And ready are they to pass o'er the river,
che' la divina giustizia li sprona,	Because celestial Justice spurs them on,
si` che la tema si volve in disio.	So that their fear is turned into desire.
Quinci non passa mai anima buona;	This way there never passes a good soul;
e pero`, se Caron di te si lagna,	And hence if Charon doth complain of thee,
ben puoi sapere omai che 'l suo dir suona""".	Well mayst thou know now what his speech im-
	ports."
Finito questo, la buia campagna	This being finished, all the dusk champaign
tremo` si` forte, che de lo spavento	Trembled so violently, that of that terror
la mente di sudore ancor mi bagna.	The recollection bathes me still with sweat.
La terra lagrimosa diede vento,	The land of tears gave forth a blast of wind,
che baleno` una luce vermiglia	And fulminated a vermilion light,
la qual mi vinse ciascun sentimento;	Which overmastered in me every sense,
e caddi come l'uom cui sonno piglia.	And as a man whom sleep hath seized I fell.

Inferno: Canto IV

The First Circle, Limbo: Virtuous Pagans and the Unbaptized. The Four Poets, Homer, Horace, Ovid, and Lucan. The Noble Castle of Philosophy.

Ruppemi l'alto sonno ne la testa
  un greve truono, si` ch'io mi riscossi
  come persona ch'e` per forza desta;

e l'occhio riposato intorno mossi,
  dritto levato, e fiso riguardai
  per conoscer lo loco dov'io fossi.

Vero e` che 'n su la proda mi trovai
  de la valle d'abisso dolorosa
  che 'ntrono accoglie d'infiniti guai.

Oscura e profonda era e nebulosa
  tanto che, per ficcar lo viso a fondo,
  io non vi discernea alcuna cosa.

""Or discendiam qua giu` nel cieco mondo"",
  comincio` il poeta tutto smorto.
  ""Io saro` primo, e tu sarai secondo"".

E io, che del color mi fui accorto,
  dissi: ""Come verro`, se tu paventi
  che suoli al mio dubbiare esser conforto?"".

Ed elli a me: ""L'angoscia de le genti
  che son qua giu`, nel viso mi dipigne
  quella pieta` che tu per tema senti.

Andiam, che' la via lunga ne sospigne"".
  Cosi` si mise e cosi` mi fe' intrare
  nel primo cerchio che l'abisso cigne.

Broke the deep lethargy within my head
  A heavy thunder, so that I upstarted,
  Like to a person who by force is wakened;

And round about I moved my rested eyes,
  Uprisen erect, and steadfastly I gazed,
  To recognise the place wherein I was.

True is it, that upon the verge I found me
  Of the abysmal valley dolorous,
  That gathers thunder of infinite ululations.

Obscure, profound it was, and nebulous,
  So that by fixing on its depths my sight
  Nothing whatever I discerned therein.

"Let us descend now into the blind world,"
  Began the Poet, pallid utterly;
  "I will be first, and thou shalt second be."

And I, who of his colour was aware,
  Said: "How shall I come, if thou art afraid,
  Who'rt wont to be a comfort to my fears?"

And he to me: "The anguish of the people
  Who are below here in my face depicts
  That pity which for terror thou hast taken.

Let us go on, for the long way impels us."
  Thus he went in, and thus he made me enter
  The foremost circle that surrounds the abyss.

Quivi, secondo che per ascoltare,
  non avea pianto mai che di sospiri,
  che l'aura etterna facevan tremare;
	There, as it seemed to me from listening,
	  Were lamentations none, but only sighs,
	  That tremble made the everlasting air.

cio` avvenia di duol sanza martiri
  ch'avean le turbe, ch'eran molte e grandi,
  d'infanti e di femmine e di viri.
	And this arose from sorrow without torment,
	  Which the crowds had, that many were and great,
	  Of infants and of women and of men.

Lo buon maestro a me: ““Tu non dimandi
  che spiriti son questi che tu vedi?
  Or vo' che sappi, innanzi che piu` andi,
	To me the Master good: "Thou dost not ask
	  What spirits these, which thou beholdest, are?
	  Now will I have thee know, ere thou go farther,

ch'ei non peccaro; e s'elli hanno mercedi,
  non basta, perche' non ebber battesmo,
  ch'e` porta de la fede che tu credi;
	That they sinned not; and if they merit had,
	  'Tis not enough, because they had not baptism
	  Which is the portal of the Faith thou holdest;

e s'e' furon dinanzi al cristianesmo,
  non adorar debitamente a Dio:
  e di questi cotai son io medesmo.
	And if they were before Christianity,
	  In the right manner they adored not God;
	  And among such as these am I myself.

Per tai difetti, non per altro rio,
  semo perduti, e sol di tanto offesi,
  che sanza speme vivemo in disio”“.
	For such defects, and not for other guilt,
	  Lost are we and are only so far punished,
	  That without hope we live on in desire."

Gran duol mi prese al cor quando lo 'ntesi,
  pero` che gente di molto valore
  conobbi che 'n quel limbo eran sospesi.
	Great grief seized on my heart when this I heard,
	  Because some people of much worthiness
	  I knew, who in that Limbo were suspended.

““Dimmi, maestro mio, dimmi, segnore”“,
  comincia' io per voler esser certo
  di quella fede che vince ogne errore:
	"Tell me, my Master, tell me, thou my Lord,"
	  Began I, with desire of being certain
	  Of that Faith which o'ercometh every error,

““uscicci mai alcuno, o per suo merto
  o per altrui, che poi fosse beato?”“.
  E quei che 'ntese il mio parlar coverto,
	"Came any one by his own merit hence,
	  Or by another's, who was blessed thereafter?"
	  And he, who understood my covert speech,

rispuose: ““Io era nuovo in questo stato,
  quando ci vidi venire un possente,
  con segno di vittoria coronato.
	Replied: "I was a novice in this state,
	  When I saw hither come a Mighty One,
	  With sign of victory incoronate.

Trasseci l'ombra del primo parente, d'Abel suo figlio e quella di Noe`,   di Moise` legista e ubidente;	Hence he drew forth the shade of the First Parent, And that of his son Abel, and of Noah, Of Moses the lawgiver, and the obedient

Abraam patriarca e David re,
  Israel con lo padre e co' suoi nati
  e con Rachele, per cui tanto fe';
	Abraham, patriarch, and David, king,
	  Israel with his father and his children,
	  And Rachel, for whose sake he did so much,

e altri molti, e feceli beati.
  E vo' che sappi che, dinanzi ad essi,
  spiriti umani non eran salvati”“.
	And others many, and he made them blessed;
	  And thou must know, that earlier than these
	  Never were any human spirits saved."

Non lasciavam l'andar perch'ei dicessi,
 ma passavam la selva tuttavia,
 la selva, dico, di spiriti spessi.

Non era lunga ancor la nostra via
 di qua dal sonno, quand'io vidi un foco
 ch'emisperio di tenebre vincia.

Di lungi n'eravamo ancora un poco,
 ma non si` ch'io non discernessi in parte
 ch'orrevol gente possedea quel loco.

""O tu ch'onori scienzia e arte,
 questi chi son c'hanno cotanta onranza,
 che dal modo de li altri li diparte?"".

E quelli a me: ""L'onrata nominanza
 che di lor suona su` ne la tua vita,
 grazia acquista in ciel che si` li avanza"".

Intanto voce fu per me udita:
 ""Onorate l'altissimo poeta:
 l'ombra sua torna, ch'era dipartita"".

Poi che la voce fu restata e queta,
 vidi quattro grand'ombre a noi venire:
 sembianz'avevan ne' trista ne' lieta.

Lo buon maestro comincio` a dire:
 ""Mira colui con quella spada in mano,
 che vien dinanzi ai tre si` come sire:

quelli e` Omero poeta sovrano;
 l'altro e` Orazio satiro che vene;
 Ovidio e` 'l terzo, e l'ultimo Lucano.

Pero` che ciascun meco si convene
 nel nome che sono` la voce sola,
 fannomi onore, e di cio` fanno bene"".

Cosi` vid'i' adunar la bella scola
 di quel segnor de l'altissimo canto
 che sovra li altri com'aquila vola.

Da ch'ebber ragionato insieme alquanto,
 volsersi a me con salutevol cenno,
 e 'l mio maestro sorrise di tanto;

e piu` d'onore ancora assai mi fenno,
 ch'e' si` mi fecer de la loro schiera,
 si` ch'io fui sesto tra cotanto senno.

We ceased not to advance because he spake,
 But still were passing onward through the forest,
 The forest, say I, of thick-crowded ghosts.

Not very far as yet our way had gone
 This side the summit, when I saw a fire
 That overcame a hemisphere of darkness.

We were a little distant from it still,
 But not so far that I in part discerned not
 That honourable people held that place.

"O thou who honourest every art and science,
 Who may these be, which such great honour have,
 That from the fashion of the rest it parts them?"

And he to me: "The honourable name,
 That sounds of them above there in thy life,
 Wins grace in Heaven, that so advances them."

In the mean time a voice was heard by me:
 "All honour be to the pre-eminent Poet;
 His shade returns again, that was departed."

After the voice had ceased and quiet was,
 Four mighty shades I saw approaching us;
 Semblance had they nor sorrowful nor glad.

To say to me began my gracious Master:
 "Him with that falchion in his hand behold,
 Who comes before the three, even as their lord.

That one is Homer, Poet sovereign;
 He who comes next is Horace, the satirist;
 The third is Ovid, and the last is Lucan.

Because to each of these with me applies
 The name that solitary voice proclaimed,
 They do me honour, and in that do well."

Thus I beheld assemble the fair school
 Of that lord of the song pre-eminent,
 Who o'er the others like an eagle soars.

When they together had discoursed somewhat,
 They turned to me with signs of salutation,
 And on beholding this, my Master smiled;

And more of honour still, much more, they did me,
 In that they made me one of their own band;
 So that the sixth was I, 'mid so much wit.

Cosi` andammo infino a la lumera,
  parlando cose che 'l tacere e` bello,
  si` com'era 'l parlar cola` dov'era.

Venimmo al pie` d'un nobile castello,
  sette volte cerchiato d'alte mura,
  difeso intorno d'un bel fiumicello.

Questo passammo come terra dura;
  per sette porte intrai con questi savi:
  giugnemmo in prato di fresca verdura.

Genti v'eran con occhi tardi e gravi,
  di grande autorita` ne' lor sembianti:
  parlavan rado, con voci soavi.

Traemmoci cosi` da l'un de' canti,
  in loco aperto, luminoso e alto,
  si` che veder si potien tutti quanti.

Cola` diritto, sovra 'l verde smalto,
  mi fuor mostrati li spiriti magni,
  che del vedere in me stesso m'essalto.

I' vidi Eletra con molti compagni,
  tra ' quai conobbi Ettor ed Enea,
  Cesare armato con li occhi grifagni.

Vidi Cammilla e la Pantasilea;
  da l'altra parte, vidi 'l re Latino
  che con Lavina sua figlia sedea.

Vidi quel Bruto che caccio` Tarquino,
  Lucrezia, Iulia, Marzia e Corniglia;
  e solo, in parte, vidi 'l Saladino.

Poi ch'innalzai un poco piu` le ciglia,
  vidi 'l maestro di color che sanno
  seder tra filosofica famiglia.

Tutti lo miran, tutti onor li fanno:
  quivi vid'io Socrate e Platone,
  che 'nnanzi a li altri piu` presso li stanno;

Democrito, che 'l mondo a caso pone,
  Diogenes, Anassagora e Tale,
  Empedocles, Eraclito e Zenone;

e vidi il buono accoglitor del quale,
  Diascoride dico; e vidi Orfeo,
  Tulio e Lino e Seneca morale;

Thus we went on as far as to the light,
  Things saying 'tis becoming to keep silent,
  As was the saying of them where I was.

We came unto a noble castle's foot,
  Seven times encompassed with lofty walls,
  Defended round by a fair rivulet;

This we passed over even as firm ground;
  Through portals seven I entered with these Sages;
  We came into a meadow of fresh verdure.

People were there with solemn eyes and slow,
  Of great authority in their countenance;
  They spake but seldom, and with gentle voices.

Thus we withdrew ourselves upon one side
  Into an opening luminous and lofty,
  So that they all of them were visible.

There opposite, upon the green enamel,
  Were pointed out to me the mighty spirits,
  Whom to have seen I feel myself exalted.

I saw Electra with companions many,
  'Mongst whom I knew both Hector and Aeneas,
  Caesar in armour with gerfalcon eyes;

I saw Camilla and Penthesilea
  On the other side, and saw the King Latinus,
  Who with Lavinia his daughter sat;

I saw that Brutus who drove Tarquin forth,
  Lucretia, Julia, Marcia, and Cornelia,
  And saw alone, apart, the Saladin.

When I had lifted up my brows a little,
  The Master I beheld of those who know,
  Sit with his philosophic family.

All gaze upon him, and all do him honour.
  There I beheld both Socrates and Plato,
  Who nearer him before the others stand;

Democritus, who puts the world on chance,
  Diogenes, Anaxagoras, and Thales,
  Zeno, Empedocles, and Heraclitus;

Of qualities I saw the good collector,
  Hight Dioscorides; and Orpheus saw I,
  Tully and Livy, and moral Seneca,

Euclide geometra e Tolomeo,
  Ipocrate, Avicenna e Galieno,
  Averois, che 'l gran comento feo.
	Euclid, geometrician, and Ptolemy,
	  Galen, Hippocrates, and Avicenna,
	  Averroes, who the great Comment made.

Io non posso ritrar di tutti a pieno,
  pero` che si` mi caccia il lungo tema,
  che molte volte al fatto il dir vien meno.
	I cannot all of them pourtray in full,
	  Because so drives me onward the long theme,
	  That many times the word comes short of fact.

La sesta compagnia in due si scema:
  per altra via mi mena il savio duca,
  fuor de la queta, ne l'aura che trema.
	The sixfold company in two divides;
	  Another way my sapient Guide conducts me
	  Forth from the quiet to the air that trembles;

E vegno in parte ove non e` che luca.	And to a place I come where nothing shines.

Inferno: Canto V

The Second Circle: The Wanton. Minos. The Infernal Hurricane. Francesca da Rimini.

Cosi` discesi del cerchio primaio
  giu` nel secondo, che men loco cinghia,
  e tanto piu` dolor, che punge a guaio.

Stavvi Minos orribilmente, e ringhia:
  essamina le colpe ne l'intrata;
  giudica e manda secondo ch'avvinghia.

Dico che quando l'anima mal nata
  li vien dinanzi, tutta si confessa;
  e quel conoscitor de le peccata

vede qual loco d'inferno e` da essa;
  cignesi con la coda tante volte
  quantunque gradi vuol che giu` sia messa.

Sempre dinanzi a lui ne stanno molte;
  vanno a vicenda ciascuna al giudizio;
  dicono e odono, e poi son giu` volte.

““O tu che vieni al doloroso ospizio””,
  disse Minos a me quando mi vide,
  lasciando l'atto di cotanto offizio,

““guarda com'entri e di cui tu ti fide;
  non t'inganni l'ampiezza de l'intrare!””.
  E 'l duca mio a lui: ““Perche' pur gride?

Non impedir lo suo fatale andare:
  vuolsi cosi` cola` dove si puote
  cio` che si vuole, e piu` non dimandare””.

Or incomincian le dolenti note
  a farmisi sentire; or son venuto
  la` dove molto pianto mi percuote.

Thus I descended out of the first circle
  Down to the second, that less space begirds,
  And so much greater dole, that goads to wailing.

There standeth Minos horribly, and snarls;
  Examines the transgressions at the entrance;
  Judges, and sends according as he girds him.

I say, that when the spirit evil-born
  Cometh before him, wholly it confesses;
  And this discriminator of transgressions

Seeth what place in Hell is meet for it;
  Girds himself with his tail as many times
  As grades he wishes it should be thrust down.

Always before him many of them stand;
  They go by turns each one unto the judgment;
  They speak, and hear, and then are downward
    hurled.

"O thou, that to this dolorous hostelry
  Comest," said Minos to me, when he saw me,
  Leaving the practice of so great an office,

"Look how thou enterest, and in whom thou trustest;
  Let not the portal's amplitude deceive thee."
  And unto him my Guide: "Why criest thou too?

Do not impede his journey fate-ordained;
  It is so willed there where is power to do
  That which is willed; and ask no further question."

And now begin the dolesome notes to grow
  Audible unto me; now am I come
  There where much lamentation strikes upon me.

Io venni in loco d'ogne luce muto,
  che mugghia come fa mar per tempesta,
  se da contrari venti e` combattuto.

La bufera infernal, che mai non resta,
  mena li spirti con la sua rapina;
  voltando e percotendo li molesta.

Quando giungon davanti a la ruina,
  quivi le strida, il compianto, il lamento;
  bestemmian quivi la virtu` divina.

Intesi ch'a cosi` fatto tormento
  enno dannati i peccator carnali,
  che la ragion sommettono al talento.

E come li stornei ne portan l'ali
  nel freddo tempo, a schiera larga e piena,
  cosi` quel fiato li spiriti mali

di qua, di la`, di giu`, di su` li mena;
  nulla speranza li conforta mai,
  non che di posa, ma di minor pena.

E come i gru van cantando lor lai,
  faccendo in aere di se' lunga riga,
  cosi` vid'io venir, traendo guai,

ombre portate da la detta briga;
  per ch'i' dissi: ""Maestro, chi son quelle
  genti che l'aura nera si` gastiga?"".

""La prima di color di cui novelle
  tu vuo' saper"", mi disse quelli allotta,
  ""fu imperadrice di molte favelle.

A vizio di lussuria fu si` rotta,
  che libito fe' licito in sua legge,
  per torre il biasmo in che era condotta.

Ell'e` Semiramis, di cui si legge
  che succedette a Nino e fu sua sposa:
  tenne la terra che 'l Soldan corregge.

L'altra e` colei che s'ancise amorosa,
  e ruppe fede al cener di Sicheo;
  poi e` Cleopatras lussuriosa.

Elena vedi, per cui tanto reo
  tempo si volse, e vedi 'l grande Achille,
  che con amore al fine combatteo.

I came into a place mute of all light,
  Which bellows as the sea does in a tempest,
  If by opposing winds 't is combated.

The infernal hurricane that never rests
  Hurtles the spirits onward in its rapine;
  Whirling them round, and smiting, it molests them.

When they arrive before the precipice,
  There are the shrieks, the plaints, and the laments,
  There they blaspheme the puissance divine.

I understood that unto such a torment
  The carnal malefactors were condemned,
  Who reason subjugate to appetite.

And as the wings of starlings bear them on
  In the cold season in large band and full,
  So doth that blast the spirits maledict;

It hither, thither, downward, upward, drives them;
  No hope doth comfort them for evermore,
  Not of repose, but even of lesser pain.

And as the cranes go chanting forth their lays,
  Making in air a long line of themselves,
  So saw I coming, uttering lamentations,

Shadows borne onward by the aforesaid stress.
  Whereupon said I: "Master, who are those
  People, whom the black air so castigates?"

"The first of those, of whom intelligence
  Thou fain wouldst have," then said he unto me,
  "The empress was of many languages.

To sensual vices she was so abandoned,
  That lustful she made licit in her law,
  To remove the blame to which she had been led.

She is Semiramis, of whom we read
  That she succeeded Ninus, and was his spouse;
  She held the land which now the Sultan rules.

The next is she who killed herself for love,
  And broke faith with the ashes of Sichaeus;
  Then Cleopatra the voluptuous."

Helen I saw, for whom so many ruthless
  Seasons revolved; and saw the great Achilles,
  Who at the last hour combated with Love.

Vedi Paris, Tristano"""; e piu` di mille
  ombre mostrommi e nominommi a dito,
  ch'amor di nostra vita dipartille.

Poscia ch'io ebbi il mio dottore udito
  nomar le donne antiche e ' cavalieri,
  pieta` mi giunse, e fui quasi smarrito.

I' cominciai: """Poeta, volontieri
  parlerei a quei due che 'nsieme vanno,
  e paion si` al vento esser leggeri""".

Ed elli a me: """Vedrai quando saranno
  piu` presso a noi; e tu allor li priega
  per quello amor che i mena, ed ei verranno""".

Si` tosto come il vento a noi li piega,
  mossi la voce: """O anime affannate,
  venite a noi parlar, s'altri nol niega!""".

Quali colombe dal disio chiamate
  con l'ali alzate e ferme al dolce nido
  vegnon per l'aere dal voler portate;

cotali uscir de la schiera ov'e` Dido,
  a noi venendo per l'aere maligno,
  si` forte fu l'affettuoso grido.

"""O animal grazioso e benigno
  che visitando vai per l'aere perso
  noi che tignemmo il mondo di sanguigno,

se fosse amico il re de l'universo,
  noi pregheremmo lui de la tua pace,
  poi c'hai pieta` del nostro mal perverso.

Di quel che udire e che parlar vi piace,
  noi udiremo e parleremo a voi,
  mentre che 'l vento, come fa, ci tace.

Siede la terra dove nata fui
  su la marina dove 'l Po discende
  per aver pace co' seguaci sui.

Amor, ch'al cor gentil ratto s'apprende
  prese costui de la bella persona
  che mi fu tolta; e 'l modo ancor m'offende.

Paris I saw, Tristan; and more than a thousand
  Shades did he name and point out with his finger,
  Whom Love had separated from our life.

After that I had listened to my Teacher,
  Naming the dames of eld and cavaliers,
  Pity prevailed, and I was nigh bewildered.

And I began: "O Poet, willingly
  Speak would I to those two, who go together,
  And seem upon the wind to be so light."

And, he to me: "Thou'lt mark, when they shall be
  Nearer to us; and then do thou implore them
  By love which leadeth them, and they will come."

Soon as the wind in our direction sways them,
  My voice uplift I: "O ye weary souls!
  Come speak to us, if no one interdicts it."

As turtle-doves, called onward by desire,
  With open and steady wings to the sweet nest
  Fly through the air by their volition borne,

So came they from the band where Dido is,
  Approaching us athwart the air malign,
  So strong was the affectionate appeal.

"O living creature gracious and benignant,
  Who visiting goest through the purple air
  Us, who have stained the world incarnadine,

If were the King of the Universe our friend,
  We would pray unto him to give thee peace,
  Since thou hast pity on our woe perverse.

Of what it pleases thee to hear and speak,
  That will we hear, and we will speak to you,
  While silent is the wind, as it is now.

Sitteth the city, wherein I was born,
  Upon the sea-shore where the Po descends
  To rest in peace with all his retinue.

Love, that on gentle heart doth swiftly seize,
  Seized this man for the person beautiful
  That was ta'en from me, and still the mode offends
    me.

Amor, ch'a nullo amato amar perdona,
  mi prese del costui piacer si` forte,
  che, come vedi, ancor non m'abbandona.
	Love, that exempts no one beloved from loving,
	  Seized me with pleasure of this man so strongly,
	  That, as thou seest, it doth not yet desert me;

Amor condusse noi ad una morte:
  Caina attende chi a vita ci spense"".
  Queste parole da lor ci fuor porte.
	Love has conducted us unto one death;
	  Caina waiteth him who quenched our life!"
	  These words were borne along from them to us.

Quand'io intesi quell'anime offense,
  china' il viso e tanto il tenni basso,
  fin che 'l poeta mi disse: ""Che pense?"".
	As soon as I had heard those souls tormented,
	  I bowed my face, and so long held it down
	  Until the Poet said to me: "What thinkest?"

Quando rispuosi, cominciai: ""Oh lasso,
  quanti dolci pensier, quanto disio
  meno` costoro al doloroso passo!"".
	When I made answer, I began: "Alas!
	  How many pleasant thoughts, how much desire,
	  Conducted these unto the dolorous pass!"

Poi mi rivolsi a loro e parla' io,
  e cominciai: ""Francesca, i tuoi martiri
  a lagrimar mi fanno tristo e pio.
	Then unto them I turned me, and I spake,
	  And I began: "Thine agonies, Francesca,
	  Sad and compassionate to weeping make me.

Ma dimmi: al tempo d'i dolci sospiri,
  a che e come concedette Amore
  che conosceste i dubbiosi disiri?"".
	But tell me, at the time of those sweet sighs,
	  By what and in what manner Love conceded,
	  That you should know your dubious desires?"

E quella a me: ""Nessun maggior dolore
  che ricordarsi del tempo felice
  ne la miseria; e cio` sa 'l tuo dottore.
	And she to me: "There is no greater sorrow
	  Than to be mindful of the happy time
	  In misery, and that thy Teacher knows.

Ma s'a conoscer la prima radice
  del nostro amor tu hai cotanto affetto,
  diro` come colui che piange e dice.
	But, if to recognise the earliest root
	  Of love in us thou hast so great desire,
	  I will do even as he who weeps and speaks.

Noi leggiavamo un giorno per diletto
  di Lancialotto come amor lo strinse;
  soli eravamo e sanza alcun sospetto.
	One day we reading were for our delight
	  Of Launcelot, how Love did him enthral.
	  Alone we were and without any fear.

Per piu` fiate li occhi ci sospinse
  quella lettura, e scolorocci il viso;
  ma solo un punto fu quel che ci vinse.
	Full many a time our eyes together drew
	  That reading, and drove the colour from our faces;
	  But one point only was it that o'ercame us.

Quando leggemmo il disiato riso
  esser basciato da cotanto amante,
  questi, che mai da me non fia diviso,
	When as we read of the much-longed-for smile
	  Being by such a noble lover kissed,
	  This one, who ne'er from me shall be divided,

la bocca mi bascio` tutto tremante.   Galeotto fu 'l libro e chi lo scrisse:   quel giorno piu` non vi leggemmo avante"".	Kissed me upon the mouth all palpitating. Galeotto was the book and he who wrote it. That day no farther did we read therein."
Mentre che l'uno spirto questo disse, l'altro piangea; si` che di pietade   io venni men cosi` com'io morisse.	And all the while one spirit uttered this, The other one did weep so, that, for pity, I swooned away as if I had been dying,

E caddi come corpo morto cade.

And fell, even as a dead body falls.

Inferno: Canto VI

The Third Circle: The Gluttonous. Cerberus. The Eternal Rain. Ciacco. Florence.

Al tornar de la mente, che si chiuse
  dinanzi a la pieta` d'i due cognati,
  che di trestizia tutto mi confuse,
	At the return of consciousness, that closed
	  Before the pity of those two relations,
	  Which utterly with sadness had confused me,

novi tormenti e novi tormentati
  mi veggio intorno, come ch'io mi mova
  e ch'io mi volga, e come che io guati.
	New torments I behold, and new tormented
	  Around me, whichsoever way I move,
	  And whichsoever way I turn, and gaze.

Io sono al terzo cerchio, de la piova
  etterna, maladetta, fredda e greve;
  regola e qualita` mai non l'e` nova.
	In the third circle am I of the rain
	  Eternal, maledict, and cold, and heavy;
	  Its law and quality are never new.

Grandine grossa, acqua tinta e neve
  per l'aere tenebroso si riversa;
  pute la terra che questo riceve.
	Huge hail, and water sombre-hued, and snow,
	  Athwart the tenebrous air pour down amain;
	  Noisome the earth is, that receiveth this.

Cerbero, fiera crudele e diversa,
  con tre gole caninamente latra
  sovra la gente che quivi e` sommersa.
	Cerberus, monster cruel and uncouth,
	  With his three gullets like a dog is barking
	  Over the people that are there submerged.

Li occhi ha vermigli, la barba unta e atra,
  e 'l ventre largo, e unghiate le mani;
  graffia li spirti, ed iscoia ed isquatra.
	Red eyes he has, and unctuous beard and black,
	  And belly large, and armed with claws his hands;
	  He rends the spirits, flays, and quarters them.

Urlar li fa la pioggia come cani;
  de l'un de' lati fanno a l'altro schermo;
  volgonsi spesso i miseri profani.
	Howl the rain maketh them like unto dogs;
	  One side they make a shelter for the other;
	  Oft turn themselves the wretched reprobates.

Quando ci scorse Cerbero, il gran vermo,
  le bocche aperse e mostrocci le sanne;
  non avea membro che tenesse fermo.
	When Cerberus perceived us, the great worm!
	  His mouths he opened, and displayed his tusks;
	  Not a limb had he that was motionless.

E 'l duca mio distese le sue spanne,
  prese la terra, e con piene le pugna
  la gitto` dentro a le bramose canne.
	And my Conductor, with his spans extended,
	  Took of the earth, and with his fists well filled,
	  He threw it into those rapacious gullets.

Qual e` quel cane ch'abbaiando agogna,
  e si racqueta poi che 'l pasto morde,
  che' solo a divorarlo intende e pugna,
	Such as that dog is, who by barking craves,
	  And quiet grows soon as his food he gnaws,
	  For to devour it he but thinks and struggles,

cotai si fecer quelle facce lorde
  de lo demonio Cerbero, che 'ntrona
  l'anime si`, ch'esser vorrebber sorde.
	The like became those muzzles filth-begrimed
	  Of Cerberus the demon, who so thunders
	  Over the souls that they would fain be deaf.

Noi passavam su per l'ombre che adona
  la greve pioggia, e ponavam le piante
  sovra lor vanita` che par persona.
	We passed across the shadows, which subdues
	  The heavy rain-storm, and we placed our feet
	  Upon their vanity that person seems.

Elle giacean per terra tutte quante,
  fuor d'una ch'a seder si levo`, ratto
  ch'ella ci vide passarsi davante.
	They all were lying prone upon the earth,
	  Excepting one, who sat upright as soon
	  As he beheld us passing on before him.

""O tu che se' per questo 'nferno tratto"",
  mi disse, ""riconoscimi, se sai:
  tu fosti, prima ch'io disfatto, fatto"".
	"O thou that art conducted through this Hell,"
	  He said to me, "recall me, if thou canst;
	  Thyself wast made before I was unmade."

E io a lui: ""L'angoscia che tu hai
  forse ti tira fuor de la mia mente,
  si` che non par ch'i' ti vedessi mai.
	And I to him: "The anguish which thou hast
	  Perhaps doth draw thee out of my remembrance,
	  So that it seems not I have ever seen thee.

Ma dimmi chi tu se' che 'n si` dolente   loco se' messo e hai si` fatta pena, che, s'altra e` maggio, nulla e` si` spiacente"".	But tell me who thou art, that in so doleful A place art put, and in such punishment, If some are greater, none is so displeasing."

Ed elli a me: ""La tua citta`, ch'e` piena
  d'invidia si` che gia` trabocca il sacco,
  seco mi tenne in la vita serena.
	And he to me: "Thy city, which is full
	  Of envy so that now the sack runs over,
	  Held me within it in the life serene.

Voi cittadini mi chiamaste Ciacco:
  per la dannosa colpa de la gola,
  come tu vedi, a la pioggia mi fiacco.
	You citizens were wont to call me Ciacco;
	  For the pernicious sin of gluttony
	  I, as thou seest, am battered by this rain.

E io anima trista non son sola,
  che' tutte queste a simil pena stanno
  per simil colpa"". E piu` non fe' parola.
	And I, sad soul, am not the only one,
	  For all these suffer the like penalty
	  For the like sin;" and word no more spake he.

Io li rispuosi: ""Ciacco, il tuo affanno
  mi pesa si`, ch'a lagrimar mi 'nvita;
  ma dimmi, se tu sai, a che verranno
	I answered him: "Ciacco, thy wretchedness
	  Weighs on me so that it to weep invites me;
	  But tell me, if thou knowest, to what shall come

li cittadin de la citta` partita;   s'alcun v'e` giusto; e dimmi la cagione per che l'ha tanta discordia assalita"".	The citizens of the divided city; If any there be just; and the occasion Tell me why so much discord has assailed it."

E quelli a me: ""Dopo lunga tencione
  verranno al sangue, e la parte selvaggia
  caccera` l'altra con molta offensione.
	And he to me: "They, after long contention,
	  Will come to bloodshed; and the rustic party
	  Will drive the other out with much offence.

26

Poi appresso convien che questa caggia
  infra tre soli, e che l'altra sormonti
  con la forza di tal che teste' piaggia.

Alte terra` lungo tempo le fronti,
  tenendo l'altra sotto gravi pesi,
  come che di cio` pianga o che n'aonti.

Giusti son due, e non vi sono intesi;
  superbia, invidia e avarizia sono
  le tre faville c'hanno i cuori accesi"".

Qui puose fine al lagrimabil suono.
  E io a lui: ""Ancor vo' che mi 'nsegni,
  e che di piu` parlar mi facci dono.

Farinata e 'l Tegghiaio, che fuor si` degni,
  Iacopo Rusticucci, Arrigo e 'l Mosca
  e li altri ch'a ben far puoser li 'ngegni,

dimmi ove sono e fa ch'io li conosca;
  che' gran disio mi stringe di savere
  se 'l ciel li addolcia, o lo 'nferno li attosca"".

E quelli: ""Ei son tra l'anime piu` nere:
  diverse colpe giu` li grava al fondo:
  se tanto scendi, la` i potrai vedere.

Ma quando tu sarai nel dolce mondo,
  priegoti ch'a la mente altrui mi rechi:
  piu` non ti dico e piu` non ti rispondo"".

Li diritti occhi torse allora in biechi;
  guardommi un poco, e poi chino` la testa:
  cadde con essa a par de li altri ciechi.

E 'l duca disse a me: ""Piu` non si desta
  di qua dal suon de l'angelica tromba,
  quando verra` la nimica podesta:

ciascun rivedera` la trista tomba,
  ripigliera` sua carne e sua figura,
  udira` quel ch'in etterno rimbomba"".

Si` trapassammo per sozza mistura
  de l'ombre e de la pioggia, a passi lenti,
  toccando un poco la vita futura;

per ch'io dissi: ""Maestro, esti tormenti
  crescerann'ei dopo la gran sentenza,
  o fier minori, o saran si` cocenti?"".

Then afterwards behoves it this one fall
  Within three suns, and rise again the other
  By force of him who now is on the coast.

High will it hold its forehead a long while,
  Keeping the other under heavy burdens,
  Howe'er it weeps thereat and is indignant.

The just are two, and are not understood there;
  Envy and Arrogance and Avarice
  Are the three sparks that have all hearts enkindled."

Here ended he his tearful utterance;
  And I to him: "I wish thee still to teach me,
  And make a gift to me of further speech.

Farinata and Tegghiaio, once so worthy,
  Jacopo Rusticucci, Arrigo, and Mosca,
  And others who on good deeds set their thoughts,

Say where they are, and cause that I may know them;
  For great desire constraineth me to learn
  If Heaven doth sweeten them, or Hell envenom."

And he: "They are among the blacker souls;
  A different sin downweighs them to the bottom;
  If thou so far descendest, thou canst see them.

But when thou art again in the sweet world,
  I pray thee to the mind of others bring me;
  No more I tell thee and no more I answer."

Then his straightforward eyes he turned askance,
  Eyed me a little, and then bowed his head;
  He fell therewith prone like the other blind.

And the Guide said to me: "He wakes no more
  This side the sound of the angelic trumpet;
  When shall approach the hostile Potentate,

Each one shall find again his dismal tomb,
  Shall reassume his flesh and his own figure,
  Shall hear what through eternity re-echoes."

So we passed onward o'er the filthy mixture
  Of shadows and of rain with footsteps slow,
  Touching a little on the future life.

Wherefore I said: "Master, these torments here,
  Will they increase after the mighty sentence,
  Or lesser be, or will they be as burning?"

Ed elli a me: ""Ritorna a tua scienza,
  che vuol, quanto la cosa e` piu` perfetta,
  piu` senta il bene, e cosi` la doglienza.

Tutto che questa gente maladetta
  in vera perfezion gia` mai non vada,
  di la` piu` che di qua essere aspetta"".

Noi aggirammo a tondo quella strada,
  parlando piu` assai ch'i' non ridico;
  venimmo al punto dove si digrada:

quivi trovammo Pluto, il gran nemico.

And he to me: "Return unto thy science,
  Which wills, that as the thing more perfect is,
  The more it feels of pleasure and of pain.

Albeit that this people maledict
  To true perfection never can attain,
  Hereafter more than now they look to be."

Round in a circle by that road we went,
  Speaking much more, which I do not repeat;
  We came unto the point where the descent is;

There we found Plutus the great enemy.

Inferno: Canto VII

The Fourth Circle: The Avaricious and the Prodigal. Plutus. Fortune and her Wheel. The Fifth Circle: The Irascible and the Sullen. Styx.

""Pape Satan, pape Satan aleppe!"",
  comincio` Pluto con la voce chioccia;
  e quel savio gentil, che tutto seppe,

disse per confortarmi: ""Non ti noccia
  la tua paura; che', poder ch'elli abbia,
  non ci torra` lo scender questa roccia"".

Poi si rivolse a quella 'nfiata labbia,
  e disse: ""Taci, maladetto lupo!
  consuma dentro te con la tua rabbia.

Non e` sanza cagion l'andare al cupo:
  vuolsi ne l'alto, la` dove Michele
  fe' la vendetta del superbo strupo"".

Quali dal vento le gonfiate vele
  caggiono avvolte, poi che l'alber fiacca,
  tal cadde a terra la fiera crudele.

Cosi` scendemmo ne la quarta lacca
  pigliando piu` de la dolente ripa
  che 'l mal de l'universo tutto insacca.

Ahi giustizia di Dio! tante chi stipa
  nove travaglie e pene quant'io viddi?
  e perche' nostra colpa si` ne scipa?

Come fa l'onda la` sovra Cariddi,
  che si frange con quella in cui s'intoppa,
  cosi` convien che qui la gente riddi.

Qui vid'i' gente piu` ch'altrove troppa,
  e d'una parte e d'altra, con grand'urli,
  voltando pesi per forza di poppa.

"Pape Satan, Pape Satan, Aleppe!"
  Thus Plutus with his clucking voice began;
  And that benignant Sage, who all things knew,

Said, to encourage me: "Let not thy fear
  Harm thee; for any power that he may have
  Shall not prevent thy going down this crag."

Then he turned round unto that bloated lip,
  And said: "Be silent, thou accursed wolf;
  Consume within thyself with thine own rage.

Not causeless is this journey to the abyss;
  Thus is it willed on high, where Michael wrought
  Vengeance upon the proud adultery."

Even as the sails inflated by the wind
  Involved together fall when snaps the mast,
  So fell the cruel monster to the earth.

Thus we descended into the fourth chasm,
  Gaining still farther on the dolesome shore
  Which all the woe of the universe insacks.

Justice of God, ah! who heaps up so many
  New toils and sufferings as I beheld?
  And why doth our transgression waste us so?

As doth the billow there upon Charybdis,
  That breaks itself on that which it encounters,
  So here the folk must dance their roundelay.

Here saw I people, more than elsewhere, many,
  On one side and the other, with great howls,
  Rolling weights forward by main force of chest.

Percoteansi 'ncontro; e poscia pur li`
  si rivolgea ciascun, voltando a retro,
  gridando: ““Perche' tieni?”“ e ““Perche' burli?”“.

Cosi` tornavan per lo cerchio tetro
  da ogne mano a l'opposito punto,
  gridandosi anche loro ontoso metro;

poi si volgea ciascun, quand'era giunto,
  per lo suo mezzo cerchio a l'altra giostra.
  E io, ch'avea lo cor quasi compunto,

dissi: ““Maestro mio, or mi dimostra
  che gente e` questa, e se tutti fuor cherci
  questi chercuti a la sinistra nostra”“.

Ed elli a me: ““Tutti quanti fuor guerci
  si` de la mente in la vita primaia,
  che con misura nullo spendio ferci.

Assai la voce lor chiaro l'abbaia
  quando vegnono a' due punti del cerchio
  dove colpa contraria li dispaia.

Questi fuor cherci, che non han coperchio
  piloso al capo, e papi e cardinali,
  in cui usa avarizia il suo soperchio”“.

E io: ““Maestro, tra questi cotali
  dovre' io ben riconoscere alcuni
  che furo immondi di cotesti mali”“.

Ed elli a me: ““Vano pensiero aduni:
  la sconoscente vita che i fe' sozzi
  ad ogne conoscenza or li fa bruni.

In etterno verranno a li due cozzi:
  questi resurgeranno del sepulcro
  col pugno chiuso, e questi coi crin mozzi.

Mal dare e mal tener lo mondo pulcro
  ha tolto loro, e posti a questa zuffa:
  qual ella sia, parole non ci appulcro.

Or puoi, figliuol, veder la corta buffa
  d'i ben che son commessi a la fortuna,
  per che l'umana gente si rabbuffa;

They clashed together, and then at that point
  Each one turned backward, rolling retrograde,
  Crying, "Why keepest?" and, "Why squanderest
    thou?"

Thus they returned along the lurid circle
  On either hand unto the opposite point,
  Shouting their shameful metre evermore.

Then each, when he arrived there, wheeled about
  Through his half-circle to another joust;
  And I, who had my heart pierced as it were,

Exclaimed: "My Master, now declare to me
  What people these are, and if all were clerks,
  These shaven crowns upon the left of us."

And he to me: "All of them were asquint
  In intellect in the first life, so much
  That there with measure they no spending made.

Clearly enough their voices bark it forth,
  Whene'er they reach the two points of the circle,
  Where sunders them the opposite defect.

Clerks those were who no hairy covering
  Have on the head, and Popes and Cardinals,
  In whom doth Avarice practise its excess."

And I: "My Master, among such as these
  I ought forsooth to recognise some few,
  Who were infected with these maladies."

And he to me: "Vain thought thou entertainest;
  The undiscerning life which made them sordid
  Now makes them unto all discernment dim.

Forever shall they come to these two buttings;
  These from the sepulchre shall rise again
  With the fist closed, and these with tresses shorn.

Ill giving and ill keeping the fair world
  Have ta'en from them, and placed them in this scuf-
    fle;
  Whate'er it be, no words adorn I for it.

Now canst thou, Son, behold the transient farce
  Of goods that are committed unto Fortune,
  For which the human race each other buffet;

che' tutto l'oro ch'e` sotto la luna 　e che gia` fu, di quest'anime stanche 　non poterebbe farne posare una"".	For all the gold that is beneath the moon, 　Or ever has been, of these weary souls 　Could never make a single one repose."
""Maestro mio"", diss'io, ""or mi di` anche: 　questa fortuna di che tu mi tocche, 　che e`, che i ben del mondo ha si` tra branche?"".	"Master," I said to him, "now tell me also 　What is this Fortune which thou speakest of, 　That has the world's goods so within its clutches?"
E quelli a me: ""Oh creature sciocche, 　quanta ignoranza e` quella che v'offende! 　Or vo' che tu mia sentenza ne 'mbocche.	And he to me: "O creatures imbecile, 　What ignorance is this which doth beset you? 　Now will I have thee learn my judgment of her.
Colui lo cui saver tutto trascende, 　fece li cieli e die` lor chi conduce 　si` ch'ogne parte ad ogne parte splende,	He whose omniscience everything transcends 　The heavens created, and gave who should guide 　　them, 　That every part to every part may shine,
distribuendo igualmente la luce. 　Similemente a li splendor mondani 　ordino` general ministra e duce	Distributing the light in equal measure; 　He in like manner to the mundane splendours 　Ordained a general ministress and guide,
che permutasse a tempo li ben vani 　di gente in gente e d'uno in altro sangue, 　oltre la difension d'i senni umani;	That she might change at times the empty treasures 　From race to race, from one blood to another, 　Beyond resistance of all human wisdom.
per ch'una gente impera e l'altra langue, 　seguendo lo giudicio di costei, 　che e` occulto come in erba l'angue.	Therefore one people triumphs, and another 　Languishes, in pursuance of her judgment, 　Which hidden is, as in the grass a serpent.
Vostro saver non ha contasto a lei: 　questa provede, giudica, e persegue 　suo regno come il loro li altri dei.	Your knowledge has no counterstand against her; 　She makes provision, judges, and pursues 　Her governance, as theirs the other gods.
Le sue permutazion non hanno triegue; 　necessita` la fa esser veloce; 　si` spesso vien chi vicenda consegue.	Her permutations have not any truce; 　Necessity makes her precipitate, 　So often cometh who his turn obtains.
Quest'e` colei ch'e` tanto posta in croce 　pur da color che le dovrien dar lode, 　dandole biasmo a torto e mala voce;	And this is she who is so crucified 　Even by those who ought to give her praise, 　Giving her blame amiss, and bad repute.
ma ella s'e` beata e cio` non ode: 　con l'altre prime creature lieta 　volve sua spera e beata si gode.	But she is blissful, and she hears it not; 　Among the other primal creatures gladsome 　She turns her sphere, and blissful she rejoices.
Or discendiamo omai a maggior pieta; 　gia` ogne stella cade che saliva 　quand'io mi mossi, e 'l troppo star si vieta"".	Let us descend now unto greater woe; 　Already sinks each star that was ascending 　When I set out, and loitering is forbidden."

Noi ricidemmo il cerchio a l'altra riva
  sovr'una fonte che bolle e riversa
  per un fossato che da lei deriva.

L'acqua era buia assai piu` che persa;
  e noi, in compagnia de l'onde bige,
  intrammo giu` per una via diversa.

In la palude va c'ha nome Stige
  questo tristo ruscel, quand'e` disceso
  al pie` de le maligne piagge grige.

E io, che di mirare stava inteso,
  vidi genti fangose in quel pantano,
  ignude tutte, con sembiante offeso.

Queste si percotean non pur con mano,
  ma con la testa e col petto e coi piedi,
  troncandosi co' denti a brano a brano.

Lo buon maestro disse: ““Figlio, or vedi
  l'anime di color cui vinse l'ira;
  e anche vo' che tu per certo credi

che sotto l'acqua e` gente che sospira,
  e fanno pullular quest'acqua al summo,
  come l'occhio ti dice, u' che s'aggira.

Fitti nel limo, dicon: "Tristi fummo
  ne l'aere dolce che dal sol s'allegra,
  portando dentro accidioso fummo:

or ci attristiam ne la belletta negra".
  Quest'inno si gorgoglian ne la strozza,
  che' dir nol posson con parola integra”“.

Cosi` girammo de la lorda pozza
  grand'arco tra la ripa secca e 'l mezzo,
  con li occhi volti a chi del fango ingozza.

Venimmo al pie` d'una torre al da sezzo.

We crossed the circle to the other bank,
  Near to a fount that boils, and pours itself
  Along a gully that runs out of it.

The water was more sombre far than perse;
  And we, in company with the dusky waves,
  Made entrance downward by a path uncouth.

A marsh it makes, which has the name of Styx,
  This tristful brooklet, when it has descended
  Down to the foot of the malign gray shores.

And I, who stood intent upon beholding,
  Saw people mud-besprent in that lagoon,
  All of them naked and with angry look.

They smote each other not alone with hands,
  But with the head and with the breast and feet,
  Tearing each other piecemeal with their teeth.

Said the good Master: "Son, thou now beholdest
  The souls of those whom anger overcame;
  And likewise I would have thee know for certain

Beneath the water people are who sigh
  And make this water bubble at the surface,
  As the eye tells thee wheresoe'er it turns.

Fixed in the mire they say, 'We sullen were
  In the sweet air, which by the sun is gladdened,
  Bearing within ourselves the sluggish reek;

Now we are sullen in this sable mire.'
  This hymn do they keep gurgling in their throats,
  For with unbroken words they cannot say it."

Thus we went circling round the filthy fen
  A great arc 'twixt the dry bank and the swamp,
  With eyes turned unto those who gorge the mire;

Unto the foot of a tower we came at last.

Inferno: Canto VIII

Phlegyas. Philippo Argenti. The Gate of the City of Dis.

Io dico, seguitando, ch'assai prima
  che noi fossimo al pie` de l'alta torre,
  li occhi nostri n'andar suso a la cima

per due fiammette che i vedemmo porre
  e un'altra da lungi render cenno
  tanto ch'a pena il potea l'occhio torre.

E io mi volsi al mar di tutto 'l senno;
  dissi: ""Questo che dice? e che risponde
  quell'altro foco? e chi son quei che 'l fenno?"".

Ed elli a me: ""Su per le sucide onde
  gia` scorgere puoi quello che s'aspetta,
  se 'l fummo del pantan nol ti nasconde"".

Corda non pinse mai da se' saetta
  che si` corresse via per l'aere snella,
  com'io vidi una nave piccioletta

venir per l'acqua verso noi in quella,
  sotto 'l governo d'un sol galeoto,
  che gridava: ""Or se' giunta, anima fella!"".

""Flegias, Flegias, tu gridi a voto"",
  disse lo mio segnore ""a questa volta:
  piu` non ci avrai che sol passando il loto"".

Qual e` colui che grande inganno ascolta
  che li sia fatto, e poi se ne rammarca,
  fecesi Flegias ne l'ira accolta.

Lo duca mio discese ne la barca,
  e poi mi fece intrare appresso lui;
  e sol quand'io fui dentro parve carca.

I say, continuing, that long before
  We to the foot of that high tower had come,
  Our eyes went upward to the summit of it,

By reason of two flamelets we saw placed there,
  And from afar another answer them,
  So far, that hardly could the eye attain it.

And, to the sea of all discernment turned,
  I said: "What sayeth this, and what respondeth
  That other fire? and who are they that made it?"

And he to me: "Across the turbid waves
  What is expected thou canst now discern,
  If reek of the morass conceal it not."

Cord never shot an arrow from itself
  That sped away athwart the air so swift,
  As I beheld a very little boat

Come o'er the water tow'rds us at that moment,
  Under the guidance of a single pilot,
  Who shouted, "Now art thou arrived, fell soul?"

"Phlegyas, Phlegyas, thou criest out in vain
  For this once," said my Lord; "thou shalt not have
    us
  Longer than in the passing of the slough."

As he who listens to some great deceit
  That has been done to him, and then resents it,
  Such became Phlegyas, in his gathered wrath.

My Guide descended down into the boat,
  And then he made me enter after him,
  And only when I entered seemed it laden.

Tosto che 'l duca e io nel legno fui,
  segando se ne va l'antica prora
  de l'acqua piu` che non suol con altrui.

Mentre noi corravam la morta gora,
  dinanzi mi si fece un pien di fango,
  e disse: ""Chi se' tu che vieni anzi ora?"".

E io a lui: ""S'i' vegno, non rimango;
  ma tu chi se', che si` se' fatto brutto?"".
  Rispuose: ""Vedi che son un che piango"".

E io a lui: ""Con piangere e con lutto,
  spirito maladetto, ti rimani;
  ch'i' ti conosco, ancor sie lordo tutto"".

Allor distese al legno ambo le mani;
  per che 'l maestro accorto lo sospinse,
  dicendo: ""Via costa` con li altri cani!"".

Lo collo poi con le braccia mi cinse;
  basciommi 'l volto, e disse: ""Alma sdegnosa,
  benedetta colei che 'n te s'incinse!

Quei fu al mondo persona orgogliosa;
  bonta` non e` che sua memoria fregi:
  cosi` s'e` l'ombra sua qui furiosa.

Quanti si tegnon or la` su` gran regi
  che qui staranno come porci in brago,
  di se' lasciando orribili dispregi!"".

E io: ""Maestro, molto sarei vago
  di vederlo attuffare in questa broda
  prima che noi uscissimo del lago"".

Ed elli a me: ""Avante che la proda
  ti si lasci veder, tu sarai sazio:
  di tal disio convien che tu goda"".

Dopo cio` poco vid'io quello strazio
  far di costui a le fangose genti,
  che Dio ancor ne lodo e ne ringrazio.

Tutti gridavano: ""A Filippo Argenti!"";
  e 'l fiorentino spirito bizzarro
  in se' medesmo si volvea co' denti.

Soon as the Guide and I were in the boat,
  The antique prow goes on its way, dividing
  More of the water than 'tis wont with others.

While we were running through the dead canal,
  Uprose in front of me one full of mire,
  And said, "Who 'rt thou that comest ere the hour?"

And I to him: "Although I come, I stay not;
  But who art thou that hast become so squalid?"
  "Thou seest that I am one who weeps," he answered.

And I to him: "With weeping and with wailing,
  Thou spirit maledict, do thou remain;
  For thee I know, though thou art all defiled."

Then stretched he both his hands unto the boat;
  Whereat my wary Master thrust him back,
  Saying, "Away there with the other dogs!"

Thereafter with his arms he clasped my neck;
  He kissed my face, and said: "Disdainful soul,
  Blessed be she who bore thee in her bosom.

That was an arrogant person in the world;
  Goodness is none, that decks his memory;
  So likewise here his shade is furious.

How many are esteemed great kings up there,
  Who here shall be like unto swine in mire,
  Leaving behind them horrible dispraises!"

And I: "My Master, much should I be pleased,
  If I could see him soused into this broth,
  Before we issue forth out of the lake."

And he to me: "Ere unto thee the shore
  Reveal itself, thou shalt be satisfied;
  Such a desire 'tis meet thou shouldst enjoy."

A little after that, I saw such havoc
  Made of him by the people of the mire,
  That still I praise and thank my God for it.

They all were shouting, "At Philippo Argenti!"
  And that exasperate spirit Florentine
  Turned round upon himself with his own teeth.

Inferno: Canto VIII

Quivi il lasciammo, che piu` non ne narro;
  ma ne l'orecchie mi percosse un duolo,
  per ch'io avante l'occhio intento sbarro.
	We left him there, and more of him I tell not;
	  But on mine ears there smote a lamentation,
	  Whence forward I intent unbar mine eyes.

Lo buon maestro disse: ""Omai, figliuolo,
  s'appressa la citta` c'ha nome Dite,
  coi gravi cittadin, col grande stuolo"".
	And the good Master said: "Even now, my Son,
	  The city draweth near whose name is Dis,
	  With the grave citizens, with the great throng."

E io: ""Maestro, gia` le sue meschite   la` entro certe ne la valle cerno, vermiglie come se di foco uscite	And I: "Its mosques already, Master, clearly Within there in the valley I discern Vermilion, as if issuing from the fire

fossero"". Ed ei mi disse: ""Il foco etterno
  ch'entro l'affoca le dimostra rosse,
  come tu vedi in questo basso inferno"".
	They were." And he to me: "The fire eternal
	  That kindles them within makes them look red,
	  As thou beholdest in this nether Hell."

Noi pur giugnemmo dentro a l'alte fosse
  che vallan quella terra sconsolata:
  le mura mi parean che ferro fosse.
	Then we arrived within the moats profound,
	  That circumvallate that disconsolate city;
	  The walls appeared to me to be of iron.

Non sanza prima far grande aggirata,
  venimmo in parte dove il nocchier forte
  ""Usciteci"", grido`: ""qui e` l'intrata"".
	Not without making first a circuit wide,
	  We came unto a place where loud the pilot
	  Cried out to us, "Debark, here is the entrance."

Io vidi piu` di mille in su le porte   da ciel piovuti, che stizzosamente   dicean: ""Chi e` costui che sanza morte	More than a thousand at the gates I saw Out of the Heavens rained down, who angrily Were saying, "Who is this that without death

va per lo regno de la morta gente?"".
  E 'l savio mio maestro fece segno
  di voler lor parlar segretamente.
	Goes through the kingdom of the people dead?"
	  And my sagacious Master made a sign
	  Of wishing secretly to speak with them.

Allor chiusero un poco il gran disdegno,
  e disser: ""Vien tu solo, e quei sen vada,
  che si` ardito intro` per questo regno.
	A little then they quelled their great disdain,
	  And said: "Come thou alone, and he begone
	  Who has so boldly entered these dominions.

Sol si ritorni per la folle strada:
  pruovi, se sa; che' tu qui rimarrai
  che li ha' iscorta si` buia contrada"".
	Let him return alone by his mad road;
	  Try, if he can; for thou shalt here remain,
	  Who hast escorted him through such dark regions."

Pensa, lettor, se io mi sconfortai
  nel suon de le parole maladette,
  che' non credetti ritornarci mai.
	Think, Reader, if I was discomforted
	  At utterance of the accursed words;
	  For never to return here I believed.

""O caro duca mio, che piu` di sette   volte m'hai sicurta` renduta e tratto d'alto periglio che 'ncontra mi stette,	"O my dear Guide, who more than seven times Hast rendered me security, and drawn me From imminent peril that before me stood,
non mi lasciar"", diss'io, ""cosi` disfatto;   e se 'l passar piu` oltre ci e` negato, ritroviam l'orme nostre insieme ratto"".	Do not desert me," said I, "thus undone; And if the going farther be denied us, Let us retrace our steps together swiftly."

E quel segnor che li` m'avea menato,
  mi disse: ""'Non temer; che' 'l nostro passo
  non ci puo` torre alcun: da tal n'e` dato.

Ma qui m'attendi, e lo spirito lasso
  conforta e ciba di speranza buona,
  ch'i' non ti lascero` nel mondo basso"'".

Cosi` sen va, e quivi m'abbandona
  lo dolce padre, e io rimagno in forse,
  che si` e no nel capo mi tenciona.

Udir non potti quello ch'a lor porse;
  ma ei non stette la` con essi guari,
  che ciascun dentro a pruova si ricorse.

Chiuser le porte que' nostri avversari
  nel petto al mio segnor, che fuor rimase,
  e rivolsesi a me con passi rari.

Li occhi a la terra e le ciglia avea rase
  d'ogne baldanza, e dicea ne' sospiri:
  ""'Chi m'ha negate le dolenti case!'".

E a me disse: ""'Tu, perch'io m'adiri,
  non sbigottir, ch'io vincero` la prova,
  qual ch'a la difension dentro s'aggiri.

Questa lor tracotanza non e` nova;
  che' gia` l'usaro a men segreta porta,
  la qual sanza serrame ancor si trova.

Sovr'essa vedestu` la scritta morta:
  e gia` di qua da lei discende l'erta,
  passando per li cerchi sanza scorta,

tal che per lui ne fia la terra aperta"'".

And that Lord, who had led me thitherward,
  Said unto me: "Fear not; because our passage
  None can take from us, it by Such is given.

But here await me, and thy weary spirit
  Comfort and nourish with a better hope;
  For in this nether world I will not leave thee."

So onward goes and there abandons me
  My Father sweet, and I remain in doubt,
  For No and Yes within my head contend.

I could not hear what he proposed to them;
  But with them there he did not linger long,
  Ere each within in rivalry ran back.

They closed the portals, those our adversaries,
  On my Lord's breast, who had remained without
  And turned to me with footsteps far between.

His eyes cast down, his forehead shorn had he
  Of all its boldness, and he said, with sighs,
  "Who has denied to me the dolesome houses?"

And unto me: "Thou, because I am angry,
  Fear not, for I will conquer in the trial,
  Whatever for defence within be planned.

This arrogance of theirs is nothing new;
  For once they used it at less secret gate,
  Which finds itself without a fastening still.

O'er it didst thou behold the dead inscription;
  And now this side of it descends the steep,
  Passing across the circles without escort,

One by whose means the city shall be opened."

Inferno: Canto IX

The Furies and Medusa. The Angel. The City of Dis. The Sixth Circle: Heresiarchs.

Quel color che vilta` di fuor mi pinse
  veggendo il duca mio tornare in volta,
  piu` tosto dentro il suo novo ristrinse.

Attento si fermo` com'uom ch'ascolta;
  che' l'occhio nol potea menare a lunga
  per l'aere nero e per la nebbia folta.

““Pur a noi converra` vincer la punga”“,
  comincio` el, ““se non… Tal ne s'offerse.
  Oh quanto tarda a me ch'altri qui giunga!”“.

I' vidi ben si` com'ei ricoperse
  lo cominciar con l'altro che poi venne,
  che fur parole a le prime diverse;

ma nondimen paura il suo dir dienne,
  perch'io traeva la parola tronca
  forse a peggior sentenzia che non tenne.

““In questo fondo de la trista conca
  discende mai alcun del primo grado,
  che sol per pena ha la speranza cionca?”“.

Questa question fec'io; e quei ““Di rado
  incontra”“, mi rispuose, ““che di noi
  faccia il cammino alcun per qual io vado.

Ver e` ch'altra fiata qua giu` fui,
  congiurato da quella Eriton cruda
  che richiamava l'ombre a' corpi sui.

Di poco era di me la carne nuda,
  ch'ella mi fece intrar dentr'a quel muro,
  per trarne un spirto del cerchio di Giuda.

That hue which cowardice brought out on me,
  Beholding my Conductor backward turn,
  Sooner repressed within him his new colour.

He stopped attentive, like a man who listens,
  Because the eye could not conduct him far
  Through the black air, and through the heavy fog.

"Still it behoveth us to win the fight,"
  Began he; "Else. . .Such offered us herself. . .
  O how I long that some one here arrive!"

Well I perceived, as soon as the beginning
  He covered up with what came afterward,
  That they were words quite different from the first;

But none the less his saying gave me fear,
  Because I carried out the broken phrase,
  Perhaps to a worse meaning than he had.

"Into this bottom of the doleful conch
  Doth any e'er descend from the first grade,
  Which for its pain has only hope cut off?"

This question put I; and he answered me:
  "Seldom it comes to pass that one of us
  Maketh the journey upon which I go.

True is it, once before I here below
  Was conjured by that pitiless Erictho,
  Who summoned back the shades unto their bodies.

Naked of me short while the flesh had been,
  Before within that wall she made me enter,
  To bring a spirit from the circle of Judas;

Quell'e` 'l piu` basso loco e 'l piu` oscuro,
  e 'l piu` lontan dal ciel che tutto gira:
  ben so 'l cammin; pero` ti fa sicuro.

Questa palude che 'l gran puzzo spira
  cigne dintorno la citta` dolente,
  u' non potemo intrare omai sanz'ira"".

E altro disse, ma non l'ho a mente;
  pero` che l'occhio m'avea tutto tratto
  ver' l'alta torre a la cima rovente,

dove in un punto furon dritte ratto
  tre furie infernal di sangue tinte,
  che membra feminine avieno e atto,

e con idre verdissime eran cinte;
  serpentelli e ceraste avien per crine,
  onde le fiere tempie erano avvinte.

E quei, che ben conobbe le meschine
  de la regina de l'etterno pianto,
  ""Guarda"", mi disse, ""le feroci Erine.

Quest'e` Megera dal sinistro canto;
  quella che piange dal destro e` Aletto;
  Tesifon e` nel mezzo""; e tacque a tanto.

Con l'unghie si fendea ciascuna il petto;
  battiensi a palme, e gridavan si` alto,
  ch'i' mi strinsi al poeta per sospetto.

""Vegna Medusa: si` 'l farem di smalto"",
  dicevan tutte riguardando in giuso;
  ""mal non vengiammo in Teseo l'assalto"".

""Volgiti 'n dietro e tien lo viso chiuso;
  che' se 'l Gorgon si mostra e tu 'l vedessi,
  nulla sarebbe di tornar mai suso"".

Cosi` disse 'l maestro; ed elli stessi
  mi volse, e non si tenne a le mie mani,
  che con le sue ancor non mi chiudessi.

O voi ch'avete li 'ntelletti sani,
  mirate la dottrina che s'asconde
  sotto 'l velame de li versi strani.

That is the lowest region and the darkest,
  And farthest from the heaven which circles all.
  Well know I the way; therefore be reassured.

This fen, which a prodigious stench exhales,
  Encompasses about the city dolent,
  Where now we cannot enter without anger."

And more he said, but not in mind I have it;
  Because mine eye had altogether drawn me
  Tow'rds the high tower with the red-flaming sum-
    mit,

Where in a moment saw I swift uprisen
  The three infernal Furies stained with blood,
  Who had the limbs of women and their mien,

And with the greenest hydras were begirt;
  Small serpents and cerastes were their tresses,
  Wherewith their horrid temples were entwined.

And he who well the handmaids of the Queen
  Of everlasting lamentation knew,
  Said unto me: "Behold the fierce Erinnys.

This is Megaera, on the left-hand side;
  She who is weeping on the right, Alecto;
  Tisiphone is between;" and then was silent.

Each one her breast was rending with her nails;
  They beat them with their palms, and cried so loud,
  That I for dread pressed close unto the Poet.

"Medusa come, so we to stone will change him!"
  All shouted looking down; "in evil hour
  Avenged we not on Theseus his assault!"

"Turn thyself round, and keep thine eyes close shut,
  For if the Gorgon appear, and thou shouldst see it,
  No more returning upward would there be."

Thus said the Master; and he turned me round
  Himself, and trusted not unto my hands
  So far as not to blind me with his own.

O ye who have undistempered intellects,
  Observe the doctrine that conceals itself
  Beneath the veil of the mysterious verses!

E gia` venia su per le torbide onde
  un fracasso d'un suon, pien di spavento,
  per cui tremavano amendue le sponde,
	And now there came across the turbid waves
	  The clangour of a sound with terror fraught,
	  Because of which both of the margins trembled;

non altrimenti fatto che d'un vento
  impetuoso per li avversi ardori,
  che fier la selva e sanz'alcun rattento
	Not otherwise it was than of a wind
	  Impetuous on account of adverse heats,
	  That smites the forest, and, without restraint,

li rami schianta, abbatte e porta fori;
  dinanzi polveroso va superbo,
  e fa fuggir le fiere e li pastori.
	The branches rends, beats down, and bears away;
	  Right onward, laden with dust, it goes superb,
	  And puts to flight the wild beasts and the shepherds.

Gli occhi mi sciolse e disse: ""Or drizza il nerbo
  del viso su per quella schiuma antica
  per indi ove quel fummo e` piu` acerbo"".
	Mine eyes he loosed, and said: "Direct the nerve
	  Of vision now along that ancient foam,
	  There yonder where that smoke is most intense."

Come le rane innanzi a la nimica
  biscia per l'acqua si dileguan tutte,
  fin ch'a la terra ciascuna s'abbica,
	Even as the frogs before the hostile serpent
	  Across the water scatter all abroad,
	  Until each one is huddled in the earth.

vid'io piu` di mille anime distrutte   fuggir cosi` dinanzi ad un ch'al passo passava Stige con le piante asciutte.	More than a thousand ruined souls I saw, Thus fleeing from before one who on foot Was passing o'er the Styx with soles unwet.

Dal volto rimovea quell'aere grasso,
  menando la sinistra innanzi spesso;
  e sol di quell'angoscia parea lasso.
	From off his face he fanned that unctuous air,
	  Waving his left hand oft in front of him,
	  And only with that anguish seemed he weary.

Ben m'accorsi ch'elli era da ciel messo,
  e volsimi al maestro; e quei fe' segno
  ch'i' stessi queto ed inchinassi ad esso.
	Well I perceived one sent from Heaven was he,
	  And to the Master turned; and he made sign
	  That I should quiet stand, and bow before him.

Ahi quanto mi parea pien di disdegno!
  Venne a la porta, e con una verghetta
  l'aperse, che non v'ebbe alcun ritegno.
	Ah! how disdainful he appeared to me!
	  He reached the gate, and with a little rod
	  He opened it, for there was no resistance.

""O cacciati del ciel, gente dispetta"",
  comincio` elli in su l'orribil soglia,
  ""ond'esta oltracotanza in voi s'alletta?
	"O banished out of Heaven, people despised!"
	  Thus he began upon the horrid threshold;
	  "Whence is this arrogance within you couched?

Perche' recalcitrate a quella voglia
  a cui non puote il fin mai esser mozzo,
  e che piu` volte v'ha cresciuta doglia?
	Wherefore recalcitrate against that will,
	  From which the end can never be cut off,
	  And which has many times increased your pain?

Che giova ne le fata dar di cozzo?
  Cerbero vostro, se ben vi ricorda,
  ne porta ancor pelato il mento e 'l gozzo"".
	What helpeth it to butt against the fates?
	  Your Cerberus, if you remember well,
	  For that still bears his chin and gullet peeled."

Poi si rivolse per la strada lorda,
  e non fe' motto a noi, ma fe' sembiante
  d'omo cui altra cura stringa e morda

che quella di colui che li e` davante;
  e noi movemmo i piedi inver' la terra,
  sicuri appresso le parole sante.

Dentro li 'ntrammo sanz'alcuna guerra;
  e io, ch'avea di riguardar disio
  la condizion che tal fortezza serra,

com'io fui dentro, l'occhio intorno invio;
  e veggio ad ogne man grande campagna
  piena di duolo e di tormento rio.

Si` come ad Arli, ove Rodano stagna,
  si` com'a Pola, presso del Carnaro
  ch'Italia chiude e suoi termini bagna,

fanno i sepulcri tutt'il loco varo,
  cosi` facevan quivi d'ogne parte,
  salvo che 'l modo v'era piu` amaro;

che' tra gli avelli fiamme erano sparte,
  per le quali eran si` del tutto accesi,
  che ferro piu` non chiede verun'arte.

Tutti li lor coperchi eran sospesi,
  e fuor n'uscivan si` duri lamenti,
  che ben parean di miseri e d'offesi.

E io: ““Maestro, quai son quelle genti
  che, seppellite dentro da quell'arche,
  si fan sentir coi sospiri dolenti?”“.

Ed elli a me: ““Qui son li eresiarche
  con lor seguaci, d'ogne setta, e molto
  piu` che non credi son le tombe carche.

Simile qui con simile e` sepolto,
  e i monimenti son piu` e men caldi”“.
  E poi ch'a la man destra si fu volto,

passammo tra i martiri e li alti spaldi.

Then he returned along the miry road,
  And spake no word to us, but had the look
  Of one whom other care constrains and goads

Than that of him who in his presence is;
  And we our feet directed tow'rds the city,
  After those holy words all confident.

Within we entered without any contest;
  And I, who inclination had to see
  What the condition such a fortress holds,

Soon as I was within, cast round mine eye,
  And see on every hand an ample plain,
  Full of distress and torment terrible.

Even as at Arles, where stagnant grows the Rhone,
  Even as at Pola near to the Quarnaro,
  That shuts in Italy and bathes its borders,

The sepulchres make all the place uneven;
  So likewise did they there on every side,
  Saving that there the manner was more bitter;

For flames between the sepulchres were scattered,
  By which they so intensely heated were,
  That iron more so asks not any art.

All of their coverings uplifted were,
  And from them issued forth such dire laments,
  Sooth seemed they of the wretched and tormented.

And I: "My Master, what are all those people
  Who, having sepulture within those tombs,
  Make themselves audible by doleful sighs?"

And he to me: "Here are the Heresiarchs,
  With their disciples of all sects, and much
  More than thou thinkest laden are the tombs.

Here like together with its like is buried;
  And more and less the monuments are heated."
  And when he to the right had turned, we passed

Between the torments and high parapets.

40

Inferno: Canto X

Farinata and Cavalcante de' Cavalcanti. Discourse on the Knowledge of the Damned.

Ora sen va per un secreto calle,
 tra 'l muro de la terra e li martiri,
 lo mio maestro, e io dopo le spalle.

""O virtu` somma, che per li empi giri
 mi volvi""', cominciai, ""com'a te piace,
 parlami, e sodisfammi a' miei disiri.

La gente che per li sepolcri giace
 potrebbesi veder? gia` son levati
 tutt'i coperchi, e nessun guardia face""'.

E quelli a me: ""Tutti saran serrati
 quando di Iosafat qui torneranno
 coi corpi che la` su` hanno lasciati.

Suo cimitero da questa parte hanno
 con Epicuro tutti suoi seguaci,
 che l'anima col corpo morta fanno.

Pero` a la dimanda che mi faci
 quinc'entro satisfatto sara` tosto,
 e al disio ancor che tu mi taci""'.

E io: ""Buon duca, non tegno riposto
 a te mio cuor se non per dicer poco,
 e tu m'hai non pur mo a cio` disposto""'.

""O Tosco che per la citta` del foco
 vivo ten vai cosi` parlando onesto,
 piacciati di restare in questo loco.

La tua loquela ti fa manifesto
 di quella nobil patria natio
 a la qual forse fui troppo molesto""'.

Now onward goes, along a narrow path
 Between the torments and the city wall,
 My Master, and I follow at his back.

"O power supreme, that through these impious circles
 Turnest me," I began, "as pleases thee,
 Speak to me, and my longings satisfy;

The people who are lying in these tombs,
 Might they be seen? already are uplifted
 The covers all, and no one keepeth guard."

And he to me: "They all will be closed up
 When from Jehoshaphat they shall return
 Here with the bodies they have left above.

Their cemetery have upon this side
 With Epicurus all his followers,
 Who with the body mortal make the soul;

But in the question thou dost put to me,
 Within here shalt thou soon be satisfied,
 And likewise in the wish thou keepest silent."

And I: "Good Leader, I but keep concealed
 From thee my heart, that I may speak the less,
 Nor only now hast thou thereto disposed me."

"O Tuscan, thou who through the city of fire
 Goest alive, thus speaking modestly,
 Be pleased to stay thy footsteps in this place.

Thy mode of speaking makes thee manifest
 A native of that noble fatherland,
 To which perhaps I too molestful was."

Subitamente questo suono uscio
  d'una de l'arche; pero` m'accostai,
  temendo, un poco piu` al duca mio.

Ed el mi disse: ""Volgiti! Che fai?
  Vedi la` Farinata che s'e` dritto:
  da la cintola in su` tutto 'l vedrai"".

Io avea gia` il mio viso nel suo fitto;
  ed el s'ergea col petto e con la fronte
  com'avesse l'inferno a gran dispitto.

E l'animose man del duca e pronte
  mi pinser tra le sepulture a lui,
  dicendo: ""Le parole tue sien conte"".

Com'io al pie` de la sua tomba fui,
  guardommi un poco, e poi, quasi sdegnoso,
  mi dimando`: ""Chi fuor li maggior tui?"".

Io ch'era d'ubidir disideroso,
  non gliel celai, ma tutto gliel'apersi;
  ond'ei levo` le ciglia un poco in suso;

poi disse: ""Fieramente furo avversi
  a me e a miei primi e a mia parte,
  si` che per due fiate li dispersi"".

""S'ei fur cacciati, ei tornar d'ogne parte"",
  rispuos'io lui, ""l'una e l'altra fiata;
  ma i vostri non appreser ben quell'arte"".

Allor surse a la vista scoperchiata
  un'ombra, lungo questa, infino al mento:
  credo che s'era in ginocchie levata.

Dintorno mi guardo`, come talento
  avesse di veder s'altri era meco;
  e poi che 'l sospecciar fu tutto spento,

piangendo disse: ""Se per questo cieco
  carcere vai per altezza d'ingegno,
  mio figlio ov'e`? e perche' non e` teco?"".

E io a lui: ""Da me stesso non vegno:
  colui ch'attende la`, per qui mi mena
  forse cui Guido vostro ebbe a disdegno"".

Le sue parole e 'l modo de la pena
  m'avean di costui gia` letto il nome;
  pero` fu la risposta cosi` piena.

Upon a sudden issued forth this sound
  From out one of the tombs; wherefore I pressed,
  Fearing, a little nearer to my Leader.

And unto me he said: "Turn thee; what dost thou?
  Behold there Farinata who has risen;
  From the waist upwards wholly shalt thou see him."

I had already fixed mine eyes on his,
  And he uprose erect with breast and front
  E'en as if Hell he had in great despite.

And with courageous hands and prompt my Leader
  Thrust me between the sepulchres towards him,
  Exclaiming, "Let thy words explicit be."

As soon as I was at the foot of his tomb
  Somewhat he eyed me, and, as if disdainful,
  Then asked of me, "Who were thine ancestors?"

I, who desirous of obeying was,
  Concealed it not, but all revealed to him;
  Whereat he raised his brows a little upward.

Then said he: "Fiercely adverse have they been
  To me, and to my fathers, and my party;
  So that two several times I scattered them."

"If they were banished, they returned on all sides,"
  I answered him, "the first time and the second;
  But yours have not acquired that art aright."

Then there uprose upon the sight, uncovered
  Down to the chin, a shadow at his side;
  I think that he had risen on his knees.

Round me he gazed, as if solicitude
  He had to see if some one else were with me,
  But after his suspicion was all spent,

Weeping, he said to me: "If through this blind
  Prison thou goest by loftiness of genius,
  Where is my son? and why is he not with thee?"

And I to him: "I come not of myself;
  He who is waiting yonder leads me here,
  Whom in disdain perhaps your Guido had."

His language and the mode of punishment
  Already unto me had read his name;
  On that account my answer was so full.

Di subito drizzato grido`: ““Come?
  dicesti "elli ebbe"? non viv'elli ancora?
  non fiere li occhi suoi lo dolce lume?”“.

Quando s'accorse d'alcuna dimora
  ch'io facea dinanzi a la risposta,
  supin ricadde e piu` non parve fora.

Ma quell'altro magnanimo, a cui posta
  restato m'era, non muto` aspetto,
  ne' mosse collo, ne' piego` sua costa:

e se' continuando al primo detto,
  ”“S'elli han quell'arte”“, disse, ““male appresa,
  cio` mi tormenta piu` che questo letto.

Ma non cinquanta volte fia raccesa
  la faccia de la donna che qui regge,
  che tu saprai quanto quell'arte pesa.

E se tu mai nel dolce mondo regge,
  dimmi: perche' quel popolo e` si` empio
  incontr'a' miei in ciascuna sua legge?”“.

Ond'io a lui: ““Lo strazio e 'l grande scempio
  che fece l'Arbia colorata in rosso,
  tal orazion fa far nel nostro tempio”“.

Poi ch'ebbe sospirando il capo mosso,
  ”“A cio` non fu' io sol”“, disse, ““ne' certo
  sanza cagion con li altri sarei mosso.

Ma fu' io solo, la` dove sofferto
  fu per ciascun di torre via Fiorenza,
  colui che la difesi a viso aperto”“.

““Deh, se riposi mai vostra semenza”“,
  prega' io lui, ““solvetemi quel nodo
  che qui ha 'nviluppata mia sentenza.

El par che voi veggiate, se ben odo,
  dinanzi quel che 'l tempo seco adduce,
  e nel presente tenete altro modo”“.

““Noi veggiam, come quei c'ha mala luce,
  le cose”“, disse, ““che ne son lontano;
  cotanto ancor ne splende il sommo duce.

Quando s'appressano o son, tutto e` vano
  nostro intelletto; e s'altri non ci apporta,
  nulla sapem di vostro stato umano.

Up starting suddenly, he cried out: "How
  Saidst thou,—he had? Is he not still alive?
  Does not the sweet light strike upon his eyes?"

When he became aware of some delay,
  Which I before my answer made, supine
  He fell again, and forth appeared no more.

But the other, magnanimous, at whose desire
  I had remained, did not his aspect change,
  Neither his neck he moved, nor bent his side.

"And if," continuing his first discourse,
  "They have that art," he said, "not learned aright,
  That more tormenteth me, than doth this bed.

But fifty times shall not rekindled be
  The countenance of the Lady who reigns here,
  Ere thou shalt know how heavy is that art;

And as thou wouldst to the sweet world return,
  Say why that people is so pitiless
  Against my race in each one of its laws?"

Whence I to him: "The slaughter and great carnage
  Which have with crimson stained the Arbia, cause
  Such orisons in our temple to be made."

After his head he with a sigh had shaken,
  "There I was not alone," he said, "nor surely
  Without a cause had with the others moved.

But there I was alone, where every one
  Consented to the laying waste of Florence,
  He who defended her with open face."

"Ah! so hereafter may your seed repose,"
  I him entreated, "solve for me that knot,
  Which has entangled my conceptions here.

It seems that you can see, if I hear rightly,
  Beforehand whatsoe'er time brings with it,
  And in the present have another mode."

"We see, like those who have imperfect sight,
  The things," he said, "that distant are from us;
  So much still shines on us the Sovereign Ruler.

When they draw near, or are, is wholly vain
  Our intellect, and if none brings it to us,
  Not anything know we of your human state.

Pero` comprender puoi che tutta morta
  fia nostra conoscenza da quel punto
  che del futuro fia chiusa la porta"".

Allor, come di mia colpa compunto,
  dissi: ""Or direte dunque a quel caduto
  che 'l suo nato e` co'vivi ancor congiunto;

e s'i' fui, dianzi, a la risposta muto,
  fate i saper che 'l fei perche' pensava
  gia` ne l'error che m'avete soluto"".

E gia` 'l maestro mio mi richiamava;
  per ch'i' pregai lo spirto piu` avaccio
  che mi dicesse chi con lu' istava.

Dissemi: ""Qui con piu` di mille giaccio:
  qua dentro e` 'l secondo Federico,
  e 'l Cardinale; e de li altri mi taccio"".

Indi s'ascose; e io inver' l'antico
  poeta volsi i passi, ripensando
  a quel parlar che mi parea nemico.

Elli si mosse; e poi, cosi` andando,
  mi disse: ""Perche' se' tu si` smarrito?"".
  E io li sodisfeci al suo dimando.

""La mente tua conservi quel ch'udito
  hai contra te"", mi comando` quel saggio.
  ""E ora attendi qui"", e drizzo` 'l dito:

""quando sarai dinanzi al dolce raggio
  di quella il cui bell'occhio tutto vede,
  da lei saprai di tua vita il viaggio"".

Appresso mosse a man sinistra il piede:
  lasciammo il muro e gimmo inver' lo mezzo
  per un sentier ch'a una valle fiede,

che 'nfin la` su` facea spiacer suo lezzo.

Hence thou canst understand, that wholly dead
  Will be our knowledge from the moment when
  The portal of the future shall be closed."

Then I, as if compunctious for my fault,
  Said: "Now, then, you will tell that fallen one,
  That still his son is with the living joined.

And if just now, in answering, I was dumb,
  Tell him I did it because I was thinking
  Already of the error you have solved me."

And now my Master was recalling me,
  Wherefore more eagerly I prayed the spirit
  That he would tell me who was with him there.

He said: "With more than a thousand here I lie;
  Within here is the second Frederick,
  And the Cardinal, and of the rest I speak not."

Thereon he hid himself; and I towards
  The ancient poet turned my steps, reflecting
  Upon that saying, which seemed hostile to me.

He moved along; and afterward thus going,
  He said to me, "Why art thou so bewildered?"
  And I in his inquiry satisfied him.

"Let memory preserve what thou hast heard
  Against thyself," that Sage commanded me,
  "And now attend here;" and he raised his finger.

"When thou shalt be before the radiance sweet
  Of her whose beauteous eyes all things behold,
  From her thou'lt know the journey of thy life."

Unto the left hand then he turned his feet;
  We left the wall, and went towards the middle,
  Along a path that strikes into a valley,

Which even up there unpleasant made its stench.

Inferno: Canto XI

The Broken Rocks. Pope Anastasius. General Description of the Inferno and its Divisions.

In su l'estremita` d'un'alta ripa
  che facevan gran pietre rotte in cerchio
  venimmo sopra piu` crudele stipa;

e quivi, per l'orribile soperchio
  del puzzo che 'l profondo abisso gitta,
  ci raccostammo, in dietro, ad un coperchio

d'un grand'avello, ov'io vidi una scritta
  che dicea: "Anastasio papa guardo,
  lo qual trasse Fotin de la via dritta".

““Lo nostro scender conviene esser tardo,
  si` che s'ausi un poco in prima il senso
  al tristo fiato; e poi no i fia riguardo”“.

Cosi` 'l maestro; e io ““Alcun compenso”“,
  dissi lui, ““trova che 'l tempo non passi
  perduto”“. Ed elli: ““Vedi ch'a cio` penso”“.

““Figliuol mio, dentro da cotesti sassi”“,
  comincio` poi a dir, ““son tre cerchietti
  di grado in grado, come que' che lassi.

Tutti son pien di spirti maladetti;
  ma perche' poi ti basti pur la vista,
  intendi come e perche' son costretti.

D'ogne malizia, ch'odio in cielo acquista,
  ingiuria e` 'l fine, ed ogne fin cotale
  o con forza o con frode altrui contrista.

Ma perche' frode e` de l'uom proprio male,
  piu` spiace a Dio; e pero` stan di sotto
  li frodolenti, e piu` dolor li assale.

Upon the margin of a lofty bank
  Which great rocks broken in a circle made,
  We came upon a still more cruel throng;

And there, by reason of the horrible
  Excess of stench the deep abyss throws out,
  We drew ourselves aside behind the cover

Of a great tomb, whereon I saw a writing,
  Which said: "Pope Anastasius I hold,
  Whom out of the right way Photinus drew."

"Slow it behoveth our descent to be,
  So that the sense be first a little used
  To the sad blast, and then we shall not heed it."

The Master thus; and unto him I said,
  "Some compensation find, that the time pass not
  Idly;" and he: "Thou seest I think of that.

My son, upon the inside of these rocks,"
  Began he then to say, "are three small circles,
  From grade to grade, like those which thou art leaving.

They all are full of spirits maledict;
  But that hereafter sight alone suffice thee,
  Hear how and wherefore they are in constraint.

Of every malice that wins hate in Heaven,
  Injury is the end; and all such end
  Either by force or fraud afflicteth others.

But because fraud is man's peculiar vice,
  More it displeases God; and so stand lowest
  The fraudulent, and greater dole assails them.

Di violenti il primo cerchio e` tutto;
  ma perche' si fa forza a tre persone,
  in tre gironi e` distinto e costrutto.

A Dio, a se', al prossimo si pone
  far forza, dico in loro e in lor cose,
  come udirai con aperta ragione.

Morte per forza e ferute dogliose
  nel prossimo si danno, e nel suo avere
  ruine, incendi e tollette dannose;

onde omicide e ciascun che mal fiere,
  guastatori e predon, tutti tormenta
  lo giron primo per diverse schiere.

Puote omo avere in se' man violenta
  e ne' suoi beni; e pero` nel secondo
  giron convien che sanza pro si penta

qualunque priva se' del vostro mondo,
  biscazza e fonde la sua facultade,
  e piange la` dov'esser de' giocondo.

Puossi far forza nella deitade,
  col cor negando e bestemmiando quella,
  e spregiando natura e sua bontade;

e pero` lo minor giron suggella
  del segno suo e Soddoma e Caorsa
  e chi, spregiando Dio col cor, favella.

La frode, ond'ogne coscienza e` morsa,
  puo` l'omo usare in colui che 'n lui fida
  e in quel che fidanza non imborsa.

Questo modo di retro par ch'incida
  pur lo vinco d'amor che fa natura;
  onde nel cerchio secondo s'annida

ipocresia, lusinghe e chi affattura,
  falsita`, ladroneccio e simonia,
  ruffian, baratti e simile lordura.

Per l'altro modo quell'amor s'oblia
  che fa natura, e quel ch'e` poi aggiunto,
  di che la fede spezial si cria;

onde nel cerchio minore, ov'e` 'l punto
  de l'universo in su che Dite siede,
  qualunque trade in etterno e` consunto"".

All the first circle of the Violent is;
  But since force may be used against three persons,
  In three rounds 'tis divided and constructed.

To God, to ourselves, and to our neighbour can we
  Use force; I say on them and on their things,
  As thou shalt hear with reason manifest.

A death by violence, and painful wounds,
  Are to our neighbour given; and in his substance
  Ruin, and arson, and injurious levies;

Whence homicides, and he who smites unjustly,
  Marauders, and freebooters, the first round
  Tormenteth all in companies diverse.

Man may lay violent hands upon himself
  And his own goods; and therefore in the second
  Round must perforce without avail repent

Whoever of your world deprives himself,
  Who games, and dissipates his property,
  And weepeth there, where he should jocund be.

Violence can be done the Deity,
  In heart denying and blaspheming Him,
  And by disdaining Nature and her bounty.

And for this reason doth the smallest round
  Seal with its signet Sodom and Cahors,
  And who, disdaining God, speaks from the heart.

Fraud, wherewithal is every conscience stung,
  A man may practise upon him who trusts,
  And him who doth no confidence imburse.

This latter mode, it would appear, dissevers
  Only the bond of love which Nature makes;
  Wherefore within the second circle nestle

Hypocrisy, flattery, and who deals in magic,
  Falsification, theft, and simony,
  Panders, and barrators, and the like filth.

By the other mode, forgotten is that love
  Which Nature makes, and what is after added,
  From which there is a special faith engendered.

Hence in the smallest circle, where the point is
  Of the Universe, upon which Dis is seated,
  Whoe'er betrays for ever is consumed."

E io: ""Maestro, assai chiara procede
 la tua ragione, e assai ben distingue
 questo baratro e 'l popol ch'e' possiede.

Ma dimmi: quei de la palude pingue,
 che mena il vento, e che batte la pioggia,
 e che s'incontran con si` aspre lingue,

perche' non dentro da la citta` roggia
 sono ei puniti, se Dio li ha in ira?
 e se non li ha, perche' sono a tal foggia?"".

Ed elli a me ""Perche' tanto delira"",
 disse ""lo 'ngegno tuo da quel che sole?
 o ver la mente dove altrove mira?

Non ti rimembra di quelle parole
 con le quai la tua Etica pertratta
 le tre disposizion che 'l ciel non vole,

incontenenza, malizia e la matta
 bestialitade? e come incontenenza
 men Dio offende e men biasimo accatta?

Se tu riguardi ben questa sentenza,
 e rechiti a la mente chi son quelli
 che su` di fuor sostegnon penitenza,

tu vedrai ben perche' da questi felli
 sien dipartiti, e perche' men crucciata
 la divina vendetta li martelli"".

""O sol che sani ogni vista turbata,
 tu mi contenti si` quando tu solvi,
 che, non men che saver, dubbiar m'aggrata.

Ancora in dietro un poco ti rivolvi"",
 diss'io, ""la` dove di' ch'usura offende
 la divina bontade, e 'l groppo solvi"".

""Filosofia"", mi disse, ""a chi la 'ntende,
 nota, non pure in una sola parte,
 come natura lo suo corso prende

dal divino 'ntelletto e da sua arte;
 e se tu ben la tua Fisica note,
 tu troverai, non dopo molte carte,

And I: "My Master, clear enough proceeds
 Thy reasoning, and full well distinguishes
 This cavern and the people who possess it.

But tell me, those within the fat lagoon,
 Whom the wind drives, and whom the rain doth beat,
 And who encounter with such bitter tongues,

Wherefore are they inside of the red city
 Not punished, if God has them in his wrath,
 And if he has not, wherefore in such fashion?"

And unto me he said: "Why wanders so
 Thine intellect from that which it is wont?
 Or, sooth, thy mind where is it elsewhere looking?

Hast thou no recollection of those words
 With which thine Ethics thoroughly discusses
 The dispositions three, that Heaven abides not,—

Incontinence, and Malice, and insane
 Bestiality? and how Incontinence
 Less God offendeth, and less blame attracts?

If thou regardest this conclusion well,
 And to thy mind recallest who they are
 That up outside are undergoing penance,

Clearly wilt thou perceive why from these felons
 They separated are, and why less wroth
 Justice divine doth smite them with its hammer."

"O Sun, that healest all distempered vision,
 Thou dost content me so, when thou resolvest,
 That doubting pleases me no less than knowing!

Once more a little backward turn thee," said I,
 "There where thou sayest that usury offends
 Goodness divine, and disengage the knot."

"Philosophy," he said, "to him who heeds it,
 Noteth, not only in one place alone,
 After what manner Nature takes her course

From Intellect Divine, and from its art;
 And if thy Physics carefully thou notest,
 After not many pages shalt thou find,

che l'arte vostra quella, quanto pote,
  segue, come 'l maestro fa 'l discente;
  si` che vostr'arte a Dio quasi e` nepote.

Da queste due, se tu ti rechi a mente
  lo Genesi` dal principio, convene
  prender sua vita e avanzar la gente;

e perche' l'usuriere altra via tene,
  per se' natura e per la sua seguace
  dispregia, poi ch'in altro pon la spene.

Ma seguimi oramai, che 'l gir mi piace;
  che' i Pesci guizzan su per l'orizzonta,
  e 'l Carro tutto sovra 'l Coro giace,

e 'l balzo via la` oltra si dismonta"".

That this your art as far as possible
  Follows, as the disciple doth the master;
  So that your art is, as it were, God's grandchild.

From these two, if thou bringest to thy mind
  Genesis at the beginning, it behoves
  Mankind to gain their life and to advance;

And since the usurer takes another way,
  Nature herself and in her follower
  Disdains he, for elsewhere he puts his hope.

But follow, now, as I would fain go on,
  For quivering are the Fishes on the horizon,
  And the Wain wholly over Caurus lies,

And far beyond there we descend the crag."

Inferno: Canto XII

The Minotaur. The Seventh Circle: The Violent. The River Phlegethon. The Violent against their Neighbours. The Centaurs. Tyrants.

Era lo loco ov'a scender la riva
  venimmo, alpestro e, per quel che v'er'anco,
  tal, ch'ogne vista ne sarebbe schiva.
	The place where to descend the bank we came
	  Was alpine, and from what was there, moreover,
	  Of such a kind that every eye would shun it.

Qual e` quella ruina che nel fianco
  di qua da Trento l'Adice percosse,
  o per tremoto o per sostegno manco,
	Such as that ruin is which in the flank
	  Smote, on this side of Trent, the Adige,
	  Either by earthquake or by failing stay,

che da cima del monte, onde si mosse,
  al piano e` si` la roccia discoscesa,
  ch'alcuna via darebbe a chi su` fosse:
	For from the mountain's top, from which it moved,
	  Unto the plain the cliff is shattered so,
	  Some path 'twould give to him who was above;

cotal di quel burrato era la scesa;
  e 'n su la punta de la rotta lacca
  l'infamia di Creti era distesa
	Even such was the descent of that ravine,
	  And on the border of the broken chasm
	  The infamy of Crete was stretched along,

che fu concetta ne la falsa vacca;
  e quando vide noi, se' stesso morse,
  si` come quei cui l'ira dentro fiacca.
	Who was conceived in the fictitious cow;
	  And when he us beheld, he bit himself,
	  Even as one whom anger racks within.

Lo savio mio inver' lui grido`: ""Forse   tu credi che qui sia 'l duca d'Atene,   che su` nel mondo la morte ti porse?	My Sage towards him shouted: "Peradventure Thou think'st that here may be the Duke of Athens, Who in the world above brought death to thee?

Partiti, bestia: che' questi non vene
  ammaestrato da la tua sorella,
  ma vassi per veder le vostre pene""".
	Get thee gone, beast, for this one cometh not
	  Instructed by thy sister, but he comes
	  In order to behold your punishments."

Qual e` quel toro che si slaccia in quella   c'ha ricevuto gia` 'l colpo mortale, che gir non sa, ma qua e la` saltella,	As is that bull who breaks loose at the moment In which he has received the mortal blow, Who cannot walk, but staggers here and there,
vid'io lo Minotauro far cotale; e quello accorto grido`: ""Corri al varco:   mentre ch'e' 'nfuria, e` buon che tu ti cale""".	The Minotaur beheld I do the like; And he, the wary, cried: "Run to the passage; While he wroth, 'tis well thou shouldst descend."

Così prendemmo via giù per lo scarco
  di quelle pietre, che spesso moviensi
  sotto i miei piedi per lo novo carco.

Io gia pensando; e quei disse: ““Tu pensi
  forse a questa ruina ch'e` guardata
  da quell'ira bestial ch'i' ora spensi.

Or vo' che sappi che l'altra fiata
  ch'i' discesi qua giù nel basso inferno,
  questa roccia non era ancor cascata.

Ma certo poco pria, se ben discerno,
  che venisse colui che la gran preda
  levo` a Dite del cerchio superno,

da tutte parti l'alta valle feda
  tremo` si`, ch'i' pensai che l'universo
  sentisse amor, per lo qual e` chi creda

piu` volte il mondo in caosso converso;
  e in quel punto questa vecchia roccia
  qui e altrove, tal fece riverso.

Ma ficca li occhi a valle, che' s'approccia
  la riviera del sangue in la qual bolle
  qual che per violenza in altrui noccia”“.

Oh cieca cupidigia e ira folle,
  che si` ci sproni ne la vita corta,
  e ne l'etterna poi si` mal c'immolle!

Io vidi un'ampia fossa in arco torta,
  come quella che tutto 'l piano abbraccia,
  secondo ch'avea detto la mia scorta;

e tra 'l pie` de la ripa ed essa, in traccia
  corrien centauri, armati di saette,
  come solien nel mondo andare a caccia.

Veggendoci calar, ciascun ristette,
  e de la schiera tre si dipartiro
  con archi e asticciuole prima elette;

e l'un gridò da lungi: ““A qual martiro
  venite voi che scendete la costa?
  Ditel costinci; se non, l'arco tiro”“.

Thus down we took our way o'er that discharge
  Of stones, which oftentimes did move themselves
  Beneath my feet, from the unwonted burden.

Thoughtful I went; and he said: "Thou art thinking
  Perhaps upon this ruin, which is guarded
  By that brute anger which just now I quenched.

Now will I have thee know, the other time
  I here descended to the nether Hell,
  This precipice had not yet fallen down.

But truly, if I well discern, a little
  Before His coming who the mighty spoil
  Bore off from Dis, in the supernal circle,

Upon all sides the deep and loathsome valley
  Trembled so, that I thought the Universe
  Was thrilled with love, by which there are who
    think

The world ofttimes converted into chaos;
  And at that moment this primeval crag
  Both here and elsewhere made such overthrow.

But fix thine eyes below; for draweth near
  The river of blood, within which boiling is
  Whoe'er by violence doth injure others."

O blind cupidity, O wrath insane,
  That spurs us onward so in our short life,
  And in the eternal then so badly steeps us!

I saw an ample moat bent like a bow,
  As one which all the plain encompasses,
  Conformable to what my Guide had said.

And between this and the embankment's foot
  Centaurs in file were running, armed with arrows,
  As in the world they used the chase to follow.

Beholding us descend, each one stood still,
  And from the squadron three detached themselves,
  With bows and arrows in advance selected;

And from afar one cried: "Unto what torment
  Come ye, who down the hillside are descending?
  Tell us from there; if not, I draw the bow."

Lo mio maestro disse: ""La risposta
  farem noi a Chiron costa` di presso:
  mal fu la voglia tua sempre si` tosta"".

Poi mi tento`, e disse: ""Quelli e` Nesso,
  che mori` per la bella Deianira
  e fe' di se' la vendetta elli stesso.

E quel di mezzo, ch'al petto si mira,
  e` il gran Chiron, il qual nodri` Achille;
  quell'altro e` Folo, che fu si` pien d'ira.

Dintorno al fosso vanno a mille a mille,
  saettando qual anima si svelle
  del sangue piu` che sua colpa sortille"".

Noi ci appressammo a quelle fiere isnelle:
  Chiron prese uno strale, e con la cocca
  fece la barba in dietro a le mascelle.

Quando s'ebbe scoperta la gran bocca,
  disse a' compagni: ""Siete voi accorti
  che quel di retro move cio` ch'el tocca?

Cosi` non soglion far li pie` d'i morti"".
  E 'l mio buon duca, che gia` li er'al petto,
  dove le due nature son consorti,

rispuose: ""Ben e` vivo, e si` soletto
  mostrar li mi convien la valle buia;
  necessita` 'l ci 'nduce, e non diletto.

Tal si parti` da cantare alleluia
  che mi commise quest'officio novo:
  non e` ladron, ne' io anima fuia.

Ma per quella virtu` per cu' io movo
  li passi miei per si` selvaggia strada,
  danne un de' tuoi, a cui noi siamo a provo,

e che ne mostri la` dove si guada
  e che porti costui in su la groppa,
  che' non e` spirto che per l'aere vada"".

Chiron si volse in su la destra poppa,
  e disse a Nesso: ""Torna, e si` li guida,
  e fa cansar s'altra schiera v'intoppa"".

Or ci movemmo con la scorta fida
  lungo la proda del bollor vermiglio,
  dove i bolliti facieno alte strida.

My Master said: "Our answer will we make
  To Chiron, near you there; in evil hour,
  That will of thine was evermore so hasty."

Then touched he me, and said: "This one is Nessus,
  Who perished for the lovely Dejanira,
  And for himself, himself did vengeance take.

And he in the midst, who at his breast is gazing,
  Is the great Chiron, who brought up Achilles;
  That other Pholus is, who was so wrathful.

Thousands and thousands go about the moat
  Shooting with shafts whatever soul emerges
  Out of the blood, more than his crime allots."

Near we approached unto those monsters fleet;
  Chiron an arrow took, and with the notch
  Backward upon his jaws he put his beard.

After he had uncovered his great mouth,
  He said to his companions: "Are you ware
  That he behind moveth whate'er he touches?

Thus are not wont to do the feet of dead men."
  And my good Guide, who now was at his breast,
  Where the two natures are together joined,

Replied: "Indeed he lives, and thus alone
  Me it behoves to show him the dark valley;
  Necessity, and not delight, impels us.

Some one withdrew from singing Halleluja,
  Who unto me committed this new office;
  No thief is he, nor I a thievish spirit.

But by that virtue through which I am moving
  My steps along this savage thoroughfare,
  Give us some one of thine, to be with us,

And who may show us where to pass the ford,
  And who may carry this one on his back;
  For 'tis no spirit that can walk the air."

Upon his right breast Chiron wheeled about,
  And said to Nessus: "Turn and do thou guide them,
  And warn aside, if other band may meet you."

We with our faithful escort onward moved
  Along the brink of the vermilion boiling,
  Wherein the boiled were uttering loud laments.

Io vidi gente sotto infino al ciglio;
  e 'l gran centauro disse: ""E' son tiranni
  che dier nel sangue e ne l'aver di piglio.

Quivi si piangon li spietati danni;
  quivi e` Alessandro, e Dionisio fero,
  che fe' Cicilia aver dolorosi anni.

E quella fronte c'ha 'l pel cosi` nero,
  e` Azzolino; e quell'altro ch'e` biondo,
  e` Opizzo da Esti, il qual per vero

fu spento dal figliastro su` nel mondo"".
  Allor mi volsi al poeta, e quei disse:
  ""Questi ti sia or primo, e io secondo"".

Poco piu` oltre il centauro s'affisse
  sovr'una gente che 'nfino a la gola
  parea che di quel bulicame uscisse.

Mostrocci un'ombra da l'un canto sola,
  dicendo: ""Colui fesse in grembo a Dio
  lo cor che 'n su Tamisi ancor si cola"".

Poi vidi gente che di fuor del rio
  tenean la testa e ancor tutto 'l casso;
  e di costoro assai riconobb'io.

Cosi` a piu` a piu` si facea basso
  quel sangue, si` che cocea pur li piedi;
  e quindi fu del fosso il nostro passo.

""Si` come tu da questa parte vedi
  lo bulicame che sempre si scema"",
  disse 'l centauro, ""voglio che tu credi

che da quest'altra a piu` a piu` giu` prema
  lo fondo suo, infin ch'el si raggiunge
  ove la tirannia convien che gema.

La divina giustizia di qua punge
  quell'Attila che fu flagello in terra
  e Pirro e Sesto; e in etterno munge

le lagrime, che col bollor diserra,
  a Rinier da Corneto, a Rinier Pazzo,
  che fecero a le strade tanta guerra"".

Poi si rivolse, e ripassossi 'l guazzo.

People I saw within up to the eyebrows,
  And the great Centaur said: "Tyrants are these,
  Who dealt in bloodshed and in pillaging.

Here they lament their pitiless mischiefs; here
  Is Alexander, and fierce Dionysius
  Who upon Sicily brought dolorous years.

That forehead there which has the hair so black
  Is Azzolin; and the other who is blond,
  Obizzo is of Esti, who, in truth,

Up in the world was by his stepson slain."
  Then turned I to the Poet; and he said,
  "Now he be first to thee, and second I."

A little farther on the Centaur stopped
  Above a folk, who far down as the throat
  Seemed from that boiling stream to issue forth.

A shade he showed us on one side alone,
  Saying: "He cleft asunder in God's bosom
  The heart that still upon the Thames is honoured."

Then people saw I, who from out the river
  Lifted their heads and also all the chest;
  And many among these I recognised.

Thus ever more and more grew shallower
  That blood, so that the feet alone it covered;
  And there across the moat our passage was.

"Even as thou here upon this side beholdest
  The boiling stream, that aye diminishes,"
  The Centaur said, "I wish thee to believe

That on this other more and more declines
  Its bed, until it reunites itself
  Where it behoveth tyranny to groan.

Justice divine, upon this side, is goading
  That Attila, who was a scourge on earth,
  And Pyrrhus, and Sextus; and for ever milks

The tears which with the boiling it unseals
  In Rinier da Corneto and Rinier Pazzo,
  Who made upon the highways so much war."

Then back he turned, and passed again the ford.

Inferno: Canto XIII

The Wood of Thorns. The Harpies. The Violent against themselves. Suicides. Pier della Vigna. Lano and Jacopo da Sant' Andrea.

Non era ancor di la` Nesso arrivato,
  quando noi ci mettemmo per un bosco
  che da neun sentiero era segnato.

Non fronda verde, ma di color fosco;
  non rami schietti, ma nodosi e 'nvolti;
  non pomi v'eran, ma stecchi con tosco:

non han si` aspri sterpi ne' si` folti
  quelle fiere selvagge che 'n odio hanno
  tra Cecina e Corneto i luoghi colti.

Quivi le brutte Arpie lor nidi fanno,
  che cacciar de le Strofade i Troiani
  con tristo annunzio di futuro danno.

Ali hanno late, e colli e visi umani,
  pie` con artigli, e pennuto 'l gran ventre;
  fanno lamenti in su li alberi strani.

E 'l buon maestro ““Prima che piu` entre,
  sappi che se' nel secondo girone”“,
  mi comincio` a dire, ““e sarai mentre

che tu verrai ne l'orribil sabbione.
  Pero` riguarda ben; si` vederai
  cose che torrien fede al mio sermone”“.

Io sentia d'ogne parte trarre guai,
  e non vedea persona che 'l facesse;
  per ch'io tutto smarrito m'arrestai.

Cred'io ch'ei credette ch'io credesse
  che tante voci uscisser, tra quei bronchi
  da gente che per noi si nascondesse.

Not yet had Nessus reached the other side,
  When we had put ourselves within a wood,
  That was not marked by any path whatever.

Not foliage green, but of a dusky colour,
  Not branches smooth, but gnarled and intertangled,
  Not apple-trees were there, but thorns with poison.

Such tangled thickets have not, nor so dense,
  Those savage wild beasts, that in hatred hold
  'Twixt Cecina and Corneto the tilled places.

There do the hideous Harpies make their nests,
  Who chased the Trojans from the Strophades,
  With sad announcement of impending doom;

Broad wings have they, and necks and faces human,
  And feet with claws, and their great bellies fledged;
  They make laments upon the wondrous trees.

And the good Master: "Ere thou enter farther,
  Know that thou art within the second round,"
  Thus he began to say, "and shalt be, till

Thou comest out upon the horrible sand;
  Therefore look well around, and thou shalt see
  Things that will credence give unto my speech."

I heard on all sides lamentations uttered,
  And person none beheld I who might make them,
  Whence, utterly bewildered, I stood still.

I think he thought that I perhaps might think
  So many voices issued through those trunks
  From people who concealed themselves from us;

Pero` disse 'l maestro: ““Se tu tronchi
  qualche fraschetta d'una d'este piante,
  li pensier c'hai si faran tutti monchi”“.

Allor porsi la mano un poco avante,
  e colsi un ramicel da un gran pruno;
  e 'l tronco suo grido`: ““Perche' mi schiante?”“.

Da che fatto fu poi di sangue bruno,
  ricomincio` a dir: ““Perche' mi scerpi?
  non hai tu spirto di pietade alcuno?

Uomini fummo, e or siam fatti sterpi:
  ben dovrebb'esser la tua man piu` pia,
  se state fossimo anime di serpi”“.

Come d'un stizzo verde ch'arso sia
  da l'un de'capi, che da l'altro geme
  e cigola per vento che va via,

si` de la scheggia rotta usciva insieme
  parole e sangue; ond'io lasciai la cima
  cadere, e stetti come l'uom che teme.

““S'elli avesse potuto creder prima”“,
  rispuose 'l savio mio, ““anima lesa,
  cio` c'ha veduto pur con la mia rima,

non averebbe in te la man distesa;
  ma la cosa incredibile mi fece
  indurlo ad ovra ch'a me stesso pesa.

Ma dilli chi tu fosti, si` che 'n vece
  d'alcun'ammenda tua fama rinfreschi
  nel mondo su`, dove tornar li lece”“.

E 'l tronco: ““Si` col dolce dir m'adeschi,
  ch'i' non posso tacere; e voi non gravi
  perch'io un poco a ragionar m'inveschi.

Io son colui che tenni ambo le chiavi
  del cor di Federigo, e che le volsi,
  serrando e diserrando, si` soavi,

che dal secreto suo quasi ogn'uom tolsi:
  fede portai al glorioso offizio,
  tanto ch'i' ne perde' li sonni e ' polsi.

La meretrice che mai da l'ospizio
  di Cesare non torse li occhi putti,
  morte comune e de le corti vizio,

Therefore the Master said: "If thou break off
  Some little spray from any of these trees,
  The thoughts thou hast will wholly be made vain."

Then stretched I forth my hand a little forward,
  And plucked a branchlet off from a great thorn;
  And the trunk cried, "Why dost thou mangle me?"

After it had become embrowned with blood,
  It recommenced its cry: "Why dost thou rend me?
  Hast thou no spirit of pity whatsoever?

Men once we were, and now are changed to trees;
  Indeed, thy hand should be more pitiful,
  Even if the souls of serpents we had been."

As out of a green brand, that is on fire
  At one of the ends, and from the other drips
  And hisses with the wind that is escaping;

So from that splinter issued forth together
  Both words and blood; whereat I let the tip
  Fall, and stood like a man who is afraid.

"Had he been able sooner to believe,"
  My Sage made answer, "O thou wounded soul,
  What only in my verses he has seen,

Not upon thee had he stretched forth his hand;
  Whereas the thing incredible has caused me
  To put him to an act which grieveth me.

But tell him who thou wast, so that by way
  Of some amends thy fame he may refresh
  Up in the world, to which he can return."

And the trunk said: "So thy sweet words allure me,
  I cannot silent be; and you be vexed not,
  That I a little to discourse am tempted.

I am the one who both keys had in keeping
  Of Frederick's heart, and turned them to and fro
  So softly in unlocking and in locking,

That from his secrets most men I withheld;
  Fidelity I bore the glorious office
  So great, I lost thereby my sleep and pulses.

The courtesan who never from the dwelling
  Of Caesar turned aside her strumpet eyes,
  Death universal and the vice of courts,

infiammo` contra me li animi tutti;
  e li 'nfiammati infiammar si` Augusto,
  che ' lieti onor tornaro in tristi lutti.

L'animo mio, per disdegnoso gusto,
  credendo col morir fuggir disdegno,
  ingiusto fece me contra me giusto.

Per le nove radici d'esto legno
  vi giuro che gia` mai non ruppi fede
  al mio segnor, che fu d'onor si` degno.

E se di voi alcun nel mondo riede,
  conforti la memoria mia, che giace
  ancor del colpo che 'nvidia le diede"".

Un poco attese, e poi ""Da ch'el si tace"",
  disse 'l poeta a me, ""non perder l'ora;
  ma parla, e chiedi a lui, se piu` ti piace"".

Ond'io a lui: ""Domandal tu ancora
  di quel che credi ch'a me satisfaccia;
  ch'i' non potrei, tanta pieta` m'accora"".

Percio` ricomincio`: ""Se l'om ti faccia
  liberamente cio` che 'l tuo dir priega,
  spirito incarcerato, ancor ti piaccia

di dirne come l'anima si lega
  in questi nocchi; e dinne, se tu puoi,
  s'alcuna mai di tai membra si spiega"".

Allor soffio` il tronco forte, e poi
  si converti` quel vento in cotal voce:
  ""Brievemente sara` risposto a voi.

Quando si parte l'anima feroce
  dal corpo ond'ella stessa s'e` disvelta,
  Minos la manda a la settima foce.

Cade in la selva, e non l'e` parte scelta;
  ma la` dove fortuna la balestra,
  quivi germoglia come gran di spelta.

Surge in vermena e in pianta silvestra:
  l'Arpie, pascendo poi de le sue foglie,
  fanno dolore, e al dolor fenestra.

Inflamed against me all the other minds,
  And they, inflamed, did so inflame Augustus,
  That my glad honours turned to dismal mournings.

My spirit, in disdainful exultation,
  Thinking by dying to escape disdain,
  Made me unjust against myself, the just.

I, by the roots unwonted of this wood,
  Do swear to you that never broke I faith
  Unto my lord, who was so worthy of honour;

And to the world if one of you return,
  Let him my memory comfort, which is lying
  Still prostrate from the blow that envy dealt it."

Waited awhile, and then: "Since he is silent,"
  The Poet said to me, "lose not the time,
  But speak, and question him, if more may please
    thee."

Whence I to him: "Do thou again inquire
  Concerning what thou thinks't will satisfy me;
  For I cannot, such pity is in my heart."

Therefore he recommenced: "So may the man
  Do for thee freely what thy speech implores,
  Spirit incarcerate, again be pleased

To tell us in what way the soul is bound
  Within these knots; and tell us, if thou canst,
  If any from such members e'er is freed."

Then blew the trunk amain, and afterward
  The wind was into such a voice converted:
  "With brevity shall be replied to you.

When the exasperated soul abandons
  The body whence it rent itself away,
  Minos consigns it to the seventh abyss.

It falls into the forest, and no part
  Is chosen for it; but where Fortune hurls it,
  There like a grain of spelt it germinates.

It springs a sapling, and a forest tree;
  The Harpies, feeding then upon its leaves,
  Do pain create, and for the pain an outlet.

Come l'altre verrem per nostre spoglie, ma non pero` ch'alcuna sen rivesta,   che' non e` giusto aver cio` ch'om si toglie.	Like others for our spoils shall we return; But not that any one may them revest, For 'tis not just to have what one casts off.

Qui le trascineremo, e per la mesta
  selva saranno i nostri corpi appesi,
  ciascuno al prun de l'ombra sua molesta'''.
	Here we shall drag them, and along the dismal
	  Forest our bodies shall suspended be,
	  Each to the thorn of his molested shade."

Noi eravamo ancora al tronco attesi,
  credendo ch'altro ne volesse dire,
  quando noi fummo d'un romor sorpresi,
	We were attentive still unto the trunk,
	  Thinking that more it yet might wish to tell us,
	  When by a tumult we were overtaken,

similemente a colui che venire
  sente 'l porco e la caccia a la sua posta,
  ch'ode le bestie, e le frasche stormire.
	In the same way as he is who perceives
	  The boar and chase approaching to his stand,
	  Who hears the crashing of the beasts and branches;

Ed ecco due da la sinistra costa,
  nudi e graffiati, fuggendo si` forte,
  che de la selva rompieno ogni rosta.
	And two behold! upon our left-hand side,
	  Naked and scratched, fleeing so furiously,
	  That of the forest, every fan they broke.

Quel dinanzi: ""Or accorri, accorri, morte!"".
  E l'altro, cui pareva tardar troppo,
  gridava: ""Lano, si` non furo accorte
	He who was in advance: "Now help, Death, help!"
	  And the other one, who seemed to lag too much,
	  Was shouting: "Lano, were not so alert

le gambe tue a le giostre dal Toppo!"".
  E poi che forse li fallia la lena,
  di se' e d'un cespuglio fece un groppo.
	Those legs of thine at joustings of the Toppo!"
	  And then, perchance because his breath was failing,
	  He grouped himself together with a bush.

Di rietro a loro era la selva piena
  di nere cagne, bramose e correnti
  come veltri ch'uscisser di catena.
	Behind them was the forest full of black
	  She-mastiffs, ravenous, and swift of foot
	  As greyhounds, who are issuing from the chain.

In quel che s'appiatto` miser li denti,
  e quel dilaceraro a brano a brano;
  poi sen portar quelle membra dolenti.
	On him who had crouched down they set their teeth,
	  And him they lacerated piece by piece,
	  Thereafter bore away those aching members.

Presemi allor la mia scorta per mano,
  e menommi al cespuglio che piangea,
  per le rotture sanguinenti in vano.
	Thereat my Escort took me by the hand,
	  And led me to the bush, that all in vain
	  Was weeping from its bloody lacerations.

""O Iacopo"", dicea, ""da Santo Andrea,
  che t'e` giovato di me fare schermo?
  che colpa ho io de la tua vita rea?"".
	"O Jacopo," it said, "of Sant' Andrea,
	  What helped it thee of me to make a screen?
	  What blame have I in thy nefarious life?"

Quando 'l maestro fu sovr'esso fermo,
  disse ""Chi fosti, che per tante punte
  soffi con sangue doloroso sermo?"".
	When near him had the Master stayed his steps,
	  He said: "Who wast thou, that through wounds so
	      many
	  Art blowing out with blood thy dolorous speech?"

Ed elli a noi: ““O anime che giunte
  siete a veder lo strazio disonesto
  c'ha le mie fronde si` da me disgiunte,

raccoglietele al pie` del tristo cesto.
  I' fui de la citta` che nel Batista
  muto` il primo padrone; ond'ei per questo

sempre con l'arte sua la fara` trista;
  e se non fosse che 'n sul passo d'Arno
  rimane ancor di lui alcuna vista,

que' cittadin che poi la rifondarno
  sovra 'l cener che d'Attila rimase,
  avrebber fatto lavorare indarno.

Io fei gibbetto a me de le mie case”“.

And he to us: "O souls, that hither come
  To look upon the shameful massacre
  That has so rent away from me my leaves,

Gather them up beneath the dismal bush;
  I of that city was which to the Baptist
  Changed its first patron, wherefore he for this

Forever with his art will make it sad.
  And were it not that on the pass of Arno
  Some glimpses of him are remaining still,

Those citizens, who afterwards rebuilt it
  Upon the ashes left by Attila,
  In vain had caused their labour to be done.

Of my own house I made myself a gibbet."

Inferno: Canto XIV

The Sand Waste and the Rain of Fire. The Violent against God. Capaneus. The Statue of Time, and the Four Infernal Rivers.

Poi che la carita` del natio loco
  mi strinse, raunai le fronde sparte,
  e rende'le a colui, ch'era gia` fioco.

Indi venimmo al fine ove si parte
  lo secondo giron dal terzo, e dove
  si vede di giustizia orribil arte.

A ben manifestar le cose nove,
  dico che arrivammo ad una landa
  che dal suo letto ogne pianta rimove.

La dolorosa selva l'e` ghirlanda
  intorno, come 'l fosso tristo ad essa:
  quivi fermammo i passi a randa a randa.

Lo spazzo era una rena arida e spessa,
  non d'altra foggia fatta che colei
  che fu da' pie` di Caton gia` soppressa.

O vendetta di Dio, quanto tu dei
  esser temuta da ciascun che legge
  cio` che fu manifesto a li occhi miei!

D'anime nude vidi molte gregge
  che piangean tutte assai miseramente,
  e parea posta lor diversa legge.

Supin giacea in terra alcuna gente,
  alcuna si sedea tutta raccolta,
  e altra andava continuamente.

Quella che giva intorno era piu` molta,
  e quella men che giacea al tormento,
  ma piu` al duolo avea la lingua sciolta.

Because the charity of my native place
  Constrained me, gathered I the scattered leaves,
  And gave them back to him, who now was hoarse.

Then came we to the confine, where disparted
  The second round is from the third, and where
  A horrible form of Justice is beheld.

Clearly to manifest these novel things,
  I say that we arrived upon a plain,
  Which from its bed rejecteth every plant;

The dolorous forest is a garland to it
  All round about, as the sad moat to that;
  There close upon the edge we stayed our feet.

The soil was of an arid and thick sand,
  Not of another fashion made than that
  Which by the feet of Cato once was pressed.

Vengeance of God, O how much oughtest thou
  By each one to be dreaded, who doth read
  That which was manifest unto mine eyes!

Of naked souls beheld I many herds,
  Who all were weeping very miserably,
  And over them seemed set a law diverse.

Supine upon the ground some folk were lying;
  And some were sitting all drawn up together,
  And others went about continually.

Those who were going round were far the more,
  And those were less who lay down to their torment,
  But had their tongues more loosed to lamentation.

Sovra tutto 'l sabbion, d'un cader lento,
 piovean di foco dilatate falde,
 come di neve in alpe sanza vento.

Quali Alessandro in quelle parti calde
 d'India vide sopra 'l suo stuolo
 fiamme cadere infino a terra salde,

per ch'ei provide a scalpitar lo suolo
 con le sue schiere, accio` che lo vapore
 mei si stingueva mentre ch'era solo:

tale scendeva l'etternale ardore;
 onde la rena s'accendea, com'esca
 sotto focile, a doppiar lo dolore.

Sanza riposo mai era la tresca
 de le misere mani, or quindi or quinci
 escotendo da se' l'arsura fresca.

I' cominciai: ""Maestro, tu che vinci
 tutte le cose, fuor che ' demon duri
 ch'a l'intrar de la porta incontra uscinci,

chi e` quel grande che non par che curi
 lo 'ncendio e giace dispettoso e torto,
 si` che la pioggia non par che 'l marturi?""'.

E quel medesmo, che si fu accorto
 ch'io domandava il mio duca di lui,
 grido`: ""Qual io fui vivo, tal son morto.

Se Giove stanchi 'l suo fabbro da cui
 crucciato prese la folgore aguta
 onde l'ultimo di` percosso fui;

o s'elli stanchi li altri a muta a muta
 in Mongibello a la focina negra,
 chiamando "Buon Vulcano, aiuta, aiuta!",

si` com'el fece a la pugna di Flegra,
 e me saetti con tutta sua forza,
 non ne potrebbe aver vendetta allegra""'.

Allora il duca mio parlo` di forza
 tanto, ch'i' non l'avea si` forte udito:
 ""O Capaneo, in cio` che non s'ammorza

la tua superbia, se' tu piu` punito:
 nullo martiro, fuor che la tua rabbia,
 sarebbe al tuo furor dolor compito""'.

O'er all the sand-waste, with a gradual fall,
 Were raining down dilated flakes of fire,
 As of the snow on Alp without a wind.

As Alexander, in those torrid parts
 Of India, beheld upon his host
 Flames fall unbroken till they reached the ground.

Whence he provided with his phalanxes
 To trample down the soil, because the vapour
 Better extinguished was while it was single;

Thus was descending the eternal heat,
 Whereby the sand was set on fire, like tinder
 Beneath the steel, for doubling of the dole.

Without repose forever was the dance
 Of miserable hands, now there, now here,
 Shaking away from off them the fresh gleeds.

"Master," began I, "thou who overcomest
 All things except the demons dire, that issued
 Against us at the entrance of the gate,

Who is that mighty one who seems to heed not
 The fire, and lieth lowering and disdainful,
 So that the rain seems not to ripen him?"

And he himself, who had become aware
 That I was questioning my Guide about him,
 Cried: "Such as I was living, am I, dead.

If Jove should weary out his smith, from whom
 He seized in anger the sharp thunderbolt,
 Wherewith upon the last day I was smitten,

And if he wearied out by turns the others
 In Mongibello at the swarthy forge,
 Vociferating, 'Help, good Vulcan, help!'

Even as he did there at the fight of Phlegra,
 And shot his bolts at me with all his might,
 He would not have thereby a joyous vengeance."

Then did my Leader speak with such great force,
 That I had never heard him speak so loud:
 "O Capaneus, in that is not extinguished

Thine arrogance, thou punished art the more;
 Not any torment, saving thine own rage,
 Would be unto thy fury pain complete."

Poi si rivolse a me con miglior labbia
  dicendo: ““Quei fu l'un d'i sette regi
  ch'assiser Tebe; ed ebbe e par ch'elli abbia

Dio in disdegno, e poco par che 'l pregi;
  ma, com'io dissi lui, li suoi dispetti
  sono al suo petto assai debiti fregi.

Or mi vien dietro, e guarda che non metti,
  ancor, li piedi ne la rena arsiccia;
  ma sempre al bosco tien li piedi stretti”“.

Tacendo divenimmo la` 've spiccia
  fuor de la selva un picciol fiumicello,
  lo cui rossore ancor mi raccapriccia.

Quale del Bulicame esce ruscello
  che parton poi tra lor le peccatrici,
  tal per la rena giu` sen giva quello.

Lo fondo suo e ambo le pendici
  fatt'era 'n pietra, e ' margini dallato;
  per ch'io m'accorsi che 'l passo era lici.

““Tra tutto l'altro ch'i' t'ho dimostrato,
  poscia che noi intrammo per la porta
  lo cui sogliare a nessuno e` negato,

cosa non fu da li tuoi occhi scorta
  notabile com'e` 'l presente rio,
  che sovra se' tutte fiammelle ammorta”“.

Queste parole fuor del duca mio;
  per ch'io 'l pregai che mi largisse 'l pasto
  di cui largito m'avea il disio.

““In mezzo mar siede un paese guasto”“,
  diss'elli allora, ““che s'appella Creta,
  sotto 'l cui rege fu gia` 'l mondo casto.

Una montagna v'e` che gia` fu lieta
  d'acqua e di fronde, che si chiamo` Ida:
  or e` diserta come cosa vieta.

Rea la scelse gia` per cuna fida
  del suo figliuolo, e per celarlo meglio,
  quando piangea, vi facea far le grida.

Then he turned round to me with better lip,
  Saying: "One of the Seven Kings was he
  Who Thebes besieged, and held, and seems to hold

God in disdain, and little seems to prize him;
  But, as I said to him, his own despites
  Are for his breast the fittest ornaments.

Now follow me, and mind thou do not place
  As yet thy feet upon the burning sand,
  But always keep them close unto the wood."

Speaking no word, we came to where there gushes
  Forth from the wood a little rivulet,
  Whose redness makes my hair still stand on end.

As from the Bulicame springs the brooklet,
  The sinful women later share among them,
  So downward through the sand it went its way.

The bottom of it, and both sloping banks,
  Were made of stone, and the margins at the side;
  Whence I perceived that there the passage was.

"In all the rest which I have shown to thee
  Since we have entered in within the gate
  Whose threshold unto no one is denied,

Nothing has been discovered by thine eyes
  So notable as is the present river,
  Which all the little flames above it quenches."

These words were of my Leader; whence I prayed him
  That he would give me largess of the food,
  For which he had given me largess of desire.

"In the mid-sea there sits a wasted land,"
  Said he thereafterward, "whose name is Crete,
  Under whose king the world of old was chaste.

There is a mountain there, that once was glad
  With waters and with leaves, which was called Ida;
  Now 'tis deserted, as a thing worn out.

Rhea once chose it for the faithful cradle
  Of her own son; and to conceal him better,
  Whene'er he cried, she there had clamours made.

Dentro dal monte sta dritto un gran veglio,
  che tien volte le spalle inver' Dammiata
  e Roma guarda come suo speglio.

La sua testa e` di fin oro formata,
  e puro argento son le braccia e 'l petto,
  poi e` di rame infino a la forcata;

da indi in giuso e` tutto ferro eletto,
  salvo che 'l destro piede e` terra cotta;
  e sta 'n su quel piu` che 'n su l'altro, eretto.

Ciascuna parte, fuor che l'oro, e` rotta
  d'una fessura che lagrime goccia,
  le quali, accolte, foran quella grotta.

Lor corso in questa valle si diroccia:
  fanno Acheronte, Stige e Flegetonta;
  poi sen van giu` per questa stretta doccia

infin, la` ove piu` non si dismonta
  fanno Cocito; e qual sia quello stagno
  tu lo vedrai, pero` qui non si conta"".

E io a lui: ""Se 'l presente rigagno
  si diriva cosi` dal nostro mondo,
  perche' ci appar pur a questo vivagno?"".

Ed elli a me: ""Tu sai che 'l loco e` tondo;
  e tutto che tu sie venuto molto,
  pur a sinistra, giu` calando al fondo,

non se' ancor per tutto il cerchio volto:
  per che, se cosa n'apparisce nova,
  non de' addur maraviglia al tuo volto"".

E io ancor: ""Maestro, ove si trova
  Flegetonta e Lete`? che' de l'un taci,
  e l'altro di' che si fa d'esta piova"".

""In tutte tue question certo mi piaci"",
  rispuose; ""ma 'l bollor de l'acqua rossa
  dovea ben solver l'una che tu faci.

Lete` vedrai, ma fuor di questa fossa,
  la` dove vanno l'anime a lavarsi
  quando la colpa pentuta e` rimossa"".

Poi disse: ""Omai e` tempo da scostarsi
  dal bosco; fa che di retro a me vegne:
  li margini fan via, che non son arsi,

A grand old man stands in the mount erect,
  Who holds his shoulders turned tow'rds Damietta,
  And looks at Rome as if it were his mirror.

His head is fashioned of refined gold,
  And of pure silver are the arms and breast;
  Then he is brass as far down as the fork.

From that point downward all is chosen iron,
  Save that the right foot is of kiln-baked clay,
  And more he stands on that than on the other.

Each part, except the gold, is by a fissure
  Asunder cleft, that dripping is with tears,
  Which gathered together perforate that cavern.

From rock to rock they fall into this valley;
  Acheron, Styx, and Phlegethon they form;
  Then downward go along this narrow sluice

Unto that point where is no more descending.
  They form Cocytus; what that pool may be
  Thou shalt behold, so here 'tis not narrated."

And I to him: "If so the present runnel
  Doth take its rise in this way from our world,
  Why only on this verge appears it to us?"

And he to me: "Thou knowest the place is round,
  And notwithstanding thou hast journeyed far,
  Still to the left descending to the bottom,

Thou hast not yet through all the circle turned.
  Therefore if something new appear to us,
  It should not bring amazement to thy face."

And I again: "Master, where shall be found
  Lethe and Phlegethon, for of one thou'rt silent,
  And sayest the other of this rain is made?"

"In all thy questions truly thou dost please me,"
  Replied he; "but the boiling of the red
  Water might well solve one of them thou makest.

Thou shalt see Lethe, but outside this moat,
  There where the souls repair to lave themselves,
  When sin repented of has been removed."

Then said he: "It is time now to abandon
  The wood; take heed that thou come after me;
  A way the margins make that are not burning,

e sopra loro ogne vapor si spegne"".

And over them all vapours are extinguished."

Inferno: Canto XV

The Violent against Nature. Brunetto Latini.

Ora cen porta l'un de' duri margini;
  e 'l fummo del ruscel di sopra aduggia,
  si` che dal foco salva l'acqua e li argini.

Quali Fiamminghi tra Guizzante e Bruggia,
  temendo 'l fiotto che 'nver lor s'avventa,
  fanno lo schermo perche' 'l mar si fuggia;

e quali Padoan lungo la Brenta,
  per difender lor ville e lor castelli,
  anzi che Carentana il caldo senta:

a tale imagine eran fatti quelli,
  tutto che ne' si` alti ne' si` grossi,
  qual che si fosse, lo maestro felli.

Gia` eravam da la selva rimossi
  tanto, ch'i' non avrei visto dov'era,
  perch'io in dietro rivolto mi fossi,

quando incontrammo d'anime una schiera
  che venian lungo l'argine, e ciascuna
  ci riguardava come suol da sera

guardare uno altro sotto nuova luna;
  e si` ver' noi aguzzavan le ciglia
  come 'l vecchio sartor fa ne la cruna.

Cosi` adocchiato da cotal famiglia,
  fui conosciuto da un, che mi prese
  per lo lembo e grido`: ""Qual maraviglia!"".

E io, quando 'l suo braccio a me distese,
  ficcai li occhi per lo cotto aspetto,
  si` che 'l viso abbrusciato non difese

Now bears us onward one of the hard margins,
  And so the brooklet's mist o'ershadows it,
  From fire it saves the water and the dikes.

Even as the Flemings, 'twixt Cadsand and Bruges,
  Fearing the flood that tow'rds them hurls itself,
  Their bulwarks build to put the sea to flight;

And as the Paduans along the Brenta,
  To guard their villas and their villages,
  Or ever Chiarentana feel the heat;

In such similitude had those been made,
  Albeit not so lofty nor so thick,
  Whoever he might be, the master made them.

Now were we from the forest so remote,
  I could not have discovered where it was,
  Even if backward I had turned myself,

When we a company of souls encountered,
  Who came beside the dike, and every one
  Gazed at us, as at evening we are wont

To eye each other under a new moon,
  And so towards us sharpened they their brows
  As an old tailor at the needle's eye.

Thus scrutinised by such a family,
  By some one I was recognised, who seized
  My garment's hem, and cried out, "What a marvel!"

And I, when he stretched forth his arm to me,
  On his baked aspect fastened so mine eyes,
  That the scorched countenance prevented not

la conoscenza sua al mio 'ntelletto;
 e chinando la mano a la sua faccia,
 rispuosi: ""Siete voi qui, ser Brunetto?"".

E quelli: ""O figliuol mio, non ti dispiaccia
 se Brunetto Latino un poco teco
 ritorna 'n dietro e lascia andar la traccia"".

I' dissi lui: ""Quanto posso, ven preco;
 e se volete che con voi m'asseggia,
 farol, se piace a costui che vo seco"".

""O figliuol"", disse, ""qual di questa greggia
 s'arresta punto, giace poi cent'anni
 sanz'arrostarsi quando 'l foco il feggia.

Pero` va oltre: i' ti verro` a' panni;
 e poi rigiugnero` la mia masnada,
 che va piangendo i suoi etterni danni"".

I' non osava scender de la strada
 per andar par di lui; ma 'l capo chino
 tenea com'uom che reverente vada.

El comincio`: ""Qual fortuna o destino
 anzi l'ultimo di` qua giu` ti mena?
 e chi e` questi che mostra 'l cammino?"".

""La` su` di sopra, in la vita serena"",
 rispuos'io lui, ""mi smarri' in una valle,
 avanti che l'eta` mia fosse piena.

Pur ier mattina le volsi le spalle:
 questi m'apparve, tornand'io in quella,
 e reducemi a ca per questo calle"".

Ed elli a me: ""Se tu segui tua stella,
 non puoi fallire a glorioso porto,
 se ben m'accorsi ne la vita bella;

e s'io non fossi si` per tempo morto,
 veggendo il cielo a te cosi` benigno,
 dato t'avrei a l'opera conforto.

Ma quello ingrato popolo maligno
 che discese di Fiesole ab antico,
 e tiene ancor del monte e del macigno,

ti si fara`, per tuo ben far, nimico:
 ed e` ragion, che' tra li lazzi sorbi
 si disconvien fruttare al dolce fico.

His recognition by my intellect;
 And bowing down my face unto his own,
 I made reply, "Are you here, Ser Brunetto?"

And he: "May't not displease thee, O my son,
 If a brief space with thee Brunetto Latini
 Backward return and let the trail go on."

I said to him: "With all my power I ask it;
 And if you wish me to sit down with you,
 I will, if he please, for I go with him."

"O son," he said, "whoever of this herd
 A moment stops, lies then a hundred years,
 Nor fans himself when smiteth him the fire.

Therefore go on; I at thy skirts will come,
 And afterward will I rejoin my band,
 Which goes lamenting its eternal doom."

I did not dare to go down from the road
 Level to walk with him; but my head bowed
 I held as one who goeth reverently.

And he began: "What fortune or what fate
 Before the last day leadeth thee down here?
 And who is this that showeth thee the way?"

"Up there above us in the life serene,"
 I answered him, "I lost me in a valley,
 Or ever yet my age had been completed.

But yestermorn I turned my back upon it;
 This one appeared to me, returning thither,
 And homeward leadeth me along this road."

And he to me: "If thou thy star do follow,
 Thou canst not fail thee of a glorious port,
 If well I judged in the life beautiful.

And if I had not died so prematurely,
 Seeing Heaven thus benignant unto thee,
 I would have given thee comfort in the work.

But that ungrateful and malignant people,
 Which of old time from Fesole descended,
 And smacks still of the mountain and the granite,

Will make itself, for thy good deeds, thy foe;
 And it is right; for among crabbed sorbs
 It ill befits the sweet fig to bear fruit.

Vecchia fama nel mondo li chiama orbi;	Old rumour in the world proclaims them blind;
gent'e` avara, invidiosa e superba:	A people avaricious, envious, proud;
dai lor costumi fa che tu ti forbi.	Take heed that of their customs thou do cleanse thee.
La tua fortuna tanto onor ti serba,	Thy fortune so much honour doth reserve thee,
che l'una parte e l'altra avranno fame	One party and the other shall be hungry
di te; ma lungi fia dal becco l'erba.	For thee; but far from goat shall be the grass.
Faccian le bestie fiesolane strame	Their litter let the beasts of Fesole
di lor medesme, e non tocchin la pianta,	Make of themselves, nor let them touch the plant,
s'alcuna surge ancora in lor letame,	If any still upon their dunghill rise,
in cui riviva la sementa santa	In which may yet revive the consecrated
di que' Roman che vi rimaser quando	Seed of those Romans, who remained there when
fu fatto il nido di malizia tanta"".	The nest of such great malice it became."
""Se fosse tutto pieno il mio dimando"",	"If my entreaty wholly were fulfilled,"
rispuos'io lui, ""voi non sareste ancora	Replied I to him, "not yet would you be
de l'umana natura posto in bando;	In banishment from human nature placed;
che' 'n la mente m'e` fitta, e or m'accora,	For in my mind is fixed, and touches now
la cara e buona imagine paterna	My heart the dear and good paternal image
di voi quando nel mondo ad ora ad ora	Of you, when in the world from hour to hour
m'insegnavate come l'uom s'etterna:	You taught me how a man becomes eternal;
e quant'io l'abbia in grado, mentr'io vivo	And how much I am grateful, while I live
convien che ne la mia lingua si scerna.	Behoves that in my language be discerned.
Cio` che narrate di mio corso scrivo,	What you narrate of my career I write,
e serbolo a chiosar con altro testo	And keep it to be glossed with other text
a donna che sapra`, s'a lei arrivo.	By a Lady who can do it, if I reach her.
Tanto vogl'io che vi sia manifesto,	This much will I have manifest to you;
pur che mia coscienza non mi garra,	Provided that my conscience do not chide me,
che a la Fortuna, come vuol, son presto.	For whatsoever Fortune I am ready.
Non e` nuova a li orecchi miei tal arra:	Such handsel is not new unto mine ears;
pero` giri Fortuna la sua rota	Therefore let Fortune turn her wheel around
come le piace, e 'l villan la sua marra"".	As it may please her, and the churl his mattock."
Lo mio maestro allora in su la gota	My Master thereupon on his right cheek
destra si volse in dietro, e riguardommi;	Did backward turn himself, and looked at me;
poi disse: ""Bene ascolta chi la nota"".	Then said: "He listeneth well who noteth it."
Ne' per tanto di men parlando vommi	Nor speaking less on that account, I go
con ser Brunetto, e dimando chi sono	With Ser Brunetto, and I ask who are
li suoi compagni piu` noti e piu` sommi.	His most known and most eminent companions.

La Divina Commedia - The Divine Comedy

Ed elli a me: ""Saper d'alcuno e` buono;
  de li altri fia laudabile tacerci,
  che' 'l tempo saria corto a tanto suono.

In somma sappi che tutti fur cherci
  e litterati grandi e di gran fama,
  d'un peccato medesmo al mondo lerci.

Priscian sen va con quella turba grama,
  e Francesco d'Accorso anche; e vedervi,
  s'avessi avuto di tal tigna brama,

colui potei che dal servo de' servi
  fu trasmutato d'Arno in Bacchiglione,
  dove lascio` li mal protesi nervi.

Di piu` direi; ma 'l venire e 'l sermone
  piu` lungo esser non puo`, pero` ch'i' veggio
  la` surger nuovo fummo del sabbione.

Gente vien con la quale esser non deggio.
  Sieti raccomandato il mio Tesoro
  nel qual io vivo ancora, e piu` non cheggio"".

Poi si rivolse, e parve di coloro
  che corrono a Verona il drappo verde
  per la campagna; e parve di costoro

quelli che vince, non colui che perde.

And he to me: "To know of some is well;
  Of others it were laudable to be silent,
  For short would be the time for so much speech.

Know them in sum, that all of them were clerks,
  And men of letters great and of great fame,
  In the world tainted with the selfsame sin.

Priscian goes yonder with that wretched crowd,
  And Francis of Accorso; and thou hadst seen there
  If thou hadst had a hankering for such scurf,

That one, who by the Servant of the Servants
  From Arno was transferred to Bacchiglione,
  Where he has left his sin-excited nerves.

More would I say, but coming and discoursing
  Can be no longer; for that I behold
  New smoke uprising yonder from the sand.

A people comes with whom I may not be;
  Commended unto thee be my Tesoro,
  In which I still live, and no more I ask."

Then he turned round, and seemed to be of those
  Who at Verona run for the Green Mantle
  Across the plain; and seemed to be among them

The one who wins, and not the one who loses.

Inferno: Canto XVI

Guidoguerra, Aldobrandi, and Rusticucci. Cataract of the River of Blood.

Gia` era in loco onde s'udia 'l rimbombo
  de l'acqua che cadea ne l'altro giro,
  simile a quel che l'arnie fanno rombo,

quando tre ombre insieme si partiro,
  correndo, d'una torma che passava
  sotto la pioggia de l'aspro martiro.

Venian ver noi, e ciascuna gridava:
  ""Sostati tu ch'a l'abito ne sembri
  esser alcun di nostra terra prava"".

Ahime`, che piaghe vidi ne' lor membri
  ricenti e vecchie, da le fiamme incese!
  Ancor men duol pur ch'i' me ne rimembri.

A le lor grida il mio dottor s'attese;
  volse 'l viso ver me, e: ""Or aspetta"",
  disse ""a costor si vuole esser cortese.

E se non fosse il foco che saetta
  la natura del loco, i' dicerei
  che meglio stesse a te che a lor la fretta"".

Ricominciar, come noi restammo, ei
  l'antico verso; e quando a noi fuor giunti,
  fenno una rota di se' tutti e trei.

Qual sogliono i campion far nudi e unti,
  avvisando lor presa e lor vantaggio,
  prima che sien tra lor battuti e punti,

cosi` rotando, ciascuno il visaggio
  drizzava a me, si` che 'n contraro il collo
  faceva ai pie` continuo viaggio.

Now was I where was heard the reverberation
  Of water falling into the next round,
  Like to that humming which the beehives make,

When shadows three together started forth,
  Running, from out a company that passed
  Beneath the rain of the sharp martyrdom.

Towards us came they, and each one cried out:
  "Stop, thou; for by thy garb to us thou seemest
  To be some one of our depraved city."

Ah me! what wounds I saw upon their limbs,
  Recent and ancient by the flames burnt in!
  It pains me still but to remember it.

Unto their cries my Teacher paused attentive;
  He turned his face towards me, and "Now wait,"
  He said; "to these we should be courteous.

And if it were not for the fire that darts
  The nature of this region, I should say
  That haste were more becoming thee than them."

As soon as we stood still, they recommenced
  The old refrain, and when they overtook us,
  Formed of themselves a wheel, all three of them.

As champions stripped and oiled are wont to do,
  Watching for their advantage and their hold,
  Before they come to blows and thrusts between
    them,

Thus, wheeling round, did every one his visage
  Direct to me, so that in opposite wise
  His neck and feet continual journey made.

E ""Se miseria d'esto loco sollo
  rende in dispetto noi e nostri prieghi"",
  comincio' l'uno ""e 'l tinto aspetto e brollo,

la fama nostra il tuo animo pieghi
  a dirne chi tu se', che i vivi piedi
  cosi' sicuro per lo 'nferno freghi.

Questi, l'orme di cui pestar mi vedi,
  tutto che nudo e dipelato vada,
  fu di grado maggior che tu non credi:

nepote fu de la buona Gualdrada;
  Guido Guerra ebbe nome, e in sua vita
  fece col senno assai e con la spada.

L'altro, ch'appresso me la rena trita,
  e' Tegghiaio Aldobrandi, la cui voce
  nel mondo su' dovria esser gradita.

E io, che posto son con loro in croce,
  Iacopo Rusticucci fui; e certo
  la fiera moglie piu' ch'altro mi nuoce"".

S'i' fossi stato dal foco coperto,
  gittato mi sarei tra lor di sotto,
  e credo che 'l dottor l'avria sofferto;

ma perch'io mi sarei brusciato e cotto,
  vinse paura la mia buona voglia
  che di loro abbracciar mi facea ghiotto.

Poi cominciai: ""Non dispetto, ma doglia
  la vostra condizion dentro mi fisse,
  tanta che tardi tutta si dispoglia,

tosto che questo mio segnor mi disse
  parole per le quali i' mi pensai
  che qual voi siete, tal gente venisse.

Di vostra terra sono, e sempre mai
  l'ovra di voi e li onorati nomi
  con affezion ritrassi e ascoltai.

Lascio lo fele e vo per dolci pomi
  promessi a me per lo verace duca;
  ma 'nfino al centro pria convien ch'i' tomi"".

And, "If the misery of this soft place
  Bring in disdain ourselves and our entreaties,"
  Began one, "and our aspect black and blistered,

Let the renown of us thy mind incline
  To tell us who thou art, who thus securely
  Thy living feet dost move along through Hell.

He in whose footprints thou dost see me treading,
  Naked and skinless though he now may go,
  Was of a greater rank than thou dost think;

He was the grandson of the good Gualdrada;
  His name was Guidoguerra, and in life
  Much did he with his wisdom and his sword.

The other, who close by me treads the sand,
  Tegghiaio Aldobrandi is, whose fame
  Above there in the world should welcome be.

And I, who with them on the cross am placed,
  Jacopo Rusticucci was; and truly
  My savage wife, more than aught else, doth harm
    me."

Could I have been protected from the fire,
  Below I should have thrown myself among them,
  And think the Teacher would have suffered it;

But as I should have burned and baked myself,
  My terror overmastered my good will,
  Which made me greedy of embracing them.

Then I began: "Sorrow and not disdain
  Did your condition fix within me so,
  That tardily it wholly is stripped off,

As soon as this my Lord said unto me
  Words, on account of which I thought within me
  That people such as you are were approaching.

I of your city am; and evermore
  Your labours and your honourable names
  I with affection have retraced and heard.

I leave the gall, and go for the sweet fruits
  Promised to me by the veracious Leader;
  But to the centre first I needs must plunge."

""Se lungamente l'anima conduca
  le membra tue"", rispuose quelli ancora,
  ""e se la fama tua dopo te luca,

cortesia e valor di` se dimora
  ne la nostra citta` si` come suole,
  o se del tutto se n'e` gita fora;

che' Guiglielmo Borsiere, il qual si duole
  con noi per poco e va la` coi compagni,
  assai ne cruccia con le sue parole"".

""La gente nuova e i subiti guadagni
  orgoglio e dismisura han generata,
  Fiorenza, in te, si` che tu gia` ten piagni"".

Cosi` gridai con la faccia levata;
  e i tre, che cio` inteser per risposta,
  guardar l'un l'altro com'al ver si guata.

""Se l'altre volte si` poco ti costa"",
  rispuoser tutti ""il satisfare altrui,
  felice te se si` parli a tua posta!

Pero`, se campi d'esti luoghi bui
  e torni a riveder le belle stelle,
  quando ti giovera` dicere "I' fui",

fa che di noi a la gente favelle"".
  Indi rupper la rota, e a fuggirsi
  ali sembiar le gambe loro isnelle.

Un amen non saria potuto dirsi
  tosto cosi` com'e' fuoro spariti;
  per ch'al maestro parve di partirsi.

Io lo seguiva, e poco eravam iti,
  che 'l suon de l'acqua n'era si` vicino,
  che per parlar saremmo a pena uditi.

Come quel fiume c'ha proprio cammino
  prima dal Monte Viso 'nver' levante,
  da la sinistra costa d'Apennino,

che si chiama Acquacheta suso, avante
  che si divalli giu` nel basso letto,
  e a Forli` di quel nome e` vacante,

rimbomba la` sovra San Benedetto
  de l'Alpe per cadere ad una scesa
  ove dovea per mille esser recetto;

"So may the soul for a long while conduct
  Those limbs of thine," did he make answer then,
  "And so may thy renown shine after thee,

Valour and courtesy, say if they dwell
  Within our city, as they used to do,
  Or if they wholly have gone out of it;

For Guglielmo Borsier, who is in torment
  With us of late, and goes there with his comrades,
  Doth greatly mortify us with his words."

"The new inhabitants and the sudden gains,
  Pride and extravagance have in thee engendered,
  Florence, so that thou weep'st thereat already!"

In this wise I exclaimed with face uplifted;
  And the three, taking that for my reply,
  Looked at each other, as one looks at truth.

"If other times so little it doth cost thee,"
  Replied they all, "to satisfy another,
  Happy art thou, thus speaking at thy will!

Therefore, if thou escape from these dark places,
  And come to rebehold the beauteous stars,
  When it shall pleasure thee to say, 'I was,'

See that thou speak of us unto the people."
  Then they broke up the wheel, and in their flight
  It seemed as if their agile legs were wings.

Not an Amen could possibly be said
  So rapidly as they had disappeared;
  Wherefore the Master deemed best to depart.

I followed him, and little had we gone,
  Before the sound of water was so near us,
  That speaking we should hardly have been heard.

Even as that stream which holdeth its own course
  The first from Monte Veso tow'rds the East,
  Upon the left-hand slope of Apennine,

Which is above called Acquacheta, ere
  It down descendeth into its low bed,
  And at Forli is vacant of that name,

Reverberates there above San Benedetto
  From Alps, by falling at a single leap,
  Where for a thousand there were room enough;

cosi`, giu` d'una ripa discoscesa,
  trovammo risonar quell'acqua tinta,
  si` che 'n poc'ora avria l'orecchia offesa.
	Thus downward from a bank precipitate,
	  We found resounding that dark-tinted water,
	  So that it soon the ear would have offended.

Io avea una corda intorno cinta,
  e con essa pensai alcuna volta
  prender la lonza a la pelle dipinta.
	I had a cord around about me girt,
	  And therewithal I whilom had designed
	  To take the panther with the painted skin.

Poscia ch'io l'ebbi tutta da me sciolta,
  si` come 'l duca m'avea comandato,
  porsila a lui aggroppata e ravvolta.
	After I this had all from me unloosed,
	  As my Conductor had commanded me,
	  I reached it to him, gathered up and coiled,

Ond'ei si volse inver' lo destro lato,
  e alquanto di lunge da la sponda
  la gitto` giuso in quell'alto burrato.
	Whereat he turned himself to the right side,
	  And at a little distance from the verge,
	  He cast it down into that deep abyss.

'E' pur convien che novita` risponda'   dicea fra me medesmo 'al novo cenno   che 'l maestro con l'occhio si` seconda'.	"It must needs be some novelty respond," I said within myself, "to the new signal The Master with his eye is following so."

Ahi quanto cauti li uomini esser dienno
  presso a color che non veggion pur l'ovra,
  ma per entro i pensier miran col senno!
	Ah me! how very cautious men should be
	  With those who not alone behold the act,
	  But with their wisdom look into the thoughts!

El disse a me: ""Tosto verra` di sovra   cio` ch'io attendo e che il tuo pensier sogna: tosto convien ch'al tuo viso si scovra"".	He said to me: "Soon there will upward come What I await; and what thy thought is dreaming Must soon reveal itself unto thy sight."

Sempre a quel ver c'ha faccia di menzogna
  de' l'uom chiuder le labbra fin ch'el puote,
  pero` che sanza colpa fa vergogna;
	Aye to that truth which has the face of falsehood,
	  A man should close his lips as far as may be,
	  Because without his fault it causes shame;

ma qui tacer nol posso; e per le note
  di questa comedia, lettor, ti giuro,
  s'elle non sien di lunga grazia vote,
	But here I cannot; and, Reader, by the notes
	  Of this my Comedy to thee I swear,
	  So may they not be void of lasting favour,

ch'i' vidi per quell'aere grosso e scuro
  venir notando una figura in suso,
  maravigliosa ad ogne cor sicuro,
	Athwart that dense and darksome atmosphere
	  I saw a figure swimming upward come,
	  Marvellous unto every steadfast heart,

si` come torna colui che va giuso   talora a solver l'ancora ch'aggrappa   o scoglio o altro che nel mare e` chiuso,	Even as he returns who goeth down Sometimes to clear an anchor, which has grappled Reef, or aught else that in the sea is hidden,
che 'n su` si stende, e da pie` si rattrappa.	Who upward stretches, and draws in his feet.

Inferno: Canto XVII

Geryon. The Violent against Art. Usurers. Descent into the Abyss of Malebolge.

""Ecco la fiera con la coda aguzza, che passa i monti, e rompe i muri e l'armi! Ecco colei che tutto 'l mondo appuzza!"".	"Behold the monster with the pointed tail, Who cleaves the hills, and breaketh walls and weapons, Behold him who infecteth all the world."
Si` comincio` lo mio duca a parlarmi; e accennolle che venisse a proda vicino al fin d'i passeggiati marmi.	Thus unto me my Guide began to say, And beckoned him that he should come to shore, Near to the confine of the trodden marble;
E quella sozza imagine di froda sen venne, e arrivo` la testa e 'l busto, ma 'n su la riva non trasse la coda.	And that uncleanly image of deceit Came up and thrust ashore its head and bust, But on the border did not drag its tail.
La faccia sua era faccia d'uom giusto, tanto benigna avea di fuor la pelle, e d'un serpente tutto l'altro fusto;	The face was as the face of a just man, Its semblance outwardly was so benign, And of a serpent all the trunk beside.
due branche avea pilose insin l'ascelle; lo dosso e 'l petto e ambedue le coste dipinti avea di nodi e di rotelle.	Two paws it had, hairy unto the armpits; The back, and breast, and both the sides it had Depicted o'er with nooses and with shields.
Con piu` color, sommesse e sovraposte non fer mai drappi Tartari ne' Turchi, ne' fuor tai tele per Aragne imposte.	With colours more, groundwork or broidery Never in cloth did Tartars make nor Turks, Nor were such tissues by Arachne laid.
Come tal volta stanno a riva i burchi, che parte sono in acqua e parte in terra, e come la` tra li Tedeschi lurchi	As sometimes wherries lie upon the shore, That part are in the water, part on land; And as among the guzzling Germans there,
lo bivero s'assetta a far sua guerra, cosi` la fiera pessima si stava su l'orlo ch'e` di pietra e 'l sabbion serra.	The beaver plants himself to wage his war; So that vile monster lay upon the border, Which is of stone, and shutteth in the sand.
Nel vano tutta sua coda guizzava, torcendo in su` la venenosa forca ch'a guisa di scorpion la punta armava.	His tail was wholly quivering in the void, Contorting upwards the envenomed fork, That in the guise of scorpion armed its point.

Lo duca disse: ""Or convien che si torca
la nostra via un poco insino a quella
bestia malvagia che cola` si corca""`.

Pero` scendemmo a la destra mammella,
e diece passi femmo in su lo stremo,
per ben cessar la rena e la fiammella.

E quando noi a lei venuti semo,
poco piu` oltre veggio in su la rena
gente seder propinqua al loco scemo.

Quivi 'l maestro ""Accio` che tutta piena
esperienza d'esto giron porti""`,
mi disse, ""va, e vedi la lor mena.

Li tuoi ragionamenti sian la` corti:
mentre che torni, parlero` con questa,
che ne conceda i suoi omeri forti""`.

Cosi` ancor su per la strema testa
di quel settimo cerchio tutto solo
andai, dove sedea la gente mesta.

Per li occhi fora scoppiava lor duolo;
e` di qua, di la` soccorrien con le mani
quando a' vapori, e quando al caldo suolo:

non altrimenti fan di state i cani
or col ceffo, or col pie`, quando son morsi
o da pulci o da mosche o da tafani.

Poi che nel viso a certi li occhi porsi,
ne' quali 'l doloroso foco casca,
non ne conobbi alcun; ma io m'accorsi

che dal collo a ciascun pendea una tasca
ch'avea certo colore e certo segno,
e quindi par che 'l loro occhio si pasca.

E com'io riguardando tra lor vegno,
in una borsa gialla vidi azzurro
che d'un leone avea faccia e contegno.

Poi, procedendo di mio sguardo il curro,
vidine un'altra come sangue rossa,
mostrando un'oca bianca piu` che burro.

The Guide said: "Now perforce must turn aside
Our way a little, even to that beast
Malevolent, that yonder coucheth him."

We therefore on the right side descended,
And made ten steps upon the outer verge,
Completely to avoid the sand and flame;

And after we are come to him, I see
A little farther off upon the sand
A people sitting near the hollow place.

Then said to me the Master: "So that full
Experience of this round thou bear away,
Now go and see what their condition is.

There let thy conversation be concise;
Till thou returnest I will speak with him,
That he concede to us his stalwart shoulders."

Thus farther still upon the outermost
Head of that seventh circle all alone
I went, where sat the melancholy folk.

Out of their eyes was gushing forth their woe;
This way, that way, they helped them with their
hands
Now from the flames and now from the hot soil.

Not otherwise in summer do the dogs,
Now with the foot, now with the muzzle, when
By fleas, or flies, or gadflies, they are bitten.

When I had turned mine eyes upon the faces
Of some, on whom the dolorous fire is falling,
Not one of them I knew; but I perceived

That from the neck of each there hung a pouch,
Which certain colour had, and certain blazon;
And thereupon it seems their eyes are feeding.

And as I gazing round me come among them,
Upon a yellow pouch I azure saw
That had the face and posture of a lion.

Proceeding then the current of my sight,
Another of them saw I, red as blood,
Display a goose more white than butter is.

E un che d'una scrofa azzurra e grossa
  segnato avea lo suo sacchetto bianco,
  mi disse: ""Che fai tu in questa fossa?

Or te ne va; e perche' se' vivo anco,
  sappi che 'l mio vicin Vitaliano
  sedera` qui dal mio sinistro fianco.

Con questi Fiorentin son padoano:
  spesse fiate mi 'ntronan li orecchi
  gridando: "Vegna 'l cavalier sovrano,

che rechera` la tasca con tre becchi!""".
  Qui distorse la bocca e di fuor trasse
  la lingua, come bue che 'l naso lecchi.

E io, temendo no 'l piu` star crucciasse
  lui che di poco star m'avea 'mmonito,
  torna'mi in dietro da l'anime lasse.

Trova' il duca mio ch'era salito
  gia` su la groppa del fiero animale,
  e disse a me: ""Or sie forte e ardito.

Omai si scende per si` fatte scale:
  monta dinanzi, ch'i' voglio esser mezzo,
  si` che la coda non possa far male"".

Qual e` colui che si` presso ha 'l riprezzo
  de la quartana, c'ha gia` l'unghie smorte,
  e triema tutto pur guardando 'l rezzo,

tal divenn'io a le parole porte;
  ma vergogna mi fe' le sue minacce,
  che innanzi a buon segnor fa servo forte.

I' m'assettai in su quelle spallacce;
  si` volli dir, ma la voce non venne
  com'io credetti: 'Fa che tu m'abbracce'.

Ma esso, ch'altra volta mi sovvenne
  ad altro forse, tosto ch'i' montai
  con le braccia m'avvinse e mi sostenne;

e disse: ""Gerion, moviti omai:
  le rote larghe e lo scender sia poco:
  pensa la nova soma che tu hai"".

Come la navicella esce di loco
  in dietro in dietro, si` quindi si tolse;
  e poi ch'al tutto si senti` a gioco,

And one, who with an azure sow and gravid
  Emblazoned had his little pouch of white,
  Said unto me: "What dost thou in this moat?

Now get thee gone; and since thou'rt still alive,
  Know that a neighbour of mine, Vitaliano,
  Will have his seat here on my left-hand side.

A Paduan am I with these Florentines;
  Full many a time they thunder in mine ears,
  Exclaiming, 'Come the sovereign cavalier,

He who shall bring the satchel with three goats;'"
  Then twisted he his mouth, and forth he thrust
  His tongue, like to an ox that licks its nose.

And fearing lest my longer stay might vex
  Him who had warned me not to tarry long,
  Backward I turned me from those weary souls.

I found my Guide, who had already mounted
  Upon the back of that wild animal,
  And said to me: "Now be both strong and bold.

Now we descend by stairways such as these;
  Mount thou in front, for I will be midway,
  So that the tail may have no power to harm thee."

Such as he is who has so near the ague
  Of quartan that his nails are blue already,
  And trembles all, but looking at the shade;

Even such became I at those proffered words;
  But shame in me his menaces produced,
  Which maketh servant strong before good master.

I seated me upon those monstrous shoulders;
  I wished to say, and yet the voice came not
  As I believed, "Take heed that thou embrace me."

But he, who other times had rescued me
  In other peril, soon as I had mounted,
  Within his arms encircled and sustained me,

And said: "Now, Geryon, bestir thyself;
  The circles large, and the descent be little;
  Think of the novel burden which thou hast."

Even as the little vessel shoves from shore,
  Backward, still backward, so he thence withdrew;
  And when he wholly felt himself afloat,

la` 'v'era 'l petto, la coda rivolse,
  e quella tesa, come anguilla, mosse,
  e con le branche l'aere a se' raccolse.

Maggior paura non credo che fosse
  quando Fetonte abbandono` li freni,
  per che 'l ciel, come pare ancor, si cosse;

ne' quando Icaro misero le reni
  senti` spennar per la scaldata cera,
  gridando il padre a lui ““Mala via tieni!”“,

che fu la mia, quando vidi ch'i' era
  ne l'aere d'ogne parte, e vidi spenta
  ogne veduta fuor che de la fera.

Ella sen va notando lenta lenta:
  rota e discende, ma non me n'accorgo
  se non che al viso e di sotto mi venta.

Io sentia gia` da la man destra il gorgo
  far sotto noi un orribile scroscio,
  per che con li occhi 'n giu` la testa sporgo.

Allor fu' io piu` timido a lo stoscio,
  pero` ch'i' vidi fuochi e senti' pianti;
  ond'io tremando tutto mi raccoscio.

E vidi poi, che' nol vedea davanti,
  lo scendere e 'l girar per li gran mali
  che s'appressavan da diversi canti.

Come 'l falcon ch'e` stato assai su l'ali,
  che sanza veder logoro o uccello
  fa dire al falconiere ““Ome`, tu cali!”“,

discende lasso onde si move isnello,
  per cento rote, e da lunge si pone
  dal suo maestro, disdegnoso e fello;

cosi` ne puose al fondo Gerione
  al pie` al pie` de la stagliata rocca
  e, discarcate le nostre persone,

si dileguo` come da corda cocca.

There where his breast had been he turned his tail,
  And that extended like an eel he moved,
  And with his paws drew to himself the air.

A greater fear I do not think there was
  What time abandoned Phaeton the reins,
  Whereby the heavens, as still appears, were scorched;

Nor when the wretched Icarus his flanks
  Felt stripped of feathers by the melting wax,
  His father crying, "An ill way thou takest!"

Than was my own, when I perceived myself
  On all sides in the air, and saw extinguished
  The sight of everything but of the monster.

Onward he goeth, swimming slowly, slowly;
  Wheels and descends, but I perceive it only
  By wind upon my face and from below.

I heard already on the right the whirlpool
  Making a horrible crashing under us;
  Whence I thrust out my head with eyes cast downward.

Then was I still more fearful of the abyss;
  Because I fires beheld, and heard laments,
  Whereat I, trembling, all the closer cling.

I saw then, for before I had not seen it,
  The turning and descending, by great horrors
  That were approaching upon divers sides.

As falcon who has long been on the wing,
  Who, without seeing either lure or bird,
  Maketh the falconer say, "Ah me, thou stoopest,"

Descendeth weary, whence he started swiftly,
  Thorough a hundred circles, and alights
  Far from his master, sullen and disdainful;

Even thus did Geryon place us on the bottom,
  Close to the bases of the rough-hewn rock,
  And being disencumbered of our persons,

He sped away as arrow from the string.

Inferno: Canto XVIII

The Eighth Circle, Malebolge: The Fraudulent and the Malicious. The First Bolgia: Seducers and Panders. Venedico Caccianimico. Jason. The Second Bolgia: Flatterers. Allessio Interminelli. Thais.

Luogo e` in inferno detto Malebolge,
 tutto di pietra di color ferrigno,
 come la cerchia che dintorno il volge.

Nel dritto mezzo del campo maligno
 vaneggia un pozzo assai largo e profondo,
 di cui suo loco dicero` l'ordigno.

Quel cinghio che rimane adunque e` tondo
 tra 'l pozzo e 'l pie` de l'alta ripa dura,
 e ha distinto in dieci valli il fondo.

Quale, dove per guardia de le mura
 piu` e piu` fossi cingon li castelli,
 la parte dove son rende figura,

tale imagine quivi facean quelli;
 e come a tai fortezze da' lor sogli
 a la ripa di fuor son ponticelli,

cosi` da imo de la roccia scogli
 movien che ricidien li argini e ' fossi
 infino al pozzo che i tronca e raccogli.

In questo luogo, de la schiena scossi
 di Gerion, trovammoci; e 'l poeta
 tenne a sinistra, e io dietro mi mossi.

A la man destra vidi nova pieta,
 novo tormento e novi frustatori,
 di che la prima bolgia era repleta.

There is a place in Hell called Malebolge,
 Wholly of stone and of an iron colour,
 As is the circle that around it turns.

Right in the middle of the field malign
 There yawns a well exceeding wide and deep,
 Of which its place the structure will recount.

Round, then, is that enclosure which remains
 Between the well and foot of the high, hard bank,
 And has distinct in valleys ten its bottom.

As where for the protection of the walls
 Many and many moats surround the castles,
 The part in which they are a figure forms,

Just such an image those presented there;
 And as about such strongholds from their gates
 Unto the outer bank are little bridges,

So from the precipice's base did crags
 Project, which intersected dikes and moats,
 Unto the well that truncates and collects them.

Within this place, down shaken from the back
 Of Geryon, we found us; and the Poet
 Held to the left, and I moved on behind.

Upon my right hand I beheld new anguish,
 New torments, and new wielders of the lash,
 Wherewith the foremost Bolgia was replete.

Nel fondo erano ignudi i peccatori;
  dal mezzo in qua ci venien verso 'l volto,
  di la` con noi, ma con passi maggiori,

come i Roman per l'essercito molto,
  l'anno del giubileo, su per lo ponte
  hanno a passar la gente modo colto,

che da l'un lato tutti hanno la fronte
  verso 'l castello e vanno a Santo Pietro;
  da l'altra sponda vanno verso 'l monte.

Di qua, di la`, su per lo sasso tetro
  vidi demon cornuti con gran ferze,
  che li battien crudelmente di retro.

Ahi come facean lor levar le berze
  a le prime percosse! gia` nessuno
  le seconde aspettava ne' le terze.

Mentr'io andava, li occhi miei in uno
  furo scontrati; e io si` tosto dissi:
  "“Gia` di veder costui non son digiuno”“.

Per ch'io a figurarlo i piedi affissi;
  e 'l dolce duca meco si ristette,
  e assentio ch'alquanto in dietro gissi.

E quel frustato celar si credette
  bassando 'l viso; ma poco li valse,
  ch'io dissi: "“O tu che l'occhio a terra gette,

se le fazion che porti non son false,
  Venedico se' tu Caccianemico.
  Ma che ti mena a si` pungenti salse?”“.

Ed elli a me: "“Mal volentier lo dico;
  ma sforzami la tua chiara favella,
  che mi fa sovvenir del mondo antico.

I' fui colui che la Ghisolabella
  condussi a far la voglia del marchese,
  come che suoni la sconcia novella.

E non pur io qui piango bolognese;
  anzi n'e` questo luogo tanto pieno,
  che tante lingue non son ora apprese

a dicer 'sipa' tra Savena e Reno;
  e se di cio` vuoi fede o testimonio,
  recati a mente il nostro avaro seno”"“.

Down at the bottom were the sinners naked;
  This side the middle came they facing us,
  Beyond it, with us, but with greater steps;

Even as the Romans, for the mighty host,
  The year of Jubilee, upon the bridge,
  Have chosen a mode to pass the people over;

For all upon one side towards the Castle
  Their faces have, and go unto St. Peter's;
  On the other side they go towards the Mountain.

This side and that, along the livid stone
  Beheld I horned demons with great scourges,
  Who cruelly were beating them behind.

Ah me! how they did make them lift their legs
  At the first blows! and sooth not any one
  The second waited for, nor for the third.

While I was going on, mine eyes by one
  Encountered were; and straight I said: "Already
  With sight of this one I am not unfed."

Therefore I stayed my feet to make him out,
  And with me the sweet Guide came to a stand,
  And to my going somewhat back assented;

And he, the scourged one, thought to hide himself,
  Lowering his face, but little it availed him;
  For said I: "Thou that castest down thine eyes,

If false are not the features which thou bearest,
  Thou art Venedico Caccianimico;
  But what doth bring thee to such pungent sauces?"

And he to me: "Unwillingly I tell it;
  But forces me thine utterance distinct,
  Which makes me recollect the ancient world.

I was the one who the fair Ghisola
  Induced to grant the wishes of the Marquis,
  Howe'er the shameless story may be told.

Not the sole Bolognese am I who weeps here;
  Nay, rather is this place so full of them,
  That not so many tongues to-day are taught

'Twixt Reno and Savena to say 'sipa;'
  And if thereof thou wishest pledge or proof,
  Bring to thy mind our avaricious heart."

Cosi` parlando il percosse un demonio
  de la sua scuriada, e disse: ""Via,
  ruffian! qui non son femmine da conio"".

I' mi raggiunsi con la scorta mia;
  poscia con pochi passi divenimmo
  la` 'v'uno scoglio de la ripa uscia.

Assai leggeramente quel salimmo;
  e volti a destra su per la sua scheggia,
  da quelle cerchie etterne ci partimmo.

Quando noi fummo la` dov'el vaneggia
  di sotto per dar passo a li sferzati,
  lo duca disse: ""Attienti, e fa che feggia

lo viso in te di quest'altri mal nati,
  ai quali ancor non vedesti la faccia
  pero` che son con noi insieme andati"".

Del vecchio ponte guardavam la traccia
  che venia verso noi da l'altra banda,
  e che la ferza similmente scaccia.

E 'l buon maestro, sanza mia dimanda,
  mi disse: ""Guarda quel grande che vene,
  e per dolor non par lagrime spanda:

quanto aspetto reale ancor ritene!
  Quelli e` Iason, che per cuore e per senno
  li Colchi del monton privati fene.

Ello passo` per l'isola di Lenno,
  poi che l'ardite femmine spietate
  tutti li maschi loro a morte dienno.

Ivi con segni e con parole ornate
  Isifile inganno`, la giovinetta
  che prima avea tutte l'altre ingannate.

Lasciolla quivi, gravida, soletta;
  tal colpa a tal martiro lui condanna;
  e anche di Medea si fa vendetta.

Con lui sen va chi da tal parte inganna:
  e questo basti de la prima valle
  sapere e di color che 'n se' assanna"".

Gia` eravam la` 've lo stretto calle
  con l'argine secondo s'incrocicchia,
  e fa di quello ad un altr'arco spalle.

While speaking in this manner, with his scourge
  A demon smote him, and said: "Get thee gone
  Pander, there are no women here for coin."

I joined myself again unto mine Escort;
  Thereafterward with footsteps few we came
  To where a crag projected from the bank.

This very easily did we ascend,
  And turning to the right along its ridge,
  From those eternal circles we departed.

When we were there, where it is hollowed out
  Beneath, to give a passage to the scourged,
  The Guide said: "Wait, and see that on thee strike

The vision of those others evil-born,
  Of whom thou hast not yet beheld the faces,
  Because together with us they have gone."

From the old bridge we looked upon the train
  Which tow'rds us came upon the other border,
  And which the scourges in like manner smite.

And the good Master, without my inquiring,
  Said to me: "See that tall one who is coming,
  And for his pain seems not to shed a tear;

Still what a royal aspect he retains!
  That Jason is, who by his heart and cunning
  The Colchians of the Ram made destitute.

He by the isle of Lemnos passed along
  After the daring women pitiless
  Had unto death devoted all their males.

There with his tokens and with ornate words
  Did he deceive Hypsipyle, the maiden
  Who first, herself, had all the rest deceived.

There did he leave her pregnant and forlorn;
  Such sin unto such punishment condemns him,
  And also for Medea is vengeance done.

With him go those who in such wise deceive;
  And this sufficient be of the first valley
  To know, and those that in its jaws it holds."

We were already where the narrow path
  Crosses athwart the second dike, and forms
  Of that a buttress for another arch.

Quindi sentimmo gente che si nicchia
  ne l'altra bolgia e che col muso scuffa,
  e se' medesma con le palme picchia.

Le ripe eran grommate d'una muffa,
  per l'alito di giu` che vi s'appasta,
  che con li occhi e col naso facea zuffa.

Lo fondo e` cupo si`, che non ci basta
  loco a veder sanza montare al dosso
  de l'arco, ove lo scoglio piu` sovrasta.

Quivi venimmo; e quindi giu` nel fosso
  vidi gente attuffata in uno sterco
  che da li uman privadi parea mosso.

E mentre ch'io la` giu` con l'occhio cerco,
  vidi un col capo si` di merda lordo,
  che non parea s'era laico o cherco.

Quei mi sgrido`: ""Perche' se' tu si` gordo
  di riguardar piu` me che li altri brutti?"".
  E io a lui: ""Perche', se ben ricordo,

gia` t'ho veduto coi capelli asciutti,
  e se' Alessio Interminei da Lucca:
  pero` t'adocchio piu` che li altri tutti"".

Ed elli allor, battendosi la zucca:
  ""Qua giu` m'hanno sommerso le lusinghe
  ond'io non ebbi mai la lingua stucca"".

Appresso cio` lo duca ""Fa che pinghe"",
  mi disse ""il viso un poco piu` avante,
  si` che la faccia ben con l'occhio attinghe

di quella sozza e scapigliata fante
  che la` si graffia con l'unghie merdose,
  e or s'accoscia e ora e` in piedi stante.

Taide e`, la puttana che rispuose
  al drudo suo quando disse "Ho io grazie
  grandi apo te?": "Anzi maravigliose!".

E quinci sien le nostre viste sazie"".

Thence we heard people, who are making moan
  In the next Bolgia, snorting with their muzzles,
  And with their palms beating upon themselves

The margins were incrusted with a mould
  By exhalation from below, that sticks there,
  And with the eyes and nostrils wages war.

The bottom is so deep, no place suffices
  To give us sight of it, without ascending
  The arch's back, where most the crag impends.

Thither we came, and thence down in the moat
  I saw a people smothered in a filth
  That out of human privies seemed to flow;

And whilst below there with mine eye I search,
  I saw one with his head so foul with ordure,
  It was not clear if he were clerk or layman.

He screamed to me: "Wherefore art thou so eager
  To look at me more than the other foul ones?"
  And I to him: "Because, if I remember,

I have already seen thee with dry hair,
  And thou'rt Alessio Interminei of Lucca;
  Therefore I eye thee more than all the others."

And he thereon, belabouring his pumpkin:
  "The flatteries have submerged me here below,
  Wherewith my tongue was never surfeited."

Then said to me the Guide: "See that thou thrust
  Thy visage somewhat farther in advance,
  That with thine eyes thou well the face attain

Of that uncleanly and dishevelled drab,
  Who there doth scratch herself with filthy nails,
  And crouches now, and now on foot is standing.

Thais the harlot is it, who replied
  Unto her paramour, when he said, 'Have I
  Great gratitude from thee?'—'Nay, marvellous;'

And herewith let our sight be satisfied."

Inferno: Canto XIX

The Third Bolgia: Simoniacs. Pope Nicholas III. Dante's Reproof of corrupt Prelates.

O Simon mago, o miseri seguaci
  che le cose di Dio, che di bontate
  deon essere spose, e voi rapaci

per oro e per argento avolterate,
  or convien che per voi suoni la tromba,
  pero` che ne la terza bolgia state.

Gia` eravamo, a la seguente tomba,
  montati de lo scoglio in quella parte
  ch'a punto sovra mezzo 'l fosso piomba.

O somma sapienza, quanta e` l'arte
  che mostri in cielo, in terra e nel mal mondo,
  e quanto giusto tua virtu` comparte!

Io vidi per le coste e per lo fondo
  piena la pietra livida di fori,
  d'un largo tutti e ciascun era tondo.

Non mi parean men ampi ne' maggiori
  che que' che son nel mio bel San Giovanni,
  fatti per loco d'i battezzatori;

l'un de li quali, ancor non e` molt'anni,
  rupp'io per un che dentro v'annegava:
  e questo sia suggel ch'ogn'omo sganni.

Fuor de la bocca a ciascun soperchiava
  d'un peccator li piedi e de le gambe
  infino al grosso, e l'altro dentro stava.

Le piante erano a tutti accese intrambe;
  per che si` forte guizzavan le giunte,
  che spezzate averien ritorte e strambe.

O Simon Magus, O forlorn disciples,
  Ye who the things of God, which ought to be
  The brides of holiness, rapaciously

For silver and for gold do prostitute,
  Now it behoves for you the trumpet sound,
  Because in this third Bolgia ye abide.

We had already on the following tomb
  Ascended to that portion of the crag
  Which o'er the middle of the moat hangs plumb.

Wisdom supreme, O how great art thou showest
  In heaven, in earth, and in the evil world,
  And with what justice doth thy power distribute!

I saw upon the sides and on the bottom
  The livid stone with perforations filled,
  All of one size, and every one was round.

To me less ample seemed they not, nor greater
  Than those that in my beautiful Saint John
  Are fashioned for the place of the baptisers,

And one of which, not many years ago,
  I broke for some one, who was drowning in it;
  Be this a seal all men to undeceive.

Out of the mouth of each one there protruded
  The feet of a transgressor, and the legs
  Up to the calf, the rest within remained.

In all of them the soles were both on fire;
  Wherefore the joints so violently quivered,
  They would have snapped asunder withes and bands.

Qual suole il fiammeggiar de le cose unte
  muoversi pur su per la strema buccia,
  tal era li` dai calcagni a le punte.

""Chi e` colui, maestro, che si cruccia
  guizzando piu` che li altri suoi consorti"",
  diss'io, ""e cui piu` roggia fiamma succia?"".

Ed elli a me: ""Se tu vuo' ch'i' ti porti
  la` giu` per quella ripa che piu` giace,
  da lui saprai di se' e de' suoi torti"".

E io: ""Tanto m'e` bel, quanto a te piace:
  tu se' segnore, e sai ch'i' non mi parto
  dal tuo volere, e sai quel che si tace"".

Allor venimmo in su l'argine quarto:
  volgemmo e discendemmo a mano stanca
  la` giu` nel fondo foracchiato e arto.

Lo buon maestro ancor de la sua anca
  non mi dipuose, si` mi giunse al rotto
  di quel che si piangeva con la zanca.

""O qual che se' che 'l di su` tien di sotto,
  anima trista come pal commessa"",
  comincia' io a dir, ""se puoi, fa motto"".

Io stava come 'l frate che confessa
  lo perfido assessin, che, poi ch'e` fitto,
  richiama lui, per che la morte cessa.

Ed el grido`: ""Se' tu gia` costi` ritto,
  se' tu gia` costi` ritto, Bonifazio?
  Di parecchi anni mi menti` lo scritto.

Se' tu si` tosto di quell'aver sazio
  per lo qual non temesti torre a 'nganno
  la bella donna, e poi di farne strazio?"".

Tal mi fec'io, quai son color che stanno,
  per non intender cio` ch'e` lor risposto,
  quasi scornati, e risponder non sanno.

Allor Virgilio disse: ""Dilli tosto:
  "Non son colui, non son colui che credi""";
  e io rispuosi come a me fu imposto.

Per che lo spirto tutti storse i piedi;
  poi, sospirando e con voce di pianto,
  mi disse: ""Dunque che a me richiedi?

Even as the flame of unctuous things is wont
  To move upon the outer surface only,
  So likewise was it there from heel to point.

"Master, who is that one who writhes himself,
  More than his other comrades quivering,"
  I said, "and whom a redder flame is sucking?"

And he to me: "If thou wilt have me bear thee
  Down there along that bank which lowest lies,
  From him thou'lt know his errors and himself."

And I: "What pleases thee, to me is pleasing;
  Thou art my Lord, and knowest that I depart not
  From thy desire, and knowest what is not spoken."

Straightway upon the fourth dike we arrived;
  We turned, and on the left-hand side descended
  Down to the bottom full of holes and narrow.

And the good Master yet from off his haunch
  Deposed me not, till to the hole he brought me
  Of him who so lamented with his shanks.

"Whoe'er thou art, that standest upside down,
  O doleful soul, implanted like a stake,"
  To say began I, "if thou canst, speak out."

I stood even as the friar who is confessing
  The false assassin, who, when he is fixed,
  Recalls him, so that death may be delayed.

And he cried out: "Dost thou stand there already,
  Dost thou stand there already, Boniface?
  By many years the record lied to me.

Art thou so early satiate with that wealth,
  For which thou didst not fear to take by fraud
  The beautiful Lady, and then work her woe?"

Such I became, as people are who stand,
  Not comprehending what is answered them,
  As if bemocked, and know not how to answer.

Then said Virgilius: "Say to him straightway,
  'I am not he, I am not he thou thinkest.'"
  And I replied as was imposed on me.

Whereat the spirit writhed with both his feet,
  Then, sighing, with a voice of lamentation
  Said to me: "Then what wantest thou of me?

Se di saper ch'i' sia ti cal cotanto,
  che tu abbi pero` la ripa corsa,
  sappi ch'i' fui vestito del gran manto;

e veramente fui figliuol de l'orsa,
  cupido si` per avanzar li orsatti,
  che su` l'avere e qui me misi in borsa.

Di sotto al capo mio son li altri tratti
  che precedetter me simoneggiando,
  per le fessure de la pietra piatti.

La` giu` caschero` io altresi` quando
  verra` colui ch'i' credea che tu fossi
  allor ch'i' feci 'l subito dimando.

Ma piu` e` 'l tempo gia` che i pie` mi cossi
  e ch'i' son stato cosi` sottosopra,
  ch'el non stara` piantato coi pie` rossi:

che' dopo lui verra` di piu` laida opra
  di ver' ponente, un pastor sanza legge,
  tal che convien che lui e me ricuopra.

Novo Iason sara`, di cui si legge
  ne' Maccabei; e come a quel fu molle
  suo re, cosi` fia lui chi Francia regge"".

Io non so s'i' mi fui qui troppo folle,
  ch'i' pur rispuosi lui a questo metro:
  ""Deh, or mi di`: quanto tesoro volle

Nostro Segnore in prima da san Pietro
  ch'ei ponesse le chiavi in sua balia?
  Certo non chiese se non "Viemmi retro".

Ne' Pier ne' li altri tolsero a Matia
  oro od argento, quando fu sortito
  al loco che perde' l'anima ria.

Pero` ti sta, che' tu se' ben punito;
  e guarda ben la mal tolta moneta
  ch'esser ti fece contra Carlo ardito.

E se non fosse ch'ancor lo mi vieta
  la reverenza delle somme chiavi
  che tu tenesti ne la vita lieta,

io userei parole ancor piu` gravi;
  che' la vostra avarizia il mondo attrista,
  calcando i buoni e sollevando i pravi.

If who I am thou carest so much to know,
  That thou on that account hast crossed the bank,
  Know that I vested was with the great mantle;

And truly was I son of the She-bear,
  So eager to advance the cubs, that wealth
  Above, and here myself, I pocketed.

Beneath my head the others are dragged down
  Who have preceded me in simony,
  Flattened along the fissure of the rock.

Below there I shall likewise fall, whenever
  That one shall come who I believed thou wast,
  What time the sudden question I proposed.

But longer I my feet already toast,
  And here have been in this way upside down,
  Than he will planted stay with reddened feet;

For after him shall come of fouler deed
  From tow'rds the west a Pastor without law,
  Such as befits to cover him and me.

New Jason will he be, of whom we read
  In Maccabees; and as his king was pliant,
  So he who governs France shall be to this one."

I do not know if I were here too bold,
  That him I answered only in this metre:
  "I pray thee tell me now how great a treasure

Our Lord demanded of Saint Peter first,
  Before he put the keys into his keeping?
  Truly he nothing asked but 'Follow me.'

Nor Peter nor the rest asked of Matthias
  Silver or gold, when he by lot was chosen
  Unto the place the guilty soul had lost.

Therefore stay here, for thou art justly punished,
  And keep safe guard o'er the ill-gotten money,
  Which caused thee to be valiant against Charles.

And were it not that still forbids it me
  The reverence for the keys superlative
  Thou hadst in keeping in the gladsome life,

I would make use of words more grievous still;
  Because your avarice afflicts the world,
  Trampling the good and lifting the depraved.

Di voi pastor s'accorse il Vangelista,	The Evangelist you Pastors had in mind,
quando colei che siede sopra l'acque	When she who sitteth upon many waters
puttaneggiar coi regi a lui fu vista;	To fornicate with kings by him was seen;
quella che con le sette teste nacque,	The same who with the seven heads was born,
e da le diece corna ebbe argomento,	And power and strength from the ten horns re-
	ceived,
fin che virtute al suo marito piacque.	So long as virtue to her spouse was pleasing.
Fatto v'avete Dio d'oro e d'argento;	Ye have made yourselves a god of gold and silver;
e che altro e` da voi a l'idolatre,	And from the idolater how differ ye,
se non ch'elli uno, e voi ne orate cento?	Save that he one, and ye a hundred worship?
Ahi, Costantin, di quanto mal fu matre,	Ah, Constantine! of how much ill was mother,
non la tua conversion, ma quella dote	Not thy conversion, but that marriage dower
che da te prese il primo ricco patre!"".	Which the first wealthy Father took from thee!"
E mentr'io li cantava cotai note,	And while I sang to him such notes as these,
o ira o coscienza che 'l mordesse,	Either that anger or that conscience stung him,
forte spingava con ambo le piote.	He struggled violently with both his feet.
I' credo ben ch'al mio duca piacesse,	I think in sooth that it my Leader pleased,
con si` contenta labbia sempre attese	With such contented lip he listened ever
lo suon de le parole vere espresse.	Unto the sound of the true words expressed.
Pero` con ambo le braccia mi prese;	Therefore with both his arms he took me up,
e poi che tutto su mi s'ebbe al petto,	And when he had me all upon his breast,
rimonto` per la via onde discese.	Remounted by the way where he descended.
Ne' si stanco` d'avermi a se' distretto,	Nor did he tire to have me clasped to him;
si` men porto` sovra 'l colmo de l'arco	But bore me to the summit of the arch
che dal quarto al quinto argine e` tragetto.	Which from the fourth dike to the fifth is passage.
Quivi soavemente spuose il carco,	There tenderly he laid his burden down,
soave per lo scoglio sconcio ed erto	Tenderly on the crag uneven and steep,
che sarebbe a le capre duro varco.	That would have been hard passage for the goats:
Indi un altro vallon mi fu scoperto.	Thence was unveiled to me another valley.

Inferno: Canto XX

The Fourth Bolgia: Soothsayers. Amphiaraus, Tiresias, Aruns, Manto, Eryphylus, Michael Scott, Guido Bonatti, and Asdente. Virgil reproaches Dante's Pity. Mantua's Foundation.

Di nova pena mi conven far versi
  e dar matera al ventesimo canto
  de la prima canzon ch'e` d'i sommersi.
	Of a new pain behoves me to make verses
	  And give material to the twentieth canto
	  Of the first song, which is of the submerged.

Io era gia` disposto tutto quanto
  a riguardar ne lo scoperto fondo,
  che si bagnava d'angoscioso pianto;
	I was already thoroughly disposed
	  To peer down into the uncovered depth,
	  Which bathed itself with tears of agony;

e vidi gente per lo vallon tondo
  venir, tacendo e lagrimando, al passo
  che fanno le letane in questo mondo.
	And people saw I through the circular valley,
	  Silent and weeping, coming at the pace
	  Which in this world the Litanies assume.

Come 'l viso mi scese in lor piu` basso,
  mirabilmente apparve esser travolto
  ciascun tra 'l mento e 'l principio del casso;
	As lower down my sight descended on them,
	  Wondrously each one seemed to be distorted
	  From chin to the beginning of the chest;

che' da le reni era tornato 'l volto,
  e in dietro venir li convenia,
  perche' 'l veder dinanzi era lor tolto.
	For tow'rds the reins the countenance was turned,
	  And backward it behoved them to advance,
	  As to look forward had been taken from them.

Forse per forza gia` di parlasia   si travolse cosi` alcun del tutto; ma io nol vidi, ne' credo che sia.	Perchance indeed by violence of palsy Some one has been thus wholly turned awry; But I ne'er saw it, nor believe it can be.

Se Dio ti lasci, lettor, prender frutto
  di tua lezione, or pensa per te stesso
  com'io potea tener lo viso asciutto,
	As God may let thee, Reader, gather fruit
	  From this thy reading, think now for thyself
	  How I could ever keep my face unmoistened,

quando la nostra imagine di presso
  vidi si` torta, che 'l pianto de li occhi
  le natiche bagnava per lo fesso.
	When our own image near me I beheld
	  Distorted so, the weeping of the eyes
	  Along the fissure bathed the hinder parts.

Certo io piangea, poggiato a un de' rocchi
 del duro scoglio, si` che la mia scorta
 mi disse: ""Ancor se' tu de li altri sciocchi?

Qui vive la pieta` quand'e` ben morta;
 chi e` piu` scellerato che colui
 che al giudicio divin passion comporta?

Drizza la testa, drizza, e vedi a cui
 s'aperse a li occhi d'i Teban la terra;
 per ch'ei gridavan tutti: "Dove rui,

Anfiarao? perche' lasci la guerra?".
 E non resto` di ruinare a valle
 fino a Minos che ciascheduno afferra.

Mira c'ha fatto petto de le spalle:
 perche' volle veder troppo davante,
 di retro guarda e fa retroso calle.

Vedi Tiresia, che muto` sembiante
 quando di maschio femmina divenne
 cangiandosi le membra tutte quante;

e prima, poi, ribatter li convenne
 li duo serpenti avvolti, con la verga,
 che riavesse le maschili penne.

Aronta e` quel ch'al ventre li s'atterga,
 che ne' monti di Luni, dove ronca
 lo Carrarese che di sotto alberga,

ebbe tra ' bianchi marmi la spelonca
 per sua dimora; onde a guardar le stelle
 e 'l mar no li era la veduta tronca.

E quella che ricuopre le mammelle,
 che tu non vedi, con le trecce sciolte,
 e ha di la` ogne pilosa pelle,

Manto fu, che cerco` per terre molte;
 poscia si puose la` dove nacqu'io;
 onde un poco mi piace che m'ascolte.

Poscia che 'l padre suo di vita uscio,
 e venne serva la citta` di Baco,
 questa gran tempo per lo mondo gio.

Suso in Italia bella giace un laco,
 a pie` de l'Alpe che serra Lamagna
 sovra Tiralli, c'ha nome Benaco.

Truly I wept, leaning upon a peak
 Of the hard crag, so that my Escort said
 To me: "Art thou, too, of the other fools?

Here pity lives when it is wholly dead;
 Who is a greater reprobate than he
 Who feels compassion at the doom divine?

Lift up, lift up thy head, and see for whom
 Opened the earth before the Thebans' eyes;
 Wherefore they all cried: 'Whither rushest thou,

Amphiaraus? Why dost leave the war?'
 And downward ceased he not to fall amain
 As far as Minos, who lays hold on all.

See, he has made a bosom of his shoulders!
 Because he wished to see too far before him
 Behind he looks, and backward goes his way:

Behold Tiresias, who his semblance changed,
 When from a male a female he became,
 His members being all of them transformed;

And afterwards was forced to strike once more
 The two entangled serpents with his rod,
 Ere he could have again his manly plumes.

That Aruns is, who backs the other's belly,
 Who in the hills of Luni, there where grubs
 The Carrarese who houses underneath,

Among the marbles white a cavern had
 For his abode; whence to behold the stars
 And sea, the view was not cut off from him.

And she there, who is covering up her breasts,
 Which thou beholdest not, with loosened tresses,
 And on that side has all the hairy skin,

Was Manto, who made quest through many lands,
 Afterwards tarried there where I was born;
 Whereof I would thou list to me a little.

After her father had from life departed,
 And the city of Bacchus had become enslaved,
 She a long season wandered through the world.

Above in beauteous Italy lies a lake
 At the Alp's foot that shuts in Germany
 Over Tyrol, and has the name Benaco.

84

Per mille fonti, credo, e piu` si bagna
  tra Garda e Val Camonica e Pennino
  de l'acqua che nel detto laco stagna.
	By a thousand springs, I think, and more, is bathed,
	  'Twixt Garda and Val Camonica, Pennino,
	  With water that grows stagnant in that lake.

Loco e` nel mezzo la` dove 'l trentino
  pastore e quel di Brescia e 'l veronese
  segnar poria, s'e' fesse quel cammino.
	Midway a place is where the Trentine Pastor,
	  And he of Brescia, and the Veronese
	  Might give his blessing, if he passed that way.

Siede Peschiera, bello e forte arnese
  da fronteggiar Bresciani e Bergamaschi,
  ove la riva 'ntorno piu` discese.
	Sitteth Peschiera, fortress fair and strong,
	  To front the Brescians and the Bergamasks,
	  Where round about the bank descendeth lowest.

Ivi convien che tutto quanto caschi
  cio` che 'n grembo a Benaco star non puo`,
  e fassi fiume giu` per verdi paschi.
	There of necessity must fall whatever
	  In bosom of Benaco cannot stay,
	  And grows a river down through verdant pastures.

Tosto che l'acqua a correr mette co,
  non piu` Benaco, ma Mencio si chiama
  fino a Governol, dove cade in Po.
	Soon as the water doth begin to run,
	  No more Benaco is it called, but Mincio,
	  Far as Governo, where it falls in Po.

Non molto ha corso, ch'el trova una lama,
  ne la qual si distende e la 'mpaluda;
  e suol di state talor essere grama.
	Not far it runs before it finds a plain
	  In which it spreads itself, and makes it marshy,
	  And oft 'tis wont in summer to be sickly.

Quindi passando la vergine cruda
  vide terra, nel mezzo del pantano,
  sanza coltura e d'abitanti nuda.
	Passing that way the virgin pitiless
	  Land in the middle of the fen descried,
	  Untilled and naked of inhabitants;

Li`, per fuggire ogne consorzio umano,   ristette con suoi servi a far sue arti,   e visse, e vi lascio` suo corpo vano.	There to escape all human intercourse, She with her servants stayed, her arts to practise And lived, and left her empty body there.

Li uomini poi che 'ntorno erano sparti
  s'accolsero a quel loco, ch'era forte
  per lo pantan ch'avea da tutte parti.
	The men, thereafter, who were scattered round,
	  Collected in that place, which was made strong
	  By the lagoon it had on every side;

Fer la citta` sovra quell'ossa morte;
  e per colei che 'l loco prima elesse,
  Mantua l'appellar sanz'altra sorte.
	They built their city over those dead bones,
	  And, after her who first the place selected,
	  Mantua named it, without other omen.

Gia` fuor le genti sue dentro piu` spesse,
  prima che la mattia da Casalodi
  da Pinamonte inganno ricevesse.
	Its people once within more crowded were,
	  Ere the stupidity of Casalodi
	  From Pinamonte had received deceit.

Pero` t'assenno che, se tu mai odi   originar la mia terra altrimenti,   la verita` nulla menzogna frodi'"".	Therefore I caution thee, if e'er thou hearest Originate my city otherwise, No falsehood may the verity defraud."

E io: ""Maestro, i tuoi ragionamenti
  mi son si` certi e prendon si` mia fede,
  che li altri mi sarien carboni spenti.
	And I: "My Master, thy discourses are
	  To me so certain, and so take my faith,
	  That unto me the rest would be spent coals.

Ma dimmi, de la gente che procede,
  se tu ne vedi alcun degno di nota;
  che' solo a cio` la mia mente rifiede"".

Allor mi disse: ""Quel che da la gota
  porge la barba in su le spalle brune,
  fu - quando Grecia fu di maschi vota,

si` ch'a pena rimaser per le cune -
  augure, e diede 'l punto con Calcanta
  in Aulide a tagliar la prima fune.

Euripilo ebbe nome, e cosi` 'l canta
  l'alta mia tragedia in alcun loco:
  ben lo sai tu che la sai tutta quanta.

Quell'altro che ne' fianchi e` cosi` poco,
  Michele Scotto fu, che veramente
  de le magiche frode seppe 'l gioco.

Vedi Guido Bonatti; vedi Asdente,
  ch'avere inteso al cuoio e a lo spago
  ora vorrebbe, ma tardi si pente.

Vedi le triste che lasciaron l'ago,
  la spuola e 'l fuso, e fecersi 'ndivine;
  fecer malie con erbe e con imago.

Ma vienne omai, che' gia` tiene 'l confine
  d'amendue li emisperi e tocca l'onda
  sotto Sobilia Caino e le spine;

e gia` iernotte fu la luna tonda:
  ben ten de' ricordar, che' non ti nocque
  alcuna volta per la selva fonda"".

Si` mi parlava, e andavamo introcque.

But tell me of the people who are passing,
  If any one note-worthy thou beholdest,
  For only unto that my mind reverts."

Then said he to me: "He who from the cheek
  Thrusts out his beard upon his swarthy shoulders
  Was, at the time when Greece was void of males,

So that there scarce remained one in the cradle,
  An augur, and with Calchas gave the moment,
  In Aulis, when to sever the first cable.

Eryphylus his name was, and so sings
  My lofty Tragedy in some part or other;
  That knowest thou well, who knowest the whole of
      it.

The next, who is so slender in the flanks,
  Was Michael Scott, who of a verity
  Of magical illusions knew the game.

Behold Guido Bonatti, behold Asdente,
  Who now unto his leather and his thread
  Would fain have stuck, but he too late repents.

Behold the wretched ones, who left the needle,
  The spool and rock, and made them fortune-tellers;
  They wrought their magic spells with herb and im-
      age.

But come now, for already holds the confines
  Of both the hemispheres, and under Seville
  Touches the ocean-wave, Cain and the thorns,

And yesternight the moon was round already;
  Thou shouldst remember well it did not harm thee
  From time to time within the forest deep."

Thus spake he to me, and we walked the while.

Inferno: Canto XXI

The Fifth Bolgia: Peculators. The Elder of Santa Zita. Malacoda and other Devils.

Cosi` di ponte in ponte, altro parlando
  che la mia comedia cantar non cura,
  venimmo; e tenavamo il colmo, quando

restammo per veder l'altra fessura
  di Malebolge e li altri pianti vani;
  e vidila mirabilmente oscura.

Quale ne l'arzana` de' Viniziani
  bolle l'inverno la tenace pece
  a rimpalmare i legni lor non sani,

che' navicar non ponno - in quella vece
  chi fa suo legno novo e chi ristoppa
  le coste a quel che piu` viaggi fece;

chi ribatte da proda e chi da poppa;
  altri fa remi e altri volge sarte;
  chi terzeruolo e artimon rintoppa -;

tal, non per foco, ma per divin'arte,
  bollia la` giuso una pegola spessa,
  che 'nviscava la ripa d'ogne parte.

I' vedea lei, ma non vedea in essa
  mai che le bolle che 'l bollor levava,
  e gonfiar tutta, e riseder compressa.

Mentr'io la` giu` fisamente mirava,
  lo duca mio, dicendo ""Guarda, guarda!"",
  mi trasse a se' del loco dov'io stava.

Allor mi volsi come l'uom cui tarda
  di veder quel che li convien fuggire
  e cui paura subita sgagliarda,

From bridge to bridge thus, speaking other things
  Of which my Comedy cares not to sing,
  We came along, and held the summit, when

We halted to behold another fissure
  Of Malebolge and other vain laments;
  And I beheld it marvellously dark.

As in the Arsenal of the Venetians
  Boils in the winter the tenacious pitch
  To smear their unsound vessels o'er again,

For sail they cannot; and instead thereof
  One makes his vessel new, and one recaulks
  The ribs of that which many a voyage has made;

One hammers at the prow, one at the stern,
  This one makes oars, and that one cordage twists,
  Another mends the mainsail and the mizzen;

Thus, not by fire, but by the art divine,
  Was boiling down below there a dense pitch
  Which upon every side the bank belimed.

I saw it, but I did not see within it
  Aught but the bubbles that the boiling raised,
  And all swell up and resubside compressed.

The while below there fixedly I gazed,
  My Leader, crying out: "Beware, beware!"
  Drew me unto himself from where I stood.

Then I turned round, as one who is impatient
  To see what it behoves him to escape,
  And whom a sudden terror doth unman,

che, per veder, non indugia 'l partire:
 e vidi dietro a noi un diavol nero
 correndo su per lo scoglio venire.

Ahi quant'elli era ne l'aspetto fero!
 e quanto mi parea ne l'atto acerbo,
 con l'ali aperte e sovra i pie` leggero!

L'omero suo, ch'era aguto e superbo,
 carcava un peccator con ambo l'anche,
 e quei tenea de' pie` ghermito 'l nerbo.

Del nostro ponte disse: ""O Malebranche,
 ecco un de li anzian di Santa Zita!
 Mettetel sotto, ch'i' torno per anche

a quella terra che n'e` ben fornita:
 ogn'uom v'e` barattier, fuor che Bonturo;
 del no, per li denar vi si fa ita"".

La` giu` 'l butto`, e per lo scoglio duro
 si volse; e mai non fu mastino sciolto
 con tanta fretta a seguitar lo furo.

Quel s'attuffo`, e torno` su` convolto;
 ma i demon che del ponte avean coperchio,
 gridar: ""Qui non ha loco il Santo Volto:

qui si nuota altrimenti che nel Serchio!
 Pero`, se tu non vuo' di nostri graffi,
 non far sopra la pegola soverchio"".

Poi l'addentar con piu` di cento raffi,
 disser: ""Coverto convien che qui balli,
 si` che, se puoi, nascosamente accaffi"".

Non altrimenti i cuoci a' lor vassalli
 fanno attuffare in mezzo la caldaia
 la carne con li uncin, perche' non galli.

Lo buon maestro ""Accio` che non si paia
 che tu ci sia"", mi disse, ""giu` t'acquatta
 dopo uno scheggio, ch'alcun schermo t'aia;

e per nulla offension che mi sia fatta,
 non temer tu, ch'i' ho le cose conte,
 perch'altra volta fui a tal baratta"".

Who, while he looks, delays not his departure;
 And I beheld behind us a black devil,
 Running along upon the crag, approach.

Ah, how ferocious was he in his aspect!
 And how he seemed to me in action ruthless,
 With open wings and light upon his feet!

His shoulders, which sharp-pointed were and high,
 A sinner did encumber with both haunches,
 And he held clutched the sinews of the feet.

From off our bridge, he said: "O Malebranche,
 Behold one of the elders of Saint Zita;
 Plunge him beneath, for I return for others

Unto that town, which is well furnished with them.
 All there are barrators, except Bonturo;
 No into Yes for money there is changed."

He hurled him down, and over the hard crag
 Turned round, and never was a mastiff loosened
 In so much hurry to pursue a thief.

The other sank, and rose again face downward;
 But the demons, under cover of the bridge,
 Cried: "Here the Santo Volto has no place!

Here swims one otherwise than in the Serchio;
 Therefore, if for our gaffs thou wishest not,
 Do not uplift thyself above the pitch."

They seized him then with more than a hundred
   rakes;
 They said: "It here behoves thee to dance covered,
 That, if thou canst, thou secretly mayest pilfer."

Not otherwise the cooks their scullions make
 Immerse into the middle of the caldron
 The meat with hooks, so that it may not float.

Said the good Master to me: "That it be not
 Apparent thou art here, crouch thyself down
 Behind a jag, that thou mayest have some screen;

And for no outrage that is done to me
 Be thou afraid, because these things I know,
 For once before was I in such a scuffle."

Poscia passo` di la` dal co del ponte;
  e com'el giunse in su la ripa sesta,
  mestier li fu d'aver sicura fronte.

Con quel furore e con quella tempesta
  ch'escono i cani a dosso al poverello
  che di subito chiede ove s'arresta,

usciron quei di sotto al ponticello,
  e volser contra lui tutt'i runcigli;
  ma el grido`: ““Nessun di voi sia fello!

Innanzi che l'uncin vostro mi pigli,
  traggasi avante l'un di voi che m'oda,
  e poi d'arruncigliarmi si consigli”“.

Tutti gridaron: ““Vada Malacoda!”“;
  per ch'un si mosse - e li altri stetter fermi -,
  e venne a lui dicendo: ““Che li approda?”“.

““Credi tu, Malacoda, qui vedermi
  esser venuto”“, disse 'l mio maestro,
  ”“sicuro gia` da tutti vostri schermi,

sanza voler divino e fato destro?
  Lascian'andar, che' nel cielo e` voluto
  ch'i' mostri altrui questo cammin silvestro”“.

Allor li fu l'orgoglio si` caduto,
  ch'e' si lascio` cascar l'uncino a' piedi,
  e disse a li altri: ““Omai non sia feruto”“.

E 'l duca mio a me: ““O tu che siedi
  tra li scheggion del ponte quatto quatto,
  sicuramente omai a me ti riedi”“.

Per ch'io mi mossi, e a lui venni ratto;
  e i diavoli si fecer tutti avanti,
  si` ch'io temetti ch'ei tenesser patto;

cosi` vid'io gia` temer li fanti
  ch'uscivan patteggiati di Caprona,
  veggendo se' tra nemici cotanti.

I' m'accostai con tutta la persona
  lungo 'l mio duca, e non torceva li occhi
  da la sembianza lor ch'era non buona.

Then he passed on beyond the bridge's head,
  And as upon the sixth bank he arrived,
  Need was for him to have a steadfast front.

With the same fury, and the same uproar,
  As dogs leap out upon a mendicant,
  Who on a sudden begs, where'er he stops,

They issued from beneath the little bridge,
  And turned against him all their grappling-irons;
  But he cried out: "Be none of you malignant!

Before those hooks of yours lay hold of me,
  Let one of you step forward, who may hear me,
  And then take counsel as to grappling me."

They all cried out: "Let Malacoda go;"
  Whereat one started, and the rest stood still,
  And he came to him, saying: "What avails it?"

"Thinkest thou, Malacoda, to behold me
  Advanced into this place," my Master said,
  "Safe hitherto from all your skill of fence,

Without the will divine, and fate auspicious?
  Let me go on, for it in Heaven is willed
  That I another show this savage road."

Then was his arrogance so humbled in him,
  That he let fall his grapnel at his feet,
  And to the others said: "Now strike him not."

And unto me my Guide: "O thou, who sittest
  Among the splinters of the bridge crouched down,
  Securely now return to me again."

Wherefore I started and came swiftly to him;
  And all the devils forward thrust themselves,
  So that I feared they would not keep their compact.

And thus beheld I once afraid the soldiers
  Who issued under safeguard from Caprona,
  Seeing themselves among so many foes.

Close did I press myself with all my person
  Beside my Leader, and turned not mine eyes
  From off their countenance, which was not good.

Ei chinavan li raffi e ““Vuo' che 'l tocchi”“,
  diceva l'un con l'altro, ““in sul groppone?”“.
  E rispondien: ““Si`, fa che gliel'accocchi!”“.

They lowered their rakes, and "Wilt thou have me hit
    him,"
  They said to one another, "on the rump?"
  And answered: "Yes; see that thou nick him with
    it."

Ma quel demonio che tenea sermone
  col duca mio, si volse tutto presto,
  e disse: ““Posa, posa, Scarmiglione!”“.

But the same demon who was holding parley
  With my Conductor turned him very quickly,
  And said: "Be quiet, be quiet, Scarmiglione;"

Poi disse a noi: ““Piu` oltre andar per questo
  iscoglio non si puo`, pero` che giace
  tutto spezzato al fondo l'arco sesto.

Then said to us: "You can no farther go
  Forward upon this crag, because is lying
  All shattered, at the bottom, the sixth arch.

E se l'andare avante pur vi piace,
  andatevene su per questa grotta;
  presso e` un altro scoglio che via face.

And if it still doth please you to go onward,
  Pursue your way along upon this rock;
  Near is another crag that yields a path.

Ier, piu` oltre cinqu'ore che quest'otta,
  mille dugento con sessanta sei
  anni compie' che qui la via fu rotta.

Yesterday, five hours later than this hour,
  One thousand and two hundred sixty-six
  Years were complete, that here the way was bro-
    ken.

Io mando verso la` di questi miei
  a riguardar s'alcun se ne sciorina;
  gite con lor, che non saranno rei”“.

I send in that direction some of mine
  To see if any one doth air himself;
  Go ye with them; for they will not be vicious.

““Tra'ti avante, Alichino, e Calcabrina”“,
  comincio` elli a dire, ““e tu, Cagnazzo;
  e Barbariccia guidi la decina.

Step forward, Alichino and Calcabrina,"
  Began he to cry out, "and thou, Cagnazzo;
  And Barbariccia, do thou guide the ten.

Libicocco vegn'oltre e Draghignazzo,
  Ciriatto sannuto e Graffiacane
  e Farfarello e Rubicante pazzo.

Come forward, Libicocco and Draghignazzo,
  And tusked Ciriatto and Graffiacane,
  And Farfarello and mad Rubicante;

Cercate 'ntorno le boglienti pane;
  costor sian salvi infino a l'altro scheggio
  che tutto intero va sovra le tane”“.

Search ye all round about the boiling pitch;
  Let these be safe as far as the next crag,
  That all unbroken passes o'er the dens."

““Ome`, maestro, che e` quel ch'i' veggio?”“,
  diss'io, ““deh, sanza scorta andianci soli,
  se tu sa' ir; ch'i' per me non la cheggio.

"O me! what is it, Master, that I see?
  Pray let us go," I said, "without an escort,
  If thou knowest how, since for myself I ask none.

Se tu se' si` accorto come suoli,
  non vedi tu ch'e' digrignan li denti,
  e con le ciglia ne minaccian duoli?”“.

If thou art as observant as thy wont is,
  Dost thou not see that they do gnash their teeth,
  And with their brows are threatening woe to us?"

Ed elli a me: ““Non vo' che tu paventi;
  lasciali digrignar pur a lor senno,
  ch'e' fanno cio` per li lessi dolenti”“.

And he to me: "I will not have thee fear;
  Let them gnash on, according to their fancy,
  Because they do it for those boiling wretches."

Per l'argine sinistro volta dienno;
  ma prima avea ciascun la lingua stretta
  coi denti, verso lor duca, per cenno;

ed elli avea del cul fatto trombetta.

Along the left-hand dike they wheeled about;
  But first had each one thrust his tongue between
  His teeth towards their leader for a signal;

And he had made a trumpet of his rump.

Inferno: Canto XXII

Ciampolo, Friar Gomita, and Michael Zanche. The Malabranche quarrel.

Io vidi gia` cavalier muover campo,
  e cominciare stormo e far lor mostra,
  e talvolta partir per loro scampo;

corridor vidi per la terra vostra,
  o Aretini, e vidi gir gualdane,
  fedir torneamenti e correr giostra;

quando con trombe, e quando con campane,
  con tamburi e con cenni di castella,
  e con cose nostrali e con istrane;

ne' gia` con si` diversa cennamella
  cavalier vidi muover ne' pedoni,
  ne' nave a segno di terra o di stella.

Noi andavam con li diece demoni.
  Ahi fiera compagnia! ma ne la chiesa
  coi santi, e in taverna coi ghiottoni.

Pur a la pegola era la mia 'ntesa, .
  per veder de la bolgia ogne contegno
  e de la gente ch'entro v'era incesa.

Come i dalfini, quando fanno segno
  a' marinar con l'arco de la schiena,
  che s'argomentin di campar lor legno,

talor cosi`, ad alleggiar la pena,
  mostrav'alcun de' peccatori il dosso
  e nascondea in men che non balena.

E come a l'orlo de l'acqua d'un fosso
  stanno i ranocchi pur col muso fuori,
  si` che celano i piedi e l'altro grosso,

I have erewhile seen horsemen moving camp,
  Begin the storming, and their muster make,
  And sometimes starting off for their escape;

Vaunt-couriers have I seen upon your land,
  O Aretines, and foragers go forth,
  Tournaments stricken, and the joustings run,

Sometimes with trumpets and sometimes with bells,
  With kettle-drums, and signals of the castles,
  And with our own, and with outlandish things,

But never yet with bagpipe so uncouth
  Did I see horsemen move, nor infantry,
  Nor ship by any sign of land or star.

We went upon our way with the ten demons;
  Ah, savage company! but in the church
  With saints, and in the tavern with the gluttons!

Ever upon the pitch was my intent,
  To see the whole condition of that Bolgia,
  And of the people who therein were burned.

Even as the dolphins, when they make a sign
  To mariners by arching of the back,
  That they should counsel take to save their vessel,

Thus sometimes, to alleviate his pain,
  One of the sinners would display his back,
  And in less time conceal it than it lightens.

As on the brink of water in a ditch
  The frogs stand only with their muzzles out,
  So that they hide their feet and other bulk,

si` stavan d'ogne parte i peccatori;
  ma come s'appressava Barbariccia,
  cosi` si ritraen sotto i bollori.

I' vidi, e anco il cor me n'accapriccia,
  uno aspettar cosi`, com'elli 'ncontra
  ch'una rana rimane e l'altra spiccia;

e Graffiacan, che li era piu` di contra,
  li arrunciglio` le 'mpegolate chiome
  e trassel su`, che mi parve una lontra.

I' sapea gia` di tutti quanti 'l nome,
  si` li notai quando fuorono eletti,
  e poi ch'e' si chiamaro, attesi come.

""O Rubicante, fa che tu li metti
  li unghioni a dosso, si` che tu lo scuoi!"",
  gridavan tutti insieme i maladetti.

E io: ""Maestro mio, fa, se tu puoi,
  che tu sappi chi e` lo sciagurato
  venuto a man de li avversari suoi"".

Lo duca mio li s'accosto` allato;
  domandollo ond'ei fosse, e quei rispuose:
  ""I' fui del regno di Navarra nato.

Mia madre a servo d'un segnor mi puose,
  che m'avea generato d'un ribaldo,
  distruggitor di se' e di sue cose.

Poi fui famiglia del buon re Tebaldo:
  quivi mi misi a far baratteria;
  di ch'io rendo ragione in questo caldo"".

E Ciriatto, a cui di bocca uscia
  d'ogne parte una sanna come a porco,
  li fe' sentir come l'una sdruscia.

Tra male gatte era venuto 'l sorco;
  ma Barbariccia il chiuse con le braccia,
  e disse: ""State in la`, mentr'io lo 'nforco"".

E al maestro mio volse la faccia:
  ""Domanda"", disse, ""ancor, se piu` disii
  saper da lui, prima ch'altri 'l disfaccia"".

Lo duca dunque: ""Or di`: de li altri rii
  conosci tu alcun che sia latino
  sotto la pece?"". E quelli: ""I' mi partii,

So upon every side the sinners stood;
  But ever as Barbariccia near them came,
  Thus underneath the boiling they withdrew.

I saw, and still my heart doth shudder at it,
  One waiting thus, even as it comes to pass
  One frog remains, and down another dives;

And Graffiacan, who most confronted him,
  Grappled him by his tresses smeared with pitch,
  And drew him up, so that he seemed an otter.

I knew, before, the names of all of them,
  So had I noted them when they were chosen,
  And when they called each other, listened how.

"O Rubicante, see that thou do lay
  Thy claws upon him, so that thou mayst flay him,"
  Cried all together the accursed ones.

And I: "My Master, see to it, if thou canst,
  That thou mayst know who is the luckless wight,
  Thus come into his adversaries' hands."

Near to the side of him my Leader drew,
  Asked of him whence he was; and he replied:
  "I in the kingdom of Navarre was born;

My mother placed me servant to a lord,
  For she had borne me to a ribald knave,
  Destroyer of himself and of his things.

Then I domestic was of good King Thibault;
  I set me there to practise barratry,
  For which I pay the reckoning in this heat."

And Ciriatto, from whose mouth projected,
  On either side, a tusk, as in a boar,
  Caused him to feel how one of them could rip.

Among malicious cats the mouse had come;
  But Barbariccia clasped him in his arms,
  And said: "Stand ye aside, while I enfork him."

And to my Master he turned round his head;
  "Ask him again," he said, "if more thou wish
  To know from him, before some one destroy him."

The Guide: "Now tell then of the other culprits;
  Knowest thou any one who is a Latian,
  Under the pitch?" And he: "I separated

poco e`, da un che fu di la` vicino.
  Cosi` foss'io ancor con lui coperto,
  ch'i' non temerei unghia ne' uncino!"".

E Libicocco ""Troppo avem sofferto"",
  disse; e preseli 'l braccio col runciglio,
  si` che, stracciando, ne porto` un lacerto.

Draghignazzo anco i volle dar di piglio
  giuso a le gambe; onde 'l decurio loro
  si volse intorno intorno con mal piglio.

Quand'elli un poco rappaciati fuoro,
  a lui, ch'ancor mirava sua ferita,
  domando` 'l duca mio sanza dimoro:

""Chi fu colui da cui mala partita
  di' che facesti per venire a proda?"".
  Ed ei rispuose: ""Fu frate Gomita,

quel di Gallura, vasel d'ogne froda,
  ch'ebbe i nemici di suo donno in mano,
  e fe' si` lor, che ciascun se ne loda.

Danar si tolse, e lasciolli di piano,
  si` com'e' dice; e ne li altri offici anche
  barattier fu non picciol, ma sovrano.

Usa con esso donno Michel Zanche
  di Logodoro; e a dir di Sardigna
  le lingue lor non si sentono stanche.

Ome`, vedete l'altro che digrigna:
  i' direi anche, ma i' temo ch'ello
  non s'apparecchi a grattarmi la tigna"".

E 'l gran proposto, volto a Farfarello
  che stralunava li occhi per fedire,
  disse: ""Fatti 'n costa`, malvagio uccello!"".

""Se voi volete vedere o udire"",
  ricomincio` lo spaurato appresso
  ""Toschi o Lombardi, io ne faro` venire;

ma stieno i Malebranche un poco in cesso,
  si` ch'ei non teman de le lor vendette;
  e io, seggendo in questo loco stesso,

per un ch'io son, ne faro` venir sette
  quand'io suffolero`, com'e` nostro uso
  di fare allor che fori alcun si mette"".

Lately from one who was a neighbour to it;
  Would that I still were covered up with him,
  For I should fear not either claw nor hook!"

And Libicocco: "We have borne too much;"
  And with his grapnel seized him by the arm,
  So that, by rending, he tore off a tendon.

Eke Draghignazzo wished to pounce upon him
  Down at the legs; whence their Decurion
  Turned round and round about with evil look.

When they again somewhat were pacified,
  Of him, who still was looking at his wound,
  Demanded my Conductor without stay:

"Who was that one, from whom a luckless parting
  Thou sayest thou hast made, to come ashore?"
  And he replied: "It was the Friar Gomita,

He of Gallura, vessel of all fraud,
  Who had the enemies of his Lord in hand,
  And dealt so with them each exults thereat;

Money he took, and let them smoothly off,
  As he says; and in other offices
  A barrator was he, not mean but sovereign.

Foregathers with him one Don Michael Zanche
  Of Logodoro; and of Sardinia
  To gossip never do their tongues feel tired.

O me! see that one, how he grinds his teeth;
  Still farther would I speak, but am afraid
  Lest he to scratch my itch be making ready."

And the grand Provost, turned to Farfarello,
  Who rolled his eyes about as if to strike,
  Said: "Stand aside there, thou malicious bird."

"If you desire either to see or hear,"
  The terror-stricken recommenced thereon,
  "Tuscans or Lombards, I will make them come.

But let the Malebranche cease a little,
  So that these may not their revenges fear,
  And I, down sitting in this very place,

For one that I am will make seven come,
  When I shall whistle, as our custom is
  To do whenever one of us comes out."

Cagnazzo a cotal motto levo` 'l muso,	Cagnazzo at these words his muzzle lifted,
crollando 'l capo, e disse: ""Odi malizia	Shaking his head, and said: "Just hear the trick
ch'elli ha pensata per gittarsi giuso!"".	Which he has thought of, down to throw himself!"
Ond'ei, ch'avea lacciuoli a gran divizia,	Whence he, who snares in great abundance had,
rispuose: ""Malizioso son io troppo,	Responded: "I by far too cunning am,
quand'io procuro a' mia maggior trestizia"".	When I procure for mine a greater sadness."
Alichin non si tenne e, di rintoppo	Alichin held not in, but running counter
a li altri, disse a lui: ""Se tu ti cali,	Unto the rest, said to him: "If thou dive,
io non ti verro` dietro di gualoppo,	I will not follow thee upon the gallop,
ma battero` sovra la pece l'ali.	But I will beat my wings above the pitch;
Lascisi 'l collo, e sia la ripa scudo,	The height be left, and be the bank a shield
a veder se tu sol piu` di noi vali"".	To see if thou alone dost countervail us."
O tu che leggi, udirai nuovo ludo:	O thou who readest, thou shalt hear new sport!
ciascun da l'altra costa li occhi volse;	Each to the other side his eyes averted;
quel prima, ch'a cio` fare era piu` crudo.	He first, who most reluctant was to do it.
Lo Navarrese ben suo tempo colse;	The Navarrese selected well his time;
fermo` le piante a terra, e in un punto	Planted his feet on land, and in a moment
salto` e dal proposto lor si sciolse.	Leaped, and released himself from their design.
Di che ciascun di colpa fu compunto,	Whereat each one was suddenly stung with shame,
ma quei piu` che cagion fu del difetto;	But he most who was cause of the defeat;
pero` si mosse e grido`: ""Tu se' giunto!"".	Therefore he moved, and cried: "Thou art o'ertak-ern."
Ma poco i valse: che' l'ali al sospetto	But little it availed, for wings could not
non potero avanzar: quelli ando` sotto,	Outstrip the fear; the other one went under,
e quei drizzo` volando suso il petto:	And, flying, upward he his breast directed;
non altrimenti l'anitra di botto,	Not otherwise the duck upon a sudden
quando 'l falcon s'appressa, giu` s'attuffa,	Dives under, when the falcon is approaching,
ed ei ritorna su` crucciato e rotto.	And upward he returneth cross and weary.
Irato Calcabrina de la buffa,	Infuriate at the mockery, Calcabrina
volando dietro li tenne, invaghito	Flying behind him followed close, desirous
che quei campasse per aver la zuffa;	The other should escape, to have a quarrel.
e come 'l barattier fu disparito,	And when the barrator had disappeared,
cosi` volse li artigli al suo compagno,	He turned his talons upon his companion,
e fu con lui sopra 'l fosso ghermito.	And grappled with him right above the moat.
Ma l'altro fu bene sparvier grifagno	But sooth the other was a doughty sparhawk
ad artigliar ben lui, e amendue	To clapperclaw him well; and both of them
cadder nel mezzo del bogliente stagno.	Fell in the middle of the boiling pond.

Lo caldo sghermitor subito fue;
  ma pero` di levarsi era neente,
  si` avieno inviscate l'ali sue.

Barbariccia, con li altri suoi dolente,
  quattro ne fe' volar da l'altra costa
  con tutt'i raffi, e assai prestamente

di qua, di la` discesero a la posta;
  porser li uncini verso li 'mpaniati,
  ch'eran gia` cotti dentro da la crosta;

e noi lasciammo lor cosi` 'mpacciati.

A sudden intercessor was the heat;
  But ne'ertheless of rising there was naught,
  To such degree they had their wings belimed.

Lamenting with the others, Barbariccia
  Made four of them fly to the other side
  With all their gaffs, and very speedily

This side and that they to their posts descended;
  They stretched their hooks towards the pitch-
    ensnared,
  Who were already baked within the crust,

And in this manner busied did we leave them.

Inferno: Canto XXIII

Escape from the Malabranche. The Sixth Bolgia: Hypocrites. Catalano and Loderingo. Caiaphas.

Taciti, soli, sanza compagnia
  n'andavam l'un dinanzi e l'altro dopo,
  come frati minor vanno per via.

Volt'era in su la favola d'Isopo
  lo mio pensier per la presente rissa,
  dov'el parlo` de la rana e del topo;

che' piu` non si pareggia 'mo' e 'issa'
  che l'un con l'altro fa, se ben s'accoppia
  principio e fine con la mente fissa.

E come l'un pensier de l'altro scoppia,
  cosi` nacque di quello un altro poi,
  che la prima paura mi fe' doppia.

Io pensava cosi`: 'Questi per noi
  sono scherniti con danno e con beffa
  si` fatta, ch'assai credo che lor noi.

Se l'ira sovra 'l mal voler s'aggueffa,
  ei ne verranno dietro piu` crudeli
  che 'l cane a quella lievre ch'elli acceffa'.

Gia` mi sentia tutti arricciar li peli
  de la paura e stava in dietro intento,
  quand'io dissi: ""Maestro, se non celi

te e me tostamente, i' ho pavento
  d'i Malebranche. Noi li avem gia` dietro;
  io li 'magino si`, che gia` li sento"".

E quei: ""S'i' fossi di piombato vetro,
  l'imagine di fuor tua non trarrei
  piu` tosto a me, che quella dentro 'mpetro.

Silent, alone, and without company
  We went, the one in front, the other after,
  As go the Minor Friars along their way.

Upon the fable of Aesop was directed
  My thought, by reason of the present quarrel,
  Where he has spoken of the frog and mouse;

For 'mo' and 'issa' are not more alike
  Than this one is to that, if well we couple
  End and beginning with a steadfast mind.

And even as one thought from another springs,
  So afterward from that was born another,
  Which the first fear within me double made.

Thus did I ponder: "These on our account
  Are laughed to scorn, with injury and scoff
  So great, that much I think it must annoy them.

If anger be engrafted on ill-will,
  They will come after us more merciless
  Than dog upon the leveret which he seizes,"

I felt my hair stand all on end already
  With terror, and stood backwardly intent,
  When said I: "Master, if thou hidest not

Thyself and me forthwith, of Malebranche
  I am in dread; we have them now behind us;
  I so imagine them, I already feel them."

And he: "If I were made of leaded glass,
  Thine outward image I should not attract
  Sooner to me than I imprint the inner.

Pur mo venieno i tuo' pensier tra ' miei,
  con simile atto e con simile faccia,
  si` che d'intrambi un sol consiglio fei.
	Just now thy thoughts came in among my own,
	  With similar attitude and similar face,
	  So that of both one counsel sole I made.

S'elli e` che si` la destra costa giaccia,
  che noi possiam ne l'altra bolgia scendere,
  noi fuggirem l'imaginata caccia"".
	If peradventure the right bank so slope
	  That we to the next Bolgia can descend,
	  We shall escape from the imagined chase."

Gia` non compie' di tal consiglio rendere,
  ch'io li vidi venir con l'ali tese
  non molto lungi, per volerne prendere.
	Not yet he finished rendering such opinion,
	  When I beheld them come with outstretched wings,
	  Not far remote, with will to seize upon us.

Lo duca mio di subito mi prese,
  come la madre ch'al romore e` desta
  e vede presso a se' le fiamme accese,
	My Leader on a sudden seized me up,
	  Even as a mother who by noise is wakened,
	  And close beside her sees the enkindled flames,

che prende il figlio e fugge e non s'arresta,
  avendo piu` di lui che di se' cura,
  tanto che solo una camiscia vesta;
	Who takes her son, and flies, and does not stop,
	  Having more care of him than of herself,
	  So that she clothes her only with a shift;

e giu` dal collo de la ripa dura
  supin si diede a la pendente roccia,
  che l'un de' lati a l'altra bolgia tura.
	And downward from the top of the hard bank
	  Supine he gave him to the pendent rock,
	  That one side of the other Bolgia walls.

Non corse mai si` tosto acqua per doccia   a volger ruota di molin terragno,   quand'ella piu` verso le pale approccia,	Ne'er ran so swiftly water through a sluice To turn the wheel of any land-built mill, When nearest to the paddles it approaches,

come 'l maestro mio per quel vivagno,
  portandosene me sovra 'l suo petto,
  come suo figlio, non come compagno.
	As did my Master down along that border,
	  Bearing me with him on his breast away,
	  As his own son, and not as a companion.

A pena fuoro i pie` suoi giunti al letto   del fondo giu`, ch'e' furon in sul colle sovresso noi; ma non li` era sospetto;	Hardly the bed of the ravine below His feet had reached, ere they had reached the hill Right over us; but he was not afraid;

che' l'alta provedenza che lor volle
  porre ministri de la fossa quinta,
  poder di partirs'indi a tutti tolle.
	For the high Providence, which had ordained
	  To place them ministers of the fifth moat,
	  The power of thence departing took from all.

La` giu` trovammo una gente dipinta
  che giva intorno assai con lenti passi,
  piangendo e nel sembiante stanca e vinta.
	A painted people there below we found,
	  Who went about with footsteps very slow,
	  Weeping and in their semblance tired and van-
	    quished.

Elli avean cappe con cappucci bassi
  dinanzi a li occhi, fatte de la taglia
  che in Clugni` per li monaci fassi.
	They had on mantles with the hoods low down
	  Before their eyes, and fashioned of the cut
	  That in Cologne they for the monks are made.

Di fuor dorate son, si` ch'elli abbaglia;
  ma dentro tutte piombo, e gravi tanto,
  che Federigo le mettea di paglia.

Oh in etterno faticoso manto!
  Noi ci volgemmo ancor pur a man manca
  con loro insieme, intenti al tristo pianto;

ma per lo peso quella gente stanca
  venia si` pian, che noi eravam nuovi
  di compagnia ad ogne mover d'anca.

Per ch'io al duca mio: ""Fa che tu trovi
  alcun ch'al fatto o al nome si conosca,
  e li occhi, si` andando, intorno movi"".

E un che 'ntese la parola tosca,
  di retro a noi grido`: ""Tenete i piedi,
  voi che correte si` per l'aura fosca!

Forse ch'avrai da me quel che tu chiedi"".
  Onde 'l duca si volse e disse: ""Aspetta
  e poi secondo il suo passo procedi"".

Ristetti, e vidi due mostrar gran fretta
  de l'animo, col viso, d'esser meco;
  ma tardavali 'l carco e la via stretta.

Quando fuor giunti, assai con l'occhio bieco
  mi rimiraron sanza far parola;
  poi si volsero in se', e dicean seco:

""Costui par vivo a l'atto de la gola;
  e s'e' son morti, per qual privilegio
  vanno scoperti de la grave stola?"".

Poi disser me: ""O Tosco, ch'al collegio
  de l'ipocriti tristi se' venuto,
  dir chi tu se' non avere in dispregio"".

E io a loro: ""I' fui nato e cresciuto
  sovra 'l bel fiume d'Arno a la gran villa,
  e son col corpo ch'i' ho sempre avuto.

Ma voi chi siete, a cui tanto distilla
  quant'i' veggio dolor giu` per le guance?
  e che pena e` in voi che si` sfavilla?"".

E l'un rispuose a me: ""Le cappe rance
  son di piombo si` grosse, che li pesi
  fan cosi` cigolar le lor bilance.

Without, they gilded are so that it dazzles;
  But inwardly all leaden and so heavy
  That Frederick used to put them on of straw.

O everlastingly fatiguing mantle!
  Again we turned us, still to the left hand
  Along with them, intent on their sad plaint;

But owing to the weight, that weary folk
  Came on so tardily, that we were new
  In company at each motion of the haunch.

Whence I unto my Leader: "See thou find
  Some one who may by deed or name be known,
  And thus in going move thine eye about."

And one, who understood the Tuscan speech,
  Cried to us from behind: "Stay ye your feet,
  Ye, who so run athwart the dusky air!

Perhaps thou'lt have from me what thou demandest."
  Whereat the Leader turned him, and said: "Wait,
  And then according to his pace proceed."

I stopped, and two beheld I show great haste
  Of spirit, in their faces, to be with me;
  But the burden and the narrow way delayed them.

When they came up, long with an eye askance
  They scanned me without uttering a word.
  Then to each other turned, and said together:

"He by the action of his throat seems living;
  And if they dead are, by what privilege
  Go they uncovered by the heavy stole?"

Then said to me: "Tuscan, who to the college
  Of miserable hypocrites art come,
  Do not disdain to tell us who thou art."

And I to them: "Born was I, and grew up
  In the great town on the fair river of Arno,
  And with the body am I've always had.

But who are ye, in whom there trickles down
  Along your cheeks such grief as I behold?
  And what pain is upon you, that so sparkles?"

And one replied to me: "These orange cloaks
  Are made of lead so heavy, that the weights
  Cause in this way their balances to creak.

Frati godenti fummo, e bolognesi;
  io Catalano e questi Loderingo
  nomati, e da tua terra insieme presi,

come suole esser tolto un uom solingo,
  per conservar sua pace; e fummo tali,
  ch'ancor si pare intorno dal Gardingo'".

Io cominciai: ""O frati, i vostri mali…"";
  ma piu` non dissi, ch'a l'occhio mi corse
  un, crucifisso in terra con tre pali.

Quando mi vide, tutto si distorse,
  soffiando ne la barba con sospiri;
  e 'l frate Catalan, ch'a cio` s'accorse,

mi disse: ""Quel confitto che tu miri,
  consiglio` i Farisei che convenia
  porre un uom per lo popolo a' martiri.

Attraversato e`, nudo, ne la via,
  come tu vedi, ed e` mestier ch'el senta
  qualunque passa, come pesa, pria.

E a tal modo il socero si stenta
  in questa fossa, e li altri dal concilio
  che fu per li Giudei mala sementa"".

Allor vid'io maravigliar Virgilio
  sovra colui ch'era disteso in croce
  tanto vilmente ne l'etterno essilio.

Poscia drizzo` al frate cotal voce:
  ""Non vi dispiaccia, se vi lece, dirci
  s'a la man destra giace alcuna foce

onde noi amendue possiamo uscirci,
  sanza costrigner de li angeli neri
  che vegnan d'esto fondo a dipartirci"".

Rispuose adunque: ""Piu` che tu non speri
  s'appressa un sasso che de la gran cerchia
  si move e varca tutt'i vallon feri,

salvo che 'n questo e` rotto e nol coperchia:
  montar potrete su per la ruina,
  che giace in costa e nel fondo soperchia"".

Lo duca stette un poco a testa china;
  poi disse: ""Mal contava la bisogna
  colui che i peccator di qua uncina"".

Frati Gaudenti were we, and Bolognese;
  I Catalano, and he Loderingo
  Named, and together taken by thy city,

As the wont is to take one man alone,
  For maintenance of its peace; and we were such
  That still it is apparent round Gardingo."

"O Friars," began I, "your iniquitous. . ."
  But said no more; for to mine eyes there rushed
  One crucified with three stakes on the ground.

When me he saw, he writhed himself all over,
  Blowing into his beard with suspirations;
  And the Friar Catalan, who noticed this,

Said to me: "This transfixed one, whom thou seest,
  Counselled the Pharisees that it was meet
  To put one man to torture for the people.

Crosswise and naked is he on the path,
  As thou perceivest; and he needs must feel,
  Whoever passes, first how much he weighs;

And in like mode his father-in-law is punished
  Within this moat, and the others of the council,
  Which for the Jews was a malignant seed."

And thereupon I saw Virgilius marvel
  O'er him who was extended on the cross
  So vilely in eternal banishment.

Then he directed to the Friar this voice:
  "Be not displeased, if granted thee, to tell us
  If to the right hand any pass slope down

By which we two may issue forth from here,
  Without constraining some of the black angels
  To come and extricate us from this deep."

Then he made answer: "Nearer than thou hopest
  There is a rock, that forth from the great circle
  Proceeds, and crosses all the cruel valleys,

Save that at this 'tis broken, and does not bridge it;
  You will be able to mount up the ruin,
  That sidelong slopes and at the bottom rises."

The Leader stood awhile with head bowed down;
  Then said: "The business badly he recounted
  Who grapples with his hook the sinners yonder."

E 'l frate: ""Io udi' gia` dire a Bologna
 del diavol vizi assai, tra ' quali udi'
 ch'elli e` bugiardo, e padre di menzogna"".

Appresso il duca a gran passi sen gi`,
 turbato un poco d'ira nel sembiante;
 ond'io da li 'ncarcati mi parti'

dietro a le poste de le care piante.

And the Friar: "Many of the Devil's vices
 Once heard I at Bologna, and among them,
 That he's a liar and the father of lies."

Thereat my Leader with great strides went on,
 Somewhat disturbed with anger in his looks;
 Whence from the heavy-laden I departed

After the prints of his beloved feet.

Inferno: Canto XXIV

The Seventh Bolgia: Thieves. Vanni Fucci. Serpents.

In quella parte del giovanetto anno
  che 'l sole i crin sotto l'Aquario tempra
  e gia` le notti al mezzo di` sen vanno,

quando la brina in su la terra assempra
  l'imagine di sua sorella bianca,
  ma poco dura a la sua penna tempra,

lo villanello a cui la roba manca,
  si leva, e guarda, e vede la campagna
  biancheggiar tutta; ond'ei si batte l'anca,

ritorna in casa, e qua e la` si lagna,
  come 'l tapin che non sa che si faccia;
  poi riede, e la speranza ringavagna,

veggendo 'l mondo aver cangiata faccia
  in poco d'ora, e prende suo vincastro,
  e fuor le pecorelle a pascer caccia.

Cosi` mi fece sbigottir lo mastro
  quand'io li vidi si` turbar la fronte,
  e cosi` tosto al mal giunse lo 'mpiastro;

che', come noi venimmo al guasto ponte,
  lo duca a me si volse con quel piglio
  dolce ch'io vidi prima a pie` del monte.

Le braccia aperse, dopo alcun consiglio
  eletto seco riguardando prima
  ben la ruina, e diedemi di piglio.

E come quei ch'adopera ed estima,
  che sempre par che 'nnanzi si proveggia,
  cosi`, levando me su` ver la cima

In that part of the youthful year wherein
  The Sun his locks beneath Aquarius tempers,
  And now the nights draw near to half the day,

What time the hoar-frost copies on the ground
  The outward semblance of her sister white,
  But little lasts the temper of her pen,

The husbandman, whose forage faileth him,
  Rises, and looks, and seeth the champaign
  All gleaming white, whereat he beats his flank,

Returns in doors, and up and down laments,
  Like a poor wretch, who knows not what to do;
  Then he returns and hope revives again,

Seeing the world has changed its countenance
  In little time, and takes his shepherd's crook,
  And forth the little lambs to pasture drives.

Thus did the Master fill me with alarm,
  When I beheld his forehead so disturbed,
  And to the ailment came as soon the plaster.

For as we came unto the ruined bridge,
  The Leader turned to me with that sweet look
  Which at the mountain's foot I first beheld.

His arms he opened, after some advisement
  Within himself elected, looking first
  Well at the ruin, and laid hold of me.

And even as he who acts and meditates,
  For aye it seems that he provides beforehand,
  So upward lifting me towards the summit

d'un ronchione, avvisava un'altra scheggia
dicendo: ""Sovra quella poi t'aggrappa;
ma tenta pria s'e` tal ch'ella ti reggia"".

Non era via da vestito di cappa,
che' noi a pena, ei lieve e io sospinto,
potavam su` montar di chiappa in chiappa.

E se non fosse che da quel precinto
piu` che da l'altro era la costa corta,
non so di lui, ma io sarei ben vinto.

Ma perche' Malebolge inver' la porta
del bassissimo pozzo tutta pende,
lo sito di ciascuna valle porta

che l'una costa surge e l'altra scende;
noi pur venimmo al fine in su la punta
onde l'ultima pietra si scoscende.

La lena m'era del polmon si` munta
quand'io fui su`, ch'i' non potea piu` oltre,
anzi m'assisi ne la prima giunta.

""Omai convien che tu cosi` ti spoltre"",
disse 'l maestro; ""che', seggendo in piuma,
in fama non si vien, ne' sotto coltre;

sanza la qual chi sua vita consuma,
cotal vestigio in terra di se' lascia,
qual fummo in aere e in acqua la schiuma.

E pero` leva su`: vinci l'ambascia
con l'animo che vince ogne battaglia,
se col suo grave corpo non s'accascia.

Piu` lunga scala convien che si saglia;
non basta da costoro esser partito.
Se tu mi 'ntendi, or fa si` che ti vaglia"".

Leva'mi allor, mostrandomi fornito
meglio di lena ch'i' non mi sentia;
e dissi: ""Va, ch'i' son forte e ardito"".

Su per lo scoglio prendemmo la via,
ch'era ronchioso, stretto e malagevole,
ed erto piu` assai che quel di pria.

Parlando andava per non parer fievole;
onde una voce usci` de l'altro fosso,
a parole formar disconvenevole.

Of a huge rock, he scanned another crag,
Saying: "To that one grapple afterwards,
But try first if 'tis such that it will hold thee."

This was no way for one clothed with a cloak;
For hardly we, he light, and I pushed upward,
Were able to ascend from jag to jag.

And had it not been, that upon that precinct
Shorter was the ascent than on the other,
He I know not, but I had been dead beat.

But because Malebolge tow'rds the mouth
Of the profoundest well is all inclining,
The structure of each valley doth import

That one bank rises and the other sinks.
Still we arrived at length upon the point
Wherefrom the last stone breaks itself asunder.

The breath was from my lungs so milked away,
When I was up, that I could go no farther,
Nay, I sat down upon my first arrival.

"Now it behoves thee thus to put off sloth,"
My Master said; "for sitting upon down,
Or under quilt, one cometh not to fame,

Withouten which whoso his life consumes
Such vestige leaveth of himself on earth,
As smoke in air or in the water foam.

And therefore raise thee up, o'ercome the anguish
With spirit that o'ercometh every battle,
If with its heavy body it sink not.

A longer stairway it behoves thee mount;
'Tis not enough from these to have departed;
Let it avail thee, if thou understand me."

Then I uprose, showing myself provided
Better with breath than I did feel myself,
And said: "Go on, for I am strong and bold."

Upward we took our way along the crag,
Which jagged was, and narrow, and difficult,
And more precipitous far than that before.

Speaking I went, not to appear exhausted;
Whereat a voice from the next moat came forth,
Not well adapted to articulate words.

Non so che disse, ancor che sovra 'l dosso
  fossi de l'arco gia` che varca quivi;
  ma chi parlava ad ire parea mosso.

Io era volto in giu`, ma li occhi vivi
  non poteano ire al fondo per lo scuro;
  per ch'io: ““Maestro, fa che tu arrivi

da l'altro cinghio e dismontiam lo muro;
  che', com'i' odo quinci e non intendo,
  cosi` giu` veggio e neente affiguro”“.

““Altra risposta”“, disse, ““non ti rendo
  se non lo far; che' la dimanda onesta
  si de' seguir con l'opera tacendo”“.

Noi discendemmo il ponte da la testa
  dove s'aggiugne con l'ottava ripa,
  e poi mi fu la bolgia manifesta:

e vidivi entro terribile stipa
  di serpenti, e di si` diversa mena
  che la memoria il sangue ancor mi scipa.

Piu` non si vanti Libia con sua rena;
  che' se chelidri, iaculi e faree
  produce, e cencri con anfisibena,

ne' tante pestilenzie ne' si` ree
  mostro` gia` mai con tutta l'Etiopia
  ne' con cio` che di sopra al Mar Rosso ee.

Tra questa cruda e tristissima copia
  correan genti nude e spaventate,
  sanza sperar pertugio o elitropia:

con serpi le man dietro avean legate;
  quelle ficcavan per le ren la coda
  e 'l capo, ed eran dinanzi aggroppate.

Ed ecco a un ch'era da nostra proda,
  s'avvento` un serpente che 'l trafisse
  la` dove 'l collo a le spalle s'annoda.

Ne' O si` tosto mai ne' I si scrisse,
  com'el s'accese e arse, e cener tutto
  convenne che cascando divenisse;

I know not what it said, though o'er the back
  I now was of the arch that passes there;
  But he seemed moved to anger who was speaking.

I was bent downward, but my living eyes
  Could not attain the bottom, for the dark;
  Wherefore I: "Master, see that thou arrive

At the next round, and let us descend the wall;
  For as from hence I hear and understand not,
  So I look down and nothing I distinguish."

"Other response," he said, "I make thee not,
  Except the doing; for the modest asking
  Ought to be followed by the deed in silence."

We from the bridge descended at its head,
  Where it connects itself with the eighth bank,
  And then was manifest to me the Bolgia;

And I beheld therein a terrible throng
  Of serpents, and of such a monstrous kind,
  That the remembrance still congeals my blood

Let Libya boast no longer with her sand;
  For if Chelydri, Jaculi, and Phareae
  She breeds, with Cenchri and with Amphisbaena,

Neither so many plagues nor so malignant
  E'er showed she with all Ethiopia,
  Nor with whatever on the Red Sea is!

Among this cruel and most dismal throng
  People were running naked and affrighted.
  Without the hope of hole or heliotrope.

They had their hands with serpents bound behind
    them;
  These riveted upon their reins the tail
  And head, and were in front of them entwined.

And lo! at one who was upon our side
  There darted forth a serpent, which transfixed him
  There where the neck is knotted to the shoulders.

Nor 'O' so quickly e'er, nor 'I' was written,
  As he took fire, and burned; and ashes wholly
  Behoved it that in falling he became.

e poi che fu a terra si` distrutto,
  la polver si raccolse per se' stessa,
  e 'n quel medesmo ritorno` di butto.

Cosi` per li gran savi si confessa
  che la fenice more e poi rinasce,
  quando al cinquecentesimo anno appressa;

erba ne' biado in sua vita non pasce,
  ma sol d'incenso lagrime e d'amomo,
  e nardo e mirra son l'ultime fasce.

E qual e` quel che cade, e non sa como,
  per forza di demon ch'a terra il tira,
  o d'altra oppilazion che lega l'omo,

quando si leva, che 'ntorno si mira
  tutto smarrito de la grande angoscia
  ch'elli ha sofferta, e guardando sospira:

tal era il peccator levato poscia.
  Oh potenza di Dio, quant'e` severa,
  che cotai colpi per vendetta croscia!

Lo duca il domando` poi chi ello era;
  per ch'ei rispuose: ““Io piovvi di Toscana,
  poco tempo e`, in questa gola fiera.

Vita bestial mi piacque e non umana,
  si` come a mul ch'i' fui; son Vanni Fucci
  bestia, e Pistoia mi fu degna tana”“.

E io al duca: ““Dilli che non mucci,
  e domanda che colpa qua giu` 'l pinse;
  ch'io 'l vidi uomo di sangue e di crucci”“.

E 'l peccator, che 'ntese, non s'infinse,
  ma drizzo` verso me l'animo e 'l volto,
  e di trista vergogna si dipinse;

poi disse: ““Piu` mi duol che tu m'hai colto
  ne la miseria dove tu mi vedi,
  che quando fui de l'altra vita tolto.

Io non posso negar quel che tu chiedi;
  in giu` son messo tanto perch'io fui
  ladro a la sagrestia d'i belli arredi,

And when he on the ground was thus destroyed,
  The ashes drew together, and of themselves
  Into himself they instantly returned.

Even thus by the great sages 'tis confessed
  The phoenix dies, and then is born again,
  When it approaches its five-hundredth year;

On herb or grain it feeds not in its life,
  But only on tears of incense and amomum,
  And nard and myrrh are its last winding-sheet.

And as he is who falls, and knows not how,
  By force of demons who to earth down drag him,
  Or other oppilation that binds man,

When he arises and around him looks,
  Wholly bewildered by the mighty anguish
  Which he has suffered, and in looking sighs;

Such was that sinner after he had risen.
  Justice of God! O how severe it is,
  That blows like these in vengeance poureth down!

The Guide thereafter asked him who he was;
  Whence he replied: "I rained from Tuscany
  A short time since into this cruel gorge.

A bestial life, and not a human, pleased me,
  Even as the mule I was; I'm Vanni Fucci,
  Beast, and Pistoia was my worthy den."

And I unto the Guide: "Tell him to stir not,
  And ask what crime has thrust him here below,
  For once a man of blood and wrath I saw him."

And the sinner, who had heard, dissembled not,
  But unto me directed mind and face,
  And with a melancholy shame was painted.

Then said: "It pains me more that thou hast caught
    me
  Amid this misery where thou seest me,
  Than when I from the other life was taken.

What thou demandest I cannot deny;
  So low am I put down because I robbed
  The sacristy of the fair ornaments,

e falsamente gia` fu apposto altrui.
  Ma perche' di tal vista tu non godi,
  se mai sarai di fuor da' luoghi bui,

apri li orecchi al mio annunzio, e odi:
  Pistoia in pria d'i Neri si dimagra;
  poi Fiorenza rinova gente e modi.

Tragge Marte vapor di Val di Magra
  ch'e` di torbidi nuvoli involuto;
  e con tempesta impetuosa e agra

sovra Campo Picen fia combattuto;
  ond'ei repente spezzera` la nebbia,
  si` ch'ogne Bianco ne sara` feruto.

E detto l'ho perche' doler ti debbia!"".

And falsely once 'twas laid upon another;
  But that thou mayst not such a sight enjoy,
  If thou shalt e'er be out of the dark places,

Thine ears to my announcement ope and hear:
  Pistoia first of Neri groweth meagre;
  Then Florence doth renew her men and manners;

Mars draws a vapour up from Val di Magra,
  Which is with turbid clouds enveloped round,
  And with impetuous and bitter tempest

Over Campo Picen shall be the battle;
  When it shall suddenly rend the mist asunder,
  So that each Bianco shall thereby be smitten.

And this I've said that it may give thee pain."

Inferno: Canto XXV

Vanni Fucci's Punishment. Agnello Brunelleschi, Buoso degli Abati, Puccio Sciancato, Cianfa de' Donati, and Guercio Cavalcanti.

Al fine de le sue parole il ladro
  le mani alzo` con amendue le fiche,
  gridando: ""Togli, Dio, ch'a te le squadro!"".

Da indi in qua mi fuor le serpi amiche,
  perch'una li s'avvolse allora al collo,
  come dicesse 'Non vo' che piu` diche';

e un'altra a le braccia, e rilegollo,
  ribadendo se' stessa si` dinanzi,
  che non potea con esse dare un crollo.

Ahi Pistoia, Pistoia, che' non stanzi
  d'incenerarti si` che piu` non duri,
  poi che 'n mal fare il seme tuo avanzi?

Per tutt'i cerchi de lo 'nferno scuri
  non vidi spirto in Dio tanto superbo,
  non quel che cadde a Tebe giu` da' muri.

El si fuggi` che non parlo` piu` verbo;
  e io vidi un centauro pien di rabbia
  venir chiamando: ""Ov'e`, ov'e` l'acerbo?"".

Maremma non cred'io che tante n'abbia,
  quante bisce elli avea su per la groppa
  infin ove comincia nostra labbia.

Sovra le spalle, dietro da la coppa,
  con l'ali aperte li giacea un draco;
  e quello affuoca qualunque s'intoppa.

Lo mio maestro disse: ""Questi e` Caco,
  che sotto 'l sasso di monte Aventino
  di sangue fece spesse volte laco.

At the conclusion of his words, the thief
  Lifted his hands aloft with both the figs,
  Crying: "Take that, God, for at thee I aim them."

From that time forth the serpents were my friends;
  For one entwined itself about his neck
  As if it said: "I will not thou speak more;"

And round his arms another, and rebound him,
  Clinching itself together so in front,
  That with them he could not a motion make.

Pistoia, ah, Pistoia! why resolve not
  To burn thyself to ashes and so perish,
  Since in ill-doing thou thy seed excellest?

Through all the sombre circles of this Hell,
  Spirit I saw not against God so proud,
  Not he who fell at Thebes down from the walls!

He fled away, and spake no further word;
  And I beheld a Centaur full of rage
  Come crying out: "Where is, where is the scoffer?"

I do not think Maremma has so many
  Serpents as he had all along his back,
  As far as where our countenance begins.

Upon the shoulders, just behind the nape,
  With wings wide open was a dragon lying,
  And he sets fire to all that he encounters.

My Master said: "That one is Cacus, who
  Beneath the rock upon Mount Aventine
  Created oftentimes a lake of blood.

Non va co' suoi fratei per un cammino,
  per lo furto che frodolente fece
  del grande armento ch'elli ebbe a vicino;

onde cessar le sue opere biece
  sotto la mazza d'Ercule, che forse
  gliene die` cento, e non senti` le diece"".

Mentre che si` parlava, ed el trascorse
  e tre spiriti venner sotto noi,
  de' quali ne' io ne' 'l duca mio s'accorse,

se non quando gridar: ""Chi siete voi?"";
  per che nostra novella si ristette,
  e intendemmo pur ad essi poi.

Io non li conoscea; ma ei seguette,
  come suol seguitar per alcun caso,
  che l'un nomar un altro convenette,

dicendo: ""Cianfa dove fia rimaso?"";
  per ch'io, accio` che 'l duca stesse attento,
  mi puosi 'l dito su dal mento al naso.

Se tu se' or, lettore, a creder lento
  cio` ch'io diro`, non sara` maraviglia,
  che' io che 'l vidi, a pena il mi consento.

Com'io tenea levate in lor le ciglia,
  e un serpente con sei pie` si lancia
  dinanzi a l'uno, e tutto a lui s'appiglia.

Co' pie` di mezzo li avvinse la pancia,
  e con li anterior le braccia prese;
  poi li addento` e l'una e l'altra guancia;

li diretani a le cosce distese,
  e miseli la coda tra 'mbedue,
  e dietro per le ren su` la ritese.

Ellera abbarbicata mai non fue
  ad alber si`, come l'orribil fiera
  per l'altrui membra avviticchio` le sue.

Poi s'appiccar, come di calda cera
  fossero stati, e mischiar lor colore,
  ne' l'un ne' l'altro gia` parea quel ch'era:

He goes not on the same road with his brothers,
  By reason of the fraudulent theft he made
  Of the great herd, which he had near to him;

Whereat his tortuous actions ceased beneath
  The mace of Hercules, who peradventure
  Gave him a hundred, and he felt not ten."

While he was speaking thus, he had passed by,
  And spirits three had underneath us come,
  Of which nor I aware was, nor my Leader,

Until what time they shouted: "Who are you?"
  On which account our story made a halt,
  And then we were intent on them alone.

I did not know them; but it came to pass,
  As it is wont to happen by some chance,
  That one to name the other was compelled,

Exclaiming: "Where can Cianfa have remained?"
  Whence I, so that the Leader might attend,
  Upward from chin to nose my finger laid.

If thou art, Reader, slow now to believe
  What I shall say, it will no marvel be,
  For I who saw it hardly can admit it.

As I was holding raised on them my brows,
  Behold! a serpent with six feet darts forth
  In front of one, and fastens wholly on him.

With middle feet it bound him round the paunch,
  And with the forward ones his arms it seized;
  Then thrust its teeth through one cheek and the oth-
    er;

The hindermost it stretched upon his thighs,
  And put its tail through in between the two,
  And up behind along the reins outspread it.

Ivy was never fastened by its barbs
  Unto a tree so, as this horrible reptile
  Upon the other's limbs entwined its own.

Then they stuck close, as if of heated wax
  They had been made, and intermixed their colour;
  Nor one nor other seemed now what he was;

come procede innanzi da l'ardore,
  per lo papiro suso, un color bruno
  che non e` nero ancora e 'l bianco more.

Li altri due 'l riguardavano, e ciascuno
  gridava: ""Ome`, Agnel, come ti muti!
  Vedi che gia` non se' ne' due ne' uno"".

Gia` eran li due capi un divenuti,
  quando n'apparver due figure miste
  in una faccia, ov'eran due perduti.

Fersi le braccia due di quattro liste;
  le cosce con le gambe e 'l ventre e 'l casso
  divenner membra che non fuor mai viste.

Ogne primaio aspetto ivi era casso:
  due e nessun l'imagine perversa
  parea; e tal sen gio con lento passo.

Come 'l ramarro sotto la gran fersa
  dei di` canicular, cangiando sepe,
  folgore par se la via attraversa,

si` pareva, venendo verso l'epe
  de li altri due, un serpentello acceso,
  livido e nero come gran di pepe;

e quella parte onde prima e` preso
  nostro alimento, a l'un di lor trafisse;
  poi cadde giuso innanzi lui disteso.

Lo trafitto 'l miro`, ma nulla disse;
  anzi, co' pie` fermati, sbadigliava
  pur come sonno o febbre l'assalisse.

Elli 'l serpente, e quei lui riguardava;
  l'un per la piaga, e l'altro per la bocca
  fummavan forte, e 'l fummo si scontrava.

Taccia Lucano ormai la` dove tocca
  del misero Sabello e di Nasidio,
  e attenda a udir quel ch'or si scocca.

Taccia di Cadmo e d'Aretusa Ovidio;
  che' se quello in serpente e quella in fonte
  converte poetando, io non lo 'nvidio;

E'en as proceedeth on before the flame
  Upward along the paper a brown colour,
  Which is not black as yet, and the white dies.

The other two looked on, and each of them
  Cried out: "O me, Agnello, how thou changest!
  Behold, thou now art neither two nor one."

Already the two heads had one become,
  When there appeared to us two figures mingled
  Into one face, wherein the two were lost.

Of the four lists were fashioned the two arms,
  The thighs and legs, the belly and the chest
  Members became that never yet were seen.

Every original aspect there was cancelled;
  Two and yet none did the perverted image
  Appear, and such departed with slow pace.

Even as a lizard, under the great scourge
  Of days canicular, exchanging hedge,
  Lightning appeareth if the road it cross;

Thus did appear, coming towards the bellies
  Of the two others, a small fiery serpent,
  Livid and black as is a peppercorn.

And in that part whereat is first received
  Our aliment, it one of them transfixed;
  Then downward fell in front of him extended.

The one transfixed looked at it, but said naught;
  Nay, rather with feet motionless he yawned,
  Just as if sleep or fever had assailed him.

He at the serpent gazed, and it at him;
  One through the wound, the other through the
    mouth
  Smoked violently, and the smoke commingled.

Henceforth be silent Lucan, where he mentions
  Wretched Sabellus and Nassidius,
  And wait to hear what now shall be shot forth.

Be silent Ovid, of Cadmus and Arethusa;
  For if him to a snake, her to fountain,
  Converts he fabling, that I grudge him not;

che' due nature mai a fronte a fronte
  non trasmuto` si` ch'amendue le forme
  a cambiar lor matera fosser pronte.

Insieme si rispuosero a tai norme,
  che 'l serpente la coda in forca fesse,
  e il feruto ristrinse insieme l'orme.

Le gambe con le cosce seco stesse
  s'appiccar si`, che 'n poco la giuntura
  non facea segno alcun che si paresse.

Togliea la coda fessa la figura
  che si perdeva la`, e la sua pelle
  si facea molle, e quella di la` dura.

Io vidi intrar le braccia per l'ascelle,
  e i due pie` de la fiera, ch'eran corti,
  tanto allungar quanto accorciavan quelle.

Poscia li pie` di retro, insieme attorti,
  diventaron lo membro che l'uom cela,
  e 'l misero del suo n'avea due porti.

Mentre che 'l fummo l'uno e l'altro vela
  di color novo, e genera 'l pel suso
  per l'una parte e da l'altra il dipela,

l'un si levo` e l'altro cadde giuso,
  non torcendo pero` le lucerne empie,
  sotto le quai ciascun cambiava muso.

Quel ch'era dritto, il trasse ver' le tempie,
  e di troppa matera ch'in la` venne
  uscir li orecchi de le gote scempie;

cio` che non corse in dietro e si ritenne
  di quel soverchio, fe' naso a la faccia
  e le labbra ingrosso` quanto convenne.

Quel che giacea, il muso innanzi caccia,
  e li orecchi ritira per la testa
  come face le corna la lumaccia;

e la lingua, ch'avea unita e presta
  prima a parlar, si fende, e la forcuta
  ne l'altro si richiude; e 'l fummo resta.

L'anima ch'era fiera divenuta,
  suffolando si fugge per la valle,
  e l'altro dietro a lui parlando sputa.

Because two natures never front to front
  Has he transmuted, so that both the forms
  To interchange their matter ready were.

Together they responded in such wise,
  That to a fork the serpent cleft his tail,
  And eke the wounded drew his feet together.

The legs together with the thighs themselves
  Adhered so, that in little time the juncture
  No sign whatever made that was apparent.

He with the cloven tail assumed the figure
  The other one was losing, and his skin
  Became elastic, and the other's hard.

I saw the arms draw inward at the armpits,
  And both feet of the reptile, that were short,
  Lengthen as much as those contracted were.

Thereafter the hind feet, together twisted,
  Became the member that a man conceals,
  And of his own the wretch had two created.

While both of them the exhalation veils
  With a new colour, and engenders hair
  On one of them and depilates the other,

The one uprose and down the other fell,
  Though turning not away their impious lamps,
  Underneath which each one his muzzle changed.

He who was standing drew it tow'rds the temples,
  And from excess of matter, which came thither,
  Issued the ears from out the hollow cheeks;

What did not backward run and was retained
  Of that excess made to the face a nose,
  And the lips thickened far as was befitting.

He who lay prostrate thrusts his muzzle forward,
  And backward draws the ears into his head,
  In the same manner as the snail its horns;

And so the tongue, which was entire and apt
  For speech before, is cleft, and the bi-forked
  In the other closes up, and the smoke ceases.

The soul, which to a reptile had been changed,
  Along the valley hissing takes to flight,
  And after him the other speaking sputters.

Poscia li volse le novelle spalle,
  e disse a l'altro: ““I' vo' che Buoso corra,
  com'ho fatt'io, carpon per questo calle””.

Cosi` vid'io la settima zavorra
  mutare e trasmutare; e qui mi scusi
  la novita` se fior la penna abborra.

E avvegna che li occhi miei confusi
  fossero alquanto e l'animo smagato,
  non poter quei fuggirsi tanto chiusi,

ch'i' non scorgessi ben Puccio Sciancato;
  ed era quel che sol, di tre compagni
  che venner prima, non era mutato;

l'altr'era quel che tu, Gaville, piagni.

Then did he turn upon him his new shoulders,
  And said to the other: "I'll have Buoso run,
  Crawling as I have done, along this road."

In this way I beheld the seventh ballast
  Shift and reshift, and here be my excuse
  The novelty, if aught my pen transgress.

And notwithstanding that mine eyes might be
  Somewhat bewildered, and my mind dismayed,
  They could not flee away so secretly

But that I plainly saw Puccio Sciancato;
  And he it was who sole of three companions,
  Which came in the beginning, was not changed;

The other was he whom thou, Gaville, weepest.

Inferno: Canto XXVI

The Eighth Bolgia: Evil Counsellors. Ulysses and Diomed. Ulysses' Last Voyage.

Godi, Fiorenza, poi che se' si` grande,
  che per mare e per terra batti l'ali,
  e per lo 'nferno tuo nome si spande!

Tra li ladron trovai cinque cotali
  tuoi cittadini onde mi ven vergogna,
  e tu in grande orranza non ne sali.

Ma se presso al mattin del ver si sogna,
  tu sentirai di qua da picciol tempo
  di quel che Prato, non ch'altri, t'agogna.

E se gia` fosse, non saria per tempo.
  Cosi` foss'ei, da che pur esser dee!
  che' piu` mi gravera`, com'piu` m'attempo.

Noi ci partimmo, e su per le scalee
  che n'avea fatto iborni a scender pria,
  rimonto` 'l duca mio e trasse mee;

e proseguendo la solinga via,
  tra le schegge e tra ' rocchi de lo scoglio
  lo pie` sanza la man non si spedia.

Allor mi dolsi, e ora mi ridoglio
  quando drizzo la mente a cio` ch'io vidi,
  e piu` lo 'ngegno affreno ch'i' non soglio,

perche' non corra che virtu` nol guidi;
  si` che, se stella bona o miglior cosa
  m'ha dato 'l ben, ch'io stessi nol m'invidi.

Quante 'l villan ch'al poggio si riposa,
  nel tempo che colui che 'l mondo schiara
  la faccia sua a noi tien meno ascosa,

Rejoice, O Florence, since thou art so great,
  That over sea and land thou beatest thy wings,
  And throughout Hell thy name is spread abroad!

Among the thieves five citizens of thine
  Like these I found, whence shame comes unto me,
  And thou thereby to no great honour risest.

But if when morn is near our dreams are true,
  Feel shalt thou in a little time from now
  What Prato, if none other, craves for thee.

And if it now were, it were not too soon;
  Would that it were, seeing it needs must be,
  For 'twill aggrieve me more the more I age.

We went our way, and up along the stairs
  The bourns had made us to descend before,
  Remounted my Conductor and drew me.

And following the solitary path
  Among the rocks and ridges of the crag,
  The foot without the hand sped not at all.

Then sorrowed I, and sorrow now again,
  When I direct my mind to what I saw,
  And more my genius curb than I am wont,

That it may run not unless virtue guide it;
  So that if some good star, or better thing,
  Have given me good, I may myself not grudge it.

As many as the hind (who on the hill
  Rests at the time when he who lights the world
  His countenance keeps least concealed from us,

come la mosca cede alla zanzara,
  vede lucciole giu` per la vallea,
  forse cola` dov'e' vendemmia e ara:

di tante fiamme tutta risplendea
  l'ottava bolgia, si` com'io m'accorsi
  tosto che fui la` 've 'l fondo parea.

E qual colui che si vengio` con li orsi
  vide 'l carro d'Elia al dipartire,
  quando i cavalli al cielo erti levorsi,

che nol potea si` con li occhi seguire,
  ch'el vedesse altro che la fiamma sola,
  si` come nuvoletta, in su` salire:

tal si move ciascuna per la gola
  del fosso, che' nessuna mostra 'l furto,
  e ogne fiamma un peccatore invola.

Io stava sovra 'l ponte a veder surto,
  si` che s'io non avessi un ronchion preso,
  caduto sarei giu` sanz'esser urto.

E 'l duca che mi vide tanto atteso,
  disse: ““Dentro dai fuochi son li spirti;
  catun si fascia di quel ch'elli e` inceso”“.

““Maestro mio”“, rispuos'io, ““per udirti
  son io piu` certo; ma gia` m'era avviso
  che cosi` fosse, e gia` voleva dirti:

chi e` 'n quel foco che vien si` diviso
  di sopra, che par surger de la pira
  dov'Eteocle col fratel fu miso?”“.

Rispuose a me: ““La` dentro si martira
  Ulisse e Diomede, e cosi` insieme
  a la vendetta vanno come a l'ira;

e dentro da la lor fiamma si geme
  l'agguato del caval che fe' la porta
  onde usci` de' Romani il gentil seme.

Piangevisi entro l'arte per che, morta,
  Deidamia ancor si duol d'Achille,
  e del Palladio pena vi si porta”“.

While as the fly gives place unto the gnat)
  Seeth the glow-worms down along the valley,
  Perchance there where he ploughs and makes his vintage;

With flames as manifold resplendent all
  Was the eighth Bolgia, as I grew aware
  As soon as I was where the depth appeared.

And such as he who with the bears avenged him
  Beheld Elijah's chariot at departing,
  What time the steeds to heaven erect uprose,

For with his eye he could not follow it
  So as to see aught else than flame alone,
  Even as a little cloud ascending upward,

Thus each along the gorge of the intrenchment
  Was moving; for not one reveals the theft,
  And every flame a sinner steals away.

I stood upon the bridge uprisen to see,
  So that, if I had seized not on a rock,
  Down had I fallen without being pushed.

And the Leader, who beheld me so attent,
  Exclaimed: "Within the fires the spirits are;
  Each swathes himself with that wherewith he burns."

"My Master," I replied, "by hearing thee
  I am more sure; but I surmised already
  It might be so, and already wished to ask thee

Who is within that fire, which comes so cleft
  At top, it seems uprising from the pyre
  Where was Eteocles with his brother placed."

He answered me: "Within there are tormented
  Ulysses and Diomed, and thus together
  They unto vengeance run as unto wrath.

And there within their flame do they lament
  The ambush of the horse, which made the door
  Whence issued forth the Romans' gentle seed;

Therein is wept the craft, for which being dead
  Deidamia still deplores Achilles,
  And pain for the Palladium there is borne."

““S'ei posson dentro da quelle faville
parlar”“, diss'io, ““maestro, assai ten priego
e ripriego, che 'l priego vaglia mille,

che non mi facci de l'attender niego
fin che la fiamma cornuta qua vegna;
vedi che del disio ver' lei mi piego!”“.

Ed elli a me: ““La tua preghiera e` degna
di molta loda, e io pero` l'accetto;
ma fa che la tua lingua si sostegna.

Lascia parlare a me, ch'i' ho concetto
cio` che tu vuoi; ch'ei sarebbero schivi,
perch'e' fuor greci, forse del tuo detto”“.

Poi che la fiamma fu venuta quivi
dove parve al mio duca tempo e loco,
in questa forma lui parlare audivi:

““O voi che siete due dentro ad un foco,
s'io meritai di voi mentre ch'io vissi,
s'io meritai di voi assai o poco

quando nel mondo li alti versi scrissi,
non vi movete; ma l'un di voi dica
dove, per lui, perduto a morir gissi”“.

Lo maggior corno de la fiamma antica
comincio` a crollarsi mormorando
pur come quella cui vento affatica;

indi la cima qua e la` menando,
come fosse la lingua che parlasse,
gitto` voce di fuori, e disse: ““Quando

mi diparti' da Circe, che sottrasse
me piu` d'un anno la` presso a Gaeta,
prima che si` Enea la nomasse,

ne' dolcezza di figlio, ne' la pieta
del vecchio padre, ne' 'l debito amore
lo qual dovea Penelope' far lieta,

vincer potero dentro a me l'ardore
ch'i' ebbi a divenir del mondo esperto,
e de li vizi umani e del valore;

"If they within those sparks possess the power
To speak," I said, "thee, Master, much I pray,
And re-pray, that the prayer be worth a thousand,

That thou make no denial of awaiting
Until the horned flame shall hither come;
Thou seest that with desire I lean towards it."

And he to me: "Worthy is thy entreaty
Of much applause, and therefore I accept it;
But take heed that thy tongue restrain itself.

Leave me to speak, because I have conceived
That which thou wishest; for they might disdain
Perchance, since they were Greeks, discourse of
thine."

When now the flame had come unto that point,
Where to my Leader it seemed time and place,
After this fashion did I hear him speak:

"O ye, who are twofold within one fire,
If I deserved of you, while I was living,
If I deserved of you or much or little

When in the world I wrote the lofty verses,
Do not move on, but one of you declare
Whither, being lost, he went away to die."

Then of the antique flame the greater horn,
Murmuring, began to wave itself about
Even as a flame doth which the wind fatigues.

Thereafterward, the summit to and fro
Moving as if it were the tongue that spake,
It uttered forth a voice, and said: "When I

From Circe had departed, who concealed me
More than a year there near unto Gaeta,
Or ever yet Aeneas named it so,

Nor fondness for my son, nor reverence
For my old father, nor the due affection
Which joyous should have made Penelope,

Could overcome within me the desire
I had to be experienced of the world,
And of the vice and virtue of mankind;

ma misi me per l'alto mare aperto
  sol con un legno e con quella compagna
  picciola da la qual non fui diserto.

L'un lito e l'altro vidi infin la Spagna,
  fin nel Morrocco, e l'isola d'i Sardi,
  e l'altre che quel mare intorno bagna.

Io e ' compagni eravam vecchi e tardi
  quando venimmo a quella foce stretta
  dov'Ercule segno` li suoi riguardi,

accio` che l'uom piu` oltre non si metta:
  da la man destra mi lasciai Sibilia,
  da l'altra gia` m'avea lasciata Setta.

"O frati", dissi "che per cento milia
  perigli siete giunti a l'occidente,
  a questa tanto picciola vigilia

d'i nostri sensi ch'e` del rimanente,
  non vogliate negar l'esperienza,
  di retro al sol, del mondo sanza gente.

Considerate la vostra semenza:
  fatti non foste a viver come bruti,
  ma per seguir virtute e canoscenza".

Li miei compagni fec'io si` aguti,
  con questa orazion picciola, al cammino,
  che a pena poscia li avrei ritenuti;

e volta nostra poppa nel mattino,
  de' remi facemmo ali al folle volo,
  sempre acquistando dal lato mancino.

Tutte le stelle gia` de l'altro polo
  vedea la notte e 'l nostro tanto basso,
  che non surgea fuor del marin suolo.

Cinque volte racceso e tante casso
  lo lume era di sotto da la luna,
  poi che 'ntrati eravam ne l'alto passo,

quando n'apparve una montagna, bruna
  per la distanza, e parvemi alta tanto
  quanto veduta non avea alcuna.

Noi ci allegrammo, e tosto torno` in pianto,
  che' de la nova terra un turbo nacque,
  e percosse del legno il primo canto.

But I put forth on the high open sea
  With one sole ship, and that small company
  By which I never had deserted been.

Both of the shores I saw as far as Spain,
  Far as Morocco, and the isle of Sardes,
  And the others which that sea bathes round about.

I and my company were old and slow
  When at that narrow passage we arrived
  Where Hercules his landmarks set as signals,

That man no farther onward should adventure.
  On the right hand behind me left I Seville,
  And on the other already had left Ceuta.

'O brothers, who amid a hundred thousand
  Perils,' I said, 'have come unto the West,
  To this so inconsiderable vigil

Which is remaining of your senses still
  Be ye unwilling to deny the knowledge,
  Following the sun, of the unpeopled world.

Consider ye the seed from which ye sprang;
  Ye were not made to live like unto brutes,
  But for pursuit of virtue and of knowledge.'

So eager did I render my companions,
  With this brief exhortation, for the voyage,
  That then I hardly could have held them back.

And having turned our stern unto the morning,
  We of the oars made wings for our mad flight,
  Evermore gaining on the larboard side.

Already all the stars of the other pole
  The night beheld, and ours so very low
  It did not rise above the ocean floor.

Five times rekindled and as many quenched
  Had been the splendour underneath the moon,
  Since we had entered into the deep pass,

When there appeared to us a mountain, dim
  From distance, and it seemed to me so high
  As I had never any one beheld.

Joyful were we, and soon it turned to weeping;
  For out of the new land a whirlwind rose,
  And smote upon the fore part of the ship.

Tre volte il fe' girar con tutte l'acque;   Three times it made her whirl with all the waters,
 a la quarta levar la poppa in suso   At the fourth time it made the stern uplift,
 e la prora ire in giu`, com'altrui piacque,   And the prow downward go, as pleased Another,

infin che 'l mar fu sovra noi richiuso"".   Until the sea above us closed again."

Inferno: Canto XXVII

Guido da Montefeltro. His deception by Pope Boniface VIII.

Gia` era dritta in su` la fiamma e queta
  per non dir piu`, e gia` da noi sen gia
  con la licenza del dolce poeta,

quand'un'altra, che dietro a lei venia,
  ne fece volger li occhi a la sua cima
  per un confuso suon che fuor n'uscia.

Come 'l bue cicilian che mugghio` prima
  col pianto di colui, e cio` fu dritto,
  che l'avea temperato con sua lima,

mugghiava con la voce de l'afflitto,
  si` che, con tutto che fosse di rame,
  pur el pareva dal dolor trafitto;

cosi`, per non aver via ne' forame
  dal principio nel foco, in suo linguaggio
  si convertian le parole grame.

Ma poscia ch'ebber colto lor viaggio
  su per la punta, dandole quel guizzo
  che dato avea la lingua in lor passaggio,

udimmo dire: ""O tu a cu' io drizzo
  la voce e che parlavi mo lombardo,
  dicendo "Istra ten va, piu` non t'adizzo",

perch'io sia giunto forse alquanto tardo,
  non t'incresca restare a parlar meco;
  vedi che non incresce a me, e ardo!

Se tu pur mo in questo mondo cieco
  caduto se' di quella dolce terra
  latina ond'io mia colpa tutta reco,

Already was the flame erect and quiet,
  To speak no more, and now departed from us
  With the permission of the gentle Poet;

When yet another, which behind it came,
  Caused us to turn our eyes upon its top
  By a confused sound that issued from it.

As the Sicilian bull (that bellowed first
  With the lament of him, and that was right,
  Who with his file had modulated it)

Bellowed so with the voice of the afflicted,
  That, notwithstanding it was made of brass,
  Still it appeared with agony transfixed;

Thus, by not having any way or issue
  At first from out the fire, to its own language
  Converted were the melancholy words.

But afterwards, when they had gathered way
  Up through the point, giving it that vibration
  The tongue had given them in their passage out,

We heard it said: "O thou, at whom I aim
  My voice, and who but now wast speaking Lombard,
  Saying, 'Now go thy way, no more I urge thee,'

Because I come perchance a little late,
  To stay and speak with me let it not irk thee;
  Thou seest it irks not me, and I am burning.

If thou but lately into this blind world
  Hast fallen down from that sweet Latian land,
  Wherefrom I bring the whole of my transgression,

dimmi se Romagnuoli han pace o guerra;
  ch'io fui d'i monti la` intra Orbino
  e 'l giogo di che Tever si diserra'"".

Io era in giuso ancora attento e chino,
  quando il mio duca mi tento` di costa,
  dicendo: ""Parla tu; questi e` latino"".

E io, ch'avea gia` pronta la risposta,
  sanza indugio a parlare incominciai:
  ""O anima che se' la` giu` nascosta,

Romagna tua non e`, e non fu mai,
  sanza guerra ne' cuor de' suoi tiranni;
  ma 'n palese nessuna or vi lasciai.

Ravenna sta come stata e` molt'anni:
  l'aguglia da Polenta la si cova,
  si` che Cervia ricuopre co' suoi vanni.

La terra che fe' gia` la lunga prova
  e di Franceschi sanguinoso mucchio,
  sotto le branche verdi si ritrova.

E 'l mastin vecchio e 'l nuovo da Verrucchio,
  che fecer di Montagna il mal governo,
  la` dove soglion fan d'i denti succhio.

Le citta` di Lamone e di Santerno
  conduce il lioncel dal nido bianco,
  che muta parte da la state al verno.

E quella cu' il Savio bagna il fianco,
  cosi` com'ella sie' tra 'l piano e 'l monte
  tra tirannia si vive e stato franco.

Ora chi se', ti priego che ne conte;
  non esser duro piu` ch'altri sia stato,
  se 'l nome tuo nel mondo tegna fronte'"".

Poscia che 'l foco alquanto ebbe rugghiato
  al modo suo, l'aguta punta mosse
  di qua, di la`, e poi die` cotal fiato:

""S'i' credesse che mia risposta fosse
  a persona che mai tornasse al mondo,
  questa fiamma staria sanza piu` scosse;

Say, if the Romagnuols have peace or war,
  For I was from the mountains there between
  Urbino and the yoke whence Tiber bursts."

I still was downward bent and listening,
  When my Conductor touched me on the side,
  Saying: "Speak thou: this one a Latian is."

And I, who had beforehand my reply
  In readiness, forthwith began to speak:
  "O soul, that down below there art concealed,

Romagna thine is not and never has been
  Without war in the bosom of its tyrants;
  But open war I none have left there now.

Ravenna stands as it long years has stood;
  The Eagle of Polenta there is brooding,
  So that she covers Cervia with her vans.

The city which once made the long resistance,
  And of the French a sanguinary heap,
  Beneath the Green Paws finds itself again;

Verrucchio's ancient Mastiff and the new,
  Who made such bad disposal of Montagna,
  Where they are wont make wimbles of their teeth.

The cities of Lamone and Santerno
  Governs the Lioncel of the white lair,
  Who changes sides 'twixt summer-time and winter;

And that of which the Savio bathes the flank,
  Even as it lies between the plain and mountain,
  Lives between tyranny and a free state.

Now I entreat thee tell us who thou art;
  Be not more stubborn than the rest have been,
  So may thy name hold front there in the world."

After the fire a little more had roared
  In its own fashion, the sharp point it moved
  This way and that, and then gave forth such breath:

"If I believed that my reply were made
  To one who to the world would e'er return,
  This flame without more flickering would stand
     still;

ma pero` che gia` mai di questo fondo
  non torno` vivo alcun, s'i' odo il vero,
  sanza tema d'infamia ti rispondo.

Io fui uom d'arme, e poi fui cordigliero,
  credendomi, si` cinto, fare ammenda;
  e certo il creder mio venia intero,

se non fosse il gran prete, a cui mal prenda!,
  che mi rimise ne le prime colpe;
  e come e quare, voglio che m'intenda.

Mentre ch'io forma fui d'ossa e di polpe
  che la madre mi die`, l'opere mie
  non furon leonine, ma di volpe.

Li accorgimenti e le coperte vie
  io seppi tutte, e si` menai lor arte,
  ch'al fine de la terra il suono uscie.

Quando mi vidi giunto in quella parte
  di mia etade ove ciascun dovrebbe
  calar le vele e raccoglier le sarte,

cio` che pria mi piacea, allor m'increbbe,
  e pentuto e confesso mi rendei;
  ahi miser lasso! e giovato sarebbe.

Lo principe d'i novi Farisei,
  avendo guerra presso a Laterano,
  e non con Saracin ne' con Giudei,

che' ciascun suo nimico era cristiano,
  e nessun era stato a vincer Acri
  ne' mercatante in terra di Soldano;

ne' sommo officio ne' ordini sacri
  guardo` in se', ne' in me quel capestro
  che solea fare i suoi cinti piu` macri.

Ma come Costantin chiese Silvestro
  d'entro Siratti a guerir de la lebbre;
  cosi` mi chiese questi per maestro

a guerir de la sua superba febbre:
  domandommi consiglio, e io tacetti
  perche' le sue parole parver ebbre.

But inasmuch as never from this depth
  Did any one return, if I hear true,
  Without the fear of infamy I answer,

I was a man of arms, then Cordelier,
  Believing thus begirt to make amends;
  And truly my belief had been fulfilled

But for the High Priest, whom may ill betide,
  Who put me back into my former sins;
  And how and wherefore I will have thee hear.

While I was still the form of bone and pulp
  My mother gave to me, the deeds I did
  Were not those of a lion, but a fox.

The machinations and the covert ways
  I knew them all, and practised so their craft,
  That to the ends of earth the sound went forth.

When now unto that portion of mine age
  I saw myself arrived, when each one ought
  To lower the sails, and coil away the ropes,

That which before had pleased me then displeased
    me;
  And penitent and confessing I surrendered,
  Ah woe is me! and it would have bestead me;

The Leader of the modern Pharisees
  Having a war near unto Lateran,
  And not with Saracens nor with the Jews,

For each one of his enemies was Christian,
  And none of them had been to conquer Acre,
  Nor merchandising in the Sultan's land,

Nor the high office, nor the sacred orders,
  In him regarded, nor in me that cord
  Which used to make those girt with it more meagre;

But even as Constantine sought out Sylvester
  To cure his leprosy, within Soracte,
  So this one sought me out as an adept

To cure him of the fever of his pride.
  Counsel he asked of me, and I was silent,
  Because his words appeared inebriate.

E' poi ridisse: "Tuo cuor non sospetti;
  finor t'assolvo, e tu m'insegna fare
  si` come Penestrino in terra getti.

Lo ciel poss'io serrare e diserrare,
  come tu sai; pero` son due le chiavi
  che 'l mio antecessor non ebbe care".

Allor mi pinser li argomenti gravi
  la` 've 'l tacer mi fu avviso 'l peggio,
  e dissi: "Padre, da che tu mi lavi

di quel peccato ov'io mo cader deggio,
  lunga promessa con l'attender corto
  ti fara` triunfar ne l'alto seggio".

Francesco venne poi com'io fu' morto,
  per me; ma un d'i neri cherubini
  li disse: "Non portar: non mi far torto.

Venir se ne dee giu` tra ' miei meschini
  perche' diede 'l consiglio frodolente,
  dal quale in qua stato li sono a' crini;

ch'assolver non si puo` chi non si pente,
  ne' pentere e volere insieme puossi
  per la contradizion che nol consente".

Oh me dolente! come mi riscossi
  quando mi prese dicendomi: "Forse
  tu non pensavi ch'io loico fossi!".

A Minos mi porto`; e quelli attorse
  otto volte la coda al dosso duro;
  e poi che per gran rabbia la si morse,

disse: "Questi e` d'i rei del foco furo";
  per ch'io la` dove vedi son perduto,
  e si` vestito, andando, mi rancuro"".

Quand'elli ebbe 'l suo dir cosi` compiuto,
  la fiamma dolorando si partio,
  torcendo e dibattendo 'l corno aguto.

Noi passamm'oltre, e io e 'l duca mio,
  su per lo scoglio infino in su l'altr'arco
  che cuopre 'l fosso in che si paga il fio

a quei che scommettendo acquistan carco.

And then he said: 'Be not thy heart afraid;
  Henceforth I thee absolve; and thou instruct me
  How to raze Palestrina to the ground.

Heaven have I power to lock and to unlock,
  As thou dost know; therefore the keys are two,
  The which my predecessor held not dear.'

Then urged me on his weighty arguments
  There, where my silence was the worst advice;
  And said I: 'Father, since thou washest me

Of that sin into which I now must fall,
  The promise long with the fulfilment short
  Will make thee triumph in thy lofty seat.'

Francis came afterward, when I was dead,
  For me; but one of the black Cherubim
  Said to him: 'Take him not; do me no wrong;

He must come down among my servitors,
  Because he gave the fraudulent advice
  From which time forth I have been at his hair;

For who repents not cannot be absolved,
  Nor can one both repent and will at once,
  Because of the contradiction which consents not.'

O miserable me! how I did shudder
  When he seized on me, saying: 'Peradventure
  Thou didst not think that I was a logician!'

He bore me unto Minos, who entwined
  Eight times his tail about his stubborn back,
  And after he had bitten it in great rage,

Said: 'Of the thievish fire a culprit this;'
  Wherefore, here where thou seest, am I lost,
  And vested thus in going I bemoan me."

When it had thus completed its recital,
  The flame departed uttering lamentations,
  Writhing and flapping its sharp-pointed horn.

Onward we passed, both I and my Conductor,
  Up o'er the crag above another arch,
  Which the moat covers, where is paid the fee

By those who, sowing discord, win their burden.

Inferno: Canto XXVIII

The Ninth Bolgia: Schismatics. Mahomet and Ali. Pier da Medicina, Curio, Mosca, and Bertrand de Born.

Chi poria mai pur con parole sciolte
  dicer del sangue e de le piaghe a pieno
  ch'i' ora vidi, per narrar piu` volte?
	Who ever could, e'en with untrammelled words,
	  Tell of the blood and of the wounds in full
	  Which now I saw, by many times narrating?

Ogne lingua per certo verria meno
  per lo nostro sermone e per la mente
  c'hanno a tanto comprender poco seno.
	Each tongue would for a certainty fall short
	  By reason of our speech and memory,
	  That have small room to comprehend so much.

S'el s'aunasse ancor tutta la gente
  che gia` in su la fortunata terra
  di Puglia, fu del suo sangue dolente
	If were again assembled all the people
	  Which formerly upon the fateful land
	  Of Puglia were lamenting for their blood

per li Troiani e per la lunga guerra
  che de l'anella fe' si` alte spoglie,
  come Livio scrive, che non erra,
	Shed by the Romans and the lingering war
	  That of the rings made such illustrious spoils,
	  As Livy has recorded, who errs not,

con quella che sentio di colpi doglie
  per contastare a Ruberto Guiscardo;
  e l'altra il cui ossame ancor s'accoglie
	With those who felt the agony of blows
	  By making counterstand to Robert Guiscard,
	  And all the rest, whose bones are gathered still

a Ceperan, la` dove fu bugiardo   ciascun Pugliese, e la` da Tagliacozzo, dove sanz'arme vinse il vecchio Alardo;	At Ceperano, where a renegade Was each Apulian, and at Tagliacozzo, Where without arms the old Alardo conquered,

e qual forato suo membro e qual mozzo
  mostrasse, d'aequar sarebbe nulla
  il modo de la nona bolgia sozzo.
	And one his limb transpierced, and one lopped off,
	  Should show, it would be nothing to compare
	  With the disgusting mode of the ninth Bolgia.

Gia` veggia, per mezzul perdere o lulla,   com'io vidi un, cosi` non si pertugia, rotto dal mento infin dove si trulla.	A cask by losing centre-piece or cant Was never shattered so, as I saw one Rent from the chin to where one breaketh wind.

Tra le gambe pendevan le minugia;
  la corata pareva e 'l tristo sacco
  che merda fa di quel che si trangugia.
	Between his legs were hanging down his entrails;
	  His heart was visible, and the dismal sack
	  That maketh excrement of what is eaten.

Mentre che tutto in lui veder m'attacco,
  guardommi, e con le man s'aperse il petto,
  dicendo: ""Or vedi com'io mi dilacco!

vedi come storpiato e` Maometto!
  Dinanzi a me sen va piangendo Ali`,
  fesso nel volto dal mento al ciuffetto.

E tutti li altri che tu vedi qui,
  seminator di scandalo e di scisma
  fuor vivi, e pero` son fessi cosi`.

Un diavolo e` qua dietro che n'accisma
  si` crudelmente, al taglio de la spada
  rimettendo ciascun di questa risma,

quand'avem volta la dolente strada;
  pero` che le ferite son richiuse
  prima ch'altri dinanzi li rivada.

Ma tu chi se' che 'n su lo scoglio muse,
  forse per indugiar d'ire a la pena
  ch'e` giudicata in su le tue accuse?"".

""Ne' morte 'l giunse ancor, ne' colpa 'l mena"",
  rispuose 'l mio maestro ""a tormentarlo;
  ma per dar lui esperienza piena,

a me, che morto son, convien menarlo
  per lo 'nferno qua giu` di giro in giro;
  e quest'e` ver cosi` com'io ti parlo"".

Piu` fuor di cento che, quando l'udiro,
  s'arrestaron nel fosso a riguardarmi
  per maraviglia obliando il martiro.

""Or di` a fra Dolcin dunque che s'armi,
  tu che forse vedra' il sole in breve,
  s'ello non vuol qui tosto seguitarmi,

si` di vivanda, che stretta di neve
  non rechi la vittoria al Noarese,
  ch'altrimenti acquistar non saria leve"".

Poi che l'un pie` per girsene sospese,
  Maometto mi disse esta parola;
  indi a partirsi in terra lo distese.

While I was all absorbed in seeing him,
  He looked at me, and opened with his hands
  His bosom, saying: "See now how I rend me;

How mutilated, see, is Mahomet;
  In front of me doth Ali weeping go,
  Cleft in the face from forelock unto chin;

And all the others whom thou here beholdest,
  Disseminators of scandal and of schism
  While living were, and therefore are cleft thus.

A devil is behind here, who doth cleave us
  Thus cruelly, unto the falchion's edge
  Putting again each one of all this ream,

When we have gone around the doleful road;
  By reason that our wounds are closed again
  Ere any one in front of him repass.

But who art thou, that musest on the crag,
  Perchance to postpone going to the pain
  That is adjudged upon thine accusations?"

"Nor death hath reached him yet, nor guilt doth bring
  him,"
  My Master made reply, "to be tormented;
  But to procure him full experience,

Me, who am dead, behoves it to conduct him
  Down here through Hell, from circle unto circle;
  And this is true as that I speak to thee."

More than a hundred were there when they heard
  him,
  Who in the moat stood still to look at me,
  Through wonderment oblivious of their torture.

"Now say to Fra Dolcino, then, to arm him,
  Thou, who perhaps wilt shortly see the sun,
  If soon he wish not here to follow me,

So with provisions, that no stress of snow
  May give the victory to the Novarese,
  Which otherwise to gain would not be easy."

After one foot to go away he lifted,
  This word did Mahomet say unto me,
  Then to depart upon the ground he stretched it.

Un altro, che forata avea la gola	Another one, who had his throat pierced through,
e tronco 'l naso infin sotto le ciglia,	And nose cut off close underneath the brows,
e non avea mai ch'una orecchia sola,	And had no longer but a single ear,
ristato a riguardar per maraviglia	Staying to look in wonder with the others,
con li altri, innanzi a li altri apri` la canna,	Before the others did his gullet open,
ch'era di fuor d'ogni parte vermiglia,	Which outwardly was red in every part,
e disse: ""O tu cui colpa non condanna	And said: "O thou, whom guilt doth not condemn,
e cu' io vidi su in terra latina,	And whom I once saw up in Latian land,
se troppa simiglianza non m'inganna,	Unless too great similitude deceive me,
rimembriti di Pier da Medicina,	Call to remembrance Pier da Medicina,
se mai torni a veder lo dolce piano	If e'er thou see again the lovely plain
che da Vercelli a Marcabo` dichina.	That from Vercelli slopes to Marcabo,
E fa saper a' due miglior da Fano,	And make it known to the best two of Fano,
a messer Guido e anco ad Angiolello,	To Messer Guido and Angiolello likewise,
che, se l'antiveder qui non e` vano,	That if foreseeing here be not in vain,
gittati saran fuor di lor vasello	Cast over from their vessel shall they be,
e mazzerati presso a la Cattolica	And drowned near unto the Cattolica,
per tradimento d'un tiranno fello.	By the betrayal of a tyrant fell.
Tra l'isola di Cipri e di Maiolica	Between the isles of Cyprus and Majorca
non vide mai si` gran fallo Nettuno,	Neptune ne'er yet beheld so great a crime,
non da pirate, non da gente argolica.	Neither of pirates nor Argolic people.
Quel traditor che vede pur con l'uno,	That traitor, who sees only with one eye,
e tien la terra che tale qui meco	And holds the land, which some one here with me
vorrebbe di vedere esser digiuno,	Would fain be fasting from the vision of,
fara` venirli a parlamento seco;	Will make them come unto a parley with him;
poi fara` si`, ch'al vento di Focara	Then will do so, that to Focara's wind
non sara` lor mestier voto ne' preco"".	They will not stand in need of vow or prayer."
E io a lui: ""Dimostrami e dichiara,	And I to him: "Show to me and declare,
se vuo' ch'i' porti su` di te novella,	If thou wouldst have me bear up news of thee,
chi e` colui da la veduta amara"".	Who is this person of the bitter vision."
Allor puose la mano a la mascella	Then did he lay his hand upon the jaw
d'un suo compagno e la bocca li aperse,	Of one of his companions, and his mouth
gridando: ""Questi e` desso, e non favella.	Oped, crying: "This is he, and he speaks not.
Questi, scacciato, il dubitar sommerse	This one, being banished, every doubt submerged
in Cesare, affermando che 'l fornito	In Caesar by affirming the forearmed
sempre con danno l'attender sofferse"".	Always with detriment allowed delay."
Oh quanto mi pareva sbigottito	O how bewildered unto me appeared,
con la lingua tagliata ne la strozza	With tongue asunder in his windpipe slit,
Curio, ch'a dir fu cosi` ardito!	Curio, who in speaking was so bold!

E un ch'avea l'una e l'altra man mozza,
  levando i moncherin per l'aura fosca,
  si` che 'l sangue facea la faccia sozza,

grido`: ““Ricordera'ti anche del Mosca,
  che disse, lasso!, "Capo ha cosa fatta",
  che fu mal seme per la gente tosca”“.

E io li aggiunsi: ““E morte di tua schiatta”“;
  per ch'elli, accumulando duol con duolo,
  sen gio come persona trista e matta.

Ma io rimasi a riguardar lo stuolo,
  e vidi cosa, ch'io avrei paura,
  sanza piu` prova, di contarla solo;

se non che coscienza m'assicura,
  la buona compagnia che l'uom francheggia
  sotto l'asbergo del sentirsi pura.

Io vidi certo, e ancor par ch'io 'l veggia,
  un busto sanza capo andar si` come
  andavan li altri de la trista greggia;

e 'l capo tronco tenea per le chiome,
  pesol con mano a guisa di lanterna;
  e quel mirava noi e dicea: ““Oh me!”“.

Di se' facea a se' stesso lucerna,
  ed eran due in uno e uno in due:
  com'esser puo`, quei sa che si` governa.

Quando diritto al pie` del ponte fue,
  levo` 'l braccio alto con tutta la testa,
  per appressarne le parole sue,

che fuoro: ““Or vedi la pena molesta
  tu che, spirando, vai veggendo i morti:
  vedi s'alcuna e` grande come questa.

E perche' tu di me novella porti,
  sappi ch'i' son Bertram dal Bornio, quelli
  che diedi al re giovane i ma' conforti.

Io feci il padre e 'l figlio in se' ribelli:
  Achitofel non fe' piu` d'Absalone
  e di David coi malvagi punzelli.

Perch'io parti' cosi` giunte persone,
  partito porto il mio cerebro, lasso!,
  dal suo principio ch'e` in questo troncone.

And one, who both his hands dissevered had,
  The stumps uplifting through the murky air,
  So that the blood made horrible his face,

Cried out: "Thou shalt remember Mosca also,
  Who said, alas! 'A thing done has an end!'
  Which was an ill seed for the Tuscan people."

"And death unto thy race," thereto I added;
  Whence he, accumulating woe on woe,
  Departed, like a person sad and crazed.

But I remained to look upon the crowd;
  And saw a thing which I should be afraid,
  Without some further proof, even to recount,

If it were not that conscience reassures me,
  That good companion which emboldens man
  Beneath the hauberk of its feeling pure.

I truly saw, and still I seem to see it,
  A trunk without a head walk in like manner
  As walked the others of the mournful herd.

And by the hair it held the head dissevered,
  Hung from the hand in fashion of a lantern,
  And that upon us gazed and said: "O me!"

It of itself made to itself a lamp,
  And they were two in one, and one in two;
  How that can be, He knows who so ordains it.

When it was come close to the bridge's foot,
  It lifted high its arm with all the head,
  To bring more closely unto us its words,

Which were: "Behold now the sore penalty,
  Thou, who dost breathing go the dead beholding;
  Behold if any be as great as this.

And so that thou may carry news of me,
  Know that Bertram de Born am I, the same
  Who gave to the Young King the evil comfort.

I made the father and the son rebellious;
  Achitophel not more with Absalom
  And David did with his accursed goadings.

Because I parted persons so united,
  Parted do I now bear my brain, alas!
  From its beginning, which is in this trunk.

Cosi` s'osserva in me lo contrapasso"".   Thus is observed in me the counterpoise."

Inferno: Canto XXIX

Geri del Bello. The Tenth Bolgia: Alchemists. Griffolino d' Arezzo and Capocchino.

La molta gente e le diverse piaghe
  avean le luci mie si` inebriate,
  che de lo stare a piangere eran vaghe.

Ma Virgilio mi disse: ""Che pur guate?
  perche' la vista tua pur si soffolge
  la` giu` tra l'ombre triste smozzicate?

Tu non hai fatto si` a l'altre bolge;
  pensa, se tu annoverar le credi,
  che miglia ventidue la valle volge.

E gia` la luna e` sotto i nostri piedi:
  lo tempo e` poco omai che n'e` concesso,
  e altro e` da veder che tu non vedi"".

""Se tu avessi"", rispuos'io appresso,
  ""atteso a la cagion perch'io guardava,
  forse m'avresti ancor lo star dimesso"".

Parte sen giva, e io retro li andava,
  lo duca, gia` faccendo la risposta,
  e soggiugnendo: ""Dentro a quella cava

dov'io tenea or li occhi si` a posta,
  credo ch'un spirto del mio sangue pianga
  la colpa che la` giu` cotanto costa"".

Allor disse 'l maestro: ""Non si franga
  lo tuo pensier da qui innanzi sovr'ello.
  Attendi ad altro, ed ei la` si rimanga;

ch'io vidi lui a pie` del ponticello
  mostrarti, e minacciar forte, col dito,
  e udi' 'l nominar Geri del Bello.

The many people and the divers wounds
  These eyes of mine had so inebriated,
  That they were wishful to stand still and weep;

But said Virgilius: "What dost thou still gaze at?
  Why is thy sight still riveted down there
  Among the mournful, mutilated shades?

Thou hast not done so at the other Bolge;
  Consider, if to count them thou believest,
  That two-and-twenty miles the valley winds,

And now the moon is underneath our feet;
  Henceforth the time allotted us is brief,
  And more is to be seen than what thou seest."

"If thou hadst," I made answer thereupon,
  "Attended to the cause for which I looked,
  Perhaps a longer stay thou wouldst have pardoned."

Meanwhile my Guide departed, and behind him
  I went, already making my reply,
  And superadding: "In that cavern where

I held mine eyes with such attention fixed,
  I think a spirit of my blood laments
  The sin which down below there costs so much."

Then said the Master: "Be no longer broken
  Thy thought from this time forward upon him;
  Attend elsewhere, and there let him remain;

For him I saw below the little bridge,
  Pointing at thee, and threatening with his finger
  Fiercely, and heard him called Geri del Bello.

Tu eri allor si` del tutto impedito	So wholly at that time wast thou impeded
sovra colui che gia` tenne Altaforte,	By him who formerly held Altaforte,
che non guardasti in la`, si` fu partito"".	Thou didst not look that way; so he departed."
""O duca mio, la violenta morte	"O my Conductor, his own violent death,
che non li e` vendicata ancor"", diss'io,	Which is not yet avenged for him," I said,
""per alcun che de l'onta sia consorte,	"By any who is sharer in the shame,
fece lui disdegnoso; ond'el sen gio	Made him disdainful; whence he went away,
sanza parlarmi, si` com'io estimo:	As I imagine, without speaking to me,
e in cio` m'ha el fatto a se' piu` pio"".	And thereby made me pity him the more."
Cosi` parlammo infino al loco primo	Thus did we speak as far as the first place
che de lo scoglio l'altra valle mostra,	Upon the crag, which the next valley shows
se piu` lume vi fosse, tutto ad imo.	Down to the bottom, if there were more light.
Quando noi fummo sor l'ultima chiostra	When we were now right over the last cloister
di Malebolge, si` che i suoi conversi	Of Malebolge, so that its lay-brothers
potean parere a la veduta nostra,	Could manifest themselves unto our sight,
lamenti saettaron me diversi,	Divers lamentings pierced me through and through,
che di pieta` ferrati avean li strali;	Which with compassion had their arrows barbed,
ond'io li orecchi con le man copersi.	Whereat mine ears I covered with my hands.
Qual dolor fora, se de li spedali,	What pain would be, if from the hospitals
di Valdichiana tra 'l luglio e 'l settembre	Of Valdichiana, 'twixt July and September,
e di Maremma e di Sardigna i mali	And of Maremma and Sardinia
fossero in una fossa tutti 'nsembre,	All the diseases in one moat were gathered,
tal era quivi, e tal puzzo n'usciva	Such was it here, and such a stench came from it
qual suol venir de le marcite membre.	As from putrescent limbs is wont to issue.
Noi discendemmo in su l'ultima riva	We had descended on the furthest bank
del lungo scoglio, pur da man sinistra;	From the long crag, upon the left hand still,
e allor fu la mia vista piu` viva	And then more vivid was my power of sight
giu` ver lo fondo, la 've la ministra	Down tow'rds the bottom, where the ministress
de l'alto Sire infallibil giustizia	Of the high Lord, Justice infallible,
punisce i falsador che qui registra.	Punishes forgers, which she here records.
Non credo ch'a veder maggior tristizia	I do not think a sadder sight to see
fosse in Egina il popol tutto infermo,	Was in Aegina the whole people sick,
quando fu l'aere si` pien di malizia,	(When was the air so full of pestilence,
che li animali, infino al picciol vermo,	The animals, down to the little worm,
cascaron tutti, e poi le genti antiche,	All fell, and afterwards the ancient people,
secondo che i poeti hanno per fermo,	According as the poets have affirmed,
si ristorar di seme di formiche;	Were from the seed of ants restored again,)
ch'era a veder per quella oscura valle	Than was it to behold through that dark valley
languir li spirti per diverse biche.	The spirits languishing in divers heaps.

Qual sovra 'l ventre, e qual sovra le spalle
  l'un de l'altro giacea, e qual carpone
  si trasmutava per lo tristo calle.

Passo passo andavam sanza sermone,
  guardando e ascoltando li ammalati,
  che non potean levar le lor persone.

Io vidi due sedere a se' poggiati,
  com'a scaldar si poggia tegghia a tegghia,
  dal capo al pie` di schianze macolati;

e non vidi gia` mai menare stregghia
  a ragazzo aspettato dal segnorso,
  ne' a colui che mal volontier vegghia,

come ciascun menava spesso il morso
  de l'unghie sopra se' per la gran rabbia
  del pizzicor, che non ha piu` soccorso;

e si` traevan giu` l'unghie la scabbia,
  come coltel di scardova le scaglie
  o d'altro pesce che piu` larghe l'abbia.

""O tu che con le dita ti dismaglie"",
  comincio` 'l duca mio a l'un di loro,
  ""e che fai d'esse talvolta tanaglie,

dinne s'alcun Latino e` tra costoro
  che son quinc'entro, se l'unghia ti basti
  etternalmente a cotesto lavoro"".

""Latin siam noi, che tu vedi si` guasti
  qui ambedue"", rispuose l'un piangendo;
  ""ma tu chi se' che di noi dimandasti?"".

E 'l duca disse: ""I' son un che discendo
  con questo vivo giu` di balzo in balzo,
  e di mostrar lo 'nferno a lui intendo"".

Allor si ruppe lo comun rincalzo;
  e tremando ciascuno a me si volse
  con altri che l'udiron di rimbalzo.

Lo buon maestro a me tutto s'accolse,
  dicendo: ""Di` a lor cio` che tu vuoli"";
  e io incominciai, poscia ch'ei volse:

""Se la vostra memoria non s'imboli
  nel primo mondo da l'umane menti,
  ma s'ella viva sotto molti soli,

This on the belly, that upon the back
  One of the other lay, and others crawling
  Shifted themselves along the dismal road.

We step by step went onward without speech,
  Gazing upon and listening to the sick
  Who had not strength enough to lift their bodies.

I saw two sitting leaned against each other,
  As leans in heating platter against platter,
  From head to foot bespotted o'er with scabs;

And never saw I plied a currycomb
  By stable-boy for whom his master waits,
  Or him who keeps awake unwillingly,

As every one was plying fast the bite
  Of nails upon himself, for the great rage
  Of itching which no other succour had.

And the nails downward with them dragged the scab,
  In fashion as a knife the scales of bream,
  Or any other fish that has them largest.

"O thou, that with thy fingers dost dismail thee,"
  Began my Leader unto one of them,
  "And makest of them pincers now and then,

Tell me if any Latian is with those
  Who are herein; so may thy nails suffice thee
  To all eternity unto this work."

"Latians are we, whom thou so wasted seest,
  Both of us here," one weeping made reply;
  "But who art thou, that questionest about us?"

And said the Guide: "One am I who descends
  Down with this living man from cliff to cliff,
  And I intend to show Hell unto him."

Then broken was their mutual support,
  And trembling each one turned himself to me,
  With others who had heard him by rebound.

Wholly to me did the good Master gather,
  Saying: "Say unto them whate'er thou wishest."
  And I began, since he would have it so:

"So may your memory not steal away
  In the first world from out the minds of men,
  But so may it survive 'neath many suns,

ditemi chi voi siete e di che genti;
  la vostra sconcia e fastidiosa pena
  di palesarvi a me non vi spaventi"".

""Io fui d'Arezzo, e Albero da Siena"",
  rispuose l'un, ""mi fe' mettere al foco;
  ma quel per ch'io mori' qui non mi mena.

Vero e` ch'i' dissi lui, parlando a gioco:
  "I' mi saprei levar per l'aere a volo";
  e quei, ch'avea vaghezza e senno poco,

volle ch'i' li mostrassi l'arte; e solo
  perch'io nol feci Dedalo, mi fece
  ardere a tal che l'avea per figliuolo.

Ma nell 'ultima bolgia de le diece
  me per l'alchimia che nel mondo usai
  danno` Minos, a cui fallar non lece"".

E io dissi al poeta: ""Or fu gia` mai
  gente si` vana come la sanese?
  Certo non la francesca si` d'assai!"".

Onde l'altro lebbroso, che m'intese,
  rispuose al detto mio: ""Tra'mene Stricca
  che seppe far le temperate spese,

e Niccolo` che la costuma ricca
  del garofano prima discoverse
  ne l'orto dove tal seme s'appicca;

e tra'ne la brigata in che disperse
  Caccia d'Ascian la vigna e la gran fonda,
  e l'Abbagliato suo senno proferse.

Ma perche' sappi chi si` ti seconda
  contra i Sanesi, aguzza ver me l'occhio,
  si` che la faccia mia ben ti risponda:

si` vedrai ch'io son l'ombra di Capocchio,
  che falsai li metalli con l'alchimia;
  e te dee ricordar, se ben t'adocchio,

com'io fui di natura buona scimia"".

Say to me who ye are, and of what people;
  Let not your foul and loathsome punishment
  Make you afraid to show yourselves to me."

"I of Arezzo was," one made reply,
  "And Albert of Siena had me burned;
  But what I died for does not bring me here.

'Tis true I said to him, speaking in jest,
  That I could rise by flight into the air,
  And he who had conceit, but little wit,

Would have me show to him the art; and only
  Because no Daedalus I made him, made me
  Be burned by one who held him as his son.

But unto the last Bolgia of the ten,
  For alchemy, which in the world I practised,
  Minos, who cannot err, has me condemned."

And to the Poet said I: "Now was ever
  So vain a people as the Sienese?
  Not for a certainty the French by far."

Whereat the other leper, who had heard me,
  Replied unto my speech: "Taking out Stricca,
  Who knew the art of moderate expenses,

And Niccolo, who the luxurious use
  Of cloves discovered earliest of all
  Within that garden where such seed takes root;

And taking out the band, among whom squandered
  Caccia d'Ascian his vineyards and vast woods,
  And where his wit the Abbagliato proffered!

But, that thou know who thus doth second thee
  Against the Sienese, make sharp thine eye
  Tow'rds me, so that my face well answer thee,

And thou shalt see I am Capocchio's shade,
  Who metals falsified by alchemy;
  Thou must remember, if I well descry thee,

How I a skilful ape of nature was."

Inferno: Canto XXX

Other Falsifiers or Forgers. Gianni Schicchi, Myrrha, Adam of Brescia, Potiphar's Wife, and Sinon of Troy.

Nel tempo che Iunone era crucciata
  per Semele` contra 'l sangue tebano,
  come mostro` una e altra fiata,

Atamante divenne tanto insano,
  che veggendo la moglie con due figli
  andar carcata da ciascuna mano,

grido`: ""Tendiam le reti, si` ch'io pigli
  la leonessa e ' leoncini al varco""";
  e poi distese i dispietati artigli,

prendendo l'un ch'avea nome Learco,
  e rotollo e percosselo ad un sasso;
  e quella s'annego` con l'altro carco.

E quando la fortuna volse in basso
  l'altezza de' Troian che tutto ardiva,
  si` che 'nsieme col regno il re fu casso,

Ecuba trista, misera e cattiva,
  poscia che vide Polissena morta,
  e del suo Polidoro in su la riva

del mar si fu la dolorosa accorta,
  forsennata latro` si` come cane;
  tanto il dolor le fe' la mente torta.

Ma ne' di Tebe furie ne' troiane
  si vider mai in alcun tanto crude,
  non punger bestie, nonche' membra umane,

quant'io vidi in due ombre smorte e nude,
  che mordendo correvan di quel modo
  che 'l porco quando del porcil si schiude.

'Twas at the time when Juno was enraged,
  For Semele, against the Theban blood,
  As she already more than once had shown,

So reft of reason Athamas became,
  That, seeing his own wife with children twain
  Walking encumbered upon either hand,

He cried: "Spread out the nets, that I may take
  The lioness and her whelps upon the passage;"
  And then extended his unpitying claws,

Seizing the first, who had the name Learchus,
  And whirled him round, and dashed him on a rock;
  And she, with the other burthen, drowned her-
    self;—

And at the time when fortune downward hurled
  The Trojan's arrogance, that all things dared,
  So that the king was with his kingdom crushed,

Hecuba sad, disconsolate, and captive,
  When lifeless she beheld Polyxena,
  And of her Polydorus on the shore

Of ocean was the dolorous one aware,
  Out of her senses like a dog she barked,
  So much the anguish had her mind distorted;

But not of Thebes the furies nor the Trojan
  Were ever seen in any one so cruel
  In goading beasts, and much more human members,

As I beheld two shadows pale and naked,
  Who, biting, in the manner ran along
  That a boar does, when from the sty turned loose.

L'una giunse a Capocchio, e in sul nodo
  del collo l'assanno`, si` che, tirando,
  grattar li fece il ventre al fondo sodo.

E l'Aretin che rimase, tremando
  mi disse: ""Quel folletto e` Gianni Schicchi,
  e va rabbioso altrui cosi` conciando"".

""Oh!"", diss'io lui, ""se l'altro non ti ficchi
  li denti a dosso, non ti sia fatica
  a dir chi e`, pria che di qui si spicchi"".

Ed elli a me: ""Quell'e` l'anima antica
  di Mirra scellerata, che divenne
  al padre fuor del dritto amore amica.

Questa a peccar con esso cosi` venne,
  falsificando se' in altrui forma,
  come l'altro che la` sen va, sostenne,

per guadagnar la donna de la torma,
  falsificare in se' Buoso Donati,
  testando e dando al testamento norma"".

E poi che i due rabbiosi fuor passati
  sovra cu' io avea l'occhio tenuto,
  rivolsilo a guardar li altri mal nati.

Io vidi un, fatto a guisa di leuto,
  pur ch'elli avesse avuta l'anguinaia
  tronca da l'altro che l'uomo ha forcuto.

La grave idropesi`, che si` dispaia
  le membra con l'omor che mal converte,
  che 'l viso non risponde a la ventraia,

facea lui tener le labbra aperte
  come l'etico fa, che per la sete
  l'un verso 'l mento e l'altro in su` rinverte.

""O voi che sanz'alcuna pena siete,
  e non so io perche', nel mondo gramo"",
  diss'elli a noi, ""guardate e attendete

a la miseria del maestro Adamo:
  io ebbi vivo assai di quel ch'i' volli,
  e ora, lasso!, un gocciol d'acqua bramo.

Li ruscelletti che d'i verdi colli
  del Casentin discendon giuso in Arno,
  faccendo i lor canali freddi e molli,

One to Capocchio came, and by the nape
  Seized with its teeth his neck, so that in dragging
  It made his belly grate the solid bottom.

And the Aretine, who trembling had remained,
  Said to me: "That mad sprite is Gianni Schicchi,
  And raving goes thus harrying other people."

"O," said I to him, "so may not the other
  Set teeth on thee, let it not weary thee
  To tell us who it is, ere it dart hence."

And he to me: "That is the ancient ghost
  Of the nefarious Myrrha, who became
  Beyond all rightful love her father's lover.

She came to sin with him after this manner,
  By counterfeiting of another's form;
  As he who goeth yonder undertook,

That he might gain the lady of the herd,
  To counterfeit in himself Buoso Donati,
  Making a will and giving it due form."

And after the two maniacs had passed
  On whom I held mine eye, I turned it back
  To look upon the other evil-born.

I saw one made in fashion of a lute,
  If he had only had the groin cut off
  Just at the point at which a man is forked.

The heavy dropsy, that so disproportions
  The limbs with humours, which it ill concocts,
  That the face corresponds not to the belly,

Compelled him so to hold his lips apart
  As does the hectic, who because of thirst
  One tow'rds the chin, the other upward turns.

"O ye, who without any torment are,
  And why I know not, in the world of woe,"
  He said to us, "behold, and be attentive

Unto the misery of Master Adam;
  I had while living much of what I wished,
  And now, alas! a drop of water crave.

The rivulets, that from the verdant hills
  Of Cassentin descend down into Arno,
  Making their channels to be cold and moist,

sempre mi stanno innanzi, e non indarno,	Ever before me stand, and not in vain;
che' l'imagine lor vie piu` m'asciuga	For far more doth their image dry me up
che 'l male ond'io nel volto mi discarno.	Than the disease which strips my face of flesh.
La rigida giustizia che mi fruga	The rigid justice that chastises me
tragge cagion del loco ov'io peccai	Draweth occasion from the place in which
a metter piu` li miei sospiri in fuga.	I sinned, to put the more my sighs in flight.
Ivi e` Romena, la` dov'io falsai	There is Romena, where I counterfeited
la lega suggellata del Batista;	The currency imprinted with the Baptist,
per ch'io il corpo su` arso lasciai.	For which I left my body burned above.
Ma s'io vedessi qui l'anima trista	But if I here could see the tristful soul
di Guido o d'Alessandro o di lor frate,	Of Guido, or Alessandro, or their brother,
per Fonte Branda non darei la vista.	For Branda's fount I would not give the sight.
Dentro c'e` l'una gia`, se l'arrabbiate	One is within already, if the raving
ombre che vanno intorno dicon vero;	Shades that are going round about speak truth;
ma che mi val, c'ho le membra legate?	But what avails it me, whose limbs are tied?
S'io fossi pur di tanto ancor leggero	If I were only still so light, that in
ch'i' potessi in cent'anni andare un'oncia,	A hundred years I could advance one inch,
io sarei messo gia` per lo sentiero,	I had already started on the way,
cercando lui tra questa gente sconcia,	Seeking him out among this squalid folk,
con tutto ch'ella volge undici miglia,	Although the circuit be eleven miles,
e men d'un mezzo di traverso non ci ha.	And be not less than half a mile across.
Io son per lor tra si` fatta famiglia:	For them am I in such a family;
e' m'indussero a batter li fiorini	They did induce me into coining florins,
ch'avevan tre carati di mondiglia"".	Which had three carats of impurity."
E io a lui: ""Chi son li due tapini	And I to him: "Who are the two poor wretches
che fumman come man bagnate 'l verno,	That smoke like unto a wet hand in winter,
giacendo stretti a' tuoi destri confini?"".	Lying there close upon thy right-hand confines?"
""Qui li trovai - e poi volta non dierno - "",	"I found them here," replied he, "when I rained
rispuose, ""quando piovvi in questo greppo,	Into this chasm, and since they have not turned,
e non credo che dieno in sempiterno.	Nor do I think they will for evermore.
L'una e` la falsa ch'accuso` Gioseppo;	One the false woman is who accused Joseph,
l'altr'e` 'l falso Sinon greco di Troia:	The other the false Sinon, Greek of Troy;
per febbre aguta gittan tanto leppo"".	From acute fever they send forth such reek."
E l'un di lor, che si reco` a noia	And one of them, who felt himself annoyed
forse d'esser nomato si` oscuro,	At being, peradventure, named so darkly,
col pugno li percosse l'epa croia.	Smote with the fist upon his hardened paunch.
Quella sono` come fosse un tamburo;	It gave a sound, as if it were a drum;
e mastro Adamo li percosse il volto	And Master Adam smote him in the face,
col braccio suo, che non parve men duro,	With arm that did not seem to be less hard,

dicendo a lui: ""'Ancor che mi sia tolto
lo muover per le membra che son gravi,
ho io il braccio a tal mestiere sciolto"'".

Ond'ei rispuose: ""'Quando tu andavi
al fuoco, non l'avei tu cosi` presto;
ma si` e piu` l'avei quando coniavi"'".

E l'idropico: ""'Tu di' ver di questo:
ma tu non fosti si` ver testimonio
la` 've del ver fosti a Troia richesto"'".

""'S'io dissi falso, e tu falsasti il conio"'",
disse Sinon; ""'e son qui per un fallo,
e tu per piu` ch'alcun altro demonio!'"".

""'Ricorditi, spergiuro, del cavallo"'",
rispuose quel ch'avea infiata l'epa;
"'"e sieti reo che tutto il mondo sallo!'"".

""'E te sia rea la sete onde ti crepa"'",
disse 'l Greco, ""'la lingua, e l'acqua marcia
che 'l ventre innanzi a li occhi si` t'assiepa!'"".

Allora il monetier: ""'Cosi` si squarcia
la bocca tua per tuo mal come suole;
che' s'i' ho sete e omor mi rinfarcia,

tu hai l'arsura e 'l capo che ti duole,
e per leccar lo specchio di Narciso,
non vorresti a 'nvitar molte parole"'".

Ad ascoltarli er'io del tutto fisso,
quando 'l maestro mi disse: ""'Or pur mira,
che per poco che teco non mi risso!'"".

Quand'io 'l senti' a me parlar con ira,
volsimi verso lui con tal vergogna,
ch'ancor per la memoria mi si gira.

Qual e` colui che suo dannaggio sogna,
che sognando desidera sognare,
si` che quel ch'e`, come non fosse, agogna,

tal mi fec'io, non possendo parlare,
che disiava scusarmi, e scusava
me tuttavia, e nol mi credea fare.

""'Maggior difetto men vergogna lava"'",
disse 'l maestro, ""'che 'l tuo non e` stato;
pero` d'ogne trestizia ti disgrava.

Saying to him: "Although be taken from me
All motion, for my limbs that heavy are,
I have an arm unfettered for such need."

Whereat he answer made: "When thou didst go
Unto the fire, thou hadst it not so ready:
But hadst it so and more when thou wast coining."

The dropsical: "Thou sayest true in that;
But thou wast not so true a witness there,
Where thou wast questioned of the truth at Troy."

"If I spake false, thou falsifiedst the coin,"
Said Sinon; "and for one fault I am here,
And thou for more than any other demon."

"Remember, perjurer, about the horse,"
He made reply who had the swollen belly,
"And rueful be it thee the whole world knows it."

"Rueful to thee the thirst be wherewith cracks
Thy tongue," the Greek said, "and the putrid water
That hedges so thy paunch before thine eyes."

Then the false-coiner: "So is gaping wide
Thy mouth for speaking evil, as 'tis wont;
Because if I have thirst, and humour stuff me

Thou hast the burning and the head that aches,
And to lick up the mirror of Narcissus
Thou wouldst not want words many to invite thee."

In listening to them was I wholly fixed,
When said the Master to me: "Now just look,
For little wants it that I quarrel with thee."

When him I heard in anger speak to me,
I turned me round towards him with such shame
That still it eddies through my memory.

And as he is who dreams of his own harm,
Who dreaming wishes it may be a dream,
So that he craves what is, as if it were not;

Such I became, not having power to speak,
For to excuse myself I wished, and still
Excused myself, and did not think I did it.

"Less shame doth wash away a greater fault,"
The Master said, "than this of thine has been;
Therefore thyself disburden of all sadness,

E fa ragion ch'io ti sia sempre allato,
  se piu` avvien che fortuna t'accoglia
  dove sien genti in simigliante piato:

che' voler cio` udire e` bassa voglia"".

And make account that I am aye beside thee,
  If e'er it come to pass that fortune bring thee
  Where there are people in a like dispute;

For a base wish it is to wish to hear it."

Inferno: Canto XXXI

The Giants, Nimrod, Ephialtes, and Antaeus. Descent to Cocytus.

Una medesma lingua pria mi morse,
 si` che mi tinse l'una e l'altra guancia,
 e poi la medicina mi riporse;

cosi` od'io che solea far la lancia
 d'Achille e del suo padre esser cagione
 prima di trista e poi di buona mancia.

Noi demmo il dosso al misero vallone
 su per la ripa che 'l cinge dintorno,
 attraversando sanza alcun sermone.

Quiv'era men che notte e men che giorno,
 si` che 'l viso m'andava innanzi poco;
 ma io senti' sonare un alto corno,

tanto ch'avrebbe ogne tuon fatto fioco,
 che, contra se' la sua via seguitando,
 dirizzo` li occhi miei tutti ad un loco.

Dopo la dolorosa rotta, quando
 Carlo Magno perde' la santa gesta,
 non sono` si` terribilmente Orlando.

Poco portai in la` volta la testa,
 che me parve veder molte alte torri;
 ond'io: ““Maestro, di', che terra e` questa?”“.

Ed elli a me: ““Pero` che tu trascorri
 per le tenebre troppo da la lungi,
 avvien che poi nel maginare abborri.

Tu vedrai ben, se tu la` ti congiungi,
 quanto 'l senso s'inganna di lontano;
 pero` alquanto piu` te stesso pungi”“.

One and the selfsame tongue first wounded me,
 So that it tinged the one cheek and the other,
 And then held out to me the medicine;

Thus do I hear that once Achilles' spear,
 His and his father's, used to be the cause
 First of a sad and then a gracious boon.

We turned our backs upon the wretched valley,
 Upon the bank that girds it round about,
 Going across it without any speech.

There it was less than night, and less than day,
 So that my sight went little in advance;
 But I could hear the blare of a loud horn,

So loud it would have made each thunder faint,
 Which, counter to it following its way,
 Mine eyes directed wholly to one place.

After the dolorous discomfiture
 When Charlemagne the holy emprise lost,
 So terribly Orlando sounded not.

Short while my head turned thitherward I held
 When many lofty towers I seemed to see,
 Whereat I: "Master, say, what town is this?"

And he to me: "Because thou peerest forth
 Athwart the darkness at too great a distance,
 It happens that thou errest in thy fancy.

Well shalt thou see, if thou arrivest there,
 How much the sense deceives itself by distance;
 Therefore a little faster spur thee on."

Poi caramente mi prese per mano,
  e disse: ""Pria che noi siamo piu` avanti,
  accio` che 'l fatto men ti paia strano,

sappi che non son torri, ma giganti,
  e son nel pozzo intorno da la ripa
  da l'umbilico in giuso tutti quanti"".

Come quando la nebbia si dissipa,
  lo sguardo a poco a poco raffigura
  cio` che cela 'l vapor che l'aere stipa,

cosi` forando l'aura grossa e scura,
  piu` e piu` appressando ver' la sponda,
  fuggiemi errore e cresciemi paura;

pero` che come su la cerchia tonda
  Montereggion di torri si corona,
  cosi` la proda che 'l pozzo circonda

torreggiavan di mezza la persona
  li orribili giganti, cui minaccia
  Giove del cielo ancora quando tuona.

E io scorgeva gia` d'alcun la faccia,
  le spalle e 'l petto e del ventre gran parte,
  e per le coste giu` ambo le braccia.

Natura certo, quando lascio` l'arte
  di si` fatti animali, assai fe' bene
  per torre tali essecutori a Marte.

E s'ella d'elefanti e di balene
  non si pente, chi guarda sottilmente,
  piu` giusta e piu` discreta la ne tene;

che' dove l'argomento de la mente
  s'aggiugne al mal volere e a la possa,
  nessun riparo vi puo` far la gente.

La faccia sua mi parea lunga e grossa
  come la pina di San Pietro a Roma,
  e a sua proporzione eran l'altre ossa;

si` che la ripa, ch'era perizoma
  dal mezzo in giu`, ne mostrava ben tanto
  di sovra, che di giugnere a la chioma

Then tenderly he took me by the hand,
  And said: "Before we farther have advanced,
  That the reality may seem to thee

Less strange, know that these are not towers, but giants,
  And they are in the well, around the bank,
  From navel downward, one and all of them."

As, when the fog is vanishing away,
  Little by little doth the sight refigure
  Whate'er the mist that crowds the air conceals,

So, piercing through the dense and darksome air,
  More and more near approaching tow'rd the verge,
  My error fled, and fear came over me;

Because as on its circular parapets
  Montereggione crowns itself with towers,
  E'en thus the margin which surrounds the well

With one half of their bodies turreted
  The horrible giants, whom Jove menaces
  E'en now from out the heavens when he thunders.

And I of one already saw the face,
  Shoulders, and breast, and great part of the belly,
  And down along his sides both of the arms.

Certainly Nature, when she left the making
  Of animals like these, did well indeed,
  By taking such executors from Mars;

And if of elephants and whales she doth not
  Repent her, whosoever looketh subtly
  More just and more discreet will hold her for it;

For where the argument of intellect
  Is added unto evil will and power,
  No rampart can the people make against it.

His face appeared to me as long and large
  As is at Rome the pine-cone of Saint Peter's,
  And in proportion were the other bones;

So that the margin, which an apron was
  Down from the middle, showed so much of him
  Above it, that to reach up to his hair

tre Frison s'averien dato mal vanto;
  pero` ch'i' ne vedea trenta gran palmi
  dal loco in giu` dov'omo affibbia 'l manto.

""'Raphel mai` ameche zabi` almi'"",
  comincio` a gridar la fiera bocca,
  cui non si convenia piu` dolci salmi.

E 'l duca mio ver lui: ""'Anima sciocca,
  tienti col corno, e con quel ti disfoga
  quand'ira o altra passion ti tocca!

Cercati al collo, e troverai la soga
  che 'l tien legato, o anima confusa,
  e vedi lui che 'l gran petto ti doga'"".

Poi disse a me: ""'Elli stessi s'accusa;
  questi e` Nembrotto per lo cui mal coto
  pur un linguaggio nel mondo non s'usa.

Lascianlo stare e non parliamo a voto;
  che' cosi` e` a lui ciascun linguaggio
  come 'l suo ad altrui, ch'a nullo e` noto'"".

Facemmo adunque piu` lungo viaggio,
  volti a sinistra; e al trar d'un balestro,
  trovammo l'altro assai piu` fero e maggio.

A cigner lui qual che fosse 'l maestro,
  non so io dir, ma el tenea soccinto
  dinanzi l'altro e dietro il braccio destro

d'una catena che 'l tenea avvinto
  dal collo in giu`, si` che 'n su lo scoperto
  si ravvolgea infino al giro quinto.

""'Questo superbo volle esser esperto
  di sua potenza contra 'l sommo Giove'"",
  disse 'l mio duca, ""'ond'elli ha cotal merto.

Fialte ha nome, e fece le gran prove
  quando i giganti fer paura a' dei;
  le braccia ch'el meno`, gia` mai non move'"".

E io a lui: ""'S'esser puote, io vorrei
  che de lo smisurato Briareo
  esperienza avesser li occhi miei'"".

Three Frieslanders in vain had vaunted them;
  For I beheld thirty great palms of him
  Down from the place where man his mantle buckles.

"Raphael mai amech izabi almi,"
  Began to clamour the ferocious mouth,
  To which were not befitting sweeter psalms.

And unto him my Guide: "Soul idiotic,
  Keep to thy horn, and vent thyself with that,
  When wrath or other passion touches thee.

Search round thy neck, and thou wilt find the belt
  Which keeps it fastened, O bewildered soul,
  And see it, where it bars thy mighty breast."

Then said to me: "He doth himself accuse;
  This one is Nimrod, by whose evil thought
  One language in the world is not still used.

Here let us leave him and not speak in vain;
  For even such to him is every language
  As his to others, which to none is known."

Therefore a longer journey did we make,
  Turned to the left, and a crossbow-shot off
  We found another far more fierce and large.

In binding him, who might the master be
  I cannot say; but he had pinioned close
  Behind the right arm, and in front the other,

With chains, that held him so begirt about
  From the neck down, that on the part uncovered
  It wound itself as far as the fifth gyre.

"This proud one wished to make experiment
  Of his own power against the Supreme Jove,"
  My Leader said, "whence he has such a guerdon.

Ephialtes is his name; he showed great prowess.
  What time the giants terrified the gods;
  The arms he wielded never more he moves."

And I to him: "If possible, I should wish
  That of the measureless Briareus
  These eyes of mine might have experience."

Ond'ei rispuose: ““Tu vedrai Anteo
 presso di qui che parla ed e` disciolto,
 che ne porra` nel fondo d'ogne reo.

Quel che tu vuo' veder, piu` la` e` molto,
 ed e` legato e fatto come questo,
 salvo che piu` feroce par nel volto”“.

Non fu tremoto gia` tanto rubesto,
 che scotesse una torre cosi` forte,
 come Fialte a scuotersi fu presto.

Allor temett'io piu` che mai la morte,
 e non v'era mestier piu` che la dotta,
 s'io non avessi viste le ritorte.

Noi procedemmo piu` avante allotta,
 e venimmo ad Anteo, che ben cinque alle,
 sanza la testa, uscia fuor de la grotta.

““O tu che ne la fortunata valle
 che fece Scipion di gloria reda,
 quand'Anibal co' suoi diede le spalle,

recasti gia` mille leon per preda,
 e che, se fossi stato a l'alta guerra
 de'tuoi fratelli, ancor par che si creda

ch'avrebber vinto i figli de la terra;
 mettine giu`, e non ten vegna schifo,
 dove Cocito la freddura serra.

Non ci fare ire a Tizio ne' a Tifo:
 questi puo` dar di quel che qui si brama;
 pero` ti china, e non torcer lo grifo.

Ancor ti puo` nel mondo render fama,
 ch'el vive, e lunga vita ancor aspetta
 se 'nnanzi tempo grazia a se' nol chiama”“.

Cosi` disse 'l maestro; e quelli in fretta
 le man distese, e prese 'l duca mio,
 ond'Ercule senti` gia` grande stretta.

Virgilio, quando prender si sentio,
 disse a me: ““Fatti qua, si` ch'io ti prenda”“;
 poi fece si` ch'un fascio era elli e io.

Qual pare a riguardar la Carisenda
 sotto 'l chinato, quando un nuvol vada
 sovr'essa si`, ched ella incontro penda;

Whence he replied: "Thou shalt behold Antaeus
 Close by here, who can speak and is unbound,
 Who at the bottom of all crime shall place us.

Much farther yon is he whom thou wouldst see,
 And he is bound, and fashioned like to this one,
 Save that he seems in aspect more ferocious."

There never was an earthquake of such might
 That it could shake a tower so violently,
 As Ephialtes suddenly shook himself.

Then was I more afraid of death than ever,
 For nothing more was needful than the fear,
 If I had not beheld the manacles.

Then we proceeded farther in advance,
 And to Antaeus came, who, full five ells
 Without the head, forth issued from the cavern.

"O thou, who in the valley fortunate,
 Which Scipio the heir of glory made,
 When Hannibal turned back with all his hosts,

Once brought'st a thousand lions for thy prey,
 And who, hadst thou been at the mighty war
 Among thy brothers, some it seems still think

The sons of Earth the victory would have gained:
 Place us below, nor be disdainful of it,
 There where the cold doth lock Cocytus up.

Make us not go to Tityus nor Typhoeus;
 This one can give of that which here is longed for;
 Therefore stoop down, and do not curl thy lip.

Still in the world can he restore thy fame;
 Because he lives, and still expects long life,
 If to itself Grace call him not untimely."

So said the Master; and in haste the other
 His hands extended and took up my Guide,—
 Hands whose great pressure Hercules once felt.

Virgilius, when he felt himself embraced,
 Said unto me: "Draw nigh, that I may take thee;"
 Then of himself and me one bundle made.

As seems the Carisenda, to behold
 Beneath the leaning side, when goes a cloud
 Above it so that opposite it hangs;

tal parve Anteo a me che stava a bada
  di vederlo chinare, e fu tal ora
  ch'i' avrei voluto ir per altra strada.

Ma lievemente al fondo che divora
  Lucifero con Giuda, ci sposo`;
  ne' si` chinato, li` fece dimora,

e come albero in nave si levo`.

Such did Antaeus seem to me, who stood
  Watching to see him stoop, and then it was
  I could have wished to go some other way.

But lightly in the abyss, which swallows up
  Judas with Lucifer, he put us down;
  Nor thus bowed downward made he there delay,

But, as a mast does in a ship, uprose.

Inferno: Canto XXXII

The Ninth Circle: Traitors. The Frozen Lake of Cocytus. First Division, Caina: Traitors to their Kindred. Camicion de' Pazzi. Second Division, Antenora: Traitors to their Country. Dante questions Bocca degli Abati. Buoso da Duera.

S'io avessi le rime aspre e chiocce,
  come si converrebbe al tristo buco
  sovra 'l qual pontan tutte l'altre rocce,
	If I had rhymes both rough and stridulous,
	  As were appropriate to the dismal hole
	  Down upon which thrust all the other rocks,

io premerei di mio concetto il suco
  piu` pienamente; ma perch'io non l'abbo,
  non sanza tema a dicer mi conduco;
	I would press out the juice of my conception
	  More fully; but because I have them not,
	  Not without fear I bring myself to speak;

che' non e` impresa da pigliare a gabbo
  discriver fondo a tutto l'universo,
  ne' da lingua che chiami mamma o babbo.
	For 'tis no enterprise to take in jest,
	  To sketch the bottom of all the universe,
	  Nor for a tongue that cries Mamma and Babbo.

Ma quelle donne aiutino il mio verso
  ch'aiutaro Anfione a chiuder Tebe,
  si` che dal fatto il dir non sia diverso.
	But may those Ladies help this verse of mine,
	  Who helped Amphion in enclosing Thebes,
	  That from the fact the word be not diverse.

Oh sovra tutte mal creata plebe
  che stai nel loco onde parlare e` duro,
  mei foste state qui pecore o zebe!
	O rabble ill-begotten above all,
	  Who're in the place to speak of which is hard,
	  'Twere better ye had here been sheep or goats!

Come noi fummo giu` nel pozzo scuro   sotto i pie` del gigante assai piu` bassi, e io mirava ancora a l'alto muro,	When we were down within the darksome well, Beneath the giant's feet, but lower far, And I was scanning still the lofty wall,

dicere udi'mi: ""Guarda come passi:
  va si`, che tu non calchi con le piante
  le teste de' fratei miseri lassi"".
	I heard it said to me: "Look how thou steppest!
	  Take heed thou do not trample with thy feet
	  The heads of the tired, miserable brothers!"

Per ch'io mi volsi, e vidimi davante
  e sotto i piedi un lago che per gelo
  avea di vetro e non d'acqua sembiante.
	Whereat I turned me round, and saw before me
	  And underfoot a lake, that from the frost
	  The semblance had of glass, and not of water.

Non fece al corso suo si` grosso velo
  di verno la Danoia in Osterlicchi,
  ne' Tanai la` sotto 'l freddo cielo,

com'era quivi; che se Tambernicchi
  vi fosse su` caduto, o Pietrapana,
  non avria pur da l'orlo fatto cricchi.

E come a gracidar si sta la rana
  col muso fuor de l'acqua, quando sogna
  di spigolar sovente la villana;

livide, insin la` dove appar vergogna
  eran l'ombre dolenti ne la ghiaccia,
  mettendo i denti in nota di cicogna.

Ognuna in giu` tenea volta la faccia;
  da bocca il freddo, e da li occhi il cor tristo
  tra lor testimonianza si procaccia.

Quand'io m'ebbi dintorno alquanto visto,
  volsimi a' piedi, e vidi due si` stretti,
  che 'l pel del capo avieno insieme misto.

""Ditemi, voi che si` strignete i petti"",
  diss'io, ""chi siete?"". E quei piegaro i colli;
  e poi ch'ebber li visi a me eretti,

li occhi lor, ch'eran pria pur dentro molli,
  gocciar su per le labbra, e 'l gelo strinse
  le lagrime tra essi e riserrolli.

Con legno legno spranga mai non cinse
  forte cosi`; ond'ei come due becchi
  cozzaro insieme, tanta ira li vinse.

E un ch'avea perduti ambo li orecchi
  per la freddura, pur col viso in giue,
  disse: ""Perche' cotanto in noi ti specchi?

Se vuoi saper chi son cotesti due,
  la valle onde Bisenzo si dichina
  del padre loro Alberto e di lor fue.

D'un corpo usciro; e tutta la Caina
  potrai cercare, e non troverai ombra
  degna piu` d'esser fitta in gelatina;

So thick a veil ne'er made upon its current
  In winter-time Danube in Austria,
  Nor there beneath the frigid sky the Don,

As there was here; so that if Tambernich
  Had fallen upon it, or Pietrapana,
  E'en at the edge 'twould not have given a creak.

And as to croak the frog doth place himself
  With muzzle out of water,—when is dreaming
  Of gleaning oftentimes the peasant-girl,—

Livid, as far down as where shame appears,
  Were the disconsolate shades within the ice,
  Setting their teeth unto the note of storks.

Each one his countenance held downward bent;
  From mouth the cold, from eyes the doleful heart
  Among them witness of itself procures.

When round about me somewhat I had looked,
  I downward turned me, and saw two so close,
  The hair upon their heads together mingled.

"Ye who so strain your breasts together, tell me,"
  I said, "who are you;" and they bent their necks,
  And when to me their faces they had lifted,

Their eyes, which first were only moist within,
  Gushed o'er the eyelids, and the frost congealed
  The tears between, and locked them up again.

Clamp never bound together wood with wood
  So strongly; whereat they, like two he-goats,
  Butted together, so much wrath o'ercame them.

And one, who had by reason of the cold
  Lost both his ears, still with his visage downward,
  Said: "Why dost thou so mirror thyself in us?

If thou desire to know who these two are,
  The valley whence Bisenzio descends
  Belonged to them and to their father Albert.

They from one body came, and all Caina
  Thou shalt search through, and shalt not find a shade
  More worthy to be fixed in gelatine;

non quelli a cui fu rotto il petto e l'ombra
  con esso un colpo per la man d'Artu`;
  non Focaccia; non questi che m'ingombra
	Not he in whom were broken breast and shadow
	  At one and the same blow by Arthur's hand;
	  Focaccia not; not he who me encumbers

col capo si`, ch'i' non veggio oltre piu`,
  e fu nomato Sassol Mascheroni;
  se tosco se', ben sai omai chi fu.
	So with his head I see no farther forward,
	  And bore the name of Sassol Mascheroni;
	  Well knowest thou who he was, if thou art Tuscan.

E perche' non mi metti in piu` sermoni,
  sappi ch'i' fu' il Camiscion de' Pazzi;
  e aspetto Carlin che mi scagioni"".
	And that thou put me not to further speech,
	  Know that I Camicion de' Pazzi was,
	  And wait Carlino to exonerate me."

Poscia vid'io mille visi cagnazzi
  fatti per freddo; onde mi vien riprezzo,
  e verra` sempre, de' gelati guazzi.
	Then I beheld a thousand faces, made
	  Purple with cold; whence o'er me comes a shudder,
	  And evermore will come, at frozen ponds.

E mentre ch'andavamo inver' lo mezzo
  al quale ogne gravezza si rauna,
  e io tremava ne l'etterno rezzo;
	And while we were advancing tow'rds the middle,
	  Where everything of weight unites together,
	  And I was shivering in the eternal shade,

se voler fu o destino o fortuna,
  non so; ma, passeggiando tra le teste,
  forte percossi 'l pie` nel viso ad una.
	Whether 'twere will, or destiny, or chance,
	  I know not; but in walking 'mong the heads
	  I struck my foot hard in the face of one.

Piangendo mi sgrido`: ""Perche' mi peste?
  se tu non vieni a crescer la vendetta
  di Montaperti, perche' mi moleste?"".
	Weeping he growled: "Why dost thou trample me?
	  Unless thou comest to increase the vengeance
	  of Montaperti, why dost thou molest me?"

E io: ""Maestro mio, or qui m'aspetta,
  si ch'io esca d'un dubbio per costui;
  poi mi farai, quantunque vorrai, fretta"".
	And I: "My Master, now wait here for me,
	  That I through him may issue from a doubt;
	  Then thou mayst hurry me, as thou shalt wish."

Lo duca stette, e io dissi a colui
  che bestemmiava duramente ancora:
  ""Qual se' tu che cosi` rampogni altrui?"".
	The Leader stopped; and to that one I said
	  Who was blaspheming vehemently still:
	  "Who art thou, that thus reprehendest others?"

""Or tu chi se' che vai per l'Antenora,
  percotendo"", rispuose, ""altrui le gote,
  si` che, se fossi vivo, troppo fora?"".
	"Now who art thou, that goest through Antenora
	  Smiting," replied he, "other people's cheeks,
	  So that, if thou wert living, 'twere too much?"

""Vivo son io, e caro esser ti puote"",
  fu mia risposta, ""se dimandi fama,
  ch'io metta il nome tuo tra l'altre note"".
	"Living I am, and dear to thee it may be,"
	  Was my response, "if thou demandest fame,
	  That 'mid the other notes thy name I place."

Ed elli a me: ""Del contrario ho io brama.
  Levati quinci e non mi dar piu` lagna,
  che' mal sai lusingar per questa lama!"".
	And he to me: "For the reverse I long;
	  Take thyself hence, and give me no more trouble;
	  For ill thou knowest to flatter in this hollow."

Allor lo presi per la cuticagna, e dissi: ""El converra` che tu ti nomi,   o che capel qui su` non ti rimagna"".	Then by the scalp behind I seized upon him, And said: "It must needs be thou name thyself, Or not a hair remain upon thee here."

Ond'elli a me: ""Perche' tu mi dischiomi,
 ne' ti diro` ch'io sia, ne' mosterrolti,
 se mille fiate in sul capo mi tomi"".

Io avea gia` i capelli in mano avvolti,
 e tratto glien'avea piu` d'una ciocca,
 latrando lui con li occhi in giu` raccolti,

quando un altro grido`: ""Che hai tu, Bocca?
 non ti basta sonar con le mascelle,
 se tu non latri? qual diavol ti tocca?"".

""Omai"", diss'io, ""non vo' che piu` favelle,
 malvagio traditor; ch'a la tua onta
 io portero` di te vere novelle"".

""Va via"", rispuose, ""e cio` che tu vuoi conta;
 ma non tacer, se tu di qua entro eschi,
 di quel ch'ebbe or cosi` la lingua pronta.

El piange qui l'argento de' Franceschi:
 "Io vidi", potrai dir, "quel da Duera
 la` dove i peccatori stanno freschi".

Se fossi domandato "Altri chi v'era?",
 tu hai dallato quel di Beccheria
 di cui sego` Fiorenza la gorgiera.

Gianni de' Soldanier credo che sia
 piu` la` con Ganellone e Tebaldello,
 ch'apri` Faenza quando si dormia"".

Noi eravam partiti gia` da ello,
 ch'io vidi due ghiacciati in una buca,
 si` che l'un capo a l'altro era cappello;

e come 'l pan per fame si manduca,
 cosi` 'l sovran li denti a l'altro pose
 la` 've 'l cervel s'aggiugne con la nuca:

non altrimenti Tideo si rose
 le tempie a Menalippo per disdegno,
 che quei faceva il teschio e l'altre cose.

""O tu che mostri per si` bestial segno
 odio sovra colui che tu ti mangi,
 dimmi 'l perche'"", diss'io, ""per tal convegno,

che se tu a ragion di lui ti piangi,
 sappiendo chi voi siete e la sua pecca,
 nel mondo suso ancora io te ne cangi,

Whence he to me: "Though thou strip off my hair,
 I will not tell thee who I am, nor show thee,
 If on my head a thousand times thou fall."

I had his hair in hand already twisted,
 And more than one shock of it had pulled out,
 He barking, with his eyes held firmly down,

When cried another: "What doth ail thee, Bocca?
 Is't not enough to clatter with thy jaws,
 But thou must bark? what devil touches thee?"

"Now," said I, "I care not to have thee speak,
 Accursed traitor; for unto thy shame
 I will report of thee veracious news."

"Begone," replied he, "and tell what thou wilt,
 But be not silent, if thou issue hence,
 Of him who had just now his tongue so prompt;

He weepeth here the silver of the French;
 'I saw,' thus canst thou phrase it, 'him of Duera
 There where the sinners stand out in the cold.'

If thou shouldst questioned be who else was there,
 Thou hast beside thee him of Beccaria,
 Of whom the gorget Florence slit asunder;

Gianni del Soldanier, I think, may be
 Yonder with Ganellon, and Tebaldello
 Who oped Faenza when the people slep."

Already we had gone away from him,
 When I beheld two frozen in one hole,
 So that one head a hood was to the other;

And even as bread through hunger is devoured,
 The uppermost on the other set his teeth,
 There where the brain is to the nape united.

Not in another fashion Tydeus gnawed
 The temples of Menalippus in disdain,
 Than that one did the skull and the other things.

"O thou, who showest by such bestial sign
 Thy hatred against him whom thou art eating,
 Tell me the wherefore," said I, "with this compact,

That if thou rightfully of him complain,
 In knowing who ye are, and his transgression,
 I in the world above repay thee for it,

se quella con ch'io parlo non si secca"".

If that wherewith I speak be not dried up."

Inferno: Canto XXXIII

Count Ugolino and the Archbishop Ruggieri. The Death of Count Ugolino's Sons. Third Division of the Ninth Circle, Ptolomaea: Traitors to their Friends. Friar Alberigo, Branco d' Oria.

La bocca sollevo` dal fiero pasto
  quel peccator, forbendola a'capelli
  del capo ch'elli avea di retro guasto.

Poi comincio`: ""Tu vuo' ch'io rinovelli
  disperato dolor che 'l cor mi preme
  gia` pur pensando, pria ch'io ne favelli.

Ma se le mie parole esser dien seme
  che frutti infamia al traditor ch'i' rodo,
  parlar e lagrimar vedrai insieme.

Io non so chi tu se' ne' per che modo
  venuto se' qua giu`; ma fiorentino
  mi sembri veramente quand'io t'odo.

Tu dei saper ch'i' fui conte Ugolino,
  e questi e` l'arcivescovo Ruggieri:
  or ti diro` perche' i son tal vicino.

Che per l'effetto de' suo' mai pensieri,
  fidandomi di lui, io fossi preso
  e poscia morto, dir non e` mestieri;

pero` quel che non puoi avere inteso,
  cioe` come la morte mia fu cruda,
  udirai, e saprai s'e' m'ha offeso.

Breve pertugio dentro da la Muda
  la qual per me ha 'l titol de la fame,
  e che conviene ancor ch'altrui si chiuda,

His mouth uplifted from his grim repast,
  That sinner, wiping it upon the hair
  Of the same head that he behind had wasted.

Then he began: "Thou wilt that I renew
  The desperate grief, which wrings my heart already
  To think of only, ere I speak of it;

But if my words be seed that may bear fruit
  Of infamy to the traitor whom I gnaw,
  Speaking and weeping shalt thou see together.

I know not who thou art, nor by what mode
  Thou hast come down here; but a Florentine
  Thou seemest to me truly, when I hear thee.

Thou hast to know I was Count Ugolino,
  And this one was Ruggieri the Archbishop;
  Now I will tell thee why I am such a neighbour.

That, by effect of his malicious thoughts,
  Trusting in him I was made prisoner,
  And after put to death, I need not say;

But ne'ertheless what thou canst not have heard,
  That is to say, how cruel was my death,
  Hear shalt thou, and shalt know if he has wronged
    me.

A narrow perforation in the mew,
  Which bears because of me the title of Famine,
  And in which others still must be locked up,

m'avea mostrato per lo suo forame
  piu` lune gia`, quand'io feci 'l mal sonno
  che del futuro mi squarcio` 'l velame.

Questi pareva a me maestro e donno,
  cacciando il lupo e ' lupicini al monte
  per che i Pisan veder Lucca non ponno.

Con cagne magre, studiose e conte
  Gualandi con Sismondi e con Lanfranchi
  s'avea messi dinanzi da la fronte.

In picciol corso mi parieno stanchi
  lo padre e ' figli, e con l'agute scane
  mi parea lor veder fender li fianchi.

Quando fui desto innanzi la dimane,
  pianger senti' fra 'l sonno i miei figliuoli
  ch'eran con meco, e dimandar del pane.

Ben se' crudel, se tu gia` non ti duoli
  pensando cio` che 'l mio cor s'annunziava;
  e se non piangi, di che pianger suoli?

Gia` eran desti, e l'ora s'appressava
  che 'l cibo ne solea essere addotto,
  e per suo sogno ciascun dubitava;

e io senti' chiavar l'uscio di sotto
  a l'orribile torre; ond'io guardai
  nel viso a' mie' figliuoi sanza far motto.

Io non piangea, si` dentro impetrai:
  piangevan elli; e Anselmuccio mio
  disse: "Tu guardi si`, padre! che hai?".

Percio` non lacrimai ne' rispuos'io
  tutto quel giorno ne' la notte appresso,
  infin che l'altro sol nel mondo uscio.

Come un poco di raggio si fu messo
  nel doloroso carcere, e io scorsi
  per quattro visi il mio aspetto stesso,

ambo le man per lo dolor mi morsi;
  ed ei, pensando ch'io 'l fessi per voglia
  di manicar, di subito levorsi

Had shown me through its opening many moons
  Already, when I dreamed the evil dream
  Which of the future rent for me the veil.

This one appeared to me as lord and master,
  Hunting the wolf and whelps upon the mountain
  For which the Pisans cannot Lucca see.

With sleuth-hounds gaunt, and eager, and well
    trained,
  Gualandi with Sismondi and Lanfianchi
  He had sent out before him to the front.

After brief course seemed unto me forespent
  The father and the sons, and with sharp tushes
  It seemed to me I saw their flanks ripped open.

When I before the morrow was awake,
  Moaning amid their sleep I heard my sons
  Who with me were, and asking after bread.

Cruel indeed art thou, if yet thou grieve not,
  Thinking of what my heart foreboded me,
  And weep'st thou not, what art thou wont to weep
    at?

They were awake now, and the hour drew nigh
  At which our food used to be brought to us,
  And through his dream was each one apprehensive;

And I heard locking up the under door
  Of the horrible tower; whereat without a word
  I gazed into the faces of my sons.

I wept not, I within so turned to stone;
  They wept; and darling little Anselm mine
  Said: 'Thou dost gaze so, father, what doth ail thee?'

Still not a tear I shed, nor answer made
  All of that day, nor yet the night thereafter,
  Until another sun rose on the world.

As now a little glimmer made its way
  Into the dolorous prison, and I saw
  Upon four faces my own very aspect,

Both of my hands in agony I bit;
  And, thinking that I did it from desire
  Of eating, on a sudden they uprose,

e disser: "Padre, assai ci fia men doglia
  se tu mangi di noi: tu ne vestisti
  queste misere carni, e tu le spoglia".

Queta'mi allor per non farli piu` tristi;
  lo di` e l'altro stemmo tutti muti;
  ahi dura terra, perche' non t'apristi?

Poscia che fummo al quarto di` venuti,
  Gaddo mi si gitto` disteso a' piedi,
  dicendo: "Padre mio, che' non mi aiuti?".

Quivi mori`; e come tu mi vedi,
  vid'io cascar li tre ad uno ad uno
  tra 'l quinto di` e 'l sesto; ond'io mi diedi,

gia` cieco, a brancolar sovra ciascuno,
  e due di` li chiamai, poi che fur morti.
  Poscia, piu` che 'l dolor, pote' 'l digiuno"".

Quand'ebbe detto cio`, con li occhi torti
  riprese 'l teschio misero co'denti,
  che furo a l'osso, come d'un can, forti.

Ahi Pisa, vituperio de le genti
  del bel paese la` dove 'l si` suona,
  poi che i vicini a te punir son lenti,

muovasi la Capraia e la Gorgona,
  e faccian siepe ad Arno in su la foce,
  si` ch'elli annieghi in te ogne persona!

Che' se 'l conte Ugolino aveva voce
  d'aver tradita te de le castella,
  non dovei tu i figliuoi porre a tal croce.

Innocenti facea l'eta` novella,
  novella Tebe, Uguiccione e 'l Brigata
  e li altri due che 'l canto suso appella.

Noi passammo oltre, la` 've la gelata
  ruvidamente un'altra gente fascia,
  non volta in giu`, ma tutta riversata.

Lo pianto stesso li` pianger non lascia,
  e 'l duol che truova in su li occhi rintoppo,
  si volge in entro a far crescer l'ambascia;

che' le lagrime prime fanno groppo,
  e si` come visiere di cristallo,
  riempion sotto 'l ciglio tutto il coppo.

And said they: 'Father, much less pain 'twill give us
  If thou do eat of us; thyself didst clothe us
  With this poor flesh, and do thou strip it off.'

I calmed me then, not to make them more sad.
  That day we all were silent, and the next.
  Ah! obdurate earth, wherefore didst thou not open?

When we had come unto the fourth day, Gaddo
  Threw himself down outstretched before my feet,
  Saying, 'My father, why dost thou not help me?'

And there he died; and, as thou seest me,
  I saw the three fall, one by one, between
  The fifth day and the sixth; whence I betook me,

Already blind, to groping over each,
  And three days called them after they were dead;
  Then hunger did what sorrow could not do."

When he had said this, with his eyes distorted,
  The wretched skull resumed he with his teeth,
  Which, as a dog's, upon the bone were strong.

Ah! Pisa, thou opprobrium of the people
  Of the fair land there where the 'Si' doth sound,
  Since slow to punish thee thy neighbours are,

Let the Capraia and Gorgona move,
  And make a hedge across the mouth of Arno
  That every person in thee it may drown!

For if Count Ugolino had the fame
  Of having in thy castles thee betrayed,
  Thou shouldst not on such cross have put his sons.

Guiltless of any crime, thou modern Thebes!
  Their youth made Uguccione and Brigata,
  And the other two my song doth name above!

We passed still farther onward, where the ice
  Another people ruggedly enswathes,
  Not downward turned, but all of them reversed.

Weeping itself there does not let them weep,
  And grief that finds a barrier in the eyes
  Turns itself inward to increase the anguish;

Because the earliest tears a cluster form,
  And, in the manner of a crystal visor,
  Fill all the cup beneath the eyebrow full.

E avvegna che, si` come d'un callo,
  per la freddura ciascun sentimento
  cessato avesse del mio viso stallo,

gia` mi parea sentire alquanto vento:
  per ch'io: ““Maestro mio, questo chi move?
  non e` qua giu` ogne vapore spento?”“.

Ond'elli a me: ““Avaccio sarai dove
  di cio` ti fara` l'occhio la risposta,
  veggendo la cagion che 'l fiato piove”“.

E un de' tristi de la fredda crosta
  grido` a noi: ““O anime crudeli,
  tanto che data v'e` l'ultima posta,

levatemi dal viso i duri veli,
  si` ch'io sfoghi 'l duol che 'l cor m'impregna,
  un poco, pria che 'l pianto si raggeli”“.

Per ch'io a lui: ““Se vuo' ch'i' ti sovvegna,
  dimmi chi se', e s'io non ti disbrigo,
  al fondo de la ghiaccia ir mi convegna”“.

Rispuose adunque: ““I' son frate Alberigo;
  i' son quel da le frutta del mal orto,
  che qui riprendo dattero per figo”“.

““Oh!”“, diss'io lui, ““or se' tu ancor morto?”“.
  Ed elli a me: ““Come 'l mio corpo stea
  nel mondo su`, nulla scienza porto.

Cotal vantaggio ha questa Tolomea,
  che spesse volte l'anima ci cade
  innanzi ch'Atropos mossa le dea.

E perche' tu piu` volentier mi rade
  le 'nvetriate lagrime dal volto,
  sappie che, tosto che l'anima trade

come fec'io, il corpo suo l'e` tolto
  da un demonio, che poscia il governa
  mentre che 'l tempo suo tutto sia volto.

Ella ruina in si` fatta cisterna;
  e forse pare ancor lo corpo suso
  de l'ombra che di qua dietro mi verna.

And notwithstanding that, as in a callus,
  Because of cold all sensibility
  Its station had abandoned in my face,

Still it appeared to me I felt some wind;
  Whence I: "My Master, who sets this in motion?
  Is not below here every vapour quenched?"

Whence he to me: "Full soon shalt thou be where
  Thine eye shall answer make to thee of this,
  Seeing the cause which raineth down the blast."

And one of the wretches of the frozen crust
  Cried out to us: "O souls so merciless
  That the last post is given unto you,

Lift from mine eyes the rigid veils, that I
  May vent the sorrow which impregns my heart
  A little, e'er the weeping recongeal."

Whence I to him: "If thou wouldst have me help thee
  Say who thou wast; and if I free thee not,
  May I go to the bottom of the ice."

Then he replied: "I am Friar Alberigo;
  He am I of the fruit of the bad garden,
  Who here a date am getting for my fig."

"O," said I to him, "now art thou, too, dead?"
  And he to me: "How may my body fare
  Up in the world, no knowledge I possess.

Such an advantage has this Ptolomaea,
  That oftentimes the soul descendeth here
  Sooner than Atropos in motion sets it.

And, that thou mayest more willingly remove
  From off my countenance these glassy tears,
  Know that as soon as any soul betrays

As I have done, his body by a demon
  Is taken from him, who thereafter rules it,
  Until his time has wholly been revolved.

Itself down rushes into such a cistern;
  And still perchance above appears the body
  Of yonder shade, that winters here behind me.

Tu 'l dei saper, se tu vien pur mo giuso:
  elli e` ser Branca Doria, e son piu` anni
  poscia passati ch'el fu si` racchiuso"".

""Io credo"", diss'io lui, ""che tu m'inganni;
  che' Branca Doria non mori` unquanche,
  e mangia e bee e dorme e veste panni"".

""Nel fosso su`"", diss'el, ""de' Malebranche,
  la` dove bolle la tenace pece,
  non era ancor giunto Michel Zanche,

che questi lascio` il diavolo in sua vece
  nel corpo suo, ed un suo prossimano
  che 'l tradimento insieme con lui fece.

Ma distendi oggimai in qua la mano;
  aprimi li occhi"". E io non gliel'apersi;
  e cortesia fu lui esser villano.

Ahi Genovesi, uomini diversi
  d'ogne costume e pien d'ogne magagna,
  perche' non siete voi del mondo spersi?

Che' col peggiore spirto di Romagna
  trovai di voi un tal, che per sua opra
  in anima in Cocito gia` si bagna,

e in corpo par vivo ancor di sopra.

This thou shouldst know, if thou hast just come
    down;
  It is Ser Branca d' Oria, and many years
  Have passed away since he was thus locked up."

"I think," said I to him, "thou dost deceive me;
  For Branca d' Oria is not dead as yet,
  And eats, and drinks, and sleeps, and puts on
    clothes."

"In moat above," said he, "of Malebranche,
  There where is boiling the tenacious pitch,
  As yet had Michel Zanche not arrived,

When this one left a devil in his stead
  In his own body and one near of kin,
  Who made together with him the betrayal.

But hitherward stretch out thy hand forthwith,
  Open mine eyes;"—and open them I did not,
  And to be rude to him was courtesy.

Ah, Genoese! ye men at variance
  With every virtue, full of every vice
  Wherefore are ye not scattered from the world?

For with the vilest spirit of Romagna
  I found of you one such, who for his deeds
  In soul already in Cocytus bathes,

And still above in body seems alive!

Inferno: Canto XXXIV

Fourth Division of the Ninth Circle, the Judecca: Traitors to their Lords and Benefactors. Lucifer, Judas Iscariot, Brutus, and Cassius. The Chasm of Lethe. The Ascent.

""Vexilla regis prodeunt inferni
  verso di noi; pero` dinanzi mira"",
  disse 'l maestro mio ""se tu 'l discerni"".

Come quando una grossa nebbia spira,
  o quando l'emisperio nostro annotta,
  par di lungi un molin che 'l vento gira,

veder mi parve un tal dificio allotta;
  poi per lo vento mi ristrinsi retro
  al duca mio; che' non li` era altra grotta.

Gia` era, e con paura il metto in metro,
  la` dove l'ombre tutte eran coperte,
  e trasparien come festuca in vetro.

Altre sono a giacere; altre stanno erte,
  quella col capo e quella con le piante;
  altra, com'arco, il volto a' pie` rinverte.

Quando noi fummo fatti tanto avante,
  ch'al mio maestro piacque di mostrarmi
  la creatura ch'ebbe il bel sembiante,

d'innanzi mi si tolse e fe' restarmi,
  ""Ecco Dite"", dicendo, ""ed ecco il loco
  ove convien che di fortezza t'armi"".

Com'io divenni allor gelato e fioco,
  nol dimandar, lettor, ch'i' non lo scrivo,
  pero` ch'ogne parlar sarebbe poco.

"'Vexilla Regis prodeunt Inferni'
  Towards us; therefore look in front of thee,"
  My Master said, "if thou discernest him."

As, when there breathes a heavy fog, or when
  Our hemisphere is darkening into night,
  Appears far off a mill the wind is turning,

Methought that such a building then I saw;
  And, for the wind, I drew myself behind
  My Guide, because there was no other shelter.

Now was I, and with fear in verse I put it,
  There where the shades were wholly covered up,
  And glimmered through like unto straws in glass.

Some prone are lying, others stand erect,
  This with the head, and that one with the soles;
  Another, bow-like, face to feet inverts.

When in advance so far we had proceeded,
  That it my Master pleased to show to me
  The creature who once had the beauteous sem-
      blance,

He from before me moved and made me stop,
  Saying: "Behold Dis, and behold the place
  Where thou with fortitude must arm thyself."

How frozen I became and powerless then,
  Ask it not, Reader, for I write it not,
  Because all language would be insufficient.

Io non mori' e non rimasi vivo:
  pensa oggimai per te, s'hai fior d'ingegno,
  qual io divenni, d'uno e d'altro privo.

Lo 'mperador del doloroso regno
  da mezzo 'l petto uscia fuor de la ghiaccia;
  e piu` con un gigante io mi convegno,

che i giganti non fan con le sue braccia:
  vedi oggimai quant'esser dee quel tutto
  ch'a cosi` fatta parte si confaccia.

S'el fu si` bel com'elli e` ora brutto,
  e contra 'l suo fattore alzo` le ciglia,
  ben dee da lui proceder ogne lutto.

Oh quanto parve a me gran maraviglia
  quand'io vidi tre facce a la sua testa!
  L'una dinanzi, e quella era vermiglia;

l'altr'eran due, che s'aggiugnieno a questa
  sovresso 'l mezzo di ciascuna spalla,
  e se' giugnieno al loco de la cresta:

e la destra parea tra bianca e gialla;
  la sinistra a vedere era tal, quali
  vegnon di la` onde 'l Nilo s'avvalla.

Sotto ciascuna uscivan due grand'ali,
  quanto si convenia a tanto uccello:
  vele di mar non vid'io mai cotali.

Non avean penne, ma di vispistrello
  era lor modo; e quelle svolazzava,
  si` che tre venti si movean da ello:

quindi Cocito tutto s'aggelava.
  Con sei occhi piangea, e per tre menti
  gocciava 'l pianto e sanguinosa bava.

Da ogne bocca dirompea co' denti
  un peccatore, a guisa di maciulla,
  si` che tre ne facea cosi` dolenti.

A quel dinanzi il mordere era nulla
  verso 'l graffiar, che talvolta la schiena
  rimanea de la pelle tutta brulla.

I did not die, and I alive remained not;
  Think for thyself now, hast thou aught of wit,
  What I became, being of both deprived.

The Emperor of the kingdom dolorous
  From his mid-breast forth issued from the ice;
  And better with a giant I compare

Than do the giants with those arms of his;
  Consider now how great must be that whole,
  Which unto such a part conforms itself.

Were he as fair once, as he now is foul,
  And lifted up his brow against his Maker,
  Well may proceed from him all tribulation.

O, what a marvel it appeared to me,
  When I beheld three faces on his head!
  The one in front, and that vermilion was;

Two were the others, that were joined with this
  Above the middle part of either shoulder,
  And they were joined together at the crest;

And the right-hand one seemed 'twixt white and yel-
      low;
  The left was such to look upon as those
  Who come from where the Nile falls valley-ward.

Underneath each came forth two mighty wings,
  Such as befitting were so great a bird;
  Sails of the sea I never saw so large.

No feathers had they, but as of a bat
  Their fashion was; and he was waving them,
  So that three winds proceeded forth therefrom.

Thereby Cocytus wholly was congealed.
  With six eyes did he weep, and down three chins
  Trickled the tear-drops and the bloody drivel.

At every mouth he with his teeth was crunching
  A sinner, in the manner of a brake,
  So that he three of them tormented thus.

To him in front the biting was as naught
  Unto the clawing, for sometimes the spine
  Utterly stripped of all the skin remained.

““Quell'anima la` su` c'ha maggior pena””“,
  disse 'l maestro, ““e` Giuda Scariotto,
  che 'l capo ha dentro e fuor le gambe mena.

De li altri due c'hanno il capo di sotto,
  quel che pende dal nero ceffo e` Bruto:
  vedi come si storce, e non fa motto!;

e l'altro e` Cassio che par si` membruto.
  Ma la notte risurge, e oramai
  e` da partir, che' tutto avem veduto””“.

Com'a lui piacque, il collo li avvinghiai;
  ed el prese di tempo e loco poste,
  e quando l'ali fuoro aperte assai,

appiglio` se' a le vellute coste;
  di vello in vello giu` discese poscia
  tra 'l folto pelo e le gelate croste.

Quando noi fummo la` dove la coscia
  si volge, a punto in sul grosso de l'anche,
  lo duca, con fatica e con angoscia,

volse la testa ov'elli avea le zanche,
  e aggrappossi al pel com'om che sale,
  si` che 'n inferno i' credea tornar anche.

““Attienti ben, che' per cotali scale””“,
  disse 'l maestro, ansando com'uom lasso,
  ”“conviensi dipartir da tanto male””“.

Poi usci` fuor per lo foro d'un sasso,
  e puose me in su l'orlo a sedere;
  appresso porse a me l'accorto passo.

Io levai li occhi e credetti vedere
  Lucifero com'io l'avea lasciato,
  e vidili le gambe in su` tenere;

e s'io divenni allora travagliato,
  la gente grossa il pensi, che non vede
  qual e` quel punto ch'io avea passato.

““Levati su`”“, disse 'l maestro, ““in piede:
  la via e` lunga e 'l cammino e` malvagio,
  e gia` il sole a mezza terza riede””“.

"That soul up there which has the greatest pain,"
  The Master said, "is Judas Iscariot;
  With head inside, he plies his legs without.

Of the two others, who head downward are,
  The one who hangs from the black jowl is Brutus;
  See how he writhes himself, and speaks no word.

And the other, who so stalwart seems, is Cassius.
  But night is reascending, and 'tis time
  That we depart, for we have seen the whole."

As seemed him good, I clasped him round the neck,
  And he the vantage seized of time and place,
  And when the wings were opened wide apart,

He laid fast hold upon the shaggy sides;
  From fell to fell descended downward then
  Between the thick hair and the frozen crust.

When we were come to where the thigh revolves
  Exactly on the thickness of the haunch,
  The Guide, with labour and with hard-drawn breath,

Turned round his head where he had had his legs,
  And grappled to the hair, as one who mounts,
  So that to Hell I thought we were returning.

"Keep fast thy hold, for by such stairs as these,"
  The Master said, panting as one fatigued,
  "Must we perforce depart from so much evil."

Then through the opening of a rock he issued,
  And down upon the margin seated me;
  Then tow'rds me he outstretched his wary step.

I lifted up mine eyes and thought to see
  Lucifer in the same way I had left him;
  And I beheld him upward hold his legs.

And if I then became disquieted,
  Let stolid people think who do not see
  What the point is beyond which I had passed.

"Rise up," the Master said, "upon thy feet;
  The way is long, and difficult the road,
  And now the sun to middle-tierce returns."

Non era camminata di palagio
  la` 'v'eravam, ma natural burella
  ch'avea mal suolo e di lume disagio.

““Prima ch'io de l'abisso mi divella,
  maestro mio”“, diss'io quando fui dritto,
  ”“a trarmi d'erro un poco mi favella:

ov'e` la ghiaccia? e questi com'e` fitto
  si` sottosopra? e come, in si` poc'ora,
  da sera a mane ha fatto il sol tragitto?”“.

Ed elli a me: ““Tu imagini ancora
  d'esser di la` dal centro, ov'io mi presi
  al pel del vermo reo che 'l mondo fora.

Di la` fosti cotanto quant'io scesi;
  quand'io mi volsi, tu passasti 'l punto
  al qual si traggon d'ogne parte i pesi.

E se' or sotto l'emisperio giunto
  ch'e` contraposto a quel che la gran secca
  coverchia, e sotto 'l cui colmo consunto

fu l'uom che nacque e visse sanza pecca:
  tu hai i piedi in su picciola spera
  che l'altra faccia fa de la Giudecca.

Qui e` da man, quando di la` e` sera;
  e questi, che ne fe' scala col pelo,
  fitto e` ancora si` come prim'era.

Da questa parte cadde giu` dal cielo;
  e la terra, che pria di qua si sporse,
  per paura di lui fe' del mar velo,

e venne a l'emisperio nostro; e forse
  per fuggir lui lascio` qui loco voto
  quella ch'appar di qua, e su` ricorse”“.

Luogo e` la` giu` da Belzebu` remoto
  tanto quanto la tomba si distende,
  che non per vista, ma per suono e` noto

d'un ruscelletto che quivi discende
  per la buca d'un sasso, ch'elli ha roso,
  col corso ch'elli avvolge, e poco pende.

It was not any palace corridor
  There where we were, but dungeon natural,
  With floor uneven and unease of light.

"Ere from the abyss I tear myself away,
  My Master," said I when I had arisen,
  "To draw me from an error speak a little;

Where is the ice? and how is this one fixed
  Thus upside down? and how in such short time
  From eve to morn has the sun made his transit?"

And he to me: "Thou still imaginest
  Thou art beyond the centre, where I grasped
  The hair of the fell worm, who mines the world.

That side thou wast, so long as I descended;
  When round I turned me, thou didst pass the point
  To which things heavy draw from every side,

And now beneath the hemisphere art come
  Opposite that which overhangs the vast
  Dry-land, and 'neath whose cope was put to death

The Man who without sin was born and lived.
  Thou hast thy feet upon the little sphere
  Which makes the other face of the Judecca.

Here it is morn when it is evening there;
  And he who with his hair a stairway made us
  Still fixed remaineth as he was before.

Upon this side he fell down out of heaven;
  And all the land, that whilom here emerged,
  For fear of him made of the sea a veil,

And came to our hemisphere; and peradventure
  To flee from him, what on this side appears
  Left the place vacant here, and back recoiled."

A place there is below, from Beelzebub
  As far receding as the tomb extends,
  Which not by sight is known, but by the sound

Of a small rivulet, that there descendeth
  Through chasm within the stone, which it has
      gnawed
  With course that winds about and slightly falls.

Lo duca e io per quel cammino ascoso
  intrammo a ritornar nel chiaro mondo;
  e sanza cura aver d'alcun riposo,

salimmo su`, el primo e io secondo,
  tanto ch'i' vidi de le cose belle
  che porta 'l ciel, per un pertugio tondo.

E quindi uscimmo a riveder le stelle.

The Guide and I into that hidden road
  Now entered, to return to the bright world;
  And without care of having any rest

We mounted up, he first and I the second,
  Till I beheld through a round aperture
  Some of the beauteous things that Heaven doth
        bear;

Thence we came forth to rebehold the stars.

PURGATORIO

Purgatorio: Canto I

The Shores of Purgatory. The Four Stars. Cato of Utica. The Rush

Per correr miglior acque alza le vele
  omai la navicella del mio ingegno,
  che lascia dietro a se' mar si` crudele;

e cantero` di quel secondo regno
  dove l'umano spirito si purga
  e di salire al ciel diventa degno.

Ma qui la morta poesi` resurga,
  o sante Muse, poi che vostro sono;
  e qui Caliope` alquanto surga,

seguitando il mio canto con quel suono
  di cui le Piche misere sentiro
  lo colpo tal, che disperar perdono.

Dolce color d'oriental zaffiro,
  che s'accoglieva nel sereno aspetto
  del mezzo, puro infino al primo giro,

a li occhi miei ricomincio` diletto,
  tosto ch'io usci' fuor de l'aura morta
  che m'avea contristati li occhi e 'l petto.

Lo bel pianeto che d'amar conforta
  faceva tutto rider l'oriente,
  velando i Pesci ch'erano in sua scorta.

I' mi volsi a man destra, e puosi mente
  a l'altro polo, e vidi quattro stelle
  non viste mai fuor ch'a la prima gente.

Goder pareva 'l ciel di lor fiammelle:
  oh settentrional vedovo sito,
  poi che privato se' di mirar quelle!

To run o'er better waters hoists its sail
  The little vessel of my genius now,
  That leaves behind itself a sea so cruel;

And of that second kingdom will I sing
  Wherein the human spirit doth purge itself,
  And to ascend to heaven becometh worthy.

But let dead Poesy here rise again,
  O holy Muses, since that I am yours,
  And here Calliope somewhat ascend,

My song accompanying with that sound,
  Of which the miserable magpies felt
  The blow so great, that they despaired of pardon.

Sweet colour of the oriental sapphire,
  That was upgathered in the cloudless aspect
  Of the pure air, as far as the first circle,

Unto mine eyes did recommence delight
  Soon as I issued forth from the dead air,
  Which had with sadness filled mine eyes and
    breast.

The beauteous planet, that to love incites,
  Was making all the orient to laugh,
  Veiling the Fishes that were in her escort.

To the right hand I turned, and fixed my mind
  Upon the other pole, and saw four stars
  Ne'er seen before save by the primal people.

Rejoicing in their flamelets seemed the heaven.
  O thou septentrional and widowed site,
  Because thou art deprived of seeing these!

Com'io da loro sguardo fui partito,
  un poco me volgendo a l 'altro polo,
  la` onde il Carro gia` era sparito,

vidi presso di me un veglio solo,
  degno di tanta reverenza in vista,
  che piu` non dee a padre alcun figliuolo.

Lunga la barba e di pel bianco mista
  portava, a' suoi capelli simigliante,
  de' quai cadeva al petto doppia lista.

Li raggi de le quattro luci sante
  fregiavan si` la sua faccia di lume,
  ch'i' 'l vedea come 'l sol fosse davante.

““Chi siete voi che contro al cieco fiume
  fuggita avete la pregione etterna?”“,
  diss'el, movendo quelle oneste piume.

““Chi v'ha guidati, o che vi fu lucerna,
  uscendo fuor de la profonda notte
  che sempre nera fa la valle inferna?

Son le leggi d'abisso cosi` rotte?
  o e` mutato in ciel novo consiglio,
  che, dannati, venite a le mie grotte?”“.

Lo duca mio allor mi die` di piglio,
  e con parole e con mani e con cenni
  reverenti mi fe' le gambe e 'l ciglio.

Poscia rispuose lui: ““Da me non venni:
  donna scese del ciel, per li cui prieghi
  de la mia compagnia costui sovvenni.

Ma da ch'e` tuo voler che piu` si spieghi
  di nostra condizion com'ell'e` vera,
  esser non puote il mio che a te si nieghi.

Questi non vide mai l'ultima sera;
  ma per la sua follia le fu si` presso,
  che molto poco tempo a volger era.

Si` com'io dissi, fui mandato ad esso
  per lui campare; e non li` era altra via
  che questa per la quale i' mi son messo.

Mostrata ho lui tutta la gente ria;
  e ora intendo mostrar quelli spirti
  che purgan se' sotto la tua balia.

When from regarding them I had withdrawn,
  Turning a little to the other pole,
  There where the Wain had disappeared already,

I saw beside me an old man alone,
  Worthy of so much reverence in his look,
  That more owes not to father any son.

A long beard and with white hair intermingled
  He wore, in semblance like unto the tresses,
  Of which a double list fell on his breast.

The rays of the four consecrated stars
  Did so adorn his countenance with light,
  That him I saw as were the sun before him.

"Who are you? ye who, counter the blind river,
  Have fled away from the eternal prison?"
  Moving those venerable plumes, he said:

"Who guided you? or who has been your lamp
  In issuing forth out of the night profound,
  That ever black makes the infernal valley?

The laws of the abyss, are they thus broken?
  Or is there changed in heaven some council new,
  That being damned ye come unto my crags?"

Then did my Leader lay his grasp upon me,
  And with his words, and with his hands and signs,
  Reverent he made in me my knees and brow;

Then answered him: "I came not of myself;
  A Lady from Heaven descended, at whose prayers
  I aided this one with my company.

But since it is thy will more be unfolded
  Of our condition, how it truly is,
  Mine cannot be that this should be denied thee.

This one has never his last evening seen,
  But by his folly was so near to it
  That very little time was there to turn.

As I have said, I unto him was sent
  To rescue him, and other way was none
  Than this to which I have myself betaken.

I've shown him all the people of perdition,
  And now those spirits I intend to show
  Who purge themselves beneath thy guardianship.

Com'io l'ho tratto, saria lungo a dirti;
  de l'alto scende virtu` che m'aiuta
  conducerlo a vederti e a udirti.

Or ti piaccia gradir la sua venuta:
  liberta` va cercando, ch'e` si` cara,
  come sa chi per lei vita rifiuta.

Tu 'l sai, che' non ti fu per lei amara
  in Utica la morte, ove lasciasti
  la vesta ch'al gran di` sara` si` chiara.

Non son li editti etterni per noi guasti,
  che' questi vive, e Minos me non lega;
  ma son del cerchio ove son li occhi casti

di Marzia tua, che 'n vista ancor ti priega,
  o santo petto, che per tua la tegni:
  per lo suo amore adunque a noi ti piega.

Lasciane andar per li tuoi sette regni;
  grazie riportero` di te a lei,
  se d'esser mentovato la` giu` degni'''".

""Marzia piacque tanto a li occhi miei
  mentre ch'i' fu' di la`''", diss'elli allora,
  ""che quante grazie volse da me, fei.

Or che di la` dal mal fiume dimora,
  piu` muover non mi puo`, per quella legge
  che fatta fu quando me n'usci' fora.

Ma se donna del ciel ti muove e regge,
  come tu di', non c'e` mestier lusinghe:
  bastisi ben che per lei mi richegge.

Va dunque, e fa che tu costui ricinghe
  d'un giunco schietto e che li lavi 'l viso,
  si` ch'ogne sucidume quindi stinghe;

che' non si converria, l'occhio sorpriso
  d'alcuna nebbia, andar dinanzi al primo
  ministro, ch'e` di quei di paradiso.

Questa isoletta intorno ad imo ad imo,
  la` giu` cola` dove la batte l'onda,
  porta di giunchi sovra 'l molle limo;

null'altra pianta che facesse fronda
  o indurasse, vi puote aver vita,
  pero` ch'a le percosse non seconda.

How I have brought him would be long to tell thee.
  Virtue descendeth from on high that aids me
  To lead him to behold thee and to hear thee.

Now may it please thee to vouchsafe his coming;
  He seeketh Liberty, which is so dear,
  As knoweth he who life for her refuses.

Thou know'st it; since, for her, to thee not bitter
  Was death in Utica, where thou didst leave
  The vesture, that will shine so, the great day.

By us the eternal edicts are not broken;
  Since this one lives, and Minos binds not me;
  But of that circle I, where are the chaste

Eyes of thy Marcia, who in looks still prays thee,
  O holy breast, to hold her as thine own;
  For her love, then, incline thyself to us.

Permit us through thy sevenfold realm to go;
  I will take back this grace from thee to her,
  If to be mentioned there below thou deignest."

"Marcia so pleasing was unto mine eyes
  While I was on the other side," then said he,
  "That every grace she wished of me I granted;

Now that she dwells beyond the evil river,
  She can no longer move me, by that law
  Which, when I issued forth from there, was made.

But if a Lady of Heaven do move and rule thee,
  As thou dost say, no flattery is needful;
  Let it suffice thee that for her thou ask me.

Go, then, and see thou gird this one about
  With a smooth rush, and that thou wash his face,
  So that thou cleanse away all stain therefrom,

For 'twere not fitting that the eye o'ercast
  By any mist should go before the first
  Angel, who is of those of Paradise.

This little island round about its base
  Below there, yonder, where the billow beats it,
  Doth rushes bear upon its washy ooze;

No other plant that putteth forth the leaf,
  Or that doth indurate, can there have life,
  Because it yieldeth not unto the shocks.

Poscia non sia di qua vostra reddita;
  lo sol vi mosterra`, che surge omai,
  prendere il monte a piu` lieve salita"".

Cosi` spari`; e io su` mi levai
  sanza parlare, e tutto mi ritrassi
  al duca mio, e li occhi a lui drizzai.

El comincio`: ""Figliuol, segui i miei passi:
  volgianci in dietro, che' di qua dichina
  questa pianura a' suoi termini bassi"".

L'alba vinceva l'ora mattutina
  che fuggia innanzi, si` che di lontano
  conobbi il tremolar de la marina.

Noi andavam per lo solingo piano
  com'om che torna a la perduta strada,
  che 'nfino ad essa li pare ire in vano.

Quando noi fummo la` 've la rugiada
  pugna col sole, per essere in parte
  dove, ad orezza, poco si dirada,

ambo le mani in su l'erbetta sparte
  soavemente 'l mio maestro pose:
  ond'io, che fui accorto di sua arte,

porsi ver' lui le guance lagrimose:
  ivi mi fece tutto discoverto
  quel color che l'inferno mi nascose.

Venimmo poi in sul lito diserto,
  che mai non vide navicar sue acque
  omo, che di tornar sia poscia esperto.

Quivi mi cinse si` com'altrui piacque:
  oh maraviglia! che' qual elli scelse
  l'umile pianta, cotal si rinacque

subitamente la` onde l'avelse.

Thereafter be not this way your return;
  The sun, which now is rising, will direct you
  To take the mount by easier ascent."

With this he vanished; and I raised me up
  Without a word, and wholly drew myself
  Unto my Guide, and turned mine eyes to him.

And he began: "Son, follow thou my steps;
  Let us turn back, for on this side declines
  The plain unto its lower boundaries."

The dawn was vanquishing the matin hour
  Which fled before it, so that from afar
  I recognised the trembling of the sea.

Along the solitary plain we went
  As one who unto the lost road returns,
  And till he finds it seems to go in vain.

As soon as we were come to where the dew
  Fights with the sun, and, being in a part
  Where shadow falls, little evaporates,

Both of his hands upon the grass outspread
  In gentle manner did my Master place;
  Whence I, who of his action was aware,

Extended unto him my tearful cheeks;
  There did he make in me uncovered wholly
  That hue which Hell had covered up in me.

Then came we down upon the desert shore
  Which never yet saw navigate its waters
  Any that afterward had known return.

There he begirt me as the other pleased;
  O marvellous! for even as he culled
  The humble plant, such it sprang up again

Suddenly there where he uprooted it.

Purgatorio: Canto II

The Celestial Pilot. Casella. The Departure.

Gia` era 'l sole a l'orizzonte giunto   lo cui meridian cerchio coverchia   Ierusalem col suo piu` alto punto;	Already had the sun the horizon reached Whose circle of meridian covers o'er Jerusalem with its most lofty point,

e la notte, che opposita a lui cerchia,
  uscia di Gange fuor con le Bilance,
  che le caggion di man quando soverchia;
	And night that opposite to him revolves
	  Was issuing forth from Ganges with the Scales
	  That fall from out her hand when she exceedeth;

si` che le bianche e le vermiglie guance,   la` dov'i' era, de la bella Aurora per troppa etate divenivan rance.	So that the white and the vermilion cheeks Of beautiful Aurora, where I was, By too great age were changing into orange.

Noi eravam lunghesso mare ancora,
  come gente che pensa a suo cammino,
  che va col cuore e col corpo dimora.
	We still were on the border of the sea,
	  Like people who are thinking of their road,
	  Who go in heart and with the body stay;

Ed ecco, qual, sorpreso dal mattino,
  per li grossi vapor Marte rosseggia
  giu` nel ponente sovra 'l suol marino,
	And lo! as when, upon the approach of morning,
	  Through the gross vapours Mars grows fiery red
	  Down in the West upon the ocean floor,

cotal m'apparve, s'io ancor lo veggia,
  un lume per lo mar venir si` ratto,
  che 'l muover suo nessun volar pareggia.
	Appeared to me—may I again behold it!—
	  A light along the sea so swiftly coming,
	  Its motion by no flight of wing is equalled;

Dal qual com'io un poco ebbi ritratto
  l'occhio per domandar lo duca mio,
  rividil piu` lucente e maggior fatto.
	From which when I a little had withdrawn
	  Mine eyes, that I might question my Conductor,
	  Again I saw it brighter grown and larger.

Poi d'ogne lato ad esso m'appario
  un non sapeva che bianco, e di sotto
  a poco a poco un altro a lui uscio.
	Then on each side of it appeared to me
	  I knew not what of white, and underneath it
	  Little by little there came forth another.

Lo mio maestro ancor non facea motto,
  mentre che i primi bianchi apparver ali;
  allor che ben conobbe il galeotto,
	My Master yet had uttered not a word
	  While the first whiteness into wings unfolded;
	  But when he clearly recognised the pilot,

grido`: ““Fa, fa che le ginocchia cali.	He cried: "Make haste, make haste to bow the knee!
Ecco l'angel di Dio: piega le mani;	Behold the Angel of God! fold thou thy hands!
omai vedrai di si` fatti officiali.	Henceforward shalt thou see such officers!
Vedi che sdegna li argomenti umani,	See how he scorneth human arguments,
si` che remo non vuol, ne' altro velo	So that nor oar he wants, nor other sail
che l'ali sue, tra liti si` lontani.	Than his own wings, between so distant shores.
Vedi come l'ha dritte verso 'l cielo,	See how he holds them pointed up to heaven,
trattando l'aere con l'etterne penne,	Fanning the air with the eternal pinions,
che non si mutan come mortal pelo”“.	That do not moult themselves like mortal hair!"
Poi, come piu` e piu` verso noi venne	Then as still nearer and more near us came
l'uccel divino, piu` chiaro appariva:	The Bird Divine, more radiant he appeared,
per che l'occhio da presso nol sostenne,	So that near by the eye could not endure him,
ma chinail giuso; e quei sen venne a riva	But down I cast it; and he came to shore
con un vasello snelletto e leggero,	With a small vessel, very swift and light,
tanto che l'acqua nulla ne 'nghiottiva.	So that the water swallowed naught thereof.
Da poppa stava il celestial nocchiero,	Upon the stern stood the Celestial Pilot;
tal che faria beato pur descripto;	Beatitude seemed written in his face,
e piu` di cento spirti entro sediero.	And more than a hundred spirits sat within.
'In exitu Israel de Aegypto'	"In exitu Israel de Aegypto!"
cantavan tutti insieme ad una voce	They chanted all together in one voice,
con quanto di quel salmo e` poscia scripto.	With whatso in that psalm is after written.
Poi fece il segno lor di santa croce;	Then made he sign of holy rood upon them,
ond'ei si gittar tutti in su la piaggia;	Whereat all cast themselves upon the shore,
ed el sen gi`, come venne, veloce.	And he departed swiftly as he came.
La turba che rimase li`, selvaggia	The throng which still remained there unfamiliar
parea del loco, rimirando intorno	Seemed with the place, all round about them gaz-
come colui che nove cose assaggia.	ing,
	As one who in new matters makes essay.
Da tutte parti saettava il giorno	On every side was darting forth the day.
lo sol, ch'avea con le saette conte	The sun, who had with his resplendent shafts
di mezzo 'l ciel cacciato Capricorno,	From the mid-heaven chased forth the Capricorn,
quando la nova gente alzo` la fronte	When the new people lifted up their faces
ver' noi, dicendo a noi: ““Se voi sapete,	Towards us, saying to us: "If ye know,
mostratene la via di gire al monte”“.	Show us the way to go unto the mountain."
E Virgilio rispuose: ““Voi credete	And answer made Virgilius: "Ye believe
forse che siamo esperti d'esto loco;	Perchance that we have knowledge of this place,
ma noi siam peregrin come voi siete.	But we are strangers even as yourselves.

Dianzi venimmo, innanzi a voi un poco,
  per altra via, che fu si` aspra e forte,
  che lo salire omai ne parra` gioco"".

L'anime, che si fuor di me accorte,
  per lo spirare, ch'i' era ancor vivo,
  maravigliando diventaro smorte.

E come a messagger che porta ulivo
  tragge la gente per udir novelle,
  e di calcar nessun si mostra schivo,

cosi` al viso mio s'affisar quelle
  anime fortunate tutte quante,
  quasi obliando d'ire a farsi belle.

Io vidi una di lor trarresi avante
  per abbracciarmi con si` grande affetto,
  che mosse me a far lo somigliante.

Ohi ombre vane, fuor che ne l'aspetto!
  tre volte dietro a lei le mani avvinsi,
  e tante mi tornai con esse al petto.

Di maraviglia, credo, mi dipinsi;
  per che l'ombra sorrise e si ritrasse,
  e io, seguendo lei, oltre mi pinsi.

Soavemente disse ch'io posasse;
  allor conobbi chi era, e pregai
  che, per parlarmi, un poco s'arrestasse.

Rispuosemi: ""Cosi` com'io t'amai
  nel mortal corpo, cosi` t'amo sciolta:
  pero` m'arresto; ma tu perche' vai?"".

""Casella mio, per tornar altra volta
  la` dov'io son, fo io questo viaggio"",
  diss'io; ""ma a te com'e` tanta ora tolta?"".

Ed elli a me: ""Nessun m'e` fatto oltraggio,
  se quei che leva quando e cui li piace,
  piu` volte m'ha negato esto passaggio;

che' di giusto voler lo suo si face:
  veramente da tre mesi elli ha tolto
  chi ha voluto intrar, con tutta pace.

Ond'io, ch'era ora a la marina volto
  dove l'acqua di Tevero s'insala,
  benignamente fu' da lui ricolto.

Just now we came, a little while before you,
  Another way, which was so rough and steep,
  That mounting will henceforth seem sport to us."

The souls who had, from seeing me draw breath,
  Become aware that I was still alive,
  Pallid in their astonishment became;

And as to messenger who bears the olive
  The people throng to listen to the news,
  And no one shows himself afraid of crowding,

So at the sight of me stood motionless
  Those fortunate spirits, all of them, as if
  Oblivious to go and make them fair.

One from among them saw I coming forward,
  As to embrace me, with such great affection,
  That it incited me to do the like.

O empty shadows, save in aspect only!
  Three times behind it did I clasp my hands,
  As oft returned with them to my own breast!

I think with wonder I depicted me;
  Whereat the shadow smiled and backward drew;
  And I, pursuing it, pressed farther forward.

Gently it said that I should stay my steps;
  Then knew I who it was, and I entreated
  That it would stop awhile to speak with me.

It made reply to me: "Even as I loved thee
  In mortal body, so I love thee free;
  Therefore I stop; but wherefore goest thou?"

"My own Casella! to return once more
  There where I am, I make this journey," said I;
  "But how from thee has so much time be taken?"

And he to me: "No outrage has been done me,
  If he who takes both when and whom he pleases
  Has many times denied to me this passage,

For of a righteous will his own is made.
  He, sooth to say, for three months past has taken
  Whoever wished to enter with all peace;

Whence I, who now had turned unto that shore
  Where salt the waters of the Tiber grow,
  Benignantly by him have been received.

163

A quella foce ha elli or dritta l'ala,
 pero` che sempre quivi si ricoglie
 qual verso Acheronte non si cala"".

E io: ""Se nuova legge non ti toglie
 memoria o uso a l'amoroso canto
 che mi solea quetar tutte mie doglie,

di cio` ti piaccia consolare alquanto
 l'anima mia, che, con la sua persona
 venendo qui, e` affannata tanto!"".

'Amor che ne la mente mi ragiona'
 comincio` elli allor si` dolcemente,
 che la dolcezza ancor dentro mi suona.

Lo mio maestro e io e quella gente
 ch'eran con lui parevan si` contenti,
 come a nessun toccasse altro la mente.

Noi eravam tutti fissi e attenti
 a le sue note; ed ecco il veglio onesto
 gridando: ""Che e` cio`, spiriti lenti?

qual negligenza, quale stare e` questo?
 Correte al monte a spogliarvi lo scoglio
 ch'esser non lascia a voi Dio manifesto"".

Come quando, cogliendo biado o loglio,
 li colombi adunati a la pastura,
 queti, sanza mostrar l'usato orgoglio,

se cosa appare ond'elli abbian paura,
 subitamente lasciano star l'esca,
 perch'assaliti son da maggior cura;

cosi` vid'io quella masnada fresca
 lasciar lo canto, e fuggir ver' la costa,
 com'om che va, ne' sa dove riesca:

ne' la nostra partita fu men tosta.

Unto that outlet now his wing is pointed,
 Because for evermore assemble there
 Those who tow'rds Acheron do not descend."

And I: "If some new law take not from thee
 Memory or practice of the song of love,
 Which used to quiet in me all my longings,

Thee may it please to comfort therewithal
 Somewhat this soul of mine, that with its body
 Hitherward coming is so much distressed."

"Love, that within my mind discourses with me,"
 Forthwith began he so melodiously,
 The melody within me still is sounding.

My Master, and myself, and all that people
 Which with him were, appeared as satisfied
 As if naught else might touch the mind of any.

We all of us were moveless and attentive
 Unto his notes; and lo! the grave old man,
 Exclaiming: "What is this, ye laggard spirits?

What negligence, what standing still is this?
 Run to the mountain to strip off the slough,
 That lets not God be manifest to you."

Even as when, collecting grain or tares,
 The doves, together at their pasture met,
 Quiet, nor showing their accustomed pride,

If aught appear of which they are afraid,
 Upon a sudden leave their food alone,
 Because they are assailed by greater care;

So that fresh company did I behold
 The song relinquish, and go tow'rds the hill,
 As one who goes, and knows not whitherward;

Nor was our own departure less in haste.

Purgatorio: Canto III

Discourse on the Limits of Reason. The Foot of the Mountain. Those who died in Contumacy of Holy Church. Manfredi.

Avvegna che la subitana fuga
  dispergesse color per la campagna,
  rivolti al monte ove ragion ne fruga,

i' mi ristrinsi a la fida compagna:
  e come sare' io sanza lui corso?
  chi m'avria tratto su per la montagna?

El mi parea da se' stesso rimorso:
  o dignitosa coscienza e netta,
  come t'e` picciol fallo amaro morso!

Quando li piedi suoi lasciar la fretta,
  che l'onestade ad ogn'atto dismaga,
  la mente mia, che prima era ristretta,

lo 'ntento rallargo`, si` come vaga,
  e diedi 'l viso mio incontr'al poggio
  che 'nverso 'l ciel piu` alto si dislaga.

Lo sol, che dietro fiammeggiava roggio,
  rotto m'era dinanzi a la figura,
  ch'avea in me de' suoi raggi l'appoggio.

Io mi volsi dallato con paura
  d'essere abbandonato, quand'io vidi
  solo dinanzi a me la terra oscura;

e 'l mio conforto: ""Perche' pur diffidi?"",
  a dir mi comincio` tutto rivolto;
  ""non credi tu me teco e ch'io ti guidi?

Vespero e` gia` cola` dov'e` sepolto
  lo corpo dentro al quale io facea ombra:
  Napoli l'ha, e da Brandizio e` tolto.

Inasmuch as the instantaneous flight
  Had scattered them asunder o'er the plain,
  Turned to the mountain whither reason spurs us,

I pressed me close unto my faithful comrade,
  And how without him had I kept my course?
  Who would have led me up along the mountain?

He seemed to me within himself remorseful;
  O noble conscience, and without a stain,
  How sharp a sting is trivial fault to thee!

After his feet had laid aside the haste
  Which mars the dignity of every act,
  My mind, that hitherto had been restrained,

Let loose its faculties as if delighted,
  And I my sight directed to the hill
  That highest tow'rds the heaven uplifts itself.

The sun, that in our rear was flaming red,
  Was broken in front of me into the figure
  Which had in me the stoppage of its rays;

Unto one side I turned me, with the fear
  Of being left alone, when I beheld
  Only in front of me the ground obscured.

"Why dost thou still mistrust?" my Comforter
  Began to say to me turned wholly round;
  "Dost thou not think me with thee, and that I guide
    thee?

'Tis evening there already where is buried
  The body within which I cast a shadow;
  'Tis from Brundusium ta'en, and Naples has it.

Ora, se innanzi a me nulla s'aombra,
  non ti maravigliar piu` che d'i cieli
  che l'uno a l'altro raggio non ingombra.
	Now if in front of me no shadow fall,
	  Marvel not at it more than at the heavens,
	  Because one ray impedeth not another

A sofferir tormenti, caldi e geli
  simili corpi la Virtu` dispone
  che, come fa, non vuol ch'a noi si sveli.
	To suffer torments, both of cold and heat,
	  Bodies like this that Power provides, which wills
	  That how it works be not unveiled to us.

Matto e` chi spera che nostra ragione
  possa trascorrer la infinita via
  che tiene una sustanza in tre persone.
	Insane is he who hopeth that our reason
	  Can traverse the illimitable way,
	  Which the one Substance in three Persons follows!

State contenti, umana gente, al quia;
  che' se potuto aveste veder tutto,
  mestier non era parturir Maria;
	Mortals, remain contented at the 'Quia;'
	  For if ye had been able to see all,
	  No need there were for Mary to give birth;

e disiar vedeste sanza frutto
  tai che sarebbe lor disio quetato,
  ch'etternalmente e` dato lor per lutto:
	And ye have seen desiring without fruit,
	  Those whose desire would have been quieted,
	  Which evermore is given them for a grief.

io dico d'Aristotile e di Plato e di molt'altri""; e qui chino` la fronte,   e piu` non disse, e rimase turbato.	I speak of Aristotle and of Plato, And many others;"—and here bowed his head, And more he said not, and remained disturbed.
Noi divenimmo intanto a pie` del monte;   quivi trovammo la roccia si` erta, che 'ndarno vi sarien le gambe pronte.	We came meanwhile unto the mountain's foot; There so precipitate we found the rock, That nimble legs would there have been in vain.
Tra Lerice e Turbia la piu` diserta,   la piu` rotta ruina e` una scala, verso di quella, agevole e aperta.	'Twixt Lerici and Turbia, the most desert, The most secluded pathway is a stair Easy and open, if compared with that.

""Or chi sa da qual man la costa cala"",
  disse 'l maestro mio fermando 'l passo,
  ""si` che possa salir chi va sanz'ala?"".
	"Who knoweth now upon which hand the hill
	  Slopes down," my Master said, his footsteps stay-
	     ing,
	  "So that who goeth without wings may mount?"

E mentre ch'e' tenendo 'l viso basso
  essaminava del cammin la mente,
  e io mirava suso intorno al sasso,
	And while he held his eyes upon the ground
	  Examining the nature of the path,
	  And I was looking up around the rock,

da man sinistra m'appari` una gente   d'anime, che movieno i pie` ver' noi, e non pareva, si` venian lente.	On the left hand appeared to me a throng Of souls, that moved their feet in our direction, And did not seem to move, they came so slowly.

""Leva"", diss'io, ""maestro, li occhi tuoi:
  ecco di qua chi ne dara` consiglio,
  se tu da te medesmo aver nol puoi"".
	"Lift up thine eyes," I to the Master said;
	  "Behold, on this side, who will give us counsel,
	  If thou of thine own self can have it not."

Guardo` allora, e con libero piglio
  rispuose: ""Andiamo in la`, ch'ei vegnon piano;
  e tu ferma la spene, dolce figlio"".

Ancora era quel popol di lontano,
  i' dico dopo i nostri mille passi,
  quanto un buon gittator trarria con mano,

quando si strinser tutti ai duri massi
  de l'alta ripa, e stetter fermi e stretti
  com'a guardar, chi va dubbiando, stassi.

""O ben finiti, o gia` spiriti eletti"",
  Virgilio incomincio`, ""per quella pace
  ch'i' credo che per voi tutti s'aspetti,

ditene dove la montagna giace
  si` che possibil sia l'andare in suso;
  che' perder tempo a chi piu` sa piu` spiace"".

Come le pecorelle escon del chiuso
  a una, a due, a tre, e l'altre stanno
  timidette atterrando l'occhio e 'l muso;

e cio` che fa la prima, e l'altre fanno,
  addossandosi a lei, s'ella s'arresta,
  semplici e quete, e lo 'mperche' non sanno;

si` vid'io muovere a venir la testa
  di quella mandra fortunata allotta,
  pudica in faccia e ne l'andare onesta.

Come color dinanzi vider rotta
  la luce in terra dal mio destro canto,
  si` che l'ombra era da me a la grotta,

restaro, e trasser se' in dietro alquanto,
  e tutti li altri che venieno appresso,
  non sappiendo 'l perche', fenno altrettanto.

""Sanza vostra domanda io vi confesso
  che questo e` corpo uman che voi vedete;
  per che 'l lume del sole in terra e` fesso.

Non vi maravigliate, ma credete
  che non sanza virtu` che da ciel vegna
  cerchi di soverchiar questa parete"".

Then he looked at me, and with frank expression
  Replied: "Let us go there, for they come slowly,
  And thou be steadfast in thy hope, sweet son."

Still was that people as far off from us,
  After a thousand steps of ours I say,
  As a good thrower with his hand would reach,

When they all crowded unto the hard masses
  Of the high bank, and motionless stood and close,
  As he stands still to look who goes in doubt.

"O happy dead! O spirits elect already!"
  Virgilius made beginning, "by that peace
  Which I believe is waiting for you all,

Tell us upon what side the mountain slopes,
  So that the going up be possible,
  For to lose time irks him most who most knows."

As sheep come issuing forth from out the fold
  By ones and twos and threes, and the others stand
  Timidly, holding down their eyes and nostrils,

And what the foremost does the others do,
  Huddling themselves against her, if she stop,
  Simple and quiet and the wherefore know not;

So moving to approach us thereupon
  I saw the leader of that fortunate flock,
  Modest in face and dignified in gait.

As soon as those in the advance saw broken
  The light upon the ground at my right side,
  So that from me the shadow reached the rock,

They stopped, and backward drew themselves
    somewhat;
  And all the others, who came after them,
  Not knowing why nor wherefore, did the same.

"Without your asking, I confess to you
  This is a human body which you see,
  Whereby the sunshine on the ground is cleft.

Marvel ye not thereat, but be persuaded
  That not without a power which comes from Heav-
    en
  Doth he endeavour to surmount this wall."

Cosi` 'l maestro; e quella gente degna
"Tornate"", disse, ""intrate innanzi dunque"",
coi dossi de le man faccendo insegna.

E un di loro incomincio`: ""Chiunque
tu se', cosi` andando, volgi 'l viso:
pon mente se di la` mi vedesti unque"".

Io mi volsi ver lui e guardail fiso:
biondo era e bello e di gentile aspetto,
ma l'un de' cigli un colpo avea diviso.

Quand'io mi fui umilmente disdetto
d'averlo visto mai, el disse: ""Or vedi"";
e mostrommi una piaga a sommo 'l petto.

Poi sorridendo disse: ""Io son Manfredi,
nepote di Costanza imperadrice;
ond'io ti priego che, quando tu riedi,

vadi a mia bella figlia, genitrice
de l'onor di Cicilia e d'Aragona,
e dichi 'l vero a lei, s'altro si dice.

Poscia ch'io ebbi rotta la persona
di due punte mortali, io mi rendei,
piangendo, a quei che volontier perdona.

Orribil furon li peccati miei;
ma la bonta` infinita ha si` gran braccia,
che prende cio` che si rivolge a lei.

Se 'l pastor di Cosenza, che a la caccia
di me fu messo per Clemente allora,
avesse in Dio ben letta questa faccia,

l'ossa del corpo mio sarieno ancora
in co del ponte presso a Benevento,
sotto la guardia de la grave mora.

Or le bagna la pioggia e move il vento
di fuor dal regno, quasi lungo 'l Verde,
dov'e' le trasmuto` a lume spento.

Per lor maladizion si` non si perde,
che non possa tornar, l'etterno amore,
mentre che la speranza ha fior del verde.

Vero e` che quale in contumacia more
di Santa Chiesa, ancor ch'al fin si penta,
star li convien da questa ripa in fore,

The Master thus; and said those worthy people:
"Return ye then, and enter in before us,"
Making a signal with the back o' the hand

And one of them began: "Whoe'er thou art,
Thus going turn thine eyes, consider well
If e'er thou saw me in the other world."

I turned me tow'rds him, and looked at him closely;
Blond was he, beautiful, and of noble aspect,
But one of his eyebrows had a blow divided.

When with humility I had disclaimed
E'er having seen him, "Now behold!" he said,
And showed me high upon his breast a wound.

Then said he with a smile: "I am Manfredi,
The grandson of the Empress Costanza;
Therefore, when thou returnest, I beseech thee

Go to my daughter beautiful, the mother
Of Sicily's honour and of Aragon's,
And the truth tell her, if aught else be told.

After I had my body lacerated
By these two mortal stabs, I gave myself
Weeping to Him, who willingly doth pardon.

Horrible my iniquities had been;
But Infinite Goodness hath such ample arms,
That it receives whatever turns to it.

Had but Cosenza's pastor, who in chase
Of me was sent by Clement at that time,
In God read understandingly this page,

The bones of my dead body still would be
At the bridge-head, near unto Benevento,
Under the safeguard of the heavy cairn.

Now the rain bathes and moveth them the wind,
Beyond the realm, almost beside the Verde,
Where he transported them with tapers quenched.

By malison of theirs is not so lost
Eternal Love, that it cannot return,
So long as hope has anything of green.

True is it, who in contumacy dies
Of Holy Church, though penitent at last,
Must wait upon the outside this bank

per ognun tempo ch'elli e` stato, trenta,
  in sua presunzion, se tal decreto
  piu` corto per buon prieghi non diventa.

Vedi oggimai se tu mi puoi far lieto,
  revelando a la mia buona Costanza
  come m'hai visto, e anco esto divieto;

che' qui per quei di la` molto s'avanza'"".

Thirty times told the time that he has been
  In his presumption, unless such decree
  Shorter by means of righteous prayers become.

See now if thou hast power to make me happy,
  By making known unto my good Costanza
  How thou hast seen me, and this ban beside,

For those on earth can much advance us here."

Purgatorio: Canto IV

Farther Ascent. Nature of the Mountain. The Negligent, who postponed Repentance till the last Hour. Belacqua.

Quando per dilettanze o ver per doglie,
  che alcuna virtu` nostra comprenda
  l'anima bene ad essa si raccoglie,

par ch'a nulla potenza piu` intenda;
  e questo e` contra quello error che crede
  ch'un'anima sovr'altra in noi s'accenda.

E pero`, quando s'ode cosa o vede
  che tegna forte a se' l'anima volta,
  vassene 'l tempo e l'uom non se n'avvede;

ch'altra potenza e` quella che l'ascolta,
  e altra e` quella c'ha l'anima intera:
  questa e` quasi legata, e quella e` sciolta.

Di cio` ebb'io esperienza vera,
  udendo quello spirto e ammirando;
  che' ben cinquanta gradi salito era

lo sole, e io non m'era accorto, quando
  venimmo ove quell'anime ad una
  gridaro a noi: ""Qui e` vostro dimando"".

Maggiore aperta molte volte impruna
  con una forcatella di sue spine
  l'uom de la villa quando l'uva imbruna,

che non era la calla onde saline
  lo duca mio, e io appresso, soli,
  come da noi la schiera si partine.

Vassi in Sanleo e discendesi in Noli,
  montasi su in Bismantova 'n Cacume
  con esso i pie`; ma qui convien ch'om voli;

Whenever by delight or else by pain,
  That seizes any faculty of ours,
  Wholly to that the soul collects itself,

It seemeth that no other power it heeds;
  And this against that error is which thinks
  One soul above another kindles in us.

And hence, whenever aught is heard or seen
  Which keeps the soul intently bent upon it,
  Time passes on, and we perceive it not,

Because one faculty is that which listens,
  And other that which the soul keeps entire;
  This is as if in bonds, and that is free.

Of this I had experience positive
  In hearing and in gazing at that spirit;
  For fifty full degrees uprisen was

The sun, and I had not perceived it, when
  We came to where those souls with one accord
  Cried out unto us: "Here is what you ask."

A greater opening ofttimes hedges up
  With but a little forkful of his thorns
  The villager, what time the grape imbrowns,

Than was the passage-way through which ascended
  Only my Leader and myself behind him,
  After that company departed from us.

One climbs Sanleo and descends in Noli,
  And mounts the summit of Bismantova,
  With feet alone; but here one needs must fly;

dico con l'ale snelle e con le piume
  del gran disio, di retro a quel condotto
  che speranza mi dava e facea lume.

Noi salavam per entro 'l sasso rotto,
  e d'ogne lato ne stringea lo stremo,
  e piedi e man volea il suol di sotto.

Poi che noi fummo in su l'orlo suppremo
  de l'alta ripa, a la scoperta piaggia,
  ""Maestro mio"", diss'io, ""che via faremo?"".

Ed elli a me: ""Nessun tuo passo caggia;
  pur su al monte dietro a me acquista,
  fin che n'appaia alcuna scorta saggia"".

Lo sommo er'alto che vincea la vista,
  e la costa superba piu` assai
  che da mezzo quadrante a centro lista.

Io era lasso, quando cominciai:
  ""O dolce padre, volgiti, e rimira
  com'io rimango sol, se non restai"".

""Figliuol mio"", disse, ""infin quivi ti tira"",
  additandomi un balzo poco in sue
  che da quel lato il poggio tutto gira.

Si` mi spronaron le parole sue,
  ch'i' mi sforzai carpando appresso lui,
  tanto che 'l cinghio sotto i pie` mi fue.

A seder ci ponemmo ivi ambedui
  volti a levante ond'eravam saliti,
  che suole a riguardar giovare altrui.

Li occhi prima drizzai ai bassi liti;
  poscia li alzai al sole, e ammirava
  che da sinistra n'eravam feriti.

Ben s'avvide il poeta ch'io stava
  stupido tutto al carro de la luce,
  ove tra noi e Aquilone intrava.

Ond'elli a me: ""Se Castore e Poluce
  fossero in compagnia di quello specchio
  che su` e giu` del suo lume conduce,

tu vedresti il Zodiaco rubecchio
  ancora a l'Orse piu` stretto rotare,
  se non uscisse fuor del cammin vecchio.

With the swift pinions and the plumes I say
  Of great desire, conducted after him
  Who gave me hope, and made a light for me.

We mounted upward through the rifted rock,
  And on each side the border pressed upon us,
  And feet and hands the ground beneath required.

When we were come upon the upper rim
  Of the high bank, out on the open slope,
  "My Master," said I, "what way shall we take?"

And he to me: "No step of thine descend;
  Still up the mount behind me win thy way,
  Till some sage escort shall appear to us."

The summit was so high it vanquished sight,
  And the hillside precipitous far more
  Than line from middle quadrant to the centre.

Spent with fatigue was I, when I began:
  "O my sweet Father! turn thee and behold
  How I remain alone, unless thou stay!"

"O son," he said, "up yonder drag thyself,"
  Pointing me to a terrace somewhat higher,
  Which on that side encircles all the hill.

These words of his so spurred me on, that I
  Strained every nerve, behind him scrambling up,
  Until the circle was beneath my feet.

Thereon ourselves we seated both of us
  Turned to the East, from which we had ascended,
  For all men are delighted to look back.

To the low shores mine eyes I first directed,
  Then to the sun uplifted them, and wondered
  That on the left hand we were smitten by it.

The Poet well perceived that I was wholly
  Bewildered at the chariot of the light,
  Where 'twixt us and the Aquilon it entered.

Whereon he said to me: "If Castor and Pollux
  Were in the company of yonder mirror,
  That up and down conducteth with its light,

Thou wouldst behold the zodiac's jagged wheel
  Revolving still more near unto the Bears,
  Unless it swerved aside from its old track.

Come cio` sia, se 'l vuoi poter pensare,
  dentro raccolto, imagina Sion
  con questo monte in su la terra stare

si`, ch'amendue hanno un solo orizzon
  e diversi emisperi; onde la strada
  che mal non seppe carreggiar Feton,

vedrai come a costui convien che vada
  da l'un, quando a colui da l'altro fianco,
  se lo 'ntelletto tuo ben chiaro bada"".

""Certo, maestro mio,"" diss'io, ""unquanco
  non vid'io chiaro si` com'io discerno
  la` dove mio ingegno parea manco,

che 'l mezzo cerchio del moto superno,
  che si chiama Equatore in alcun'arte,
  e che sempre riman tra 'l sole e 'l verno,

per la ragion che di', quinci si parte
  verso settentrion, quanto li Ebrei
  vedevan lui verso la calda parte.

Ma se a te piace, volontier saprei
  quanto avemo ad andar; che' 'l poggio sale
  piu` che salir non posson li occhi miei"".

Ed elli a me: ""Questa montagna e` tale,
  che sempre al cominciar di sotto e` grave;
  e quant'om piu` va su`, e men fa male.

Pero`, quand'ella ti parra` soave
  tanto, che su` andar ti fia leggero
  com'a seconda giu` andar per nave,

allor sarai al fin d'esto sentiero;
  quivi di riposar l'affanno aspetta.
  Piu` non rispondo, e questo so per vero"".

E com'elli ebbe sua parola detta,
  una voce di presso sono`: ""Forse
  che di sedere in pria avrai distretta!"".

Al suon di lei ciascun di noi si torse,
  e vedemmo a mancina un gran petrone,
  del qual ne' io ne' ei prima s'accorse.

La` ci traemmo; e ivi eran persone
  che si stavano a l'ombra dietro al sasso
  come l'uom per negghienza a star si pone.

How that may be wouldst thou have power to think,
  Collected in thyself, imagine Zion
  Together with this mount on earth to stand,

So that they both one sole horizon have,
  And hemispheres diverse; whereby the road
  Which Phaeton, alas! knew not to drive,

Thou'lt see how of necessity must pass
  This on one side, when that upon the other,
  If thine intelligence right clearly heed."

"Truly, my Master," said I, "never yet
  Saw I so clearly as I now discern,
  There where my wit appeared incompetent,

That the mid-circle of supernal motion,
  Which in some art is the Equator called,
  And aye remains between the Sun and Winter,

For reason which thou sayest, departeth hence
  Tow'rds the Septentrion, what time the Hebrews
  Beheld it tow'rds the region of the heat.

But, if it pleaseth thee, I fain would learn
  How far we have to go; for the hill rises
  Higher than eyes of mine have power to rise."

And he to me: "This mount is such, that ever
  At the beginning down below 'tis tiresome,
  And aye the more one climbs, the less it hurts.

Therefore, when it shall seem so pleasant to thee,
  That going up shall be to thee as easy
  As going down the current in a boat,

Then at this pathway's ending thou wilt be;
  There to repose thy panting breath expect;
  No more I answer; and this I know for true."

And as he finished uttering these words,
  A voice close by us sounded: "Peradventure
  Thou wilt have need of sitting down ere that."

At sound thereof each one of us turned round,
  And saw upon the left hand a great rock,
  Which neither I nor he before had noticed.

Thither we drew; and there were persons there
  Who in the shadow stood behind the rock,
  As one through indolence is wont to stand.

E un di lor, che mi sembiava lasso,
  sedeva e abbracciava le ginocchia,
  tenendo 'l viso giu` tra esse basso.

““O dolce segnor mio”“, diss'io, ““adocchia
  colui che mostra se' piu` negligente
  che se pigrizia fosse sua serocchia”“.

Allor si volse a noi e puose mente,
  movendo 'l viso pur su per la coscia,
  e disse: ““Or va tu su`, che se' valente!”“.

Conobbi allor chi era, e quella angoscia
  che m'avacciava un poco ancor la lena,
  non m'impedi` l'andare a lui; e poscia

ch'a lui fu' giunto, alzo` la testa a pena,
  dicendo: ““Hai ben veduto come 'l sole
  da l'omero sinistro il carro mena?”“.

Li atti suoi pigri e le corte parole
  mosser le labbra mie un poco a riso;
  poi cominciai: ““Belacqua, a me non dole

di te omai; ma dimmi: perche' assiso
  quiritto se'? attendi tu iscorta,
  o pur lo modo usato t'ha' ripriso?”“.

Ed elli: ““O frate, andar in su` che porta?
  che' non mi lascerebbe ire a' martiri
  l'angel di Dio che siede in su la porta.

Prima convien che tanto il ciel m'aggiri
  di fuor da essa, quanto fece in vita,
  perch'io 'ndugiai al fine i buon sospiri,

se orazione in prima non m'aita
  che surga su` di cuor che in grazia viva;
  l'altra che val, che 'n ciel non e` udita?”“.

E gia` il poeta innanzi mi saliva,
  e dicea: ““Vienne omai; vedi ch'e` tocco
  meridian dal sole e a la riva

cuopre la notte gia` col pie` Morrocco”“.

And one of them, who seemed to me fatigued,
  Was sitting down, and both his knees embraced,
  Holding his face low down between them bowed.

"O my sweet Lord," I said, "do turn thine eye
  On him who shows himself more negligent
  Then even Sloth herself his sister were."

Then he turned round to us, and he gave heed,
  Just lifting up his eyes above his thigh,
  And said: "Now go thou up, for thou art valiant."

Then knew I who he was; and the distress,
  That still a little did my breathing quicken,
  My going to him hindered not; and after

I came to him he hardly raised his head,
  Saying: "Hast thou seen clearly how the sun
  O'er thy left shoulder drives his chariot?"

His sluggish attitude and his curt words
  A little unto laughter moved my lips;
  Then I began: "Belacqua, I grieve not

For thee henceforth; but tell me, wherefore seated
  In this place art thou? Waitest thou an escort?
  Or has thy usual habit seized upon thee?"

And he: "O brother, what's the use of climbing?
  Since to my torment would not let me go
  The Angel of God, who sitteth at the gate.

First heaven must needs so long revolve me round
  Outside thereof, as in my life it did,
  Since the good sighs I to the end postponed,

Unless, e'er that, some prayer may bring me aid
  Which rises from a heart that lives in grace;
  What profit others that in heaven are heard not?"

Meanwhile the Poet was before me mounting,
  And saying: "Come now; see the sun has touched
  Meridian, and from the shore the night

Covers already with her foot Morocco."

Purgatorio: Canto V

Those who died by Violence, but repentant. Buonconte di Monfeltro. La Pia.

Io era gia` da quell'ombre partito,
  e seguitava l'orme del mio duca,
  quando di retro a me, drizzando 'l dito,

una grido`: ""Ve' che non par che luca
  lo raggio da sinistra a quel di sotto,
  e come vivo par che si conduca!"".

Li occhi rivolsi al suon di questo motto,
  e vidile guardar per maraviglia
  pur me, pur me, e 'l lume ch'era rotto.

""Perche' l'animo tuo tanto s'impiglia"",
  disse 'l maestro, ""che l'andare allenti?
  che ti fa cio` che quivi si pispiglia?

Vien dietro a me, e lascia dir le genti:
  sta come torre ferma, che non crolla
  gia` mai la cima per soffiar di venti;

che' sempre l'omo in cui pensier rampolla
  sovra pensier, da se' dilunga il segno,
  perche' la foga l'un de l'altro insolla"".

Che potea io ridir, se non ""Io vegno""?
  Dissilo, alquanto del color consperso
  che fa l'uom di perdon talvolta degno.

E 'ntanto per la costa di traverso
  venivan genti innanzi a noi un poco,
  cantando 'Miserere' a verso a verso.

Quando s'accorser ch'i' non dava loco
  per lo mio corpo al trapassar d'i raggi,
  mutar lor canto in un ""oh!"" lungo e roco;

I had already from those shades departed,
  And followed in the footsteps of my Guide,
  When from behind, pointing his finger at me,

One shouted: "See, it seems as if shone not
  The sunshine on the left of him below,
  And like one living seems he to conduct him."

Mine eyes I turned at utterance of these words,
  And saw them watching with astonishment
  But me, but me, and the light which was broken!

"Why doth thy mind so occupy itself,"
  The Master said, "that thou thy pace dost slacken?
  What matters it to thee what here is whispered?

Come after me, and let the people talk;
  Stand like a steadfast tower, that never wags
  Its top for all the blowing of the winds;

For evermore the man in whom is springing
  Thought upon thought, removes from him the mark,
  Because the force of one the other weakens."

What could I say in answer but "I come"?
  I said it somewhat with that colour tinged
  Which makes a man of pardon sometimes worthy.

Meanwhile along the mountain-side across
  Came people in advance of us a little,
  Singing the Miserere verse by verse.

When they became aware I gave no place
  For passage of the sunshine through my body,
  They changed their song into a long, hoarse "Oh!"

e due di loro, in forma di messaggi,
  corsero incontr'a noi e dimandarne:
  ""Di vostra condizion fatene saggi"".

E 'l mio maestro: ""Voi potete andarne
  e ritrarre a color che vi mandaro
  che 'l corpo di costui e` vera carne.

Se per veder la sua ombra restaro,
  com'io avviso, assai e` lor risposto:
  faccianli onore, ed essere puo` lor caro"".

Vapori accesi non vid'io si` tosto
  di prima notte mai fender sereno,
  ne', sol calando, nuvole d'agosto,

che color non tornasser suso in meno;
  e, giunti la`, con li altri a noi dier volta
  come schiera che scorre sanza freno.

""Questa gente che preme a noi e` molta,
  e vegnonti a pregar"", disse 'l poeta:
  ""pero` pur va, e in andando ascolta"".

""O anima che vai per esser lieta
  con quelle membra con le quai nascesti"",
  venian gridando, ""un poco il passo queta.

Guarda s'alcun di noi unqua vedesti,
  si` che di lui di la` novella porti:
  deh, perche' vai? deh, perche' non t'arresti?

Noi fummo tutti gia` per forza morti,
  e peccatori infino a l'ultima ora;
  quivi lume del ciel ne fece accorti,

si` che, pentendo e perdonando, fora
  di vita uscimmo a Dio pacificati,
  che del disio di se' veder n'accora"".

E io: ""Perche' ne' vostri visi guati,
  non riconosco alcun; ma s'a voi piace
  cosa ch'io possa, spiriti ben nati,

voi dite, e io faro` per quella pace
  che, dietro a' piedi di si` fatta guida
  di mondo in mondo cercar mi si face"".

And two of them, in form of messengers,
  Ran forth to meet us, and demanded of us,
  "Of your condition make us cognisant."

And said my Master: "Ye can go your way
  And carry back again to those who sent you,
  That this one's body is of very flesh.

If they stood still because they saw his shadow,
  As I suppose, enough is answered them;
  Him let them honour, it may profit them."

Vapours enkindled saw I ne'er so swiftly
  At early nightfall cleave the air serene,
  Nor, at the set of sun, the clouds of August,

But upward they returned in briefer time,
  And, on arriving, with the others wheeled
  Tow'rds us, like troops that run without a rein.

"This folk that presses unto us is great,
  And cometh to implore thee," said the Poet;
  "So still go onward, and in going listen."

"O soul that goest to beatitude
  With the same members wherewith thou wast
      born,"
  Shouting they came, "a little stay thy steps,

Look, if thou e'er hast any of us seen,
  So that o'er yonder thou bear news of him;
  Ah, why dost thou go on? Ah, why not stay?

Long since we all were slain by violence,
  And sinners even to the latest hour;
  Then did a light from heaven admonish us,

So that, both penitent and pardoning, forth
  From life we issued reconciled to God,
  Who with desire to see Him stirs our hearts."

And I: "Although I gaze into your faces,
  No one I recognize; but if may please you
  Aught I have power to do, ye well-born spirits,

Speak ye, and I will do it, by that peace
  Which, following the feet of such a Guide,
  From world to world makes itself sought by me."

E uno incomincio`: ““Ciascun si fida
  del beneficio tuo sanza giurarlo,
  pur che 'l voler nonpossa non ricida.

Ond'io, che solo innanzi a li altri parlo,
  ti priego, se mai vedi quel paese
  che siede tra Romagna e quel di Carlo,

che tu mi sie di tuoi prieghi cortese
  in Fano, si` che ben per me s'adori
  pur ch'i' possa purgar le gravi offese.

Quindi fu' io; ma li profondi fori
  ond'usci` 'l sangue in sul quale io sedea,
  fatti mi fuoro in grembo a li Antenori,

la` dov'io piu` sicuro esser credea:
  quel da Esti il fe' far, che m'avea in ira
  assai piu` la` che dritto non volea.

Ma s'io fosse fuggito inver' la Mira,
  quando fu' sovragiunto ad Oriaco,
  ancor sarei di la` dove si spira.

Corsi al palude, e le cannucce e 'l braco
  m'impigliar si` ch'i' caddi; e li` vid'io
  de le mie vene farsi in terra laco”“.

Poi disse un altro: ““Deh, se quel disio
  si compia che ti tragge a l'alto monte,
  con buona pietate aiuta il mio!

Io fui di Montefeltro, io son Boncone;
  Giovanna o altri non ha di me cura;
  per ch'io vo tra costor con bassa fronte”“.

E io a lui: ““Qual forza o qual ventura
  ti travio` si` fuor di Campaldino,
  che non si seppe mai tua sepultura?”“.

““Oh!”“, rispuos'elli, ““a pie` del Casentino
  traversa un'acqua c'ha nome l'Archiano,
  che sovra l'Ermo nasce in Apennino.

La` 've 'l vocabol suo diventa vano,
  arriva' io forato ne la gola,
  fuggendo a piede e sanguinando il piano.

And one began: "Each one has confidence
  In thy good offices without an oath,
  Unless the I cannot cut off the I will;

Whence I, who speak alone before the others,
  Pray thee, if ever thou dost see the land
  That 'twixt Romagna lies and that of Charles,

Thou be so courteous to me of thy prayers
  In Fano, that they pray for me devoutly,
  That I may purge away my grave offences.

From thence was I; but the deep wounds, through
    which
  Issued the blood wherein I had my seat,
  Were dealt me in bosom of the Antenori,

There where I thought to be the most secure;
  'Twas he of Este had it done, who held me
  In hatred far beyond what justice willed.

But if towards the Mira I had fled,
  When I was overtaken at Oriaco,
  I still should be o'er yonder where men breathe.

I ran to the lagoon, and reeds and mire
  Did so entangle me I fell, and saw there
  A lake made from my veins upon the ground."

Then said another: "Ah, be that desire
  Fulfilled that draws thee to the lofty mountain,
  As thou with pious pity aidest mine.

I was of Montefeltro, and am Buonconte;
  Giovanna, nor none other cares for me;
  Hence among these I go with downcast front."

And I to him: "What violence or what chance
  Led thee astray so far from Campaldino,
  That never has thy sepulture been known?"

"Oh," he replied, "at Casentino's foot
  A river crosses named Archiano, born
  Above the Hermitage in Apennine.

There where the name thereof becometh void
  Did I arrive, pierced through and through the throat,
  Fleeing on foot, and bloodying the plain;

Quivi perdei la vista e la parola
  nel nome di Maria fini', e quivi
  caddi, e rimase la mia carne sola.

Io diro` vero e tu 'l ridi` tra ' vivi:
  l'angel di Dio mi prese, e quel d'inferno
  gridava: "O tu del ciel, perche' mi privi?

Tu te ne porti di costui l'etterno
  per una lagrimetta che 'l mi toglie;
  ma io faro` de l'altro altro governo!".

Ben sai come ne l'aere si raccoglie
  quell'umido vapor che in acqua riede,
  tosto che sale dove 'l freddo il coglie.

Giunse quel mal voler che pur mal chiede
  con lo 'ntelletto, e mosse il fummo e 'l vento
  per la virtu` che sua natura diede.

Indi la valle, come 'l di` fu spento,
  da Pratomagno al gran giogo coperse
  di nebbia; e 'l ciel di sopra fece intento,

si` che 'l pregno aere in acqua si converse;
  la pioggia cadde e a' fossati venne
  di lei cio` che la terra non sofferse;

e come ai rivi grandi si convenne,
  ver' lo fiume real tanto veloce
  si ruino`, che nulla la ritenne.

Lo corpo mio gelato in su la foce
  trovo` l'Archian rubesto; e quel sospinse
  ne l'Arno, e sciolse al mio petto la croce

ch'i' fe' di me quando 'l dolor mi vinse;
  voltommi per le ripe e per lo fondo,
  poi di sua preda mi coperse e cinse"".

""Deh, quando tu sarai tornato al mondo,
  e riposato de la lunga via"",
  seguito` 'l terzo spirito al secondo,

""ricorditi di me, che son la Pia:
  Siena mi fe', disfecemi Maremma:
  salsi colui che 'nnanellata pria

disposando m'avea con la sua gemma"".

There my sight lost I, and my utterance
  Ceased in the name of Mary, and thereat
  I fell, and tenantless my flesh remained.

Truth will I speak, repeat it to the living;
  God's Angel took me up, and he of hell
  Shouted: 'O thou from heaven, why dost thou rob
    me?

Thou bearest away the eternal part of him,
  For one poor little tear, that takes him from me;
  But with the rest I'll deal in other fashion!'

Well knowest thou how in the air is gathered
  That humid vapour which to water turns,
  Soon as it rises where the cold doth grasp it.

He joined that evil will, which aye seeks evil,
  To intellect, and moved the mist and wind
  By means of power, which his own nature gave;

Thereafter, when the day was spent, the valley
  From Pratomagno to the great yoke covered
  With fog, and made the heaven above intent,

So that the pregnant air to water changed;
  Down fell the rain, and to the gullies came
  Whate'er of it earth tolerated not;

And as it mingled with the mighty torrents,
  Towards the royal river with such speed
  It headlong rushed, that nothing held it back.

My frozen body near unto its outlet
  The robust Archian found, and into Arno
  Thrust it, and loosened from my breast the cross

I made of me, when agony o'ercame me;
  It rolled me on the banks and on the bottom,
  Then with its booty covered and begirt me."

"Ah, when thou hast returned unto the world,
  And rested thee from thy long journeying,"
  After the second followed the third spirit,

"Do thou remember me who am the Pia;
  Siena made me, unmade me Maremma;
  He knoweth it, who had encircled first,

Espousing me, my finger with his gem."

Purgatorio: Canto VI

Dante's Inquiry on Prayers for the Dead. Sordello. Italy.

Quando si parte il gioco de la zara,
  colui che perde si riman dolente,
  repetendo le volte, e tristo impara;

con l'altro se ne va tutta la gente;
  qual va dinanzi, e qual di dietro il prende,
  e qual dallato li si reca a mente;

el non s'arresta, e questo e quello intende;
  a cui porge la man, piu` non fa pressa;
  e cosi` da la calca si difende.

Tal era io in quella turba spessa,
  volgendo a loro, e qua e la`, la faccia,
  e promettendo mi sciogliea da essa.

Quiv'era l'Aretin che da le braccia
  fiere di Ghin di Tacco ebbe la morte,
  e l'altro ch'annego` correndo in caccia.

Quivi pregava con le mani sporte
  Federigo Novello, e quel da Pisa
  che fe' parer lo buon Marzucco forte.

Vidi conte Orso e l'anima divisa
  dal corpo suo per astio e per inveggia,
  com'e' dicea, non per colpa commisa;

Pier da la Broccia dico; e qui proveggia,
  mentr'e` di qua, la donna di Brabante,
  si` che pero` non sia di peggior greggia.

Come libero fui da tutte quante
  quell'ombre che pregar pur ch'altri prieghi,
  si` che s'avacci lor divenir sante,

Whene'er is broken up the game of Zara,
  He who has lost remains behind despondent,
  The throws repeating, and in sadness learns;

The people with the other all depart;
  One goes in front, and one behind doth pluck him,
  And at his side one brings himself to mind;

He pauses not, and this and that one hears;
  They crowd no more to whom his hand he stretch-
    es,
  And from the throng he thus defends himself.

Even such was I in that dense multitude,
  Turning to them this way and that my face,
  And, promising, I freed myself therefrom.

There was the Aretine, who from the arms
  Untamed of Ghin di Tacco had his death,
  And he who fleeing from pursuit was drowned.

There was imploring with his hands outstretched
  Frederick Novello, and that one of Pisa
  Who made the good Marzucco seem so strong.

I saw Count Orso; and the soul divided
  By hatred and by envy from its body,
  As it declared, and not for crime committed,

Pierre de la Brosse I say; and here provide
  While still on earth the Lady of Brabant,
  So that for this she be of no worse flock!

As soon as I was free from all those shades
  Who only prayed that some one else may pray,
  So as to hasten their becoming holy,

io cominciai: ""El par che tu mi nieghi,
  o luce mia, espresso in alcun testo
  che decreto del cielo orazion pieghi;

e questa gente prega pur di questo:
  sarebbe dunque loro speme vana,
  o non m'e` 'l detto tuo ben manifesto?"".

Ed elli a me: ""La mia scrittura e` piana;
  e la speranza di costor non falla,
  se ben si guarda con la mente sana;

che' cima di giudicio non s'avvalla
  perche' foco d'amor compia in un punto
  cio` che de' sodisfar chi qui s'astalla;

e la` dov'io fermai cotesto punto,
  non s'ammendava, per pregar, difetto,
  perche' 'l priego da Dio era disgiunto.

Veramente a cosi` alto sospetto
  non ti fermar, se quella nol ti dice
  che lume fia tra 'l vero e lo 'ntelletto.

Non so se 'ntendi: io dico di Beatrice;
  tu la vedrai di sopra, in su la vetta
  di questo monte, ridere e felice"".

E io: ""Segnore, andiamo a maggior fretta,
  che' gia` non m'affatico come dianzi,
  e vedi omai che 'l poggio l'ombra getta"".

""Noi anderem con questo giorno innanzi"",
  rispuose, ""quanto piu` potremo omai;
  ma 'l fatto e` d'altra forma che non stanzi.

Prima che sie la` su`, tornar vedrai
  colui che gia` si cuopre de la costa,
  si` che ' suoi raggi tu romper non fai.

Ma vedi la` un'anima che, posta
  sola soletta, inverso noi riguarda:
  quella ne 'nsegnera` la via piu` tosta"".

Venimmo a lei: o anima lombarda,
  come ti stavi altera e disdegnosa
  e nel mover de li occhi onesta e tarda!

Ella non ci dicea alcuna cosa,
  ma lasciavane gir, solo sguardando
  a guisa di leon quando si posa.

Began I: "It appears that thou deniest,
  O light of mine, expressly in some text,
  That orison can bend decree of Heaven;

And ne'ertheless these people pray for this.
  Might then their expectation bootless be?
  Or is to me thy saying not quite clear?"

And he to me: "My writing is explicit,
  And not fallacious is the hope of these,
  If with sane intellect 'tis well regarded;

For top of judgment doth not vail itself,
  Because the fire of love fulfils at once
  What he must satisfy who here installs him.

And there, where I affirmed that proposition,
  Defect was not amended by a prayer,
  Because the prayer from God was separate.

Verily, in so deep a questioning
  Do not decide, unless she tell it thee,
  Who light 'twixt truth and intellect shall be.

I know not if thou understand; I speak
  Of Beatrice; her shalt thou see above,
  Smiling and happy, on this mountain's top."

And I: "Good Leader, let us make more haste,
  For I no longer tire me as before;
  And see, e'en now the hill a shadow casts."

"We will go forward with this day" he answered,
  "As far as now is possible for us;
  But otherwise the fact is than thou thinkest.

Ere thou art up there, thou shalt see return
  Him, who now hides himself behind the hill,
  So that thou dost not interrupt his rays.

But yonder there behold! a soul that stationed
  All, all alone is looking hitherward;
  It will point out to us the quickest way."

We came up unto it; O Lombard soul,
  How lofty and disdainful thou didst bear thee,
  And grand and slow in moving of thine eyes!

Nothing whatever did it say to us,
  But let us go our way, eying us only
  After the manner of a couchant lion;

Pur Virgilio si trasse a lei, pregando
  che ne mostrasse la miglior salita;
  e quella non rispuose al suo dimando,

ma di nostro paese e de la vita
  ci 'nchiese; e 'l dolce duca incominciava
  '"“Mantua…”"', e l'ombra, tutta in se' romita,

surse ver' lui del loco ove pria stava,
  dicendo: '"“O Mantoano, io son Sordello
  de la tua terra!”"'; e l'un l'altro abbracciava.

Ahi serva Italia, di dolore ostello,
  nave sanza nocchiere in gran tempesta,
  non donna di province, ma bordello!

Quell'anima gentil fu così` presta,
  sol per lo dolce suon de la sua terra,
  di fare al cittadin suo quivi festa;

e ora in te non stanno sanza guerra
  li vivi tuoi, e l'un l'altro si rode
  di quei ch'un muro e una fossa serra.

Cerca, misera, intorno da le prode
  le tue marine, e poi ti guarda in seno,
  s'alcuna parte in te di pace gode.

Che val perche' ti racconciasse il freno
  Iustiniano, se la sella e` vota?
  Sanz'esso fora la vergogna meno.

Ahi gente che dovresti esser devota,
  e lasciar seder Cesare in la sella,
  se bene intendi cio` che Dio ti nota,

guarda come esta fiera e` fatta fella
  per non esser corretta da li sproni,
  poi che ponesti mano a la predella.

O Alberto tedesco ch'abbandoni
  costei ch'e` fatta indomita e selvaggia,
  e dovresti inforcar li suoi arcioni,

giusto giudicio da le stelle caggia
  sovra 'l tuo sangue, e sia novo e aperto,
  tal che 'l tuo successor temenza n'aggia!

Ch'avete tu e 'l tuo padre sofferto,
  per cupidigia di costa` distretti,
  che 'l giardin de lo 'mperio sia diserto.

Still near to it Virgilius drew, entreating
  That it would point us out the best ascent;
  And it replied not unto his demand,

But of our native land and of our life
  It questioned us; and the sweet Guide began:
  "Mantua,"—and the shade, all in itself recluse,

Rose tow'rds him from the place where first it was,
  Saying: "O Mantuan, I am Sordello
  Of thine own land!" and one embraced the other.

Ah! servile Italy, grief's hostelry!
  A ship without a pilot in great tempest!
  No Lady thou of Provinces, but brothel!

That noble soul was so impatient, only
  At the sweet sound of his own native land,
  To make its citizen glad welcome there;

And now within thee are not without war
  Thy living ones, and one doth gnaw the other
  Of those whom one wall and one fosse shut in!

Search, wretched one, all round about the shores
  Thy seaboard, and then look within thy bosom,
  If any part of thee enjoyeth peace!

What boots it, that for thee Justinian
  The bridle mend, if empty be the saddle?
  Withouten this the shame would be the less.

Ah! people, thou that oughtest to be devout,
  And to let Caesar sit upon the saddle,
  If well thou hearest what God teacheth thee,

Behold how fell this wild beast has become,
  Being no longer by the spur corrected,
  Since thou hast laid thy hand upon the bridle.

O German Albert! who abandonest
  Her that has grown recalcitrant and savage,
  And oughtest to bestride her saddle-bow,

May a just judgment from the stars down fall
  Upon thy blood, and be it new and open,
  That thy successor may have fear thereof;

Because thy father and thyself have suffered,
  By greed of those transalpine lands distrained,
  The garden of the empire to be waste.

Vieni a veder Montecchi e Cappelletti,
Monaldi e Filippeschi, uom sanza cura:
color gia` tristi, e questi con sospetti!

Vien, crudel, vieni, e vedi la pressura
d'i tuoi gentili, e cura lor magagne;
e vedrai Santafior com'e` oscura!

Vieni a veder la tua Roma che piagne
vedova e sola, e di` e notte chiama:
""«Cesare mio, perche' non m'accompagne?»"".

Vieni a veder la gente quanto s'ama!
e se nulla di noi pieta` ti move,
a vergognar ti vien de la tua fama.

E se licito m'e`, o sommo Giove
che fosti in terra per noi crucifisso,
son li giusti occhi tuoi rivolti altrove?

O e` preparazion che ne l'abisso
del tuo consiglio fai per alcun bene
in tutto de l'accorger nostro scisso?

Che' le citta` d'Italia tutte piene
son di tiranni, e un Marcel diventa
ogne villan che parteggiando viene.

Fiorenza mia, ben puoi esser contenta
di questa digression che non ti tocca,
merce' del popol tuo che si argomenta.

Molti han giustizia in cuore, e tardi scocca
per non venir sanza consiglio a l'arco;
ma il popol tuo l'ha in sommo de la bocca.

Molti rifiutan lo comune incarco;
ma il popol tuo solicito risponde
sanza chiamare, e grida: ""«I' mi sobbarco!»"".

Or ti fa lieta, che' tu hai ben onde:
tu ricca, tu con pace, e tu con senno!
S'io dico 'l ver, l'effetto nol nasconde.

Atene e Lacedemona, che fenno
l'antiche leggi e furon si` civili,
fecero al viver bene un picciol cenno

verso di te, che fai tanto sottili
provedimenti, ch'a mezzo novembre
non giugne quel che tu d'ottobre fili.

Come and behold Montecchi and Cappelletti,
Monaldi and Fillippeschi, careless man!
Those sad already, and these doubt-depressed!

Come, cruel one! come and behold the oppression
Of thy nobility, and cure their wounds,
And thou shalt see how safe is Santafiore!

Come and behold thy Rome, that is lamenting,
Widowed, alone, and day and night exclaims,
"My Caesar, why hast thou forsaken me?"

Come and behold how loving are the people;
And if for us no pity moveth thee,
Come and be made ashamed of thy renown!

And if it lawful be, O Jove Supreme!
Who upon earth for us wast crucified,
Are thy just eyes averted otherwhere?

Or preparation is 't, that, in the abyss
Of thine own counsel, for some good thou makest
From our perception utterly cut off?

For all the towns of Italy are full
Of tyrants, and becometh a Marcellus
Each peasant churl who plays the partisan!

My Florence! well mayst thou contented be
With this digression, which concerns thee not,
Thanks to thy people who such forethought take!

Many at heart have justice, but shoot slowly,
That unadvised they come not to the bow,
But on their very lips thy people have it!

Many refuse to bear the common burden;
But thy solicitous people answereth
Without being asked, and crieth: "I submit."

Now be thou joyful, for thou hast good reason;
Thou affluent, thou in peace, thou full of wisdom!
If I speak true, the event conceals it not.

Athens and Lacedaemon, they who made
The ancient laws, and were so civilized,
Made towards living well a little sign

Compared with thee, who makest such fine-spun
Provisions, that to middle of November
Reaches not what thou in October spinnest.

Quante volte, del tempo che rimembre,
  legge, moneta, officio e costume
  hai tu mutato e rinovate membre!

E se ben ti ricordi e vedi lume,
  vedrai te somigliante a quella inferma
  che non puo` trovar posa in su le piume,

ma con dar volta suo dolore scherma.

How oft, within the time of thy remembrance,
  Laws, money, offices, and usages
  Hast thou remodelled, and renewed thy members?

And if thou mind thee well, and see the light,
  Thou shalt behold thyself like a sick woman,
  Who cannot find repose upon her down,

But by her tossing wardeth off her pain.

Purgatorio: Canto VII

The Valley of Flowers. Negligent Princes.

Poscia che l'accoglienze oneste e liete
  furo iterate tre e quattro volte,
  Sordel si trasse, e disse: ""Voi, chi siete?"".

""Anzi che a questo monte fosser volte
  l'anime degne di salire a Dio,
  fur l'ossa mie per Ottavian sepolte.

Io son Virgilio; e per null'altro rio
  lo ciel perdei che per non aver fe"".
  Cosi` rispuose allora il duca mio.

Qual e` colui che cosa innanzi se'
  subita vede ond'e' si maraviglia,
  che crede e non, dicendo ""Ella e`... non e`...""",

tal parve quelli; e poi chino` le ciglia,
  e umilmente ritorno` ver' lui,
  e abbracciol la` 've 'l minor s'appiglia.

""O gloria di Latin"", disse, ""per cui
  mostro` cio` che potea la lingua nostra,
  o pregio etterno del loco ond'io fui,

qual merito o qual grazia mi ti mostra?
  S'io son d'udir le tue parole degno,
  dimmi se vien d'inferno, e di qual chiostra"".

""Per tutt'i cerchi del dolente regno"",
  rispuose lui, ""son io di qua venuto;
  virtu` del ciel mi mosse, e con lei vegno.

Non per far, ma per non fare ho perduto
  a veder l'alto Sol che tu disiri
  e che fu tardi per me conosciuto.

After the gracious and glad salutations
  Had three and four times been reiterated,
  Sordello backward drew and said, "Who are you?"

"Or ever to this mountain were directed
  The souls deserving to ascend to God,
  My bones were buried by Octavian.

I am Virgilius; and for no crime else
  Did I lose heaven, than for not having faith;"
  In this wise then my Leader made reply.

As one who suddenly before him sees
  Something whereat he marvels, who believes
  And yet does not, saying, "It is! it is not!"

So he appeared; and then bowed down his brow,
  And with humility returned towards him,
  And, where inferiors embrace, embraced him.

"O glory of the Latians, thou," he said,
  "Through whom our language showed what it could
    do
  O pride eternal of the place I came from,

What merit or what grace to me reveals thee?
  If I to hear thy words be worthy, tell me
  If thou dost come from Hell, and from what clois-
    ter."

"Through all the circles of the doleful realm,"
  Responded he, "have I come hitherward;
  Heaven's power impelled me, and with that I come.

I by not doing, not by doing, lost
  The sight of that high sun which thou desirest,
  And which too late by me was recognized.

Luogo e` la` giu` non tristo di martiri,
  ma di tenebre solo, ove i lamenti
  non suonan come guai, ma son sospiri.

Quivi sto io coi pargoli innocenti
  dai denti morsi de la morte avante
  che fosser da l'umana colpa essenti;

quivi sto io con quei che le tre sante
  virtu` non si vestiro, e sanza vizio
  conobber l'altre e seguir tutte quante.

Ma se tu sai e puoi, alcuno indizio
  da` noi per che venir possiam piu` tosto
  la` dove purgatorio ha dritto inizio"".

Rispuose: ""Loco certo non c'e` posto;
  licito m'e` andar suso e intorno;
  per quanto ir posso, a guida mi t'accosto.

Ma vedi gia` come dichina il giorno,
  e andar su` di notte non si puote;
  pero` e` buon pensar di bel soggiorno.

Anime sono a destra qua remote:
  se mi consenti, io ti merro` ad esse,
  e non sanza diletto ti fier note"".

""Com'e` cio`?"", fu risposto. ""Chi volesse
  salir di notte, fora elli impedito
  d'altrui, o non sarria che' non potesse?"".

E 'l buon Sordello in terra frego` 'l dito,
  dicendo: ""Vedi? sola questa riga
  non varcheresti dopo 'l sol partito:

non pero` ch'altra cosa desse briga,
  che la notturna tenebra, ad ir suso;
  quella col nonpoder la voglia intriga.

Ben si poria con lei tornare in giuso
  e passeggiar la costa intorno errando,
  mentre che l'orizzonte il di` tien chiuso"".

Allora il mio segnor, quasi ammirando,
  ""Menane"", disse, ""dunque la` 've dici
  ch'aver si puo` diletto dimorando"".

Poco allungati c'eravam di lici,
  quand'io m'accorsi che 'l monte era scemo,
  a guisa che i vallon li sceman quici.

A place there is below not sad with torments,
  But darkness only, where the lamentations
  Have not the sound of wailing, but are sighs.

There dwell I with the little innocents
  Snatched by the teeth of Death, or ever they
  Were from our human sinfulness exempt.

There dwell I among those who the three saintly
  Virtues did not put on, and without vice
  The others knew and followed all of them.

But if thou know and can, some indication
  Give us by which we may the sooner come
  Where Purgatory has its right beginning."

He answered: "No fixed place has been assigned us;
  'Tis lawful for me to go up and round;
  So far as I can go, as guide I join thee.

But see already how the day declines,
  And to go up by night we are not able;
  Therefore 'tis well to think of some fair sojourn.

Souls are there on the right hand here withdrawn;
  If thou permit me I will lead thee to them,
  And thou shalt know them not without delight."

"How is this?" was the answer; "should one wish
  To mount by night would he prevented be
  By others? or mayhap would not have power?"

And on the ground the good Sordello drew
  His finger, saying, "See, this line alone
  Thou couldst not pass after the sun is gone;

Not that aught else would hindrance give, however,
  To going up, save the nocturnal darkness;
  This with the want of power the will perplexes.

We might indeed therewith return below,
  And, wandering, walk the hill-side round about,
  While the horizon holds the day imprisoned."

Thereon my Lord, as if in wonder, said:
  "Do thou conduct us thither, where thou sayest
  That we can take delight in tarrying."

Little had we withdrawn us from that place,
  When I perceived the mount was hollowed out
  In fashion as the valleys here are hollowed.

""Cola`"", disse quell'ombra, ""'n'anderemo   dove la costa face di se' grembo;   e la` il novo giorno attenderemo"".	"Thitherward," said that shade, "will we repair, Where of itself the hill-side makes a lap, And there for the new day will we await."

Tra erto e piano era un sentiero schembo,
  che ne condusse in fianco de la lacca,
  la` dove piu` ch'a mezzo muore il lembo.
	'Twixt hill and plain there was a winding path
	  Which led us to the margin of that dell,
	  Where dies the border more than half away.

Oro e argento fine, cocco e biacca,
  indaco, legno lucido e sereno,
  fresco smeraldo in l'ora che si fiacca,
	Gold and fine silver, and scarlet and pearl-white,
	  The Indian wood resplendent and serene,
	  Fresh emerald the moment it is broken,

da l'erba e da li fior, dentr'a quel seno
  posti, ciascun saria di color vinto,
  come dal suo maggiore e` vinto il meno.
	By herbage and by flowers within that hollow
	  Planted, each one in colour would be vanquished,
	  As by its greater vanquished is the less.

Non avea pur natura ivi dipinto,
  ma di soavita` di mille odori
  vi facea uno incognito e indistinto.
	Nor in that place had nature painted only,
	  But of the sweetness of a thousand odours
	  Made there a mingled fragrance and unknown.

'Salve, Regina' in sul verde e 'n su' fiori
  quindi seder cantando anime vidi,
  che per la valle non parean di fuori.
	"Salve Regina," on the green and flowers
	  There seated, singing, spirits I beheld,
	  Which were not visible outside the valley.

""Prima che 'l poco sole omai s'annidi"",
  comincio` 'l Mantoan che ci avea volti,
  ""tra color non vogliate ch'io vi guidi.
	"Before the scanty sun now seeks his nest,"
	  Began the Mantuan who had led us thither,
	  "Among them do not wish me to conduct you.

Di questo balzo meglio li atti e ' volti
  conoscerete voi di tutti quanti,
  che ne la lama giu` tra essi accolti.
	Better from off this ledge the acts and faces
	  Of all of them will you discriminate,
	  Than in the plain below received among them.

Colui che piu` siede alto e fa sembianti   d'aver negletto cio` che far dovea, e che non move bocca a li altrui canti,	He who sits highest, and the semblance bears Of having what he should have done neglected, And to the others' song moves not his lips,

Rodolfo imperador fu, che potea
  sanar le piaghe c'hanno Italia morta,
  si` che tardi per altri si ricrea.
	Rudolph the Emperor was, who had the power
	  To heal the wounds that Italy have slain,
	  So that through others slowly she revives.

L'altro che ne la vista lui conforta,
  resse la terra dove l'acqua nasce
  che Molta in Albia, e Albia in mar ne porta:
	The other, who in look doth comfort him,
	  Governed the region where the water springs,
	  The Moldau bears the Elbe, and Elbe the sea.

Ottacchero ebbe nome, e ne le fasce
  fu meglio assai che Vincislao suo figlio
  barbuto, cui lussuria e ozio pasce.
	His name was Ottocar; and in swaddling-clothes
	  Far better he than bearded Winceslaus
	  His son, who feeds in luxury and ease.

E quel nasetto che stretto a consiglio par con colui c'ha si` benigno aspetto,   mori` fuggendo e disfiorando il giglio:	And the small-nosed, who close in council seems With him that has an aspect so benign, Died fleeing and disflowering the lily;

guardate la` come si batte il petto!
  L'altro vedete c'ha fatto a la guancia
  de la sua palma, sospirando, letto.

Padre e suocero son del mal di Francia:
  sanno la vita sua viziata e lorda,
  e quindi viene il duol che si` li lancia.

Quel che par si` membruto e che s'accorda,
  cantando, con colui dal maschio naso,
  d'ogne valor porto` cinta la corda;

e se re dopo lui fosse rimaso
  lo giovanetto che retro a lui siede,
  ben andava il valor di vaso in vaso,

che non si puote dir de l'altre rede;
  Iacomo e Federigo hanno i reami;
  del retaggio miglior nessun possiede.

Rade volte risurge per li rami
  l'umana probitate; e questo vole
  quei che la da`, perche' da lui si chiami.

Anche al nasuto vanno mie parole
  non men ch'a l'altro, Pier, che con lui canta,
  onde Puglia e Proenza gia` si dole.

Tant'e` del seme suo minor la pianta,
  quanto piu` che Beatrice e Margherita,
  Costanza di marito ancor si vanta.

Vedete il re de la semplice vita
  seder la` solo, Arrigo d'Inghilterra:
  questi ha ne' rami suoi migliore uscita.

Quel che piu` basso tra costor s'atterra,
  guardando in suso, e` Guiglielmo marchese,
  per cui e Alessandria e la sua guerra

fa pianger Monferrato e Canavese"".

Look there, how he is beating at his breast!
  Behold the other one, who for his cheek
  Sighing has made of his own palm a bed;

Father and father-in-law of France's Pest
  Are they, and know his vicious life and lewd,
  And hence proceeds the grief that so doth pierce
    them.

He who appears so stalwart, and chimes in,
  Singing, with that one of the manly nose,
  The cord of every valour wore begirt;

And if as King had after him remained
  The stripling who in rear of him is sitting,
  Well had the valour passed from vase to vase,

Which cannot of the other heirs be said.
  Frederick and Jacomo possess the realms,
  But none the better heritage possesses.

Not oftentimes upriseth through the branches
  The probity of man; and this He wills
  Who gives it, so that we may ask of Him.

Eke to the large-nosed reach my words, no less
  Than to the other, Pier, who with him sings;
  Whence Provence and Apulia grieve already

The plant is as inferior to its seed,
  As more than Beatrice and Margaret
  Costanza boasteth of her husband still.

Behold the monarch of the simple life,
  Harry of England, sitting there alone;
  He in his branches has a better issue.

He who the lowest on the ground among them
  Sits looking upward, is the Marquis William,
  For whose sake Alessandria and her war

Make Monferrat and Canavese weep."

Purgatorio: Canto VIII

The Guardian Angels and the Serpent. Nino di Gallura. The Three Stars. Currado Malaspina.

Era gia` l'ora che volge il disio
  ai navicanti e 'ntenerisce il core
  lo di` c'han detto ai dolci amici addio;

e che lo novo peregrin d'amore
  punge, se ode squilla di lontano
  che paia il giorno pianger che si more;

quand'io incominciai a render vano
  l'udire e a mirare una de l'alme
  surta, che l'ascoltar chiedea con mano.

Ella giunse e levo` ambo le palme,
  ficcando li occhi verso l'oriente,
  come dicesse a Dio: 'D'altro non calme'.

'Te lucis ante' si` devotamente
  le uscio di bocca e con si` dolci note,
  che fece me a me uscir di mente;

e l'altre poi dolcemente e devote
  seguitar lei per tutto l'inno intero,
  avendo li occhi a le superne rote.

Aguzza qui, lettor, ben li occhi al vero,
  che' 'l velo e` ora ben tanto sottile,
  certo che 'l trapassar dentro e` leggero.

Io vidi quello essercito gentile
  tacito poscia riguardare in sue
  quasi aspettando, palido e umile;

e vidi uscir de l'alto e scender giue
  due angeli con due spade affocate,
  tronche e private de le punte sue.

'Twas now the hour that turneth back desire
  In those who sail the sea, and melts the heart,
  The day they've said to their sweet friends farewell,

And the new pilgrim penetrates with love,
  If he doth hear from far away a bell
  That seemeth to deplore the dying day,

When I began to make of no avail
  My hearing, and to watch one of the souls
  Uprisen, that begged attention with its hand.

It joined and lifted upward both its palms,
  Fixing its eyes upon the orient,
  As if it said to God, "Naught else I care for."

"Te lucis ante" so devoutly issued
  Forth from its mouth, and with such dulcet notes,
  It made me issue forth from my own mind.

And then the others, sweetly and devoutly,
  Accompanied it through all the hymn entire,
  Having their eyes on the supernal wheels.

Here, Reader, fix thine eyes well on the truth,
  For now indeed so subtile is the veil,
  Surely to penetrate within is easy.

I saw that army of the gentle-born
  Thereafterward in silence upward gaze,
  As if in expectation, pale and humble;

And from on high come forth and down descend,
  I saw two Angels with two flaming swords,
  Truncated and deprived of their points.

Verdi come fogliette pur mo nate
  erano in veste, che da verdi penne
  percosse traean dietro e ventilate.

L'un poco sovra noi a star si venne,
  e l'altro scese in l'opposita sponda,
  si` che la gente in mezzo si contenne.

Ben discernea in lor la testa bionda;
  ma ne la faccia l'occhio si smarria,
  come virtu` ch'a troppo si confonda.

""Ambo vegnon del grembo di Maria"",
  disse Sordello, ""a guardia de la valle,
  per lo serpente che verra` vie via"".

Ond'io, che non sapeva per qual calle,
  mi volsi intorno, e stretto m'accostai,
  tutto gelato, a le fidate spalle.

E Sordello anco: ""Or avvalliamo omai
  tra le grandi ombre, e parleremo ad esse;
  grazioso fia lor vedervi assai"".

Solo tre passi credo ch'i' scendesse,
  e fui di sotto, e vidi un che mirava
  pur me, come conoscer mi volesse.

Temp'era gia` che l'aere s'annerava,
  ma non si` che tra li occhi suoi e ' miei
  non dichiarisse cio` che pria serrava.

Ver' me si fece, e io ver' lui mi fei:
  giudice Nin gentil, quanto mi piacque
  quando ti vidi non esser tra ' rei!

Nullo bel salutar tra noi si tacque;
  poi dimando`: ""Quant'e` che tu venisti
  a pie` del monte per le lontane acque?"".

""Oh!"", diss'io lui, ""per entro i luoghi tristi
  venni stamane, e sono in prima vita,
  ancor che l'altra, si` andando, acquisti"".

E come fu la mia risposta udita,
  Sordello ed elli in dietro si raccolse
  come gente di subito smarrita.

Green as the little leaflets just now born
  Their garments were, which, by their verdant pin-
    ions
  Beaten and blown abroad, they trailed behind.

One just above us came to take his station,
  And one descended to the opposite bank,
  So that the people were contained between them.

Clearly in them discerned I the blond head;
  But in their faces was the eye bewildered,
  As faculty confounded by excess.

"From Mary's bosom both of them have come,"
  Sordello said, "as guardians of the valley
  Against the serpent, that will come anon."

Whereupon I, who knew not by what road,
  Turned round about, and closely drew myself,
  Utterly frozen, to the faithful shoulders.

And once again Sordello: "Now descend we
  'Mid the grand shades, and we will speak to them;
  Right pleasant will it be for them to see you."

Only three steps I think that I descended,
  And was below, and saw one who was looking
  Only at me, as if he fain would know me.

Already now the air was growing dark,
  But not so that between his eyes and mine
  It did not show what it before locked up.

Tow'rds me he moved, and I tow'rds him did move;
  Noble Judge Nino! how it me delighted,
  When I beheld thee not among the damned!

No greeting fair was left unsaid between us;
  Then asked he: "How long is it since thou camest
  O'er the far waters to the mountain's foot?"

"Oh!" said I to him, "through the dismal places
  I came this morn; and am in the first life,
  Albeit the other, going thus, I gain."

And on the instant my reply was heard,
  He and Sordello both shrank back from me,
  Like people who are suddenly bewildered.

L'uno a Virgilio e l'altro a un si volse
  che sedea li`, gridando: ""Su`, Currado!
  vieni a veder che Dio per grazia volse"".

Poi, volto a me: ""Per quel singular grado
  che tu dei a colui che si` nasconde
  lo suo primo perche', che non li` e` guado,

quando sarai di la` da le larghe onde,
  di` a Giovanna mia che per me chiami
  la` dove a li 'nnocenti si risponde.

Non credo che la sua madre piu` m'ami,
  poscia che trasmuto` le bianche bende,
  le quai convien che, misera!, ancor brami.

Per lei assai di lieve si comprende
  quanto in femmina foco d'amor dura,
  se l'occhio o 'l tatto spesso non l'accende.

Non le fara` si` bella sepultura
  la vipera che Melanesi accampa,
  com'avria fatto il gallo di Gallura"".

Cosi` dicea, segnato de la stampa,
  nel suo aspetto, di quel dritto zelo
  che misuratamente in core avvampa.

Li occhi miei ghiotti andavan pur al cielo,
  pur la` dove le stelle son piu` tarde,
  si` come rota piu` presso a lo stelo.

E 'l duca mio: ""Figliuol, che la` su` guarde?"".
  E io a lui: ""A quelle tre facelle
  di che 'l polo di qua tutto quanto arde"".

Ond'elli a me: ""Le quattro chiare stelle
  che vedevi staman, son di la` basse,
  e queste son salite ov'eran quelle"".

Com'ei parlava, e Sordello a se' il trasse
  dicendo: ""Vedi la` 'l nostro avversaro"";
  e drizzo` il dito perche' 'n la` guardasse.

Da quella parte onde non ha riparo
  la picciola vallea, era una biscia,
  forse qual diede ad Eva il cibo amaro.

Tra l'erba e ' fior venia la mala striscia,
  volgendo ad ora ad or la testa, e 'l dosso
  leccando come bestia che si liscia.

One to Virgilius, and the other turned
  To one who sat there, crying, "Up, Currado!
  Come and behold what God in grace has willed!"

Then, turned to me: "By that especial grace
  Thou owest unto Him, who so conceals
  His own first wherefore, that it has no ford,

When thou shalt be beyond the waters wide,
  Tell my Giovanna that she pray for me,
  Where answer to the innocent is made.

I do not think her mother loves me more,
  Since she has laid aside her wimple white,
  Which she, unhappy, needs must wish again.

Through her full easily is comprehended
  How long in woman lasts the fire of love,
  If eye or touch do not relight it often.

So fair a hatchment will not make for her
  The Viper marshalling the Milanese
  A-field, as would have made Gallura's Cock."

In this wise spake he, with the stamp impressed
  Upon his aspect of that righteous zeal
  Which measurably burneth in the heart.

My greedy eyes still wandered up to heaven,
  Still to that point where slowest are the stars,
  Even as a wheel the nearest to its axle.

And my Conductor: "Son, what dost thou gaze at
  Up there?" And I to him: "At those three torches
  With which this hither pole is all on fire."

And he to me: "The four resplendent stars
  Thou sawest this morning are down yonder low,
  And these have mounted up to where those were."

As he was speaking, to himself Sordello
  Drew him, and said, "Lo there our Adversary!"
  And pointed with his finger to look thither.

Upon the side on which the little valley
  No barrier hath, a serpent was; perchance
  The same which gave to Eve the bitter food.

'Twixt grass and flowers came on the evil streak,
  Turning at times its head about, and licking
  Its back like to a beast that smoothes itself.

Io non vidi, e pero` dicer non posso,
  come mosser li astor celestiali;
  ma vidi bene e l'uno e l'altro mosso.

Sentendo fender l'aere a le verdi ali,
  fuggi` 'l serpente, e li angeli dier volta,
  suso a le poste rivolando iguali.

L'ombra che s'era al giudice raccolta
  quando chiamo`, per tutto quello assalto
  punto non fu da me guardare sciolta.

""Se la lucerna che ti mena in alto
  truovi nel tuo arbitrio tanta cera
  quant'e` mestiere infino al sommo smalto""",

comincio` ella, ""se novella vera
  di Val di Magra o di parte vicina
  sai, dillo a me, che gia` grande la` era.

Fui chiamato Currado Malaspina;
  non son l'antico, ma di lui discesi;
  a' miei portai l'amor che qui raffina""".

""Oh!""", diss'io lui, ""per li vostri paesi
  gia` mai non fui; ma dove si dimora
  per tutta Europa ch'ei non sien palesi?

La fama che la vostra casa onora,
  grida i segnori e grida la contrada,
  si` che ne sa chi non vi fu ancora;

e io vi giuro, s'io di sopra vada,
  che vostra gente onrata non si sfregia
  del pregio de la borsa e de la spada.

Uso e natura si` la privilegia,
  che, perche' il capo reo il mondo torca,
  sola va dritta e 'l mal cammin dispregia""".

Ed elli: ""Or va; che 'l sol non si ricorca
  sette volte nel letto che 'l Montone
  con tutti e quattro i pie` cuopre e inforca,

che cotesta cortese oppinione
  ti fia chiavata in mezzo de la testa
  con maggior chiovi che d'altrui sermone,

se corso di giudicio non s'arresta""".

I did not see, and therefore cannot say
  How the celestial falcons 'gan to move,
  But well I saw that they were both in motion.

Hearing the air cleft by their verdant wings,
  The serpent fled, and round the Angels wheeled,
  Up to their stations flying back alike.

The shade that to the Judge had near approached
  When he had called, throughout that whole assault
  Had not a moment loosed its gaze on me.

"So may the light that leadeth thee on high
  Find in thine own free-will as much of wax
  As needful is up to the highest azure,"

Began it, "if some true intelligence
  Of Valdimagra or its neighbourhood
  Thou knowest, tell it me, who once was great there.

Currado Malaspina was I called;
  I'm not the elder, but from him descended;
  To mine I bore the love which here refineth."

"O," said I unto him, "through your domains
  I never passed, but where is there a dwelling
  Throughout all Europe, where they are not known?

That fame, which doeth honour to your house,
  Proclaims its Signors and proclaims its land,
  So that he knows of them who ne'er was there.

And, as I hope for heaven, I swear to you
  Your honoured family in naught abates
  The glory of the purse and of the sword.

It is so privileged by use and nature,
  That though a guilty head misguide the world,
  Sole it goes right, and scorns the evil way."

And he: "Now go; for the sun shall not lie
  Seven times upon the pillow which the Ram
  With all his four feet covers and bestrides,

Before that such a courteous opinion
  Shall in the middle of thy head be nailed
  With greater nails than of another's speech,

Unless the course of justice standeth still."

Purgatorio: Canto IX

Dante's Dream of the Eagle. The Gate of Purgatory and the Angel. Seven P's. The Keys.

La concubina di Titone antico
  gia` s'imbiancava al balco d'oriente,
  fuor de le braccia del suo dolce amico;

di gemme la sua fronte era lucente,
  poste in figura del freddo animale
  che con la coda percuote la gente;

e la notte, de' passi con che sale,
  fatti avea due nel loco ov'eravamo,
  e 'l terzo gia` chinava in giuso l'ale;

quand'io, che meco avea di quel d'Adamo,
  vinto dal sonno, in su l'erba inchinai
  la` 've gia` tutti e cinque sedavamo.

Ne l'ora che comincia i tristi lai
  la rondinella presso a la mattina,
  forse a memoria de' suo' primi guai,

e che la mente nostra, peregrina
  piu` da la carne e men da' pensier presa,
  a le sue vision quasi e` divina,

in sogno mi parea veder sospesa
  un'aguglia nel ciel con penne d'oro,
  con l'ali aperte e a calare intesa;

ed esser mi parea la` dove fuoro
  abbandonati i suoi da Ganimede,
  quando fu ratto al sommo consistoro.

Fra me pensava: 'Forse questa fiede
  pur qui per uso, e forse d'altro loco
  disdegna di portarne suso in piede'.

The concubine of old Tithonus now
  Gleamed white upon the eastern balcony,
  Forth from the arms of her sweet paramour;

With gems her forehead all relucent was,
  Set in the shape of that cold animal
  Which with its tail doth smite amain the nations,

And of the steps, with which she mounts, the Night
  Had taken two in that place where we were,
  And now the third was bending down its wings;

When I, who something had of Adam in me,
  Vanquished by sleep, upon the grass reclined,
  There were all five of us already sat.

Just at the hour when her sad lay begins
  The little swallow, near unto the morning,
  Perchance in memory of her former woes,

And when the mind of man, a wanderer
  More from the flesh, and less by thought impris-
    oned,
  Almost prophetic in its visions is,

In dreams it seemed to me I saw suspended
  An eagle in the sky, with plumes of gold,
  With wings wide open, and intent to stoop,

And this, it seemed to me, was where had been
  By Ganymede his kith and kin abandoned,
  When to the high consistory he was rapt.

I thought within myself, perchance he strikes
  From habit only here, and from elsewhere
  Disdains to bear up any in his feet.

Poi mi parea che, poi rotata un poco,
 terribil come folgor discendesse,
 e me rapisse suso infino al foco.

Ivi parea che ella e io ardesse;
 e si` lo 'ncendio imaginato cosse,
 che convenne che 'l sonno si rompesse.

Non altrimenti Achille si riscosse,
 li occhi svegliati rivolgendo in giro
 e non sappiendo la` dove si fosse,

quando la madre da Chiron a Schiro
 trafuggo` lui dormendo in le sue braccia,
 la` onde poi li Greci il dipartiro;

che mi scoss'io, si` come da la faccia
 mi fuggi` 'l sonno, e diventa' ismorto,
 come fa l'uom che, spaventato, agghiaccia.

Dallato m'era solo il mio conforto,
 e 'l sole er'alto gia` piu` che due ore,
 e 'l viso m'era a la marina torto.

““Non aver tema”“, disse il mio segnore;
 ”“fatti sicur, che' noi semo a buon punto;
 non stringer, ma rallarga ogne vigore.

Tu se' omai al purgatorio giunto:
 vedi la` il balzo che 'l chiude dintorno;
 vedi l'entrata la` 've par digiunto.

Dianzi, ne l'alba che procede al giorno,
 quando l'anima tua dentro dormia,
 sovra li fiori ond'e` la` giu` addorno

venne una donna, e disse: "I' son Lucia;
 lasciatemi pigliar costui che dorme;
 si` l'agevolero` per la sua via".

Sordel rimase e l'altre genti forme;
 ella ti tolse, e come 'l di` fu chiaro,
 sen venne suso; e io per le sue orme.

Qui ti poso`, ma pria mi dimostraro
 li occhi suoi belli quella intrata aperta;
 poi ella e 'l sonno ad una se n'andaro”“.

A guisa d'uom che 'n dubbio si raccerta
 e che muta in conforto sua paura,
 poi che la verita` li e` discoperta,

Then wheeling somewhat more, it seemed to me,
 Terrible as the lightning he descended,
 And snatched me upward even to the fire.

Therein it seemed that he and I were burning,
 And the imagined fire did scorch me so,
 That of necessity my sleep was broken.

Not otherwise Achilles started up,
 Around him turning his awakened eyes,
 And knowing not the place in which he was,

What time from Chiron stealthily his mother
 Carried him sleeping in her arms to Scyros,
 Wherefrom the Greeks withdrew him afterwards,

Than I upstarted, when from off my face
 Sleep fled away; and pallid I became,
 As doth the man who freezes with affright.

Only my Comforter was at my side,
 And now the sun was more than two hours high,
 And turned towards the sea-shore was my face.

"Be not intimidated," said my Lord,
 "Be reassured, for all is well with us;
 Do not restrain, but put forth all thy strength.

Thou hast at length arrived at Purgatory;
 See there the cliff that closes it around;
 See there the entrance, where it seems disjoined.

Whilom at dawn, which doth precede the day,
 When inwardly thy spirit was asleep
 Upon the flowers that deck the land below,

There came a Lady and said: 'I am Lucia;
 Let me take this one up, who is asleep;
 So will I make his journey easier for him.'

Sordello and the other noble shapes
 Remained; she took thee, and, as day grew bright,
 Upward she came, and I upon her footsteps.

She laid thee here; and first her beauteous eyes
 That open entrance pointed out to me;
 Then she and sleep together went away."

In guise of one whose doubts are reassured,
 And who to confidence his fear doth change,
 After the truth has been discovered to him,

mi cambia' io; e come sanza cura
  vide me 'l duca mio, su per lo balzo
  si mosse, e io di rietro inver' l'altura.

Lettor, tu vedi ben com'io innalzo
  la mia matera, e pero` con piu` arte
  non ti maravigliar s'io la rincalzo.

Noi ci appressammo, ed eravamo in parte,
  che la` dove pareami prima rotto,
  pur come un fesso che muro diparte,

vidi una porta, e tre gradi di sotto
  per gire ad essa, di color diversi,
  e un portier ch'ancor non facea motto.

E come l'occhio piu` e piu` v'apersi,
  vidil seder sovra 'l grado sovrano,
  tal ne la faccia ch'io non lo soffersi;

e una spada nuda avea in mano,
  che reflettea i raggi si` ver' noi,
  ch'io drizzava spesso il viso in vano.

““Dite costinci: che volete voi?”“,
  comincio` elli a dire, ““ov'e` la scorta?
  Guardate che 'l venir su` non vi noi”“.

““Donna del ciel, di queste cose accorta”“,
  rispuose 'l mio maestro a lui, ““pur dianzi
  ne disse: "Andate la`: quivi e` la porta"”“.

““Ed ella i passi vostri in bene avanzi”“,
  ricomincio` il cortese portinaio:
  ”“Venite dunque a' nostri gradi innanzi”“.

La` ne venimmo; e lo scaglion primaio
  bianco marmo era si` pulito e terso,
  ch'io mi specchiai in esso qual io paio.

Era il secondo tinto piu` che perso,
  d'una petrina ruvida e arsiccia,
  crepata per lo lungo e per traverso.

Lo terzo, che di sopra s'ammassiccia,
  porfido mi parea, si` fiammeggiante,
  come sangue che fuor di vena spiccia.

Sovra questo tenea ambo le piante
  l'angel di Dio, sedendo in su la soglia,
  che mi sembiava pietra di diamante.

So did I change; and when without disquiet
  My Leader saw me, up along the cliff
  He moved, and I behind him, tow'rd the height.

Reader, thou seest well how I exalt
  My theme, and therefore if with greater art
  I fortify it, marvel not thereat.

Nearer approached we, and were in such place,
  That there, where first appeared to me a rift
  Like to a crevice that disparts a wall,

I saw a portal, and three stairs beneath,
  Diverse in colour, to go up to it,
  And a gate-keeper, who yet spake no word.

And as I opened more and more mine eyes,
  I saw him seated on the highest stair,
  Such in the face that I endured it not.

And in his hand he had a naked sword,
  Which so reflected back the sunbeams tow'rds us,
  That oft in vain I lifted up mine eyes.

"Tell it from where you are, what is't you wish?"
  Began he to exclaim; "where is the escort?
  Take heed your coming hither harm you not!"

"A Lady of Heaven, with these things conversant,"
  My Master answered him, "but even now
  Said to us, 'Thither go; there is the portal.'"

"And may she speed your footsteps in all good,"
  Again began the courteous janitor;
  "Come forward then unto these stairs of ours."

Thither did we approach; and the first stair
  Was marble white, so polished and so smooth,
  I mirrored myself therein as I appear.

The second, tinct of deeper hue than perse,
  Was of a calcined and uneven stone,
  Cracked all asunder lengthwise and across.

The third, that uppermost rests massively,
  Porphyry seemed to me, as flaming red
  As blood that from a vein is spirting forth.

Both of his feet was holding upon this
  The Angel of God, upon the threshold seated,
  Which seemed to me a stone of diamond.

Per li tre gradi su` di buona voglia
  mi trasse il duca mio, dicendo: ""Chiedi
  umilemente che 'l serrame scioglia"".

Divoto mi gittai a' santi piedi;
  misericordia chiesi e ch'el m'aprisse,
  ma tre volte nel petto pria mi diedi.

Sette P ne la fronte mi descrisse
  col punton de la spada, e ""Fa che lavi,
  quando se' dentro, queste piaghe"", disse.

Cenere, o terra che secca si cavi,
  d'un color fora col suo vestimento;
  e di sotto da quel trasse due chiavi.

L'una era d'oro e l'altra era d'argento;
  pria con la bianca e poscia con la gialla
  fece a la porta si`, ch'i' fu' contento.

""Quandunque l'una d'este chiavi falla,
  che non si volga dritta per la toppa"",
  diss'elli a noi, ""non s'apre questa calla.

Piu` cara e` l'una; ma l'altra vuol troppa
  d'arte e d'ingegno avanti che diserri,
  perch'ella e` quella che 'l nodo digroppa.

Da Pier le tegno; e dissemi ch'i' erri
  anzi ad aprir ch'a tenerla serrata,
  pur che la gente a' piedi mi s'atterri"".

Poi pinse l'uscio a la porta sacrata,
  dicendo: ""Intrate; ma facciovi accorti
  che di fuor torna chi 'n dietro si guata"".

E quando fuor ne' cardini distorti
  li spigoli di quella regge sacra,
  che di metallo son sonanti e forti,

non rugghio` si` ne' si mostro` si` acra
  Tarpea, come tolto le fu il buono
  Metello, per che poi rimase macra.

Io mi rivolsi attento al primo tuono,
  e 'Te Deum laudamus' mi parea
  udire in voce mista al dolce suono.

Along the three stairs upward with good will
  Did my Conductor draw me, saying: "Ask
  Humbly that he the fastening may undo."

Devoutly at the holy feet I cast me,
  For mercy's sake besought that he would open,
  But first upon my breast three times I smote.

Seven P's upon my forehead he described
  With the sword's point, and, "Take heed that thou wash
  These wounds, when thou shalt be within," he said.

Ashes, or earth that dry is excavated,
  Of the same colour were with his attire,
  And from beneath it he drew forth two keys.

One was of gold, and the other was of silver;
  First with the white, and after with the yellow,
  Plied he the door, so that I was content.

"Whenever faileth either of these keys
  So that it turn not rightly in the lock,"
  He said to us, "this entrance doth not open.

More precious one is, but the other needs
  More art and intellect ere it unlock,
  For it is that which doth the knot unloose.

From Peter I have them; and he bade me err
  Rather in opening than in keeping shut,
  If people but fall down before my feet."

Then pushed the portals of the sacred door,
  Exclaiming: "Enter; but I give you warning
  That forth returns whoever looks behind."

And when upon their hinges were turned round
  The swivels of that consecrated gate,
  Which are of metal, massive and sonorous,

Roared not so loud, nor so discordant seemed
  Tarpeia, when was ta'en from it the good
  Metellus, wherefore meagre it remained.

At the first thunder-peal I turned attentive,
  And "Te Deum laudamus" seemed to hear
  In voices mingled with sweet melody.

Tale imagine a punto mi rendea
  cio` ch'io udiva, qual prender si suole
  quando a cantar con organi si stea;

ch'or si` or no s'intendon le parole.

Exactly such an image rendered me
  That which I heard, as we are wont to catch,
  When people singing with the organ stand;

For now we hear, and now hear not, the words.

Purgatorio: Canto X

The Needle's Eye. The First Circle: The Proud.   The Sculptures on the Wall.

Poi fummo dentro al soglio de la porta
  che 'l mal amor de l'anime disusa,
  perche' fa parer dritta la via torta,
	When we had crossed the threshold of the door
	  Which the perverted love of souls disuses,
	  Because it makes the crooked way seem straight,

sonando la senti' esser richiusa;
  e s'io avesse li occhi volti ad essa,
  qual fora stata al fallo degna scusa?
	Re-echoing I heard it closed again;
	  And if I had turned back mine eyes upon it,
	  What for my failing had been fit excuse?

Noi salavam per una pietra fessa,
  che si moveva e d'una e d'altra parte,
  si` come l'onda che fugge e s'appressa.
	We mounted upward through a rifted rock,
	  Which undulated to this side and that,
	  Even as a wave receding and advancing.

""Qui si conviene usare un poco d'arte"",
  comincio` 'l duca mio, ""in accostarsi
  or quinci, or quindi al lato che si parte"".
	"Here it behoves us use a little art,"
	  Began my Leader, "to adapt ourselves
	  Now here, now there, to the receding side."

E questo fece i nostri passi scarsi,
  tanto che pria lo scemo de la luna
  rigiunse al letto suo per ricorcarsi,
	And this our footsteps so infrequent made,
	  That sooner had the moon's decreasing disk
	  Regained its bed to sink again to rest,

che noi fossimo fuor di quella cruna;
  ma quando fummo liberi e aperti
  su` dove il monte in dietro si rauna,
	Than we were forth from out that needle's eye;
	  But when we free and in the open were,
	  There where the mountain backward piles itself,

io stancato e amendue incerti
  di nostra via, restammo in su un piano
  solingo piu` che strade per diserti.
	I wearied out, and both of us uncertain
	  About our way, we stopped upon a plain
	  More desolate than roads across the deserts.

Da la sua sponda, ove confina il vano,
  al pie` de l'alta ripa che pur sale,
  misurrebbe in tre volte un corpo umano;
	From where its margin borders on the void,
	  To foot of the high bank that ever rises,
	  A human body three times told would measure;

e quanto l'occhio mio potea trar d'ale,
  or dal sinistro e or dal destro fianco,
  questa cornice mi parea cotale.
	And far as eye of mine could wing its flight,
	  Now on the left, and on the right flank now,
	  The same this cornice did appear to me.

La` su` non eran mossi i pie` nostri anco,	Thereon our feet had not been moved as yet,
quand'io conobbi quella ripa intorno	When I perceived the embankment round about,
che dritto di salita aveva manco,	Which all right of ascent had interdicted,
esser di marmo candido e addorno	To be of marble white, and so adorned
d'intagli si`, che non pur Policleto,	With sculptures, that not only Polycletus,
ma la natura li` avrebbe scorno.	But Nature's self, had there been put to shame.
L'angel che venne in terra col decreto	The Angel, who came down to earth with tidings
de la molt'anni lagrimata pace,	Of peace, that had been wept for many a year,
ch'aperse il ciel del suo lungo divieto,	And opened Heaven from its long interdict,
dinanzi a noi pareva si` verace	In front of us appeared so truthfully
quivi intagliato in un atto soave,	There sculptured in a gracious attitude,
che non sembiava imagine che tace.	He did not seem an image that is silent.
Giurato si saria ch'el dicesse 'Ave!';	One would have sworn that he was saying, "Ave;"
perche' iv'era imaginata quella	For she was there in effigy portrayed
ch'ad aprir l'alto amor volse la chiave;	Who turned the key to ope the exalted love,
e avea in atto impressa esta favella	And in her mien this language had impressed,
'Ecce ancilla Dei', propriamente	"Ecce ancilla Dei," as distinctly
come figura in cera si suggella.	As any figure stamps itself in wax.
""Non tener pur ad un loco la mente"",	"Keep not thy mind upon one place alone,"
disse 'l dolce maestro, che m'avea	The gentle Master said, who had me standing
da quella parte onde 'l cuore ha la gente.	Upon that side where people have their hearts;
Per ch'i' mi mossi col viso, e vedea	Whereat I moved mine eyes, and I beheld
di retro da Maria, da quella costa	In rear of Mary, and upon that side
onde m'era colui che mi movea,	Where he was standing who conducted me,
un'altra storia ne la roccia imposta;	Another story on the rock imposed;
per ch'io varcai Virgilio, e fe'mi presso,	Wherefore I passed Virgilius and drew near,
accio` che fosse a li occhi miei disposta.	So that before mine eyes it might be set.
Era intagliato li` nel marmo stesso	There sculptured in the self-same marble were
lo carro e ' buoi, traendo l'arca santa,	The cart and oxen, drawing the holy ark,
per che si teme officio non commesso.	Wherefore one dreads an office not appointed.
Dinanzi parea gente; e tutta quanta,	People appeared in front, and all of them
partita in sette cori, a' due mie' sensi	In seven choirs divided, of two senses
faceva dir l'un ""No"", l'altro ""Si`, canta"".	Made one say "No," the other, "Yes, they sing."
Similemente al fummo de li 'ncensi	Likewise unto the smoke of the frankincense,
che v'era imaginato, li occhi e 'l naso	Which there was imaged forth, the eyes and nose
e al si` e al no discordi fensi.	Were in the yes and no discordant made.
Li` precedeva al benedetto vaso,	Preceded there the vessel benedight,
trescando alzato, l'umile salmista,	Dancing with girded loins, the humble Psalmist,
e piu` e men che re era in quel caso.	And more and less than King was he in this.

Di contra, effigiata ad una vista
 d'un gran palazzo, Micol ammirava
 si` come donna dispettosa e trista.

I' mossi i pie` del loco dov'io stava,
 per avvisar da presso un'altra istoria,
 che di dietro a Micol mi biancheggiava.

Quiv'era storiata l'alta gloria
 del roman principato, il cui valore
 mosse Gregorio a la sua gran vittoria;

i' dico di Traiano imperadore;
 e una vedovella li era al freno,
 di lagrime atteggiata e di dolore.

Intorno a lui parea calcato e pieno
 di cavalieri, e l'aguglie ne l'oro
 sovr'essi in vista al vento si movieno.

La miserella intra tutti costoro
 pareva dir: ““Segnor, fammi vendetta
 di mio figliuol ch'e` morto, ond'io m'accoro”“;

ed elli a lei rispondere: ““Or aspetta
 tanto ch'i' torni”“; e quella: ““Segnor mio”“,
 come persona in cui dolor s'affretta,

““se tu non torni?”“; ed ei: ““Chi fia dov'io,
 la ti fara`”“; ed ella: ““L'altrui bene
 a te che fia, se 'l tuo metti in oblio?”“;

ond'elli: ““Or ti conforta; ch'ei convene
 ch'i' solva il mio dovere anzi ch'i' mova:
 giustizia vuole e pieta` mi ritene”“.

Colui che mai non vide cosa nova
 produsse esto visibile parlare,
 novello a noi perche' qui non si trova.

Mentr'io mi dilettava di guardare
 l'imagini di tante umilitadi,
 e per lo fabbro loro a veder care,

““Ecco di qua, ma fanno i passi radi”“,
 mormorava il poeta, ““molte genti:
 questi ne 'nvieranno a li alti gradi”“.

Li occhi miei ch'a mirare eran contenti
 per veder novitadi ond'e' son vaghi,
 volgendosi ver' lui non furon lenti.

Opposite, represented at the window
 Of a great palace, Michal looked upon him,
 Even as a woman scornful and afflicted.

I moved my feet from where I had been standing,
 To examine near at hand another story,
 Which after Michal glimmered white upon me.

There the high glory of the Roman Prince
 Was chronicled, whose great beneficence
 Moved Gregory to his great victory;

'Tis of the Emperor Trajan I am speaking;
 And a poor widow at his bridle stood,
 In attitude of weeping and of grief.

Around about him seemed it thronged and full
 Of cavaliers, and the eagles in the gold
 Above them visibly in the wind were moving.

The wretched woman in the midst of these
 Seemed to be saying: "Give me vengeance, Lord,
 For my dead son, for whom my heart is breaking."

And he to answer her: "Now wait until
 I shall return." And she: "My Lord," like one
 In whom grief is impatient, "shouldst thou not

Return?" And he: "Who shall be where I am
 Will give it thee." And she: "Good deed of others
 What boots it thee, if thou neglect thine own?"

Whence he: "Now comfort thee, for it behoves me
 That I discharge my duty ere I move;
 Justice so wills, and pity doth retain me."

He who on no new thing has ever looked
 Was the creator of this visible language,
 Novel to us, for here it is not found.

While I delighted me in contemplating
 The images of such humility,
 And dear to look on for their Maker's sake,

"Behold, upon this side, but rare they make
 Their steps," the Poet murmured, "many people;
 These will direct us to the lofty stairs."

Mine eyes, that in beholding were intent
 To see new things, of which they curious are,
 In turning round towards him were not slow.

Non vo' pero`, lettor, che tu ti smaghi
  di buon proponimento per udire
  come Dio vuol che 'l debito si paghi.

Non attender la forma del martire:
  pensa la succession; pensa ch'al peggio,
  oltre la gran sentenza non puo` ire.

Io cominciai: ""Maestro, quel ch'io veggio
  muovere a noi, non mi sembian persone,
  e non so che, si` nel veder vaneggio"".

Ed elli a me: ""La grave condizione
  di lor tormento a terra li rannicchia,
  si` che ' miei occhi pria n'ebber tencione.

Ma guarda fiso la`, e disviticchia
  col viso quel che vien sotto a quei sassi:
  gia` scorger puoi come ciascun si picchia"".

O superbi cristian, miseri lassi,
  che, de la vista de la mente infermi,
  fidanza avete ne' retrosi passi,

non v'accorgete voi che noi siam vermi
  nati a formar l'angelica farfalla,
  che vola a la giustizia sanza schermi?

Di che l'animo vostro in alto galla,
  poi siete quasi antomata in difetto,
  si` come vermo in cui formazion falla?

Come per sostentar solaio o tetto,
  per mensola talvolta una figura
  si vede giugner le ginocchia al petto,

la qual fa del non ver vera rancura
  nascere 'n chi la vede; cosi` fatti
  vid'io color, quando puosi ben cura.

Vero e` che piu` e meno eran contratti
  secondo ch'avien piu` e meno a dosso;
  e qual piu` pazienza avea ne li atti,

piangendo parea dicer: 'Piu` non posso'.

But still I wish not, Reader, thou shouldst swerve
  From thy good purposes, because thou hearest
  How God ordaineth that the debt be paid;

Attend not to the fashion of the torment,
  Think of what follows; think that at the worst
  It cannot reach beyond the mighty sentence.

"Master," began I, "that which I behold
  Moving towards us seems to me not persons,
  And what I know not, so in sight I waver."

And he to me: "The grievous quality
  Of this their torment bows them so to earth,
  That my own eyes at first contended with it;

But look there fixedly, and disentangle
  By sight what cometh underneath those stones;
  Already canst thou see how each is stricken."

O ye proud Christians! wretched, weary ones!
  Who, in the vision of the mind infirm
  Confidence have in your backsliding steps,

Do ye not comprehend that we are worms,
  Born to bring forth the angelic butterfly
  That flieth unto judgment without screen?

Why floats aloft your spirit high in air?
  Like are ye unto insects undeveloped,
  Even as the worm in whom formation fails!

As to sustain a ceiling or a roof,
  In place of corbel, oftentimes a figure
  Is seen to join its knees unto its breast,

Which makes of the unreal real anguish
  Arise in him who sees it, fashioned thus
  Beheld I those, when I had ta'en good heed.

True is it, they were more or less bent down,
  According as they more or less were laden;
  And he who had most patience in his looks

Weeping did seem to say, "I can no more!"

199

Purgatorio: Canto XI

The Humble Prayer. Omberto di Santafiore. Oderisi d' Agobbio. Provenzan Salvani.

““O Padre nostro, che ne' cieli stai,
  non circunscritto, ma per piu` amore
  ch'ai primi effetti di la` su` tu hai,

laudato sia 'l tuo nome e 'l tuo valore
  da ogni creatura, com'e` degno
  di render grazie al tuo dolce vapore.

Vegna ver' noi la pace del tuo regno,
  che' noi ad essa non potem da noi,
  s'ella non vien, con tutto nostro ingegno.

Come del suo voler li angeli tuoi
  fan sacrificio a te, cantando osanna,
  cosi` facciano li uomini de' suoi.

Da` oggi a noi la cotidiana manna,
  sanza la qual per questo aspro diserto
  a retro va chi piu` di gir s'affanna.

E come noi lo mal ch'avem sofferto
  perdoniamo a ciascuno, e tu perdona
  benigno, e non guardar lo nostro merto.

Nostra virtu` che di legger s'adona,
  non spermentar con l'antico avversaro,
  ma libera da lui che si` la sprona.

Quest'ultima preghiera, segnor caro,
  gia` non si fa per noi, che' non bisogna,
  ma per color che dietro a noi restaro”“.

Cosi` a se' e noi buona ramogna
  quell'ombre orando, andavan sotto 'l pondo,
  simile a quel che tal volta si sogna,

"Our Father, thou who dwellest in the heavens,
  Not circumscribed, but from the greater love
  Thou bearest to the first effects on high,

Praised be thy name and thine omnipotence
  By every creature, as befitting is
  To render thanks to thy sweet effluence.

Come unto us the peace of thy dominion,
  For unto it we cannot of ourselves,
  If it come not, with all our intellect.

Even as thine own Angels of their will
  Make sacrifice to thee, Hosanna singing,
  So may all men make sacrifice of theirs.

Give unto us this day our daily manna,
  Withouten which in this rough wilderness
  Backward goes he who toils most to advance.

And even as we the trespass we have suffered
  Pardon in one another, pardon thou
  Benignly, and regard not our desert.

Our virtue, which is easily o'ercome,
  Put not to proof with the old Adversary,
  But thou from him who spurs it so, deliver.

This last petition verily, dear Lord,
  Not for ourselves is made, who need it not,
  But for their sake who have remained behind us."

Thus for themselves and us good furtherance
  Those shades imploring, went beneath a weight
  Like unto that of which we sometimes dream,

disparmente angosciate tutte a tondo
  e lasse su per la prima cornice,
  purgando la caligine del mondo.

Se di la` sempre ben per noi si dice,
  di qua che dire e far per lor si puote
  da quei ch'hanno al voler buona radice?

Ben si de' loro atar lavar le note
  che portar quinci, si` che, mondi e lievi,
  possano uscire a le stellate ruote.

““Deh, se giustizia e pieta` vi disgrievi
  tosto, si` che possiate muover l'ala,
  che secondo il disio vostro vi lievi,

mostrate da qual mano inver' la scala
  si va piu` corto; e se c'e` piu` d'un varco,
  quel ne 'nsegnate che men erto cala;

che' questi che vien meco, per lo 'ncarco
  de la carne d'Adamo onde si veste,
  al montar su`, contra sua voglia, e` parco”“.

Le lor parole, che rendero a queste
  che dette avea colui cu' io seguiva,
  non fur da cui venisser manifeste;

ma fu detto: ““A man destra per la riva
  con noi venite, e troverete il passo
  possibile a salir persona viva.

E s'io non fossi impedito dal sasso
  che la cervice mia superba doma,
  onde portar convienmi il viso basso,

cotesti, ch'ancor vive e non si noma,
  guardere' io, per veder s'i' 'l conosco,
  e per farlo pietoso a questa soma.

Io fui latino e nato d'un gran Tosco:
  Guiglielmo Aldobrandesco fu mio padre;
  non so se 'l nome suo gia` mai fu vosco.

L'antico sangue e l'opere leggiadre
  d'i miei maggior mi fer si` arrogante,
  che, non pensando a la comune madre,

ogn'uomo ebbi in despetto tanto avante,
  ch'io ne mori', come i Sanesi sanno
  e sallo in Campagnatico ogne fante.

Unequally in anguish round and round
  And weary all, upon that foremost cornice,
  Purging away the smoke-stains of the world.

If there good words are always said for us,
  What may not here be said and done for them,
  By those who have a good root to their will?

Well may we help them wash away the marks
  That hence they carried, so that clean and light
  They may ascend unto the starry wheels!

"Ah! so may pity and justice you disburden
  Soon, that ye may have power to move the wing,
  That shall uplift you after your desire,

Show us on which hand tow'rd the stairs the way
  Is shortest, and if more than one the passes,
  Point us out that which least abruptly falls;

For he who cometh with me, through the burden
  Of Adam's flesh wherewith he is invested,
  Against his will is chary of his climbing."

The words of theirs which they returned to those
  That he whom I was following had spoken,
  It was not manifest from whom they came,

But it was said: "To the right hand come with us
  Along the bank, and ye shall find a pass
  Possible for living person to ascend.

And were I not impeded by the stone,
  Which this proud neck of mine doth subjugate,
  Whence I am forced to hold my visage down,

Him, who still lives and does not name himself,
  Would I regard, to see if I may know him
  And make him piteous unto this burden.

A Latian was I, and born of a great Tuscan;
  Guglielmo Aldobrandeschi was my father;
  I know not if his name were ever with you.

The ancient blood and deeds of gallantry
  Of my progenitors so arrogant made me
  That, thinking not upon the common mother,

All men I held in scorn to such extent
  I died therefor, as know the Sienese,
  And every child in Campagnatico.

Io sono Omberto; e non pur a me danno
  superbia fa, che' tutti miei consorti
  ha ella tratti seco nel malanno.

E qui convien ch'io questo peso porti
  per lei, tanto che a Dio si sodisfaccia,
  poi ch'io nol fe' tra ' vivi, qui tra ' morti"".

Ascoltando chinai in giu` la faccia;
  e un di lor, non questi che parlava,
  si torse sotto il peso che li 'mpaccia,

e videmi e conobbemi e chiamava,
  tenendo li occhi con fatica fisi
  a me che tutto chin con loro andava.

""Oh!"", diss'io lui, ""non se' tu Oderisi,
  l'onor d'Agobbio e l'onor di quell'arte
  ch'alluminar chiamata e` in Parisi?"".

""Frate"", diss'elli, ""piu` ridon le carte
  che pennelleggia Franco Bolognese;
  l'onore e` tutto or suo, e mio in parte.

Ben non sare' io stato si` cortese
  mentre ch'io vissi, per lo gran disio
  de l'eccellenza ove mio core intese.

Di tal superbia qui si paga il fio;
  e ancor non sarei qui, se non fosse
  che, possendo peccar, mi volsi a Dio.

Oh vana gloria de l'umane posse!
  com'poco verde in su la cima dura,
  se non e` giunta da l'etati grosse!

Credette Cimabue ne la pittura
  tener lo campo, e ora ha Giotto il grido,
  si` che la fama di colui e` scura:

cosi` ha tolto l'uno a l'altro Guido
  la gloria de la lingua; e forse e` nato
  chi l'uno e l'altro caccera` del nido.

Non e` il mondan romore altro ch'un fiato
  di vento, ch'or vien quinci e or vien quindi,
  e muta nome perche' muta lato.

I am Omberto; and not to me alone
  Has pride done harm, but all my kith and kin
  Has with it dragged into adversity.

And here must I this burden bear for it
  Till God be satisfied, since I did not
  Among the living, here among the dead."

Listening I downward bent my countenance;
  And one of them, not this one who was speaking,
  Twisted himself beneath the weight that cramps
      him,

And looked at me, and knew me, and called out,
  Keeping his eyes laboriously fixed
  On me, who all bowed down was going with them.

"O," asked I him, "art thou not Oderisi,
  Agobbio's honour, and honour of that art
  Which is in Paris called illuminating?"

"Brother," said he, "more laughing are the leaves
  Touched by the brush of Franco Bolognese;
  All his the honour now, and mine in part.

In sooth I had not been so courteous
  While I was living, for the great desire
  Of excellence, on which my heart was bent.

Here of such pride is paid the forfeiture;
  And yet I should not be here, were it not
  That, having power to sin, I turned to God.

O thou vain glory of the human powers,
  How little green upon thy summit lingers,
  If't be not followed by an age of grossness!

In painting Cimabue thought that he
  Should hold the field, now Giotto has the cry,
  So that the other's fame is growing dim.

So has one Guido from the other taken
  The glory of our tongue, and he perchance
  Is born, who from the nest shall chase them both.

Naught is this mundane rumour but a breath
  Of wind, that comes now this way and now that,
  And changes name, because it changes side.

Che voce avrai tu piu`, se vecchia scindi
  da te la carne, che se fossi morto
  anzi che tu lasciassi il 'pappo' e 'l 'dindi',

pria che passin mill'anni? ch'e` piu` corto
  spazio a l'etterno, ch'un muover di ciglia
  al cerchio che piu` tardi in cielo e` torto.

Colui che del cammin si` poco piglia
  dinanzi a me, Toscana sonò tutta;
  e ora a pena in Siena sen pispiglia,

ond'era sire quando fu distrutta
  la rabbia fiorentina, che superba
  fu a quel tempo si` com'ora e` putta.

La vostra nominanza e` color d'erba,
  che viene e va, e quei la discolora
  per cui ella esce de la terra acerba"".

E io a lui: ""Tuo vero dir m'incora
  bona umilta`, e gran tumor m'appiani;
  ma chi e` quei di cui tu parlavi ora?"".

""Quelli e`"", rispuose, ""Provenzan Salvani;
  ed e` qui perche' fu presuntuoso
  a recar Siena tutta a le sue mani.

Ito e` cosi` e va, sanza riposo,
  poi che mori`; cotal moneta rende
  a sodisfar chi e` di la` troppo oso"".

E io: ""Se quello spirito ch'attende,
  pria che si penta, l'orlo de la vita,
  qua giu` dimora e qua su` non ascende,

se buona orazion lui non aita,
  prima che passi tempo quanto visse,
  come fu la venuta lui largita?"".

""Quando vivea piu` glorioso"", disse,
  ""liberamente nel Campo di Siena,
  ogne vergogna diposta, s'affisse;

e li`, per trar l'amico suo di pena
  ch'e' sostenea ne la prigion di Carlo,
  si condusse a tremar per ogne vena.

Piu` non diro`, e scuro so che parlo;
  ma poco tempo andra`, che ' tuoi vicini
  faranno si` che tu potrai chiosarlo.

What fame shalt thou have more, if old peel off
  From thee thy flesh, than if thou hadst been dead
  Before thou left the 'pappo' and the 'dindi,'

Ere pass a thousand years? which is a shorter
  Space to the eterne, than twinkling of an eye
  Unto the circle that in heaven wheels slowest.

With him, who takes so little of the road
  In front of me, all Tuscany resounded;
  And now he scarce is lisped of in Siena,

Where he was lord, what time was overthrown
  The Florentine delirium, that superb
  Was at that day as now 'tis prostitute.

Your reputation is the colour of grass
  Which comes and goes, and that discolours it
  By which it issues green from out the earth."

And I: "Thy true speech fills my heart with good
  Humility, and great tumour thou assuagest;
  But who is he, of whom just now thou spakest?"

"That," he replied, "is Provenzan Salvani,
  And he is here because he had presumed
  To bring Siena all into his hands.

He has gone thus, and goeth without rest
  E'er since he died; such money renders back
  In payment he who is on earth too daring."

And I: "If every spirit who awaits
  The verge of life before that he repent,
  Remains below there and ascends not hither,

(Unless good orison shall him bestead,)
  Until as much time as he lived be passed,
  How was the coming granted him in largess?"

"When he in greatest splendour lived," said he,
  "Freely upon the Campo of Siena,
  All shame being laid aside, he placed himself;

And there to draw his friend from the duress
  Which in the prison-house of Charles he suffered,
  He brought himself to tremble in each vein.

I say no more, and know that I speak darkly;
  Yet little time shall pass before thy neighbours
  Will so demean themselves that thou canst gloss it.

Quest'opera li tolse quei confini"".

This action has released him from those confines."

Purgatorio: Canto XII

The Sculptures on the Pavement. Ascent to the Second Circle.

Di pari, come buoi che vanno a giogo,
  m'andava io con quell'anima carca,
  fin che 'l sofferse il dolce pedagogo.

Ma quando disse: ""Lascia lui e varca;
  che' qui e` buono con l'ali e coi remi,
  quantunque puo`, ciascun pinger sua barca"";

dritto si` come andar vuolsi rife'mi
  con la persona, avvegna che i pensieri
  mi rimanessero e chinati e scemi.

Io m'era mosso, e seguia volontieri
  del mio maestro i passi, e amendue
  gia` mostravam com'eravam leggeri;

ed el mi disse: ""Volgi li occhi in giue:
  buon ti sara`, per tranquillar la via,
  veder lo letto de le piante tue"".

Come, perche' di lor memoria sia,
  sovra i sepolti le tombe terragne
  portan segnato quel ch'elli eran pria,

onde li` molte volte si ripiagne
  per la puntura de la rimembranza,
  che solo a' pii da` de le calcagne;

si` vid'io li`, ma di miglior sembianza
  secondo l'artificio, figurato
  quanto per via di fuor del monte avanza.

Vedea colui che fu nobil creato
  piu` ch'altra creatura, giu` dal cielo
  folgoreggiando scender, da l'un lato.

Abreast, like oxen going in a yoke,
  I with that heavy-laden soul went on,
  As long as the sweet pedagogue permitted;

But when he said, "Leave him, and onward pass,
  For here 'tis good that with the sail and oars,
  As much as may be, each push on his barque;"

Upright, as walking wills it, I redressed
  My person, notwithstanding that my thoughts
  Remained within me downcast and abashed.

I had moved on, and followed willingly
  The footsteps of my Master, and we both
  Already showed how light of foot we were,

When unto me he said: "Cast down thine eyes;
  'Twere well for thee, to alleviate the way,
  To look upon the bed beneath thy feet."

As, that some memory may exist of them,
  Above the buried dead their tombs in earth
  Bear sculptured on them what they were before;

Whence often there we weep for them afresh,
  From pricking of remembrance, which alone
  To the compassionate doth set its spur;

So saw I there, but of a better semblance
  In point of artifice, with figures covered
  Whate'er as pathway from the mount projects.

I saw that one who was created noble
  More than all other creatures, down from heaven
  Flaming with lightnings fall upon one side.

La Divina Commedia - The Divine Comedy

Vedea Briareo, fitto dal telo
celestial giacer, da l'altra parte,
grave a la terra per lo mortal gelo.

Vedea Timbreo, vedea Pallade e Marte,
armati ancora, intorno al padre loro,
mirar le membra d'i Giganti sparte.

Vedea Nembrot a pie` del gran lavoro
quasi smarrito, e riguardar le genti
che 'n Sennaar con lui superbi fuoro.

O Niobe`, con che occhi dolenti
vedea io te segnata in su la strada,
tra sette e sette tuoi figliuoli spenti!

O Saul, come in su la propria spada
quivi parevi morto in Gelboe`,
che poi non senti` pioggia ne' rugiada!

O folle Aragne, si` vedea io te
gia` mezza ragna, trista in su li stracci
de l'opera che mal per te si fe'.

O Roboam, gia` non par che minacci
quivi 'l tuo segno; ma pien di spavento
nel porta un carro, sanza ch'altri il cacci.

Mostrava ancor lo duro pavimento
come Almeon a sua madre fe' caro
parer lo sventurato addornamento.

Mostrava come i figli si gittaro
sovra Sennacherib dentro dal tempio,
e come, morto lui, quivi il lasciaro.

Mostrava la ruina e 'l crudo scempio
che fe' Tamiri, quando disse a Ciro:
'"'Sangue sitisti, e io di sangue t'empio'"'.

Mostrava come in rotta si fuggiro
li Assiri, poi che fu morto Oloferne,
e anche le reliquie del martiro.

Vedeva Troia in cenere e in caverne;
o Ilion, come te basso e vile
mostrava il segno che li` si discerne!

I saw Briareus smitten by the dart
Celestial, lying on the other side,
Heavy upon the earth by mortal frost.

I saw Thymbraeus, Pallas saw, and Mars,
Still clad in armour round about their father,
Gaze at the scattered members of the giants.

I saw, at foot of his great labour, Nimrod,
As if bewildered, looking at the people
Who had been proud with him in Sennaar.

O Niobe! with what afflicted eyes
Thee I beheld upon the pathway traced,
Between thy seven and seven children slain!

O Saul! how fallen upon thy proper sword
Didst thou appear there lifeless in Gilboa,
That felt thereafter neither rain nor dew!

O mad Arachne! so I thee beheld
E'en then half spider, sad upon the shreds
Of fabric wrought in evil hour for thee!

O Rehoboam! no more seems to threaten
Thine image there; but full of consternation
A chariot bears it off, when none pursues!

Displayed moreo'er the adamantine pavement
How unto his own mother made Alcmaeon
Costly appear the luckless ornament;

Displayed how his own sons did throw themselves
Upon Sennacherib within the temple,
And how, he being dead, they left him there;

Displayed the ruin and the cruel carnage
That Tomyris wrought, when she to Cyrus said,
"Blood didst thou thirst for, and with blood I glut
thee!"

Displayed how routed fled the Assyrians
After that Holofernes had been slain,
And likewise the remainder of that slaughter.

I saw there Troy in ashes and in caverns;
O Ilion! thee, how abject and debased,
Displayed the image that is there discerned!

Qual di pennel fu maestro o di stile
  che ritraesse l'ombre e ' tratti ch'ivi
  mirar farieno uno ingegno sottile?

Morti li morti e i vivi parean vivi:
  non vide mei di me chi vide il vero,
  quant'io calcai, fin che chinato givi.

Or superbite, e via col viso altero,
  figliuoli d'Eva, e non chinate il volto
  si` che veggiate il vostro mal sentero!

Piu` era gia` per noi del monte volto
  e del cammin del sole assai piu` speso
  che non stimava l'animo non sciolto,

quando colui che sempre innanzi atteso
  andava, comincio`: ""Drizza la testa;
  non e` piu` tempo di gir si` sospeso.

Vedi cola` un angel che s'appresta
  per venir verso noi; vedi che torna
  dal servigio del di` l'ancella sesta.

Di reverenza il viso e li atti addorna,
  si` che i diletti lo 'nviarci in suso;
  pensa che questo di` mai non raggiorna!"".

Io era ben del suo ammonir uso
  pur di non perder tempo, si` che 'n quella
  materia non potea parlarmi chiuso.

A noi venia la creatura bella,
  biancovestito e ne la faccia quale
  par tremolando mattutina stella.

Le braccia aperse, e indi aperse l'ale;
  disse: ""Venite: qui son presso i gradi,
  e agevolemente omai si sale.

A questo invito vegnon molto radi:
  o gente umana, per volar su` nata,
  perche' a poco vento cosi` cadi?"".

Menocci ove la roccia era tagliata;
  quivi mi batte' l'ali per la fronte;
  poi mi promise sicura l'andata.

Come a man destra, per salire al monte
  dove siede la chiesa che soggioga
  la ben guidata sopra Rubaconte,

Whoe'er of pencil master was or stile,
  That could portray the shades and traits which there
  Would cause each subtile genius to admire?

Dead seemed the dead, the living seemed alive;
  Better than I saw not who saw the truth,
  All that I trod upon while bowed I went.

Now wax ye proud, and on with looks uplifted,
  Ye sons of Eve, and bow not down your faces
  So that ye may behold your evil ways!

More of the mount by us was now encompassed,
  And far more spent the circuit of the sun,
  Than had the mind preoccupied imagined,

When he, who ever watchful in advance
  Was going on, began: "Lift up thy head,
  'Tis no more time to go thus meditating.

Lo there an Angel who is making haste
  To come towards us; lo, returning is
  From service of the day the sixth handmaiden.

With reverence thine acts and looks adorn,
  So that he may delight to speed us upward;
  Think that this day will never dawn again."

I was familiar with his admonition
  Ever to lose no time; so on this theme
  He could not unto me speak covertly.

Towards us came the being beautiful
  Vested in white, and in his countenance
  Such as appears the tremulous morning star.

His arms he opened, and opened then his wings;
  "Come," said he, "near at hand here are the steps,
  And easy from henceforth is the ascent."

At this announcement few are they who come!
  O human creatures, born to soar aloft,
  Why fall ye thus before a little wind?

He led us on to where the rock was cleft;
  There smote upon my forehead with his wings,
  Then a safe passage promised unto me.

As on the right hand, to ascend the mount
  Where seated is the church that lordeth it
  O'er the well-guided, above Rubaconte,

si rompe del montar l'ardita foga
  per le scalee che si fero ad etade
  ch'era sicuro il quaderno e la doga;

cosi` s'allenta la ripa che cade
  quivi ben ratta da l'altro girone;
  ma quinci e quindi l'alta pietra rade.

Noi volgendo ivi le nostre persone,
  'Beati pauperes spiritu!' voci
  cantaron si`, che nol diria sermone.

Ahi quanto son diverse quelle foci
  da l'infernali! che' quivi per canti
  s'entra, e la` giu` per lamenti feroci.

Gia` montavam su per li scaglion santi,
  ed esser mi parea troppo piu` lieve
  che per lo pian non mi parea davanti.

Ond'io: ““Maestro, di`, qual cosa greve
  levata s'e` da me, che nulla quasi
  per me fatica, andando, si riceve?”“.

Rispuose: ““Quando i P che son rimasi
  ancor nel volto tuo presso che stinti,
  saranno, com'e` l'un, del tutto rasi,

fier li tuoi pie` dal buon voler si` vinti,
  che non pur non fatica sentiranno,
  ma fia diletto loro esser su` pinti”“.

Allor fec'io come color che vanno
  con cosa in capo non da lor saputa,
  se non che ' cenni altrui sospecciar fanno;

per che la mano ad accertar s'aiuta,
  e cerca e truova e quello officio adempie
  che non si puo` fornir per la veduta;

e con le dita de la destra scempie
  trovai pur sei le lettere che 'ncise
  quel da le chiavi a me sovra le tempie:

a che guardando, il mio duca sorrise.

The bold abruptness of the ascent is broken
  By stairways that were made there in the age
  When still were safe the ledger and the stave,

E'en thus attempered is the bank which falls
  Sheer downward from the second circle there;
  But on this, side and that the high rock graze.

As we were turning thitherward our persons,
  "Beati pauperes spiritu," voices
  Sang in such wise that speech could tell it not.

Ah me! how different are these entrances
  From the Infernal! for with anthems here
  One enters, and below with wild laments.

We now were hunting up the sacred stairs,
  And it appeared to me by far more easy
  Than on the plain it had appeared before.

Whence I: "My Master, say, what heavy thing
  Has been uplifted from me, so that hardly
  Aught of fatigue is felt by me in walking?"

He answered: "When the P's which have remained
  Still on thy face almost obliterate
  Shall wholly, as the first is, be erased,

Thy feet will be so vanquished by good will,
  That not alone they shall not feel fatigue,
  But urging up will be to them delight."

Then did I even as they do who are going
  With something on the head to them unknown,
  Unless the signs of others make them doubt,

Wherefore the hand to ascertain is helpful,
  And seeks and finds, and doth fulfill the office
  Which cannot be accomplished by the sight;

And with the fingers of the right hand spread
  I found but six the letters, that had carved
  Upon my temples he who bore the keys;

Upon beholding which my Leader smiled.

Purgatorio: Canto XIII

The Second Circle: The Envious. Sapia of Siena.

Noi eravamo al sommo de la scala,
  dove secondamente si risega
  lo monte che salendo altrui dismala.

Ivi cosi` una cornice lega
  dintorno il poggio, come la primaia;
  se non che l'arco suo piu` tosto piega.

Ombra non li` e` ne' segno che si paia:
  parsi la ripa e parsi la via schietta
  col livido color de la petraia.

""Se qui per dimandar gente s'aspetta"",
  ragionava il poeta, ""io temo forse
  che troppo avra` d'indugio nostra eletta"".

Poi fisamente al sole li occhi porse;
  fece del destro lato a muover centro,
  e la sinistra parte di se' torse.

""O dolce lume a cui fidanza i' entro
  per lo novo cammin, tu ne conduci"",
  dicea, ""come condur si vuol quinc'entro.

Tu scaldi il mondo, tu sovr'esso luci;
  s'altra ragione in contrario non ponta,
  esser dien sempre li tuoi raggi duci"".

Quanto di qua per un migliaio si conta,
  tanto di la` eravam noi gia` iti,
  con poco tempo, per la voglia pronta;

e verso noi volar furon sentiti,
  non pero` visti, spiriti parlando
  a la mensa d'amor cortesi inviti.

We were upon the summit of the stairs,
  Where for the second time is cut away
  The mountain, which ascending shriveth all.

There in like manner doth a cornice bind
  The hill all round about, as does the first,
  Save that its arc more suddenly is curved.

Shade is there none, nor sculpture that appears;
  So seems the bank, and so the road seems smooth,
  With but the livid colour of the stone.

"If to inquire we wait for people here,"
  The Poet said, "I fear that peradventure
  Too much delay will our election have."

Then steadfast on the sun his eyes he fixed,
  Made his right side the centre of his motion,
  And turned the left part of himself about.

"O thou sweet light! with trust in whom I enter
  Upon this novel journey, do thou lead us,"
  Said he, "as one within here should be led.

Thou warmest the world, thou shinest over it;
  If other reason prompt not otherwise,
  Thy rays should evermore our leaders be!"

As much as here is counted for a mile,
  So much already there had we advanced
  In little time, by dint of ready will;

And tow'rds us there were heard to fly, albeit
  They were not visible, spirits uttering
  Unto Love's table courteous invitations,

La prima voce che passo` volando
  'Vinum non habent' altamente disse,
  e dietro a noi l'ando` reiterando.

E prima che del tutto non si udisse
  per allungarsi, un'altra 'I' sono Oreste'
  passo` gridando, e anco non s'affisse.

““Oh!”“, diss'io, ““padre, che voci son queste?”“.
  E com'io domandai, ecco la terza
  dicendo: 'Amate da cui male aveste'.

E 'l buon maestro: ““Questo cinghio sferza
  la colpa de la invidia, e pero` sono
  tratte d'amor le corde de la ferza.

Lo fren vuol esser del contrario suono;
  credo che l'udirai, per mio avviso,
  prima che giunghi al passo del perdono.

Ma ficca li occhi per l'aere ben fiso,
  e vedrai gente innanzi a noi sedersi,
  e ciascun e` lungo la grotta assiso”“.

Allora piu` che prima li occhi apersi;
  guarda'mi innanzi, e vidi ombre con manti
  al color de la pietra non diversi.

E poi che fummo un poco piu` avanti,
  udia gridar: 'Maria, ora per noi':
  gridar 'Michele' e 'Pietro', e 'Tutti santi'.

Non credo che per terra vada ancoi
  omo si` duro, che non fosse punto
  per compassion di quel ch'i' vidi poi;

che', quando fui si` presso di lor giunto,
  che li atti loro a me venivan certi,
  per li occhi fui di grave dolor munto.

Di vil ciliccio mi parean coperti,
  e l'un sofferia l'altro con la spalla,
  e tutti da la ripa eran sofferti.

Cosi` li ciechi a cui la roba falla
  stanno a' perdoni a chieder lor bisogna,
  e l'uno il capo sopra l'altro avvalla,

perche' 'n altrui pieta` tosto si pogna,
  non pur per lo sonar de le parole,
  ma per la vista che non meno agogna.

The first voice that passed onward in its flight,
  "Vinum non habent," said in accents loud,
  And went reiterating it behind us.

And ere it wholly grew inaudible
  Because of distance, passed another, crying,
  "I am Orestes!" and it also stayed not.

"O," said I, "Father, these, what voices are they?"
  And even as I asked, behold the third,
  Saying: "Love those from whom ye have had evil!"

And the good Master said: "This circle scourges
  The sin of envy, and on that account
  Are drawn from love the lashes of the scourge.

The bridle of another sound shall be;
  I think that thou wilt hear it, as I judge,
  Before thou comest to the Pass of Pardon.

But fix thine eyes athwart the air right steadfast,
  And people thou wilt see before us sitting,
  And each one close against the cliff is seated."

Then wider than at first mine eyes I opened;
  I looked before me, and saw shades with mantles
  Not from the colour of the stone diverse.

And when we were a little farther onward,
  I heard a cry of, "Mary, pray for us!"
  A cry of, "Michael, Peter, and all Saints!"

I do not think there walketh still on earth
  A man so hard, that he would not be pierced
  With pity at what afterward I saw.

For when I had approached so near to them
  That manifest to me their acts became,
  Drained was I at the eyes by heavy grief.

Covered with sackcloth vile they seemed to me,
  And one sustained the other with his shoulder,
  And all of them were by the bank sustained.

Thus do the blind, in want of livelihood,
  Stand at the doors of churches asking alms,
  And one upon another leans his head,

So that in others pity soon may rise,
  Not only at the accent of their words,
  But at their aspect, which no less implores.

E come a li orbi non approda il sole,
  così a l'ombre quivi, ond'io parlo ora,
  luce del ciel di sé largir non vole;

che' a tutti un fil di ferro i cigli fora
  e cusce sì, come a sparvier selvaggio
  si fa però che queto non dimora.

A me pareva, andando, fare oltraggio,
  veggendo altrui, non essendo veduto:
  per ch'io mi volsi al mio consiglio saggio.

Ben sapev'ei che volea dir lo muto;
  e però non attese mia dimanda,
  ma disse: ""Parla, e sie breve e arguto"".

Virgilio mi venia da quella banda
  de la cornice onde cader si puote,
  perche' da nulla sponda s'inghirlanda;

da l'altra parte m'eran le divote
  ombre, che per l'orribile costura
  premevan sì, che bagnavan le gote.

Volsimi a loro e ""O gente sicura"",
  incominciai, ""di veder l'alto lume
  che 'l disio vostro solo ha in sua cura,

se tosto grazia resolva le schiume
  di vostra coscienza sì che chiaro
  per essa scenda de la mente il fiume,

ditemi, che' mi fia grazioso e caro,
  s'anima è qui tra voi che sia latina;
  e forse lei sarà buon s'i' l'apparo"".

""O frate mio, ciascuna è cittadina
  d'una vera città; ma tu vuo' dire
  che vivesse in Italia peregrina"".

Questo mi parve per risposta udire
  più innanzi alquanto che là dov'io stava,
  ond'io mi feci ancor più là sentire.

Tra l'altre vidi un'ombra ch'aspettava
  in vista; e se volesse alcun dir 'Come?',
  lo mento a guisa d'orbo in su levava.

And as unto the blind the sun comes not,
  So to the shades, of whom just now I spake,
  Heaven's light will not be bounteous of itself;

For all their lids an iron wire transpierces,
  And sews them up, as to a sparhawk wild
  Is done, because it will not quiet stay.

To me it seemed, in passing, to do outrage,
  Seeing the others without being seen;
  Wherefore I turned me to my counsel sage.

Well knew he what the mute one wished to say,
  And therefore waited not for my demand,
  But said: "Speak, and be brief, and to the point."

I had Virgilius upon that side
  Of the embankment from which one may fall,
  Since by no border 'tis engarlanded;

Upon the other side of me I had
  The shades devout, who through the horrible seam
  Pressed out the tears so that they bathed their
    cheeks.

To them I turned me, and, "O people, certain,"
  Began I, "of beholding the high light,
  Which your desire has solely in its care,

So may grace speedily dissolve the scum
  Upon your consciences, that limpidly
  Through them descend the river of the mind,

Tell me, for dear 'twill be to me and gracious,
  If any soul among you here is Latian,
  And 'twill perchance be good for him I learn it."

"O brother mine, each one is citizen
  Of one true city; but thy meaning is,
  Who may have lived in Italy a pilgrim."

By way of answer this I seemed to hear
  A little farther on than where I stood,
  Whereat I made myself still nearer heard.

Among the rest I saw a shade that waited
  In aspect, and should any one ask how,
  Its chin it lifted upward like a blind man.

""Spirto"", diss'io, ""che per salir ti dome,
  se tu se' quelli che mi rispondesti,
  fammiti conto o per luogo o per nome"".

""Io fui sanese"", rispuose, ""e con questi
  altri rimendo qui la vita ria,
  lagrimando a colui che se' ne presti.

Savia non fui, avvegna che Sapia
  fossi chiamata, e fui de li altrui danni
  piu` lieta assai che di ventura mia.

E perche' tu non creda ch'io t'inganni,
  odi s'i' fui, com'io ti dico, folle,
  gia` discendendo l'arco d'i miei anni.

Eran li cittadin miei presso a Colle
  in campo giunti co' loro avversari,
  e io pregava Iddio di quel ch'e' volle.

Rotti fuor quivi e volti ne li amari
  passi di fuga; e veggendo la caccia,
  letizia presi a tutte altre dispari,

tanto ch'io volsi in su` l'ardita faccia,
  gridando a Dio: "Omai piu` non ti temo!",
  come fe' 'l merlo per poca bonaccia.

Pace volli con Dio in su lo stremo
  de la mia vita; e ancor non sarebbe
  lo mio dover per penitenza scemo,

se cio` non fosse, ch'a memoria m'ebbe
  Pier Pettinaio in sue sante orazioni,
  a cui di me per caritate increbbe.

Ma tu chi se', che nostre condizioni
  vai dimandando, e porti li occhi sciolti,
  si` com'io credo, e spirando ragioni?"".

""Li occhi"", diss'io, ""mi fieno ancor qui tolti,
  ma picciol tempo, che' poca e` l'offesa
  fatta per esser con invidia volti.

Troppa e` piu` la paura ond'e` sospesa
  l'anima mia del tormento di sotto,
  che gia` lo 'ncarco di la` giu` mi pesa"".

Ed ella a me: ""Chi t'ha dunque condotto
  qua su` tra noi, se giu` ritornar credi?"".
  E io: ""Costui ch'e` meco e non fa motto.

"Spirit," I said, "who stoopest to ascend,
  If thou art he who did reply to me,
  Make thyself known to me by place or name."

"Sienese was I," it replied, "and with
  The others here recleanse my guilty life,
  Weeping to Him to lend himself to us.

Sapient I was not, although I Sapia
  Was called, and I was at another's harm
  More happy far than at my own good fortune.

And that thou mayst not think that I deceive thee,
  Hear if I was as foolish as I tell thee.
  The arc already of my years descending,

My fellow-citizens near unto Colle
  Were joined in battle with their adversaries,
  And I was praying God for what he willed.

Routed were they, and turned into the bitter
  Passes of flight; and I, the chase beholding,
  A joy received unequalled by all others;

So that I lifted upward my bold face
  Crying to God, 'Henceforth I fear thee not,'
  As did the blackbird at the little sunshine.

Peace I desired with God at the extreme
  Of my existence, and as yet would not
  My debt have been by penitence discharged,

Had it not been that in remembrance held me
  Pier Pettignano in his holy prayers,
  Who out of charity was grieved for me.

But who art thou, that into our conditions
  Questioning goest, and hast thine eyes unbound
  As I believe, and breathing dost discourse?"

"Mine eyes," I said, "will yet be here ta'en from me,
  But for short space; for small is the offence
  Committed by their being turned with envy.

Far greater is the fear, wherein suspended
  My soul is, of the torment underneath,
  For even now the load down there weighs on me."

And she to me: "Who led thee, then, among us
  Up here, if to return below thou thinkest?"
  And I: "He who is with me, and speaks not;

E vivo sono; e pero` mi richiedi,
  spirito eletto, se tu vuo' ch'i' mova
  di la` per te ancor li mortai piedi"".

""Oh, questa e` a udir si` cosa nuova"",
  rispuose, ""che gran segno e` che Dio t'ami;
  pero` col priego tuo talor mi giova.

E cheggioti, per quel che tu piu` brami,
  se mai calchi la terra di Toscana,
  che a' miei propinqui tu ben mi rinfami.

Tu li vedrai tra quella gente vana
  che spera in Talamone, e perderagli
  piu` di speranza ch'a trovar la Diana;

ma piu` vi perderanno li ammiragli"".

And living am I; therefore ask of me,
  Spirit elect, if thou wouldst have me move
  O'er yonder yet my mortal feet for thee."

"O, this is such a novel thing to hear,"
  She answered, "that great sign it is God loves thee;
  Therefore with prayer of thine sometimes assist me.

And I implore, by what thou most desirest,
  If e'er thou treadest the soil of Tuscany,
  Well with my kindred reinstate my fame.

Them wilt thou see among that people vain
  Who hope in Talamone, and will lose there
  More hope than in discovering the Diana;

But there still more the admirals will lose."

Purgatorio: Canto XIV

Guido del Duca and Renier da Calboli. Cities of the Arno Valley. Denunciation of Stubbornness.

““Chi e` costui che 'l nostro monte cerchia
prima che morte li abbia dato il volo,
e apre li occhi a sua voglia e coverchia?”“.

"Who is this one that goes about our mountain,
Or ever Death has given him power of flight,
And opes his eyes and shuts them at his will?"

““Non so chi sia, ma so ch'e' non e` solo:
domandal tu che piu` li t'avvicini,
e dolcemente, si` che parli, acco'lo”“.

"I know not who, but know he's not alone;
Ask him thyself, for thou art nearer to him,
And gently, so that he may speak, accost him."

Cosi` due spirti, l'uno a l'altro chini,
ragionavan di me ivi a man dritta;
poi fer li visi, per dirmi, supini;

Thus did two spirits, leaning tow'rds each other,
Discourse about me there on the right hand;
Then held supine their faces to address me.

e disse l'uno: ““O anima che fitta
nel corpo ancora inver' lo ciel ten vai,
per carita` ne consola e ne ditta

And said the one: "O soul, that, fastened still
Within the body, tow'rds the heaven art going,
For charity console us, and declare

onde vieni e chi se'; che' tu ne fai
tanto maravigliar de la tua grazia,
quanto vuol cosa che non fu piu` mai”“.

Whence comest and who art thou; for thou mak'st us
As much to marvel at this grace of thine
As must a thing that never yet has been."

E io: ““Per mezza Toscana si spazia
un fiumicel che nasce in Falterona,
e cento miglia di corso nol sazia.

And I: "Through midst of Tuscany there wanders
A streamlet that is born in Falterona,
And not a hundred miles of course suffice it;

Di sovr'esso rech'io questa persona:
dirvi ch'i' sia, saria parlare indarno,
che' 'l nome mio ancor molto non suona”“.

From thereupon do I this body bring.
To tell you who I am were speech in vain,
Because my name as yet makes no great noise."

““Se ben lo 'ntendimento tuo accarno
con lo 'ntelletto”“, allora mi rispuose
quei che diceva pria, ““tu parli d'Arno”“.

"If well thy meaning I can penetrate
With intellect of mine," then answered me
He who first spake, "thou speakest of the Arno."

E l'altro disse lui: ““Perche' nascose
questi il vocabol di quella riviera,
pur com'om fa de l'orribili cose?”“.

And said the other to him: "Why concealed
This one the appellation of that river,
Even as a man doth of things horrible?"

E l'ombra che di cio` domandata era,
  si sdebito` cosi`: ““Non so; ma degno
  ben e` che 'l nome di tal valle pera;

che' dal principio suo, ov'e` si` pregno
  l'alpestro monte ond'e` tronco Peloro,
  che 'n pochi luoghi passa oltra quel segno,

infin la` 've si rende per ristoro
  di quel che 'l ciel de la marina asciuga,
  ond'hanno i fiumi cio` che va con loro,

vertu` cosi` per nimica si fuga
  da tutti come biscia, o per sventura
  del luogo, o per mal uso che li fruga:

ond'hanno si` mutata lor natura
  li abitator de la misera valle,
  che par che Circe li avesse in pastura.

Tra brutti porci, piu` degni di galle
  che d'altro cibo fatto in uman uso,
  dirizza prima il suo povero calle.

Botoli trova poi, venendo giuso,
  ringhiosi piu` che non chiede lor possa,
  e da lor disdegnosa torce il muso.

Vassi caggendo; e quant'ella piu` 'ngrossa,
  tanto piu` trova di can farsi lupi
  la maladetta e sventurata fossa.

Discesa poi per piu` pelaghi cupi,
  trova le volpi si` piene di froda,
  che non temono ingegno che le occupi.

Ne' lascero` di dir perch'altri m'oda;
  e buon sara` costui, s'ancor s'ammenta
  di cio` che vero spirto mi disnoda.

Io veggio tuo nepote che diventa
  cacciator di quei lupi in su la riva
  del fiero fiume, e tutti li sgomenta.

Vende la carne loro essendo viva;
  poscia li ancide come antica belva;
  molti di vita e se' di pregio priva.

Sanguinoso esce de la trista selva;
  lasciala tal, che di qui a mille anni
  ne lo stato primaio non si rinselva”“.

And thus the shade that questioned was of this
  Himself acquitted: "I know not; but truly
  'Tis fit the name of such a valley perish;

For from its fountain-head (where is so pregnant
  The Alpine mountain whence is cleft Peloro
  That in few places it that mark surpasses)

To where it yields itself in restoration
  Of what the heaven doth of the sea dry up,
  Whence have the rivers that which goes with them,

Virtue is like an enemy avoided
  By all, as is a serpent, through misfortune
  Of place, or through bad habit that impels them;

On which account have so transformed their nature
  The dwellers in that miserable valley,
  It seems that Circe had them in her pasture.

'Mid ugly swine, of acorns worthier
  Than other food for human use created,
  It first directeth its impoverished way.

Curs findeth it thereafter, coming downward,
  More snarling than their puissance demands,
  And turns from them disdainfully its muzzle.

It goes on falling, and the more it grows,
  The more it finds the dogs becoming wolves,
  This maledict and misadventurous ditch.

Descended then through many a hollow gulf,
  It finds the foxes so replete with fraud,
  They fear no cunning that may master them.

Nor will I cease because another hears me;
  And well 'twill be for him, if still he mind him
  Of what a truthful spirit to me unravels.

Thy grandson I behold, who doth become
  A hunter of those wolves upon the bank
  Of the wild stream, and terrifies them all.

He sells their flesh, it being yet alive;
  Thereafter slaughters them like ancient beeves;
  Many of life, himself of praise, deprives.

Blood-stained he issues from the dismal forest;
  He leaves it such, a thousand years from now
  In its primeval state 'tis not re-wooded."

Com'a l'annunzio di dogliosi danni
  si turba il viso di colui ch'ascolta,
  da qual che parte il periglio l'assanni,

cosi` vid'io l'altr'anima, che volta
  stava a udir, turbarsi e farsi trista,
  poi ch'ebbe la parola a se' raccolta.

Lo dir de l'una e de l'altra la vista
  mi fer voglioso di saper lor nomi,
  e dimanda ne fei con prieghi mista;

per che lo spirto che di pria parlomi
  ricomincio`: ""Tu vuo' ch'io mi deduca
  nel fare a te cio` che tu far non vuo'mi.

Ma da che Dio in te vuol che traluca
  tanto sua grazia, non ti saro` scarso;
  pero` sappi ch'io fui Guido del Duca.

Fu il sangue mio d'invidia si` riarso,
  che se veduto avesse uom farsi lieto,
  visto m'avresti di livore sparso.

Di mia semente cotal paglia mieto;
  o gente umana, perche' poni 'l core
  la` 'v'e` mestier di consorte divieto?

Questi e` Rinier; questi e` 'l pregio e l'onore
  de la casa da Calboli, ove nullo
  fatto s'e` reda poi del suo valore.

E non pur lo suo sangue e` fatto brullo,
  tra 'l Po e 'l monte e la marina e 'l Reno,
  del ben richesto al vero e al trastullo;

che' dentro a questi termini e` ripieno
  di venenosi sterpi, si` che tardi
  per coltivare omai verrebber meno.

Ov'e` 'l buon Lizio e Arrigo Mainardi?
  Pier Traversaro e Guido di Carpigna?
  Oh Romagnuoli tornati in bastardi!

Quando in Bologna un Fabbro si ralligna?
  quando in Faenza un Bernardin di Fosco,
  verga gentil di picciola gramigna?

As at the announcement of impending ills
  The face of him who listens is disturbed,
  From whate'er side the peril seize upon him;

So I beheld that other soul, which stood
  Turned round to listen, grow disturbed and sad,
  When it had gathered to itself the word.

The speech of one and aspect of the other
  Had me desirous made to know their names,
  And question mixed with prayers I made thereof,

Whereat the spirit which first spake to me
  Began again: "Thou wishest I should bring me
  To do for thee what thou'lt not do for me;

But since God willeth that in thee shine forth
  Such grace of his, I'll not be chary with thee;
  Know, then, that I Guido del Duca am.

My blood was so with envy set on fire,
  That if I had beheld a man make merry,
  Thou wouldst have seen me sprinkled o'er with pal-
    lor.

From my own sowing such the straw I reap!
  O human race! why dost thou set thy heart
  Where interdict of partnership must be?

This is Renier; this is the boast and honour
  Of the house of Calboli, where no one since
  Has made himself the heir of his desert.

And not alone his blood is made devoid,
  'Twixt Po and mount, and sea-shore and the Reno,
  Of good required for truth and for diversion;

For all within these boundaries is full
  Of venomous roots, so that too tardily
  By cultivation now would they diminish.

Where is good Lizio, and Arrigo Manardi,
  Pier Traversaro, and Guido di Carpigna,
  O Romagnuoli into bastards turned?

When in Bologna will a Fabbro rise?
  When in Faenza a Bernardin di Fosco,
  The noble scion of ignoble seed?

Non ti maravigliar s'io piango, Tosco,
  quando rimembro con Guido da Prata,
  Ugolin d'Azzo che vivette nosco,

Federigo Tignoso e sua brigata,
  la casa Traversara e li Anastagi
  (e l'una gente e l'altra e` diretata),

le donne e ' cavalier, li affanni e li agi
  che ne 'nvogliava amore e cortesia
  la` dove i cuor son fatti si` malvagi.

O Bretinoro, che' non fuggi via,
  poi che gita se n'e` la tua famiglia
  e molta gente per non esser ria?

Ben fa Bagnacaval, che non rifiglia;
  e mal fa Castrocaro, e peggio Conio,
  che di figliar tai conti piu` s'impiglia.

Ben faranno i Pagan, da che 'l demonio
  lor sen gira`; ma non pero` che puro
  gia` mai rimagna d'essi testimonio.

O Ugolin de' Fantolin, sicuro
  e` il nome tuo, da che piu` non s'aspetta
  chi far lo possa, tralignando, scuro.

Ma va via, Tosco, omai; ch'or mi diletta
  troppo di pianger piu` che di parlare,
  si` m'ha nostra ragion la mente stretta'"".

Noi sapavam che quell'anime care
  ci sentivano andar; pero`, tacendo,
  facean noi del cammin confidare.

Poi fummo fatti soli procedendo,
  folgore parve quando l'aere fende,
  voce che giunse di contra dicendo:

'Anciderammi qualunque m'apprende';
  e fuggi` come tuon che si dilegua,
  se subito la nuvola scoscende.

Come da lei l'udir nostro ebbe triegua,
  ed ecco l'altra con si` gran fracasso,
  che somiglio` tonar che tosto segua:

""Io sono Aglauro che divenni sasso'"";
  e allor, per ristrignermi al poeta,
  in destro feci e non innanzi il passo.

Be not astonished, Tuscan, if I weep,
  When I remember, with Guido da Prata,
  Ugolin d' Azzo, who was living with us,

Frederick Tignoso and his company,
  The house of Traversara, and th' Anastagi,
  And one race and the other is extinct;

The dames and cavaliers, the toils and ease
  That filled our souls with love and courtesy,
  There where the hearts have so malicious grown!

O Brettinoro! why dost thou not flee,
  Seeing that all thy family is gone,
  And many people, not to be corrupted?

Bagnacaval does well in not begetting
  And ill does Castrocaro, and Conio worse,
  In taking trouble to beget such Counts.

Will do well the Pagani, when their Devil
  Shall have departed; but not therefore pure
  Will testimony of them e'er remain.

O Ugolin de' Fantoli, secure
  Thy name is, since no longer is awaited
  One who, degenerating, can obscure it!

But go now, Tuscan, for it now delights me
  To weep far better than it does to speak,
  So much has our discourse my mind distressed."

We were aware that those beloved souls
  Heard us depart; therefore, by keeping silent,
  They made us of our pathway confident.

When we became alone by going onward,
  Thunder, when it doth cleave the air, appeared
  A voice, that counter to us came, exclaiming:

"Shall slay me whosoever findeth me!"
  And fled as the reverberation dies
  If suddenly the cloud asunder bursts.

As soon as hearing had a truce from this,
  Behold another, with so great a crash,
  That it resembled thunderings following fast:

"I am Aglaurus, who became a stone!"
  And then, to press myself close to the Poet,
  I backward, and not forward, took a step.

Gia` era l'aura d'ogne parte queta;
  ed el mi disse: ""Quel fu 'l duro camo
  che dovria l'uom tener dentro a sua meta.

Ma voi prendete l'esca, si` che l'amo
  de l'antico avversaro a se' vi tira;
  e pero` poco val freno o richiamo.

Chiamavi 'l cielo e 'ntorno vi si gira,
  mostrandovi le sue bellezze etterne,
  e l'occhio vostro pur a terra mira;

onde vi batte chi tutto discerne"".

Already on all sides the air was quiet;
  And said he to me: "That was the hard curb
  That ought to hold a man within his bounds;

But you take in the bait so that the hook
  Of the old Adversary draws you to him,
  And hence availeth little curb or call.

The heavens are calling you, and wheel around you,
  Displaying to you their eternal beauties,
  And still your eye is looking on the ground;

Whence He, who all discerns, chastises you."

Purgatorio: Canto XV

The Third Circle: The Irascible. Dante's Visions. The Smoke.

Quanto tra l'ultimar de l'ora terza
  e 'l principio del di` par de la spera
  che sempre a guisa di fanciullo scherza,
	As much as 'twixt the close of the third hour
	  And dawn of day appeareth of that sphere
	  Which aye in fashion of a child is playing,

tanto pareva gia` inver' la sera   essere al sol del suo corso rimaso;   vespero la`, e qui mezza notte era.	So much it now appeared, towards the night, Was of his course remaining to the sun; There it was evening, and 'twas midnight here;
E i raggi ne ferien per mezzo 'l naso, perche' per noi girato era si` 'l monte,   che gia` dritti andavamo inver' l'occaso,	And the rays smote the middle of our faces, Because by us the mount was so encircled, That straight towards the west we now were going

quand'io senti' a me gravar la fronte
  a lo splendore assai piu` che di prima,
  e stupor m'eran le cose non conte;
	When I perceived my forehead overpowered
	  Beneath the splendour far more than at first,
	  And stupor were to me the things unknown,

ond'io levai le mani inver' la cima
  de le mie ciglia, e fecimi 'l solecchio,
  che del soverchio visibile lima.
	Whereat towards the summit of my brow
	  I raised my hands, and made myself the visor
	  Which the excessive glare diminishes.

Come quando da l'acqua o da lo specchio
  salta lo raggio a l'opposita parte,
  salendo su per lo modo parecchio
	As when from off the water, or a mirror,
	  The sunbeam leaps unto the opposite side,
	  Ascending upward in the selfsame measure

a quel che scende, e tanto si diparte
  dal cader de la pietra in igual tratta,
  si` come mostra esperienza e arte;
	That it descends, and deviates as far
	  From falling of a stone in line direct,
	  (As demonstrate experiment and art,)

cosi` mi parve da luce rifratta
  quivi dinanzi a me esser percosso;
  per che a fuggir la mia vista fu ratta.
	So it appeared to me that by a light
	  Refracted there before me I was smitten;
	  On which account my sight was swift to flee.

""Che e` quel, dolce padre, a che non posso
  schermar lo viso tanto che mi vaglia"",
  diss'io, ""e pare inver' noi esser mosso?"".
	"What is that, Father sweet, from which I cannot
	  So fully screen my sight that it avail me,"
	  Said I, "and seems towards us to be moving?"

""'Non ti maravigliar s'ancor t'abbaglia
la famiglia del cielo''", a me rispuose:
"''messo e` che viene ad invitar ch'om saglia.

Tosto sara` ch'a veder queste cose
non ti fia grave, ma fieti diletto
quanto natura a sentir ti dispuose''".

Poi giunti fummo a l'angel benedetto,
con lieta voce disse: ""Intrate quinci
ad un scaleo vie men che li altri eretto''".

Noi montavam, gia` partiti di linci,
e 'Beati misericordes!' fue
cantato retro, e 'Godi tu che vinci!'.

Lo mio maestro e io soli amendue
suso andavamo; e io pensai, andando,
prode acquistar ne le parole sue;

e dirizza'mi a lui si` dimandando:
""Che volse dir lo spirto di Romagna,
e 'divieto' e 'consorte' menzionando?''".

Per ch'elli a me: ""Di sua maggior magagna
conosce il danno; e pero` non s'ammiri
se ne riprende perche' men si piagna.

Perche' s'appuntano i vostri disiri
dove per compagnia parte si scema,
invidia move il mantaco a' sospiri.

Ma se l'amor de la spera supprema
torcesse in suso il disiderio vostro,
non vi sarebbe al petto quella tema;

che', per quanti si dice piu` li` 'nostro',
tanto possiede piu` di ben ciascuno,
e piu` di caritate arde in quel chiostro''".

""Io son d'esser contento piu` digiuno''",
diss'io, ""che se mi fosse pria taciuto,
e piu` di dubbio ne la mente aduno.

Com'esser puote ch'un ben, distributo
in piu` posseditor, faccia piu` ricchi
di se', che se da pochi e` posseduto?''".

Ed elli a me: ""Pero` che tu rificchi
la mente pur a le cose terrene,
di vera luce tenebre dispicchi.

"Marvel thou not, if dazzle thee as yet
The family of heaven," he answered me;
"An angel 'tis, who comes to invite us upward.

Soon will it be, that to behold these things
Shall not be grievous, but delightful to thee
As much as nature fashioned thee to feel."

When we had reached the Angel benedight,
With joyful voice he said: "Here enter in
To stairway far less steep than are the others."

We mounting were, already thence departed,
And "Beati misericordes" was
Behind us sung, "Rejoice, thou that o'ercomest!"

My Master and myself, we two alone
Were going upward, and I thought, in going,
Some profit to acquire from words of his;

And I to him directed me, thus asking:
"What did the spirit of Romagna mean,
Mentioning interdict and partnership?"

Whence he to me: "Of his own greatest failing
He knows the harm; and therefore wonder not
If he reprove us, that we less may rue it.

Because are thither pointed your desires
Where by companionship each share is lessened,
Envy doth ply the bellows to your sighs.

But if the love of the supernal sphere
Should upwardly direct your aspiration,
There would not be that fear within your breast;

For there, as much the more as one says 'Our,'
So much the more of good each one possesses,
And more of charity in that cloister burns."

"I am more hungering to be satisfied,"
I said, "than if I had before been silent,
And more of doubt within my mind I gather.

How can it be, that boon distributed
The more possessors can more wealthy make
Therein, than if by few it be possessed?"

And he to me: "Because thou fixest still
Thy mind entirely upon earthly things,
Thou pluckest darkness from the very light.

Quello infinito e ineffabil bene
  che la` su` e`, cosi` corre ad amore
  com'a lucido corpo raggio vene.

Tanto si da` quanto trova d'ardore;
  si` che, quantunque carita` si stende,
  cresce sovr'essa l'etterno valore.

E quanta gente piu` la` su` s'intende,
  piu` v'e` da bene amare, e piu` vi s'ama,
  e come specchio l'uno a l'altro rende.

E se la mia ragion non ti disfama,
  vedrai Beatrice, ed ella pienamente
  ti torra` questa e ciascun'altra brama.

Procaccia pur che tosto sieno spente,
  come son gia` le due, le cinque piaghe,
  che si richiudon per esser dolente"".

Com'io voleva dicer 'Tu m'appaghe',
  vidimi giunto in su l'altro girone,
  si` che tacer mi fer le luci vaghe.

Ivi mi parve in una visione
  estatica di subito esser tratto,
  e vedere in un tempio piu` persone;

e una donna, in su l'entrar, con atto
  dolce di madre dicer: ""Figliuol mio
  perche' hai tu cosi` verso noi fatto?

Ecco, dolenti, lo tuo padre e io
  ti cercavamo"". E come qui si tacque,
  cio` che pareva prima, dispario.

Indi m'apparve un'altra con quell'acque
  giu` per le gote che 'l dolor distilla
  quando di gran dispetto in altrui nacque,

e dir: ""Se tu se' sire de la villa
  del cui nome ne' dei fu tanta lite,
  e onde ogni scienza disfavilla,

vendica te di quelle braccia ardite
  ch'abbracciar nostra figlia, o Pisistrato"".
  E 'l segnor mi parea, benigno e mite,

That goodness infinite and ineffable
  Which is above there, runneth unto love,
  As to a lucid body comes the sunbeam.

So much it gives itself as it finds ardour,
  So that as far as charity extends,
  O'er it increases the eternal valour.

And the more people thitherward aspire,
  More are there to love well, and more they love
    there,
  And, as a mirror, one reflects the other.

And if my reasoning appease thee not,
  Thou shalt see Beatrice; and she will fully
  Take from thee this and every other longing.

Endeavour, then, that soon may be extinct,
  As are the two already, the five wounds
  That close themselves again by being painful."

Even as I wished to say, "Thou dost appease me,"
  I saw that I had reached another circle,
  So that my eager eyes made me keep silence.

There it appeared to me that in a vision
  Ecstatic on a sudden I was rapt,
  And in a temple many persons saw;

And at the door a woman, with the sweet
  Behaviour of a mother, saying: "Son,
  Why in this manner hast thou dealt with us?

Lo, sorrowing, thy father and myself
  Were seeking for thee;"—and as here she ceased,
  That which appeared at first had disappeared.

Then I beheld another with those waters
  Adown her cheeks which grief distils whenever
  From great disdain of others it is born,

And saying: "If of that city thou art lord,
  For whose name was such strife among the gods,
  And whence doth every science scintillate,

Avenge thyself on those audacious arms
  That clasped our daughter, O Pisistratus;"
  And the lord seemed to me benign and mild

risponder lei con viso temperato:
  ""'Che farem noi a chi mal ne disira,
  se quei che ci ama e' per noi condannato?'"',

Poi vidi genti accese in foco d'ira
  con pietre un giovinetto ancider, forte
  gridando a se' pur: ""'Martira, martira!'"'.

E lui vedea chinarsi, per la morte
  che l'aggravava gia', inver' la terra,
  ma de li occhi facea sempre al ciel porte,

orando a l'alto Sire, in tanta guerra,
  che perdonasse a' suoi persecutori,
  con quello aspetto che pieta' diserra.

Quando l'anima mia torno' di fori
  a le cose che son fuor di lei vere,
  io riconobbi i miei non falsi errori.

Lo duca mio, che mi potea vedere
  far si` com'om che dal sonno si slega,
  disse: ""'Che hai che non ti puoi tenere,

ma se' venuto piu` che mezza lega
  velando li occhi e con le gambe avvolte,
  a guisa di cui vino o sonno piega?"'.

""'O dolce padre mio, se tu m'ascolte,
  io ti diro`'"', diss'io, ""'cio` che m'apparve
  quando le gambe mi furon si` tolte'"'.

Ed ei: ""'Se tu avessi cento larve
  sovra la faccia, non mi sarian chiuse
  le tue cogitazion, quantunque parve.

Cio` che vedesti fu perche' non scuse
  d'aprir lo core a l'acque de la pace
  che da l'etterno fonte son diffuse.

Non dimandai "Che hai?" per quel che face
  chi guarda pur con l'occhio che non vede,
  quando disanimato il corpo giace;

ma dimandai per darti forza al piede:
  cosi` frugar conviensi i pigri, lenti
  ad usar lor vigilia quando riede'"'.

To answer her with aspect temperate:
  "What shall we do to those who wish us ill,
  If he who loves us be by us condemned?"

Then saw I people hot in fire of wrath,
  With stones a young man slaying, clamorously
  Still crying to each other, "Kill him! kill him!"

And him I saw bow down, because of death
  That weighed already on him, to the earth,
  But of his eyes made ever gates to heaven,

Imploring the high Lord, in so great strife,
  That he would pardon those his persecutors,
  With such an aspect as unlocks compassion.

Soon as my soul had outwardly returned
  To things external to it which are true,
  Did I my not false errors recognize.

My Leader, who could see me bear myself
  Like to a man that rouses him from sleep,
  Exclaimed: "What ails thee, that thou canst not
    stand?

But hast been coming more than half a league
  Veiling thine eyes, and with thy legs entangled,
  In guise of one whom wine or sleep subdues?"

"O my sweet Father, if thou listen to me,
  I'll tell thee," said I, "what appeared to me,
  When thus from me my legs were ta'en away."

And he: "If thou shouldst have a hundred masks
  Upon thy face, from me would not be shut
  Thy cogitations, howsoever small.

What thou hast seen was that thou mayst not fail
  To ope thy heart unto the waters of peace,
  Which from the eternal fountain are diffused.

I did not ask, 'What ails thee?' as he does
  Who only looketh with the eyes that see not
  When of the soul bereft the body lies,

But asked it to give vigour to thy feet;
  Thus must we needs urge on the sluggards, slow
  To use their wakefulness when it returns."

Noi andavam per lo vespero, attenti
 oltre quanto potean li occhi allungarsi
 contra i raggi serotini e lucenti.

Ed ecco a poco a poco un fummo farsi
 verso di noi come la notte oscuro;
 ne' da quello era loco da cansarsi.

Questo ne tolse li occhi e l'aere puro.

We passed along, athwart the twilight peering
 Forward as far as ever eye could stretch
 Against the sunbeams serotine and lucent;

And lo! by slow degrees a smoke approached
 In our direction, sombre as the night,
 Nor was there place to hide one's self therefrom.

This of our eyes and the pure air bereft us.

Purgatorio: Canto XVI

Marco Lombardo. Lament over the State of the World.

Buio d'inferno e di notte privata
  d'ogne pianeto, sotto pover cielo,
  quant'esser puo` di nuvol tenebrata,

non fece al viso mio si` grosso velo
  come quel fummo ch'ivi ci coperse,
  ne' a sentir di cosi` aspro pelo,

che l'occhio stare aperto non sofferse;
  onde la scorta mia saputa e fida
  mi s'accosto` e l'omero m'offerse.

Si` come cieco va dietro a sua guida
  per non smarrirsi e per non dar di cozzo
  in cosa che 'l molesti, o forse ancida,

m'andava io per l'aere amaro e sozzo,
  ascoltando il mio duca che diceva
  pur: ““Guarda che da me tu non sia mozzo”“.

Io sentia voci, e ciascuna pareva
  pregar per pace e per misericordia
  l'Agnel di Dio che le peccata leva.

Pur 'Agnus Dei' eran le loro essordia;
  una parola in tutte era e un modo,
  si` che parea tra esse ogne concordia.

““Quei sono spirti, maestro, ch'i' odo?”“,
  diss'io. Ed elli a me: ““Tu vero apprendi,
  e d'iracundia van solvendo il nodo”“.

““Or tu chi se' che 'l nostro fummo fendi,
  e di noi parli pur come se tue
  partissi ancor lo tempo per calendi?”“.

Darkness of hell, and of a night deprived
  Of every planet under a poor sky,
  As much as may be tenebrous with cloud,

Ne'er made unto my sight so thick a veil,
  As did that smoke which there enveloped us,
  Nor to the feeling of so rough a texture;

For not an eye it suffered to stay open;
  Whereat mine escort, faithful and sagacious,
  Drew near to me and offered me his shoulder.

E'en as a blind man goes behind his guide,
  Lest he should wander, or should strike against
  Aught that may harm or peradventure kill him,

So went I through the bitter and foul air,
  Listening unto my Leader, who said only,
  "Look that from me thou be not separated."

Voices I heard, and every one appeared
  To supplicate for peace and misericord
  The Lamb of God who takes away our sins.

Still "Agnus Dei" their exordium was;
  One word there was in all, and metre one,
  So that all harmony appeared among them.

"Master," I said, "are spirits those I hear?"
  And he to me: "Thou apprehendest truly,
  And they the knot of anger go unloosing."

"Now who art thou, that cleavest through our smoke
  And art discoursing of us even as though
  Thou didst by calends still divide the time?"

Cosi` per una voce detto fue;
  onde 'l maestro mio disse: ““Rispondi,
  e domanda se quinci si va sue”“.

E io: ““O creatura che ti mondi
  per tornar bella a colui che ti fece,
  maraviglia udirai, se mi secondi”“.

““Io ti seguitero` quanto mi lece”“,
  rispuose; ““e se veder fummo non lascia,
  l'udir ci terra` giunti in quella vece”“.

Allora incominciai: ““Con quella fascia
  che la morte dissolve men vo suso,
  e venni qui per l'infernale ambascia.

E se Dio m'ha in sua grazia rinchiuso,
  tanto che vuol ch'i' veggia la sua corte
  per modo tutto fuor del moderno uso,

non mi celar chi fosti anzi la morte,
  ma dilmi, e dimmi s'i' vo bene al varco;
  e tue parole fier le nostre scorte”“.

““Lombardo fui, e fu' chiamato Marco;
  del mondo seppi, e quel valore amai
  al quale ha or ciascun disteso l'arco.

Per montar su` dirittamente vai”“.
  Cosi` rispuose, e soggiunse: ““I' ti prego
  che per me prieghi quando su` sarai”“.

E io a lui: ““Per fede mi ti lego
  di far cio` che mi chiedi; ma io scoppio
  dentro ad un dubbio, s'io non me ne spiego.

Prima era scempio, e ora e` fatto doppio
  ne la sentenza tua, che mi fa certo
  qui, e altrove, quello ov'io l'accoppio.

Lo mondo e` ben cosi` tutto diserto
  d'ogne virtute, come tu mi sone,
  e di malizia gravido e coverto;

ma priego che m'addite la cagione,
  si` ch'i' la veggia e ch'i' la mostri altrui;
  che' nel cielo uno, e un qua giu` la pone”“.

Alto sospir, che duolo strinse in ““uhi!”“,
  mise fuor prima; e poi comincio`: ““Frate,
  lo mondo e` cieco, e tu vien ben da lui.

After this manner by a voice was spoken;
  Whereon my Master said: "Do thou reply,
  And ask if on this side the way go upward."

And I: "O creature that dost cleanse thyself
  To return beautiful to Him who made thee,
  Thou shalt hear marvels if thou follow me."

"Thee will I follow far as is allowed me,"
  He answered; "and if smoke prevent our seeing,
  Hearing shall keep us joined instead thereof."

Thereon began I: "With that swathing band
  Which death unwindeth am I going upward,
  And hither came I through the infernal anguish.

And if God in his grace has me infolded,
  So that he wills that I behold his court
  By method wholly out of modern usage,

Conceal not from me who ere death thou wast,
  But tell it me, and tell me if I go
  Right for the pass, and be thy words our escort."

"Lombard was I, and I was Marco called;
  The world I knew, and loved that excellence,
  At which has each one now unbent his bow.

For mounting upward, thou art going right."
  Thus he made answer, and subjoined: "I pray thee
  To pray for me when thou shalt be above."

And I to him: "My faith I pledge to thee
  To do what thou dost ask me; but am bursting
  Inly with doubt, unless I rid me of it.

First it was simple, and is now made double
  By thy opinion, which makes certain to me,
  Here and elsewhere, that which I couple with it.

The world forsooth is utterly deserted
  By every virtue, as thou tellest me,
  And with iniquity is big and covered;

But I beseech thee point me out the cause,
  That I may see it, and to others show it;
  For one in the heavens, and here below one puts it."

A sigh profound, that grief forced into Ai!
  He first sent forth, and then began he: "Brother,
  The world is blind, and sooth thou comest from it!

Voi che vivete ogne cagion recate
  pur suso al cielo, pur come se tutto
  movesse seco di necessitate.
	Ye who are living every cause refer
	  Still upward to the heavens, as if all things
	  They of necessity moved with themselves.

Se cosi` fosse, in voi fora distrutto
  libero arbitrio, e non fora giustizia
  per ben letizia, e per male aver lutto.
	If this were so, in you would be destroyed
	  Free will, nor any justice would there be
	  In having joy for good, or grief for evil.

Lo cielo i vostri movimenti inizia;
  non dico tutti, ma, posto ch'i' 'l dica,
  lume v'e` dato a bene e a malizia,
	The heavens your movements do initiate,
	  I say not all; but granting that I say it,
	  Light has been given you for good and evil,

e libero voler; che, se fatica
  ne le prime battaglie col ciel dura,
  poi vince tutto, se ben si notrica.
	And free volition; which, if some fatigue
	  In the first battles with the heavens it suffers,
	  Afterwards conquers all, if well 'tis nurtured.

A maggior forza e a miglior natura
  liberi soggiacete; e quella cria
  la mente in voi, che 'l ciel non ha in sua cura.
	To greater force and to a better nature,
	  Though free, ye subject are, and that creates
	  The mind in you the heavens have not in charge.

Pero`, se 'l mondo presente disvia,   in voi e` la cagione, in voi si cheggia; e io te ne saro` or vera spia.	Hence, if the present world doth go astray, In you the cause is, be it sought in you; And I therein will now be thy true spy.

Esce di mano a lui che la vagheggia
  prima che sia, a guisa di fanciulla
  che piangendo e ridendo pargoleggia,
	Forth from the hand of Him, who fondles it
	  Before it is, like to a little girl
	  Weeping and laughing in her childish sport,

l'anima semplicetta che sa nulla,
  salvo che, mossa da lieto fattore,
  volontier torna a cio` che la trastulla.
	Issues the simple soul, that nothing knows,
	  Save that, proceeding from a joyous Maker,
	  Gladly it turns to that which gives it pleasure.

Di picciol bene in pria sente sapore;
  quivi s'inganna, e dietro ad esso corre,
  se guida o fren non torce suo amore.
	Of trivial good at first it tastes the savour;
	  Is cheated by it, and runs after it,
	  If guide or rein turn not aside its love.

Onde convenne legge per fren porre;
  convenne rege aver che discernesse
  de la vera cittade almen la torre.
	Hence it behoved laws for a rein to place,
	  Behoved a king to have, who at the least
	  Of the true city should discern the tower.

Le leggi son, ma chi pon mano ad esse? Nullo, pero` che 'l pastor che procede,   rugumar puo`, ma non ha l'unghie fesse;	The laws exist, but who sets hand to them? No one; because the shepherd who precedes Can ruminate, but cleaveth not the hoof;
per che la gente, che sua guida vede pur a quel ben fedire ond'ella e` ghiotta,   di quel si pasce, e piu` oltre non chiede.	Wherefore the people that perceives its guide Strike only at the good for which it hankers, Feeds upon that, and farther seeketh not.

Ben puoi veder che la mala condotta
  e` la cagion che 'l mondo ha fatto reo,
  e non natura che 'n voi sia corrotta.
	Clearly canst thou perceive that evil guidance
	  The cause is that has made the world depraved,
	  And not that nature is corrupt in you.

Soleva Roma, che 'l buon mondo feo,
  due soli aver, che l'una e l'altra strada
  facean vedere, e del mondo e di Deo.

L'un l'altro ha spento; ed e` giunta la spada
  col pasturale, e l'un con l'altro insieme
  per viva forza mal convien che vada;

pero` che, giunti, l'un l'altro non teme:
  se non mi credi, pon mente a la spiga,
  ch'ogn'erba si conosce per lo seme.

In sul paese ch'Adice e Po riga,
  solea valore e cortesia trovarsi,
  prima che Federigo avesse briga;

or puo` sicuramente indi passarsi
  per qualunque lasciasse, per vergogna
  di ragionar coi buoni o d'appressarsi.

Ben v'en tre vecchi ancora in cui rampogna
  l'antica eta` la nova, e par lor tardo
  che Dio a miglior vita li ripogna:

Currado da Palazzo e 'l buon Gherardo
  e Guido da Castel, che mei si noma
  francescamente, il semplice Lombardo.

Di` oggimai che la Chiesa di Roma,
  per confondere in se' due reggimenti,
  cade nel fango e se' brutta e la soma""".

""O Marco mio""", diss'io, ""bene argomenti;
  e or discerno perche' dal retaggio
  li figli di Levi` furono essenti.

Ma qual Gherardo e` quel che tu per saggio
  di' ch'e` rimaso de la gente spenta,
  in rimprovero del secol selvaggio?""".

""O tuo parlar m'inganna, o el mi tenta""",
  rispuose a me; ""che', parlandomi tosco,
  par che del buon Gherardo nulla senta.

Per altro sopranome io nol conosco,
  s'io nol togliessi da sua figlia Gaia.
  Dio sia con voi, che' piu` non vegno vosco.

Rome, that reformed the world, accustomed was
  Two suns to have, which one road and the other,
  Of God and of the world, made manifest.

One has the other quenched, and to the crosier
  The sword is joined, and ill beseemeth it
  That by main force one with the other go,

Because, being joined, one feareth not the other;
  If thou believe not, think upon the grain,
  For by its seed each herb is recognized.

In the land laved by Po and Adige,
  Valour and courtesy used to be found,
  Before that Frederick had his controversy;

Now in security can pass that way
  Whoever will abstain, through sense of shame,
  From speaking with the good, or drawing near
    them.

True, three old men are left, in whom upbraids
  The ancient age the new, and late they deem it
  That God restore them to the better life:

Currado da Palazzo, and good Gherardo,
  And Guido da Castel, who better named is,
  In fashion of the French, the simple Lombard:

Say thou henceforward that the Church of Rome,
  Confounding in itself two governments,
  Falls in the mire, and soils itself and burden."

"O Marco mine," I said, "thou reasonest well;
  And now discern I why the sons of Levi
  Have been excluded from the heritage.

But what Gherardo is it, who, as sample
  Of a lost race, thou sayest has remained
  In reprobation of the barbarous age?"

"Either thy speech deceives me, or it tempts me,"
  He answered me; "for speaking Tuscan to me,
  It seems of good Gherardo naught thou knowest.

By other surname do I know him not,
  Unless I take it from his daughter Gaia.
  May God be with you, for I come no farther.

Vedi l'albor che per lo fummo raia
  gia` biancheggiare, e me convien partirmi
  (l'angelo e` ivi) prima ch'io li paia'"".

Cosi` torno`, e piu` non volle udirmi.

Behold the dawn, that through the smoke rays out,
  Already whitening; and I must depart—
  Yonder the Angel is—ere he appear."

Thus did he speak, and would no farther hear me.

Purgatorio: Canto XVII

Dante's Dream of Anger. The Fourth Circle: The Slothful. Virgil's Discourse of Love.

Ricorditi, lettor, se mai ne l'alpe
  ti colse nebbia per la qual vedessi
  non altrimenti che per pelle talpe,
	Remember, Reader, if e'er in the Alps
	  A mist o'ertook thee, through which thou couldst
	    see
	  Not otherwise than through its membrane mole,

come, quando i vapori umidi e spessi
  a diradar cominciansi, la spera
  del sol debilemente entra per essi;
	How, when the vapours humid and condensed
	  Begin to dissipate themselves, the sphere
	  Of the sun feebly enters in among them,

e fia la tua imagine leggera
  in giugnere a veder com'io rividi
  lo sole in pria, che gia` nel corcar era.
	And thy imagination will be swift
	  In coming to perceive how I re-saw
	  The sun at first, that was already setting.

Si`, pareggiando i miei co' passi fidi   del mio maestro, usci' fuor di tal nube   ai raggi morti gia` ne' bassi lidi.	Thus, to the faithful footsteps of my Master Mating mine own, I issued from that cloud To rays already dead on the low shores.

O imaginativa che ne rube
  talvolta si` di fuor, ch'om non s'accorge
  perche' dintorno suonin mille tube,
	O thou, Imagination, that dost steal us
	  So from without sometimes, that man perceives not,
	  Although around may sound a thousand trumpets,

chi move te, se 'l senso non ti porge?
  Moveti lume che nel ciel s'informa,
  per se' o per voler che giu` lo scorge.
	Who moveth thee, if sense impel thee not?
	  Moves thee a light, which in the heaven takes form,
	  By self, or by a will that downward guides it.

De l'empiezza di lei che muto` forma   ne l'uccel ch'a cantar piu` si diletta, ne l'imagine mia apparve l'orma;	Of her impiety, who changed her form Into the bird that most delights in singing, In my imagining appeared the trace;

e qui fu la mia mente si` ristretta
  dentro da se', che di fuor non venia
  cosa che fosse allor da lei ricetta.
	And hereupon my mind was so withdrawn
	  Within itself, that from without there came
	  Nothing that then might be received by it.

Poi piovve dentro a l'alta fantasia
  un crucifisso dispettoso e fero
  ne la sua vista, e cotal si moria;
	Then reigned within my lofty fantasy
	  One crucified, disdainful and ferocious
	  In countenance, and even thus was dying.

intorno ad esso era il grande Assuero,
  Ester sua sposa e 'l giusto Mardoceo,
  che fu al dire e al far cosi` intero.
	Around him were the great Ahasuerus,
	  Esther his wife, and the just Mordecai,
	  Who was in word and action so entire.

E come questa imagine rompeo
  se' per se' stessa, a guisa d'una bulla
  cui manca l'acqua sotto qual si feo,
	And even as this image burst asunder
	  Of its own self, in fashion of a bubble
	  In which the water it was made of fails,

surse in mia visione una fanciulla
  piangendo forte, e dicea: ““O regina,
  perche' per ira hai voluto esser nulla?
	There rose up in my vision a young maiden
	  Bitterly weeping, and she said: "O queen,
	  Why hast thou wished in anger to be naught?

Ancisa t'hai per non perder Lavina;
  or m'hai perduta! Io son essa che lutto,
  madre, a la tua pria ch'a l'altrui ruina”“.
	Thou'st slain thyself, Lavinia not to lose;
	  Now hast thou lost me; I am she who mourns,
	  Mother, at thine ere at another's ruin."

Come si frange il sonno ove di butto
  nova luce percuote il viso chiuso,
  che fratto guizza pria che muoia tutto;
	As sleep is broken, when upon a sudden
	  New light strikes in upon the eyelids closed,
	  And broken quivers ere it dieth wholly,

cosi` l'imaginar mio cadde giuso   tosto che lume il volto mi percosse,   maggior assai che quel ch'e` in nostro uso.	So this imagining of mine fell down As soon as the effulgence smote my face, Greater by far than what is in our wont.

I' mi volgea per veder ov'io fosse,
  quando una voce disse ““Qui si monta”“,
  che da ogne altro intento mi rimosse;
	I turned me round to see where I might be,
	  When said a voice, "Here is the passage up;"
	  Which from all other purposes removed me,

e fece la mia voglia tanto pronta
  di riguardar chi era che parlava,
  che mai non posa, se non si raffronta.
	And made my wish so full of eagerness
	  To look and see who was it that was speaking,
	  It never rests till meeting face to face;

Ma come al sol che nostra vista grava
  e per soverchio sua figura vela,
  cosi` la mia virtu` quivi mancava.
	But as before the sun, which quells the sight,
	  And in its own excess its figure veils,
	  Even so my power was insufficient here.

““Questo e` divino spirito, che ne la   via da ir su` ne drizza sanza prego, e col suo lume se' medesmo cela.	"This is a spirit divine, who in the way Of going up directs us without asking, And who with his own light himself conceals.
Si` fa con noi, come l'uom si fa sego;   che' quale aspetta prego e l'uopo vede,   malignamente gia` si mette al nego.	He does with us as man doth with himself; For he who sees the need, and waits the asking, Malignly leans already tow'rds denial.

Or accordiamo a tanto invito il piede;
  procacciam di salir pria che s'abbui,
  che' poi non si poria, se 'l di` non riede”“.
	Accord we now our feet to such inviting,
	  Let us make haste to mount ere it grow dark;
	  For then we could not till the day return."

Cosi` disse il mio duca, e io con lui
  volgemmo i nostri passi ad una scala;
  e tosto ch'io al primo grado fui,
	Thus my Conductor said; and I and he
	  Together turned our footsteps to a stairway;
	  And I, as soon as the first step I reached,

senti'mi presso quasi un muover d'ala
 e ventarmi nel viso e dir: 'Beati
pacifici, che son sanz'ira mala!'.

Gia` eran sovra noi tanto levati
 li ultimi raggi che la notte segue,
 che le stelle apparivan da piu` lati.

'O virtu` mia, perche' si` ti dilegue?',
 fra me stesso dicea, che' mi sentiva
 la possa de le gambe posta in triegue.

Noi eravam dove piu` non saliva
 la scala su`, ed eravamo affissi,
 pur come nave ch'a la piaggia arriva.

E io attesi un poco, s'io udissi
 alcuna cosa nel novo girone;
 poi mi volsi al maestro mio, e dissi:

""Dolce mio padre, di`, quale offensione
 si purga qui nel giro dove semo?
 Se i pie` si stanno, non stea tuo sermone"".

Ed elli a me: ""L'amor del bene, scemo
 del suo dover, quiritta si ristora;
 qui si ribatte il mal tardato remo.

Ma perche' piu` aperto intendi ancora,
 volgi la mente a me, e prenderai
 alcun buon frutto di nostra dimora"".

""Ne' creator ne' creatura mai"",
 comincio` el, ""figliuol, fu sanza amore,
 o naturale o d'animo; e tu 'l sai.

Lo naturale e` sempre sanza errore,
 ma l'altro puote errar per malo obietto
 o per troppo o per poco di vigore.

Mentre ch'elli e` nel primo ben diretto,
 e ne' secondi se' stesso misura,
 esser non puo` cagion di mal diletto;

ma quando al mal si torce, o con piu` cura
 o con men che non dee corre nel bene,
 contra 'l fattore adovra sua fattura.

Near me perceived a motion as of wings,
 And fanning in the face, and saying, "'Beati
Pacifici,' who are without ill anger."

Already over us were so uplifted
 The latest sunbeams, which the night pursues,
 That upon many sides the stars appeared.

"O manhood mine, why dost thou vanish so?"
 I said within myself; for I perceived
 The vigour of my legs was put in truce.

We at the point were where no more ascends
 The stairway upward, and were motionless,
 Even as a ship, which at the shore arrives;

And I gave heed a little, if I might hear
 Aught whatsoever in the circle new;
 Then to my Master turned me round and said:

"Say, my sweet Father, what delinquency
 Is purged here in the circle where we are?
 Although our feet may pause, pause not thy
  speech."

And he to me: "The love of good, remiss
 In what it should have done, is here restored;
 Here plied again the ill-belated oar;

But still more openly to understand,
 Turn unto me thy mind, and thou shalt gather
 Some profitable fruit from our delay.

Neither Creator nor a creature ever,
 Son," he began, "was destitute of love
 Natural or spiritual; and thou knowest it.

The natural was ever without error;
 But err the other may by evil object,
 Or by too much, or by too little vigour.

While in the first it well directed is,
 And in the second moderates itself,
 It cannot be the cause of sinful pleasure;

But when to ill it turns, and, with more care
 Or lesser than it ought, runs after good,
 'Gainst the Creator works his own creation.

Quinci comprender puoi ch'esser convene
  amor sementa in voi d'ogne virtute
  e d'ogne operazion che merta pene.

Or, perche' mai non puo` da la salute
  amor del suo subietto volger viso,
  da l'odio proprio son le cose tute;

e perche' intender non si puo` diviso,
  e per se' stante, alcuno esser dal primo,
  da quello odiare ogne effetto e` deciso.

Resta, se dividendo bene stimo,
  che 'l mal che s'ama e` del prossimo; ed esso
  amor nasce in tre modi in vostro limo.

E' chi, per esser suo vicin soppresso,
  spera eccellenza, e sol per questo brama
  ch'el sia di sua grandezza in basso messo;

e` chi podere, grazia, onore e fama
  teme di perder perch'altri sormonti,
  onde s'attrista si` che 'l contrario ama;

ed e` chi per ingiuria par ch'aonti,
  si` che si fa de la vendetta ghiotto,
  e tal convien che 'l male altrui impronti.

Questo triforme amor qua giu` di sotto
  si piange; or vo' che tu de l'altro intende,
  che corre al ben con ordine corrotto.

Ciascun confusamente un bene apprende
  nel qual si queti l'animo, e disira;
  per che di giugner lui ciascun contende.

Se lento amore a lui veder vi tira
  o a lui acquistar, questa cornice,
  dopo giusto penter, ve ne martira.

Altro ben e` che non fa l'uom felice;
  non e` felicita`, non e` la buona
  essenza, d'ogne ben frutto e radice.

L'amor ch'ad esso troppo s'abbandona,
  di sovr'a noi si piange per tre cerchi;
  ma come tripartito si ragiona,

tacciolo, accio` che tu per te ne cerchi'''".

Hence thou mayst comprehend that love must be
  The seed within yourselves of every virtue,
  And every act that merits punishment.

Now inasmuch as never from the welfare
  Of its own subject can love turn its sight,
  From their own hatred all things are secure;

And since we cannot think of any being
  Standing alone, nor from the First divided,
  Of hating Him is all desire cut off.

Hence if, discriminating, I judge well,
  The evil that one loves is of one's neighbour,
  And this is born in three modes in your clay.

There are, who, by abasement of their neighbour,
  Hope to excel, and therefore only long
  That from his greatness he may be cast down;

There are, who power, grace, honour, and renown
  Fear they may lose because another rises,
  Thence are so sad that the reverse they love;

And there are those whom injury seems to chafe,
  So that it makes them greedy for revenge,
  And such must needs shape out another's harm.

This threefold love is wept for down below;
  Now of the other will I have thee hear,
  That runneth after good with measure faulty.

Each one confusedly a good conceives
  Wherein the mind may rest, and longeth for it;
  Therefore to overtake it each one strives.

If languid love to look on this attract you,
  Or in attaining unto it, this cornice,
  After just penitence, torments you for it.

There's other good that does not make man happy;
  'Tis not felicity, 'tis not the good
  Essence, of every good the fruit and root.

The love that yields itself too much to this
  Above us is lamented in three circles;
  But how tripartite it may be described,

I say not, that thou seek it for thyself."

Purgatorio: Canto XVIII

Virgil further discourses of Love and Free Will. The Abbot of San Zeno.

Posto avea fine al suo ragionamento
  l'alto dottore, e attento guardava
  ne la mia vista s'io parea contento;
	An end had put unto his reasoning
	  The lofty Teacher, and attent was looking
	  Into my face, if I appeared content;

e io, cui nova sete ancor frugava,
  di fuor tacea, e dentro dicea: 'Forse
  lo troppo dimandar ch'io fo li grava'.
	And I, whom a new thirst still goaded on,
	  Without was mute, and said within: "Perchance
	  The too much questioning I make annoys him."

Ma quel padre verace, che s'accorse
  del timido voler che non s'apriva,
  parlando, di parlare ardir mi porse.
	But that true Father, who had comprehended
	  The timid wish, that opened not itself,
	  By speaking gave me hardihood to speak.

Ond'io: "“Maestro, il mio veder s'avviva
  si` nel tuo lume, ch'io discerno chiaro
  quanto la tua ragion parta o descriva.
	Whence I: "My sight is, Master, vivified
	  So in thy light, that clearly I discern
	  Whate'er thy speech importeth or describes.

Pero` ti prego, dolce padre caro,
  che mi dimostri amore, a cui reduci
  ogne buono operare e 'l suo contraro”“.
	Therefore I thee entreat, sweet Father dear,
	  To teach me love, to which thou dost refer
	  Every good action and its contrary."

"“Drizza”“, disse, "“ver' me l'agute luci
  de lo 'ntelletto, e fieti manifesto
  l'error de' ciechi che si fanno duci.
	"Direct," he said, "towards me the keen eyes
	  Of intellect, and clear will be to thee
	  The error of the blind, who would be leaders.

L'animo, ch'e` creato ad amar presto,   ad ogne cosa e` mobile che piace, tosto che dal piacere in atto e` desto.	The soul, which is created apt to love, Is mobile unto everything that pleases, Soon as by pleasure she is waked to action.

Vostra apprensiva da esser verace
  tragge intenzione, e dentro a voi la spiega,
  si` che l'animo ad essa volger face;
	Your apprehension from some real thing
	  An image draws, and in yourselves displays it
	  So that it makes the soul turn unto it.

e se, rivolto, inver' di lei si piega,
  quel piegare e` amor, quell'e` natura
  che per piacer di novo in voi si lega.
	And if, when turned, towards it she incline,
	  Love is that inclination; it is nature,
	  Which is by pleasure bound in you anew

Poi, come 'l foco movesi in altura per la sua forma ch'e` nata a salire   la` dove piu` in sua matera dura,	Then even as the fire doth upward move By its own form, which to ascend is born, Where longest in its matter it endures,
cosi` l'animo preso entra in disire,   ch'e` moto spiritale, e mai non posa fin che la cosa amata il fa gioire.	So comes the captive soul into desire, Which is a motion spiritual, and ne'er rests Until she doth enjoy the thing beloved.

Or ti puote apparer quant'e` nascosa
  la veritate a la gente ch'avvera
  ciascun amore in se' laudabil cosa;
	Now may apparent be to thee how hidden
	  The truth is from those people, who aver
	  All love is in itself a laudable thing;

pero` che forse appar la sua matera   sempre esser buona, ma non ciascun segno   e` buono, ancor che buona sia la cera"".	Because its matter may perchance appear Aye to be good; but yet not each impression Is good, albeit good may be the wax."

""Le tue parole e 'l mio seguace ingegno"",
  rispuos'io lui, ""m'hanno amor discoverto,
  ma cio` m'ha fatto di dubbiar piu` pregno;
	"Thy words, and my sequacious intellect,"
	  I answered him, "have love revealed to me;
	  But that has made me more impregned with doubt;

che', s'amore e` di fuori a noi offerto,   e l'anima non va con altro piede,   se dritta o torta va, non e` suo merto"".	For if love from without be offered us, And with another foot the soul go not, If right or wrong she go, 'tis not her merit."
Ed elli a me: ""Quanto ragion qui vede, dir ti poss'io; da indi in la` t'aspetta   pur a Beatrice, ch'e` opra di fede.	And he to me: "What reason seeth here, Myself can tell thee; beyond that await For Beatrice, since 'tis a work of faith.

Ogne forma sustanzial, che setta
  e` da matera ed e` con lei unita,
  specifica vertute ha in se' colletta,
	Every substantial form, that segregate
	  From matter is, and with it is united,
	  Specific power has in itself collected,

la qual sanza operar non e` sentita,
  ne' si dimostra mai che per effetto,
  come per verdi fronde in pianta vita.
	Which without act is not perceptible,
	  Nor shows itself except by its effect,
	  As life does in a plant by the green leaves.

Pero`, la` onde vegna lo 'ntelletto
  de le prime notizie, omo non sape,
  e de' primi appetibili l'affetto,
	But still, whence cometh the intelligence
	  Of the first notions, man is ignorant,
	  And the affection for the first allurements,

che sono in voi si` come studio in ape
  di far lo mele; e questa prima voglia
  merto di lode o di biasmo non cape.
	Which are in you as instinct in the bee
	  To make its honey; and this first desire
	  Merit of praise or blame containeth not.

Or perche' a questa ogn'altra si raccoglia,
  innata v'e` la virtu` che consiglia,
  e de l'assenso de' tener la soglia.
	Now, that to this all others may be gathered,
	  Innate within you is the power that counsels,
	  And it should keep the threshold of assent.

Quest'e` 'l principio la` onde si piglia
  ragion di meritare in voi, secondo
  che buoni e rei amori accoglie e viglia.
	This is the principle, from which is taken
	  Occasion of desert in you, according
	  As good and guilty loves it takes and winnows.

Color che ragionando andaro al fondo,
  s'accorser d'esta innata libertate;
  pero` moralita` lasciaro al mondo.

Onde, poniam che di necessitate
  surga ogne amor che dentro a voi s'accende,
  di ritenerlo e` in voi la podestate.

La nobile virtu` Beatrice intende
  per lo libero arbitrio, e pero` guarda
  che l'abbi a mente, s'a parlar ten prende'"'.

La luna, quasi a mezza notte tarda,
  facea le stelle a noi parer piu` rade,
  fatta com'un secchion che tuttor arda;

e correa contro 'l ciel per quelle strade
  che 'l sole infiamma allor che quel da Roma
  tra Sardi e ' Corsi il vede quando cade.

E quell'ombra gentil per cui si noma
  Pietola piu` che villa mantoana,
  del mio carcar diposta avea la soma;

per ch'io, che la ragione aperta e piana
  sovra le mie quistioni avea ricolta,
  stava com'om che sonnolento vana.

Ma questa sonnolenza mi fu tolta
  subitamente da gente che dopo
  le nostre spalle a noi era gia` volta.

E quale Ismeno gia` vide e Asopo
  lungo di se` di notte furia e calca,
  pur che i Teban di Bacco avesser uopo,

cotal per quel giron suo passo falca,
  per quel ch'io vidi di color, venendo,
  cui buon volere e giusto amor cavalca.

Tosto fur sovr'a noi, perche' correndo
  si movea tutta quella turba magna;
  e due dinanzi gridavan piangendo:

""Maria corse con fretta a la montagna;
  e Cesare, per soggiogare Ilerda,
  punse Marsilia e poi corse in Ispagna'"'.

""Ratto, ratto, che 'l tempo non si perda
  per poco amor'"', gridavan li altri appresso,
  ""che studio di ben far grazia rinverda'"'.

Those who, in reasoning, to the bottom went,
  Were of this innate liberty aware,
  Therefore bequeathed they Ethics to the world.

Supposing, then, that from necessity
  Springs every love that is within you kindled,
  Within yourselves the power is to restrain it.

The noble virtue Beatrice understands
  By the free will; and therefore see that thou
  Bear it in mind, if she should speak of it."

The moon, belated almost unto midnight,
  Now made the stars appear to us more rare,
  Formed like a bucket, that is all ablaze,

And counter to the heavens ran through those paths
  Which the sun sets aflame, when he of Rome
  Sees it 'twixt Sardes and Corsicans go down;

And that patrician shade, for whom is named
  Pietola more than any Mantuan town,
  Had laid aside the burden of my lading;

Whence I, who reason manifest and plain
  In answer to my questions had received,
  Stood like a man in drowsy reverie.

But taken from me was this drowsiness
  Suddenly by a people, that behind
  Our backs already had come round to us.

And as, of old, Ismenus and Asopus
  Beside them saw at night the rush and throng,
  If but the Thebans were in need of Bacchus,

So they along that circle curve their step,
  From what I saw of those approaching us,
  Who by good-will and righteous love are ridden.

Full soon they were upon us, because running
  Moved onward all that mighty multitude,
  And two in the advance cried out, lamenting,

"Mary in haste unto the mountain ran,
  And Caesar, that he might subdue Ilerda,
  Thrust at Marseilles, and then ran into Spain."

"Quick! quick! so that the time may not be lost
  By little love!" forthwith the others cried,
  "For ardour in well-doing freshens grace!"

""O gente in cui fervore aguto adesso
  ricompie forse negligenza e indugio
  da voi per tepidezza in ben far messo,

questi che vive, e certo i' non vi bugio,
  vuole andar su`, pur che 'l sol ne riluca;
  pero` ne dite ond'e` presso il pertugio"".

Parole furon queste del mio duca;
  e un di quelli spirti disse: ""Vieni
  di retro a noi, e troverai la buca.

Noi siam di voglia a muoverci si` pieni,
  che restar non potem; pero` perdona,
  se villania nostra giustizia tieni.

Io fui abate in San Zeno a Verona
  sotto lo 'mperio del buon Barbarossa,
  di cui dolente ancor Milan ragiona.

E tale ha gia` l'un pie` dentro la fossa,
  che tosto piangera` quel monastero,
  e tristo fia d'avere avuta possa;

perche' suo figlio, mal del corpo intero,
  e de la mente peggio, e che mal nacque,
  ha posto in loco di suo pastor vero"".

Io non so se piu` disse o s'ei si tacque,
  tant'era gia` di la` da noi trascorso;
  ma questo intesi, e ritener mi piacque.

E quei che m'era ad ogne uopo soccorso
  disse: ""Volgiti qua: vedine due
  venir dando a l'accidia di morso"".

Di retro a tutti dicean: ""Prima fue
  morta la gente a cui il mar s'aperse,
  che vedesse Iordan le rede sue.

E quella che l'affanno non sofferse
  fino a la fine col figlio d'Anchise,
  se' stessa a vita sanza gloria offerse"".

Poi quando fuor da noi tanto divise
  quell'ombre, che veder piu` non potiersi,
  novo pensiero dentro a me si mise,

del qual piu` altri nacquero e diversi;
  e tanto d'uno in altro vaneggiai,
  che li occhi per vaghezza ricopersi,

"O folk, in whom an eager fervour now
  Supplies perhaps delay and negligence,
  Put by you in well-doing, through lukewarmness,

This one who lives, and truly I lie not,
  Would fain go up, if but the sun relight us;
  So tell us where the passage nearest is."

These were the words of him who was my Guide;
  And some one of those spirits said: "Come on
  Behind us, and the opening shalt thou find;

So full of longing are we to move onward,
  That stay we cannot; therefore pardon us,
  If thou for churlishness our justice take.

I was San Zeno's Abbot at Verona,
  Under the empire of good Barbarossa,
  Of whom still sorrowing Milan holds discourse;

And he has one foot in the grave already,
  Who shall erelong lament that monastery,
  And sorry be of having there had power,

Because his son, in his whole body sick,
  And worse in mind, and who was evil-born,
  He put into the place of its true pastor."

If more he said, or silent was, I know not,
  He had already passed so far beyond us;
  But this I heard, and to retain it pleased me.

And he who was in every need my succour
  Said: "Turn thee hitherward; see two of them
  Come fastening upon slothfulness their teeth."

In rear of all they shouted: "Sooner were
  The people dead to whom the sea was opened,
  Than their inheritors the Jordan saw;

And those who the fatigue did not endure
  Unto the issue, with Anchises' son,
  Themselves to life withouten glory offered."

Then when from us so separated were
  Those shades, that they no longer could be seen,
  Within me a new thought did entrance find,

Whence others many and diverse were born;
  And so I lapsed from one into another,
  That in a reverie mine eyes I closed,

e 'l pensamento in sogno trasmutai.   And meditation into dream transmuted.

Purgatorio: Canto XIX

Dante's Dream of the Siren. The Fifth Circle: The Avaricious and Prodigal. Pope Adrian V.

Ne l'ora che non puo` 'l calor diurno   intepidar piu` 'l freddo de la luna, vinto da terra, e talor da Saturno	It was the hour when the diurnal heat No more can warm the coldness of the moon, Vanquished by earth, or peradventure Saturn,

- quando i geomanti lor Maggior Fortuna
  veggiono in oriiente, innanzi a l'alba,
  surger per via che poco le sta bruna -,
	When geomancers their Fortuna Major
	  See in the orient before the dawn
	  Rise by a path that long remains not dim,

mi venne in sogno una femmina balba,
  ne li occhi guercia, e sovra i pie` distorta,
  con le man monche, e di colore scialba.
	There came to me in dreams a stammering woman,
	  Squint in her eyes, and in her feet distorted,
	  With hands dissevered and of sallow hue.

Io la mirava; e come 'l sol conforta
  le fredde membra che la notte aggrava,
  cosi` lo sguardo mio le facea scorta
	I looked at her; and as the sun restores
	  The frigid members which the night benumbs,
	  Even thus my gaze did render voluble

la lingua, e poscia tutta la drizzava
  in poco d'ora, e lo smarrito volto,
  com' amor vuol, cosi` le colorava.
	Her tongue, and made her all erect thereafter
	  In little while, and the lost countenance
	  As love desires it so in her did colour.

Poi ch'ell' avea 'l parlar cosi` disciolto,   cominciava a cantar si`, che con pena da lei avrei mio intento rivolto.	When in this wise she had her speech unloosed, She 'gan to sing so, that with difficulty Could I have turned my thoughts away from her.

""Io son"", cantava, ""io son dolce serena,
  che' marinari in mezzo mar dismago;
  tanto son di piacere a sentir piena!
	"I am," she sang, "I am the Siren sweet
	  Who mariners amid the main unman,
	  So full am I of pleasantness to hear.

Io volsi Ulisse del suo cammin vago
  al canto mio; e qual meco s'ausa,
  rado sen parte; si` tutto l'appago!"".
	I drew Ulysses from his wandering way
	  Unto my song, and he who dwells with me
	  Seldom departs so wholly I content him."

Ancor non era sua bocca richiusa,
  quand' una donna apparve santa e presta
  lunghesso me per far colei confusa.
	Her mouth was not yet closed again, before
	  Appeared a Lady saintly and alert
	  Close at my side to put her to confusion.

““O Virgilio, Virgilio, chi e` questa?”“,
  fieramente dicea; ed el venia
  con li occhi fitti pur in quella onesta.

L'altra prendea, e dinanzi l'apria
  fendendo i drappi, e mostravami 'l ventre;
  quel mi sveglio` col puzzo che n'uscia.

Io mossi li occhi, e 'l buon maestro: ““Almen tre
  voci t'ho messe!”“, dicea, ““Surgi e vieni;
  troviam l'aperta per la qual tu entre”“.

Su` mi levai, e tutti eran gia` pieni
  de l'alto di` i giron del sacro monte,
  e andavam col sol novo a le reni.

Seguendo lui, portava la mia fronte
  come colui che l'ha di pensier carca,
  che fa di se' un mezzo arco di ponte;

quand' io udi' ““Venite; qui si varca”“
  parlare in modo soave e benigno,
  qual non si sente in questa mortal marca.

Con l'ali aperte, che parean di cigno,
  volseci in su` colui che si` parlonne
  tra due pareti del duro macigno.

Mosse le penne poi e ventilonne,
  'Qui lugent' affermando esser beati,
  ch'avran di consolar l'anime donne.

““Che hai che pur inver' la terra guati?”“,
  la guida mia incomincio` a dirmi,
  poco amendue da l'angel sormontati.

E io: ““Con tanta sospeccion fa irmi
  novella visiion ch'a se' mi piega,
  si` ch'io non posso dal pensar partirmi”“.

““Vedesti”“, disse, ““quell'antica strega
  che sola sovr' a noi omai si piagne;
  vedesti come l'uom da lei si slega.

Bastiti, e batti a terra le calcagne;
  li occhi rivolgi al logoro che gira
  lo rege etterno con le rote magne”“.

Quale 'l falcon, che prima a' pie' si mira,
  indi si volge al grido e si protende
  per lo disio del pasto che la` il tira,

"Virgilius, O Virgilius! who is this?"
  Sternly she said; and he was drawing near
  With eyes still fixed upon that modest one.

She seized the other and in front laid open,
  Rending her garments, and her belly showed me;
  This waked me with the stench that issued from it.

I turned mine eyes, and good Virgilius said:
  "At least thrice have I called thee; rise and come;
  Find we the opening by which thou mayst enter."

I rose; and full already of high day
  Were all the circles of the Sacred Mountain,
  And with the new sun at our back we went.

Following behind him, I my forehead bore
  Like unto one who has it laden with thought,
  Who makes himself the half arch of a bridge,

When I heard say, "Come, here the passage is,"
  Spoken in a manner gentle and benign,
  Such as we hear not in this mortal region.

With open wings, which of a swan appeared,
  Upward he turned us who thus spake to us,
  Between the two walls of the solid granite.

He moved his pinions afterwards and fanned us,
  Affirming those 'qui lugent' to be blessed,
  For they shall have their souls with comfort filled.

"What aileth thee, that aye to earth thou gazest?"
  To me my Guide began to say, we both
  Somewhat beyond the Angel having mounted.

And I: "With such misgiving makes me go
  A vision new, which bends me to itself,
  So that I cannot from the thought withdraw me."

"Didst thou behold," he said, "that old enchantress,
  Who sole above us henceforth is lamented?
  Didst thou behold how man is freed from her?

Suffice it thee, and smite earth with thy heels,
  Thine eyes lift upward to the lure, that whirls
  The Eternal King with revolutions vast."

Even as the hawk, that first his feet surveys,
  Then turns him to the call and stretches forward,
  Through the desire of food that draws him thither,

tal mi fec' io; e tal, quanto si fende
la roccia per dar via a chi va suso,
n'andai infin dove 'l cerchiar si prende.

Com'io nel quinto giro fui dischiuso,
vidi gente per esso che piangea,
giacendo a terra tutta volta in giuso.

'Adhaesit pavimento anima mea'
sentia dir lor con si` alti sospiri,
che la parola a pena s'intendea.

““O eletti di Dio, li cui soffriri
e giustizia e speranza fa men duri,
drizzate noi verso li alti saliri”“.

““Se voi venite dal giacer sicuri,
e volete trovar la via piu` tosto,
le vostre destre sien sempre di fori”“.

Cosi` prego` 'l poeta, e si` risposto
poco dinanzi a noi ne fu; per ch'io
nel parlare avvisai l'altro nascosto,

e volsi li occhi a li occhi al segnor mio:
ond' elli m'assenti` con lieto cenno
cio` che chiedea la vista del disio.

Poi ch'io potei di me fare a mio senno,
trassimi sovra quella creatura
le cui parole pria notar mi fenno,

dicendo: ““Spirto in cui pianger matura
quel sanza 'l quale a Dio tornar non possi,
sosta un poco per me tua maggior cura.

Chi fosti e perche' volti avete i dossi
al su`, mi di`, e se vuo' ch'io t'impetri
cosa di la` ond' io vivendo mossi”“.

Ed elli a me: ““Perche' i nostri diretri
rivolga il cielo a se', saprai; ma prima
scias quod ego fui successor Petri.

Intra Siiestri e Chiaveri s'adima
una fiumana bella, e del suo nome
lo titol del mio sangue fa sua cima.

Such I became, and such, as far as cleaves
The rock to give a way to him who mounts,
Went on to where the circling doth begin.

On the fifth circle when I had come forth,
People I saw upon it who were weeping,
Stretched prone upon the ground, all downward
turned.

"Adhaesit pavimento anima mea,"
I heard them say with sighings so profound,
That hardly could the words be understood.

"O ye elect of God, whose sufferings
Justice and Hope both render less severe,
Direct ye us towards the high ascents."

"If ye are come secure from this prostration,
And wish to find the way most speedily,
Let your right hands be evermore outside."

Thus did the Poet ask, and thus was answered
By them somewhat in front of us; whence I
In what was spoken divined the rest concealed,

And unto my Lord's eyes mine eyes I turned;
Whence he assented with a cheerful sign
To what the sight of my desire implored.

When of myself I could dispose at will,
Above that creature did I draw myself,
Whose words before had caused me to take note,

Saying: "O Spirit, in whom weeping ripens
That without which to God we cannot turn,
Suspend awhile for me thy greater care.

Who wast thou, and why are your backs turned up-
wards,
Tell me, and if thou wouldst that I procure thee
Anything there whence living I departed."

And he to me: "Wherefore our backs the heaven
Turns to itself, know shalt thou; but beforehand
'Scias quod ego fui successor Petri.'

Between Siestri and Chiaveri descends
A river beautiful, and of its name
The title of my blood its summit makes.

Un mese e` poco piu` prova' io come
  pesa il gran manto a chi dal fango il guarda,
  che piuma sembran tutte l'altre some.

La mia conversiione, ome`!, fu tarda;
  ma, come fatto fui roman pastore,
  cosi` scopersi la vita bugiarda.

Vidi che li` non s'acquetava il core,
  ne' piu` salir potiesi in quella vita;
  er che di questa in me s'accese amore.

Fino a quel punto misera e partita
  da Dio anima fui, del tutto avara;
  or, come vedi, qui ne son punita.

Quel ch'avarizia fa, qui si dichiara
  in purgazion de l'anime converse;
  e nulla pena il monte ha piu` amara.

Si` come l'occhio nostro non s'aderse
  in alto, fisso a le cose terrene,
  cosi` giustizia qui a terra il merse.

Come avarizia spense a ciascun bene
  lo nostro amore, onde operar perdesi,
  cosi` giustizia qui stretti ne tene,

ne' piedi e ne le man legati e presi;
  e quanto fia piacer del giusto Sire,
  tanto staremo immobili e distesi"".

Io m'era inginocchiato e volea dire;
  ma com' io cominciai ed el s'accorse,
  solo ascoltando, del mio reverire,

""Qual cagion"", disse, ""in giu` cosi` ti torse?"".
  E io a lui: ""Per vostra dignitate
  mia cosciienza dritto mi rimorse"".

""Drizza le gambe, levati su`, frate!"",
  rispuose; ""non errar: conservo sono
  teco e con li altri ad una podestate.

Se mai quel santo evangelico suono
  che dice 'Neque nubent' intendesti,
  ben puoi veder perch'io cosi` ragiono.

A month and little more essayed I how
  Weighs the great cloak on him from mire who
      keeps it,
  For all the other burdens seem a feather.

Tardy, ah woe is me! was my conversion;
  But when the Roman Shepherd I was made,
  Then I discovered life to be a lie.

I saw that there the heart was not at rest,
  Nor farther in that life could one ascend;
  Whereby the love of this was kindled in me.

Until that time a wretched soul and parted
  From God was I, and wholly avaricious;
  Now, as thou seest, I here am punished for it.

What avarice does is here made manifest
  In the purgation of these souls converted,
  And no more bitter pain the Mountain has.

Even as our eye did not uplift itself
  Aloft, being fastened upon earthly things,
  So justice here has merged it in the earth.

As avarice had extinguished our affection
  For every good, whereby was action lost,
  So justice here doth hold us in restraint,

Bound and imprisoned by the feet and hands;
  And so long as it pleases the just Lord
  Shall we remain immovable and prostrate."

I on my knees had fallen, and wished to speak;
  But even as I began, and he was 'ware,
  Only by listening, of my reverence,

"What cause," he said, "has downward bent thee
      thus?"
  And I to him: "For your own dignity,
  Standing, my conscience stung me with remorse."

"Straighten thy legs, and upward raise thee, brother,"
  He answered: "Err not, fellow-servant am I
  With thee and with the others to one power.

If e'er that holy, evangelic sound,
  Which sayeth 'neque nubent,' thou hast heard,
  Well canst thou see why in this wise I speak.

Vattene omai: non vo' che piu` t'arresti;
  che' la tua stanza mio pianger disagia,
  col qual maturo cio` che tu dicesti.

Nepote ho io di la` c'ha nome Alagia,
  buona da se', pur che la nostra casa
  non faccia lei per essempro malvagia;

e questa sola di la` m'e` rimasa"".

Now go; no longer will I have thee linger,
  Because thy stay doth incommode my weeping,
  With which I ripen that which thou hast said.

On earth I have a grandchild named Alagia,
  Good in herself, unless indeed our house
  Malevolent may make her by example,

And she alone remains to me on earth."

Purgatorio: Canto XX

Hugh Capet. Corruption of the French Crown.   Prophecy of the Abduction of Pope Boniface VIII and the Sacrilege of Philip the Fair. The Earthquake.

Contra miglior voler voler mal pugna;
  onde contra 'l piacer mio, per piacerli,
  trassi de l'acqua non sazia la spugna.

Mossimi; e 'l duca mio si mosse per li
  luoghi spediti pur lungo la roccia,
  come si va per muro stretto a' merli;

che' la gente che fonde a goccia a goccia
  per li occhi il mal che tutto 'l mondo occupa,
  da l'altra parte in fuor troppo s'approccia.

Maladetta sie tu, antica lupa,
  che piu` che tutte l'altre bestie hai preda
  per la tua fame sanza fine cupa!

O ciel, nel cui girar par che si creda
  le condizion di qua giu` trasmutarsi,
  quando verra` per cui questa disceda?

Noi andavam con passi lenti e scarsi,
  e io attento a l'ombre, ch'i' sentia
  pietosamente piangere e lagnarsi;

e per ventura udi' ""Dolce Maria!""
  dinanzi a noi chiamar cosi` nel pianto
  come fa donna che in parturir sia;

e seguitar: ""Povera fosti tanto,
  quanto veder si puo` per quello ospizio
  dove sponesti il tuo portato santo"".

Ill strives the will against a better will;
  Therefore, to pleasure him, against my pleasure
  I drew the sponge not saturate from the water.

Onward I moved, and onward moved my Leader,
  Through vacant places, skirting still the rock,
  As on a wall close to the battlements;

For they that through their eyes pour drop by drop
  The malady which all the world pervades,
  On the other side too near the verge approach.

Accursed mayst thou be, thou old she-wolf,
  That more than all the other beasts hast prey,
  Because of hunger infinitely hollow!

O heaven, in whose gyrations some appear
  To think conditions here below are changed,
  When will he come through whom she shall depart?

Onward we went with footsteps slow and scarce,
  And I attentive to the shades I heard
  Piteously weeping and bemoaning them;

And I by peradventure heard "Sweet Mary!"
  Uttered in front of us amid the weeping
  Even as a woman does who is in child-birth;

And in continuance: "How poor thou wast
  Is manifested by that hostelry
  Where thou didst lay thy sacred burden down."

Seguentemente intesi: ""O buon Fabrizio,
  con poverta` volesti anzi virtute
  che gran ricchezza posseder con vizio""".

Queste parole m'eran si` piaciute,
  ch'io mi trassi oltre per aver contezza
  di quello spirto onde parean venute.

Esso parlava ancor de la larghezza
  che fece Niccolo` a le pulcelle,
  per condurre ad onor lor giovinezza.

""O anima che tanto ben favelle,
  dimmi chi fosti"", dissi, ""e perche' sola
  tu queste degne lode rinovelle.

Non fia sanza merce' la tua parola,
  s'io ritorno a compier lo cammin corto
  di quella vita ch'al termine vola""".

Ed elli: ""Io ti diro`, non per conforto
  ch'io attenda di la`, ma perche' tanta
  grazia in te luce prima che sie morto.

Io fui radice de la mala pianta
  che la terra cristiana tutta aduggia,
  si` che buon frutto rado se ne schianta.

Ma se Doagio, Lilla, Guanto e Bruggia
  potesser, tosto ne saria vendetta;
  e io la cheggio a lui che tutto giuggia.

Chiamato fui di la` Ugo Ciappetta;
  di me son nati i Filippi e i Luigi
  per cui novellamente e` Francia retta.

Figliuol fu' io d'un beccaio di Parigi:
  quando li regi antichi venner meno
  tutti, fuor ch'un renduto in panni bigi,

trova'mi stretto ne le mani il freno
  del governo del regno, e tanta possa
  di nuovo acquisto, e si` d'amici pieno,

ch'a la corona vedova promossa
  la testa di mio figlio fu, dal quale
  cominciar di costor le sacrate ossa.

Mentre che la gran dota provenzale
  al sangue mio non tolse la vergogna,
  poco valea, ma pur non facea male.

Thereafterward I heard: "O good Fabricius,
  Virtue with poverty didst thou prefer
  To the possession of great wealth with vice."

So pleasurable were these words to me
  That I drew farther onward to have knowledge
  Touching that spirit whence they seemed to come.

He furthermore was speaking of the largess
  Which Nicholas unto the maidens gave,
  In order to conduct their youth to honour.

"O soul that dost so excellently speak,
  Tell me who wast thou," said I, "and why only
  Thou dost renew these praises well deserved?

Not without recompense shall be thy word,
  If I return to finish the short journey
  Of that life which is flying to its end."

And he: "I'll tell thee, not for any comfort
  I may expect from earth, but that so much
  Grace shines in thee or ever thou art dead.

I was the root of that malignant plant
  Which overshadows all the Christian world,
  So that good fruit is seldom gathered from it;

But if Douay and Ghent, and Lille and Bruges
  Had Power, soon vengeance would be taken on it;
  And this I pray of Him who judges all.

Hugh Capet was I called upon the earth;
  From me were born the Louises and Philips,
  By whom in later days has France been governed.

I was the son of a Parisian butcher,
  What time the ancient kings had perished all,
  Excepting one, contrite in cloth of gray.

I found me grasping in my hands the rein
  Of the realm's government, and so great power
  Of new acquest, and so with friends abounding,

That to the widowed diadem promoted
  The head of mine own offspring was, from whom
  The consecrated bones of these began.

So long as the great dowry of Provence
  Out of my blood took not the sense of shame,
  'Twas little worth, but still it did no harm.

Li` comincio` con forza e con menzogna
 la sua rapina; e poscia, per ammenda,
 Ponti` e Normandia prese e Guascogna.

Carlo venne in Italia e, per ammenda,
 vittima fe' di Curradino; e poi
 ripinse al ciel Tommaso, per ammenda.

Tempo vegg'io, non molto dopo ancoi,
 che tragge un altro Carlo fuor di Francia,
 per far conoscer meglio e se' e ' suoi.

Sanz'arme n'esce e solo con la lancia
 con la qual giostro` Giuda, e quella ponta
 si` ch'a Fiorenza fa scoppiar la pancia.

Quindi non terra, ma peccato e onta
 guadagnera`, per se' tanto piu` grave,
 quanto piu` lieve simil danno conta.

L'altro, che gia` usci` preso di nave,
 veggio vender sua figlia e patteggiarne
 come fanno i corsar de l'altre schiave.

O avarizia, che puoi tu piu` farne,
 poscia c'ha' il mio sangue a te si` tratto,
 che non si cura de la propria carne?

Perche' men paia il mal futuro e 'l fatto,
 veggio in Alagna intrar lo fiordaliso,
 e nel vicario suo Cristo esser catto.

Veggiolo un'altra volta esser deriso;
 veggio rinovellar l'aceto e 'l fiele,
 e tra vivi ladroni esser anciso.

Veggio il novo Pilato si` crudele,
 che cio` nol sazia, ma sanza decreto
 portar nel Tempio le cupide vele.

O Segnor mio, quando saro` io lieto
 a veder la vendetta che, nascosa,
 fa dolce l'ira tua nel tuo secreto?

Cio` ch'io dicea di quell'unica sposa
 de lo Spirito Santo e che ti fece
 verso me volger per alcuna chiosa,

tanto e` risposto a tutte nostre prece
 quanto 'l di` dura; ma com'el s'annotta,
 contrario suon prendemo in quella vece.

Then it began with falsehood and with force
 Its rapine; and thereafter, for amends,
 Took Ponthieu, Normandy, and Gascony.

Charles came to Italy, and for amends
 A victim made of Conradin, and then
 Thrust Thomas back to heaven, for amends.

A time I see, not very distant now,
 Which draweth forth another Charles from France,
 The better to make known both him and his.

Unarmed he goes, and only with the lance
 That Judas jousted with; and that he thrusts
 So that he makes the paunch of Florence burst.

He thence not land, but sin and infamy,
 Shall gain, so much more grievous to himself
 As the more light such damage he accounts.

The other, now gone forth, ta'en in his ship,
 See I his daughter sell, and chaffer for her
 As corsairs do with other female slaves.

What more, O Avarice, canst thou do to us,
 Since thou my blood so to thyself hast drawn,
 It careth not for its own proper flesh?

That less may seem the future ill and past,
 I see the flower-de-luce Alagna enter,
 And Christ in his own Vicar captive made.

I see him yet another time derided;
 I see renewed the vinegar and gall,
 And between living thieves I see him slain.

I see the modern Pilate so relentless,
 This does not sate him, but without decretal
 He to the temple bears his sordid sails!

When, O my Lord! shall I be joyful made
 By looking on the vengeance which, concealed,
 Makes sweet thine anger in thy secrecy?

What I was saying of that only bride
 Of the Holy Ghost, and which occasioned thee
 To turn towards me for some commentary,

So long has been ordained to all our prayers
 As the day lasts; but when the night comes on,
 Contrary sound we take instead thereof.

Noi repetiam Pigmalion allotta,
  cui traditore e ladro e paricida
  fece la voglia sua de l'oro ghiotta;
	At that time we repeat Pygmalion,
	  Of whom a traitor, thief, and parricide
	  Made his insatiable desire of gold;

e la miseria de l'avaro Mida,
  che segui` a la sua dimanda gorda,
  per la qual sempre convien che si rida.
	And the misery of avaricious Midas,
	  That followed his inordinate demand,
	  At which forevermore one needs but laugh.

Del folle Acan ciascun poi si ricorda,
  come furo` le spoglie, si` che l'ira
  di Iosue` qui par ch'ancor lo morda.
	The foolish Achan each one then records,
	  And how he stole the spoils; so that the wrath
	  Of Joshua still appears to sting him here.

Indi accusiam col marito Saffira;
  lodiam i calci ch'ebbe Eliodoro;
  e in infamia tutto 'l monte gira
	Then we accuse Sapphira with her husband,
	  We laud the hoof-beats Heliodorus had,
	  And the whole mount in infamy encircles

Polinestor ch'ancise Polidoro;
  ultimamente ci si grida: "Crasso,
  dilci, che 'l sai: di che sapore e` l'oro?".
	Polymnestor who murdered Polydorus.
	  Here finally is cried: 'O Crassus, tell us,
	  For thou dost know, what is the taste of gold?'

Talor parla l'uno alto e l'altro basso,
  secondo l'affezion ch'ad ir ci sprona
  ora a maggiore e ora a minor passo:
	Sometimes we speak, one loud, another low,
	  According to desire of speech, that spurs us
	  To greater now and now to lesser pace.

pero` al ben che 'l di` ci si ragiona,
  dianzi non era io sol; ma qui da presso
  non alzava la voce altra persona"".
	But in the good that here by day is talked of,
	  Erewhile alone I was not; yet near by
	  No other person lifted up his voice."

Noi eravam partiti gia` da esso,
  e brigavam di soverchiar la strada
  tanto quanto al poder n'era permesso,
	From him already we departed were,
	  And made endeavour to o'ercome the road
	  As much as was permitted to our power,

quand'io senti', come cosa che cada,
  tremar lo monte; onde mi prese un gelo
  qual prender suol colui ch'a morte vada.
	When I perceived, like something that is falling,
	  The mountain tremble, whence a chill seized on
	    me,
	  As seizes him who to his death is going.

Certo non si scoteo si` forte Delo,
  pria che Latona in lei facesse 'l nido
  a parturir li due occhi del cielo.
	Certes so violently shook not Delos,
	  Before Latona made her nest therein
	  To give birth to the two eyes of the heaven.

Poi comincio` da tutte parti un grido
  tal, che 'l maestro inverso me si feo,
  dicendo: ""Non dubbiar, mentr'io ti guido"".
	Then upon all sides there began a cry,
	  Such that the Master drew himself towards me,
	  Saying, "Fear not, while I am guiding thee."

'Gloria in excelsis' tutti 'Deo'
  dicean, per quel ch'io da' vicin compresi,
  onde intender lo grido si poteo.
	"Gloria in excelsis Deo," all
	  Were saying, from what near I comprehended,
	  Where it was possible to hear the cry.

No' istavamo immobili e sospesi
  come i pastor che prima udir quel canto,
  fin che 'l tremar cesso` ed el compiesi.

Poi ripigliammo nostro cammin santo,
  guardando l'ombre che giacean per terra,
  tornate gia` in su l'usato pianto.

Nulla ignoranza mai con tanta guerra
  mi fe' desideroso di sapere,
  se la memoria mia in cio` non erra,

quanta pareami allor, pensando, avere;
  ne' per la fretta dimandare er'oso,
  ne' per me li` potea cosa vedere:

cosi` m'andava timido e pensoso.

We paused immovable and in suspense,
  Even as the shepherds who first heard that song,
  Until the trembling ceased, and it was finished.

Then we resumed again our holy path,
  Watching the shades that lay upon the ground,
  Already turned to their accustomed plaint.

No ignorance ever with so great a strife
  Had rendered me importunate to know,
  If erreth not in this my memory,

As meditating then I seemed to have;
  Nor out of haste to question did I dare,
  Nor of myself I there could aught perceive;

So I went onward timorous and thoughtful.

Purgatorio: Canto XXI

The Poet Statius. Praise of Virgil.

a sete natural che mai non sazia
  se non con l'acqua onde la femminetta
  samaritana domando` la grazia,
	The natural thirst, that ne'er is satisfied
	  Excepting with the water for whose grace
	  The woman of Samaria besought,

mi travagliava, e pungeami la fretta
  per la 'mpacciata via dietro al mio duca,
  e condoleami a la giusta vendetta.
	Put me in travail, and haste goaded me
	  Along the encumbered path behind my Leader
	  And I was pitying that righteous vengeance;

Ed ecco, si` come ne scrive Luca   che Cristo apparve a' due ch'erano in via,   gia` surto fuor de la sepulcral buca,	And lo! in the same manner as Luke writeth That Christ appeared to two upon the way From the sepulchral cave already risen,
ci apparve un'ombra, e dietro a noi venia, dal pie` guardando la turba che giace;   ne' ci addemmo di lei, si` parlo` pria,	A shade appeared to us, and came behind us, Down gazing on the prostrate multitude, Nor were we ware of it, until it spake,

dicendo; ""O frati miei, Dio vi dea pace"".
  Noi ci volgemmo subiti, e Virgilio
  rendeli 'l cenno ch'a cio` si conface.
	Saying, "My brothers, may God give you peace!"
	  We turned us suddenly, and Virgilius rendered
	  To him the countersign thereto conforming.

Poi comincio`: ""Nel beato concilio
  ti ponga in pace la verace corte
  che me rilega ne l'etterno essilio"".
	Thereon began he: "In the blessed council,
	  Thee may the court veracious place in peace,
	  That me doth banish in eternal exile!"

""Come!"", diss'elli, e parte andavam forte:
  ""se voi siete ombre che Dio su` non degni,
  chi v'ha per la sua scala tanto scorte?"".
	"How," said he, and the while we went with speed,
	  "If ye are shades whom God deigns not on high,
	  Who up his stairs so far has guided you?"

E 'l dottor mio: ""Se tu riguardi a' segni
  che questi porta e che l'angel profila,
  ben vedrai che coi buon convien ch'e' regni.
	And said my Teacher: "If thou note the marks
	  Which this one bears, and which the Angel traces
	  Well shalt thou see he with the good must reign.

Ma perche' lei che di` e notte fila
  non li avea tratta ancora la conocchia
  che Cloto impone a ciascuno e compila,
	But because she who spinneth day and night
	  For him had not yet drawn the distaff off,
	  Which Clotho lays for each one and compacts,

l'anima sua, ch'e` tua e mia serocchia,
  venendo su`, non potea venir sola,
  pero` ch'al nostro modo non adocchia.

Ond'io fui tratto fuor de l'ampia gola
  d'inferno per mostrarli, e mosterrolli
  oltre, quanto 'l potra` menar mia scola.

Ma dimmi, se tu sai, perche' tai crolli
  die` dianzi 'l monte, e perche' tutto ad una
  parve gridare infino a' suoi pie` molli'"".

Si` mi die`, dimandando, per la cruna
  del mio disio, che pur con la speranza
  si fece la mia sete men digiuna.

Quei comincio`: """Cosa non e` che sanza
  ordine senta la religione
  de la montagna, o che sia fuor d'usanza.

Libero e` qui da ogne alterazione:
  di quel che 'l ciel da se' in se' riceve
  esser ci puote, e non d'altro, cagione.

Per che non pioggia, non grando, non neve,
  non rugiada, non brina piu` su` cade
  che la scaletta di tre gradi breve;

nuvole spesse non paion ne' rade,
  ne' coruscar, ne' figlia di Taumante,
  che di la` cangia sovente contrade;

secco vapor non surge piu` avante
  ch'al sommo d'i tre gradi ch'io parlai,
  dov'ha 'l vicario di Pietro le piante.

Trema forse piu` giu` poco o assai;
  ma per vento che 'n terra si nasconda,
  non so come, qua su` non tremo` mai.

Tremaci quando alcuna anima monda
  sentesi, si` che surga o che si mova
  per salir su`; e tal grido seconda.

De la mondizia sol voler fa prova,
  che, tutto libero a mutar convento,
  l'alma sorprende, e di voler le giova.

Prima vuol ben, ma non lascia il talento
  che divina giustizia, contra voglia,
  come fu al peccar, pone al tormento.

His soul, which is thy sister and my own,
  In coming upwards could not come alone,
  By reason that it sees not in our fashion.

Whence I was drawn from out the ample throat
  Of Hell to be his guide, and I shall guide him
  As far on as my school has power to lead.

But tell us, if thou knowest, why such a shudder
  Erewhile the mountain gave, and why together
  All seemed to cry, as far as its moist feet?"

In asking he so hit the very eye
  Of my desire, that merely with the hope
  My thirst became the less unsatisfied.

"Naught is there," he began, "that without order
  May the religion of the mountain feel,
  Nor aught that may be foreign to its custom.

Free is it here from every permutation;
  What from itself heaven in itself receiveth
  Can be of this the cause, and naught beside;

Because that neither rain, nor hail, nor snow,
  Nor dew, nor hoar-frost any higher falls
  Than the short, little stairway of three steps.

Dense clouds do not appear, nor rarefied,
  Nor coruscation, nor the daughter of Thaumas,
  That often upon earth her region shifts;

No arid vapour any farther rises
  Than to the top of the three steps I spake of,
  Whereon the Vicar of Peter has his feet.

Lower down perchance it trembles less or more,
  But, for the wind that in the earth is hidden
  I know not how, up here it never trembled.

It trembles here, whenever any soul
  Feels itself pure, so that it soars, or moves
  To mount aloft, and such a cry attends it.

Of purity the will alone gives proof,
  Which, being wholly free to change its convent,
  Takes by surprise the soul, and helps it fly.

First it wills well; but the desire permits not,
  Which divine justice with the self-same will
  There was to sin, upon the torment sets.

E io, che son giaciuto a questa doglia
  cinquecent'anni e piu`, pur mo sentii
  libera volonta` di miglior soglia:

pero` sentisti il tremoto e li pii
  spiriti per lo monte render lode
  a quel Segnor, che tosto su` li 'nvii"".

Cosi` ne disse; e pero` ch'el si gode
  tanto del ber quant'e` grande la sete.
  non saprei dir quant'el mi fece prode.

E 'l savio duca: ""Omai veggio la rete
  che qui v'impiglia e come si scalappia,
  perche' ci trema e di che congaudete.

Ora chi fosti, piacciati ch'io sappia,
  e perche' tanti secoli giaciuto
  qui se', ne le parole tue mi cappia"".

""Nel tempo che 'l buon Tito, con l'aiuto
  del sommo rege, vendico` le fora
  ond'usci` 'l sangue per Giuda venduto,

col nome che piu` dura e piu` onora
  era io di la`"", rispuose quello spirto,
  ""famoso assai, ma non con fede ancora.

Tanto fu dolce mio vocale spirto,
  che, tolosano, a se' mi trasse Roma,
  dove mertai le tempie ornar di mirto.

Stazio la gente ancor di la` mi noma:
  cantai di Tebe, e poi del grande Achille;
  ma caddi in via con la seconda soma.

Al mio ardor fuor seme le faville,
  che mi scaldar, de la divina fiamma
  onde sono allumati piu` di mille;

de l'Eneida dico, la qual mamma
  fummi e fummi nutrice poetando:
  sanz'essa non fermai peso di dramma.

E per esser vivuto di la` quando
  visse Virgilio, assentirei un sole
  piu` che non deggio al mio uscir di bando"".

Volser Virgilio a me queste parole
  con viso che, tacendo, disse 'Taci';
  ma non puo` tutto la virtu` che vuole;

And I, who have been lying in this pain
  Five hundred years and more, but just now felt
  A free volition for a better seat.

Therefore thou heardst the earthquake, and the pious
  Spirits along the mountain rendering praise
  Unto the Lord, that soon he speed them upwards."

So said he to him; and since we enjoy
  As much in drinking as the thirst is great,
  I could not say how much it did me good.

And the wise Leader: "Now I see the net
  That snares you here, and how ye are set free,
  Why the earth quakes, and wherefore ye rejoice.

Now who thou wast be pleased that I may know;
  And why so many centuries thou hast here
  Been lying, let me gather from thy words."

"In days when the good Titus, with the aid
  Of the supremest King, avenged the wounds
  Whence issued forth the blood by Judas sold,

Under the name that most endures and honours,
  Was I on earth," that spirit made reply,
  "Greatly renowned, but not with faith as yet.

My vocal spirit was so sweet, that Rome
  Me, a Thoulousian, drew unto herself,
  Where I deserved to deck my brows with myrtle.

Statius the people name me still on earth;
  I sang of Thebes, and then of great Achilles;
  But on the way fell with my second burden.

The seeds unto my ardour were the sparks
  Of that celestial flame which heated me,
  Whereby more than a thousand have been fired;

Of the Aeneid speak I, which to me
  A mother was, and was my nurse in song;
  Without this weighed I not a drachma's weight.

And to have lived upon the earth what time
  Virgilius lived, I would accept one sun
  More than I must ere issuing from my ban."

These words towards me made Virgilius turn
  With looks that in their silence said, "Be silent!"
  But yet the power that wills cannot do all things;

che' riso e pianto son tanto seguaci
  a la passion di che ciascun si spicca,
  che men seguon voler ne' piu` veraci.

Io pur sorrisi come l'uom ch'ammicca;
  per che l'ombra si tacque, e riguardommi
  ne li occhi ove 'l sembiante piu` si ficca;

e ""Se tanto labore in bene assommi"",
  disse, ""perche' la tua faccia testeso
  un lampeggiar di riso dimostrommi?"".

Or son io d'una parte e d'altra preso:
  l'una mi fa tacer, l'altra scongiura
  ch'io dica; ond'io sospiro, e sono inteso

dal mio maestro, e ""Non aver paura"",
  mi dice, ""di parlar; ma parla e digli
  quel ch'e' dimanda con cotanta cura"".

Ond'io: ""Forse che tu ti maravigli,
  antico spirto, del rider ch'io fei;
  ma piu` d'ammirazion vo' che ti pigli.

Questi che guida in alto li occhi miei,
  e` quel Virgilio dal qual tu togliesti
  forza a cantar de li uomini e d'i dei.

Se cagion altra al mio rider credesti,
  lasciala per non vera, ed esser credi
  quelle parole che di lui dicesti"".

Gia` s'inchinava ad abbracciar li piedi
  al mio dottor, ma el li disse: ""Frate,
  non far, che' tu se' ombra e ombra vedi"".

Ed ei surgendo: ""Or puoi la quantitate
  comprender de l'amor ch'a te mi scalda,
  quand'io dismento nostra vanitate,

trattando l'ombre come cosa salda"".

For tears and laughter are such pursuivants
  Unto the passion from which each springs forth,
  In the most truthful least the will they follow.

I only smiled, as one who gives the wink;
  Whereat the shade was silent, and it gazed
  Into mine eyes, where most expression dwells;

And, "As thou well mayst consummate a labour
  So great," it said, "why did thy face just now
  Display to me the lightning of a smile?"

Now am I caught on this side and on that;
  One keeps me silent, one to speak conjures me,
  Wherefore I sigh, and I am understood.

"Speak," said my Master, "and be not afraid
  Of speaking, but speak out, and say to him
  What he demands with such solicitude."

Whence I: "Thou peradventure marvellest,
  O antique spirit, at the smile I gave;
  But I will have more wonder seize upon thee.

This one, who guides on high these eyes of mine,
  Is that Virgilius, from whom thou didst learn
  To sing aloud of men and of the Gods.

If other cause thou to my smile imputedst,
  Abandon it as false, and trust it was
  Those words which thou hast spoken concerning
    him."

Already he was stooping to embrace
  My Teacher's feet; but he said to him: "Brother,
  Do not; for shade thou art, and shade beholdest."

And he uprising: "Now canst thou the sum
  Of love which warms me to thee comprehend,
  When this our vanity I disremember,

Treating a shadow as substantial thing."

Purgatorio: Canto XXII

Statius' Denunciation of Avarice. The Sixth Circle: The Gluttonous. The Mystic Tree.

Gia` era l'angel dietro a noi rimaso,
   l'angel che n'avea volti al sesto giro,
   avendomi dal viso un colpo raso;

e quei c'hanno a giustizia lor disiro
   detto n'avea beati, e le sue voci
   con 'sitiunt', sanz'altro, cio` forniro.

E io piu` lieve che per l'altre foci
   m'andava, si` che sanz'alcun labore
   seguiva in su` li spiriti veloci;

quando Virgilio incomincio`: ""Amore,
   acceso di virtu`, sempre altro accese,
   pur che la fiamma sua paresse fore;

onde da l'ora che tra noi discese
   nel limbo de lo 'nferno Giovenale,
   che la tua affezion mi fe' palese,

mia benvoglienza inverso te fu quale
   piu` strinse mai di non vista persona,
   si` ch'or mi parran corte queste scale.

Ma dimmi, e come amico mi perdona
   se troppa sicurta` m'allarga il freno,
   e come amico omai meco ragiona:

come pote' trovar dentro al tuo seno
   loco avarizia, tra cotanto senno
   di quanto per tua cura fosti pieno?"".

Queste parole Stazio mover fenno
   un poco a riso pria; poscia rispuose:
   ""Ogne tuo dir d'amor m'e` caro cenno.

Already was the Angel left behind us,
   The Angel who to the sixth round had turned us,
   Having erased one mark from off my face;

And those who have in justice their desire
   Had said to us, "Beati," in their voices,
   With "sitio," and without more ended it.

And I, more light than through the other passes,
   Went onward so, that without any labour
   I followed upward the swift-footed spirits;

When thus Virgilius began: "The love
   Kindled by virtue aye another kindles,
   Provided outwardly its flame appear.

Hence from the hour that Juvenal descended
   Among us into the infernal Limbo,
   Who made apparent to me thy affection,

My kindliness towards thee was as great
   As ever bound one to an unseen person,
   So that these stairs will now seem short to me.

But tell me, and forgive me as a friend,
   If too great confidence let loose the rein,
   And as a friend now hold discourse with me;

How was it possible within thy breast
   For avarice to find place, 'mid so much wisdom
   As thou wast filled with by thy diligence?"

These words excited Statius at first
   Somewhat to laughter; afterward he answered:
   "Each word of thine is love's dear sign to me.

Veramente piu` volte appaion cose
  che danno a dubitar falsa matera
  per le vere ragion che son nascose.

La tua dimanda tuo creder m'avvera
  esser ch'i' fossi avaro in l'altra vita,
  forse per quella cerchia dov'io era.

Or sappi ch'avarizia fu partita
  troppo da me, e questa dismisura
  migliaia di lunari hanno punita.

E se non fosse ch'io drizzai mia cura,
  quand'io intesi la` dove tu chiame,
  crucciato quasi a l'umana natura:

'Per che non reggi tu, o sacra fame
  de l'oro, l'appetito de' mortali?',
  voltando sentirei le giostre grame.

Allor m'accorsi che troppo aprir l'ali
  potean le mani a spendere, e pente'mi
  cosi` di quel come de li altri mali.

Quanti risurgeran coi crini scemi
  per ignoranza, che di questa pecca
  toglie 'l penter vivendo e ne li stremi!

E sappie che la colpa che rimbecca
  per dritta opposizione alcun peccato,
  con esso insieme qui suo verde secca;

pero`, s'io son tra quella gente stato
  che piange l'avarizia, per purgarmi,
  per lo contrario suo m'e` incontrato"“.

““Or quando tu cantasti le crude armi
  de la doppia trestizia di Giocasta”“,
  disse 'l cantor de' buccolici carmi,

““per quello che Clio` teco li` tasta,
  non par che ti facesse ancor fedele
  la fede, sanza qual ben far non basta.

Se cosi` e`, qual sole o quai candele
  ti stenebraron si`, che tu drizzasti
  poscia di retro al pescator le vele?”“.

Ed elli a lui: ““Tu prima m'inviasti
  verso Parnaso a ber ne le sue grotte,
  e prima appresso Dio m'alluminasti.

Verily oftentimes do things appear
  Which give fallacious matter to our doubts,
  Instead of the true causes which are hidden!

Thy question shows me thy belief to be
  That I was niggard in the other life,
  It may be from the circle where I was;

Therefore know thou, that avarice was removed
  Too far from me; and this extravagance
  Thousands of lunar periods have punished.

And were it not that I my thoughts uplifted,
  When I the passage heard where thou exclaimest,
  As if indignant, unto human nature,

'To what impellest thou not, O cursed hunger
  Of gold, the appetite of mortal men?'
  Revolving I should feel the dismal joustings.

Then I perceived the hands could spread too wide
  Their wings in spending, and repented me
  As well of that as of my other sins;

How many with shorn hair shall rise again
  Because of ignorance, which from this sin
  Cuts off repentance living and in death!

And know that the transgression which rebuts
  By direct opposition any sin
  Together with it here its verdure dries.

Therefore if I have been among that folk
  Which mourns its avarice, to purify me,
  For its opposite has this befallen me."

"Now when thou sangest the relentless weapons
  Of the twofold affliction of Jocasta,"
  The singer of the Songs Bucolic said,

"From that which Clio there with thee preludes,
  It does not seem that yet had made thee faithful
  That faith without which no good works suffice.

If this be so, what candles or what sun
  Scattered thy darkness so that thou didst trim
  Thy sails behind the Fisherman thereafter?"

And he to him: "Thou first directedst me
  Towards Parnassus, in its grots to drink,
  And first concerning God didst me enlighten.

Facesti come quei che va di notte,	Thou didst as he who walketh in the night,
che porta il lume dietro e se' non giova,	Who bears his light behind, which helps him not,
ma dopo se' fa le persone dotte,	But wary makes the persons after him,
quando dicesti: 'Secol si rinova;	When thou didst say: 'The age renews itself,
torna giustizia e primo tempo umano,	Justice returns, and man's primeval time,
e progenie scende da ciel nova'.	And a new progeny descends from heaven.'
Per te poeta fui, per te cristiano:	Through thee I Poet was, through thee a Christian;
ma perche' veggi mei cio` ch'io disegno,	But that thou better see what I design,
a colorare stendero` la mano:	To colour it will I extend my hand.
Gia` era 'l mondo tutto quanto pregno	Already was the world in every part
de la vera credenza, seminata	Pregnant with the true creed, disseminated
per li messaggi de l'etterno regno;	By messengers of the eternal kingdom;
e la parola tua sopra toccata	And thy assertion, spoken of above,
si consonava a' nuovi predicanti;	With the new preachers was in unison;
ond'io a visitarli presi usata.	Whence I to visit them the custom took.
Vennermi poi parendo tanto santi,	Then they became so holy in my sight,
che, quando Domizian li perseguette,	That, when Domitian persecuted them,
sanza mio lagrimar non fur lor pianti;	Not without tears of mine were their laments;
e mentre che di la` per me si stette,	And all the while that I on earth remained,
io li sovvenni, e i lor dritti costumi	Them I befriended, and their upright customs
fer dispregiare a me tutte altre sette.	Made me disparage all the other sects.
E pria ch'io conducessi i Greci a' fiumi	And ere I led the Greeks unto the rivers
di Tebe poetando, ebb'io battesmo;	Of Thebes, in poetry, I was baptized,
ma per paura chiuso cristian fu'mi,	But out of fear was covertly a Christian,
lungamente mostrando paganesmo;	For a long time professing paganism;
e questa tepidezza il quarto cerchio	And this lukewarmness caused me the fourth circle
cerchiar mi fe' piu` che 'l quarto centesmo.	To circuit round more than four centuries.
Tu dunque, che levato hai il coperchio	Thou, therefore, who hast raised the covering
che m'ascondeva quanto bene io dico,	That hid from me whatever good I speak of,
mentre che del salire avem soverchio,	While in ascending we have time to spare,
dimmi dov'e` Terrenzio nostro antico,	Tell me, in what place is our friend Terentius,
Cecilio e Plauto e Varro, se lo sai:	Caecilius, Plautus, Varro, if thou knowest;
dimmi se son dannati, e in qual vico"".	Tell me if they are damned, and in what alley."
""Costoro e Persio e io e altri assai"",	"These, Persius and myself, and others many,"
rispuose il duca mio, ""siam con quel Greco	Replied my Leader, "with that Grecian are
che le Muse lattar piu` ch'altri mai,	Whom more than all the rest the Muses suckled,
nel primo cinghio del carcere cieco:	In the first circle of the prison blind;
spesse fiate ragioniam del monte	Ofttimes we of the mountain hold discourse
che sempre ha le nutrice nostre seco.	Which has our nurses ever with itself.

Euripide v'e` nosco e Antifonte,
  Simonide, Agatone e altri piue
  Greci che gia` di lauro ornar la fronte.

Quivi si veggion de le genti tue
  Antigone, Deifile e Argia,
  e Ismene si` trista come fue.

Vedeisi quella che mostro` Langia;
  evvi la figlia di Tiresia, e Teti
  e con le suore sue Deidamia"".

Tacevansi ambedue gia` li poeti,
  di novo attenti a riguardar dintorno,
  liberi da saliri e da pareti;

e gia` le quattro ancelle eran del giorno
  rimase a dietro, e la quinta era al temo,
  drizzando pur in su` l'ardente corno,

quando il mio duca: ""Io credo ch'a lo stremo
  le destre spalle volger ne convegna,
  girando il monte come far solemo"".

Cosi` l'usanza fu li` nostra insegna,
  e prendemmo la via con men sospetto
  per l'assentir di quell'anima degna.

Elli givan dinanzi, e io soletto
  di retro, e ascoltava i lor sermoni,
  ch'a poetar mi davano intelletto.

Ma tosto ruppe le dolci ragioni
  un alber che trovammo in mezza strada,
  con pomi a odorar soavi e buoni;

e come abete in alto si digrada
  di ramo in ramo, cosi` quello in giuso,
  cred'io, perche' persona su` non vada.

Dal lato onde 'l cammin nostro era chiuso,
  cadea de l'alta roccia un liquor chiaro
  e si spandeva per le foglie suso.

Li due poeti a l'alber s'appressaro;
  e una voce per entro le fronde
  grido`: ""Di questo cibo avrete caro"".

Poi disse: ""Piu` pensava Maria onde
  fosser le nozze orrevoli e intere,
  ch'a la sua bocca, ch'or per voi risponde.

Euripides is with us, Antiphon,
  Simonides, Agatho, and many other
  Greeks who of old their brows with laurel decked.

There some of thine own people may be seen,
  Antigone, Deiphile and Argia,
  And there Ismene mournful as of old.

There she is seen who pointed out Langia;
  There is Tiresias' daughter, and there Thetis,
  And there Deidamia with her sisters."

Silent already were the poets both,
  Attent once more in looking round about,
  From the ascent and from the walls released;

And four handmaidens of the day already
  Were left behind, and at the pole the fifth
  Was pointing upward still its burning horn,

What time my Guide: "I think that tow'rds the edge
  Our dexter shoulders it behoves us turn,
  Circling the mount as we are wont to do."

Thus in that region custom was our ensign;
  And we resumed our way with less suspicion
  For the assenting of that worthy soul

They in advance went on, and I alone
  Behind them, and I listened to their speech,
  Which gave me lessons in the art of song.

But soon their sweet discourses interrupted
  A tree which midway in the road we found,
  With apples sweet and grateful to the smell.

And even as a fir-tree tapers upward
  From bough to bough, so downwardly did that;
  I think in order that no one might climb it.

On that side where our pathway was enclosed
  Fell from the lofty rock a limpid water,
  And spread itself abroad upon the leaves.

The Poets twain unto the tree drew near,
  And from among the foliage a voice
  Cried: "Of this food ye shall have scarcity."

Then said: "More thoughtful Mary was of making
  The marriage feast complete and honourable,
  Than of her mouth which now for you responds;

E le Romane antiche, per lor bere,
  contente furon d'acqua; e Daniello
  dispregio` cibo e acquisto` savere.

Lo secol primo, quant'oro fu bello,
  fe' savorose con fame le ghiande,
  e nettare con sete ogne ruscello.

Mele e locuste furon le vivande
  che nodriro il Batista nel diserto;
  per ch'elli e` glorioso e tanto grande

quanto per lo Vangelio v'e` aperto"".

And for their drink the ancient Roman women
  With water were content; and Daniel
  Disparaged food, and understanding won.

The primal age was beautiful as gold;
  Acorns it made with hunger savorous,
  And nectar every rivulet with thirst.

Honey and locusts were the aliments
  That fed the Baptist in the wilderness;
  Whence he is glorious, and so magnified

As by the Evangel is revealed to you."

Purgatorio: Canto XXIII

Forese. Reproof of immodest Florentine Women.

Mentre che li occhi per la fronda verde
　ficcava io si` come far suole
　chi dietro a li uccellin sua vita perde,

lo piu` che padre mi dicea: ““Figliuole,
　vienne oramai, che' 'l tempo che n'e` imposto
　piu` utilmente compartir si vuole”“.

Io volsi 'l viso, e 'l passo non men tosto,
　appresso i savi, che parlavan sie,
　che l'andar mi facean di nullo costo.

Ed ecco piangere e cantar s'udie
　'Labia mea, Domine' per modo
　tal, che diletto e doglia parturie.

““O dolce padre, che e` quel ch'i' odo?”“,
　comincia' io; ed elli: ““Ombre che vanno
　forse di lor dover solvendo il nodo”“.

Si` come i peregrin pensosi fanno,
　giugnendo per cammin gente non nota,
　che si volgono ad essa e non restanno,

cosi` di retro a noi, piu` tosto mota,
　venendo e trapassando ci ammirava
　d'anime turba tacita e devota.

Ne li occhi era ciascuna oscura e cava,
　palida ne la faccia, e tanto scema,
　che da l'ossa la pelle s'informava.

Non credo che cosi` a buccia strema
　Erisittone fosse fatto secco,
　per digiunar, quando piu` n'ebbe tema.

The while among the verdant leaves mine eyes
　I riveted, as he is wont to do
　Who wastes his life pursuing little birds,

My more than Father said unto me: "Son,
　Come now; because the time that is ordained us
　More usefully should be apportioned out."

I turned my face and no less soon my steps
　Unto the Sages, who were speaking so
　They made the going of no cost to me;

And lo! were heard a song and a lament,
　"Labia mea, Domine," in fashion
　Such that delight and dolence it brought forth.

"O my sweet Father, what is this I hear?"
　Began I; and he answered: "Shades that go
　Perhaps the knot unloosing of their debt."

In the same way that thoughtful pilgrims do,
　Who, unknown people on the road o'ertaking,
　Turn themselves round to them, and do not stop,

Even thus, behind us with a swifter motion
　Coming and passing onward, gazed upon us
　A crowd of spirits silent and devout.

Each in his eyes was dark and cavernous,
　Pallid in face, and so emaciate
　That from the bones the skin did shape itself.

I do not think that so to merest rind
　Could Erisichthon have been withered up
　By famine, when most fear he had of it.

La Divina Commedia - The Divine Comedy

Io dicea fra me stesso pensando: 'Ecco
  la gente che perde' Ierusalemme,
  quando Maria nel figlio die` di becco!'

Parean l'occhiaie anella sanza gemme:
  chi nel viso de li uomini legge 'omo'
  ben avria quivi conosciuta l'emme.

Chi crederebbe che l'odor d'un pomo
  si` governasse, generando brama,
  e quel d'un'acqua, non sappiendo como?

Gia` era in ammirar che si` li affama,
  per la cagione ancor non manifesta
  di lor magrezza e di lor trista squama,

ed ecco del profondo de la testa
  volse a me li occhi un'ombra e guardo` fiso;
  poi grido` forte: ""Qual grazia m'e` questa?"".

Mai non l'avrei riconosciuto al viso;
  ma ne la voce sua mi fu palese
  cio` che l'aspetto in se' avea conquiso.

Questa favilla tutta mi raccese
  mia conoscenza a la cangiata labbia,
  e ravvisai la faccia di Forese.

""Deh, non contendere a l'asciutta scabbia
  che mi scolora"", pregava, ""la pelle,
  ne' a difetto di carne ch'io abbia;

ma dimmi il ver di te, di' chi son quelle
  due anime che la` ti fanno scorta;
  non rimaner che tu non mi favelle!"".

""La faccia tua, ch'io lagrimai gia` morta,
  mi da` di pianger mo non minor doglia"",
  rispuos'io lui, ""veggendola si` torta.

Pero` mi di`, per Dio, che si` vi sfoglia;
  non mi far dir mentr'io mi maraviglio,
  che' mal puo` dir chi e` pien d'altra voglia"".

Ed elli a me: ""De l'etterno consiglio
  cade vertu` ne l'acqua e ne la pianta
  rimasa dietro ond'io si` m'assottiglio.

Tutta esta gente che piangendo canta
  per seguitar la gola oltra misura,
  in fame e 'n sete qui si rifa` santa.

Thinking within myself I said: "Behold,
  This is the folk who lost Jerusalem,
  When Mary made a prey of her own son."

Their sockets were like rings without the gems;
  Whoever in the face of men reads 'omo'
  Might well in these have recognised the 'm.'

Who would believe the odour of an apple,
  Begetting longing, could consume them so,
  And that of water, without knowing how?

I still was wondering what so famished them,
  For the occasion not yet manifest
  Of their emaciation and sad squalor;

And lo! from out the hollow of his head
  His eyes a shade turned on me, and looked keenly;
  Then cried aloud: "What grace to me is this?"

Never should I have known him by his look;
  But in his voice was evident to me
  That which his aspect had suppressed within it.

This spark within me wholly re-enkindled
  My recognition of his altered face,
  And I recalled the features of Forese.

"Ah, do not look at this dry leprosy,"
  Entreated he, "which doth my skin discolour,
  Nor at default of flesh that I may have;

But tell me truth of thee, and who are those
  Two souls, that yonder make for thee an escort;
  Do not delay in speaking unto me."

"That face of thine, which dead I once bewept,
  Gives me for weeping now no lesser grief,"
  I answered him, "beholding it so changed!

But tell me, for God's sake, what thus denudes you?
  Make me not speak while I am marvelling,
  For ill speaks he who's full of other longings."

And he to me: "From the eternal council
  Falls power into the water and the tree
  Behind us left, whereby I grow so thin.

All of this people who lamenting sing,
  For following beyond measure appetite
  In hunger and thirst are here re-sanctified.

Di bere e di mangiar n'accende cura
　l'odor ch'esce del pomo e de lo sprazzo
　che si distende su per sua verdura.

E non pur una volta, questo spazzo
　girando, si rinfresca nostra pena:
　io dico pena, e dovria dir sollazzo,

che' quella voglia a li alberi ci mena
　che meno` Cristo lieto a dire 'Eli`',
　quando ne libero` con la sua vena”“.

E io a lui: ““Forese, da quel di`
　nel qual mutasti mondo a miglior vita,
　cinq'anni non son volti infino a qui.

Se prima fu la possa in te finita
　di peccar piu`, che sovvenisse l'ora
　del buon dolor ch'a Dio ne rimarita,

come se' tu qua su` venuto ancora?
　Io ti credea trovar la` giu` di sotto
　dove tempo per tempo si ristora”“.

Ond'elli a me: ““Si` tosto m'ha condotto
　a ber lo dolce assenzo d'i martiri
　la Nella mia con suo pianger dirotto.

Con suoi prieghi devoti e con sospiri
　tratto m'ha de la costa ove s'aspetta,
　e liberato m'ha de li altri giri.

Tanto e` a Dio piu` cara e piu` diletta
　la vedovella mia, che molto amai,
　quanto in bene operare e` piu` soletta;

che' la Barbagia di Sardigna assai
　ne le femmine sue piu` e` pudica
　che la Barbagia dov'io la lasciai.

O dolce frate, che vuo' tu ch'io dica?
　Tempo futuro m'e` gia` nel cospetto,
　cui non sara` quest'ora molto antica,

nel qual sara` in pergamo interdetto
　a le sfacciate donne fiorentine
　l'andar mostrando con le poppe il petto.

Desire to eat and drink enkindles in us
　The scent that issues from the apple-tree,
　And from the spray that sprinkles o'er the verdure;

And not a single time alone, this ground
　Encompassing, is refreshed our pain,—
　I say our pain, and ought to say our solace,—

For the same wish doth lead us to the tree
　Which led the Christ rejoicing to say 'Eli,'
　When with his veins he liberated us."

And I to him: "Forese, from that day
　When for a better life thou changedst worlds,
　Up to this time five years have not rolled round.

If sooner were the power exhausted in thee
　Of sinning more, than thee the hour surprised
　Of that good sorrow which to God reweds us,

How hast thou come up hitherward already?
　I thought to find thee down there underneath,
　Where time for time doth restitution make."

And he to me: "Thus speedily has led me
　To drink of the sweet wormwood of these torments,
　My Nella with her overflowing tears;

She with her prayers devout and with her sighs
　Has drawn me from the coast where one where one
　　　awaits,
　And from the other circles set me free.

So much more dear and pleasing is to God
　My little widow, whom so much I loved,
　As in good works she is the more alone;

For the Barbagia of Sardinia
　By far more modest in its women is
　Than the Barbagia I have left her in.

O brother sweet, what wilt thou have me say?
　A future time is in my sight already,
　To which this hour will not be very old,

When from the pulpit shall be interdicted
　To the unblushing womankind of Florence
　To go about displaying breast and paps.

Quai barbare fuor mai, quai saracine,
  cui bisognasse, per farle ir coperte,
  o spiritali o altre discipline?

Ma se le svergognate fosser certe
  di quel che 'l ciel veloce loro ammanna,
  gia` per urlare avrian le bocche aperte;

che' se l'antiveder qui non m'inganna,
  prima fien triste che le guance impeli
  colui che mo si consola con nanna.

Deh, frate, or fa che piu` non mi ti celi!
  vedi che non pur io, ma questa gente
  tutta rimira la` dove 'l sol veli"".

Per ch'io a lui: ""Se tu riduci a mente
  qual fosti meco, e qual io teco fui,
  ancor fia grave il memorar presente.

Di quella vita mi volse costui
  che mi va innanzi, l'altr'ier, quando tonda
  vi si mostro` la suora di colui"",

e 'l sol mostrai; ""costui per la profonda
  notte menato m'ha d'i veri morti
  con questa vera carne che 'l seconda.

Indi m'han tratto su` li suoi conforti,
  salendo e rigirando la montagna
  che drizza voi che 'l mondo fece torti.

Tanto dice di farmi sua compagna,
  che io saro` la` dove fia Beatrice;
  quivi convien che sanza lui rimagna.

Virgilio e` questi che cosi` mi dice"",
  e addita'lo; ""e quest'altro e` quell'ombra
  per cui scosse dianzi ogne pendice

lo vostro regno, che da se' lo sgombra"".

What savages were e'er, what Saracens,
  Who stood in need, to make them covered go,
  Of spiritual or other discipline?

But if the shameless women were assured
  Of what swift Heaven prepares for them, already
  Wide open would they have their mouths to howl;

For if my foresight here deceive me not,
  They shall be sad ere he has bearded cheeks
  Who now is hushed to sleep with lullaby.

O brother, now no longer hide thee from me;
  See that not only I, but all these people
  Are gazing there, where thou dost veil the sun."

Whence I to him: "If thou bring back to mind
  What thou with me hast been and I with thee,
  The present memory will be grievous still.

Out of that life he turned me back who goes
  In front of me, two days agone when round
  The sister of him yonder showed herself,"

And to the sun I pointed. "Through the deep
  Night of the truly dead has this one led me,
  With this true flesh, that follows after him.

Thence his encouragements have led me up,
  Ascending and still circling round the mount
  That you doth straighten, whom the world made
    crooked.

He says that he will bear me company,
  Till I shall be where Beatrice will be;
  There it behoves me to remain without him.

This is Virgilius, who thus says to me,"
  And him I pointed at; "the other is
  That shade for whom just now shook every slope

Your realm, that from itself discharges him."

Purgatorio: Canto XXIV

Buonagiunta da Lucca. Pope Martin IV, and others.   Inquiry into the State of Poetry.

Ne' 'l dir l'andar, ne' l'andar lui piu` lento facea, ma ragionando andavam forte, si` come nave pinta da buon vento;	Nor speech the going, nor the going that Slackened; but talking we went bravely on, Even as a vessel urged by a good wind.
e l'ombre, che parean cose rimorte, per le fosse de li occhi ammirazione traean di me, di mio vivere accorte.	And shadows, that appeared things doubly dead, From out the sepulchres of their eyes betrayed Wonder at me, aware that I was living.
E io, continuando al mio sermone, dissi: ""Ella sen va su` forse piu` tarda che non farebbe, per altrui cagione.	And I, continuing my colloquy, Said: "Peradventure he goes up more slowly Than he would do, for other people's sake.
Ma dimmi, se tu sai, dov'e` Piccarda; dimmi s'io veggio da notar persona tra questa gente che si` mi riguarda"".	But tell me, if thou knowest, where is Piccarda; Tell me if any one of note I see Among this folk that gazes at me so."
""La mia sorella, che tra bella e buona non so qual fosse piu`, triunfa lieta ne l'alto Olimpo gia` di sua corona"".	"My sister, who, 'twixt beautiful and good, I know not which was more, triumphs rejoicing Already in her crown on high Olympus."
Si` disse prima; e poi: ""Qui non si vieta di nominar ciascun, da ch'e` si` munta nostra sembianza via per la dieta.	So said he first, and then: "'Tis not forbidden To name each other here, so milked away Is our resemblance by our dieting.
Questi"", e mostro` col dito, ""e` Bonagiunta, Bonagiunta da Lucca; e quella faccia di la` da lui piu` che l'altre trapunta	This," pointing with his finger, "is Buonagiunta, Buonagiunta, of Lucca; and that face Beyond him there, more peaked than the others,
ebbe la Santa Chiesa in le sue braccia: dal Torso fu, e purga per digiuno l'anguille di Bolsena e la vernaccia"".	Has held the holy Church within his arms; From Tours was he, and purges by his fasting Bolsena's eels and the Vernaccia wine."
Molti altri mi nomo` ad uno ad uno; e del nomar parean tutti contenti, si` ch'io pero` non vidi un atto bruno.	He named me many others one by one; And all contented seemed at being named, So that for this I saw not one dark look.

Vidi per fame a voto usar li denti
  Ubaldin da la Pila e Bonifazio
  che pasturo` col rocco molte genti.

Vidi messer Marchese, ch'ebbe spazio
  gia` di bere a Forli` con men secchezza,
  e si` fu tal, che non si senti` sazio.

Ma come fa chi guarda e poi s'apprezza
  piu` d'un che d'altro, fei a quel da Lucca,
  che piu` parea di me aver contezza.

El mormorava; e non so che ““Gentucca”“
  sentiv'io la`, ov'el sentia la piaga
  de la giustizia che si` li pilucca.

““O anima”“, diss'io, ““che par si` vaga
  di parlar meco, fa si` ch'io t'intenda,
  e te e me col tuo parlare appaga”“.

““Femmina e` nata, e non porta ancor benda”“,
  comincio` el, ““che ti fara` piacere
  la mia citta`, come ch'om la riprenda.

Tu te n'andrai con questo antivedere:
  se nel mio mormorar prendesti errore,
  dichiareranti ancor le cose vere.

Ma di` s'i' veggio qui colui che fore
  trasse le nove rime, cominciando
  'Donne ch'avete intelletto d'amore'”“.

E io a lui: ““I' mi son un che, quando
  Amor mi spira, noto, e a quel modo
  ch'e' ditta dentro vo significando”“.

““O frate, issa vegg'io”“, diss'elli, ““il nodo
  che 'l Notaro e Guittone e me ritenne
  di qua dal dolce stil novo ch'i' odo!

Io veggio ben come le vostre penne
  di retro al dittator sen vanno strette,
  che de le nostre certo non avvenne;

e qual piu` a gradire oltre si mette,
  non vede piu` da l'uno a l'altro stilo”“;
  e, quasi contentato, si tacette.

Come li augei che vernan lungo 'l Nilo,
  alcuna volta in aere fanno schiera,
  poi volan piu` a fretta e vanno in filo,

I saw for hunger bite the empty air
  Ubaldin dalla Pila, and Boniface,
  Who with his crook had pastured many people.

I saw Messer Marchese, who had leisure
  Once at Forli for drinking with less dryness,
  And he was one who ne'er felt satisfied.

But as he does who scans, and then doth prize
  One more than others, did I him of Lucca,
  Who seemed to take most cognizance of me.

He murmured, and I know not what Gentucca
  From that place heard I, where he felt the wound
  Of justice, that doth macerate them so.

"O soul," I said, "that seemest so desirous
  To speak with me, do so that I may hear thee,
  And with thy speech appease thyself and me."

"A maid is born, and wears not yet the veil,"
  Began he, "who to thee shall pleasant make
  My city, howsoever men may blame it.

Thou shalt go on thy way with this prevision;
  If by my murmuring thou hast been deceived,
  True things hereafter will declare it to thee.

But say if him I here behold, who forth
  Evoked the new-invented rhymes, beginning,
  'Ladies, that have intelligence of love?'"

And I to him: "One am I, who, whenever
  Love doth inspire me, note, and in that measure
  Which he within me dictates, singing go."

"O brother, now I see," he said, "the knot
  Which me, the Notary, and Guittone held
  Short of the sweet new style that now I hear.

I do perceive full clearly how your pens
  Go closely following after him who dictates,
  Which with our own forsooth came not to pass;

And he who sets himself to go beyond,
  No difference sees from one style to another;"
  And as if satisfied, he held his peace.

Even as the birds, that winter tow'rds the Nile,
  Sometimes into a phalanx form themselves,
  Then fly in greater haste, and go in file;

cosi` tutta la gente che li` era,	In such wise all the people who were there,
volgendo 'l viso, raffretto` suo passo,	Turning their faces, hurried on their steps,
e per magrezza e per voler leggera.	Both by their leanness and their wishes light.
E come l'uom che di trottare e` lasso,	And as a man, who weary is with trotting,
lascia andar li compagni, e si` passeggia	Lets his companions onward go, and walks,
fin che si sfoghi l'affollar del casso,	Until he vents the panting of his chest;
si` lascio` trapassar la santa greggia	So did Forese let the holy flock
Forese, e dietro meco sen veniva,	Pass by, and came with me behind it, saying,
dicendo: ""Quando fia ch'io ti riveggia?"".	"When will it be that I again shall see thee?"
""Non so"", rispuos'io lui, ""quant'io mi viva;	"How long," I answered, "I may live, I know not;
ma gia` non fia il tornar mio tantosto,	Yet my return will not so speedy be,
ch'io non sia col voler prima a la riva;	But I shall sooner in desire arrive;
pero` che 'l loco u' fui a viver posto,	Because the place where I was set to live
di giorno in giorno piu` di ben si spolpa,	From day to day of good is more depleted,
e a trista ruina par disposto"".	And unto dismal ruin seems ordained."
""Or va"", diss'el; ""che quei che piu` n'ha colpa,	"Now go," he said, "for him most guilty of it
vegg'io a coda d'una bestia tratto	At a beast's tail behold I dragged along
inver' la valle ove mai non si scolpa.	Towards the valley where is no repentance.
La bestia ad ogne passo va piu` ratto,	Faster at every step the beast is going,
crescendo sempre, fin ch'ella il percuote,	Increasing evermore until it smites him,
e lascia il corpo vilmente disfatto.	And leaves the body vilely mutilated.
Non hanno molto a volger quelle ruote"",	Not long those wheels shall turn," and he uplifted
e drizzo` li ochi al ciel, ""che ti fia chiaro	His eyes to heaven, "ere shall be clear to thee
cio` che 'l mio dir piu` dichiarar non puote.	That which my speech no farther can declare.
Tu ti rimani omai; che' 'l tempo e` caro	Now stay behind; because the time so precious
in questo regno, si` ch'io perdo troppo	Is in this kingdom, that I lose too much
venendo teco si` a paro a paro"".	By coming onward thus abreast with thee."
Qual esce alcuna volta di gualoppo	As sometimes issues forth upon a gallop
lo cavalier di schiera che cavalchi,	A cavalier from out a troop that ride,
e va per farsi onor del primo intoppo,	And seeks the honour of the first encounter,
tal si parti` da noi con maggior valchi;	So he with greater strides departed from us;
e io rimasi in via con esso i due	And on the road remained I with those two,
che fuor del mondo si` gran marescalchi.	Who were such mighty marshals of the world.
E quando innanzi a noi intrato fue,	And when before us he had gone so far
che li occhi miei si fero a lui seguaci,	Mine eyes became to him such pursuivants
come la mente a le parole sue,	As was my understanding to his words,
parvermi i rami gravidi e vivaci	Appeared to me with laden and living boughs
d'un altro pomo, e non molto lontani	Another apple-tree, and not far distant,
per esser pur allora volto in laci.	From having but just then turned thitherward.

Vidi gente sott'esso alzar le mani
  e gridar non so che verso le fronde,
  quasi bramosi fantolini e vani,

che pregano, e 'l pregato non risponde,
  ma, per fare esser ben la voglia acuta,
  tien alto lor disio e nol nasconde.

Poi si parti` si` come ricreduta;
  e noi venimmo al grande arbore adesso,
  che tanti prieghi e lagrime rifiuta.

""Trapassate oltre sanza farvi presso:
  legno e` piu` su` che fu morso da Eva,
  e questa pianta si levo` da esso"".

Si` tra le frasche non so chi diceva;
  per che Virgilio e Stazio e io, ristretti,
  oltre andavam dal lato che si leva.

""Ricordivi"", dicea, ""d'i maladetti
  nei nuvoli formati, che, satolli,
  Teseo combatter co' doppi petti;

e de li Ebrei ch'al ber si mostrar molli,
  per che no i volle Gedeon compagni,
  quando inver' Madian discese i colli"".

Si` accostati a l'un d'i due vivagni
  passammo, udendo colpe de la gola
  seguite gia` da miseri guadagni.

Poi, rallargati per la strada sola,
  ben mille passi e piu` ci portar oltre,
  contemplando ciascun sanza parola.

""Che andate pensando si` voi sol tre?"".
  subita voce disse; ond'io mi scossi
  come fan bestie spaventate e poltre.

Drizzai la testa per veder chi fossi;
  e gia` mai non si videro in fornace
  vetri o metalli si` lucenti e rossi,

com'io vidi un che dicea: ""S'a voi piace
  montare in su`, qui si convien dar volta;
  quinci si va chi vuole andar per pace"".

People I saw beneath it lift their hands,
  And cry I know not what towards the leaves,
  Like little children eager and deluded,

Who pray, and he they pray to doth not answer,
  But, to make very keen their appetite,
  Holds their desire aloft, and hides it not.

Then they departed as if undeceived;
  And now we came unto the mighty tree
  Which prayers and tears so manifold refuses.

"Pass farther onward without drawing near;
  The tree of which Eve ate is higher up,
  And out of that one has this tree been raised."

Thus said I know not who among the branches;
  Whereat Virgilius, Statius, and myself
  Went crowding forward on the side that rises.

"Be mindful," said he, "of the accursed ones
  Formed of the cloud-rack, who inebriate
  Combated Theseus with their double breasts;

And of the Jews who showed them soft in drinking,
  Whence Gideon would not have them for compan-
    ions
  When he tow'rds Midian the hills descended."

Thus, closely pressed to one of the two borders,
  On passed we, hearing sins of gluttony,
  Followed forsooth by miserable gains;

Then set at large upon the lonely road,
  A thousand steps and more we onward went,
  In contemplation, each without a word.

"What go ye thinking thus, ye three alone?"
  Said suddenly a voice, whereat I started
  As terrified and timid beasts are wont.

I raised my head to see who this might be,
  And never in a furnace was there seen
  Metals or glass so lucent and so red

As one I saw who said: "If it may please you
  To mount aloft, here it behoves you turn;
  This way goes he who goeth after peace."

L'aspetto suo m'avea la vista tolta;
  per ch'io mi volsi dietro a' miei dottori,
  com'om che va secondo ch'elli ascolta.

E quale, annunziatrice de li albori,
  l'aura di maggio movesi e olezza,
  tutta impregnata da l'erba e da' fiori;

tal mi senti' un vento dar per mezza
  la fronte, e ben senti' mover la piuma,
  che fe' sentir d'ambrosia l'orezza.

E senti' dir: ""Beati cui alluma
  tanto di grazia, che l'amor del gusto
  nel petto lor troppo disir non fuma,

esuriendo sempre quanto e` giusto!""".

His aspect had bereft me of my sight,
  So that I turned me back unto my Teachers,
  Like one who goeth as his hearing guides him.

And as, the harbinger of early dawn,
  The air of May doth move and breathe out fra-
    grance,
  Impregnate all with herbage and with flowers,

So did I feel a breeze strike in the midst
  My front, and felt the moving of the plumes
  That breathed around an odour of ambrosia;

And heard it said: "Blessed are they whom grace
  So much illumines, that the love of taste
  Excites not in their breasts too great desire,

Hungering at all times so far as is just."

Purgatorio: Canto XXV

Discourse of Statius on Generation. The Seventh Circle: The Wanton.

Ora era onde 'l salir non volea storpio;	Now was it the ascent no hindrance brooked,
che' 'l sole avea il cerchio di merigge	Because the sun had his meridian circle
lasciato al Tauro e la notte a lo Scorpio:	To Taurus left, and night to Scorpio;
per che, come fa l'uom che non s'affigge	Wherefore as doth a man who tarries not,
ma vassi a la via sua, che che li appaia,	But goes his way, whate'er to him appear,
se di bisogno stimolo il trafigge,	If of necessity the sting transfix him,
cosi` intrammo noi per la callaia,	In this wise did we enter through the gap,
uno innanzi altro prendendo la scala	Taking the stairway, one before the other,
che per artezza i salitor dispaia.	Which by its narrowness divides the climbers.
E quale il cicognin che leva l'ala	And as the little stork that lifts its wing
per voglia di volare, e non s'attenta	With a desire to fly, and does not venture
d'abbandonar lo nido, e giu` la cala;	To leave the nest, and lets it downward droop,
tal era io con voglia accesa e spenta	Even such was I, with the desire of asking
di dimandar, venendo infino a l'atto	Kindled and quenched, unto the motion coming
che fa colui ch'a dicer s'argomenta.	He makes who doth address himself to speak.
Non lascio`, per l'andar che fosse ratto,	Not for our pace, though rapid it might be,
lo dolce padre mio, ma disse: ““Scocca	My father sweet forbore, but said: "Let fly
l'arco del dir, che 'nfino al ferro hai tratto”“.	The bow of speech thou to the barb hast drawn."
Allor sicuramente apri' la bocca	With confidence I opened then my mouth,
e cominciai: ““Come si puo` far magro	And I began: "How can one meagre grow
la` dove l'uopo di nodrir non tocca?”“.	There where the need of nutriment applies not?"
““Se t'ammentassi come Meleagro	"If thou wouldst call to mind how Meleager
si consumo` al consumar d'un stizzo,	Was wasted by the wasting of a brand,
non fora”“, disse, ““a te questo si` agro;	This would not," said he, "be to thee so sour;
e se pensassi come, al vostro guizzo,	And wouldst thou think how at each tremulous mo-
guizza dentro a lo specchio vostra image,	tion
cio` che par duro ti parrebbe vizzo.	Trembles within a mirror your own image;
	That which seems hard would mellow seem to thee.

Ma perche' dentro a tuo voler t'adage,
  ecco qui Stazio; e io lui chiamo e prego
  che sia or sanator de le tue piage"".

""Se la veduta etterna li dislego"",
  rispuose Stazio, ""la` dove tu sie,
  discolpi me non potert'io far nego"".

Poi comincio`: ""Se le parole mie,
  figlio, la mente tua guarda e riceve,
  lume ti fiero al come che tu die.

Sangue perfetto, che poi non si beve
  da l'assetate vene, e si rimane
  quasi alimento che di mensa leve,

prende nel core a tutte membra umane
  virtute informativa, come quello
  ch'a farsi quelle per le vene vane.

Ancor digesto, scende ov'e` piu` bello
  tacer che dire; e quindi poscia geme
  sovr'altrui sangue in natural vasello.

Ivi s'accoglie l'uno e l'altro insieme,
  l'un disposto a patire, e l'altro a fare
  per lo perfetto loco onde si preme;

e, giunto lui, comincia ad operare
  coagulando prima, e poi avviva
  cio` che per sua matera fe' constare.

Anima fatta la virtute attiva
  qual d'una pianta, in tanto differente,
  che questa e` in via e quella e` gia` a riva,

tanto ovra poi, che gia` si move e sente,
  come spungo marino; e indi imprende
  ad organar le posse ond'e` semente.

Or si spiega, figliuolo, or si distende
  la virtu` ch'e` dal cor del generante,
  dove natura a tutte membra intende.

Ma come d'animal divegna fante,
  non vedi tu ancor: quest'e` tal punto,
  che piu` savio di te fe' gia` errante,

But that thou mayst content thee in thy wish
  Lo Statius here; and him I call and pray
  He now will be the healer of thy wounds."

"If I unfold to him the eternal vengeance,"
  Responded Statius, "where thou present art,
  Be my excuse that I can naught deny thee."

Then he began: "Son, if these words of mine
  Thy mind doth contemplate and doth receive,
  They'll be thy light unto the How thou sayest.

The perfect blood, which never is drunk up
  Into the thirsty veins, and which remaineth
  Like food that from the table thou removest,

Takes in the heart for all the human members
  Virtue informative, as being that
  Which to be changed to them goes through the
    veins

Again digest, descends it where 'tis better
  Silent to be than say; and then drops thence
  Upon another's blood in natural vase.

There one together with the other mingles,
  One to be passive meant, the other active
  By reason of the perfect place it springs from;

And being conjoined, begins to operate,
  Coagulating first, then vivifying
  What for its matter it had made consistent.

The active virtue, being made a soul
  As of a plant, (in so far different,
  This on the way is, that arrived already,)

Then works so much, that now it moves and feels
  Like a sea-fungus, and then undertakes
  To organize the powers whose seed it is.

Now, Son, dilates and now distends itself
  The virtue from the generator's heart,
  Where nature is intent on all the members.

But how from animal it man becomes
  Thou dost not see as yet; this is a point
  Which made a wiser man than thou once err

si` che per sua dottrina fe' disgiunto
  da l'anima il possibile intelletto,
  perche' da lui non vide organo assunto.

Apri a la verita` che viene il petto;
  e sappi che, si` tosto come al feto
  l'articular del cerebro e` perfetto,

lo motor primo a lui si volge lieto
  sovra tant'arte di natura, e spira
  spirito novo, di vertu` repleto,

che cio` che trova attivo quivi, tira
  in sua sustanzia, e fassi un'alma sola,
  che vive e sente e se' in se' rigira.

E perche' meno ammiri la parola,
  guarda il calor del sole che si fa vino,
  giunto a l'omor che de la vite cola.

Quando Lachesis non ha piu` del lino,
  solvesi da la carne, e in virtute
  ne porta seco e l'umano e 'l divino:

l'altre potenze tutte quante mute;
  memoria, intelligenza e volontade
  in atto molto piu` che prima agute.

Sanza restarsi per se' stessa cade
  mirabilmente a l'una de le rive;
  quivi conosce prima le sue strade.

Tosto che loco li` la circunscrive,
  la virtu` formativa raggia intorno
  cosi` e quanto ne le membra vive.

E come l'aere, quand'e` ben piorno,
  per l'altrui raggio che 'n se' si reflette,
  di diversi color diventa addorno;

cosi` l'aere vicin quivi si mette
  in quella forma ch'e` in lui suggella
  virtualmente l'alma che ristette;

e simigliante poi a la fiammella
  che segue il foco la` 'vunque si muta,
  segue lo spirto sua forma novella.

Pero` che quindi ha poscia sua paruta,
  e` chiamata ombra; e quindi organa poi
  ciascun sentire infino a la veduta.

So far, that in his doctrine separate
  He made the soul from possible intellect,
  For he no organ saw by this assumed.

Open thy breast unto the truth that's coming,
  And know that, just as soon as in the foetus
  The articulation of the brain is perfect,

The primal Motor turns to it well pleased
  At so great art of nature, and inspires
  A spirit new with virtue all replete,

Which what it finds there active doth attract
  Into its substance, and becomes one soul,
  Which lives, and feels, and on itself revolves.

And that thou less may wonder at my word,
  Behold the sun's heat, which becometh wine,
  Joined to the juice that from the vine distils.

Whenever Lachesis has no more thread,
  It separates from the flesh, and virtually
  Bears with itself the human and divine;

The other faculties are voiceless all;
  The memory, the intelligence, and the will
  In action far more vigorous than before.

Without a pause it falleth of itself
  In marvellous way on one shore or the other;
  There of its roads it first is cognizant.

Soon as the place there circumscribeth it,
  The virtue informative rays round about,
  As, and as much as, in the living members.

And even as the air, when full of rain,
  By alien rays that are therein reflected,
  With divers colours shows itself adorned,

So there the neighbouring air doth shape itself
  Into that form which doth impress upon it
  Virtually the soul that has stood still.

And then in manner of the little flame,
  Which followeth the fire where'er it shifts,
  After the spirit followeth its new form.

Since afterwards it takes from this its semblance,
  It is called shade; and thence it organizes
  Thereafter every sense, even to the sight.

Quindi parliamo e quindi ridiam noi;
  quindi facciam le lagrime e ' sospiri
  che per lo monte aver sentiti puoi.

Secondo che ci affiggono i disiri
  e li altri affetti, l'ombra si figura;
  e quest'e` la cagion di che tu miri"".

E gia` venuto a l'ultima tortura
  s'era per noi, e volto a la man destra,
  ed eravamo attenti ad altra cura.

Quivi la ripa fiamma in fuor balestra,
  e la cornice spira fiato in suso
  che la reflette e via da lei sequestra;

ond'ir ne convenia dal lato schiuso
  ad uno ad uno; e io temea 'l foco
  quinci, e quindi temeva cader giuso.

Lo duca mio dicea: ""Per questo loco
  si vuol tenere a li occhi stretto il freno,
  pero` ch'errar potrebbesi per poco"".

'Summae Deus clementiae' nel seno
  al grande ardore allora udi' cantando,
  che di volger mi fe' caler non meno;

e vidi spirti per la fiamma andando;
  per ch'io guardava a loro e a' miei passi
  compartendo la vista a quando a quando.

Appresso il fine ch'a quell'inno fassi,
  gridavano alto: 'Virum non cognosco';
  indi ricominciavan l'inno bassi.

Finitolo, anco gridavano: ""Al bosco
  si tenne Diana, ed Elice caccionne
  che di Venere avea sentito il tosco"".

Indi al cantar tornavano; indi donne
  gridavano e mariti che fuor casti
  come virtute e matrimonio imponne.

E questo modo credo che lor basti
  per tutto il tempo che 'l foco li abbruscia:
  con tal cura conviene e con tai pasti

che la piaga da sezzo si ricuscia.

Thence is it that we speak, and thence we laugh;
  Thence is it that we form the tears and sighs,
  That on the mountain thou mayhap hast heard.

According as impress us our desires
  And other affections, so the shade is shaped,
  And this is cause of what thou wonderest at."

And now unto the last of all the circles
  Had we arrived, and to the right hand turned,
  And were attentive to another care.

There the embankment shoots forth flames of fire,
  And upward doth the cornice breathe a blast
  That drives them back, and from itself sequesters.

Hence we must needs go on the open side,
  And one by one; and I did fear the fire
  On this side, and on that the falling down.

My Leader said: "Along this place one ought
  To keep upon the eyes a tightened rein,
  Seeing that one so easily might err."

"Summae Deus clementiae," in the bosom
  Of the great burning chanted then I heard,
  Which made me no less eager to turn round;

And spirits saw I walking through the flame;
  Wherefore I looked, to my own steps and theirs
  Apportioning my sight from time to time.

After the close which to that hymn is made,
  Aloud they shouted, "Virum non cognosco;"
  Then recommenced the hymn with voices low.

This also ended, cried they: "To the wood
  Diana ran, and drove forth Helice
  Therefrom, who had of Venus felt the poison."

Then to their song returned they; then the wives
  They shouted, and the husbands who were chaste.
  As virtue and the marriage vow imposes.

And I believe that them this mode suffices,
  For all the time the fire is burning them;
  With such care is it needful, and such food,

That the last wound of all should be closed up.

Purgatorio: Canto XXVI

Sodomites. Guido Guinicelli and Arnaldo Daniello.

Mentre che si` per l'orlo, uno innanzi altro,
  ce n'andavamo, e spesso il buon maestro
  diceami: ““Guarda: giovi ch'io ti scaltro”“;

feriami il sole in su l'omero destro,
  che gia`, raggiando, tutto l'occidente
  mutava in bianco aspetto di cilestro;

e io facea con l'ombra piu` rovente
  parer la fiamma; e pur a tanto indizio
  vidi molt'ombre, andando, poner mente.

Questa fu la cagion che diede inizio
  loro a parlar di me; e cominciarsi
  a dir: ““Colui non par corpo fittizio”“;

poi verso me, quanto potean farsi,
  certi si fero, sempre con riguardo
  di non uscir dove non fosser arsi.

““O tu che vai, non per esser piu` tardo,
  ma forse reverente, a li altri dopo,
  rispondi a me che 'n sete e 'n foco ardo.

Ne' solo a me la tua risposta e` uopo;
  che' tutti questi n'hanno maggior sete
  che d'acqua fredda Indo o Etiopo.

Dinne com'e` che fai di te parete
  al sol, pur come tu non fossi ancora
  di morte intrato dentro da la rete”“.

Si` mi parlava un d'essi; e io mi fora
  gia` manifesto, s'io non fossi atteso
  ad altra novita` ch'apparve allora;

While on the brink thus one before the other
  We went upon our way, oft the good Master
  Said: "Take thou heed! suffice it that I warn thee."

On the right shoulder smote me now the sun,
  That, raying out, already the whole west
  Changed from its azure aspect into white.

And with my shadow did I make the flame
  Appear more red; and even to such a sign
  Shades saw I many, as they went, give heed.

This was the cause that gave them a beginning
  To speak of me; and to themselves began they
  To say: "That seems not a factitious body!"

Then towards me, as far as they could come,
  Came certain of them, always with regard
  Not to step forth where they would not be burned.

"O thou who goest, not from being slower
  But reverent perhaps, behind the others,
  Answer me, who in thirst and fire am burning.

Nor to me only is thine answer needful;
  For all of these have greater thirst for it
  Than for cold water Ethiop or Indian.

Tell us how is it that thou makest thyself
  A wall unto the sun, as if thou hadst not
  Entered as yet into the net of death."

Thus one of them addressed me, and I straight
  Should have revealed myself, were I not bent
  On other novelty that then appeared.

che' per lo mezzo del cammino acceso
  venne gente col viso incontro a questa,
  la qual mi fece a rimirar sospeso.

Li` veggio d'ogne parte farsi presta
  ciascun'ombra e basciarsi una con una
  sanza restar, contente a brieve festa;

cosi` per entro loro schiera bruna
  s'ammusa l'una con l'altra formica,
  forse a spiar lor via e lor fortuna.

Tosto che parton l'accoglienza amica,
  prima che 'l primo passo li` trascorra,
  sopragridar ciascuna s'affatica:

la nova gente: ““Soddoma e Gomorra”“;
  e l'altra: ““Ne la vacca entra Pasife,
  perche' 'l torello a sua lussuria corra”“.

Poi, come grue ch'a le montagne Rife
  volasser parte, e parte inver' l'arene,
  queste del gel, quelle del sole schife,

l'una gente sen va, l'altra sen vene;
  e tornan, lagrimando, a' primi canti
  e al gridar che piu` lor si convene;

e raccostansi a me, come davanti,
  essi medesmi che m'avean pregato,
  attenti ad ascoltar ne' lor sembianti.

Io, che due volte avea visto lor grato,
  incominciai: ““O anime sicure
  d'aver, quando che sia, di pace stato,

non son rimase acerbe ne' mature
  le membra mie di la`, ma son qui meco
  col sangue suo e con le sue giunture.

Quinci su` vo per non esser piu` cieco;
  donna e` di sopra che m'acquista grazia,
  per che 'l mortal per vostro mondo reco.

Ma se la vostra maggior voglia sazia
  tosto divegna, si` che 'l ciel v'alberghi
  ch'e` pien d'amore e piu` ampio si spazia,

For through the middle of the burning road
  There came a people face to face with these,
  Which held me in suspense with gazing at them.

There see I hastening upon either side
  Each of the shades, and kissing one another
  Without a pause, content with brief salute.

Thus in the middle of their brown battalions
  Muzzle to muzzle one ant meets another
  Perchance to spy their journey or their fortune.

No sooner is the friendly greeting ended,
  Or ever the first footstep passes onward,
  Each one endeavours to outcry the other;

The new-come people: "Sodom and Gomorrah!"
  The rest: "Into the cow Pasiphae enters,
  So that the bull unto her lust may run!"

Then as the cranes, that to Riphaean mountains
  Might fly in part, and part towards the sands,
  These of the frost, those of the sun avoidant,

One folk is going, and the other coming,
  And weeping they return to their first songs,
  And to the cry that most befitteth them;

And close to me approached, even as before,
  The very same who had entreated me,
  Attent to listen in their countenance.

I, who their inclination twice had seen,
  Began: "O souls secure in the possession,
  Whene'er it may be, of a state of peace,

Neither unripe nor ripened have remained
  My members upon earth, but here are with me
  With their own blood and their articulations.

I go up here to be no longer blind;
  A Lady is above, who wins this grace,
  Whereby the mortal through your world I bring.

But as your greatest longing satisfied
  May soon become, so that the Heaven may house
    you
  Which full of love is, and most amply spreads,

ditemi, accio` ch'ancor carte ne verghi,
  chi siete voi, e chi e` quella turba
  che se ne va di retro a' vostri terghi"".

Non altrimenti stupido si turba
  lo montanaro, e rimirando ammuta,
  quando rozzo e salvatico s'inurba,

che ciascun'ombra fece in sua paruta;
  ma poi che furon di stupore scarche,
  lo qual ne li alti cuor tosto s'attuta,

""Beato te, che de le nostre marche"",
  ricomincio` colei che pria m'inchiese,
  ""per morir meglio, esperienza imbarche!

La gente che non vien con noi, offese
  di cio` per che gia` Cesar, triunfando,
  "Regina" contra se' chiamar s'intese:

pero` si parton 'Soddoma' gridando,
  rimproverando a se', com'hai udito,
  e aiutan l'arsura vergognando.

Nostro peccato fu ermafrodito;
  ma perche' non servammo umana legge,
  seguendo come bestie l'appetito,

in obbrobrio di noi, per noi si legge,
  quando partinci, il nome di colei
  che s'imbestio` ne le 'mbestiate schegge.

Or sai nostri atti e di che fummo rei:
  se forse a nome vuo' saper chi semo,
  tempo non e` di dire, e non saprei.

Farotti ben di me volere scemo:
  son Guido Guinizzelli; e gia` mi purgo
  per ben dolermi prima ch'a lo stremo"".

Quali ne la tristizia di Ligurgo
  si fer due figli a riveder la madre,
  tal mi fec'io, ma non a tanto insurgo,

quand'io odo nomar se' stesso il padre
  mio e de li altri miei miglior che mai
  rime d'amore usar dolci e leggiadre;

Tell me, that I again in books may write it,
  Who are you, and what is that multitude
  Which goes upon its way behind your backs?"

Not otherwise with wonder is bewildered
  The mountaineer, and staring round is dumb,
  When rough and rustic to the town he goes,

Than every shade became in its appearance;
  But when they of their stupor were disburdened,
  Which in high hearts is quickly quieted,

"Blessed be thou, who of our border-lands,"
  He recommenced who first had questioned us,
  "Experience freightest for a better life.

The folk that comes not with us have offended
  In that for which once Caesar, triumphing,
  Heard himself called in contumely, 'Queen.'

Therefore they separate, exclaiming, 'Sodom!'
  Themselves reproving, even as thou hast heard,
  And add unto their burning by their shame.

Our own transgression was hermaphrodite;
  But because we observed not human law,
  Following like unto beasts our appetite,

In our opprobrium by us is read,
  When we part company, the name of her
  Who bestialized herself in bestial wood.

Now knowest thou our acts, and what our crime was;
  Wouldst thou perchance by name know who we
      are,
  There is not time to tell, nor could I do it.

Thy wish to know me shall in sooth be granted;
  I'm Guido Guinicelli, and now purge me,
  Having repented ere the hour extreme."

The same that in the sadness of Lycurgus
  Two sons became, their mother re-beholding,
  Such I became, but rise not to such height,

The moment I heard name himself the father
  Of me and of my betters, who had ever
  Practised the sweet and gracious rhymes of love;

e sanza udire e dir pensoso andai
  lunga fiata rimirando lui,
  ne', per lo foco, in la` piu` m'appressai.

Poi che di riguardar pasciuto fui,
  tutto m'offersi pronto al suo servigio
  con l'affermar che fa credere altrui.

Ed elli a me: ""Tu lasci tal vestigio,
  per quel ch'i' odo, in me, e tanto chiaro,
  che Lete' nol puo` torre ne' far bigio.

Ma se le tue parole or ver giuraro,
  dimmi che e` cagion per che dimostri
  nel dire e nel guardar d'avermi caro"".

E io a lui: ""Li dolci detti vostri,
  che, quanto durera` l'uso moderno,
  faranno cari ancora i loro incostri"".

""O frate"", disse, ""questi ch'io ti cerno
  col dito"", e addito` un spirto innanzi,
  ""fu miglior fabbro del parlar materno.

Versi d'amore e prose di romanzi
  soverchio` tutti; e lascia dir li stolti
  che quel di Lemosi` credon ch'avanzi.

A voce piu` ch'al ver drizzan li volti,
  e cosi` ferman sua oppinione
  prima ch'arte o ragion per lor s'ascolti.

Cosi` fer molti antichi di Guittone,
  di grido in grido pur lui dando pregio,
  fin che l'ha vinto il ver con piu` persone.

Or se tu hai si` ampio privilegio,
  che licito ti sia l'andare al chiostro
  nel quale e` Cristo abate del collegio,

falli per me un dir d'un paternostro,
  quanto bisogna a noi di questo mondo,
  dove poter peccar non e` piu` nostro"".

Poi, forse per dar luogo altrui secondo
  che presso avea, disparve per lo foco,
  come per l'acqua il pesce andando al fondo.

Io mi fei al mostrato innanzi un poco,
  e dissi ch'al suo nome il mio disire
  apparecchiava grazioso loco.

And without speech and hearing thoughtfully
  For a long time I went, beholding him,
  Nor for the fire did I approach him nearer.

When I was fed with looking, utterly
  Myself I offered ready for his service,
  With affirmation that compels belief.

And he to me: "Thou leavest footprints such
  In me, from what I hear, and so distinct,
  Lethe cannot efface them, nor make dim.

But if thy words just now the truth have sworn,
  Tell me what is the cause why thou displayest
  In word and look that dear thou holdest me?"

And I to him: "Those dulcet lays of yours
  Which, long as shall endure our modern fashion,
  Shall make for ever dear their very ink!"

"O brother," said he, "he whom I point out,"
  And here he pointed at a spirit in front,
  "Was of the mother tongue a better smith.

Verses of love and proses of romance,
  He mastered all; and let the idiots talk,
  Who think the Lemosin surpasses him.

To clamour more than truth they turn their faces,
  And in this way establish their opinion,
  Ere art or reason has by them been heard.

Thus many ancients with Guittone did,
  From cry to cry still giving him applause,
  Until the truth has conquered with most persons.

Now, if thou hast such ample privilege
  'Tis granted thee to go unto the cloister
  Wherein is Christ the abbot of the college,

To him repeat for me a Paternoster,
  So far as needful to us of this world,
  Where power of sinning is no longer ours."

Then, to give place perchance to one behind,
  Whom he had near, he vanished in the fire
  As fish in water going to the bottom.

I moved a little tow'rds him pointed out,
  And said that to his name my own desire
  An honourable place was making ready.

El comincio` liberamente a dire:
  ”"Tan m'abellis vostre cortes deman,
  qu'ieu no me puesc ni voill a vos cobrire.

Ieu sui Arnaut, que plor e vau cantan;
  consiros vei la passada folor,
  e vei jausen lo joi qu'esper, denan.

Ara vos prec, per aquella valor
  que vos guida al som de l'escalina,
  sovenha vos a temps de ma dolor!"".

Poi s'ascose nel foco che li affina.

He of his own free will began to say:
  'Tan m' abellis vostre cortes deman,
  Que jeu nom' puesc ni vueill a vos cobrire;

Jeu sui Arnaut, que plor e vai chantan;
  Consiros vei la passada folor,
  E vei jauzen lo jorn qu' esper denan.

Ara vus prec per aquella valor,
  Que vus condus al som de la scalina,
  Sovenga vus a temprar ma dolor[1].'

Then hid him in the fire that purifies them.

---

[1] So pleases me your courteous demand,
  I cannot and I will not hide me from you.

I am Arnaut, who weep and singing go;
  Contrite I see the folly of the past,
  And joyous see the hoped-for day before me.

Therefore do I implore you, by that power
  Which guides you to the summit of the stairs,
  Be mindful to assuage my suffering!

Purgatorio: Canto XXVII

The Wall of Fire and the Angel of God. Dante's Sleep upon the Stairway, and his Dream of Leah and Rachel. Arrival at the Terrestrial Paradise.

Si` come quando i primi raggi vibra
  la` dove il suo fattor lo sangue sparse,
  cadendo Ibero sotto l'alta Libra,

e l'onde in Gange da nona riarse,
  si` stava il sole; onde 'l giorno sen giva,
  come l'angel di Dio lieto ci apparse.

Fuor de la fiamma stava in su la riva,
  e cantava 'Beati mundo corde!'.
  in voce assai piu` che la nostra viva.

Poscia ""Piu` non si va, se pria non morde,
  anime sante, il foco: intrate in esso,
  e al cantar di la` non siate sorde"",

ci disse come noi li fummo presso;
  per ch'io divenni tal, quando lo 'ntesi,
  qual e` colui che ne la fossa e` messo.

In su le man commesse mi protesi,
  guardando il foco e imaginando forte
  umani corpi gia` veduti accesi.

Volsersi verso me le buone scorte;
  e Virgilio mi disse: ""Figliuol mio,
  qui puo` esser tormento, ma non morte.

Ricorditi, ricorditi! E se io
  sovresso Gerion ti guidai salvo,
  che faro` ora presso piu` a Dio?

As when he vibrates forth his earliest rays,
  In regions where his Maker shed his blood,
  (The Ebro falling under lofty Libra,

And waters in the Ganges burnt with noon,)
  So stood the Sun; hence was the day departing,
  When the glad Angel of God appeared to us.

Outside the flame he stood upon the verge,
  And chanted forth, "Beati mundo corde,"
  In voice by far more living than our own.

Then: "No one farther goes, souls sanctified,
  If first the fire bite not; within it enter,
  And be not deaf unto the song beyond."

When we were close beside him thus he said;
  Wherefore e'en such became I, when I heard him,
  As he is who is put into the grave.

Upon my clasped hands I straightened me,
  Scanning the fire, and vividly recalling
  The human bodies I had once seen burned.

Towards me turned themselves my good Conductors,
  And unto me Virgilius said: "My son,
  Here may indeed be torment, but not death.

Remember thee, remember! and if I
  On Geryon have safely guided thee,
  What shall I do now I am nearer God?

Credi per certo che se dentro a l'alvo
  di questa fiamma stessi ben mille anni,
  non ti potrebbe far d'un capel calvo.
	Believe for certain, shouldst thou stand a full
	  Millennium in the bosom of this flame,
	  It could not make thee bald a single hair.

E se tu forse credi ch'io t'inganni,
  fatti ver lei, e fatti far credenza
  con le tue mani al lembo d'i tuoi panni.
	And if perchance thou think that I deceive thee,
	  Draw near to it, and put it to the proof
	  With thine own hands upon thy garment's hem.

Pon giu` omai, pon giu` ogni temenza;
  volgiti in qua e vieni: entra sicuro!""`.
  E io pur fermo e contra coscienza.
	Now lay aside, now lay aside all fear,
	  Turn hitherward, and onward come securely;"
	  And I still motionless, and 'gainst my conscience!

Quando mi vide star pur fermo e duro,
  turbato un poco disse: ""Or vedi, figlio:
  tra Beatrice e te e` questo muro""`.
	Seeing me stand still motionless and stubborn,
	  Somewhat disturbed he said: "Now look thou, Son,
	  'Twixt Beatrice and thee there is this wall."

Come al nome di Tisbe aperse il ciglio
  Piramo in su la morte, e riguardolla,
  allor che 'l gelso divento` vermiglio;
	As at the name of Thisbe oped his lids
	  The dying Pyramus, and gazed upon her,
	  What time the mulberry became vermilion,

cosi`, la mia durezza fatta solla,
  mi volsi al savio duca, udendo il nome
  che ne la mente sempre mi rampolla.
	Even thus, my obduracy being softened,
	  I turned to my wise Guide, hearing the name
	  That in my memory evermore is welling.

Ond'ei crollo` la fronte e disse: ""Come!   volenci star di qua?""; indi sorrise   come al fanciul si fa ch'e` vinto al pome.	Whereat he wagged his head, and said: "How now? Shall we stay on this side?" then smiled as one Does at a child who's vanquished by an apple.

Poi dentro al foco innanzi mi si mise,
  pregando Stazio che venisse retro,
  che pria per lunga strada ci divise.
	Then into the fire in front of me he entered,
	  Beseeching Statius to come after me,
	  Who a long way before divided us.

Si` com'fui dentro, in un bogliente vetro
  gittato mi sarei per rinfrescarmi,
  tant'era ivi lo 'ncendio sanza metro.
	When I was in it, into molten glass
	  I would have cast me to refresh myself,
	  So without measure was the burning there!

Lo dolce padre mio, per confortarmi,
  pur di Beatrice ragionando andava,
  dicendo: ""Li occhi suoi gia` veder parmi""`.
	And my sweet Father, to encourage me,
	  Discoursing still of Beatrice went on,
	  Saying: "Her eyes I seem to see already!"

Guidavaci una voce che cantava di la`; e noi, attenti pur a lei,   venimmo fuor la` ove si montava.	A voice, that on the other side was singing, Directed us, and we, attent alone On that, came forth where the ascent began.

'Venite, benedicti Patris mei',
  sono` dentro a un lume che li` era,
  tal che mi vinse e guardar nol potei.
	"Venite, benedicti Patris mei,"
	  Sounded within a splendour, which was there
	  Such it o'ercame me, and I could not look.

""Lo sol sen va"", soggiunse, ""e vien la sera;
  non v'arrestate, ma studiate il passo,
  mentre che l'occidente non si annera""`.
	"The sun departs," it added, "and night cometh;
	  Tarry ye not, but onward urge your steps,
	  So long as yet the west becomes not dark."

Dritta salia la via per entro 'l sasso
  verso tal parte ch'io toglieva i raggi
  dinanzi a me del sol ch'era gia` basso.

E di pochi scaglion levammo i saggi,
  che 'l sol corcar, per l'ombra che si spense,
  sentimmo dietro e io e li miei saggi.

E pria che 'n tutte le sue parti immense
  fosse orizzonte fatto d'uno aspetto,
  e notte avesse tutte sue dispense,

ciascun di noi d'un grado fece letto;
  che' la natura del monte ci affranse
  la possa del salir piu` e 'l diletto.

Quali si stanno ruminando manse
  le capre, state rapide e proterve
  sovra le cime avante che sien pranse,

tacite a l'ombra, mentre che 'l sol ferve,
  guardate dal pastor, che 'n su la verga
  poggiato s'e` e lor di posa serve;

e quale il mandrian che fori alberga,
  lungo il peculio suo queto pernotta,
  guardando perche' fiera non lo sperga;

tali eravamo tutti e tre allotta,
  io come capra, ed ei come pastori,
  fasciati quinci e quindi d'alta grotta.

Poco parer potea li` del di fori;
  ma, per quel poco, vedea io le stelle
  di lor solere e piu` chiare e maggiori.

Si` ruminando e si` mirando in quelle,
  mi prese il sonno; il sonno che sovente,
  anzi che 'l fatto sia, sa le novelle.

Ne l'ora, credo, che de l'oriente,
  prima raggio` nel monte Citerea,
  che di foco d'amor par sempre ardente,

giovane e bella in sogno mi parea
  donna vedere andar per una landa
  cogliendo fiori; e cantando dicea:

““Sappia qualunque il mio nome dimanda
  ch'i' mi son Lia, e vo movendo intorno
  le belle mani a farmi una ghirlanda.

Straight forward through the rock the path ascended
  In such a way that I cut off the rays
  Before me of the sun, that now was low.

And of few stairs we yet had made assay,
  Ere by the vanished shadow the sun's setting
  Behind us we perceived, I and my Sages.

And ere in all its parts immeasurable
  The horizon of one aspect had become,
  And Night her boundless dispensation held,

Each of us of a stair had made his bed;
  Because the nature of the mount took from us
  The power of climbing, more than the delight.

Even as in ruminating passive grow
  The goats, who have been swift and venturesome
  Upon the mountain-tops ere they were fed,

Hushed in the shadow, while the sun is hot,
  Watched by the herdsman, who upon his staff
  Is leaning, and in leaning tendeth them;

And as the shepherd, lodging out of doors,
  Passes the night beside his quiet flock,
  Watching that no wild beast may scatter it,

Such at that hour were we, all three of us,
  I like the goat, and like the herdsmen they,
  Begirt on this side and on that by rocks.

Little could there be seen of things without;
  But through that little I beheld the stars
  More luminous and larger than their wont.

Thus ruminating, and beholding these,
  Sleep seized upon me,—sleep, that oftentimes
  Before a deed is done has tidings of it.

It was the hour, I think, when from the East
  First on the mountain Citherea beamed,
  Who with the fire of love seems always burning;

Youthful and beautiful in dreams methought
  I saw a lady walking in a meadow,
  Gathering flowers; and singing she was saying:

"Know whosoever may my name demand
  That I am Leah, and go moving round
  My beauteous hands to make myself a garland.

Per piacermi a lo specchio, qui m'addorno;
  ma mia suora Rachel mai non si smaga
  dal suo miraglio, e siede tutto giorno.

Ell'e` d'i suoi belli occhi veder vaga
  com'io de l'addornarmi con le mani;
  lei lo vedere, e me l'ovrare appaga'".

E gia` per li splendori antelucani,
  che tanto a' pellegrin surgon piu` grati,
  quanto, tornando, albergan men lontani,

le tenebre fuggian da tutti lati,
  e 'l sonno mio con esse; ond'io leva'mi,
  veggendo i gran maestri gia` levati.

""Quel dolce pome che per tanti rami
  cercando va la cura de' mortali,
  oggi porra` in pace le tue fami'".

Virgilio inverso me queste cotali
  parole uso`; e mai non furo strenne
  che fosser di piacere a queste iguali.

Tanto voler sopra voler mi venne
  de l'esser su`, ch'ad ogne passo poi
  al volo mi sentia crescer le penne.

Come la scala tutta sotto noi
  fu corsa e fummo in su 'l grado superno,
  in me ficco` Virgilio li occhi suoi,

e disse: ""Il temporal foco e l'etterno
  veduto hai, figlio; e se' venuto in parte
  dov'io per me piu` oltre non discerno.

Tratto t'ho qui con ingegno e con arte;
  lo tuo piacere omai prendi per duce;
  fuor se' de l'erte vie, fuor se' de l'arte.

Vedi lo sol che 'n fronte ti riluce;
  vedi l'erbette, i fiori e li arbuscelli
  che qui la terra sol da se' produce.

Mentre che vegnan lieti li occhi belli
  che, lagrimando, a te venir mi fenno,
  seder ti puoi e puoi andar tra elli.

To please me at the mirror, here I deck me,
  But never does my sister Rachel leave
  Her looking-glass, and sitteth all day long.

To see her beauteous eyes as eager is she,
  As I am to adorn me with my hands;
  Her, seeing, and me, doing satisfies."

And now before the antelucan splendours
  That unto pilgrims the more grateful rise,
  As, home-returning, less remote they lodge,

The darkness fled away on every side,
  And slumber with it; whereupon I rose,
  Seeing already the great Masters risen.

"That apple sweet, which through so many branches
  The care of mortals goeth in pursuit of,
  To-day shall put in peace thy hungerings."

Speaking to me, Virgilius of such words
  As these made use; and never were there guerdons
  That could in pleasantness compare with these.

Such longing upon longing came upon me
  To be above, that at each step thereafter
  For flight I felt in me the pinions growing.

When underneath us was the stairway all
  Run o'er, and we were on the highest step,
  Virgilius fastened upon me his eyes,

And said: "The temporal fire and the eternal,
  Son, thou hast seen, and to a place art come
  Where of myself no farther I discern.

By intellect and art I here have brought thee;
  Take thine own pleasure for thy guide henceforth;
  Beyond the steep ways and the narrow art thou.

Behold the sun, that shines upon thy forehead;
  Behold the grass, the flowerets, and the shrubs
  Which of itself alone this land produces.

Until rejoicing come the beauteous eyes
  Which weeping caused me to come unto thee,
  Thou canst sit down, and thou canst walk among
    them.

Non aspettar mio dir piu` ne' mio cenno;
  libero, dritto e sano e` tuo arbitrio,
  e fallo fora non fare a suo senno:

per ch'io te sovra te corono e mitrio"".

Expect no more or word or sign from me;
  Free and upright and sound is thy free-will,
  And error were it not to do its bidding;

Thee o'er thyself I therefore crown and mitre!"

Purgatorio: Canto XXVIII

The River Lethe. Matilda. The Nature of the Terrestrial Paradise.

Vago gia` di cercar dentro e dintorno
  la divina foresta spessa e viva,
  ch'a li occhi temperava il novo giorno,

sanza piu` aspettar, lasciai la riva,
  prendendo la campagna lento lento
  su per lo suol che d'ogne parte auliva.

Un'aura dolce, sanza mutamento
  avere in se', mi feria per la fronte
  non di piu` colpo che soave vento;

per cui le fronde, tremolando, pronte
  tutte quante piegavano a la parte
  u' la prim'ombra gitta il santo monte;

non pero` dal loro esser dritto sparte
  tanto, che li augelletti per le cime
  lasciasser d'operare ogne lor arte;

ma con piena letizia l'ore prime,
  cantando, ricevieno intra le foglie,
  che tenevan bordone a le sue rime,

tal qual di ramo in ramo si raccoglie
  per la pineta in su 'l lito di Chiassi,
  quand'Eolo scilocco fuor discioglie.

Gia` m'avean trasportato i lenti passi
  dentro a la selva antica tanto, ch'io
  non potea rivedere ond'io mi 'ntrassi;

ed ecco piu` andar mi tolse un rio,
  che 'nver' sinistra con sue picciole onde
  piegava l'erba che 'n sua ripa uscio.

Eager already to search in and round
  The heavenly forest, dense and living-green,
  Which tempered to the eyes the new-born day,

Withouten more delay I left the bank,
  Taking the level country slowly, slowly
  Over the soil that everywhere breathes fragrance.

A softly-breathing air, that no mutation
  Had in itself, upon the forehead smote me
  No heavier blow than of a gentle wind,

Whereat the branches, lightly tremulous,
  Did all of them bow downward toward that side
  Where its first shadow casts the Holy Mountain;

Yet not from their upright direction swayed,
  So that the little birds upon their tops
  Should leave the practice of each art of theirs;

But with full ravishment the hours of prime,
  Singing, received they in the midst of leaves,
  That ever bore a burden to their rhymes,

Such as from branch to branch goes gathering on
  Through the pine forest on the shore of Chiassi,
  When Eolus unlooses the Sirocco.

Already my slow steps had carried me
  Into the ancient wood so far, that I
  Could not perceive where I had entered it.

And lo! my further course a stream cut off,
  Which tow'rd the left hand with its little waves
  Bent down the grass that on its margin sprang.

Tutte l'acque che son di qua piu` monde,
　parrieno avere in se' mistura alcuna,
　verso di quella, che nulla nasconde,

avvegna che si mova bruna bruna
　sotto l'ombra perpetua, che mai
　raggiar non lascia sole ivi ne' luna.

Coi pie` ristretti e con li occhi passai
　di la` dal fiumicello, per mirare
　la gran variazion d'i freschi mai;

e la` m'apparve, si` com'elli appare
　subitamente cosa che disvia
　per maraviglia tutto altro pensare,

una donna soletta che si gia
　e cantando e scegliendo fior da fiore
　ond'era pinta tutta la sua via.

""Deh, bella donna, che a' raggi d'amore
　ti scaldi, s'i' vo' credere a' sembianti
　che soglion esser testimon del core,

vegnati in voglia di trarreti avanti"",
　diss'io a lei, ""verso questa rivera,
　tanto ch'io possa intender che tu canti.

Tu mi fai rimembrar dove e qual era
　Proserpina nel tempo che perdette
　la madre lei, ed ella primavera"".

Come si volge, con le piante strette
　a terra e intra se', donna che balli,
　e piede innanzi piede a pena mette,

volsesi in su i vermigli e in su i gialli
　fioretti verso me, non altrimenti
　che vergine che li occhi onesti avvalli;

e fece i prieghi miei esser contenti,
　si` appressando se', che 'l dolce suono
　veniva a me co' suoi intendimenti.

Tosto che fu la` dove l'erbe sono
　bagnate gia` da l'onde del bel fiume,
　di levar li occhi suoi mi fece dono.

All waters that on earth most limpid are
　Would seem to have within themselves some mixture
　Compared with that which nothing doth conceal,

Although it moves on with a brown, brown current
　Under the shade perpetual, that never
　Ray of the sun lets in, nor of the moon.

With feet I stayed, and with mine eyes I passed
　Beyond the rivulet, to look upon
　The great variety of the fresh may.

And there appeared to me (even as appears
　Suddenly something that doth turn aside
　Through very wonder every other thought)

A lady all alone, who went along
　Singing and culling floweret after floweret,
　With which her pathway was all painted over.

"Ah, beauteous lady, who in rays of love
　Dost warm thyself, if I may trust to looks,
　Which the heart's witnesses are wont to be,

May the desire come unto thee to draw
　Near to this river's bank," I said to her,
　"So much that I might hear what thou art singing.

Thou makest me remember where and what
　Proserpina that moment was when lost
　Her mother her, and she herself the Spring."

As turns herself, with feet together pressed
　And to the ground, a lady who is dancing,
　And hardly puts one foot before the other,

On the vermilion and the yellow flowerets
　She turned towards me, not in other wise
　Than maiden who her modest eyes casts down;

And my entreaties made to be content,
　So near approaching, that the dulcet sound
　Came unto me together with its meaning

As soon as she was where the grasses are.
　Bathed by the waters of the beauteous river,
　To lift her eyes she granted me the boon.

Non credo che splendesse tanto lume
  sotto le ciglia a Venere, trafitta
  dal figlio fuor di tutto suo costume.
	I do not think there shone so great a light
	  Under the lids of Venus, when transfixed
	  By her own son, beyond his usual custom!

Ella ridea da l'altra riva dritta,
  trattando piu` color con le sue mani,
  che l'alta terra sanza seme gitta.
	Erect upon the other bank she smiled,
	  Bearing full many colours in her hands,
	  Which that high land produces without seed.

Tre passi ci facea il fiume lontani;
  ma Elesponto, la` 've passo` Serse,
  ancora freno a tutti orgogli umani,
	Apart three paces did the river make us;
	  But Hellespont, where Xerxes passed across,
	  (A curb still to all human arrogance,)

piu` odio da Leandro non sofferse
  per mareggiare intra Sesto e Abido,
  che quel da me perch'allor non s'aperse.
	More hatred from Leander did not suffer
	  For rolling between Sestos and Abydos,
	  Than that from me, because it oped not then.

""Voi siete nuovi, e forse perch'io rido""`,   comincio` ella, ""in questo luogo eletto a l'umana natura per suo nido,	"Ye are new-comers; and because I smile," Began she, "peradventure, in this place Elect to human nature for its nest,

maravigliando tienvi alcun sospetto;
  ma luce rende il salmo Delectasti,
  che puote disnebbiar vostro intelletto.
	Some apprehension keeps you marvelling;
	  But the psalm 'Delectasti' giveth light
	  Which has the power to uncloud your intellect.

E tu che se' dinanzi e mi pregasti, di` s'altro vuoli udir; ch'i' venni presta   ad ogne tua question tanto che basti""`.	And thou who foremost art, and didst entreat me, Speak, if thou wouldst hear more; for I came ready To all thy questionings, as far as needful."
""L'acqua""`, diss'io, ""e 'l suon de la foresta   impugnan dentro a me novella fede   di cosa ch'io udi' contraria a questa""`.	"The water," said I, "and the forest's sound, Are combating within me my new faith In something which I heard opposed to this."
Ond'ella: ""Io dicero` come procede   per sua cagion cio` ch'ammirar ti face, e purghero` la nebbia che ti fiede.	Whence she: "I will relate how from its cause Proceedeth that which maketh thee to wonder, And purge away the cloud that smites upon thee.

Lo sommo Ben, che solo esso a se' piace,
  fe' l'uom buono e a bene, e questo loco
  diede per arr'a lui d'etterna pace.
	The Good Supreme, sole in itself delighting,
	  Created man good, and this goodly place
	  Gave him as hansel of eternal peace.

Per sua difalta qui dimoro` poco;   per sua difalta in pianto e in affanno   cambio` onesto riso e dolce gioco.	By his default short while he sojourned here; By his default to weeping and to toil He changed his innocent laughter and sweet play.

Perche' 'l turbar che sotto da se' fanno
  l'essalazion de l'acqua e de la terra,
  che quanto posson dietro al calor vanno,
	That the disturbance which below is made
	  By exhalations of the land and water,
	  (Which far as may be follow after heat,)

a l'uomo non facesse alcuna guerra,
  questo monte salio verso 'l ciel tanto,
  e libero n'e` d'indi ove si serra.
	Might not upon mankind wage any war,
	  This mount ascended tow'rds the heaven so high,
	  And is exempt, from there where it is locked.

Or perche' in circuito tutto quanto
  l'aere si volge con la prima volta,
  se non li e` rotto il cerchio d'alcun canto,

in questa altezza ch'e` tutta disciolta
  ne l'aere vivo, tal moto percuote,
  e fa sonar la selva perch'e` folta;

e la percossa pianta tanto puote,
  che de la sua virtute l'aura impregna,
  e quella poi, girando, intorno scuote;

e l'altra terra, secondo ch'e` degna
  per se' e per suo ciel, concepe e figlia
  di diverse virtu` diverse legna.

Non parrebbe di la` poi maraviglia,
  udito questo, quando alcuna pianta
  sanza seme palese vi s'appiglia.

E saper dei che la campagna santa
  dove tu se', d'ogne semenza e` piena,
  e frutto ha in se' che di la` non si schianta.

L'acqua che vedi non surge di vena
  che ristori vapor che gel converta,
  come fiume ch'acquista e perde lena;

ma esce di fontana salda e certa,
  che tanto dal voler di Dio riprende,
  quant'ella versa da due parti aperta.

Da questa parte con virtu` discende
  che toglie altrui memoria del peccato;
  da l'altra d'ogne ben fatto la rende.

Quinci Lete`; cosi` da l'altro lato
  Eunoe` si chiama, e non adopra
  se quinci e quindi pria non e` gustato:

a tutti altri sapori esto e` di sopra.
  E avvegna ch'assai possa esser sazia
  la sete tua perch'io piu` non ti scuopra,

darotti un corollario ancor per grazia;
  ne' credo che 'l mio dir ti sia men caro,
  se oltre promession teco si spazia.

Quelli ch'anticamente poetaro
  l'eta` de l'oro e suo stato felice,
  forse in Parnaso esto loco sognaro.

Now since the universal atmosphere
  Turns in a circuit with the primal motion
  Unless the circle is broken on some side,

Upon this height, that all is disengaged
  In living ether, doth this motion strike
  And make the forest sound, for it is dense;

And so much power the stricken plant possesses
  That with its virtue it impregns the air,
  And this, revolving, scatters it around;

And yonder earth, according as 'tis worthy
  In self or in its clime, conceives and bears
  Of divers qualities the divers trees;

It should not seem a marvel then on earth,
  This being heard, whenever any plant
  Without seed manifest there taketh root.

And thou must know, this holy table-land
  In which thou art is full of every seed,
  And fruit has in it never gathered there.

The water which thou seest springs not from vein
  Restored by vapour that the cold condenses,
  Like to a stream that gains or loses breath;

But issues from a fountain safe and certain,
  Which by the will of God as much regains
  As it discharges, open on two sides.

Upon this side with virtue it descends,
  Which takes away all memory of sin;
  On that, of every good deed done restores it.

Here Lethe, as upon the other side
  Eunoe, it is called; and worketh not
  If first on either side it be not tasted.

This every other savour doth transcend;
  And notwithstanding slaked so far may be
  Thy thirst, that I reveal to thee no more,

I'll give thee a corollary still in grace,
  Nor think my speech will be to thee less dear
  If it spread out beyond my promise to thee.

Those who in ancient times have feigned in song
  The Age of Gold and its felicity,
  Dreamed of this place perhaps upon Parnassus.

Qui fu innocente l'umana radice;
  qui primavera sempre e ogne frutto;
  nettare e` questo di che ciascun dice"".

Io mi rivolsi 'n dietro allora tutto
  a' miei poeti, e vidi che con riso
  udito avean l'ultimo costrutto;

poi a la bella donna torna' il viso.

Here was the human race in innocence;
  Here evermore was Spring, and every fruit;
  This is the nectar of which each one speaks."

Then backward did I turn me wholly round
  Unto my Poets, and saw that with a smile
  They had been listening to these closing words;

Then to the beautiful lady turned mine eyes.

Purgatorio: Canto XXIX

The Triumph of the Church.

Cantando come donna innamorata,
  continuo` col fin di sue parole:
  'Beati quorum tecta sunt peccata!'.

E come ninfe che si givan sole
  per le salvatiche ombre, disiando
  qual di veder, qual di fuggir lo sole,

allor si mosse contra 'l fiume, andando
  su per la riva; e io pari di lei,
  picciol passo con picciol seguitando.

Non eran cento tra ' suoi passi e ' miei,
  quando le ripe igualmente dier volta,
  per modo ch'a levante mi rendei.

Ne' ancor fu cosi` nostra via molta,
  quando la donna tutta a me si torse,
  dicendo: ""Frate mio, guarda e ascolta"".

Ed ecco un lustro subito trascorse
  da tutte parti per la gran foresta,
  tal che di balenar mi mise in forse.

Ma perche' 'l balenar, come vien, resta,
  e quel, durando, piu` e piu` splendeva,
  nel mio pensier dicea: 'Che cosa e` questa?'.

E una melodia dolce correva
  per l'aere luminoso; onde buon zelo
  mi fe' riprender l'ardimento d'Eva,

che la` dove ubidia la terra e 'l cielo,
  femmina, sola e pur teste' formata,
  non sofferse di star sotto alcun velo;

Singing like unto an enamoured lady
  She, with the ending of her words, continued:
  "Beati quorum tecta sunt peccata."

And even as Nymphs, that wandered all alone
  Among the sylvan shadows, sedulous
  One to avoid and one to see the sun,

She then against the stream moved onward, going
  Along the bank, and I abreast of her,
  Her little steps with little steps attending.

Between her steps and mine were not a hundred,
  When equally the margins gave a turn,
  In such a way, that to the East I faced.

Nor even thus our way continued far
  Before the lady wholly turned herself
  Unto me, saying, "Brother, look and listen!"

And lo! a sudden lustre ran across
  On every side athwart the spacious forest,
  Such that it made me doubt if it were lightning.

But since the lightning ceases as it comes,
  And that continuing brightened more and more,
  Within my thought I said, "What thing is this?"

And a delicious melody there ran
  Along the luminous air, whence holy zeal
  Made me rebuke the hardihood of Eve;

For there where earth and heaven obedient were,
  The woman only, and but just created,
  Could not endure to stay 'neath any veil;

sotto 'l qual se divota fosse stata,
  avrei quelle ineffabili delizie
  sentite prima e piu` lunga fiata.

Mentr'io m'andava tra tante primizie
  de l'etterno piacer tutto sospeso,
  e disioso ancora a piu` letizie,

dinanzi a noi, tal quale un foco acceso,
  ci si fe' l'aere sotto i verdi rami;
  e 'l dolce suon per canti era gia` inteso.

O sacrosante Vergini, se fami,
  freddi o vigilie mai per voi soffersi,
  cagion mi sprona ch'io merce' vi chiami.

Or convien che Elicona per me versi,
  e Uranie m'aiuti col suo coro
  forti cose a pensar mettere in versi.

Poco piu` oltre, sette alberi d'oro
  falsava nel parere il lungo tratto
  del mezzo ch'era ancor tra noi e loro;

ma quand'i' fui si` presso di lor fatto,
  che l'obietto comun, che 'l senso inganna,
  non perdea per distanza alcun suo atto,

la virtu` ch'a ragion discorso ammanna,
  si` com'elli eran candelabri apprese,
  e ne le voci del cantare 'Osanna'.

Di sopra fiammeggiava il bello arnese
  piu` chiaro assai che luna per sereno
  di mezza notte nel suo mezzo mese.

Io mi rivolsi d'ammirazion pieno
  al buon Virgilio, ed esso mi rispuose
  con vista carca di stupor non meno.

Indi rendei l'aspetto a l'alte cose
  che si movieno incontr'a noi si` tardi,
  che foran vinte da novelle spose.

La donna mi sgrido`: ""Perche' pur ardi
  si` ne l'affetto de le vive luci,
  e cio` che vien di retro a lor non guardi?""".

Genti vid'io allor, come a lor duci,
  venire appresso, vestite di bianco;
  e tal candor di qua gia` mai non fuci.

Underneath which had she devoutly stayed,
  I sooner should have tasted those delights
  Ineffable, and for a longer time.

While 'mid such manifold first-fruits I walked
  Of the eternal pleasure all enrapt,
  And still solicitous of more delights,

In front of us like an enkindled fire
  Became the air beneath the verdant boughs,
  And the sweet sound as singing now was heard.

O Virgins sacrosanct! if ever hunger,
  Vigils, or cold for you I have endured,
  The occasion spurs me their reward to claim!

Now Helicon must needs pour forth for me,
  And with her choir Urania must assist me,
  To put in verse things difficult to think.

A little farther on, seven trees of gold
  In semblance the long space still intervening
  Between ourselves and them did counterfeit;

But when I had approached so near to them
  The common object, which the sense deceives,
  Lost not by distance any of its marks,

The faculty that lends discourse to reason
  Did apprehend that they were candlesticks,
  And in the voices of the song "Hosanna!"

Above them flamed the harness beautiful,
  Far brighter than the moon in the serene
  Of midnight, at the middle of her month.

I turned me round, with admiration filled,
  To good Virgilius, and he answered me
  With visage no less full of wonderment.

Then back I turned my face to those high things,
  Which moved themselves towards us so sedately,
  They had been distanced by new-wedded brides.

The lady chid me: "Why dost thou burn only
  So with affection for the living lights,
  And dost not look at what comes after them?"

Then saw I people, as behind their leaders,
  Coming behind them, garmented in white,
  And such a whiteness never was on earth.

L'acqua imprendea dal sinistro fianco,
  e rendea me la mia sinistra costa,
  s'io riguardava in lei, come specchio anco.

Quand'io da la mia riva ebbi tal posta,
  che solo il fiume mi facea distante,
  per veder meglio ai passi diedi sosta,

e vidi le fiammelle andar davante,
  lasciando dietro a se' l'aere dipinto,
  e di tratti pennelli avean sembiante;

si` che li` sopra rimanea distinto
  di sette liste, tutte in quei colori
  onde fa l'arco il Sole e Delia il cinto.

Questi ostendali in dietro eran maggiori
  che la mia vista; e, quanto a mio avviso,
  diece passi distavan quei di fori.

Sotto cosi` bel ciel com'io diviso,
  ventiquattro seniori, a due a due,
  coronati venien di fiordaliso.

Tutti cantavan: ""Benedicta tue
  ne le figlie d'Adamo, e benedette
  sieno in etterno le bellezze tue!"".

Poscia che i fiori e l'altre fresche erbette
  a rimpetto di me da l'altra sponda
  libere fuor da quelle genti elette,

si` come luce luce in ciel seconda,
  vennero appresso lor quattro animali,
  coronati ciascun di verde fronda.

Ognuno era pennuto di sei ali;
  le penne piene d'occhi; e li occhi d'Argo,
  se fosser vivi, sarebber cotali.

A descriver lor forme piu` non spargo
  rime, lettor; ch'altra spesa mi strigne,
  tanto ch'a questa non posso esser largo;

ma leggi Ezechiel, che li dipigne
  come li vide da la fredda parte
  venir con vento e con nube e con igne;

e quali i troverai ne le sue carte,
  tali eran quivi, salvo ch'a le penne
  Giovanni e` meco e da lui si diparte.

The water on my left flank was resplendent,
  And back to me reflected my left side,
  E'en as a mirror, if I looked therein.

When I upon my margin had such post
  That nothing but the stream divided us,
  Better to see I gave my steps repose;

And I beheld the flamelets onward go,
  Leaving behind themselves the air depicted,
  And they of trailing pennons had the semblance,

So that it overhead remained distinct
  With sevenfold lists, all of them of the colours
  Whence the sun's bow is made, and Delia's girdle.

These standards to the rearward longer were
  Than was my sight; and, as it seemed to me,
  Ten paces were the outermost apart.

Under so fair a heaven as I describe
  The four and twenty Elders, two by two,
  Came on incoronate with flower-de-luce.

They all of them were singing: "Blessed thou
  Among the daughters of Adam art, and blessed
  For evermore shall be thy loveliness."

After the flowers and other tender grasses
  In front of me upon the other margin
  Were disencumbered of that race elect,

Even as in heaven star followeth after star,
  There came close after them four animals,
  Incoronate each one with verdant leaf.

Plumed with six wings was every one of them,
  The plumage full of eyes; the eyes of Argus
  If they were living would be such as these.

Reader! to trace their forms no more I waste
  My rhymes; for other spendings press me so,
  That I in this cannot be prodigal.

But read Ezekiel, who depicteth them
  As he beheld them from the region cold
  Coming with cloud, with whirlwind, and with fire;

And such as thou shalt find them in his pages,
  Such were they here; saving that in their plumage
  John is with me, and differeth from him.

Lo spazio dentro a lor quattro contenne
  un carro, in su due rote, triunfale,
  ch'al collo d'un grifon tirato venne.

Esso tendeva in su` l'una e l'altra ale
  tra la mezzana e le tre e tre liste,
  si` ch'a nulla, fendendo, facea male.

Tanto salivan che non eran viste;
  le membra d'oro avea quant'era uccello,
  e bianche l'altre, di vermiglio miste.

Non che Roma di carro cosi` bello
  rallegrasse Affricano, o vero Augusto,
  ma quel del Sol saria pover con ello;

quel del Sol che, sviando, fu combusto
  per l'orazion de la Terra devota,
  quando fu Giove arcanamente giusto.

Tre donne in giro da la destra rota
  venian danzando; l'una tanto rossa
  ch'a pena fora dentro al foco nota;

l'altr'era come se le carni e l'ossa
  fossero state di smeraldo fatte;
  la terza parea neve teste' mossa;

e or parean da la bianca tratte,
  or da la rossa; e dal canto di questa
  l'altre toglien l'andare e tarde e ratte.

Da la sinistra quattro facean festa,
  in porpore vestite, dietro al modo
  d'una di lor ch'avea tre occhi in testa.

Appresso tutto il pertrattato nodo
  vidi due vecchi in abito dispari,
  ma pari in atto e onesto e sodo.

L'un si mostrava alcun de' famigliari
  di quel sommo Ipocrate che natura
  a li animali fe' ch'ell'ha piu` cari;

mostrava l'altro la contraria cura
  con una spada lucida e aguta,
  tal che di qua dal rio mi fe' paura.

Poi vidi quattro in umile paruta;
  e di retro da tutti un vecchio solo
  venir, dormendo, con la faccia arguta.

The interval between these four contained
  A chariot triumphal on two wheels,
  Which by a Griffin's neck came drawn along;

And upward he extended both his wings
  Between the middle list and three and three,
  So that he injured none by cleaving it.

So high they rose that they were lost to sight;
  His limbs were gold, so far as he was bird,
  And white the others with vermilion mingled.

Not only Rome with no such splendid car
  E'er gladdened Africanus, or Augustus,
  But poor to it that of the Sun would be,—

That of the Sun, which swerving was burnt up
  At the importunate orison of Earth,
  When Jove was so mysteriously just.

Three maidens at the right wheel in a circle
  Came onward dancing; one so very red
  That in the fire she hardly had been noted.

The second was as if her flesh and bones
  Had all been fashioned out of emerald;
  The third appeared as snow but newly fallen.

And now they seemed conducted by the white,
  Now by the red, and from the song of her
  The others took their step, or slow or swift.

Upon the left hand four made holiday
  Vested in purple, following the measure
  Of one of them with three eyes m her head.

In rear of all the group here treated of
  Two old men I beheld, unlike in habit,
  But like in gait, each dignified and grave.

One showed himself as one of the disciples
  Of that supreme Hippocrates, whom nature
  Made for the animals she holds most dear;

Contrary care the other manifested,
  With sword so shining and so sharp, it caused
  Terror to me on this side of the river.

Thereafter four I saw of humble aspect,
  And behind all an aged man alone
  Walking in sleep with countenance acute.

E questi sette col primaio stuolo
 erano abituati, ma di gigli
 dintorno al capo non facean brolo,

anzi di rose e d'altri fior vermigli;
 giurato avria poco lontano aspetto
 che tutti ardesser di sopra da' cigli.

E quando il carro a me fu a rimpetto,
 un tuon s'udì, e quelle genti degne
 parvero aver l'andar più interdetto,

fermandosi ivi con le prime insegne.

And like the foremost company these seven
 Were habited; yet of the flower-de-luce
 No garland round about the head they wore,

But of the rose, and other flowers vermilion;
 At little distance would the sight have sworn
 That all were in a flame above their brows.

And when the car was opposite to me
 Thunder was heard; and all that folk august
 Seemed to have further progress interdicted,

There with the vanward ensigns standing still.

Purgatorio: Canto XXX

Virgil's Departure. Beatrice. Dante's Shame.

Quando il settentrion del primo cielo,
  che ne' occaso mai seppe ne' orto
  ne' d'altra nebbia che di colpa velo,

e che faceva li` ciascun accorto
  di suo dover, come 'l piu` basso face
  qual temon gira per venire a porto,

fermo s'affisse: la gente verace,
  venuta prima tra 'l grifone ed esso,
  al carro volse se' come a sua pace;

e un di loro, quasi da ciel messo,
  'Veni, sponsa, de Libano' cantando
  grido` tre volte, e tutti li altri appresso.

Quali i beati al novissimo bando
  surgeran presti ognun di sua caverna,
  la revestita voce alleluiando,

cotali in su la divina basterna
  si levar cento, ad vocem tanti senis,
  ministri e messaggier di vita etterna.

Tutti dicean: 'Benedictus qui venis!',
  e fior gittando e di sopra e dintorno,
  'Manibus, oh, date lilia plenis!'.

Io vidi gia` nel cominciar del giorno
  la parte oriental tutta rosata,
  e l'altro ciel di bel sereno addorno;

e la faccia del sol nascere ombrata,
  si` che per temperanza di vapori
  l'occhio la sostenea lunga fiata:

When the Septentrion of the highest heaven
  (Which never either setting knew or rising,
  Nor veil of other cloud than that of sin,

And which made every one therein aware
  Of his own duty, as the lower makes
  Whoever turns the helm to come to port)

Motionless halted, the veracious people,
  That came at first between it and the Griffin,
  Turned themselves to the car, as to their peace.

And one of them, as if by Heaven commissioned,
  Singing, "Veni, sponsa, de Libano"
  Shouted three times, and all the others after.

Even as the Blessed at the final summons
  Shall rise up quickened each one from his cavern,
  Uplifting light the reinvested flesh,

So upon that celestial chariot
  A hundred rose 'ad vocem tanti senis,'
  Ministers and messengers of life eternal.

They all were saying, "Benedictus qui venis,"
  And, scattering flowers above and round about,
  "Manibus o date lilia plenis."

Ere now have I beheld, as day began,
  The eastern hemisphere all tinged with rose,
  And the other heaven with fair serene adorned;

And the sun's face, uprising, overshadowed
  So that by tempering influence of vapours
  For a long interval the eye sustained it;

cosi` dentro una nuvola di fiori   che da le mani angeliche saliva   e ricadeva in giu` dentro e di fori,	Thus in the bosom of a cloud of flowers Which from those hands angelical ascended, And downward fell again inside and out,

sovra candido vel cinta d'uliva
  donna m'apparve, sotto verde manto
  vestita di color di fiamma viva.
	Over her snow-white veil with olive cinct
	  Appeared a lady under a green mantle,
	  Vested in colour of the living flame.

E lo spirito mio, che gia` cotanto
  tempo era stato ch'a la sua presenza
  non era di stupor, tremando, affranto,
	And my own spirit, that already now
	  So long a time had been, that in her presence
	  Trembling with awe it had not stood abashed,

sanza de li occhi aver piu` conoscenza,   per occulta virtu` che da lei mosse, d'antico amor senti` la gran potenza.	Without more knowledge having by mine eyes, Through occult virtue that from her proceeded Of ancient love the mighty influence felt.

Tosto che ne la vista mi percosse
  l'alta virtu` che gia` m'avea trafitto
  prima ch'io fuor di puerizia fosse,
	As soon as on my vision smote the power
	  Sublime, that had already pierced me through
	  Ere from my boyhood I had yet come forth,

volsimi a la sinistra col respitto
  col quale il fantolin corre a la mamma
  quando ha paura o quando elli e` afflitto,
	To the left hand I turned with that reliance
	  With which the little child runs to his mother,
	  When he has fear, or when he is afflicted,

per dicere a Virgilio: 'Men che dramma
  di sangue m'e` rimaso che non tremi:
  conosco i segni de l'antica fiamma'.
	To say unto Virgilius: "Not a drachm
	  Of blood remains in me, that does not tremble;
	  I know the traces of the ancient flame."

Ma Virgilio n'avea lasciati scemi
  di se', Virgilio dolcissimo patre,
  Virgilio a cui per mia salute die'mi;
	But us Virgilius of himself deprived
	  Had left, Virgilius, sweetest of all fathers,
	  Virgilius, to whom I for safety gave me:

ne' quantunque perdeo l'antica matre,
  valse a le guance nette di rugiada,
  che, lagrimando, non tornasser atre.
	Nor whatsoever lost the ancient mother
	  Availed my cheeks now purified from dew,
	  That weeping they should not again be darkened.

""'Dante, perche' Virgilio se ne vada,
  non pianger anco, non pianger ancora;
  che' pianger ti conven per altra spada'"".
	"Dante, because Virgilius has departed
	  Do not weep yet, do not weep yet awhile;
	  For by another sword thou need'st must weep."

Quasi ammiraglio che in poppa e in prora
  viene a veder la gente che ministra
  per li altri legni, e a ben far l'incora;
	E'en as an admiral, who on poop and prow
	  Comes to behold the people that are working
	  In other ships, and cheers them to well-doing,

in su la sponda del carro sinistra,
  quando mi volsi al suon del nome mio,
  che di necessita` qui si registra,
	Upon the left hand border of the car,
	  When at the sound I turned of my own name,
	  Which of necessity is here recorded,

vidi la donna che pria m'appario
  velata sotto l'angelica festa,
  drizzar li occhi ver' me di qua dal rio.
	I saw the Lady, who erewhile appeared
	  Veiled underneath the angelic festival,
	  Direct her eyes to me across the river.

Tutto che 'l vel che le scendea di testa,
  cerchiato de le fronde di Minerva,
  non la lasciasse parer manifesta,

Although the veil, that from her head descended,
  Encircled with the foliage of Minerva,
  Did not permit her to appear distinctly,

regalmente ne l'atto ancor proterva
  continuo` come colui che dice
  e 'l piu` caldo parlar dietro reserva:

In attitude still royally majestic
  Continued she, like unto one who speaks,
  And keeps his warmest utterance in reserve:

""Guardaci ben! Ben son, ben son Beatrice.
  Come degnasti d'accedere al monte?
  non sapei tu che qui e` l'uom felice?"".

"Look at me well; in sooth I'm Beatrice!
  How didst thou deign to come unto the Mountain?
  Didst thou not know that man is happy here?"

Li occhi mi cadder giu` nel chiaro fonte;
  ma veggendomi in esso, i trassi a l'erba,
  tanta vergogna mi gravo` la fronte.

Mine eyes fell downward into the clear fountain,
  But, seeing myself therein, I sought the grass,
  So great a shame did weigh my forehead down.

Cosi` la madre al figlio par superba,
  com'ella parve a me; perche' d'amaro
  sente il sapor de la pietade acerba.

As to the son the mother seems superb,
  So she appeared to me; for somewhat bitter
  Tasteth the savour of severe compassion.

Ella si tacque; e li angeli cantaro
  di subito 'In te, Domine, speravi';
  ma oltre 'pedes meos' non passaro.

Silent became she, and the Angels sang
  Suddenly, "In te, Domine, speravi:"
  But beyond 'pedes meos' did not pass.

Si` come neve tra le vive travi
  per lo dosso d'Italia si congela,
  soffiata e stretta da li venti schiavi,

Even as the snow among the living rafters
  Upon the back of Italy congeals,
  Blown on and drifted by Sclavonian winds,

poi, liquefatta, in se' stessa trapela,
  pur che la terra che perde ombra spiri,
  si` che par foco fonder la candela;

And then, dissolving, trickles through itself
  Whene'er the land that loses shadow breathes,
  So that it seems a fire that melts a taper;

cosi` fui sanza lagrime e sospiri
  anzi 'l cantar di quei che notan sempre
  dietro a le note de li etterni giri;

E'en thus was I without a tear or sigh,
  Before the song of those who sing for ever
  After the music of the eternal spheres.

ma poi che 'ntesi ne le dolci tempre
  lor compatire a me, par che se detto
  avesser: 'Donna, perche' si` lo stempre?',

But when I heard in their sweet melodies
  Compassion for me, more than had they said,
  "O wherefore, lady, dost thou thus upbraid him?"

lo gel che m'era intorno al cor ristretto,
  spirito e acqua fessi, e con angoscia
  de la bocca e de li occhi usci` del petto.

The ice, that was about my heart congealed,
  To air and water changed, and in my anguish
  Through mouth and eyes came gushing from my
    breast.

Ella, pur ferma in su la detta coscia
  del carro stando, a le sustanze pie
  volse le sue parole cosi` poscia:

She, on the right-hand border of the car
  Still firmly standing, to those holy beings
  Thus her discourse directed afterwards:

""'Voi vigilate ne l'etterno die,
  si` che notte ne' sonno a voi non fura
  passo che faccia il secol per sue vie;

onde la mia risposta e` con piu` cura
  che m'intenda colui che di la` piagne,
  perche' sia colpa e duol d'una misura.

Non pur per ovra de le rote magne,
  che drizzan ciascun seme ad alcun fine
  secondo che le stelle son compagne,

ma per larghezza di grazie divine,
  che si` alti vapori hanno a lor piova,
  che nostre viste la` non van vicine,

questi fu tal ne la sua vita nova
  virtualmente, ch'ogne abito destro
  fatto averebbe in lui mirabil prova.

Ma tanto piu` maligno e piu` silvestro
  si fa 'l terren col mal seme e non colto,
  quant'elli ha piu` di buon vigor terrestro.

Alcun tempo il sostenni col mio volto:
  mostrando li occhi giovanetti a lui,
  meco il menava in dritta parte volto.

Si` tosto come in su la soglia fui
  di mia seconda etade e mutai vita,
  questi si tolse a me, e diessi altrui.

Quando di carne a spirto era salita
  e bellezza e virtu` cresciuta m'era,
  fu' io a lui men cara e men gradita;

e volse i passi suoi per via non vera,
  imagini di ben seguendo false,
  che nulla promession rendono intera.

Ne' l'impetrare ispirazion mi valse,
  con le quali e in sogno e altrimenti
  lo rivocai; si` poco a lui ne calse!

Tanto giu` cadde, che tutti argomenti
  a la salute sua eran gia` corti,
  fuor che mostrarli le perdute genti.

Per questo visitai l'uscio d'i morti
  e a colui che l'ha qua su` condotto,
  li prieghi miei, piangendo, furon porti.

"Ye keep your watch in the eternal day,
  So that nor night nor sleep can steal from you
  One step the ages make upon their path;

Therefore my answer is with greater care,
  That he may hear me who is weeping yonder,
  So that the sin and dole be of one measure.

Not only by the work of those great wheels,
  That destine every seed unto some end,
  According as the stars are in conjunction,

But by the largess of celestial graces,
  Which have such lofty vapours for their rain
  That near to them our sight approaches not,

Such had this man become in his new life
  Potentially, that every righteous habit
  Would have made admirable proof in him;

But so much more malignant and more savage
  Becomes the land untilled and with bad seed,
  The more good earthly vigour it possesses.

Some time did I sustain him with my look;
  Revealing unto him my youthful eyes,
  I led him with me turned in the right way.

As soon as ever of my second age
  I was upon the threshold and changed life,
  Himself from me he took and gave to others.

When from the flesh to spirit I ascended,
  And beauty and virtue were in me increased,
  I was to him less dear and less delightful;

And into ways untrue he turned his steps,
  Pursuing the false images of good,
  That never any promises fulfil;

Nor prayer for inspiration me availed,
  By means of which in dreams and otherwise
  I called him back, so little did he heed them.

So low he fell, that all appliances
  For his salvation were already short,
  Save showing him the people of perdition.

For this I visited the gates of death,
  And unto him, who so far up has led him,
  My intercessions were with weeping borne.

Alto fato di Dio sarebbe rotto,
  se Lete' si passasse e tal vivanda
  fosse gustata sanza alcuno scotto

di pentimento che lagrime spanda'"".

God's lofty fiat would be violated,
  If Lethe should be passed, and if such viands
  Should tasted be, withouten any scot

Of penitence, that gushes forth in tears."

Purgatorio: Canto XXXI

Reproaches of Beatrice and Confession of Dante. The Passage of Lethe. The Seven Virtues. The Griffon.

"" O tu che se' di la` dal fiume sacro"",
  volgendo suo parlare a me per punta,
  che pur per taglio m'era paruto acro,

ricomincio`, seguendo sanza cunta,
  ""di`, di` se questo e` vero: a tanta accusa
  tua confession conviene esser congiunta"".

Era la mia virtu` tanto confusa,
  che la voce si mosse, e pria si spense
  che da li organi suoi fosse dischiusa.

Poco sofferse; poi disse: ""Che pense?
  Rispondi a me; che' le memorie triste
  in te non sono ancor da l'acqua offense"".

Confusione e paura insieme miste
  mi pinsero un tal ""si`"" fuor de la bocca,
  al quale intender fuor mestier le viste.

Come balestro frange, quando scocca
  da troppa tesa la sua corda e l'arco,
  e con men foga l'asta il segno tocca,

si` scoppia' io sottesso grave carco,
  fuori sgorgando lagrime e sospiri,
  e la voce allento` per lo suo varco.

Ond'ella a me: ""Per entro i mie' disiri,
  che ti menavano ad amar lo bene
  di la` dal qual non e` a che s'aspiri,

quai fossi attraversati o quai catene
  trovasti, per che del passare innanzi
  dovessiti cosi` spogliar la spene?

"O thou who art beyond the sacred river,"
  Turning to me the point of her discourse,
  That edgewise even had seemed to me so keen,

She recommenced, continuing without pause,
  "Say, say if this be true; to such a charge,
  Thy own confession needs must be conjoined."

My faculties were in so great confusion,
  That the voice moved, but sooner was extinct
  Than by its organs it was set at large.

Awhile she waited; then she said: "What thinkest?
  Answer me; for the mournful memories
  In thee not yet are by the waters injured."

Confusion and dismay together mingled
  Forced such a Yes! from out my mouth, that sight
  Was needful to the understanding of it.

Even as a cross-bow breaks, when 'tis discharged
  Too tensely drawn the bowstring and the bow,
  And with less force the arrow hits the mark,

So I gave way beneath that heavy burden,
  Outpouring in a torrent tears and sighs,
  And the voice flagged upon its passage forth.

Whence she to me: "In those desires of mine
  Which led thee to the loving of that good,
  Beyond which there is nothing to aspire to,

What trenches lying traverse or what chains
  Didst thou discover, that of passing onward
  Thou shouldst have thus despoiled thee of the
        hope?

E quali agevolezze o quali avanzi
  ne la fronte de li altri si mostraro,
  per che dovessi lor passeggiare anzi?"".

Dopo la tratta d'un sospiro amaro,
  a pena ebbi la voce che rispuose,
  e le labbra a fatica la formaro.

Piangendo dissi: ""Le presenti cose
  col falso lor piacer volser miei passi,
  tosto che 'l vostro viso si nascose"".

Ed ella: ""Se tacessi o se negassi
  cio` che confessi, non fora men nota
  la colpa tua: da tal giudice sassi!

Ma quando scoppia de la propria gota
  l'accusa del peccato, in nostra corte
  rivolge se' contra 'l taglio la rota.

Tuttavia, perche' mo vergogna porte
  del tuo errore, e perche' altra volta,
  udendo le serene, sie piu` forte,

pon giu` il seme del piangere e ascolta:
  si` udirai come in contraria parte
  mover dovieti mia carne sepolta.

Mai non t'appresento` natura o arte
  piacer, quanto le belle membra in ch'io
  rinchiusa fui, e che so' 'n terra sparte;

e se 'l sommo piacer si` ti fallio
  per la mia morte, qual cosa mortale
  dovea poi trarre te nel suo disio?

Ben ti dovevi, per lo primo strale
  de le cose fallaci, levar suso
  di retro a me che non era piu` tale.

Non ti dovea gravar le penne in giuso,
  ad aspettar piu` colpo, o pargoletta
  o altra vanita` con si` breve uso.

Novo augelletto due o tre aspetta;
  ma dinanzi da li occhi d'i pennuti
  rete si spiega indarno o si saetta"".

And what allurements or what vantages
  Upon the forehead of the others showed,
  That thou shouldst turn thy footsteps unto them?"

After the heaving of a bitter sigh,
  Hardly had I the voice to make response,
  And with fatigue my lips did fashion it.

Weeping I said: "The things that present were
  With their false pleasure turned aside my steps,
  Soon as your countenance concealed itself."

And she: "Shouldst thou be silent, or deny
  What thou confessest, not less manifest
  Would be thy fault, by such a Judge 'tis known.

But when from one's own cheeks comes bursting
    forth
  The accusal of the sin, in our tribunal
  Against the edge the wheel doth turn itself.

But still, that thou mayst feel a greater shame
  For thy transgression, and another time
  Hearing the Sirens thou mayst be more strong,

Cast down the seed of weeping and attend;
  So shalt thou hear, how in an opposite way
  My buried flesh should have directed thee.

Never to thee presented art or nature
  Pleasure so great as the fair limbs wherein
  I was enclosed, which scattered are in earth.

And if the highest pleasure thus did fail thee
  By reason of my death, what mortal thing
  Should then have drawn thee into its desire?

Thou oughtest verily at the first shaft
  Of things fallacious to have risen up
  To follow me, who was no longer such.

Thou oughtest not to have stooped thy pinions
    downward
  To wait for further blows, or little girl,
  Or other vanity of such brief use.

The callow birdlet waits for two or three,
  But to the eyes of those already fledged,
  In vain the net is spread or shaft is shot."

Quali fanciulli, vergognando, muti
  con li occhi a terra stannosi, ascoltando
  e se' riconoscendo e ripentuti,

tal mi stav'io; ed ella disse: ""Quando
  per udir se' dolente, alza la barba,
  e prenderai piu` doglia riguardando"".

Con men di resistenza si dibarba
  robusto cerro, o vero al nostral vento
  o vero a quel de la terra di Iarba,

ch'io non levai al suo comando il mento;
  e quando per la barba il viso chiese,
  ben conobbi il velen de l'argomento.

E come la mia faccia si distese,
  posarsi quelle prime creature
  da loro aspersion l'occhio comprese;

e le mie luci, ancor poco sicure,
  vider Beatrice volta in su la fiera
  ch'e` sola una persona in due nature.

Sotto 'l suo velo e oltre la rivera
  vincer pariemi piu` se' stessa antica,
  vincer che l'altre qui, quand'ella c'era.

Di penter si` mi punse ivi l'ortica
  che di tutte altre cose qual mi torse
  piu` nel suo amor, piu` mi si fe' nemica.

Tanta riconoscenza il cor mi morse,
  ch'io caddi vinto; e quale allora femmi,
  salsi colei che la cagion mi porse.

Poi, quando il cor virtu` di fuor rendemmi,
  la donna ch'io avea trovata sola
  sopra me vidi, e dicea: ""Tiemmi, tiemmi!"".

Tratto m'avea nel fiume infin la gola,
  e tirandosi me dietro sen giva
  sovresso l'acqua lieve come scola.

Quando fui presso a la beata riva,
  'Asperges me' si` dolcemente udissi,
  che nol so rimembrar, non ch'io lo scriva.

La bella donna ne le braccia aprissi;
  abbracciommi la testa e mi sommerse
  ove convenne ch'io l'acqua inghiottissi.

Even as children silent in their shame
  Stand listening with their eyes upon the ground,
  And conscious of their fault, and penitent;

So was I standing; and she said: "If thou
  In hearing sufferest pain, lift up thy beard
  And thou shalt feel a greater pain in seeing."

With less resistance is a robust holm
  Uprooted, either by a native wind
  Or else by that from regions of Iarbas,

Than I upraised at her command my chin;
  And when she by the beard the face demanded,
  Well I perceived the venom of her meaning.

And as my countenance was lifted up,
  Mine eye perceived those creatures beautiful
  Had rested from the strewing of the flowers;

And, still but little reassured, mine eyes
  Saw Beatrice turned round towards the monster,
  That is one person only in two natures.

Beneath her veil, beyond the margent green,
  She seemed to me far more her ancient self
  To excel, than others here, when she was here.

So pricked me then the thorn of penitence,
  That of all other things the one which turned me
  Most to its love became the most my foe.

Such self-conviction stung me at the heart
  O'erpowered I fell, and what I then became
  She knoweth who had furnished me the cause.

Then, when the heart restored my outward sense,
  The lady I had found alone, above me
  I saw, and she was saying, "Hold me, hold me."

Up to my throat she in the stream had drawn me,
  And, dragging me behind her, she was moving
  Upon the water lightly as a shuttle.

When I was near unto the blessed shore,
  "Asperges me," I heard so sweetly sung,
  Remember it I cannot, much less write it.

The beautiful lady opened wide her arms,
  Embraced my head, and plunged me underneath,
  Where I was forced to swallow of the water.

Indi mi tolse, e bagnato m'offerse
dentro a la danza de le quattro belle;
e ciascuna del braccio mi coperse.

"Noi siam qui ninfe e nel ciel siamo stelle:
pria che Beatrice discendesse al mondo,
fummo ordinate a lei per sue ancelle.

Merrenti a li occhi suoi; ma nel giocondo
lume ch'e` dentro aguzzeranno i tuoi
le tre di la`, che miran piu` profondo"".

Cosi` cantando cominciaro; e poi
al petto del grifon seco menarmi,
ove Beatrice stava volta a noi.

Disser: ""Fa che le viste non risparmi;
posto t'avem dinanzi a li smeraldi
ond'Amor gia` ti trasse le sue armi"".

Mille disiri piu` che fiamma caldi
strinsermi li occhi a li occhi rilucenti,
che pur sopra 'l grifone stavan saldi.

Come in lo specchio il sol, non altrimenti
la doppia fiera dentro vi raggiava,
or con altri, or con altri reggimenti.

Pensa, lettor, s'io mi maravigliava,
quando vedea la cosa in se' star queta,
e ne l'idolo suo si trasmutava.

Mentre che piena di stupore e lieta
l'anima mia gustava di quel cibo
che, saziando di se', di se' asseta,

se' dimostrando di piu` alto tribo
ne li atti, l'altre tre si fero avanti,
danzando al loro angelico caribo.

""Volgi, Beatrice, volgi li occhi santi"",
era la sua canzone, ""al tuo fedele
che, per vederti, ha mossi passi tanti!

Per grazia fa noi grazia che disvele
a lui la bocca tua, si` che discerna
la seconda bellezza che tu cele"".

Then forth she drew me, and all dripping brought
Into the dance of the four beautiful,
And each one with her arm did cover me.

'We here are Nymphs, and in the Heaven are stars;
Ere Beatrice descended to the world,
We as her handmaids were appointed her.

We'll lead thee to her eyes; but for the pleasant
Light that within them is, shall sharpen thine
The three beyond, who more profoundly look.'

Thus singing they began; and afterwards
Unto the Griffin's breast they led me with them,
Where Beatrice was standing, turned towards us.

"See that thou dost not spare thine eyes," they said;
"Before the emeralds have we stationed thee,
Whence Love aforetime drew for thee his weapons."

A thousand longings, hotter than the flame,
Fastened mine eyes upon those eyes relucent,
That still upon the Griffin steadfast stayed.

As in a glass the sun, not otherwise
Within them was the twofold monster shining,
Now with the one, now with the other nature.

Think, Reader, if within myself I marvelled,
When I beheld the thing itself stand still,
And in its image it transformed itself.

While with amazement filled and jubilant,
My soul was tasting of the food, that while
It satisfies us makes us hunger for it,

Themselves revealing of the highest rank
In bearing, did the other three advance,
Singing to their angelic saraband.

"Turn, Beatrice, O turn thy holy eyes,"
Such was their song, "unto thy faithful one,
Who has to see thee ta'en so many steps.

In grace do us the grace that thou unveil
Thy face to him, so that he may discern
The second beauty which thou dost conceal."

O isplendor di viva luce etterna,
  chi palido si fece sotto l'ombra
  si` di Parnaso, o bevve in sua cisterna,

che non paresse aver la mente ingombra,
  tentando a render te qual tu paresti
  la` dove armonizzando il ciel t'adombra,

quando ne l'aere aperto ti solvesti?

O splendour of the living light eternal!
  Who underneath the shadow of Parnassus
  Has grown so pale, or drunk so at its cistern,

He would not seem to have his mind encumbered
  Striving to paint thee as thou didst appear,
  Where the harmonious heaven o'ershadowed thee,

When in the open air thou didst unveil?

Purgatorio: Canto XXXII

The Tree of Knowledge. Allegory of the Chariot.

Tant'eran li occhi miei fissi e attenti
  a disbramarsi la decenne sete,
  che li altri sensi m'eran tutti spenti.

Ed essi quinci e quindi avien parete
  di non caler - così lo santo riso
  a se' traeli con l'antica rete! -;

quando per forza mi fu volto il viso
  ver' la sinistra mia da quelle dee,
  perch'io udi' da loro un ""Troppo fiso!"";

e la disposizion ch'a veder ee
  ne li occhi pur teste' dal sol percossi,
  sanza la vista alquanto esser mi fee.

Ma poi ch'al poco il viso riformossi
  (e dico 'al poco' per rispetto al molto
  sensibile onde a forza mi rimossi),

vidi 'n sul braccio destro esser rivolto
  lo glorioso essercito, e tornarsi
  col sole e con le sette fiamme al volto.

Come sotto li scudi per salvarsi
  volgesi schiera, e se' gira col segno,
  prima che possa tutta in se' mutarsi;

quella milizia del celeste regno
  che procedeva, tutta trapassonne
  pria che piegasse il carro il primo legno.

Indi a le rote si tornar le donne,
  e 'l grifon mosse il benedetto carco
  si`, che però nulla penna crollonne.

So steadfast and attentive were mine eyes
  In satisfying their decennial thirst,
  That all my other senses were extinct,

And upon this side and on that they had
  Walls of indifference, so the holy smile
  Drew them unto itself with the old net

When forcibly my sight was turned away
  Towards my left hand by those goddesses,
  Because I heard from them a "Too intently!"

And that condition of the sight which is
  In eyes but lately smitten by the sun
  Bereft me of my vision some short while;

But to the less when sight re-shaped itself,
  I say the less in reference to the greater
  Splendour from which perforce I had withdrawn,

I saw upon its right wing wheeled about
  The glorious host returning with the sun
  And with the sevenfold flames upon their faces.

As underneath its shields, to save itself,
  A squadron turns, and with its banner wheels,
  Before the whole thereof can change its front,

That soldiery of the celestial kingdom
  Which marched in the advance had wholly passed
    us
  Before the chariot had turned its pole.

Then to the wheels the maidens turned themselves,
  And the Griffin moved his burden benedight,
  But so that not a feather of him fluttered.

La bella donna che mi trasse al varco
  e Stazio e io seguitavam la rota
  che fe' l'orbita sua con minore arco.

Si` passeggiando l'alta selva vota,
  colpa di quella ch'al serpente crese,
  temprava i passi un'angelica nota.

Forse in tre voli tanto spazio prese
  disfrenata saetta, quanto eramo
  rimossi, quando Beatrice scese.

Io senti' mormorare a tutti ""Adamo"";
  poi cerchiaro una pianta dispogliata
  di foglie e d'altra fronda in ciascun ramo.

La coma sua, che tanto si dilata
  piu` quanto piu` e` su`, fora da l'Indi
  ne' boschi lor per altezza ammirata.

""Beato se', grifon, che non discindi
  col becco d'esto legno dolce al gusto,
  poscia che mal si torce il ventre quindi"".

Cosi` dintorno a l'albero robusto
  gridaron li altri; e l'animal binato:
  ""Si` si conserva il seme d'ogne giusto"".

E volto al temo ch'elli avea tirato,
  trasselo al pie` de la vedova frasca,
  e quel di lei a lei lascio` legato.

Come le nostre piante, quando casca
  giu` la gran luce mischiata con quella
  che raggia dietro a la celeste lasca,

turgide fansi, e poi si rinovella
  di suo color ciascuna, pria che 'l sole
  giunga li suoi corsier sotto altra stella;

men che di rose e piu` che di viole
  colore aprendo, s'innovo` la pianta,
  che prima avea le ramora si` sole.

Io non lo 'ntesi, ne' qui non si canta
  l'inno che quella gente allor cantaro,
  ne' la nota soffersi tutta quanta.

S'io potessi ritrar come assonnaro
  li occhi spietati udendo di Siringa,
  li occhi a cui pur vegghiar costo` si` caro;

The lady fair who drew me through the ford
  Followed with Statius and myself the wheel
  Which made its orbit with the lesser arc.

So passing through the lofty forest, vacant
  By fault of her who in the serpent trusted,
  Angelic music made our steps keep time.

Perchance as great a space had in three flights
  An arrow loosened from the string o'erpassed,
  As we had moved when Beatrice descended.

I heard them murmur altogether, "Adam!"
  Then circled they about a tree despoiled
  Of blooms and other leafage on each bough.

Its tresses, which so much the more dilate
  As higher they ascend, had been by Indians
  Among their forests marvelled at for height.

"Blessed art thou, O Griffin, who dost not
  Pluck with thy beak these branches sweet to taste,
  Since appetite by this was turned to evil."

After this fashion round the tree robust
  The others shouted; and the twofold creature:
  "Thus is preserved the seed of all the just."

And turning to the pole which he had dragged,
  He drew it close beneath the widowed bough,
  And what was of it unto it left bound.

In the same manner as our trees (when downward
  Falls the great light, with that together mingled
  Which after the celestial Lasca shines)

Begin to swell, and then renew themselves,
  Each one with its own colour, ere the Sun
  Harness his steeds beneath another star:

Less than of rose and more than violet
  A hue disclosing, was renewed the tree
  That had erewhile its boughs so desolate.

I never heard, nor here below is sung,
  The hymn which afterward that people sang,
  Nor did I bear the melody throughout.

Had I the power to paint how fell asleep
  Those eyes compassionless, of Syrinx hearing,
  Those eyes to which more watching cost so dear,

come pintor che con essempro pinga,
  disegnerei com'io m'addormentai;
  ma qual vuol sia che l'assonnar ben finga.

Pero` trascorro a quando mi svegliai,
  e dico ch'un splendor mi squarcio` 'l velo
  del sonno e un chiamar: ""Surgi: che fai?"".

Quali a veder de' fioretti del melo
  che del suo pome li angeli fa ghiotti
  e perpetue nozze fa nel cielo,

Pietro e Giovanni e Iacopo condotti
  e vinti, ritornaro a la parola
  da la qual furon maggior sonni rotti,

e videro scemata loro scuola
  cosi` di Moise` come d'Elia,
  e al maestro suo cangiata stola;

tal torna' io, e vidi quella pia
  sovra me starsi che conducitrice
  fu de' miei passi lungo 'l fiume pria.

E tutto in dubbio dissi: ""Ov'e` Beatrice?"".
  Ond'ella: ""Vedi lei sotto la fronda
  nova sedere in su la sua radice.

Vedi la compagnia che la circonda:
  li altri dopo 'l grifon sen vanno suso
  con piu` dolce canzone e piu` profonda"".

E se piu` fu lo suo parlar diffuso,
  non so, pero` che gia` ne li occhi m'era
  quella ch'ad altro intender m'avea chiuso.

Sola sedeasi in su la terra vera,
  come guardia lasciata li` del plaustro
  che legar vidi a la biforme fera.

In cerchio le facean di se' claustro
  le sette ninfe, con quei lumi in mano
  che son sicuri d'Aquilone e d'Austro.

""Qui sarai tu poco tempo silvano;
  e sarai meco sanza fine cive
  di quella Roma onde Cristo e` romano.

Pero`, in pro del mondo che mal vive,
  al carro tieni or li occhi, e quel che vedi,
  ritornato di la`, fa che tu scrive"".

Even as a painter who from model paints
  I would portray how I was lulled asleep;
  He may, who well can picture drowsihood.

Therefore I pass to what time I awoke,
  And say a splendour rent from me the veil
  Of slumber, and a calling: "Rise, what dost thou?"

As to behold the apple-tree in blossom
  Which makes the Angels greedy for its fruit,
  And keeps perpetual bridals in the Heaven,

Peter and John and James conducted were,
  And, overcome, recovered at the word
  By which still greater slumbers have been broken,

And saw their school diminished by the loss
  Not only of Elias, but of Moses,
  And the apparel of their Master changed;

So I revived, and saw that piteous one
  Above me standing, who had been conductress
  Aforetime of my steps beside the river,

And all in doubt I said, "Where's Beatrice?"
  And she: "Behold her seated underneath
  The leafage new, upon the root of it.

Behold the company that circles her;
  The rest behind the Griffin are ascending
  With more melodious song, and more profound."

And if her speech were more diffuse I know not,
  Because already in my sight was she
  Who from the hearing of aught else had shut me.

Alone she sat upon the very earth,
  Left there as guardian of the chariot
  Which I had seen the biform monster fasten.

Encircling her, a cloister made themselves
  The seven Nymphs, with those lights in their hands
  Which are secure from Aquilon and Auster.

"Short while shalt thou be here a forester,
  And thou shalt be with me for evermore
  A citizen of that Rome where Christ is Roman.

Therefore, for that world's good which liveth ill,
  Fix on the car thine eyes, and what thou seest,
  Having returned to earth, take heed thou write."

Cosi` Beatrice; e io, che tutto ai piedi
  d'i suoi comandamenti era divoto,
  la mente e li occhi ov'ella volle diedi.

Non scese mai con si` veloce moto
  foco di spessa nube, quando piove
  da quel confine che piu` va remoto,

com'io vidi calar l'uccel di Giove
  per l'alber giu`, rompendo de la scorza,
  non che d'i fiori e de le foglie nove;

e feri` 'l carro di tutta sua forza;
  ond'el piego` come nave in fortuna,
  vinta da l'onda, or da poggia, or da orza.

Poscia vidi avventarsi ne la cuna
  del triunfal veiculo una volpe
  che d'ogne pasto buon parea digiuna;

ma, riprendendo lei di laide colpe,
  la donna mia la volse in tanta futa
  quanto sofferser l'ossa sanza polpe.

Poscia per indi ond'era pria venuta,
  l'aguglia vidi scender giu` ne l'arca
  del carro e lasciar lei di se' pennuta;

e qual esce di cuor che si rammarca,
  tal voce usci` del cielo e cotal disse:
  ""O navicella mia, com'mal se' carca!""".

Poi parve a me che la terra s'aprisse
  tr'ambo le ruote, e vidi uscirne un drago
  che per lo carro su` la coda fisse;

e come vespa che ritragge l'ago,
  a se' traendo la coda maligna,
  trasse del fondo, e gissen vago vago.

Quel che rimase, come da gramigna
  vivace terra, da la piuma, offerta
  forse con intenzion sana e benigna,

si ricoperse, e funne ricoperta
  e l'una e l'altra rota e 'l temo, in tanto
  che piu` tiene un sospir la bocca aperta.

Thus Beatrice; and I, who at the feet
  Of her commandments all devoted was,
  My mind and eyes directed where she willed.

Never descended with so swift a motion
  Fire from a heavy cloud, when it is raining
  From out the region which is most remote,

As I beheld the bird of Jove descend
  Down through the tree, rending away the bark,
  As well as blossoms and the foliage new,

And he with all his might the chariot smote,
  Whereat it reeled, like vessel in a tempest
  Tossed by the waves, now starboard and now lar-
    board.

Thereafter saw I leap into the body
  Of the triumphal vehicle a Fox,
  That seemed unfed with any wholesome food.

But for his hideous sins upbraiding him,
  My Lady put him to as swift a flight
  As such a fleshless skeleton could bear.

Then by the way that it before had come,
  Into the chariot's chest I saw the Eagle
  Descend, and leave it feathered with his plumes.

And such as issues from a heart that mourns,
  A voice from Heaven there issued, and it said:
  "My little bark, how badly art thou freighted!"

Methought, then, that the earth did yawn between
  Both wheels, and I saw rise from it a Dragon,
  Who through the chariot upward fixed his tail,

And as a wasp that draweth back its sting,
  Drawing unto himself his tail malign,
  Drew out the floor, and went his way rejoicing.

That which remained behind, even as with grass
  A fertile region, with the feathers, offered
  Perhaps with pure intention and benign,

Reclothed itself, and with them were reclothed
  The pole and both the wheels so speedily,
  A sigh doth longer keep the lips apart.

Trasformato cosi` 'l dificio santo
mise fuor teste per le parti sue,
tre sovra 'l temo e una in ciascun canto.

Le prime eran cornute come bue,
ma le quattro un sol corno avean per fronte:
simile mostro visto ancor non fue.

Sicura, quasi rocca in alto monte,
seder sovresso una puttana sciolta
m'apparve con le ciglia intorno pronte;

e come perche' non li fosse tolta,
vidi di costa a lei dritto un gigante;
e baciavansi insieme alcuna volta.

Ma perche' l'occhio cupido e vagante
a me rivolse, quel feroce drudo
la flagello` dal capo infin le piante;

poi, di sospetto pieno e d'ira crudo,
disciolse il mostro, e trassel per la selva,
tanto che sol di lei mi fece scudo

a la puttana e a la nova belva.

Transfigured thus the holy edifice
Thrust forward heads upon the parts of it,
Three on the pole and one at either corner.

The first were horned like oxen; but the four
Had but a single horn upon the forehead;
A monster such had never yet been seen!

Firm as a rock upon a mountain high,
Seated upon it, there appeared to me
A shameless whore, with eyes swift glancing round,

And, as if not to have her taken from him,
Upright beside her I beheld a giant;
And ever and anon they kissed each other.

But because she her wanton, roving eye
Turned upon me, her angry paramour
Did scourge her from her head unto her feet.

Then full of jealousy, and fierce with wrath,
He loosed the monster, and across the forest
Dragged it so far, he made of that alone

A shield unto the whore and the strange beast.

Purgatorio: Canto XXXIII

Lament over the State of the Church. Final Reproaches of Beatrice. The River Eunoe.

'Deus, venerunt gentes', alternando
  or tre or quattro dolce salmodia,
  le donne incominciaro, e lagrimando;

e Beatrice sospirosa e pia,
  quelle ascoltava si` fatta, che poco
  piu` a la croce si cambio` Maria.

Ma poi che l'altre vergini dier loco
  a lei di dir, levata dritta in pe`,
  rispuose, colorata come foco:

'Modicum, et non videbitis me;
  et iterum, sorelle mie dilette,
  modicum, et vos videbitis me'.

Poi le si mise innanzi tutte e sette,
  e dopo se', solo accennando, mosse
  me e la donna e 'l savio che ristette.

Cosi` sen giva; e non credo che fosse
  lo decimo suo passo in terra posto,
  quando con li occhi li occhi mi percosse;

e con tranquillo aspetto ""Vien piu` tosto"",
  mi disse, ""tanto che, s'io parlo teco,
  ad ascoltarmi tu sie ben disposto"".

Si` com'io fui, com'io dovea, seco,
  dissemi: ""Frate, perche' non t'attenti
  a domandarmi omai venendo meco?"".

Come a color che troppo reverenti
  dinanzi a suo maggior parlando sono,
  che non traggon la voce viva ai denti.

"Deus venerunt gentes," alternating
  Now three, now four, melodious psalmody
  The maidens in the midst of tears began;

And Beatrice, compassionate and sighing,
  Listened to them with such a countenance,
  That scarce more changed was Mary at the cross.

But when the other virgins place had given
  For her to speak, uprisen to her feet
  With colour as of fire, she made response:

"'Modicum, et non videbitis me;
  Et iterum,' my sisters predilect,
  'Modicum, et vos videbitis me.'"

Then all the seven in front of her she placed;
  And after her, by beckoning only, moved
  Me and the lady and the sage who stayed.

So she moved onward; and I do not think
  That her tenth step was placed upon the ground,
  When with her eyes upon mine eyes she smote,

And with a tranquil aspect, "Come more quickly,"
  To me she said, "that, if I speak with thee,
  To listen to me thou mayst be well placed."

As soon as I was with her as I should be,
  She said to me: "Why, brother, dost thou not
  Venture to question now, in coming with me?"

As unto those who are too reverential,
  Speaking in presence of superiors,
  Who drag no living utterance to their teeth,

avvenne a me, che sanza intero suono
  incominciai: ""Madonna, mia bisogna
  voi conoscete, e cio` ch'ad essa e` buono"".

Ed ella a me: ""Da tema e da vergogna
  voglio che tu omai ti disviluppe,
  si` che non parli piu` com'om che sogna.

Sappi che 'l vaso che 'l serpente ruppe
  fu e non e`; ma chi n'ha colpa, creda
  che vendetta di Dio non teme suppe.

Non sara` tutto tempo sanza reda
  l'aguglia che lascio` le penne al carro,
  per che divenne mostro e poscia preda;

ch'io veggio certamente, e pero` il narro,
  a darne tempo gia` stelle propinque,
  secure d'ogn'intoppo e d'ogni sbarro,

nel quale un cinquecento diece e cinque,
  messo di Dio, ancidera` la fuia
  con quel gigante che con lei delinque.

E forse che la mia narrazion buia,
  qual Temi e Sfinge, men ti persuade,
  perch'a lor modo lo 'ntelletto attuia;

ma tosto fier li fatti le Naiade,
  che solveranno questo enigma forte
  sanza danno di pecore o di biade.

Tu nota; e si` come da me son porte,
  cosi` queste parole segna a' vivi
  del viver ch'e` un correre a la morte.

E aggi a mente, quando tu le scrivi,
  di non celar qual hai vista la pianta
  ch'e` or due volte dirubata quivi.

Qualunque ruba quella o quella schianta,
  con bestemmia di fatto offende a Dio,
  che solo a l'uso suo la creo` santa.

Per morder quella, in pena e in disio
  cinquemilia anni e piu` l'anima prima
  bramo` colui che 'l morso in se' punio.

It me befell, that without perfect sound
  Began I: "My necessity, Madonna,
  You know, and that which thereunto is good."

And she to me: "Of fear and bashfulness
  Henceforward I will have thee strip thyself,
  So that thou speak no more as one who dreams.

Know that the vessel which the serpent broke
  Was, and is not; but let him who is guilty
  Think that God's vengeance does not fear a sop.

Without an heir shall not for ever be
  The Eagle that left his plumes upon the car,
  Whence it became a monster, then a prey;

For verily I see, and hence narrate it,
  The stars already near to bring the time,
  From every hindrance safe, and every bar,

Within which a Five-hundred, Ten, and Five,
  One sent from God, shall slay the thievish woman
  And that same giant who is sinning with her.

And peradventure my dark utterance,
  Like Themis and the Sphinx, may less persuade
      thee,
  Since, in their mode, it clouds the intellect;

But soon the facts shall be the Naiades
  Who shall this difficult enigma solve,
  Without destruction of the flocks and harvests.

Note thou; and even as by me are uttered
  These words, so teach them unto those who live
  That life which is a running unto death;

And bear in mind, whene'er thou writest them,
  Not to conceal what thou hast seen the plant,
  That twice already has been pillaged here.

Whoever pillages or shatters it,
  With blasphemy of deed offendeth God,
  Who made it holy for his use alone.

For biting that, in pain and in desire
  Five thousand years and more the first-born soul
  Craved Him, who punished in himself the bite.

Purgatorio: Canto XXXIII

Dorme lo 'ngegno tuo, se non estima
  per singular cagione esser eccelsa
  lei tanto e si` travolta ne la cima.

E se stati non fossero acqua d'Elsa
  li pensier vani intorno a la tua mente,
  e 'l piacer loro un Piramo a la gelsa,

per tante circostanze solamente
  la giustizia di Dio, ne l'interdetto,
  conosceresti a l'arbor moralmente.

Ma perch'io veggio te ne lo 'ntelletto
  fatto di pietra e, impetrato, tinto,
  si` che t'abbaglia il lume del mio detto,

voglio anco, e se non scritto, almen dipinto,
  che 'l te ne porti dentro a te per quello
  che si reca il bordon di palma cinto"".

E io: ""Si` come cera da suggello,
  che la figura impressa non trasmuta,
  segnato e` or da voi lo mio cervello.

Ma perche' tanto sovra mia veduta
  vostra parola disiata vola,
  che piu` la perde quanto piu` s'aiuta?"".

""Perche' conoschi"", disse, ""quella scuola
  c'hai seguitata, e veggi sua dottrina
  come puo` seguitar la mia parola;

e veggi vostra via da la divina
  distar cotanto, quanto si discorda
  da terra il ciel che piu` alto festina"".

Ond'io rispuosi lei: ""Non mi ricorda
  ch'i' straniasse me gia` mai da voi,
  ne' honne coscienza che rimorda"".

""E se tu ricordar non te ne puoi"",
  sorridendo rispuose, ""or ti rammenta
  come bevesti di Lete` ancoi;

e se dal fummo foco s'argomenta,
  cotesta oblivion chiaro conchiude
  colpa ne la tua voglia altrove attenta.

Veramente oramai saranno nude
  le mie parole, quanto converrassi
  quelle scovrire a la tua vista rude"".

Thy genius slumbers, if it deem it not
  For special reason so pre-eminent
  In height, and so inverted in its summit.

And if thy vain imaginings had not been
  Water of Elsa round about thy mind,
  And Pyramus to the mulberry, their pleasure,

Thou by so many circumstances only
  The justice of the interdict of God
  Morally in the tree wouldst recognize.

But since I see thee in thine intellect
  Converted into stone and stained with sin,
  So that the light of my discourse doth daze thee,

I will too, if not written, at least painted,
  Thou bear it back within thee, for the reason
  That cinct with palm the pilgrim's staff is borne."

And I: "As by a signet is the wax
  Which does not change the figure stamped upon it,
  My brain is now imprinted by yourself.

But wherefore so beyond my power of sight
  Soars your desirable discourse, that aye
  The more I strive, so much the more I lose it?"

"That thou mayst recognize," she said, "the school
  Which thou hast followed, and mayst see how far
  Its doctrine follows after my discourse,

And mayst behold your path from the divine
  Distant as far as separated is
  From earth the heaven that highest hastens on."

Whence her I answered: "I do not remember
  That ever I estranged myself from you,
  Nor have I conscience of it that reproves me."

"And if thou art not able to remember,"
  Smiling she answered, "recollect thee now
  That thou this very day hast drunk of Lethe;

And if from smoke a fire may be inferred,
  Such an oblivion clearly demonstrates
  Some error in thy will elsewhere intent.

Truly from this time forward shall my words
  Be naked, so far as it is befitting
  To lay them open unto thy rude gaze."

E piu` corusco e con piu` lenti passi
  teneva il sole il cerchio di merigge,
  che qua e la`, come li aspetti, fassi

quando s'affisser, si` come s'affigge
  chi va dinanzi a gente per iscorta
  se trova novitate o sue vestigge,

le sette donne al fin d'un'ombra smorta,
  qual sotto foglie verdi e rami nigri
  sovra suoi freddi rivi l'Alpe porta.

Dinanzi ad esse Eufrates e Tigri
  veder mi parve uscir d'una fontana,
  e, quasi amici, dipartirsi pigri.

““O luce, o gloria de la gente umana,
  che acqua e` questa che qui si dispiega
  da un principio e se' da se' lontana?”“.

Per cotal priego detto mi fu: ““Priega
  Matelda che 'l ti dica”“. E qui rispuose,
  come fa chi da colpa si dislega,

la bella donna: ““Questo e altre cose
  dette li son per me; e son sicura
  che l'acqua di Lete` non gliel nascose”“.

E Beatrice: ““Forse maggior cura,
  che spesse volte la memoria priva,
  fatt'ha la mente sua ne li occhi oscura.

Ma vedi Eunoe` che la` diriva:
  menalo ad esso, e come tu se' usa,
  la tramortita sua virtu` ravviva”“.

Come anima gentil, che non fa scusa,
  ma fa sua voglia de la voglia altrui
  tosto che e` per segno fuor dischiusa;

cosi`, poi che da essa preso fui,
  la bella donna mossesi, e a Stazio
  donnescamente disse: ““Vien con lui”“.

S'io avessi, lettor, piu` lungo spazio
  da scrivere, i' pur cantere' in parte
  lo dolce ber che mai non m'avria sazio;

ma perche' piene son tutte le carte
  ordite a questa cantica seconda,
  non mi lascia piu` ir lo fren de l'arte.

And more coruscant and with slower steps
  The sun was holding the meridian circle,
  Which, with the point of view, shifts here and there

When halted (as he cometh to a halt,
  Who goes before a squadron as its escort,
  If something new he find upon his way)

The ladies seven at a dark shadow's edge,
  Such as, beneath green leaves and branches black,
  The Alp upon its frigid border wears.

In front of them the Tigris and Euphrates
  Methought I saw forth issue from one fountain,
  And slowly part, like friends, from one another.

"O light, O glory of the human race!
  What stream is this which here unfolds itself
  From out one source, and from itself withdraws?"

For such a prayer, 'twas said unto me, "Pray
  Matilda that she tell thee;" and here answered,
  As one does who doth free himself from blame,

The beautiful lady: "This and other things
  Were told to him by me; and sure I am
  The water of Lethe has not hid them from him."

And Beatrice: "Perhaps a greater care,
  Which oftentimes our memory takes away,
  Has made the vision of his mind obscure.

But Eunoe behold, that yonder rises;
  Lead him to it, and, as thou art accustomed,
  Revive again the half-dead virtue in him."

Like gentle soul, that maketh no excuse,
  But makes its own will of another's will
  As soon as by a sign it is disclosed,

Even so, when she had taken hold of me,
  The beautiful lady moved, and unto Statius
  Said, in her womanly manner, "Come with him."

If, Reader, I possessed a longer space
  For writing it, I yet would sing in part
  Of the sweet draught that ne'er would satiate me;

But inasmuch as full are all the leaves
  Made ready for this second canticle,
  The curb of art no farther lets me go.

Io ritornai da la santissima onda
  rifatto si` come piante novelle
  rinnovellate di novella fronda,

puro e disposto a salire alle stelle.

From the most holy water I returned
  Regenerate, in the manner of new trees
  That are renewed with a new foliage,

Pure and disposed to mount unto the stars.

PARADISO

Paradiso: Canto I

The Ascent to the First Heaven. The Sphere of Fire.

La gloria di colui che tutto move
  per l'universo penetra, e risplende
  in una parte piu` e meno altrove.

Nel ciel che piu` de la sua luce prende
  fu' io, e vidi cose che ridire
  ne' sa ne' puo` chi di la` su` discende;

perche' appressando se' al suo disire,
  nostro intelletto si profonda tanto,
  che dietro la memoria non puo` ire.

Veramente quant'io del regno santo
  ne la mia mente potei far tesoro,
  sara` ora materia del mio canto.

O buono Appollo, a l'ultimo lavoro
  fammi del tuo valor si` fatto vaso,
  come dimandi a dar l'amato alloro.

Infino a qui l'un giogo di Parnaso
  assai mi fu; ma or con amendue
  m'e` uopo intrar ne l'aringo rimaso.

Entra nel petto mio, e spira tue
  si` come quando Marsia traesti
  de la vagina de le membra sue.

O divina virtu`, se mi ti presti
  tanto che l'ombra del beato regno
  segnata nel mio capo io manifesti,

vedra'mi al pie` del tuo diletto legno
  venire, e coronarmi de le foglie
  che la materia e tu mi farai degno.

The glory of Him who moveth everything
  Doth penetrate the universe, and shine
  In one part more and in another less.

Within that heaven which most his light receives
  Was I, and things beheld which to repeat
  Nor knows, nor can, who from above descends;

Because in drawing near to its desire
  Our intellect ingulphs itself so far,
  That after it the memory cannot go.

Truly whatever of the holy realm
  I had the power to treasure in my mind
  Shall now become the subject of my song.

O good Apollo, for this last emprise
  Make of me such a vessel of thy power
  As giving the beloved laurel asks!

One summit of Parnassus hitherto
  Has been enough for me, but now with both
  I needs must enter the arena left.

Enter into my bosom, thou, and breathe
  As at the time when Marsyas thou didst draw
  Out of the scabbard of those limbs of his.

O power divine, lend'st thou thyself to me
  So that the shadow of the blessed realm
  Stamped in my brain I can make manifest,

Thou'lt see me come unto thy darling tree,
  And crown myself thereafter with those leaves
  Of which the theme and thou shall make me worthy.

Si` rade volte, padre, se ne coglie
  per triunfare o cesare o poeta,
  colpa e vergogna de l'umane voglie,
	So seldom, Father, do we gather them
	  For triumph or of Caesar or of Poet,
	  (The fault and shame of human inclinations,)

che parturir letizia in su la lieta
  delfica deita` dovria la fronda
  peneia, quando alcun di se' asseta.
	That the Peneian foliage should bring forth
	  Joy to the joyous Delphic deity,
	  When any one it makes to thirst for it.

Poca favilla gran fiamma seconda:
  forse di retro a me con miglior voci
  si preghera` perche' Cirra risponda.
	A little spark is followed by great flame;
	  Perchance with better voices after me
	  Shall prayer be made that Cyrrha may respond!

Surge ai mortali per diverse foci
  la lucerna del mondo; ma da quella
  che quattro cerchi giugne con tre croci,
	To mortal men by passages diverse
	  Uprises the world's lamp; but by that one
	  Which circles four uniteth with three crosses,

con miglior corso e con migliore stella
  esce congiunta, e la mondana cera
  piu` a suo modo tempera e suggella.
	With better course and with a better star
	  Conjoined it issues, and the mundane wax
	  Tempers and stamps more after its own fashion.

Fatto avea di la` mane e di qua sera   tal foce, e quasi tutto era la` bianco quello emisperio, e l'altra parte nera,	Almost that passage had made morning there And evening here, and there was wholly white That hemisphere, and black the other part,

quando Beatrice in sul sinistro fianco
  vidi rivolta e riguardar nel sole:
  aquila si` non li s'affisse unquanco.
	When Beatrice towards the left-hand side
	  I saw turned round, and gazing at the sun;
	  Never did eagle fasten so upon it!

E si` come secondo raggio suole
  uscir del primo e risalire in suso,
  pur come pelegrin che tornar vuole,
	And even as a second ray is wont
	  To issue from the first and reascend,
	  Like to a pilgrim who would fain return,

cosi` de l'atto suo, per li occhi infuso
  ne l'imagine mia, il mio si fece,
  e fissi li occhi al sole oltre nostr'uso.
	Thus of her action, through the eyes infused
	  In my imagination, mine I made,
	  And sunward fixed mine eyes beyond our wont.

Molto e` licito la`, che qui non lece
  a le nostre virtu`, merce' del loco
  fatto per proprio de l'umana spece.
	There much is lawful which is here unlawful
	  Unto our powers, by virtue of the place
	  Made for the human species as its own.

Io nol soffersi molto, ne' si` poco,
  ch'io nol vedessi sfavillar dintorno,
  com'ferro che bogliente esce del foco;
	Not long I bore it, nor so little while
	  But I beheld it sparkle round about
	  Like iron that comes molten from the fire;

e di subito parve giorno a giorno
  essere aggiunto, come quei che puote
  avesse il ciel d'un altro sole addorno.
	And suddenly it seemed that day to day
	  Was added, as if He who has the power
	  Had with another sun the heaven adorned.

Beatrice tutta ne l'etterne rote
  fissa con li occhi stava; e io in lei
  le luci fissi, di la` su` rimote.
	With eyes upon the everlasting wheels
	  Stood Beatrice all intent, and I, on her
	  Fixing my vision from above removed,

Nel suo aspetto tal dentro mi fei,
  qual si fe' Glauco nel gustar de l'erba
  che 'l fe' consorto in mar de li altri dei.

Trasumanar significar per verba
  non si poria; però l'essemplo basti
  a cui esperienza grazia serba.

S'i' era sol di me quel che creasti
  novellamente, amor che 'l ciel governi,
  tu 'l sai, che col tuo lume mi levasti.

Quando la rota che tu sempiterni
  desiderato, a sé mi fece atteso
  con l'armonia che temperi e discerni,

parvemi tanto allor del cielo acceso
  de la fiamma del sol, che pioggia o fiume
  lago non fece alcun tanto disteso.

La novità del suono e 'l grande lume
  di lor cagion m'accesero un disio
  mai non sentito di cotanto acume.

Ond'ella, che vedea me sì com'io,
  a quietarmi l'animo commosso,
  pria ch'io a dimandar, la bocca aprio,

e cominciò: ""Tu stesso ti fai grosso
  col falso imaginar, sì che non vedi
  ciò che vedresti se l'avessi scosso.

Tu non se' in terra, sì come tu credi;
  ma folgore, fuggendo il proprio sito,
  non corse come tu ch'ad esso riedi"".

S'io fui del primo dubbio disvestito
  per le sorrise parolette brevi,
  dentro ad un nuovo più fu' inretito,

e dissi: ""Già contento requievi
  di grande ammirazion; ma ora ammiro
  com'io trascenda questi corpi levi"".

Ond'ella, appresso d'un pio sospiro,
  li occhi drizzò ver' me con quel sembiante
  che madre fa sovra figlio deliro,

Such at her aspect inwardly became
  As Glaucus, tasting of the herb that made him
  Peer of the other gods beneath the sea.

To represent transhumanise in words
  Impossible were; the example, then, suffice
  Him for whom Grace the experience reserves.

If I was merely what of me thou newly
  Createdst, Love who governest the heaven,
  Thou knowest, who didst lift me with thy light!

When now the wheel, which thou dost make eternal
  Desiring thee, made me attentive to it
  By harmony thou dost modulate and measure,

Then seemed to me so much of heaven enkindled
  By the sun's flame, that neither rain nor river
  E'er made a lake so widely spread abroad.

The newness of the sound and the great light
  Kindled in me a longing for their cause,
  Never before with such acuteness felt;

Whence she, who saw me as I saw myself,
  To quiet in me my perturbed mind,
  Opened her mouth, ere I did mine to ask,

And she began: "Thou makest thyself so dull
  With false imagining, that thou seest not
  What thou wouldst see if thou hadst shaken it off.

Thou art not upon earth, as thou believest;
  But lightning, fleeing its appropriate site,
  Ne'er ran as thou, who thitherward returnest."

If of my former doubt I was divested
  By these brief little words more smiled than spoken,
  I in a new one was the more ensnared;

And said: "Already did I rest content
  From great amazement; but am now amazed
  In what way I transcend these bodies light."

Whereupon she, after a pitying sigh,
  Her eyes directed tow'rds me with that look
  A mother casts on a delirious child;

e comincio`: ""Le cose tutte quante
 hanno ordine tra loro, e questo e` forma
 che l'universo a Dio fa simigliante.

Qui veggion l'alte creature l'orma
 de l'etterno valore, il qual e` fine
 al quale e` fatta la toccata norma.

Ne l'ordine ch'io dico sono accline
 tutte nature, per diverse sorti,
 piu` al principio loro e men vicine;

onde si muovono a diversi porti
 per lo gran mar de l'essere, e ciascuna
 con istinto a lei dato che la porti.

Questi ne porta il foco inver' la luna;
 questi ne' cor mortali e` permotore;
 questi la terra in se' stringe e aduna;

ne' pur le creature che son fore
 d'intelligenza quest'arco saetta
 ma quelle c'hanno intelletto e amore.

La provedenza, che cotanto assetta,
 del suo lume fa 'l ciel sempre quieto
 nel qual si volge quel c'ha maggior fretta;

e ora li`, come a sito decreto,
 cen porta la virtu` di quella corda
 che cio` che scocca drizza in segno lieto.

Vero e` che, come forma non s'accorda
 molte fiate a l'intenzion de l'arte,
 perch'a risponder la materia e` sorda,

cosi` da questo corso si diparte
 talor la creatura, c'ha podere
 di piegar, cosi` pinta, in altra parte;

e si` come veder si puo` cadere
 foco di nube, si` l'impeto primo
 l'atterra torto da falso piacere.

Non dei piu` ammirar, se bene stimo,
 lo tuo salir, se non come d'un rivo
 se d'alto monte scende giuso ad imo.

Maraviglia sarebbe in te se, privo
 d'impedimento, giu` ti fossi assiso,
 com'a terra quiete in foco vivo"".

And she began: "All things whate'er they be
 Have order among themselves, and this is form,
 That makes the universe resemble God.

Here do the higher creatures see the footprints
 Of the Eternal Power, which is the end
 Whereto is made the law already mentioned.

In the order that I speak of are inclined
 All natures, by their destinies diverse,
 More or less near unto their origin;

Hence they move onward unto ports diverse
 O'er the great sea of being; and each one
 With instinct given it which bears it on.

This bears away the fire towards the moon;
 This is in mortal hearts the motive power
 This binds together and unites the earth.

Nor only the created things that are
 Without intelligence this bow shoots forth,
 But those that have both intellect and love.

The Providence that regulates all this
 Makes with its light the heaven forever quiet,
 Wherein that turns which has the greatest haste.

And thither now, as to a site decreed,
 Bears us away the virtue of that cord
 Which aims its arrows at a joyous mark.

True is it, that as oftentimes the form
 Accords not with the intention of the art,
 Because in answering is matter deaf,

So likewise from this course doth deviate
 Sometimes the creature, who the power possesses,
 Though thus impelled, to swerve some other way,

(In the same wise as one may see the fire
 Fall from a cloud,) if the first impetus
 Earthward is wrested by some false delight.

Thou shouldst not wonder more, if well I judge,
 At thine ascent, than at a rivulet
 From some high mount descending to the lowland.

Marvel it would be in thee, if deprived
 Of hindrance, thou wert seated down below,
 As if on earth the living fire were quiet."

Quinci rivolse inver' lo cielo il viso.   Thereat she heavenward turned again her face.

Paradiso: Canto II

The First Heaven, the Moon: Spirits who, having taken Sacred Vows, were forced to violate them. The Lunar Spots.

O voi che siete in piccioletta barca,
  desiderosi d'ascoltar, seguiti
  dietro al mio legno che cantando varca,

tornate a riveder li vostri liti:
  non vi mettete in pelago, che' forse,
  perdendo me, rimarreste smarriti.

L'acqua ch'io prendo gia` mai non si corse;
  Minerva spira, e conducemi Appollo,
  e nove Muse mi dimostran l'Orse.

Voialtri pochi che drizzaste il collo
  per tempo al pan de li angeli, del quale
  vivesi qui ma non sen vien satollo,

metter potete ben per l'alto sale
  vostro navigio, servando mio solco
  dinanzi a l'acqua che ritorna equale.

Que' gloriosi che passaro al Colco
  non s'ammiraron come voi farete,
  quando Iason vider fatto bifolco.

La concreata e perpetua sete
  del deiforme regno cen portava
  veloci quasi come 'l ciel vedete.

Beatrice in suso, e io in lei guardava;
  e forse in tanto in quanto un quadrel posa
  e vola e da la noce si dischiava,

giunto mi vidi ove mirabil cosa
  mi torse il viso a se'; e pero` quella
  cui non potea mia cura essere ascosa,

O Ye, who in some pretty little boat,
  Eager to listen, have been following
  Behind my ship, that singing sails along,

Turn back to look again upon your shores;
  Do not put out to sea, lest peradventure,
  In losing me, you might yourselves be lost.

The sea I sail has never yet been passed;
  Minerva breathes, and pilots me Apollo,
  And Muses nine point out to me the Bears.

Ye other few who have the neck uplifted
  Betimes to th' bread of Angels upon which
  One liveth here and grows not sated by it,

Well may you launch upon the deep salt-sea
  Your vessel, keeping still my wake before you
  Upon the water that grows smooth again.

Those glorious ones who unto Colchos passed
  Were not so wonder-struck as you shall be,
  When Jason they beheld a ploughman made!

The con-created and perpetual thirst
  For the realm deiform did bear us on,
  As swift almost as ye the heavens behold.

Upward gazed Beatrice, and I at her;
  And in such space perchance as strikes a bolt
  And flies, and from the notch unlocks itself,

Arrived I saw me where a wondrous thing
  Drew to itself my sight; and therefore she
  From whom no care of mine could be concealed,

volta ver' me, si` lieta come bella,
  ""Drizza la mente in Dio grata"", mi disse,
  ""che n'ha congiunti con la prima stella"".

Parev'a me che nube ne coprisse
  lucida, spessa, solida e pulita,
  quasi adamante che lo sol ferisse.

Per entro se' l'etterna margarita
  ne ricevette, com'acqua recepe
  raggio di luce permanendo unita.

S'io era corpo, e qui non si concepe
  com'una dimensione altra patio,
  ch'esser convien se corpo in corpo repe,

accender ne dovria piu` il disio
  di veder quella essenza in che si vede
  come nostra natura e Dio s'unio.

Li` si vedra` cio` che tenem per fede,
  non dimostrato, ma fia per se' noto
  a guisa del ver primo che l'uom crede.

Io rispuosi: ""Madonna, si` devoto
  com'esser posso piu`, ringrazio lui
  lo qual dal mortal mondo m'ha remoto.

Ma ditemi: che son li segni bui
  di questo corpo, che la` giuso in terra
  fan di Cain favoleggiare altrui?"".

Ella sorrise alquanto, e poi ""S'elli erra
  l'oppinion"", mi disse, ""d'i mortali
  dove chiave di senso non diserra,

certo non ti dovrien punger li strali
  d'ammirazion omai, poi dietro ai sensi
  vedi che la ragione ha corte l'ali.

Ma dimmi quel che tu da te ne pensi"".
  E io: ""Cio` che n'appar qua su` diverso
  credo che fanno i corpi rari e densi"".

Ed ella: ""Certo assai vedrai sommerso
  nel falso il creder tuo, se bene ascolti
  l'argomentar ch'io li faro` avverso.

La spera ottava vi dimostra molti
  lumi, li quali e nel quale e nel quanto
  notar si posson di diversi volti.

Towards me turning, blithe as beautiful,
  Said unto me: "Fix gratefully thy mind
  On God, who unto the first star has brought us."

It seemed to me a cloud encompassed us,
  Luminous, dense, consolidate and bright
  As adamant on which the sun is striking.

Into itself did the eternal pearl
  Receive us, even as water doth receive
  A ray of light, remaining still unbroken.

If I was body, (and we here conceive not
  How one dimension tolerates another,
  Which needs must be if body enter body,)

More the desire should be enkindled in us
  That essence to behold, wherein is seen
  How God and our own nature were united.

There will be seen what we receive by faith,
  Not demonstrated, but self-evident
  In guise of the first truth that man believes.

I made reply: "Madonna, as devoutly
  As most I can do I give thanks to Him
  Who has removed me from the mortal world.

But tell me what the dusky spots may be
  Upon this body, which below on earth
  Make people tell that fabulous tale of Cain?"

Somewhat she smiled; and then, "If the opinion
  Of mortals be erroneous," she said,
  "Where'er the key of sense doth not unlock,

Certes, the shafts of wonder should not pierce thee
  Now, forasmuch as, following the senses,
  Thou seest that the reason has short wings.

But tell me what thou think'st of it thyself."
  And I: "What seems to us up here diverse,
  Is caused, I think, by bodies rare and dense."

And she: "Right truly shalt thou see immersed
  In error thy belief, if well thou hearest
  The argument that I shall make against it.

Lights many the eighth sphere displays to you
  Which in their quality and quantity
  May noted be of aspects different.

Se raro e denso cio` facesser tanto,
  una sola virtu` sarebbe in tutti,
  piu` e men distribuita e altrettanto.

Virtu` diverse esser convegnon frutti
  di principi formali, e quei, for ch'uno,
  seguiterieno a tua ragion distrutti.

Ancor, se raro fosse di quel bruno
  cagion che tu dimandi, o d'oltre in parte
  fora di sua materia si` digiuno

esto pianeto, o, si` come comparte
  lo grasso e 'l magro un corpo, cosi` questo
  nel suo volume cangerebbe carte.

Se 'l primo fosse, fora manifesto
  ne l'eclissi del sol per trasparere
  lo lume come in altro raro ingesto.

Questo non e`: pero` e` da vedere
  de l'altro; e s'elli avvien ch'io l'altro cassi,
  falsificato fia lo tuo parere.

S'elli e` che questo raro non trapassi,
  esser conviene un termine da onde
  lo suo contrario piu` passar non lassi;

e indi l'altrui raggio si rifonde
  cosi` come color torna per vetro
  lo qual di retro a se' piombo nasconde.

Or dirai tu ch'el si dimostra tetro
  ivi lo raggio piu` che in altre parti,
  per esser li` refratto piu` a retro.

Da questa instanza puo` deliberarti
  esperienza, se gia` mai la provi,
  ch'esser suol fonte ai rivi di vostr'arti.

Tre specchi prenderai; e i due rimovi
  da te d'un modo, e l'altro, piu` rimosso,
  tr'ambo li primi li occhi tuoi ritrovi.

Rivolto ad essi, fa che dopo il dosso
  ti stea un lume che i tre specchi accenda
  e torni a te da tutti ripercosso.

Ben che nel quanto tanto non si stenda
  la vista piu` lontana, li` vedrai
  come convien ch'igualmente risplenda.

If this were caused by rare and dense alone,
  One only virtue would there be in all
  Or more or less diffused, or equally.

Virtues diverse must be perforce the fruits
  Of formal principles; and these, save one,
  Of course would by thy reasoning be destroyed.

Besides, if rarity were of this dimness
  The cause thou askest, either through and through
  This planet thus attenuate were of matter,

Or else, as in a body is apportioned
  The fat and lean, so in like manner this
  Would in its volume interchange the leaves.

Were it the former, in the sun's eclipse
  It would be manifest by the shining through
  Of light, as through aught tenuous interfused.

This is not so; hence we must scan the other,
  And if it chance the other I demolish,
  Then falsified will thy opinion be.

But if this rarity go not through and through,
  There needs must be a limit, beyond which
  Its contrary prevents the further passing,

And thence the foreign radiance is reflected,
  Even as a colour cometh back from glass,
  The which behind itself concealeth lead.

Now thou wilt say the sunbeam shows itself
  More dimly there than in the other parts,
  By being there reflected farther back.

From this reply experiment will free thee
  If e'er thou try it, which is wont to be
  The fountain to the rivers of your arts.

Three mirrors shalt thou take, and two remove
  Alike from thee, the other more remote
  Between the former two shall meet thine eyes.

Turned towards these, cause that behind thy back
  Be placed a light, illuming the three mirrors
  And coming back to thee by all reflected.

Though in its quantity be not so ample
  The image most remote, there shalt thou see
  How it perforce is equally resplendent.

Or, come ai colpi de li caldi rai
  de la neve riman nudo il suggetto
  e dal colore e dal freddo primai,

cosi` rimaso te ne l'intelletto
  voglio informar di luce si` vivace,
  che ti tremolera` nel suo aspetto.

Dentro dal ciel de la divina pace
  si gira un corpo ne la cui virtute
  l'esser di tutto suo contento giace.

Lo ciel seguente, c'ha tante vedute,
  quell'esser parte per diverse essenze,
  da lui distratte e da lui contenute.

Li altri giron per varie differenze
  le distinzion che dentro da se' hanno
  dispongono a lor fini e lor semenze.

Questi organi del mondo cosi` vanno,
  come tu vedi omai, di grado in grado,
  che di su` prendono e di sotto fanno.

Riguarda bene omai si` com'io vado
  per questo loco al vero che disiri,
  si` che poi sappi sol tener lo guado.

Lo moto e la virtu` d'i santi giri,
  come dal fabbro l'arte del martello,
  da' beati motor convien che spiri;

e 'l ciel cui tanti lumi fanno bello,
  de la mente profonda che lui volve
  prende l'image e fassene suggello.

E come l'alma dentro a vostra polve
  per differenti membra e conformate
  a diverse potenze si risolve,

cosi` l'intelligenza sua bontate
  multiplicata per le stelle spiega,
  girando se' sovra sua unitate.

Virtu` diversa fa diversa lega
  col prezioso corpo ch'ella avviva,
  nel qual, si` come vita in voi, si lega.

Per la natura lieta onde deriva,
  la virtu` mista per lo corpo luce
  come letizia per pupilla viva.

Now, as beneath the touches of warm rays
  Naked the subject of the snow remains
  Both of its former colour and its cold,

Thee thus remaining in thy intellect,
  Will I inform with such a living light,
  That it shall tremble in its aspect to thee.

Within the heaven of the divine repose
  Revolves a body, in whose virtue lies
  The being of whatever it contains.

The following heaven, that has so many eyes,
  Divides this being by essences diverse,
  Distinguished from it, and by it contained.

The other spheres, by various differences,
  All the distinctions which they have within them
  Dispose unto their ends and their effects.

Thus do these organs of the world proceed,
  As thou perceivest now, from grade to grade;
  Since from above they take, and act beneath.

Observe me well, how through this place I come
  Unto the truth thou wishest, that hereafter
  Thou mayst alone know how to keep the ford

The power and motion of the holy spheres,
  As from the artisan the hammer's craft,
  Forth from the blessed motors must proceed.

The heaven, which lights so manifold make fair,
  From the Intelligence profound, which turns it,
  The image takes, and makes of it a seal.

And even as the soul within your dust
  Through members different and accommodated
  To faculties diverse expands itself,

So likewise this Intelligence diffuses
  Its virtue multiplied among the stars.
  Itself revolving on its unity.

Virtue diverse doth a diverse alloyage
  Make with the precious body that it quickens,
  In which, as life in you, it is combined.

From the glad nature whence it is derived,
  The mingled virtue through the body shines,
  Even as gladness through the living pupil.

Da essa vien cio` che da luce a luce	From this proceeds whate'er from light to light
par differente, non da denso e raro;	Appeareth different, not from dense and rare:
essa e` formal principio che produce,	This is the formal principle that produces,
conforme a sua bonta`, lo turbo e 'l chiaro"".	According to its goodness, dark and bright."

Paradiso: Canto III

Piccarda Donati and the Empress Constance.

Quel sol che pria d'amor mi scaldo` 'l petto, 　di bella verita` m'avea scoverto, 　provando e riprovando, il dolce aspetto;	That Sun, which erst with love my bosom warmed, 　Of beauteous truth had unto me discovered, 　By proving and reproving, the sweet aspect.
e io, per confessar corretto e certo 　me stesso, tanto quanto si convenne 　leva' il capo a proferer piu` erto;	And, that I might confess myself convinced 　And confident, so far as was befitting, 　I lifted more erect my head to speak.
ma visione apparve che ritenne 　a se' me tanto stretto, per vedersi, 　che di mia confession non mi sovvenne.	But there appeared a vision, which withdrew me 　So close to it, in order to be seen, 　That my confession I remembered not.
Quali per vetri trasparenti e tersi, 　o ver per acque nitide e tranquille, 　non si` profonde che i fondi sien persi,	Such as through polished and transparent glass, 　Or waters crystalline and undisturbed, 　But not so deep as that their bed be lost,
tornan d'i nostri visi le postille 　debili si`, che perla in bianca fronte 　non vien men forte a le nostre pupille;	Come back again the outlines of our faces 　So feeble, that a pearl on forehead white 　Comes not less speedily unto our eyes;
tali vid'io piu` facce a parlar pronte; 　per ch'io dentro a l'error contrario corsi 　a quel ch'accese amor tra l'omo e 'l fonte.	Such saw I many faces prompt to speak, 　So that I ran in error opposite 　To that which kindled love 'twixt man and fountain.
Subito si` com'io di lor m'accorsi, 　quelle stimando specchiati sembianti, 　per veder di cui fosser, li occhi torsi;	As soon as I became aware of them, 　Esteeming them as mirrored semblances, 　To see of whom they were, mine eyes I turned,
e nulla vidi, e ritorsili avanti 　dritti nel lume de la dolce guida, 　che, sorridendo, ardea ne li occhi santi.	And nothing saw, and once more turned them for- 　　ward 　Direct into the light of my sweet Guide, 　Who smiling kindled in her holy eyes.
""Non ti maravigliar perch'io sorrida"", 　mi disse, ""appresso il tuo pueril coto, 　poi sopra 'l vero ancor lo pie` non fida,	"Marvel thou not," she said to me, "because 　I smile at this thy puerile conceit, 　Since on the truth it trusts not yet its foot,

ma te rivolve, come suole, a voto:
  vere sustanze son cio` che tu vedi,
  qui rilegate per manco di voto.

Pero` parla con esse e odi e credi;
  che' la verace luce che li appaga
  da se' non lascia lor torcer li piedi"".

E io a l'ombra che parea piu` vaga
  di ragionar, drizza'mi, e cominciai,
  quasi com'uom cui troppa voglia smaga:

""O ben creato spirito, che a' rai
  di vita etterna la dolcezza senti
  che, non gustata, non s'intende mai,

grazioso mi fia se mi contenti
  del nome tuo e de la vostra sorte"".
  Ond'ella, pronta e con occhi ridenti:

""La nostra carita` non serra porte
  a giusta voglia, se non come quella
  che vuol simile a se' tutta sua corte.

I' fui nel mondo verginc sorella;
  e se la mente tua ben se' riguarda,
  non mi ti celera` l'esser piu` bella,

ma riconoscerai ch'i' son Piccarda,
  che, posta qui con questi altri beati,
  beata sono in la spera piu` tarda.

Li nostri affetti, che solo infiammati
  son nel piacer de lo Spirito Santo,
  letizian del suo ordine formati.

E questa sorte che par giu` cotanto,
  pero` n'e` data, perche' fuor negletti
  li nostri voti, e voti in alcun canto"".

Ond'io a lei: ""Ne' mirabili aspetti
  vostri risplende non so che divino
  che vi trasmuta da' primi concetti:

pero` non fui a rimembrar festino;
  ma or m'aiuta cio` che tu mi dici,
  si` che raffigurar m'e` piu` latino.

But turns thee, as 'tis wont, on emptiness.
  True substances are these which thou beholdest,
  Here relegate for breaking of some vow.

Therefore speak with them, listen and believe;
  For the true light, which giveth peace to them,
  Permits them not to turn from it their feet."

And I unto the shade that seemed most wishful
  To speak directed me, and I began,
  As one whom too great eagerness bewilders:

"O well-created spirit, who in the rays
  Of life eternal dost the sweetness taste
  Which being untasted ne'er is comprehended,

Grateful 'twill be to me, if thou content me
  Both with thy name and with your destiny."
  Whereat she promptly and with laughing eyes:

"Our charity doth never shut the doors
  Against a just desire, except as one
  Who wills that all her court be like herself.

I was a virgin sister in the world;
  And if thy mind doth contemplate me well,
  The being more fair will not conceal me from thee,

But thou shalt recognise I am Piccarda,
  Who, stationed here among these other blessed,
  Myself am blessed in the slowest sphere.

All our affections, that alone inflamed
  Are in the pleasure of the Holy Ghost,
  Rejoice at being of his order formed;

And this allotment, which appears so low,
  Therefore is given us, because our vows
  Have been neglected and in some part void."

Whence I to her: "In your miraculous aspects
  There shines I know not what of the divine,
  Which doth transform you from our first concep-
    tions.

Therefore I was not swift in my remembrance;
  But what thou tellest me now aids me so,
  That the refiguring is easier to me.

Ma dimmi: voi che siete qui felici,
  disiderate voi piu` alto loco
  per piu` vedere e per piu` farvi amici?"".

Con quelle altr'ombre pria sorrise un poco;
  da indi mi rispuose tanto lieta,
  ch'arder parea d'amor nel primo foco:

""Frate, la nostra volonta` quieta
  virtu` di carita`, che fa volerne
  sol quel ch'avemo, e d'altro non ci asseta.

Se disiassimo esser piu` superne,
  foran discordi li nostri disiri
  dal voler di colui che qui ne cerne;

che vedrai non capere in questi giri,
  s'essere in carita` e` qui necesse,
  e se la sua natura ben rimiri.

Anzi e` formale ad esto beato esse
  tenersi dentro a la divina voglia,
  per ch'una fansi nostre voglie stesse;

si` che, come noi sem di soglia in soglia
  per questo regno, a tutto il regno piace
  com'a lo re che 'n suo voler ne 'nvoglia.

E 'n la sua volontade e` nostra pace:
  ell'e` quel mare al qual tutto si move
  cio` ch'ella cria o che natura face"".

Chiaro mi fu allor come ogne dove
  in cielo e` paradiso, etsi la grazia
  del sommo ben d'un modo non vi piove.

Ma si` com'elli avvien, s'un cibo sazia
  e d'un altro rimane ancor la gola,
  che quel si chere e di quel si ringrazia,

cosi` fec'io con atto e con parola,
  per apprender da lei qual fu la tela
  onde non trasse infino a co la spuola.

""Perfetta vita e alto merto inciela
  donna piu` su`"", mi disse, ""a la cui norma
  nel vostro mondo giu` si veste e vela,

perche' fino al morir si vegghi e dorma
  con quello sposo ch'ogne voto accetta
  che caritate a suo piacer conforma.

But tell me, ye who in this place are happy,
  Are you desirous of a higher place,
  To see more or to make yourselves more friends?"

First with those other shades she smiled a little;
  Thereafter answered me so full of gladness,
  She seemed to burn in the first fire of love:

"Brother, our will is quieted by virtue
  Of charity, that makes us wish alone
  For what we have, nor gives us thirst for more.

If to be more exalted we aspired,
  Discordant would our aspirations be
  Unto the will of Him who here secludes us;

Which thou shalt see finds no place in these circles,
  If being in charity is needful here,
  And if thou lookest well into its nature;

Nay, 'tis essential to this blest existence
  To keep itself within the will divine,
  Whereby our very wishes are made one;

So that, as we are station above station
  Throughout this realm, to all the realm 'tis pleasing,
  As to the King, who makes his will our will.

And his will is our peace; this is the sea
  To which is moving onward whatsoever
  It doth create, and all that nature makes."

Then it was clear to me how everywhere
  In heaven is Paradise, although the grace
  Of good supreme there rain not in one measure.

But as it comes to pass, if one food sates,
  And for another still remains the longing,
  We ask for this, and that decline with thanks,

E'en thus did I; with gesture and with word,
  To learn from her what was the web wherein
  She did not ply the shuttle to the end.

"A perfect life and merit high in-heaven
  A lady o'er us," said she, "by whose rule
  Down in your world they vest and veil themselves,

That until death they may both watch and sleep
  Beside that Spouse who every vow accepts
  Which charity conformeth to his pleasure.

Dal mondo, per seguirla, giovinetta
 fuggi'mi, e nel suo abito mi chiusi
 e promisi la via de la sua setta.

Uomini poi, a mal piu` ch'a bene usi,
 fuor mi rapiron de la dolce chiostra:
 Iddio si sa qual poi mia vita fusi.

E quest'altro splendor che ti si mostra
 da la mia destra parte e che s'accende
 di tutto il lume de la spera nostra,

cio` ch'io dico di me, di se' intende;
 sorella fu, e cosi` le fu tolta
 di capo l'ombra de le sacre bende.

Ma poi che pur al mondo fu rivolta
 contra suo grado e contra buona usanza,
 non fu dal vel del cor gia` mai disciolta.

Quest'e` la luce de la gran Costanza
 che del secondo vento di Soave
 genero` 'l terzo e l'ultima possanza'"".

Cosi` parlommi, e poi comincio` 'Avc,
 Maria' cantando, e cantando vanio
 come per acqua cupa cosa grave.

La vista mia, che tanto lei seguio
 quanto possibil fu, poi che la perse,
 volsesi al segno di maggior disio,

e a Beatrice tutta si converse;
 ma quella folgoro` nel mio sguardo
 si` che da prima il viso non sofferse;

e cio` mi fece a dimandar piu` tardo.

To follow her, in girlhood from the world
 I fled, and in her habit shut myself,
 And pledged me to the pathway of her sect.

Then men accustomed unto evil more
 Than unto good, from the sweet cloister tore me;
 God knows what afterward my life became.

This other splendour, which to thee reveals
 Itself on my right side, and is enkindled
 With all the illumination of our sphere,

What of myself I say applies to her;
 A nun was she, and likewise from her head
 Was ta'en the shadow of the sacred wimple.

But when she too was to the world returned
 Against her wishes and against good usage,
 Of the heart's veil she never was divested.

Of great Costanza this is the effulgence,
 Who from the second wind of Suabia
 Brought forth the third and latest puissance."

Thus unto me she spake, and then began
 "Ave Maria" singing, and in singing
 Vanished, as through deep water something heavy.

My sight, that followed her as long a time
 As it was possible, when it had lost her
 Turned round unto the mark of more desire,

And wholly unto Beatrice reverted;
 But she such lightnings flashed into mine eyes,
 That at the first my sight endured it not;

And this in questioning more backward made me.

Paradiso: Canto IV

Questionings of the Soul and of Broken Vows.

Intra due cibi, distanti e moventi
  d'un modo, prima si morria di fame,
  che liber'omo l'un recasse ai denti;

si` si starebbe un agno intra due brame
  di fieri lupi, igualmente temendo;
  si` si starebbe un cane intra due dame:

per che, s'i' mi tacea, me non riprendo,
  da li miei dubbi d'un modo sospinto,
  poi ch'era necessario, ne' commendo.

Io mi tacea, ma 'l mio disir dipinto
  m'era nel viso, e 'l dimandar con ello,
  piu` caldo assai che per parlar distinto.

Fe' si` Beatrice qual fe' Daniello,
  Nabuccodonosor levando d'ira,
  che l'avea fatto ingiustamente fello;

e disse: ““Io veggio ben come ti tira
  uno e altro disio, si` che tua cura
  se' stessa lega si` che fuor non spira.

Tu argomenti: "Se 'l buon voler dura,
  la violenza altrui per qual ragione
  di meritar mi scema la misura?".

Ancor di dubitar ti da` cagione
  parer tornarsi l'anime a le stelle,
  secondo la sentenza di Platone.

Queste son le question che nel tuo velle
  pontano igualmente; e pero` pria
  trattero` quella che piu` ha di felle.

Between two viands, equally removed
  And tempting, a free man would die of hunger
  Ere either he could bring unto his teeth.

So would a lamb between the ravenings
  Of two fierce wolves stand fearing both alike;
  And so would stand a dog between two does.

Hence, if I held my peace, myself I blame not,
  Impelled in equal measure by my doubts,
  Since it must be so, nor do I commend.

I held my peace; but my desire was painted
  Upon my face, and questioning with that
  More fervent far than by articulate speech.

Beatrice did as Daniel had done
  Relieving Nebuchadnezzar from the wrath
  Which rendered him unjustly merciless,

And said: "Well see I how attracteth thee
  One and the other wish, so that thy care
  Binds itself so that forth it does not breathe.

Thou arguest, if good will be permanent,
  The violence of others, for what reason
  Doth it decrease the measure of my merit?

Again for doubting furnish thee occasion
  Souls seeming to return unto the stars,
  According to the sentiment of Plato.

These are the questions which upon thy wish
  Are thrusting equally; and therefore first
  Will I treat that which hath the most of gall.

D'i Serafin colui che piu` s'india,
  Moise`, Samuel, e quel Giovanni
  che prender vuoli, io dico, non Maria,

non hanno in altro cielo i loro scanni
  che questi spirti che mo t'appariro,
  ne' hanno a l'esser lor piu` o meno anni;

ma tutti fanno bello il primo giro,
  e differentemente han dolce vita
  per sentir piu` e men l'etterno spiro.

Qui si mostraro, non perche' sortita
  sia questa spera lor, ma per far segno
  de la celestial c'ha men salita.

Cosi` parlar conviensi al vostro ingegno,
  pero` che solo da sensato apprende
  cio` che fa poscia d'intelletto degno.

Per questo la Scrittura condescende
  a vostra facultate, e piedi e mano
  attribuisce a Dio, e altro intende;

e Santa Chiesa con aspetto umano
  Gabriel e Michel vi rappresenta,
  e l'altro che Tobia rifece sano.

Quel che Timeo de l'anime argomenta
  non e` simile a cio` che qui si vede,
  pero` che, come dice, par che senta.

Dice che l'alma a la sua stella riede,
  credendo quella quindi esser decisa
  quando natura per forma la diede;

e forse sua sentenza e` d'altra guisa
  che la voce non suona, ed esser puote
  con intenzion da non esser derisa.

S'elli intende tornare a queste ruote
  l'onor de la influenza e 'l biasmo, forse
  in alcun vero suo arco percuote.

Questo principio, male inteso, torse
  gia` tutto il mondo quasi, si` che Giove,
  Mercurio e Marte a nominar trascorse.

L'altra dubitazion che ti commove
  ha men velen, pero` che sua malizia
  non ti poria menar da me altrove.

He of the Seraphim most absorbed in God,
  Moses, and Samuel, and whichever John
  Thou mayst select, I say, and even Mary,

Have not in any other heaven their seats,
  Than have those spirits that just appeared to thee,
  Nor of existence more or fewer years;

But all make beautiful the primal circle,
  And have sweet life in different degrees,
  By feeling more or less the eternal breath.

They showed themselves here, not because allotted
  This sphere has been to them, but to give sign
  Of the celestial which is least exalted.

To speak thus is adapted to your mind,
  Since only through the sense it apprehendeth
  What then it worthy makes of intellect.

On this account the Scripture condescends
  Unto your faculties, and feet and hands
  To God attributes, and means something else;

And Holy Church under an aspect human
  Gabriel and Michael represent to you,
  And him who made Tobias whole again.

That which Timaeus argues of the soul
  Doth not resemble that which here is seen,
  Because it seems that as he speaks he thinks.

He says the soul unto its star returns,
  Believing it to have been severed thence
  Whenever nature gave it as a form.

Perhaps his doctrine is of other guise
  Than the words sound, and possibly may be
  With meaning that is not to be derided.

If he doth mean that to these wheels return
  The honour of their influence and the blame,
  Perhaps his bow doth hit upon some truth.

This principle ill understood once warped
  The whole world nearly, till it went astray
  Invoking Jove and Mercury and Mars.

The other doubt which doth disquiet thee
  Less venom has, for its malevolence
  Could never lead thee otherwhere from me.

Parere ingiusta la nostra giustizia
  ne li occhi d'i mortali, e` argomento
  di fede e non d'eretica nequizia.

Ma perche' puote vostro accorgimento
  ben penetrare a questa veritate,
  come disiri, ti faro` contento.

Se violenza e` quando quel che pate
  niente conferisce a quel che sforza,
  non fuor quest'alme per essa scusate;

che' volonta`, se non vuol, non s'ammorza,
  ma fa come natura face in foco,
  se mille volte violenza il torza.

Per che, s'ella si piega assai o poco,
  segue la forza; e cosi` queste fero
  possendo rifuggir nel santo loco.

Se fosse stato lor volere intero,
  come tenne Lorenzo in su la grada,
  e fece Muzio a la sua man severo,

cosi` l'avria ripinte per la strada
  ond'eran tratte, come fuoro sciolte;
  ma cosi` salda voglia e` troppo rada.

E per queste parole, se ricolte
  l'hai come dei, e` l'argomento casso
  che t'avria fatto noia ancor piu` volte.

Ma or ti s'attraversa un altro passo
  dinanzi a li occhi, tal che per te stesso
  non usciresti: pria saresti lasso.

Io t'ho per certo ne la mente messo
  ch'alma beata non poria mentire,
  pero` ch'e` sempre al primo vero appresso;

e poi potesti da Piccarda udire
  che l'affezion del vel Costanza tenne;
  si` ch'ella par qui meco contradire.

Molte fiate gia`, frate, addivenne
  che, per fuggir periglio, contra grato
  si fe' di quel che far non si convenne;

That as unjust our justice should appear
  In eyes of mortals, is an argument
  Of faith, and not of sin heretical.

But still, that your perception may be able
  To thoroughly penetrate this verity,
  As thou desirest, I will satisfy thee.

If it be violence when he who suffers
  Co-operates not with him who uses force,
  These souls were not on that account excused;

For will is never quenched unless it will,
  But operates as nature doth in fire
  If violence a thousand times distort it.

Hence, if it yieldeth more or less, it seconds
  The force; and these have done so, having power
  Of turning back unto the holy place.

If their will had been perfect, like to that
  Which Lawrence fast upon his gridiron held,
  And Mutius made severe to his own hand,

It would have urged them back along the road
  Whence they were dragged, as soon as they were
    free;
  But such a solid will is all too rare.

And by these words, if thou hast gathered them
  As thou shouldst do, the argument is refuted
  That would have still annoyed thee many times.

But now another passage runs across
  Before thine eyes, and such that by thyself
  Thou couldst not thread it ere thou wouldst be wea-
    ry.

I have for certain put into thy mind
  That soul beatified could never lie,
  For it is near the primal Truth,

And then thou from Piccarda might'st have heard
  Costanza kept affection for the veil,
  So that she seemeth here to contradict me.

Many times, brother, has it come to pass,
  That, to escape from peril, with reluctance
  That has been done it was not right to do,

come Almeone, che, di cio` pregato
  dal padre suo, la propria madre spense,
  per non perder pieta`, si fe' spietato.

A questo punto voglio che tu pense
  che la forza al voler si mischia, e fanno
  si` che scusar non si posson l'offense.

Voglia assoluta non consente al danno;
  ma consentevi in tanto in quanto teme,
  se si ritrae, cadere in piu` affanno.

Pero`, quando Piccarda quello spreme,
  de la voglia assoluta intende, e io
  de l'altra; si` che ver diciamo insieme"".

Cotal fu l'ondeggiar del santo rio
  ch'usci` del fonte ond'ogne ver deriva;
  tal puose in pace uno e altro disio.

""O amanza del primo amante, o diva"",
  diss'io appresso, ""il cui parlar m'inonda
  e scalda si`, che piu` e piu` m'avviva,

non e` l'affezion mia tanto profonda,
  che basti a render voi grazia per grazia;
  ma quei che vede e puote a cio` risponda.

Io veggio ben che gia` mai non si sazia
  nostro intelletto, se 'l ver non lo illustra
  di fuor dal qual nessun vero si spazia.

Posasi in esso, come fera in lustra,
  tosto che giunto l'ha; e giugner puollo:
  se non, ciascun disio sarebbe frustra.

Nasce per quello, a guisa di rampollo,
  a pie` del vero il dubbio; ed e` natura
  ch'al sommo pinge noi di collo in collo.

Questo m'invita, questo m'assicura
  con reverenza, donna, a dimandarvi
  d'un'altra verita` che m'e` oscura.

Io vo' saper se l'uom puo` sodisfarvi
  ai voti manchi si` con altri beni,
  ch'a la vostra statera non sien parvi"".

Beatrice mi guardo` con li occhi pieni
  di faville d'amor cosi` divini,
  che, vinta, mia virtute die` le reni,

E'en as Alcmaeon (who, being by his father
  Thereto entreated, his own mother slew)
  Not to lose pity pitiless became.

At this point I desire thee to remember
  That force with will commingles, and they cause
  That the offences cannot be excused.

Will absolute consenteth not to evil;
  But in so far consenteth as it fears,
  If it refrain, to fall into more harm.

Hence when Piccarda uses this expression,
  She meaneth the will absolute, and I
  The other, so that both of us speak truth."

Such was the flowing of the holy river
  That issued from the fount whence springs all truth;
  This put to rest my wishes one and all.

"O love of the first lover, O divine,"
  Said I forthwith, "whose speech inundates me
  And warms me so, it more and more revives me,

My own affection is not so profound
  As to suffice in rendering grace for grace;
  Let Him, who sees and can, thereto respond.

Well I perceive that never sated is
  Our intellect unless the Truth illume it,
  Beyond which nothing true expands itself.

It rests therein, as wild beast in his lair,
  When it attains it; and it can attain it;
  If not, then each desire would frustrate be.

Therefore springs up, in fashion of a shoot,
  Doubt at the foot of truth; and this is nature,
  Which to the top from height to height impels us.

This doth invite me, this assurance give me
  With reverence, Lady, to inquire of you
  Another truth, which is obscure to me.

I wish to know if man can satisfy you
  For broken vows with other good deeds, so
  That in your balance they will not be light."

Beatrice gazed upon me with her eyes
  Full of the sparks of love, and so divine,
  That, overcome my power, I turned my back

e quasi mi perdei con li occhi chini.   And almost lost myself with eyes downcast.

Paradiso: Canto V

Discourse of Beatrice on Vows and Compensations. Ascent to the Second Heaven, Mercury: Spirits who for the Love of Fame achieved great Deeds.

""S'io ti fiammeggio nel caldo d'amore
  di la` dal modo che 'n terra si vede,
  si` che del viso tuo vinco il valore,

non ti maravigliar; che' cio` procede
  da perfetto veder, che, come apprende,
  cosi` nel bene appreso move il piede.

Io veggio ben si` come gia` resplende
  ne l'intelletto tuo l'etterna luce,
  che, vista, sola e sempre amore accende;

e s'altra cosa vostro amor seduce,
  non e` se non di quella alcun vestigio,
  mal conosciuto, che quivi traluce.

Tu vuo' saper se con altro servigio,
  per manco voto, si puo` render tanto
  che l'anima sicuri di letigio"".

Si` comincio` Beatrice questo canto;
  e si` com'uom che suo parlar non spezza,
  continuo` cosi` 'l processo santo:

""Lo maggior don che Dio per sua larghezza
  fesse creando, e a la sua bontate
  piu` conformato, e quel ch'e' piu` apprezza,

fu de la volonta` la libertate;
  di che le creature intelligenti,
  e tutte e sole, fuoro e son dotate.

"If in the heat of love I flame upon thee
  Beyond the measure that on earth is seen,
  So that the valour of thine eyes I vanquish,

Marvel thou not thereat; for this proceeds
  From perfect sight, which as it apprehends
  To the good apprehended moves its feet.

Well I perceive how is already shining
  Into thine intellect the eternal light,
  That only seen enkindles always love;

And if some other thing your love seduce,
  'Tis nothing but a vestige of the same,
  Ill understood, which there is shining through.

Thou fain wouldst know if with another service
  For broken vow can such return be made
  As to secure the soul from further claim."

This Canto thus did Beatrice begin;
  And, as a man who breaks not off his speech,
  Continued thus her holy argument:

"The greatest gift that in his largess God
  Creating made, and unto his own goodness
  Nearest conformed, and that which he doth prize

Most highly, is the freedom of the will,
  Wherewith the creatures of intelligence
  Both all and only were and are endowed.

Or ti parra`, se tu quinci argomenti,
l'alto valor del voto, s'e` si` fatto
che Dio consenta quando tu consenti;

che', nel fermar tra Dio e l'uomo il patto,
vittima fassi di questo tesoro,
tal quale io dico; e fassi col suo atto.

Dunque che render puossi per ristoro?
Se credi bene usar quel c'hai offerto,
di maltolletto vuo' far buon lavoro.

Tu se' omai del maggior punto certo;
ma perche' Santa Chiesa in cio` dispensa,
che par contra lo ver ch'i' t'ho scoverto,

convienti ancor sedere un poco a mensa,
pero` che 'l cibo rigido c'hai preso,
richiede ancora aiuto a tua dispensa.

Apri la mente a quel ch'io ti paleso
e fermalvi entro; che' non fa scienza,
sanza lo ritenere, avere inteso.

Due cose si convegnono a l'essenza
di questo sacrificio: l'una e` quella
di che si fa; l'altr'e` la convenenza.

Quest'ultima gia` mai non si cancella
se non servata; e intorno di lei
si` preciso di sopra si favella:

pero` necessitato fu a li Ebrei
pur l'offerere, ancor ch'alcuna offerta
si` permutasse, come saver dei.

L'altra, che per materia t'e` aperta,
puote ben esser tal, che non si falla
se con altra materia si converta.

Ma non trasmuti carco a la sua spalla
per suo arbitrio alcun, sanza la volta
e de la chiave bianca e de la gialla;

e ogne permutanza credi stolta,
se la cosa dimessa in la sorpresa
come 'l quattro nel sei non e` raccolta.

Now wilt thou see, if thence thou reasonest,
The high worth of a vow, if it he made
So that when thou consentest God consents:

For, closing between God and man the compact,
A sacrifice is of this treasure made,
Such as I say, and made by its own act.

What can be rendered then as compensation?
Think'st thou to make good use of what thou'st of-
fered,
With gains ill gotten thou wouldst do good deed.

Now art thou certain of the greater point;
But because Holy Church in this dispenses,
Which seems against the truth which I have shown
thee,

Behoves thee still to sit awhile at table,
Because the solid food which thou hast taken
Requireth further aid for thy digestion.

Open thy mind to that which I reveal,
And fix it there within; for 'tis not knowledge,
The having heard without retaining it.

In the essence of this sacrifice two things
Convene together; and the one is that
Of which 'tis made, the other is the agreement.

This last for evermore is cancelled not
Unless complied with, and concerning this
With such precision has above been spoken.

Therefore it was enjoined upon the Hebrews
To offer still, though sometimes what was offered
Might be commuted, as thou ought'st to know.

The other, which is known to thee as matter,
May well indeed be such that one errs not
If it for other matter be exchanged.

But let none shift the burden on his shoulder
At his arbitrament, without the turning
Both of the white and of the yellow key;

And every permutation deem as foolish,
If in the substitute the thing relinquished,
As the four is in six, be not contained.

Pero` qualunque cosa tanto pesa
  per suo valor che tragga ogne bilancia,
  sodisfar non si puo` con altra spesa.

Non prendan li mortali il voto a ciancia;
  siate fedeli, e a cio` far non bieci,
  come Iepte` a la sua prima mancia;

cui piu` si convenia dicer 'Mal feci',
  che, servando, far peggio; e cosi` stolto
  ritrovar puoi il gran duca de' Greci,

onde pianse Efigenia il suo bel volto,
  e fe' pianger di se' i folli e i savi
  ch'udir parlar di cosi` fatto colto.

Siate, Cristiani, a muovervi piu` gravi:
  non siate come penna ad ogne vento,
  e non crediate ch'ogne acqua vi lavi.

Avete il novo e 'l vecchio Testamento,
  e 'l pastor de la Chiesa che vi guida;
  questo vi basti a vostro salvamento.

Se mala cupidigia altro vi grida,
  uomini siate, e non pecore matte,
  si` che 'l Giudeo di voi tra voi non rida!

Non fate com'agnel che lascia il latte
  de la sua madre, e semplice e lascivo
  seco medesmo a suo piacer combatte!"".

Cosi` Beatrice a me com'io scrivo;
  poi si rivolse tutta disiante
  a quella parte ove 'l mondo e` piu` vivo.

Lo suo tacere e 'l trasmutar sembiante
  puoser silenzio al mio cupido ingegno,
  che gia` nuove questioni avea davante;

e si` come saetta che nel segno
  percuote pria che sia la corda queta,
  cosi` corremmo nel secondo regno.

Quivi la donna mia vid'io si` lieta,
  come nel lume di quel ciel si mise,
  che piu` lucente se ne fe' 'l pianeta.

E se la stella si cambio` e rise,
  qual mi fec'io che pur da mia natura
  trasmutabile son per tutte guise!

Therefore whatever thing has so great weight
  In value that it drags down every balance,
  Cannot be satisfied with other spending.

Let mortals never take a vow in jest;
  Be faithful and not blind in doing that,
  As Jephthah was in his first offering,

Whom more beseemed to say, 'I have done wrong,
  Than to do worse by keeping; and as foolish
  Thou the great leader of the Greeks wilt find,

Whence wept Iphigenia her fair face,
  And made for her both wise and simple weep,
  Who heard such kind of worship spoken of.'

Christians, be ye more serious in your movements;
  Be ye not like a feather at each wind,
  And think not every water washes you.

Ye have the Old and the New Testament,
  And the Pastor of the Church who guideth you
  Let this suffice you unto your salvation.

If evil appetite cry aught else to you,
  Be ye as men, and not as silly sheep,
  So that the Jew among you may not mock you.

Be ye not as the lamb that doth abandon
  Its mother's milk, and frolicsome and simple
  Combats at its own pleasure with itself."

Thus Beatrice to me even as I write it;
  Then all desireful turned herself again
  To that part where the world is most alive.

Her silence and her change of countenance
  Silence imposed upon my eager mind,
  That had already in advance new questions;

And as an arrow that upon the mark
  Strikes ere the bowstring quiet hath become,
  So did we speed into the second realm.

My Lady there so joyful I beheld,
  As into the brightness of that heaven she entered,
  More luminous thereat the planet grew;

And if the star itself was changed and smiled,
  What became I, who by my nature am
  Exceeding mutable in every guise!

334

Come 'n peschiera ch'e` tranquilla e pura
 traggonsi i pesci a cio` che vien di fori
 per modo che lo stimin lor pastura,

si` vid'io ben piu` di mille splendori
 trarsi ver' noi, e in ciascun s'udia:
 ""Ecco chi crescera` li nostri amori"".

E si` come ciascuno a noi venia,
 vedeasi l'ombra piena di letizia
 nel folgor chiaro che di lei uscia.

Pensa, lettor, se quel che qui s'inizia
 non procedesse, come tu avresti
 di piu` savere angosciosa carizia;

e per te vederai come da questi
 m'era in disio d'udir lor condizioni,
 si` come a li occhi mi fur manifesti.

""O bene nato a cui veder li troni
 del triunfo etternal concede grazia
 prima che la milizia s'abbandoni,

del lume che per tutto il ciel si spazia
 noi semo accesi; e pero`, se disii
 di noi chiarirti, a tuo piacer ti sazia"".

Cosi` da un di quelli spirti pii
 detto mi fu; e da Beatrice: ""Di`, di`
 sicuramente, e credi come a dii"".

""Io veggio ben si` come tu t'annidi
 nel proprio lume, e che de li occhi il traggi,
 perch'e' coruscae si` come tu ridi;

ma non so chi tu se', ne' perche' aggi,
 anima degna, il grado de la spera
 che si vela a' mortai con altrui raggi"".

Questo diss'io diritto alla lumera
 che pria m'avea parlato; ond'ella fessi
 lucente piu` assai di quel ch'ell'era.

Si` come il sol che si cela elli stessi
 per troppa luce, come 'l caldo ha rose
 le temperanze d'i vapori spessi,

per piu` letizia si` mi si nascose
 dentro al suo raggio la figura santa;
 e cosi` chiusa chiusa mi rispuose

As, in a fish-pond which is pure and tranquil,
 The fishes draw to that which from without
 Comes in such fashion that their food they deem it;

So I beheld more than a thousand splendours
 Drawing towards us, and in each was heard:
 "Lo, this is she who shall increase our love."

And as each one was coming unto us,
 Full of beatitude the shade was seen,
 By the effulgence clear that issued from it.

Think, Reader, if what here is just beginning
 No farther should proceed, how thou wouldst have
 An agonizing need of knowing more;

And of thyself thou'lt see how I from these
 Was in desire of hearing their conditions,
 As they unto mine eyes were manifest.

"O thou well-born, unto whom Grace concedes
 To see the thrones of the eternal triumph,
 Or ever yet the warfare be abandoned

With light that through the whole of heaven is spread
 Kindled are we, and hence if thou desirest
 To know of us, at thine own pleasure sate thee."

Thus by some one among those holy spirits
 Was spoken, and by Beatrice: "Speak, speak
 Securely, and believe them even as Gods."

"Well I perceive how thou dost nest thyself
 In thine own light, and drawest it from thine eyes,
 Because they coruscate when thou dost smile,

But know not who thou art, nor why thou hast,
 Spirit august, thy station in the sphere
 That veils itself to men in alien rays."

This said I in direction of the light
 Which first had spoken to me; whence it became
 By far more lucent than it was before.

Even as the sun, that doth conceal himself
 By too much light, when heat has worn away
 The tempering influence of the vapours dense,

By greater rapture thus concealed itself
 In its own radiance the figure saintly,
 And thus close, close enfolded answered me

nel modo che 'l seguente canto canta.

In fashion as the following Canto sings.

Paradiso: Canto VI

Justinian. The Roman Eagle. The Empire. Romeo.

"'Poscia che Costantin l'aquila volse
contr'al corso del ciel, ch'ella seguio
dietro a l'antico che Lavina tolse,

cento e cent'anni e piu` l'uccel di Dio
ne lo stremo d'Europa si ritenne,
vicino a' monti de' quai prima uscio;

e sotto l'ombra de le sacre penne
governo` 'l mondo li` di mano in mano,
e, si` cangiando, in su la mia pervenne.

Cesare fui e son Iustiniano,
che, per voler del primo amor ch'i' sento,
d'entro le leggi trassi il troppo e 'l vano.

E prima ch'io a l'ovra fossi attento,
una natura in Cristo esser, non piue,
credea, e di tal fede era contento;

ma 'l benedetto Agapito, che fue
sommo pastore, a la fede sincera
mi dirizzo` con le parole sue.

Io li credetti; e cio` che 'n sua fede era,
vegg'io or chiaro si`, come tu vedi
ogni contradizione e falsa e vera.

Tosto che con la Chiesa mossi i piedi,
a Dio per grazia piacque di spirarmi
l'alto lavoro, e tutto 'n lui mi diedi;

e al mio Belisar commendai l'armi,
cui la destra del ciel fu si` congiunta,
che segno fu ch'i' dovessi posarmi.

"After that Constantine the eagle turned
Against the course of heaven, which it had followed
Behind the ancient who Lavinia took,

Two hundred years and more the bird of God
In the extreme of Europe held itself,
Near to the mountains whence it issued first;

And under shadow of the sacred plumes
It governed there the world from hand to hand,
And, changing thus, upon mine own alighted.

Caesar I was, and am Justinian,
Who, by the will of primal Love I feel,
Took from the laws the useless and redundant;

And ere unto the work I was attent,
One nature to exist in Christ, not more,
Believed, and with such faith was I contented.

But blessed Agapetus, he who was
The supreme pastor, to the faith sincere
Pointed me out the way by words of his.

Him I believed, and what was his assertion
I now see clearly, even as thou seest
Each contradiction to be false and true.

As soon as with the Church I moved my feet,
God in his grace it pleased with this high task
To inspire me, and I gave me wholly to it,

And to my Belisarius I commended
The arms, to which was heaven's right hand so
joined
It was a signal that I should repose.

Or qui a la question prima s'appunta
  la mia risposta; ma sua condizione
  mi stringe a seguitare alcuna giunta,

perche' tu veggi con quanta ragione
  si move contr'al sacrosanto segno
  e chi 'l s'appropria e chi a lui s'oppone.

Vedi quanta virtu` l'ha fatto degno
  di reverenza; e comincio` da l'ora
  che Pallante mori` per darli regno.

Tu sai ch'el fece in Alba sua dimora
  per trecento anni e oltre, infino al fine
  che i tre a' tre pugnar per lui ancora.

E sai ch'el fe' dal mal de le Sabine
  al dolor di Lucrezia in sette regi,
  vincendo intorno le genti vicine.

Sai quel ch'el fe' portato da li egregi
  Romani incontro a Brenno, incontro a Pirro,
  incontro a li altri principi e collegi;

onde Torquato e Quinzio, che dal cirro
  negletto fu nomato, i Deci e ' Fabi
  ebber la fama che volontier mirro.

Esso atterro` l'orgoglio de li Arabi
  che di retro ad Annibale passaro
  l'alpestre rocce, Po, di che tu labi.

Sott'esso giovanetti triunfaro
  Scipione e Pompeo; e a quel colle
  sotto 'l qual tu nascesti parve amaro.

Poi, presso al tempo che tutto 'l ciel volle
  redur lo mondo a suo modo sereno,
  Cesare per voler di Roma il tolle.

E quel che fe' da Varo infino a Reno,
  Isara vide ed Era e vide Senna
  e ogne valle onde Rodano e` pieno.

Quel che fe' poi ch'elli usci` di Ravenna
  e salto` Rubicon, fu di tal volo,
  che nol seguiteria lingua ne' penna.

Now here to the first question terminates
  My answer; but the character thereof
  Constrains me to continue with a sequel,

In order that thou see with how great reason
  Men move against the standard sacrosanct,
  Both who appropriate and who oppose it.

Behold how great a power has made it worthy
  Of reverence, beginning from the hour
  When Pallas died to give it sovereignty.

Thou knowest it made in Alba its abode
  Three hundred years and upward, till at last
  The three to three fought for it yet again.

Thou knowest what it achieved from Sabine wrong
  Down to Lucretia's sorrow, in seven kings
  O'ercoming round about the neighboring nations;

Thou knowest what it achieved, borne by the Ro-
  mans
  Illustrious against Brennus, against Pyrrhus,
  Against the other princes and confederates.

Torquatus thence and Quinctius, who from locks
  Unkempt was named, Decii and Fabii,
  Received the fame I willingly embalm;

It struck to earth the pride of the Arabians,
  Who, following Hannibal, had passed across
  The Alpine ridges, Po, from which thou glidest;

Beneath it triumphed while they yet were young
  Pompey and Scipio, and to the hill
  Beneath which thou wast born it bitter seemed;

Then, near unto the time when heaven had willed
  To bring the whole world to its mood serene,
  Did Caesar by the will of Rome assume it.

What it achieved from Var unto the Rhine,
  Isere beheld and Saone, beheld the Seine,
  And every valley whence the Rhone is filled;

What it achieved when it had left Ravenna,
  And leaped the Rubicon, was such a flight
  That neither tongue nor pen could follow it.

Inver' la Spagna rivolse lo stuolo,
  poi ver' Durazzo, e Farsalia percosse
  si` ch'al Nil caldo si senti` del duolo.

Antandro e Simeonta, onde si mosse,
  rivide e la` dov'Ettore si cuba;
  e mal per Tolomeo poscia si scosse.

Da indi scese folgorando a Iuba;
  onde si volse nel vostro occidente,
  ove sentia la pompeana tuba.

Di quel che fe' col baiulo seguente,
  Bruto con Cassio ne l'inferno latra,
  e Modena e Perugia fu dolente.

Piangene ancor la trista Cleopatra,
  che, fuggendoli innanzi, dal colubro
  la morte prese subitana e atra.

Con costui corse infino al lito rubro;
  con costui puose il mondo in tanta pace,
  che fu serrato a Giano il suo delubro.

Ma cio` che 'l segno che parlar mi face
  fatto avea prima e poi era fatturo
  per lo regno mortal ch'a lui soggiace,

diventa in apparenza poco e scuro,
  se in mano al terzo Cesare si mira
  con occhio chiaro e con affetto puro;

che' la viva giustizia che mi spira,
  li concedette, in mano a quel ch'i' dico,
  gloria di far vendetta a la sua ira.

Or qui t'ammira in cio` ch'io ti replico:
  poscia con Tito a far vendetta corse
  de la vendetta del peccato antico.

E quando il dente longobardo morse
  la Santa Chiesa, sotto le sue ali
  Carlo Magno, vincendo, la soccorse.

Omai puoi giudicar di quei cotali
  ch'io accusai di sopra e di lor falli,
  che son cagion di tutti vostri mali.

L'uno al pubblico segno i gigli gialli
  oppone, e l'altro appropria quello a parte,
  si` ch'e` forte a veder chi piu` si falli.

Round towards Spain it wheeled its legions; then
  Towards Durazzo, and Pharsalia smote
  That to the calid Nile was felt the pain.

Antandros and the Simois, whence it started,
  It saw again, and there where Hector lies,
  And ill for Ptolemy then roused itself.

From thence it came like lightning upon Juba;
  Then wheeled itself again into your West,
  Where the Pompeian clarion it heard.

From what it wrought with the next standard-bearer
  Brutus and Cassius howl in Hell together,
  And Modena and Perugia dolent were;

Still doth the mournful Cleopatra weep
  Because thereof, who, fleeing from before it,
  Took from the adder sudden and black death.

With him it ran even to the Red Sea shore;
  With him it placed the world in so great peace,
  That unto Janus was his temple closed.

But what the standard that has made me speak
  Achieved before, and after should achieve
  Throughout the mortal realm that lies beneath it,

Becometh in appearance mean and dim,
  If in the hand of the third Caesar seen
  With eye unclouded and affection pure,

Because the living Justice that inspires me
  Granted it, in the hand of him I speak of,
  The glory of doing vengeance for its wrath.

Now here attend to what I answer thee;
  Later it ran with Titus to do vengeance
  Upon the vengeance of the ancient sin.

And when the tooth of Lombardy had bitten
  The Holy Church, then underneath its wings
  Did Charlemagne victorious succor her.

Now hast thou power to judge of such as those
  Whom I accused above, and of their crimes,
  Which are the cause of all your miseries.

To the public standard one the yellow lilies
  Opposes, the other claims it for a party,
  So that 'tis hard to see which sins the most.

Faccian li Ghibellin, faccian lor arte
  sott'altro segno; che' mal segue quello
  sempre chi la giustizia e lui diparte;

e non l'abbatta esto Carlo novello
  coi Guelfi suoi, ma tema de li artigli
  ch'a piu` alto leon trasser lo vello.

Molte fiate gia` pianser li figli
  per la colpa del padre, e non si creda
  che Dio trasmuti l'arme per suoi gigli!

Questa picciola stella si correda
  di buoni spirti che son stati attivi
  perche' onore e fama li succeda:

e quando li disiri poggian quivi,
  si` disviando, pur convien che i raggi
  del vero amore in su` poggin men vivi.

Ma nel commensurar d'i nostri gaggi
  col merto e` parte di nostra letizia,
  perche' non li vedem minor ne' maggi.

Quindi addolcisce la viva giustizia
  in noi l'affetto si`, che non si puote
  torcer gia` mai ad alcuna nequizia.

Diverse voci fanno dolci note;
  cosi` diversi scanni in nostra vita
  rendon dolce armonia tra queste rote.

E dentro a la presente margarita
  luce la luce di Romeo, di cui
  fu l'ovra grande e bella mal gradita.

Ma i Provenzai che fecer contra lui
  non hanno riso; e pero` mal cammina
  qual si fa danno del ben fare altrui.

Quattro figlie ebbe, e ciascuna reina,
  Ramondo Beringhiere, e cio` li fece
  Romeo, persona umile e peregrina.

E poi il mosser le parole biece
  a dimandar ragione a questo giusto,
  che li assegno` sette e cinque per diece,

indi partissi povero e vetusto;
  e se 'l mondo sapesse il cor ch'elli ebbe
  mendicando sua vita a frusto a frusto,

Let, let the Ghibellines ply their handicraft
  Beneath some other standard; for this ever
  Ill follows he who it and justice parts.

And let not this new Charles e'er strike it down,
  He and his Guelfs, but let him fear the talons
  That from a nobler lion stripped the fell.

Already oftentimes the sons have wept
  The father's crime; and let him not believe
  That God will change His scutcheon for the lilies.

This little planet doth adorn itself
  With the good spirits that have active been,
  That fame and honour might come after them;

And whensoever the desires mount thither,
  Thus deviating, must perforce the rays
  Of the true love less vividly mount upward.

But in commensuration of our wages
  With our desert is portion of our joy,
  Because we see them neither less nor greater.

Herein doth living Justice sweeten so
  Affection in us, that for evermore
  It cannot warp to any iniquity.

Voices diverse make up sweet melodies;
  So in this life of ours the seats diverse
  Render sweet harmony among these spheres;

And in the compass of this present pearl
  Shineth the sheen of Romeo, of whom
  The grand and beauteous work was ill rewarded.

But the Provencals who against him wrought,
  They have not laughed, and therefore ill goes he
  Who makes his hurt of the good deeds of others.

Four daughters, and each one of them a queen,
  Had Raymond Berenger, and this for him
  Did Romeo, a poor man and a pilgrim;

And then malicious words incited him
  To summon to a reckoning this just man,
  Who rendered to him seven and five for ten.

Then he departed poor and stricken in years,
  And if the world could know the heart he had,
  In begging bit by bit his livelihood,

assai lo loda, e piu` lo loderebbe"".

Though much it laud him, it would laud him more."

Paradiso: Canto VII

Beatrice's Discourse of the Crucifixion, the Incarnation, the Immortality of the Soul, and the Resurrection of the Body.

""Osanna, sanctus Deus sabaoth,
  superillustrans claritate tua
  felices ignes horum malacoth!"".

Cosi`, volgendosi a la nota sua,
  fu viso a me cantare essa sustanza,
  sopra la qual doppio lume s'addua:

ed essa e l'altre mossero a sua danza,
  e quasi velocissime faville,
  mi si velar di subita distanza.

Io dubitava e dicea 'Dille, dille!'
  fra me, 'dille', dicea, 'a la mia donna
  che mi diseta con le dolci stille'.

Ma quella reverenza che s'indonna
  di tutto me, pur per Be e per ice,
  mi richinava come l'uom ch'assonna.

Poco sofferse me cotal Beatrice
  e comincio`, raggiandomi d'un riso
  tal, che nel foco faria l'uom felice:

""Secondo mio infallibile avviso,
  come giusta vendetta giustamente
  punita fosse, t'ha in pensier miso;

ma io ti solvero` tosto la mente;
  e tu ascolta, che' le mie parole
  di gran sentenza ti faran presente.

Per non soffrire a la virtu` che vole
  freno a suo prode, quell'uom che non nacque,
  dannando se', danno` tutta sua prole;

"Osanna sanctus Deus Sabaoth,
  Superillustrans claritate tua
  Felices ignes horum malahoth!"

In this wise, to his melody returning,
  This substance, upon which a double light
  Doubles itself, was seen by me to sing,

And to their dance this and the others moved,
  And in the manner of swift-hurrying sparks
  Veiled themselves from me with a sudden distance.

Doubting was I, and saying, "Tell her, tell her,"
  Within me, "tell her," saying, "tell my Lady,"
  Who slakes my thirst with her sweet effluences;

And yet that reverence which doth lord it over
  The whole of me only by B and ICE,
  Bowed me again like unto one who drowses.

Short while did Beatrice endure me thus;
  And she began, lighting me with a smile
  Such as would make one happy in the fire:

"According to infallible advisement,
  After what manner a just vengeance justly
  Could be avenged has put thee upon thinking,

But I will speedily thy mind unloose;
  And do thou listen, for these words of mine
  Of a great doctrine will a present make thee.

By not enduring on the power that wills
  Curb for his good, that man who ne'er was born,
  Damning himself damned all his progeny;

onde l'umana specie inferma giacque
  giu` per secoli molti in grande errore,
  fin ch'al Verbo di Dio discender piacque

u' la natura, che dal suo fattore
  s'era allungata, uni` a se' in persona
  con l'atto sol del suo etterno amore.

Or drizza il viso a quel ch'or si ragiona:
  questa natura al suo fattore unita,
  qual fu creata, fu sincera e buona;

ma per se' stessa pur fu ella sbandita
  di paradiso, pero` che si torse
  da via di verita` e da sua vita.

La pena dunque che la croce porse
  s'a la natura assunta si misura,
  nulla gia` mai si` giustamente morse;

e cosi` nulla fu di tanta ingiura,
  guardando a la persona che sofferse,
  in che era contratta tal natura.

Pero` d'un atto uscir cose diverse:
  ch'a Dio e a' Giudei piacque una morte;
  per lei tremo` la terra e 'l ciel s'aperse.

Non ti dee oramai parer piu` forte,
  quando si dice che giusta vendetta
  poscia vengiata fu da giusta corte.

Ma io veggi' or la tua mente ristretta
  di pensiero in pensier dentro ad un nodo,
  del qual con gran disio solver s'aspetta.

Tu dici: "Ben discerno cio` ch'i' odo;
  ma perche' Dio volesse, m'e` occulto,
  a nostra redenzion pur questo modo".

Questo decreto, frate, sta sepulto
  a li occhi di ciascuno il cui ingegno
  ne la fiamma d'amor non e` adulto.

Veramente, pero` ch'a questo segno
  molto si mira e poco si discerne,
  diro` perche' tal modo fu piu` degno.

La divina bonta`, che da se' sperne
  ogne livore, ardendo in se', sfavilla
  si` che dispiega le bellezze etterne.

Whereby the human species down below
  Lay sick for many centuries in great error,
  Till to descend it pleased the Word of God

To where the nature, which from its own Maker
  Estranged itself, he joined to him in person
  By the sole act of his eternal love.

Now unto what is said direct thy sight;
  This nature when united to its Maker,
  Such as created, was sincere and good;

But by itself alone was banished forth
  From Paradise, because it turned aside
  Out of the way of truth and of its life.

Therefore the penalty the cross held out,
  If measured by the nature thus assumed,
  None ever yet with so great justice stung,

And none was ever of so great injustice,
  Considering who the Person was that suffered,
  Within whom such a nature was contracted.

From one act therefore issued things diverse;
  To God and to the Jews one death was pleasing;
  Earth trembled at it and the Heaven was opened.

It should no longer now seem difficult
  To thee, when it is said that a just vengeance
  By a just court was afterward avenged.

But now do I behold thy mind entangled
  From thought to thought within a knot, from which
  With great desire it waits to free itself.

Thou sayest, 'Well discern I what I hear;
  But it is hidden from me why God willed
  For our redemption only this one mode.'

Buried remaineth, brother, this decree
  Unto the eyes of every one whose nature
  Is in the flame of love not yet adult.

Verily, inasmuch as at this mark
  One gazes long and little is discerned,
  Wherefore this mode was worthiest will I say.

Goodness Divine, which from itself doth spurn
  All envy, burning in itself so sparkles
  That the eternal beauties it unfolds.

Cio` che da lei sanza mezzo distilla
  non ha poi fine, perche' non si move
  la sua imprenta quand'ella sigilla.
	Whate'er from this immediately distils
	  Has afterwards no end, for ne'er removed
	  Is its impression when it sets its seal.

Cio` che da essa sanza mezzo piove   libero e` tutto, perche' non soggiace a la virtute de le cose nove.	Whate'er from this immediately rains down Is wholly free, because it is not subject Unto the influences of novel things.

Piu` l'e` conforme, e pero` piu` le piace;
  che' l'ardor santo ch'ogne cosa raggia,
  ne la piu` somigliante e` piu` vivace.
	The more conformed thereto, the more it pleases;
	  For the blest ardour that irradiates all things
	  In that most like itself is most vivacious.

Di tutte queste dote s'avvantaggia
  l'umana creatura; e s'una manca,
  di sua nobilita` convien che caggia.
	With all of these things has advantaged been
	  The human creature; and if one be wanting,
	  From his nobility he needs must fall.

Solo il peccato e` quel che la disfranca
  e falla dissimile al sommo bene,
  per che del lume suo poco s'imbianca;
	'Tis sin alone which doth disfranchise him,
	  And render him unlike the Good Supreme,
	  So that he little with its light is blanched,

e in sua dignita` mai non rivene,
  se non riempie, dove colpa vota,
  contra mal dilettar con giuste pene.
	And to his dignity no more returns,
	  Unless he fill up where transgression empties
	  With righteous pains for criminal delights.

Vostra natura, quando pecco` tota
  nel seme suo, da queste dignitadi,
  come di paradiso, fu remota;
	Your nature when it sinned so utterly
	  In its own seed, out of these dignities
	  Even as out of Paradise was driven,

ne' ricovrar potiensi, se tu badi
  ben sottilmente, per alcuna via,
  sanza passar per un di questi guadi:
	Nor could itself recover, if thou notest
	  With nicest subtilty, by any way,
	  Except by passing one of these two fords:

o che Dio solo per sua cortesia
  dimesso avesse, o che l'uom per se' isso
  avesse sodisfatto a sua follia.
	Either that God through clemency alone
	  Had pardon granted, or that man himself
	  Had satisfaction for his folly made.

Ficca mo l'occhio per entro l'abisso
  de l'etterno consiglio, quanto puoi
  al mio parlar distrettamente fisso.
	Fix now thine eye deep into the abyss
	  Of the eternal counsel, to my speech
	  As far as may be fastened steadfastly!

Non potea l'uomo ne' termini suoi
  mai sodisfar, per non potere ir giuso
  con umiltate obediendo poi,
	Man in his limitations had not power
	  To satisfy, not having power to sink
	  In his humility obeying then,

quanto disobediendo intese ir suso;
  e questa e` la cagion per che l'uom fue
  da poter sodisfar per se' dischiuso.
	Far as he disobeying thought to rise;
	  And for this reason man has been from power
	  Of satisfying by himself excluded.

Dunque a Dio convenia con le vie sue
  riparar l'omo a sua intera vita,
  dico con l'una, o ver con amendue.
	Therefore it God behoved in his own ways
	  Man to restore unto his perfect life,
	  I say in one, or else in both of them.

Ma perche' l'ovra tanto e` piu` gradita
  da l'operante, quanto piu` appresenta
  de la bonta` del core ond'ell'e` uscita,

la divina bonta` che 'l mondo imprenta,
  di proceder per tutte le sue vie,
  a rilevarvi suso, fu contenta.

Ne' tra l'ultima notte e 'l primo die
  si` alto o si` magnifico processo,
  o per l'una o per l'altra, fu o fie:

che' piu` largo fu Dio a dar se' stesso
  per far l'uom sufficiente a rilevarsi,
  che s'elli avesse sol da se' dimesso;

e tutti li altri modi erano scarsi
  a la giustizia, se 'l Figliuol di Dio
  non fosse umiliato ad incarnarsi.

Or per empierti bene ogni disio,
  ritorno a dichiararti in alcun loco,
  perche' tu veggi li` cosi` com'io.

Tu dici: "Io veggio l'acqua, io veggio il foco,
  l'aere e la terra e tutte lor misture
  venire a corruzione, e durar poco;

e queste cose pur furon creature;
  per che, se cio` ch'e` detto e` stato vero,
  esser dovrien da corruzion sicure".

Li angeli, frate, e 'l paese sincero
  nel qual tu se', dir si posson creati,
  si` come sono, in loro essere intero;

ma li elementi che tu hai nomati
  e quelle cose che di lor si fanno
  da creata virtu` sono informati.

Creata fu la materia ch'elli hanno;
  creata fu la virtu` informante
  in queste stelle che 'ntorno a lor vanno.

L'anima d'ogne bruto e de le piante
  di complession potenziata tira
  lo raggio e 'l moto de le luci sante;

ma vostra vita sanza mezzo spira
  la somma beninanza, e la innamora
  di se' si` che poi sempre la disira.

But since the action of the doer is
  So much more grateful, as it more presents
  The goodness of the heart from which it issues,

Goodness Divine, that doth imprint the world,
  Has been contented to proceed by each
  And all its ways to lift you up again;

Nor 'twixt the first day and the final night
  Such high and such magnificent proceeding
  By one or by the other was or shall be;

For God more bounteous was himself to give
  To make man able to uplift himself,
  Than if he only of himself had pardoned;

And all the other modes were insufficient
  For justice, were it not the Son of God
  Himself had humbled to become incarnate.

Now, to fill fully each desire of thine,
  Return I to elucidate one place,
  In order that thou there mayst see as I do.

Thou sayst: 'I see the air, I see the fire,
  The water, and the earth, and all their mixtures
  Come to corruption, and short while endure;

And these things notwithstanding were created;'
  Therefore if that which I have said were true,
  They should have been secure against corruption.

The Angels, brother, and the land sincere
  In which thou art, created may be called
  Just as they are in their entire existence;

But all the elements which thou hast named,
  And all those things which out of them are made,
  By a created virtue are informed.

Created was the matter which they have;
  Created was the informing influence
  Within these stars that round about them go.

The soul of every brute and of the plants
  By its potential temperament attracts
  The ray and motion of the holy lights;

But your own life immediately inspires
  Supreme Beneficence, and enamours it
  So with herself, it evermore desires her.

E quinci puoi argomentare ancora
vostra resurrezion, se tu ripensi
come l'umana carne fessi allora

che li primi parenti intrambo fensi"".

And thou from this mayst argue furthermore
Your resurrection, if thou think again
How human flesh was fashioned at that time

When the first parents both of them were made."

Paradiso: Canto VIII

Ascent to the Third Heaven, Venus: Lovers. Charles Martel. Discourse on diverse Natures.

Solea creder lo mondo in suo periclo
  che la bella Ciprigna il folle amore
  raggiasse, volta nel terzo epiciclo;
	The world used in its peril to believe
	  That the fair Cypria delirious love
	  Rayed out, in the third epicycle turning;

per che non pur a lei faceano onore
  di sacrificio e di votivo grido
  le genti antiche ne l'antico errore;
	Wherefore not only unto her paid honour
	  Of sacrifices and of votive cry
	  The ancient nations in the ancient error,

ma Dione onoravano e Cupido,
  quella per madre sua, questo per figlio,
  e dicean ch'el sedette in grembo a Dido;
	But both Dione honoured they and Cupid,
	  That as her mother, this one as her son,
	  And said that he had sat in Dido's lap;

e da costei ond'io principio piglio
  pigliavano il vocabol de la stella
  che 'l sol vagheggia or da coppa or da ciglio.
	And they from her, whence I beginning take,
	  Took the denomination of the star
	  That woos the sun, now following, now in front.

Io non m'accorsi del salire in ella;
  ma d'esservi entro mi fe' assai fede
  la donna mia ch'i' vidi far più bella.
	I was not ware of our ascending to it;
	  But of our being in it gave full faith
	  My Lady whom I saw more beauteous grow.

E come in fiamma favilla si vede,
  e come in voce voce si discerne,
  quand'una è ferma e altra va e riede,
	And as within a flame a spark is seen,
	  And as within a voice a voice discerned,
	  When one is steadfast, and one comes and goes,

vid'io in essa luce altre lucerne
  muoversi in giro più e men correnti,
  al modo, credo, di lor viste interne.
	Within that light beheld I other lamps
	  Move in a circle, speeding more and less,
	  Methinks in measure of their inward vision.

Di fredda nube non disceser venti,
  o visibili o no, tanto festini,
  che non paressero impediti e lenti
	From a cold cloud descended never winds,
	  Or visible or not, so rapidly
	  They would not laggard and impeded seem

a chi avesse quei lumi divini
  veduti a noi venir, lasciando il giro
  pria cominciato in li alti Serafini;
	To any one who had those lights divine
	  Seen come towards us, leaving the gyration
	  Begun at first in the high Seraphim.

e dentro a quei che piu` innanzi appariro   sonava 'Osanna' si`, che unque poi di riudir non fui sanza disiro.	And behind those that most in front appeared Sounded "Osanna!" so that never since To hear again was I without desire.
Indi si fece l'un piu` presso a noi   e solo incomincio`: ""Tutti sem presti al tuo piacer, perche' di noi ti gioi.	Then unto us more nearly one approached, And it alone began: "We all are ready Unto thy pleasure, that thou joy in us.

Noi ci volgiam coi principi celesti
  d'un giro e d'un girare e d'una sete,
  ai quali tu del mondo gia` dicesti:
	We turn around with the celestial Princes,
	  One gyre and one gyration and one thirst,
	  To whom thou in the world of old didst say,

'Voi che 'ntendendo il terzo ciel movete';
  e sem si` pien d'amor, che, per piacerti,
  non fia men dolce un poco di quiete"".
	'Ye who, intelligent, the third heaven are moving;'
	  And are so full of love, to pleasure thee
	  A little quiet will not be less sweet."

Poscia che li occhi miei si fuoro offerti
  a la mia donna reverenti, ed essa
  fatti li avea di se' contenti e certi,
	After these eyes of mine themselves had offered
	  Unto my Lady reverently, and she
	  Content and certain of herself had made them,

rivolsersi a la luce che promessa
  tanto s'avea, e ""Deh, chi siete?"" fue
  la voce mia di grande affetto impressa.
	Back to the light they turned, which so great promise
	  Made of itself, and "Say, who art thou?" was
	  My voice, imprinted with a great affection.

E quanta e quale vid'io lei far piue
  per allegrezza nova che s'accrebbe,
  quando parlai, a l'allegrezze sue!
	O how and how much I beheld it grow
	  With the new joy that superadded was
	  Unto its joys, as soon as I had spoken!

Cosi` fatta, mi disse: ""Il mondo m'ebbe   giu` poco tempo; e se piu` fosse stato,   molto sara` di mal, che non sarebbe.	Thus changed, it said to me: "The world possessed me Short time below; and, if it had been more, Much evil will be which would not have been.

La mia letizia mi ti tien celato
  che mi raggia dintorno e mi nasconde
  quasi animal di sua seta fasciato.
	My gladness keepeth me concealed from thee,
	  Which rayeth round about me, and doth hide me
	  Like as a creature swathed in its own silk.

Assai m'amasti, e avesti ben onde; che s'io fossi giu` stato, io ti mostrava   di mio amor piu` oltre che le fronde.	Much didst thou love me, and thou hadst good rea- son; For had I been below, I should have shown thee Somewhat beyond the foliage of my love.

Quella sinistra riva che si lava
  di Rodano poi ch'e` misto con Sorga,
  per suo segnore a tempo m'aspettava,
	That left-hand margin, which doth bathe itself
	  In Rhone, when it is mingled with the Sorgue,
	  Me for its lord awaited in due time,

e quel corno d'Ausonia che s'imborga
  di Bari e di Gaeta e di Catona
  da ove Tronto e Verde in mare sgorga.
	And that horn of Ausonia, which is towned
	  With Bari, with Gaeta and Catona,
	  Whence Tronto and Verde in the sea disgorge.

Fulgeami gia` in fronte la corona	Already flashed upon my brow the crown
di quella terra che 'l Danubio riga	Of that dominion which the Danube waters
poi che le ripe tedesche abbandona.	After the German borders it abandons;
E la bella Trinacria, che caliga	And beautiful Trinacria, that is murky
tra Pachino e Peloro, sopra 'l golfo	'Twixt Pachino and Peloro, (on the gulf
che riceve da Euro maggior briga,	Which greatest scath from Eurus doth receive,)
non per Tifeo ma per nascente solfo,	Not through Typhoeus, but through nascent sulphur,
attesi avrebbe li suoi regi ancora,	Would have awaited her own monarchs still,
nati per me di Carlo e di Ridolfo,	Through me from Charles descended and from Ru-dolph,
se mala segnoria, che sempre accora	If evil lordship, that exasperates ever
li popoli suggetti, non avesse	The subject populations, had not moved
mosso Palermo a gridar: "Mora, mora!".	Palermo to the outcry of 'Death! death!'
E se mio frate questo antivedesse,	And if my brother could but this foresee,
l'avara poverta` di Catalogna	The greedy poverty of Catalonia
gia` fuggeria, perche' non li offendesse;	Straight would he flee, that it might not molest him;
che' veramente proveder bisogna	For verily 'tis needful to provide,
per lui, o per altrui, si` ch'a sua barca	Through him or other, so that on his bark
carcata piu` d'incarco non si pogna.	Already freighted no more freight be placed.
La sua natura, che di larga parca	His nature, which from liberal covetous
discese, avria mestier di tal milizia	Descended, such a soldiery would need
che non curasse di mettere in arca""`.	As should not care for hoarding in a chest."
""Pero` ch'i' credo che l'alta letizia	"Because I do believe the lofty joy
che 'l tuo parlar m'infonde, segnor mio,	Thy speech infuses into me, my Lord,
la` 've ogne ben si termina e s'inizia,	Where every good thing doth begin and end
per te si veggia come la vegg'io,	Thou seest as I see it, the more grateful
grata m'e` piu`; e anco quest'ho caro	Is it to me; and this too hold I dear,
perche' 'l discerni rimirando in Dio.	That gazing upon God thou dost discern it.
Fatto m'hai lieto, e cosi` mi fa chiaro,	Glad hast thou made me; so make clear to me,
poi che, parlando, a dubitar m'hai mosso	Since speaking thou hast stirred me up to doubt,
com'esser puo`, di dolce seme, amaro""`.	How from sweet seed can bitter issue forth."
Questo io a lui; ed elli a me: ""S'io posso	This I to him; and he to me: "If I
mostrarti un vero, a quel che tu dimandi	Can show to thee a truth, to what thou askest
terrai lo viso come tien lo dosso.	Thy face thou'lt hold as thou dost hold thy back.
Lo ben che tutto il regno che tu scandi	The Good which all the realm thou art ascending
volge e contenta, fa esser virtute	Turns and contents, maketh its providence
sua provedenza in questi corpi grandi.	To be a power within these bodies vast;

E non pur le nature provedute
  sono in la mente ch'e` da se' perfetta,
  ma esse insieme con la lor salute:

per che quantunque quest'arco saetta
  disposto cade a proveduto fine,
  si` come cosa in suo segno diretta.

Se cio` non fosse, il ciel che tu cammine
  producerebbe si` li suoi effetti,
  che non sarebbero arti, ma ruine;

e cio` esser non puo`, se li 'ntelletti
  che muovon queste stelle non son manchi,
  e manco il primo, che non li ha perfetti.

Vuo' tu che questo ver piu` ti s'imbianchi?"".
  E io: ""Non gia`; che' impossibil veggio
  che la natura, in quel ch'e` uopo, stanchi"".

Ond'elli ancora: ""Or di': sarebbe il peggio
  per l'omo in terra, se non fosse cive?"".
  ""Si`"", rispuos'io; ""e qui ragion non cheggio"".

""E puot'elli esser, se giu` non si vive
  diversamente per diversi offici?
  Non, se 'l maestro vostro ben vi scrive"".

Si` venne deducendo infino a quici;
  poscia conchiuse: ""Dunque esser diverse
  convien di vostri effetti le radici:

per ch'un nasce Solone e altro Serse,
  altro Melchisedech e altro quello
  che, volando per l'aere, il figlio perse.

La circular natura, ch'e` suggello
  a la cera mortal, fa ben sua arte,
  ma non distingue l'un da l'altro ostello.

Quinci addivien ch'Esau` si diparte
  per seme da Iacob; e vien Quirino
  da si` vil padre, che si rende a Marte.

Natura generata il suo cammino
  simil farebbe sempre a' generanti,
  se non vincesse il proveder divino.

And not alone the natures are foreseen
  Within the mind that in itself is perfect,
  But they together with their preservation.

For whatsoever thing this bow shoots forth
  Falls foreordained unto an end foreseen,
  Even as a shaft directed to its mark.

If that were not, the heaven which thou dost walk
  Would in such manner its effects produce,
  That they no longer would be arts, but ruins.

This cannot be, if the Intelligences
  That keep these stars in motion are not maimed,
  And maimed the First that has not made them perfect.

Wilt thou this truth have clearer made to thee?"
  And I: "Not so; for 'tis impossible
  That nature tire, I see, in what is needful."

Whence he again: "Now say, would it be worse
  For men on earth were they not citizens?"
  "Yes," I replied; "and here I ask no reason."

"And can they be so, if below they live not
  Diversely unto offices diverse?
  No, if your master writeth well for you."

So came he with deductions to this point;
  Then he concluded: "Therefore it behoves
  The roots of your effects to be diverse.

Hence one is Solon born, another Xerxes,
  Another Melchisedec, and another he
  Who, flying through the air, his son did lose.

Revolving Nature, which a signet is
  To mortal wax, doth practise well her art,
  But not one inn distinguish from another;

Thence happens it that Esau differeth
  In seed from Jacob; and Quirinus comes
  From sire so vile that he is given to Mars.

A generated nature its own way
  Would always make like its progenitors,
  If Providence divine were not triumphant.

Or quel che t'era dietro t'e` davanti:
  ma perche' sappi che di te mi giova,
  un corollario voglio che t'ammanti.

Sempre natura, se fortuna trova
  discorde a se', com'ogne altra semente
  fuor di sua region, fa mala prova.

E se 'l mondo la` giu` ponesse mente
  al fondamento che natura pone,
  seguendo lui, avria buona la gente.

Ma voi torcete a la religione
  tal che fia nato a cignersi la spada,
  e fate re di tal ch'e` da sermone;

onde la traccia vostra e` fuor di strada""".

Now that which was behind thee is before thee;
  But that thou know that I with thee am pleased,
  With a corollary will I mantle thee.

Evermore nature, if it fortune find
  Discordant to it, like each other seed
  Out of its region, maketh evil thrift;

And if the world below would fix its mind
  On the foundation which is laid by nature,
  Pursuing that, 'twould have the people good.

But you unto religion wrench aside
  Him who was born to gird him with the sword,
  And make a king of him who is for sermons;

Therefore your footsteps wander from the road."

Paradiso: Canto IX

Cunizza da Romano, Folco of Marseilles, and Rahab. Neglect of the Holy Land.

Da poi che Carlo tuo, bella Clemenza,
  m'ebbe chiarito, mi narro` li 'nganni
  che ricever dovea la sua semenza;

ma disse: ““Taci e lascia muover li anni”“;
  si` ch'io non posso dir se non che pianto
  giusto verra` di retro ai vostri danni.

E gia` la vita di quel lume santo
  rivolta s'era al Sol che la riempie
  come quel ben ch'a ogne cosa e` tanto.

Ahi anime ingannate e fatture empie,
  che da si` fatto ben torcete i cuori,
  drizzando in vanita` le vostre tempie!

Ed ecco un altro di quelli splendori
  ver' me si fece, e 'l suo voler piacermi
  significava nel chiarir di fori.

Li occhi di Beatrice, ch'eran fermi
  sovra me, come pria, di caro assenso
  al mio disio certificato fermi.

““Deh, metti al mio voler tosto compenso,
  beato spirto”“, dissi, ““e fammi prova
  ch'i' possa in te refletter quel ch'io penso!”“.

Onde la luce che m'era ancor nova,
  del suo profondo, ond'ella pria cantava,
  seguette come a cui di ben far giova:

““In quella parte de la terra prava
  italica che siede tra Rialto
  e le fontane di Brenta e di Piava,

Beautiful Clemence, after that thy Charles
  Had me enlightened, he narrated to me
  The treacheries his seed should undergo;

But said: "Be still and let the years roll round;"
  So I can only say, that lamentation
  Legitimate shall follow on your wrongs.

And of that holy light the life already
  Had to the Sun which fills it turned again,
  As to that good which for each thing sufficeth.

Ah, souls deceived, and creatures impious,
  Who from such good do turn away your hearts,
  Directing upon vanity your foreheads!

And now, behold, another of those splendours
  Approached me, and its will to pleasure me
  It signified by brightening outwardly.

The eyes of Beatrice, that fastened were
  Upon me, as before, of dear assent
  To my desire assurance gave to me.

"Ah, bring swift compensation to my wish,
  Thou blessed spirit," I said, "and give me proof
  That what I think in thee I can reflect!"

Whereat the light, that still was new to me,
  Out of its depths, whence it before was singing,
  As one delighted to do good, continued:

"Within that region of the land depraved
  Of Italy, that lies between Rialto
  And fountain-heads of Brenta and of Piava,

si leva un colle, e non surge molt'alto,
  la` onde scese gia` una facella
  che fece a la contrada un grande assalto.

D'una radice nacqui e io ed ella:
  Cunizza fui chiamata, e qui refulgo
  perche' mi vinse il lume d'esta stella;

ma lietamente a me medesma indulgo
  la cagion di mia sorte, e non mi noia;
  che parria forse forte al vostro vulgo.

Di questa luculenta e cara gioia
  del nostro cielo che piu` m'e` propinqua,
  grande fama rimase; e pria che moia,

questo centesimo anno ancor s'incinqua:
  vedi se far si dee l'omo eccellente,
  si` ch'altra vita la prima relinqua.

E cio` non pensa la turba presente
  che Tagliamento e Adice richiude,
  ne' per esser battuta ancor si pente;

ma tosto fia che Padova al palude
  cangera` l'acqua che Vincenza bagna,
  per essere al dover le genti crude;

e dove Sile e Cagnan s'accompagna,
  tal signoreggia e va con la testa alta,
  che gia` per lui carpir si fa la ragna.

Piangera` Feltro ancora la difalta
  de l'empio suo pastor, che sara` sconcia
  si`, che per simil non s'entro` in malta.

Troppo sarebbe larga la bigoncia
  che ricevesse il sangue ferrarese,
  e stanco chi 'l pesasse a oncia a oncia,

che donera` questo prete cortese
  per mostrarsi di parte; e cotai doni
  conformi fieno al viver del paese.

Su` sono specchi, voi dicete Troni,
  onde refulge a noi Dio giudicante;
  si` che questi parlar ne paion buoni'"".

Rises a hill, and mounts not very high,
  Wherefrom descended formerly a torch
  That made upon that region great assault.

Out of one root were born both I and it;
  Cunizza was I called, and here I shine
  Because the splendour of this star o'ercame me.

But gladly to myself the cause I pardon
  Of my allotment, and it does not grieve me;
  Which would perhaps seem strong unto your vul-
    gar.

Of this so luculent and precious jewel,
  Which of our heaven is nearest unto me,
  Great fame remained; and ere it die away

This hundredth year shall yet quintupled be.
  See if man ought to make him excellent,
  So that another life the first may leave!

And thus thinks not the present multitude
  Shut in by Adige and Tagliamento,
  Nor yet for being scourged is penitent.

But soon 'twill be that Padua in the marsh
  Will change the water that Vicenza bathes,
  Because the folk are stubborn against duty;

And where the Sile and Cagnano join
  One lordeth it, and goes with lofty head,
  For catching whom e'en now the net is making.

Feltro moreover of her impious pastor
  Shall weep the crime, which shall so monstrous be
  That for the like none ever entered Malta.

Ample exceedingly would be the vat
  That of the Ferrarese could hold the blood,
  And weary who should weigh it ounce by ounce,

Of which this courteous priest shall make a gift
  To show himself a partisan; and such gifts
  Will to the living of the land conform.

Above us there are mirrors, Thrones you call them,
  From which shines out on us God Judicant,
  So that this utterance seems good to us."

Qui si tacette; e fecemi sembiante
  che fosse ad altro volta, per la rota
  in che si mise com'era davante.

L'altra letizia, che m'era gia` nota
  per cara cosa, mi si fece in vista
  qual fin balasso in che lo sol percuota.

Per letiziar la` su` fulgor s'acquista,
  si` come riso qui; ma giu` s'abbuia
  l'ombra di fuor, come la mente e` trista.

""Dio vede tutto, e tuo veder s'inluia"",
  diss'io, ""beato spirto, si` che nulla
  voglia di se' a te puot'esser fuia.

Dunque la voce tua, che 'l ciel trastulla
  sempre col canto di quei fuochi pii
  che di sei ali facen la coculla,

perche' non satisface a' miei disii?
  Gia` non attendere' io tua dimanda,
  s'io m'intuassi, come tu t'inmii"".

""La maggior valle in che l'acqua si spanda"",
  incominciaro allor le sue parole,
  ""fuor di quel mar che la terra inghirlanda,

tra ' discordanti liti contra 'l sole
  tanto sen va, che fa meridiano
  la` dove l'orizzonte pria far suole.

Di quella valle fu' io litorano
  tra Ebro e Macra, che per cammin corto
  parte lo Genovese dal Toscano.

Ad un occaso quasi e ad un orto
  Buggea siede e la terra ond'io fui,
  che fe' del sangue suo gia` caldo il porto.

Folco mi disse quella gente a cui
  fu noto il nome mio; e questo cielo
  di me s'imprenta, com'io fe' di lui;

che' piu` non arse la figlia di Belo,
  noiando e a Sicheo e a Creusa,
  di me, infin che si convenne al pelo;

ne' quella Rodopea che delusa
  fu da Demofoonte, ne' Alcide
  quando Iole nel core ebbe rinchiusa.

Here it was silent, and it had the semblance
  Of being turned elsewhither, by the wheel
  On which it entered as it was before.

The other joy, already known to me,
  Became a thing transplendent in my sight,
  As a fine ruby smitten by the sun.

Through joy effulgence is acquired above,
  As here a smile; but down below, the shade
  Outwardly darkens, as the mind is sad.

"God seeth all things, and in Him, blest spirit,
  Thy sight is," said I, "so that never will
  Of his can possibly from thee be hidden;

Thy voice, then, that for ever makes the heavens
  Glad, with the singing of those holy fires
  Which of their six wings make themselves a cowl,

Wherefore does it not satisfy my longings?
  Indeed, I would not wait thy questioning
  If I in thee were as thou art in me."

"The greatest of the valleys where the water
  Expands itself," forthwith its words began,
  "That sea excepted which the earth engarlands,

Between discordant shores against the sun
  Extends so far, that it meridian makes
  Where it was wont before to make the horizon.

I was a dweller on that valley's shore
  'Twixt Ebro and Magra that with journey short
  Doth from the Tuscan part the Genoese.

With the same sunset and same sunrise nearly
  Sit Buggia and the city whence I was,
  That with its blood once made the harbour hot.

Folco that people called me unto whom
  My name was known; and now with me this heaven
  Imprints itself, as I did once with it;

For more the daughter of Belus never burned,
  Offending both Sichaeus and Creusa,
  Than I, so long as it became my locks,

Nor yet that Rodophean, who deluded
  was by Demophoon, nor yet Alcides,
  When Iole he in his heart had locked.

Non pero` qui si pente, ma si ride,   non de la colpa, ch'a mente non torna,   ma del valor ch'ordino` e provide.	Yet here is no repenting, but we smile, Not at the fault, which comes not back to mind, But at the power which ordered and foresaw.

Qui si rimira ne l'arte ch'addorna
  cotanto affetto, e discernesi 'l bene
  per che 'l mondo di su` quel di giu` torna.
	Here we behold the art that doth adorn
	  With such affection, and the good discover
	  Whereby the world above turns that below.

Ma perche' tutte le tue voglie piene
  ten porti che son nate in questa spera,
  proceder ancor oltre mi convene.
	But that thou wholly satisfied mayst bear
	  Thy wishes hence which in this sphere are born,
	  Still farther to proceed behoveth me.

Tu vuo' saper chi e` in questa lumera   che qui appresso me cosi` scintilla, come raggio di sole in acqua mera.	Thou fain wouldst know who is within this light That here beside me thus is scintillating, Even as a sunbeam in the limpid water.

Or sappi che la` entro si tranquilla
  Raab; e a nostr'ordine congiunta,
  di lei nel sommo grado si sigilla.
	Then know thou, that within there is at rest
	  Rahab, and being to our order joined,
	  With her in its supremest grade 'tis sealed.

Da questo cielo, in cui l'ombra s'appunta
  che 'l vostro mondo face, pria ch'altr'alma
  del triunfo di Cristo fu assunta.
	Into this heaven, where ends the shadowy cone
	  Cast by your world, before all other souls
	  First of Christ's triumph was she taken up.

Ben si convenne lei lasciar per palma
  in alcun cielo de l'alta vittoria
  che s'acquisto` con l'una e l'altra palma,
	Full meet it was to leave her in some heaven,
	  Even as a palm of the high victory
	  Which he acquired with one palm and the other,

perch'ella favoro` la prima gloria   di Iosue` in su la Terra Santa, che poco tocca al papa la memoria.	Because she favoured the first glorious deed Of Joshua upon the Holy Land, That little stirs the memory of the Pope.

La tua citta`, che di colui e` pianta
  che pria volse le spalle al suo fattore
  e di cui e` la 'nvidia tanto pianta,
	Thy city, which an offshoot is of him
	  Who first upon his Maker turned his back,
	  And whose ambition is so sorely wept,

produce e spande il maladetto fiore
  c'ha disviate le pecore e li agni,
  pero` che fatto ha lupo del pastore.
	Brings forth and scatters the accursed flower
	  Which both the sheep and lambs hath led astray
	  Since it has turned the shepherd to a wolf.

Per questo l'Evangelio e i dottor magni
  son derelitti, e solo ai Decretali
  si studia, si` che pare a' lor vivagni.
	For this the Evangel and the mighty Doctors
	  Are derelict, and only the Decretals
	  So studied that it shows upon their margins.

A questo intende il papa e ' cardinali;
  non vanno i lor pensieri a Nazarette,
  la` dove Gabriello aperse l'ali.
	On this are Pope and Cardinals intent;
	  Their meditations reach not Nazareth,
	  There where his pinions Gabriel unfolded;

Ma Vaticano e l'altre parti elette
  di Roma che son state cimitero
  a la milizia che Pietro seguette,
	But Vatican and the other parts elect
	  Of Rome, which have a cemetery been
	  Unto the soldiery that followed Peter

tosto libere fien de l'avoltero"".

Shall soon be free from this adultery."

Paradiso: Canto X

The Fourth Heaven, the Sun: Theologians and Fathers of the Church. The First Circle. St. Thomas of Aquinas.

Guardando nel suo Figlio con l'Amore
  che l'uno e l'altro etternalmente spira,
  lo primo e ineffabile Valore
	Looking into his Son with all the Love
	  Which each of them eternally breathes forth,
	  The Primal and unutterable Power

quanto per mente e per loco si gira
  con tant'ordine fe', ch'esser non puote
  sanza gustar di lui chi cio` rimira.
	Whate'er before the mind or eye revolves
	  With so much order made, there can be none
	  Who this beholds without enjoying Him.

Leva dunque, lettore, a l'alte rote
  meco la vista, dritto a quella parte
  dove l'un moto e l'altro si percuote;
	Lift up then, Reader, to the lofty wheels
	  With me thy vision straight unto that part
	  Where the one motion on the other strikes,

e li` comincia a vagheggiar ne l'arte
  di quel maestro che dentro a se' l'ama,
  tanto che mai da lei l'occhio non parte.
	And there begin to contemplate with joy
	  That Master's art, who in himself so loves it
	  That never doth his eye depart therefrom.

Vedi come da indi si dirama
  l'oblico cerchio che i pianeti porta,
  per sodisfare al mondo che li chiama.
	Behold how from that point goes branching off
	  The oblique circle, which conveys the planets,
	  To satisfy the world that calls upon them;

Che se la strada lor non fosse torta, molta virtu` nel ciel sarebbe in vano,   e quasi ogne potenza qua giu` morta;	And if their pathway were not thus inflected, Much virtue in the heavens would be in vain, And almost every power below here dead.
e se dal dritto piu` o men lontano   fosse 'l partire, assai sarebbe manco   e giu` e su` de l'ordine mondano.	If from the straight line distant more or less Were the departure, much would wanting be Above and underneath of mundane order.

Or ti riman, lettor, sovra 'l tuo banco,
  dietro pensando a cio` che si preliba,
  s'esser vuoi lieto assai prima che stanco.
	Remain now, Reader, still upon thy bench,
	  In thought pursuing that which is foretasted,
	  If thou wouldst jocund be instead of weary.

Messo t'ho innanzi: omai per te ti ciba;
  che' a se' torce tutta la mia cura
  quella materia ond'io son fatto scriba.
	I've set before thee; henceforth feed thyself,
	  For to itself diverteth all my care
	  That theme whereof I have been made the scribe.

Lo ministro maggior de la natura,
  che del valor del ciel lo mondo imprenta
  e col suo lume il tempo ne misura,

con quella parte che su` si rammenta
  congiunto, si girava per le spire
  in che piu` tosto ognora s'appresenta;

e io era con lui; ma del salire
  non m'accors'io, se non com'uom s'accorge,
  anzi 'l primo pensier, del suo venire.

E' Beatrice quella che si` scorge
  di bene in meglio, si` subitamente
  che l'atto suo per tempo non si sporge.

Quant'esser convenia da se' lucente
  quel ch'era dentro al sol dov'io entra'mi,
  non per color, ma per lume parvente!

Perch'io lo 'ngegno e l'arte e l'uso chiami,
  si` nol direi che mai s'imaginasse;
  ma creder puossi e di veder si brami.

E se le fantasie nostre son basse
  a tanta altezza, non e` maraviglia;
  che' sopra 'l sol non fu occhio ch'andasse.

Tal era quivi la quarta famiglia
  de l'alto Padre, che sempre la sazia,
  mostrando come spira e come figlia.

E Beatrice comincio`: ""Ringrazia,
  ringrazia il Sol de li angeli, ch'a questo
  sensibil t'ha levato per sua grazia"".

Cor di mortal non fu mai si` digesto
  a divozione e a rendersi a Dio
  con tutto 'l suo gradir cotanto presto,

come a quelle parole mi fec'io;
  e si` tutto 'l mio amore in lui si mise,
  che Beatrice eclisso` ne l'oblio.

Non le dispiacque; ma si` se ne rise,
  che lo splendor de li occhi suoi ridenti
  mia mente unita in piu` cose divise.

Io vidi piu` folgor vivi e vincenti
  far di noi centro e di se' far corona,
  piu` dolci in voce che in vista lucenti:

The greatest of the ministers of nature,
  Who with the power of heaven the world imprints
  And measures with his light the time for us,

With that part which above is called to mind
  Conjoined, along the spirals was revolving,
  Where each time earlier he presents himself;

And I was with him; but of the ascending
  I was not conscious, saving as a man
  Of a first thought is conscious ere it come;

And Beatrice, she who is seen to pass
  From good to better, and so suddenly
  That not by time her action is expressed,

How lucent in herself must she have been!
  And what was in the sun, wherein I entered,
  Apparent not by colour but by light,

I, though I call on genius, art, and practice,
  Cannot so tell that it could be imagined;
  Believe one can, and let him long to see it.

And if our fantasies too lowly are
  For altitude so great, it is no marvel,
  Since o'er the sun was never eye could go.

Such in this place was the fourth family
  Of the high Father, who forever sates it,
  Showing how he breathes forth and how begets.

And Beatrice began: "Give thanks, give thanks
  Unto the Sun of Angels, who to this
  Sensible one has raised thee by his grace!"

Never was heart of mortal so disposed
  To worship, nor to give itself to God
  With all its gratitude was it so ready,

As at those words did I myself become;
  And all my love was so absorbed in Him,
  That in oblivion Beatrice was eclipsed.

Nor this displeased her; but she smiled at it
  So that the splendour of her laughing eyes
  My single mind on many things divided.

Lights many saw I, vivid and triumphant,
  Make us a centre and themselves a circle,
  More sweet in voice than luminous in aspect.

cosi` cinger la figlia di Latona   vedem talvolta, quando l'aere e` pregno, si` che ritenga il fil che fa la zona.	Thus girt about the daughter of Latona We sometimes see, when pregnant is the air, So that it holds the thread which makes her zone.

Ne la corte del cielo, ond'io rivegno,
  si trovan molte gioie care e belle
  tanto che non si posson trar del regno;
	Within the court of Heaven, whence I return,
	  Are many jewels found, so fair and precious
	  They cannot be transported from the realm;

e 'l canto di quei lumi era di quelle;
  chi non s'impenna si` che la` su` voli,
  dal muto aspetti quindi le novelle.
	And of them was the singing of those lights.
	  Who takes not wings that he may fly up thither,
	  The tidings thence may from the dumb await!

Poi, si` cantando, quelli ardenti soli
  si fuor girati intorno a noi tre volte,
  come stelle vicine a' fermi poli,
	As soon as singing thus those burning suns
	  Had round about us whirled themselves three times,
	  Like unto stars neighbouring the steadfast poles,

donne mi parver, non da ballo sciolte,
  ma che s'arrestin tacite, ascoltando
  fin che le nove note hanno ricolte.
	Ladies they seemed, not from the dance released,
	  But who stop short, in silence listening
	  Till they have gathered the new melody.

E dentro a l'un senti' cominciar: ""Quando
  lo raggio de la grazia, onde s'accende
  verace amore e che poi cresce amando,
	And within one I heard beginning: "When
	  The radiance of grace, by which is kindled
	  True love, and which thereafter grows by loving,

multiplicato in te tanto resplende,
  che ti conduce su per quella scala
  u' sanza risalir nessun discende;
	Within thee multiplied is so resplendent
	  That it conducts thee upward by that stair,
	  Where without reascending none descends,

qual ti negasse il vin de la sua fiala
  per la tua sete, in liberta` non fora
  se non com'acqua ch'al mar non si cala.
	Who should deny the wine out of his vial
	  Unto thy thirst, in liberty were not
	  Except as water which descends not seaward.

Tu vuo' saper di quai piante s'infiora
  questa ghirlanda che 'ntorno vagheggia
  la bella donna ch'al ciel t'avvalora.
	Fain wouldst thou know with what plants is enflow-
	      ered
	  This garland that encircles with delight
	  The Lady fair who makes thee strong for heaven.

Io fui de li agni de la santa greggia
  che Domenico mena per cammino
  u' ben s'impingua se non si vaneggia.
	Of the lambs was I of the holy flock
	  Which Dominic conducteth by a road
	  Where well one fattens if he strayeth not.

Questi che m'e` a destra piu` vicino,
  frate e maestro fummi, ed esso Alberto
  e` di Cologna, e io Thomas d'Aquino.
	He who is nearest to me on the right
	  My brother and master was; and he Albertus
	  Is of Cologne, I Thomas of Aquinum.

Se si` di tutti li altri esser vuo' certo,
  di retro al mio parlar ten vien col viso
  girando su per lo beato serto.
	If thou of all the others wouldst be certain,
	  Follow behind my speaking with thy sight
	  Upward along the blessed garland turning.

Quell'altro fiammeggiare esce del riso
  di Grazian, che l'uno e l'altro foro
  aiuto` si` che piace in paradiso.

L'altro ch'appresso addorna il nostro coro,
  quel Pietro fu che con la poverella
  offerse a Santa Chiesa suo tesoro.

La quinta luce, ch'e` tra noi piu` bella,
  spira di tal amor, che tutto 'l mondo
  la` giu` ne gola di saper novella:

entro v'e` l'alta mente u' si` profondo
  saver fu messo, che, se 'l vero e` vero
  a veder tanto non surse il secondo.

Appresso vedi il lume di quel cero
  che giu` in carne piu` a dentro vide
  l'angelica natura e 'l ministero.

Ne l'altra piccioletta luce ride
  quello avvocato de' tempi cristiani
  del cui latino Augustin si provide.

Or se tu l'occhio de la mente trani
  di luce in luce dietro a le mie lode,
  gia` de l'ottava con sete rimani.

Per vedere ogni ben dentro vi gode
  l'anima santa che 'l mondo fallace
  fa manifesto a chi di lei ben ode.

Lo corpo ond'ella fu cacciata giace
  giuso in Cieldauro; ed essa da martiro
  e da essilio venne a questa pace.

Vedi oltre fiammeggiar l'ardente spiro
  d'Isidoro, di Beda e di Riccardo,
  che a considerar fu piu` che viro.

Questi onde a me ritorna il tuo riguardo,
  e` 'l lume d'uno spirto che 'n pensieri
  gravi a morir li parve venir tardo:

essa e` la luce etterna di Sigieri,
  che, leggendo nel Vico de li Strami,
  silogizzo` invidiosi veri'"".

Indi, come orologio che ne chiami
  ne l'ora che la sposa di Dio surge
  a mattinar lo sposo perche' l'ami,

That next effulgence issues from the smile
  Of Gratian, who assisted both the courts
  In such wise that it pleased in Paradise.

The other which near by adorns our choir
  That Peter was who, e'en as the poor widow,
  Offered his treasure unto Holy Church.

The fifth light, that among us is the fairest,
  Breathes forth from such a love, that all the world
  Below is greedy to learn tidings of it.

Within it is the lofty mind, where knowledge
  So deep was put, that, if the true be true,
  To see so much there never rose a second.

Thou seest next the lustre of that taper,
  Which in the flesh below looked most within
  The angelic nature and its ministry.

Within that other little light is smiling
  The advocate of the Christian centuries,
  Out of whose rhetoric Augustine was furnished.

Now if thou trainest thy mind's eye along
  From light to light pursuant of my praise,
  With thirst already of the eighth thou waitest.

By seeing every good therein exults
  The sainted soul, which the fallacious world
  Makes manifest to him who listeneth well;

The body whence 'twas hunted forth is lying
  Down in Cieldauro, and from martyrdom
  And banishment it came unto this peace.

See farther onward flame the burning breath
  Of Isidore, of Beda, and of Richard
  Who was in contemplation more than man.

This, whence to me returneth thy regard,
  The light is of a spirit unto whom
  In his grave meditations death seemed slow.

It is the light eternal of Sigier,
  Who, reading lectures in the Street of Straw,
  Did syllogize invidious verities."

Then, as a horologe that calleth us
  What time the Bride of God is rising up
  With matins to her Spouse that he may love her,

che l'una parte e l'altra tira e urge,	Wherein one part the other draws and urges,
tin tin sonando con si` dolce nota,	Ting! ting! resounding with so sweet a note,
che 'l ben disposto spirto d'amor turge;	That swells with love the spirit well disposed,
cosi` vid'io la gloriosa rota	Thus I beheld the glorious wheel move round,
muoversi e render voce a voce in tempra	And render voice to voice, in modulation
e in dolcezza ch'esser non po` nota	And sweetness that can not be comprehended,
se non cola` dove gioir s'insempra.	Excepting there where joy is made eternal.

Paradiso: Canto XI

St. Thomas recounts the Life of St. Francis. Lament over the State of the Dominican Order.

O insensata cura de' mortali,
  quanto son difettivi silogismi
  quei che ti fanno in basso batter l'ali!

Chi dietro a iura, e chi ad amforismi
  sen giva, e chi seguendo sacerdozio,
  e chi regnar per forza o per sofismi,

e chi rubare, e chi civil negozio,
  chi nel diletto de la carne involto
  s'affaticava e chi si dava a l'ozio,

quando, da tutte queste cose sciolto,
  con Beatrice m'era suso in cielo
  cotanto gloriosamente accolto.

Poi che ciascuno fu tornato ne lo
  punto del cerchio in che avanti s'era,
  fermossi, come a candellier candelo.

E io senti' dentro a quella lumera
  che pria m'avea parlato, sorridendo
  incominciar, faccendosi piu` mera:

““Cosi` com'io del suo raggio resplendo,
  si`, riguardando ne la luce etterna,
  li tuoi pensieri onde cagioni apprendo.

Tu dubbi, e hai voler che si ricerna
  in si` aperta e 'n si` distesa lingua
  lo dicer mio, ch'al tuo sentir si sterna,

ove dinanzi dissi "U' ben s'impingua",
  e la` u' dissi "Non nacque il secondo";
  e qui e` uopo che ben si distingua.

O Thou insensate care of mortal men,
  How inconclusive are the syllogisms
  That make thee beat thy wings in downward flight!

One after laws and one to aphorisms
  Was going, and one following the priesthood,
  And one to reign by force or sophistry,

And one in theft, and one in state affairs,
  One in the pleasures of the flesh involved
  Wearied himself, one gave himself to ease;

When I, from all these things emancipate,
  With Beatrice above there in the Heavens
  With such exceeding glory was received!

When each one had returned unto that point
  Within the circle where it was before,
  It stood as in a candlestick a candle;

And from within the effulgence which at first
  Had spoken unto me, I heard begin
  Smiling while it more luminous became:

"Even as I am kindled in its ray,
  So, looking into the Eternal Light,
  The occasion of thy thoughts I apprehend.

Thou doubtest, and wouldst have me to resift
  In language so extended and so open
  My speech, that to thy sense it may be plain,

Where just before I said, 'where well one fattens,'
  And where I said, 'there never rose a second;'
  And here 'tis needful we distinguish well.

La provedenza, che governa il mondo
  con quel consiglio nel quale ogne aspetto
  creato e` vinto pria che vada al fondo,
	The Providence, which governeth the world
	  With counsel, wherein all created vision
	  Is vanquished ere it reach unto the bottom,

pero` che andasse ver' lo suo diletto   la sposa di colui ch'ad alte grida   disposo` lei col sangue benedetto,	(So that towards her own Beloved might go The bride of Him who, uttering a loud cry, Espoused her with his consecrated blood,
in se' sicura e anche a lui piu` fida,   due principi ordino` in suo favore, che quinci e quindi le fosser per guida.	Self-confident and unto Him more faithful,) Two Princes did ordain in her behoof, Which on this side and that might be her guide.

L'un fu tutto serafico in ardore;
  l'altro per sapienza in terra fue
  di cherubica luce uno splendore.
	The one was all seraphical in ardour;
	  The other by his wisdom upon earth
	  A splendour was of light cherubical.

De l'un diro`, pero` che d'amendue
  si dice l'un pregiando, qual ch'om prende,
  perch'ad un fine fur l'opere sue.
	One will I speak of, for of both is spoken
	  In praising one, whichever may be taken,
	  Because unto one end their labours were.

Intra Tupino e l'acqua che discende
  del colle eletto dal beato Ubaldo,
  fertile costa d'alto monte pende,
	Between Tupino and the stream that falls
	  Down from the hill elect of blessed Ubald,
	  A fertile slope of lofty mountain hangs,

onde Perugia sente freddo e caldo
  da Porta Sole; e di rietro le piange
  per grave giogo Nocera con Gualdo.
	From which Perugia feels the cold and heat
	  Through Porta Sole, and behind it weep
	  Gualdo and Nocera their grievous yoke.

Di questa costa, la` dov'ella frange   piu` sua rattezza, nacque al mondo un sole, come fa questo tal volta di Gange.	From out that slope, there where it breaketh most Its steepness, rose upon the world a sun As this one does sometimes from out the Ganges;

Pero` chi d'esso loco fa parole,
  non dica Ascesi, che' direbbe corto,
  ma Oriente, se proprio dir vuole.
	Therefore let him who speaketh of that place,
	  Say not Ascesi, for he would say little,
	  But Orient, if he properly would speak.

Non era ancor molto lontan da l'orto,
  ch'el comincio` a far sentir la terra
  de la sua gran virtute alcun conforto;
	He was not yet far distant from his rising
	  Before he had begun to make the earth
	  Some comfort from his mighty virtue feel.

che' per tal donna, giovinetto, in guerra
  del padre corse, a cui, come a la morte,
  la porta del piacer nessun diserra;
	For he in youth his father's wrath incurred
	  For certain Dame, to whom, as unto death,
	  The gate of pleasure no one doth unlock;

e dinanzi a la sua spirital corte
  et coram patre le si fece unito;
  poscia di di` in di` l'amo` piu` forte.
	And was before his spiritual court
	  'Et coram patre' unto her united;
	  Then day by day more fervently he loved her.

Questa, privata del primo marito,
  millecent'anni e piu` dispetta e scura
  fino a costui si stette sanza invito;
	She, reft of her first husband, scorned, obscure,
	  One thousand and one hundred years and more,
	  Waited without a suitor till he came.

ne' valse udir che la trovo` sicura
  con Amiclate, al suon de la sua voce,
  colui ch'a tutto 'l mondo fe' paura;
	Naught it availed to hear, that with Amyclas
	  Found her unmoved at sounding of his voice
	  He who struck terror into all the world;

ne' valse esser costante ne' feroce,
  si` che, dove Maria rimase giuso,
  ella con Cristo pianse in su la croce.
	Naught it availed being constant and undaunted,
	  So that, when Mary still remained below,
	  She mounted up with Christ upon the cross.

Ma perch'io non proceda troppo chiuso,
  Francesco e Poverta` per questi amanti
  prendi oramai nel mio parlar diffuso.
	But that too darkly I may not proceed,
	  Francis and Poverty for these two lovers
	  Take thou henceforward in my speech diffuse.

La lor concordia e i lor lieti sembianti,
  amore e maraviglia e dolce sguardo
  facieno esser cagion di pensier santi;
	Their concord and their joyous semblances,
	  The love, the wonder, and the sweet regard,
	  They made to be the cause of holy thoughts;

tanto che 'l venerabile Bernardo
  si scalzo` prima, e dietro a tanta pace
  corse e, correndo, li parve esser tardo.
	So much so that the venerable Bernard
	  First bared his feet, and after so great peace
	  Ran, and, in running, thought himself too slow.

Oh ignota ricchezza! oh ben ferace!
  Scalzasi Egidio, scalzasi Silvestro
  dietro a lo sposo, si` la sposa piace.
	O wealth unknown! O veritable good!
	  Giles bares his feet, and bares his feet Sylvester
	  Behind the bridegroom, so doth please the bride!

Indi sen va quel padre e quel maestro
  con la sua donna e con quella famiglia
  che gia` legava l'umile capestro.
	Then goes his way that father and that master,
	  He and his Lady and that family
	  Which now was girding on the humble cord;

Ne' li gravo` vilta` di cuor le ciglia
  per esser fi' di Pietro Bernardone,
  ne' per parer dispetto a maraviglia;
	Nor cowardice of heart weighed down his brow
	  At being son of Peter Bernardone,
	  Nor for appearing marvellously scorned;

ma regalmente sua dura intenzione
  ad Innocenzio aperse, e da lui ebbe
  primo sigillo a sua religione.
	But regally his hard determination
	  To Innocent he opened, and from him
	  Received the primal seal upon his Order.

Poi che la gente poverella crebbe
  dietro a costui, la cui mirabil vita
  meglio in gloria del ciel si canterebbe,
	After the people mendicant increased
	  Behind this man, whose admirable life
	  Better in glory of the heavens were sung,

di seconda corona redimita
  fu per Onorio da l'Etterno Spiro
  la santa voglia d'esto archimandrita.
	Incoronated with a second crown
	  Was through Honorius by the Eternal Spirit
	  The holy purpose of this Archimandrite.

E poi che, per la sete del martiro,
  ne la presenza del Soldan superba
  predico` Cristo e li altri che 'l seguiro,
	And when he had, through thirst of martyrdom,
	  In the proud presence of the Sultan preached
	  Christ and the others who came after him,

e per trovare a conversione acerba
  troppo la gente e per non stare indarno,
  redissi al frutto de l'italica erba,
	And, finding for conversion too unripe
	  The folk, and not to tarry there in vain,
	  Returned to fruit of the Italic grass,

nel crudo sasso intra Tevero e Arno
  da Cristo prese l'ultimo sigillo,
  che le sue membra due anni portarno.
	On the rude rock 'twixt Tiber and the Arno
	  From Christ did he receive the final seal,
	  Which during two whole years his members bore.

Quando a colui ch'a tanto ben sortillo
  piacque di trarlo suso a la mercede
  ch'el merito` nel suo farsi pusillo,
	When He, who chose him unto so much good,
	  Was pleased to draw him up to the reward
	  That he had merited by being lowly,

a' frati suoi, si` com'a giuste rede,   raccomando` la donna sua piu` cara,   e comando` che l'amassero a fede;	Unto his friars, as to the rightful heirs, His most dear Lady did he recommend, And bade that they should love her faithfully;

e del suo grembo l'anima preclara
  mover si volle, tornando al suo regno,
  e al suo corpo non volle altra bara.
	And from her bosom the illustrious soul
	  Wished to depart, returning to its realm,
	  And for its body wished no other bier.

Pensa oramai qual fu colui che degno
  collega fu a mantener la barca
  di Pietro in alto mar per dritto segno;
	Think now what man was he, who was a fit
	  Companion over the high seas to keep
	  The bark of Peter to its proper bearings.

e questo fu il nostro patriarca;
  per che qual segue lui, com'el comanda,
  discerner puoi che buone merce carca.
	And this man was our Patriarch; hence whoever
	  Doth follow him as he commands can see
	  That he is laden with good merchandise.

Ma 'l suo peculio di nova vivanda
  e` fatto ghiotto, si` ch'esser non puote
  che per diversi salti non si spanda;
	But for new pasturage his flock has grown
	  So greedy, that it is impossible
	  They be not scattered over fields diverse;

e quanto le sue pecore remote e vagabunde piu` da esso vanno,   piu` tornano a l'ovil di latte vote.	And in proportion as his sheep remote And vagabond go farther off from him, More void of milk return they to the fold.

Ben son di quelle che temono 'l danno
  e stringonsi al pastor; ma son si` poche,
  che le cappe fornisce poco panno.
	Verily some there are that fear a hurt,
	  And keep close to the shepherd; but so few,
	  That little cloth doth furnish forth their hoods.

Or, se le mie parole non son fioche, se la tua audienza e` stata attenta,   se cio` ch'e` detto a la mente revoche,	Now if my utterance be not indistinct, If thine own hearing hath attentive been, If thou recall to mind what I have said,

in parte fia la tua voglia contenta,
  perche' vedrai la pianta onde si scheggia,
  e vedra' il corregger che argomenta
	In part contented shall thy wishes be;
	  For thou shalt see the plant that's chipped away,
	  And the rebuke that lieth in the words,

"U' ben s'impingua, se non si vaneggia"""".	'Where well one fattens, if he strayeth not.'"

St. Buonaventura recounts the Life of St. Dominic. Lament over the State of the Franciscan Order. The Second Circle.

Si` tosto come l'ultima parola   la benedetta fiamma per dir tolse,   a rotar comincio` la santa mola;	Soon as the blessed flame had taken up The final word to give it utterance, Began the holy millstone to revolve,

e nel suo giro tutta non si volse
  prima ch'un'altra di cerchio la chiuse,
  e moto a moto e canto a canto colse;
	And in its gyre had not turned wholly round,
	  Before another in a ring enclosed it,
	  And motion joined to motion, song to song;

canto che tanto vince nostre muse,
  nostre serene in quelle dolci tube,
  quanto primo splendor quel ch'e' refuse.
	Song that as greatly doth transcend our Muses,
	  Our Sirens, in those dulcet clarions,
	  As primal splendour that which is reflected.

Come si volgon per tenera nube
  due archi paralelli e concolori,
  quando Iunone a sua ancella iube,
	And as are spanned athwart a tender cloud
	  Two rainbows parallel and like in colour,
	  When Juno to her handmaid gives command,

nascendo di quel d'entro quel di fori,
  a guisa del parlar di quella vaga
  ch'amor consunse come sol vapori;
	(The one without born of the one within,
	  Like to the speaking of that vagrant one
	  Whom love consumed as doth the sun the vapours,)

e fanno qui la gente esser presaga, per lo patto che Dio con Noe` puose,   del mondo che gia` mai piu` non s'allaga:	And make the people here, through covenant God set with Noah, presageful of the world That shall no more be covered with a flood,
cosi` di quelle sempiterne rose   volgiensi circa noi le due ghirlande,   e si` l'estrema a l'intima rispuose.	In such wise of those sempiternal roses The garlands twain encompassed us about, And thus the outer to the inner answered.

Poi che 'l tripudio e l'altra festa grande,
  si` del cantare e si` del fiammeggiarsi
  luce con luce gaudiose e blande,
	After the dance, and other grand rejoicings,
	  Both of the singing, and the flaming forth
	  Effulgence with effulgence blithe and tender,

insieme a punto e a voler quetarsi,
  pur come li occhi ch'al piacer che i move
  conviene insieme chiudere e levarsi;
	Together, at once, with one accord had stopped,
	  (Even as the eyes, that, as volition moves them,
	  Must needs together shut and lift themselves,)

del cor de l'una de le luci nove	Out of the heart of one of the new lights
si mosse voce, che l'ago a la stella	There came a voice, that needle to the star
parer mi fece in volgermi al suo dove;	Made me appear in turning thitherward.
e comincio`: ""'L'amor che mi fa bella	And it began: "The love that makes me fair
mi tragge a ragionar de l'altro duca	Draws me to speak about the other leader,
per cui del mio si` ben ci si favella.	By whom so well is spoken here of mine.
Degno e` che, dov'e` l'un, l'altro s'induca:	'Tis right, where one is, to bring in the other,
si` che, com'elli ad una militaro,	That, as they were united in their warfare,
cosi` la gloria loro insieme luca.	Together likewise may their glory shine.
L'essercito di Cristo, che si` caro	The soldiery of Christ, which it had cost
costo` a riarmar, dietro a la 'nsegna	So dear to arm again, behind the standard
si movea tardo, sospeccioso e raro,	Moved slow and doubtful and in numbers few,
quando lo 'mperador che sempre regna	When the Emperor who reigneth evermore
provide a la milizia, ch'era in forse,	Provided for the host that was in peril,
per sola grazia, non per esser degna;	Through grace alone and not that it was worthy;
e, come e` detto, a sua sposa soccorse	And, as was said, he to his Bride brought succour
con due campioni, al cui fare, al cui dire	With champions twain, at whose deed, at whose word
lo popol disviato si raccorse.	The straggling people were together drawn.
In quella parte ove surge ad aprire	Within that region where the sweet west wind
Zefiro dolce le novelle fronde	Rises to open the new leaves, wherewith
di che si vede Europa rivestire,	Europe is seen to clothe herself afresh,
non molto lungi al percuoter de l'onde	Not far off from the beating of the waves,
dietro a le quali, per la lunga foga,	Behind which in his long career the sun
lo sol talvolta ad ogne uom si nasconde,	Sometimes conceals himself from every man,
siede la fortunata Calaroga	Is situate the fortunate Calahorra,
sotto la protezion del grande scudo	Under protection of the mighty shield
in che soggiace il leone e soggioga:	In which the Lion subject is and sovereign.
dentro vi nacque l'amoroso drudo	Therein was born the amorous paramour
de la fede cristiana, il santo atleta	Of Christian Faith, the athlete consecrate,
benigno a' suoi e a' nemici crudo;	Kind to his own and cruel to his foes;
e come fu creata, fu repleta	And when it was created was his mind
si` la sua mente di viva vertute,	Replete with such a living energy,
che, ne la madre, lei fece profeta.	That in his mother her it made prophetic.
Poi che le sponsalizie fuor compiute	As soon as the espousals were complete
al sacro fonte intra lui e la Fede,	Between him and the Faith at holy font,
u' si dotar di mutua salute,	Where they with mutual safety dowered each other,

la donna che per lui l'assenso diede,	The woman, who for him had given assent,
vide nel sonno il mirabile frutto	Saw in a dream the admirable fruit
ch'uscir dovea di lui e de le rede;	That issue would from him and from his heirs;
e perche' fosse qual era in costrutto,	And that he might be construed as he was,
quinci si mosse spirito a nomarlo	A spirit from this place went forth to name him
del possessivo di cui era tutto.	With His possessive whose he wholly was.
Domenico fu detto; e io ne parlo	Dominic was he called; and him I speak of
si` come de l'agricola che Cristo	Even as of the husbandman whom Christ
elesse a l'orto suo per aiutarlo.	Elected to his garden to assist him.
Ben parve messo e famigliar di Cristo:	Envoy and servant sooth he seemed of Christ,
che 'l primo amor che 'n lui fu manifesto,	For the first love made manifest in him
fu al primo consiglio che die` Cristo.	Was the first counsel that was given by Christ.
Spesse fiate fu tacito e desto	Silent and wakeful many a time was he
trovato in terra da la sua nutrice,	Discovered by his nurse upon the ground,
come dicesse: 'Io son venuto a questo'.	As if he would have said, 'For this I came.'
Oh padre suo veramente Felice!	O thou his father, Felix verily!
oh madre sua veramente Giovanna,	O thou his mother, verily Joanna,
se, interpretata, val come si dice!	If this, interpreted, means as is said!
Non per lo mondo, per cui mo s'affanna	Not for the world which people toil for now
di retro ad Ostiense e a Taddeo,	In following Ostiense and Taddeo,
ma per amor de la verace manna	But through his longing after the true manna,
in picciol tempo gran dottor si feo;	He in short time became so great a teacher,
tal che si mise a circuir la vigna	That he began to go about the vineyard,
che tosto imbianca, se 'l vignaio e` reo.	Which fadeth soon, if faithless be the dresser;
E a la sedia che fu gia` benigna	And of the See, (that once was more benignant
piu` a' poveri giusti, non per lei,	Unto the righteous poor, not through itself,
ma per colui che siede, che traligna,	But him who sits there and degenerates,)
non dispensare o due o tre per sei,	Not to dispense or two or three for six,
non la fortuna di prima vacante,	Not any fortune of first vacancy,
non decimas, quae sunt pauperum Dei,	'Non decimas quae sunt pauperum Dei,'
addimando`, ma contro al mondo errante	He asked for, but against the errant world
licenza di combatter per lo seme	Permission to do battle for the seed,
del qual ti fascian ventiquattro piante.	Of which these four and twenty plants surround thee.
Poi, con dottrina e con volere insieme,	Then with the doctrine and the will together,
con l'officio appostolico si mosse	With office apostolical he moved,
quasi torrente ch'alta vena preme;	Like torrent which some lofty vein out-presses;

e ne li sterpi eretici percosse
　l'impeto suo, piu` vivamente quivi
　dove le resistenze eran piu` grosse.

Di lui si fecer poi diversi rivi
　onde l'orto catolico si riga,
　si` che i suoi arbuscelli stan piu` vivi.

Se tal fu l'una rota de la biga
　in che la Santa Chiesa si difese
　e vinse in campo la sua civil briga,

ben ti dovrebbe assai esser palese
　l'eccellenza de l'altra, di cui Tomma
　dinanzi al mio venir fu si` cortese.

Ma l'orbita che fe' la parte somma
　di sua circunferenza, e` derelitta,
　si` ch'e` la muffa dov'era la gromma.

La sua famiglia, che si mosse dritta
　coi piedi a le sue orme, e` tanto volta,
　che quel dinanzi a quel di retro gitta;

e tosto si vedra` de la ricolta
　de la mala coltura, quando il loglio
　si lagnera` che l'arca li sia tolta.

Ben dico, chi cercasse a foglio a foglio
　nostro volume, ancor troveria carta
　u' leggerebbe "I' mi son quel ch'i' soglio";

ma non fia da Casal ne' d'Acquasparta,
　la` onde vegnon tali a la scrittura,
　ch'uno la fugge e altro la coarta.

Io son la vita di Bonaventura
　da Bagnoregio, che ne' grandi offici
　sempre pospuosi la sinistra cura.

Illuminato e Augustin son quici,
　che fuor de' primi scalzi poverelli
　che nel capestro a Dio si fero amici.

Ugo da San Vittore e` qui con elli,
　e Pietro Mangiadore e Pietro Spano,
　lo qual giu` luce in dodici libelli;

And in among the shoots heretical
　His impetus with greater fury smote,
　Wherever the resistance was the greatest.

Of him were made thereafter divers runnels,
　Whereby the garden catholic is watered,
　So that more living its plantations stand.

If such the one wheel of the Biga was,
　In which the Holy Church itself defended
　And in the field its civic battle won,

Truly full manifest should be to thee
　The excellence of the other, unto whom
　Thomas so courteous was before my coming.

But still the orbit, which the highest part
　Of its circumference made, is derelict,
　So that the mould is where was once the crust.

His family, that had straight forward moved
　With feet upon his footprints, are turned round
　So that they set the point upon the heel.

And soon aware they will be of the harvest
　Of this bad husbandry, when shall the tares
　Complain the granary is taken from them.

Yet say I, he who searcheth leaf by leaf
　Our volume through, would still some page discov-
　　er
　Where he could read, 'I am as I am wont.'

'Twill not be from Casal nor Acquasparta,
　From whence come such unto the written word
　That one avoids it, and the other narrows.

Bonaventura of Bagnoregio's life
　Am I, who always in great offices
　Postponed considerations sinister.

Here are Illuminato and Agostino,
　Who of the first barefooted beggars were
　That with the cord the friends of God became.

Hugh of Saint Victor is among them here,
　And Peter Mangiador, and Peter of Spain,
　Who down below in volumes twelve is shining;

Natan profeta e 'l metropolitano	Nathan the seer, and metropolitan
Crisostomo e Anselmo e quel Donato	Chrysostom, and Anselmus, and Donatus
ch'a la prim'arte degno` porre mano.	Who deigned to lay his hand to the first art;
Rabano e` qui, e lucemi dallato	Here is Rabanus, and beside me here
il calavrese abate Giovacchino,	Shines the Calabrian Abbot Joachim,
di spirito profetico dotato.	He with the spirit of prophecy endowed.
Ad inveggiar cotanto paladino	To celebrate so great a paladin
mi mosse l'infiammata cortesia	Have moved me the impassioned courtesy
di fra Tommaso e 'l discreto latino;	And the discreet discourses of Friar Thomas,
e mosse meco questa compagnia"".	And with me they have moved this company."

Paradiso: Canto XIII

Of the Wisdom of Solomon. St. Thomas reproaches Dante's Judgement.

Imagini, chi bene intender cupe
  quel ch'i' or vidi - e ritegna l'image,
  mentre ch'io dico, come ferma rupe -,

quindici stelle che 'n diverse plage
  lo ciel avvivan di tanto sereno
  che soperchia de l'aere ogne compage;

imagini quel carro a cu' il seno
  basta del nostro cielo e notte e giorno,
  si` ch'al volger del temo non vien meno;

imagini la bocca di quel corno
  che si comincia in punta de lo stelo
  a cui la prima rota va dintorno,

aver fatto di se' due segni in cielo,
  qual fece la figliuola di Minoi
  allora che senti` di morte il gelo;

e l'un ne l'altro aver li raggi suoi,
  e amendue girarsi per maniera
  che l'uno andasse al primo e l'altro al poi;

e avra` quasi l'ombra de la vera
  costellazione e de la doppia danza
  che circulava il punto dov'io era:

poi ch'e` tanto di la` da nostra usanza,
  quanto di la` dal mover de la Chiana
  si move il ciel che tutti li altri avanza.

Li` si canto` non Bacco, non Peana,
  ma tre persone in divina natura,
  e in una persona essa e l'umana.

Let him imagine, who would well conceive
  What now I saw, and let him while I speak
  Retain the image as a steadfast rock,

The fifteen stars, that in their divers regions
  The sky enliven with a light so great
  That it transcends all clusters of the air;

Let him the Wain imagine unto which
  Our vault of heaven sufficeth night and day,
  So that in turning of its pole it fails not;

Let him the mouth imagine of the horn
  That in the point beginneth of the axis
  Round about which the primal wheel revolves,—

To have fashioned of themselves two signs in heav-
    en,
  Like unto that which Minos' daughter made,
  The moment when she felt the frost of death;

And one to have its rays within the other,
  And both to whirl themselves in such a manner
  That one should forward go, the other backward;

And he will have some shadowing forth of that
  True constellation and the double dance
  That circled round the point at which I was;

Because it is as much beyond our wont,
  As swifter than the motion of the Chiana
  Moveth the heaven that all the rest outspeeds.

There sang they neither Bacchus, nor Apollo,
  But in the divine nature Persons three,
  And in one person the divine and human.

Compie' 'l cantare e 'l volger sua misura;
 e attesersi a noi quei santi lumi,
 felicitando se' di cura in cura.

Ruppe il silenzio ne' concordi numi
 poscia la luce in che mirabil vita
 del poverel di Dio narrata fumi,

e disse: ""Quando l'una paglia e` trita,
 quando la sua semenza e` gia` riposta,
 a batter l'altra dolce amor m'invita.

Tu credi che nel petto onde la costa
 si trasse per formar la bella guancia
 il cui palato a tutto 'l mondo costa,

e in quel che, forato da la lancia,
 e prima e poscia tanto sodisfece,
 che d'ogne colpa vince la bilancia,

quantunque a la natura umana lece
 aver di lume, tutto fosse infuso
 da quel valor che l'uno e l'altro fece;

e pero` miri a cio` ch'io dissi suso,
 quando narrai che non ebbe 'l secondo
 lo ben che ne la quinta luce e` chiuso.

Or apri li occhi a quel ch'io ti rispondo,
 e vedrai il tuo credere e 'l mio dire
 nel vero farsi come centro in tondo.

Cio` che non more e cio` che puo` morire
 non e` se non splendor di quella idea
 che partorisce, amando, il nostro Sire;

che' quella viva luce che si` mea
 dal suo lucente, che non si disuna
 da lui ne' da l'amor ch'a lor s'intrea,

per sua bontate il suo raggiare aduna,
 quasi specchiato, in nove sussistenze,
 etternalmente rimanendosi una.

Quindi discende a l'ultime potenze
 giu` d'atto in atto, tanto divenendo,
 che piu` non fa che brevi contingenze;

e queste contingenze essere intendo
 le cose generate, che produce
 con seme e sanza seme il ciel movendo.

The singing and the dance fulfilled their measure,
 And unto us those holy lights gave need,
 Growing in happiness from care to care.

Then broke the silence of those saints concordant
 The light in which the admirable life
 Of God's own mendicant was told to me,

And said: "Now that one straw is trodden out
 Now that its seed is garnered up already,
 Sweet love invites me to thresh out the other.

Into that bosom, thou believest, whence
 Was drawn the rib to form the beauteous cheek
 Whose taste to all the world is costing dear,

And into that which, by the lance transfixed,
 Before and since, such satisfaction made
 That it weighs down the balance of all sin,

Whate'er of light it has to human nature
 Been lawful to possess was all infused
 By the same power that both of them created;

And hence at what I said above dost wonder,
 When I narrated that no second had
 The good which in the fifth light is enclosed.

Now ope thine eyes to what I answer thee,
 And thou shalt see thy creed and my discourse
 Fit in the truth as centre in a circle.

That which can die, and that which dieth not,
 Are nothing but the splendour of the idea
 Which by his love our Lord brings into being;

Because that living Light, which from its fount
 Effulgent flows, so that it disunites not
 From Him nor from the Love in them intrined,

Through its own goodness reunites its rays
 In nine subsistences, as in a mirror,
 Itself eternally remaining One.

Thence it descends to the last potencies,
 Downward from act to act becoming such
 That only brief contingencies it makes;

And these contingencies I hold to be
 Things generated, which the heaven produces
 By its own motion, with seed and without.

La cera di costoro e chi la duce
  non sta d'un modo; e pero` sotto 'l segno
  ideale poi piu` e men traluce.

Ond'elli avvien ch'un medesimo legno,
  secondo specie, meglio e peggio frutta;
  e voi nascete con diverso ingegno.

Se fosse a punto la cera dedutta
  e fosse il cielo in sua virtu` supprema,
  la luce del suggel parrebbe tutta;

ma la natura la da` sempre scema,
  similemente operando a l'artista
  ch'a l'abito de l'arte ha man che trema.

Pero` se 'l caldo amor la chiara vista
  de la prima virtu` dispone e segna,
  tutta la perfezion quivi s'acquista.

Cosi` fu fatta gia` la terra degna
  di tutta l'animal perfezione;
  cosi` fu fatta la Vergine pregna;

si` ch'io commendo tua oppinione,
  che l'umana natura mai non fue
  ne' fia qual fu in quelle due persone.

Or s'i' non procedesse avanti piue,
  'Dunque, come costui fu sanza pare?'
  comincerebber le parole tue.

Ma perche' paia ben cio` che non pare,
  pensa chi era, e la cagion che 'l mosse,
  quando fu detto "Chiedi", a dimandare.

Non ho parlato si`, che tu non posse
  ben veder ch'el fu re, che chiese senno
  accio` che re sufficiente fosse;

non per sapere il numero in che enno
  li motor di qua su`, o se necesse
  con contingente mai necesse fenno;

non si est dare primum motum esse,
  o se del mezzo cerchio far si puote
  triangol si` ch'un retto non avesse.

Onde, se cio` ch'io dissi e questo note,
  regal prudenza e` quel vedere impari
  in che lo stral di mia intenzion percuote;

Neither their wax, nor that which tempers it,
  Remains immutable, and hence beneath
  The ideal signet more and less shines through;

Therefore it happens, that the selfsame tree
  After its kind bears worse and better fruit,
  And ye are born with characters diverse.

If in perfection tempered were the wax,
  And were the heaven in its supremest virtue,
  The brilliance of the seal would all appear;

But nature gives it evermore deficient,
  In the like manner working as the artist,
  Who has the skill of art and hand that trembles.

If then the fervent Love, the Vision clear,
  Of primal Virtue do dispose and seal,
  Perfection absolute is there acquired.

Thus was of old the earth created worthy
  Of all and every animal perfection;
  And thus the Virgin was impregnate made;

So that thine own opinion I commend,
  That human nature never yet has been,
  Nor will be, what it was in those two persons.

Now if no farther forth I should proceed,
  'Then in what way was he without a peer?'
  Would be the first beginning of thy words.

But, that may well appear what now appears not,
  Think who he was, and what occasion moved him
  To make request, when it was told him, 'Ask.'

I've not so spoken that thou canst not see
  Clearly he was a king who asked for wisdom,
  That he might be sufficiently a king;

'Twas not to know the number in which are
  The motors here above, or if 'necesse'
  With a contingent e'er 'necesse' make,

'Non si est dare primum motum esse,'
  Or if in semicircle can be made
  Triangle so that it have no right angle.

Whence, if thou notest this and what I said,
  A regal prudence is that peerless seeing
  In which the shaft of my intention strikes.

e se al "surse" drizzi li occhi chiari,
  vedrai aver solamente respetto
  ai regi, che son molti, e ' buon son rari.
	And if on 'rose' thou turnest thy clear eyes,
	  Thou'lt see that it has reference alone
	  To kings who're many, and the good are rare.

Con questa distinzion prendi 'l mio detto;
  e cosi` puote star con quel che credi
  del primo padre e del nostro Diletto.
	With this distinction take thou what I said,
	  And thus it can consist with thy belief
	  Of the first father and of our Delight.

E questo ti sia sempre piombo a' piedi,
  per farti mover lento com'uom lasso
  e al si` e al no che tu non vedi:
	And lead shall this be always to thy feet,
	  To make thee, like a weary man, move slowly
	  Both to the Yes and No thou seest not;

che' quelli e` tra li stolti bene a basso,   che sanza distinzione afferma e nega   ne l'un cosi` come ne l'altro passo;	For very low among the fools is he Who affirms without distinction, or denies, As well in one as in the other case;

perch'elli 'ncontra che piu` volte piega
  l'oppinion corrente in falsa parte,
  e poi l'affetto l'intelletto lega.
	Because it happens that full often bends
	  Current opinion in the false direction,
	  And then the feelings bind the intellect.

Vie piu` che 'ndarno da riva si parte,
  perche' non torna tal qual e' si move,
  chi pesca per lo vero e non ha l'arte.
	Far more than uselessly he leaves the shore,
	  (Since he returneth not the same he went,)
	  Who fishes for the truth, and has no skill;

E di cio` sono al mondo aperte prove
  Parmenide, Melisso e Brisso e molti,
  li quali andaro e non sapean dove;
	And in the world proofs manifest thereof
	  Parmenides, Melissus, Brissus are,
	  And many who went on and knew not whither;

si` fe' Sabellio e Arrio e quelli stolti
  che furon come spade a le Scritture
  in render torti li diritti volti.
	Thus did Sabellius, Arius, and those fools
	  Who have been even as swords unto the Scriptures
	  In rendering distorted their straight faces.

Non sien le genti, ancor, troppo sicure
  a giudicar, si` come quei che stima
  le biade in campo pria che sien mature;
	Nor yet shall people be too confident
	  In judging, even as he is who doth count
	  The corn in field or ever it be ripe.

ch'i' ho veduto tutto 'l verno prima
  lo prun mostrarsi rigido e feroce;
  poscia portar la rosa in su la cima;
	For I have seen all winter long the thorn
	  First show itself intractable and fierce,
	  And after bear the rose upon its top;

e legno vidi gia` dritto e veloce
  correr lo mar per tutto suo cammino,
  perire al fine a l'intrar de la foce.
	And I have seen a ship direct and swift
	  Run o'er the sea throughout its course entire,
	  To perish at the harbour's mouth at last.

Non creda donna Berta e ser Martino,
  per vedere un furare, altro offerere,
  vederli dentro al consiglio divino;
	Let not Dame Bertha nor Ser Martin think,
	  Seeing one steal, another offering make,
	  To see them in the arbitrament divine;

che' quel puo` surgere, e quel puo` cadere"".	For one may rise, and fall the other may."

Paradiso: Canto XIV

The Third Circle. Discourse on the Resurrection of the Flesh. The Fifth Heaven, Mars: Martyrs and Crusaders who died fighting for the true Faith. The Celestial Cross.

Dal centro al cerchio, e si` dal cerchio al centro
  movesi l'acqua in un ritondo vaso,
  secondo ch'e` percosso fuori o dentro:

ne la mia mente fe' subito caso
  questo ch'io dico, si` come si tacque
  la gloriosa vita di Tommaso,

per la similitudine che nacque
  del suo parlare e di quel di Beatrice,
  a cui si` cominciar, dopo lui, piacque:

““A costui fa mestieri, e nol vi dice
  ne' con la voce ne' pensando ancora,
  d'un altro vero andare a la radice.

Diteli se la luce onde s'infiora
  vostra sustanza, rimarra` con voi
  etternalmente si` com'ell'e` ora;

e se rimane, dite come, poi
  che sarete visibili rifatti,
  esser pora` ch'al veder non vi noi”“.

Come, da piu` letizia pinti e tratti,
  a la fiata quei che vanno a rota
  levan la voce e rallegrano li atti,

cosi`, a l'orazion pronta e divota,
  li santi cerchi mostrar nova gioia
  nel torneare e ne la mira nota.

From centre unto rim, from rim to centre,
  In a round vase the water moves itself,
  As from without 'tis struck or from within.

Into my mind upon a sudden dropped
  What I am saying, at the moment when
  Silent became the glorious life of Thomas,

Because of the resemblance that was born
  Of his discourse and that of Beatrice,
  Whom, after him, it pleased thus to begin:

"This man has need (and does not tell you so,
  Nor with the voice, nor even in his thought)
  Of going to the root of one truth more.

Declare unto him if the light wherewith
  Blossoms your substance shall remain with you
  Eternally the same that it is now;

And if it do remain, say in what manner,
  After ye are again made visible,
  It can be that it injure not your sight."

As by a greater gladness urged and drawn
  They who are dancing in a ring sometimes
  Uplift their voices and their motions quicken;

So, at that orison devout and prompt,
  The holy circles a new joy displayed
  In their revolving and their wondrous song.

Qual si lamenta perche' qui si moia
  per viver cola` su`, non vide quive
  lo refrigerio de l'etterna ploia.

Quell'uno e due e tre che sempre vive
  e regna sempre in tre e 'n due e 'n uno,
  non circunscritto, e tutto circunscrive,

tre volte era cantato da ciascuno
  di quelli spirti con tal melodia,
  ch'ad ogne merto saria giusto muno.

E io udi' ne la luce piu` dia
  del minor cerchio una voce modesta,
  forse qual fu da l'angelo a Maria,

risponder: ““Quanto fia lunga la festa
  di paradiso, tanto il nostro amore
  si raggera` dintorno cotal vesta.

La sua chiarezza seguita l'ardore;
  l'ardor la visione, e quella e` tanta,
  quant'ha di grazia sovra suo valore.

Come la carne gloriosa e santa
  fia rivestita, la nostra persona
  piu` grata fia per esser tutta quanta;

per che s'accrescera` cio` che ne dona
  di gratuito lume il sommo bene,
  lume ch'a lui veder ne condiziona;

onde la vision crescer convene,
  crescer l'ardor che di quella s'accende,
  crescer lo raggio che da esso vene.

Ma si` come carbon che fiamma rende,
  e per vivo candor quella soverchia,
  si` che la sua parvenza si difende;

cosi` questo folgor che gia` ne cerchia
  fia vinto in apparenza da la carne
  che tutto di` la terra ricoperchia;

ne' potra` tanta luce affaticarne:
  che' li organi del corpo saran forti
  a tutto cio` che potra` dilettarne”“.

Tanto mi parver subiti e accorti
  e l'uno e l'altro coro a dicer ““Amme!”“,
  che ben mostrar disio d'i corpi morti:

Whoso lamenteth him that here we die
  That we may live above, has never there
  Seen the refreshment of the eternal rain.

The One and Two and Three who ever liveth,
  And reigneth ever in Three and Two and One,
  Not circumscribed and all things circumscribing,

Three several times was chanted by each one
  Among those spirits, with such melody
  That for all merit it were just reward;

And, in the lustre most divine of all
  The lesser ring, I heard a modest voice,
  Such as perhaps the Angel's was to Mary,

Answer: "As long as the festivity
  Of Paradise shall be, so long our love
  Shall radiate round about us such a vesture.

Its brightness is proportioned to the ardour,
  The ardour to the vision; and the vision
  Equals what grace it has above its worth.

When, glorious and sanctified, our flesh
  Is reassumed, then shall our persons be
  More pleasing by their being all complete;

For will increase whate'er bestows on us
  Of light gratuitous the Good Supreme,
  Light which enables us to look on Him;

Therefore the vision must perforce increase,
  Increase the ardour which from that is kindled,
  Increase the radiance which from this proceeds.

But even as a coal that sends forth flame,
  And by its vivid whiteness overpowers it
  So that its own appearance it maintains,

Thus the effulgence that surrounds us now
  Shall be o'erpowered in aspect by the flesh,
  Which still to-day the earth doth cover up;

Nor can so great a splendour weary us,
  For strong will be the organs of the body
  To everything which hath the power to please us."

So sudden and alert appeared to me
  Both one and the other choir to say Amen,
  That well they showed desire for their dead bodies;

forse non pur per lor, ma per le mamme,
  per li padri e per li altri che fuor cari
  anzi che fosser sempiterne fiamme.

Ed ecco intorno, di chiarezza pari,
  nascere un lustro sopra quel che v'era,
  per guisa d'orizzonte che rischiari.

E si` come al salir di prima sera
  comincian per lo ciel nove parvenze,
  si` che la vista pare e non par vera,

parvemi li` novelle sussistenze
  cominciare a vedere, e fare un giro
  di fuor da l'altre due circunferenze.

Oh vero sfavillar del Santo Spiro!
  come si fece subito e candente
  a li occhi miei che, vinti, nol soffriro!

Ma Beatrice si` bella e ridente
  mi si mostro`, che tra quelle vedute
  si vuol lasciar che non seguir la mente.

Quindi ripreser li occhi miei virtute
  a rilevarsi; e vidimi translato
  sol con mia donna in piu` alta salute.

Ben m'accors'io ch'io era piu` levato,
  per l'affocato riso de la stella,
  che mi parea piu` roggio che l'usato.

Con tutto 'l core e con quella favella
  ch'e` una in tutti, a Dio feci olocausto,
  qual conveniesi a la grazia novella.

E non er'anco del mio petto essausto
  l'ardor del sacrificio, ch'io conobbi
  esso litare stato accetto e fausto;

che' con tanto lucore e tanto robbi
  m'apparvero splendor dentro a due raggi,
  ch'io dissi: ""O Elios che si` li addobbi!"".

Come distinta da minori e maggi
  lumi biancheggia tra ' poli del mondo
  Galassia si`, che fa dubbiar ben saggi;

si` costellati facean nel profondo
  Marte quei raggi il venerabil segno
  che fan giunture di quadranti in tondo.

Nor sole for them perhaps, but for the mothers,
  The fathers, and the rest who had been dear
  Or ever they became eternal flames.

And lo! all round about of equal brightness
  Arose a lustre over what was there,
  Like an horizon that is clearing up.

And as at rise of early eve begin
  Along the welkin new appearances,
  So that the sight seems real and unreal,

It seemed to me that new subsistences
  Began there to be seen, and make a circle
  Outside the other two circumferences.

O very sparkling of the Holy Spirit,
  How sudden and incandescent it became
  Unto mine eyes, that vanquished bore it not!

But Beatrice so beautiful and smiling
  Appeared to me, that with the other sights
  That followed not my memory I must leave her.

Then to uplift themselves mine eyes resumed
  The power, and I beheld myself translated
  To higher salvation with my Lady only.

Well was I ware that I was more uplifted
  By the enkindled smiling of the star,
  That seemed to me more ruddy than its wont.

With all my heart, and in that dialect
  Which is the same in all, such holocaust
  To God I made as the new grace beseemed;

And not yet from my bosom was exhausted
  The ardour of sacrifice, before I knew
  This offering was accepted and auspicious;

For with so great a lustre and so red
  Splendours appeared to me in twofold rays,
  I said: "O Helios who dost so adorn them!"

Even as distinct with less and greater lights
  Glimmers between the two poles of the world
  The Galaxy that maketh wise men doubt,

Thus constellated in the depths of Mars,
  Those rays described the venerable sign
  That quadrants joining in a circle make.

Qui vince la memoria mia lo 'ngegno;
  che' quella croce lampeggiava Cristo,
  si` ch'io non so trovare essempro degno;

ma chi prende sua croce e segue Cristo,
  ancor mi scusera` di quel ch'io lasso,
  vedendo in quell'albor balenar Cristo.

Di corno in corno e tra la cima e 'l basso
  si movien lumi, scintillando forte
  nel congiugnersi insieme e nel trapasso:

cosi` si veggion qui diritte e torte,
  veloci e tarde, rinovando vista,
  le minuzie d'i corpi, lunghe e corte,

moversi per lo raggio onde si lista
  talvolta l'ombra che, per sua difesa,
  la gente con ingegno e arte acquista.

E come giga e arpa, in tempra tesa
  di molte corde, fa dolce tintinno
  a tal da cui la nota non e` intesa,

cosi` da' lumi che li` m'apparinno
  s'accogliea per la croce una melode
  che mi rapiva, sanza intender l'inno.

Ben m'accors'io ch'elli era d'alte lode,
  pero` ch'a me venia ""Resurgi"" e ""Vinci""
  come a colui che non intende e ode.

Io m'innamorava tanto quinci,
  che 'nfino a li` non fu alcuna cosa
  che mi legasse con si` dolci vinci.

Forse la mia parola par troppo osa,
  posponendo il piacer de li occhi belli,
  ne' quai mirando mio disio ha posa;

ma chi s'avvede che i vivi suggelli
  d'ogne bellezza piu` fanno piu` suso,
  e ch'io non m'era li` rivolto a quelli,

escusar puommi di quel ch'io m'accuso
  per escusarmi, e vedermi dir vero:
  che' 'l piacer santo non e` qui dischiuso,

perche' si fa, montando, piu` sincero.

Here doth my memory overcome my genius;
  For on that cross as levin gleamed forth Christ,
  So that I cannot find ensample worthy;

But he who takes his cross and follows Christ
  Again will pardon me what I omit,
  Seeing in that aurora lighten Christ.

From horn to horn, and 'twixt the top and base,
  Lights were in motion, brightly scintillating
  As they together met and passed each other;

Thus level and aslant and swift and slow
  We here behold, renewing still the sight,
  The particles of bodies long and short,

Across the sunbeam move, wherewith is listed
  Sometimes the shade, which for their own defence
  People with cunning and with art contrive.

And as a lute and harp, accordant strung
  With many strings, a dulcet tinkling make
  To him by whom the notes are not distinguished,

So from the lights that there to me appeared
  Upgathered through the cross a melody,
  Which rapt me, not distinguishing the hymn.

Well was I ware it was of lofty laud,
  Because there came to me, "Arise and conquer!"
  As unto him who hears and comprehends not.

So much enamoured I became therewith,
  That until then there was not anything
  That e'er had fettered me with such sweet bonds.

Perhaps my word appears somewhat too bold,
  Postponing the delight of those fair eyes,
  Into which gazing my desire has rest;

But who bethinks him that the living seals
  Of every beauty grow in power ascending,
  And that I there had not turned round to those,

Can me excuse, if I myself accuse
  To excuse myself, and see that I speak truly:
  For here the holy joy is not disclosed,

Because ascending it becomes more pure.

Paradiso: Canto XV

Cacciaguida. Florence in the Olden Time.

Benigna volontade in che si liqua
  sempre l'amor che drittamente spira,
  come cupidita` fa ne la iniqua,

silenzio puose a quella dolce lira,
  e fece quietar le sante corde
  che la destra del cielo allenta e tira.

Come saranno a' giusti preghi sorde
  quelle sustanze che, per darmi voglia
  ch'io le pregassi, a tacer fur concorde?

Bene e` che sanza termine si doglia
  chi, per amor di cosa che non duri,
  etternalmente quello amor si spoglia.

Quale per li seren tranquilli e puri
  discorre ad ora ad or subito foco,
  movendo li occhi che stavan sicuri,

e pare stella che tramuti loco,
  se non che da la parte ond'e' s'accende
  nulla sen perde, ed esso dura poco:

tale dal corno che 'n destro si stende
  a pie` di quella croce corse un astro
  de la costellazion che li` resplende;

ne' si parti` la gemma dal suo nastro,
  ma per la lista radial trascorse,
  che parve foco dietro ad alabastro.

Si` pia l'ombra d'Anchise si porse,
  se fede merta nostra maggior musa,
  quando in Eliso del figlio s'accorse.

A will benign, in which reveals itself
  Ever the love that righteously inspires,
  As in the iniquitous, cupidity,

Silence imposed upon that dulcet lyre,
  And quieted the consecrated chords,
  That Heaven's right hand doth tighten and relax.

How unto just entreaties shall be deaf
  Those substances, which, to give me desire
  Of praying them, with one accord grew silent?

'Tis well that without end he should lament,
  Who for the love of thing that doth not last
  Eternally despoils him of that love!

As through the pure and tranquil evening air
  There shoots from time to time a sudden fire,
  Moving the eyes that steadfast were before,

And seems to be a star that changeth place,
  Except that in the part where it is kindled
  Nothing is missed, and this endureth little;

So from the horn that to the right extends
  Unto that cross's foot there ran a star
  Out of the constellation shining there;

Nor was the gem dissevered from its ribbon,
  But down the radiant fillet ran along,
  So that fire seemed it behind alabaster.

Thus piteous did Anchises' shade reach forward,
  If any faith our greatest Muse deserve,
  When in Elysium he his son perceived.

"'O sanguis meus, o superinfusa
  gratia Dei, sicut tibi cui
  bis unquam celi ianua reclusa?"'.

Cosi` quel lume: ond'io m'attesi a lui;
  poscia rivolsi a la mia donna il viso,
  e quinci e quindi stupefatto fui;

che' dentro a li occhi suoi ardeva un riso
  tal, ch'io pensai co' miei toccar lo fondo
  de la mia gloria e del mio paradiso.

Indi, a udire e a veder giocondo,
  giunse lo spirto al suo principio cose,
  ch'io non lo 'ntesi, si` parlo` profondo;

ne' per elezion mi si nascose,
  ma per necessita`, che' 'l suo concetto
  al segno d'i mortal si soprapuose.

E quando l'arco de l'ardente affetto
  fu si` sfogato, che 'l parlar discese
  inver' lo segno del nostro intelletto,

la prima cosa che per me s'intese,
  '"Benedetto sia tu"', fu, '"trino e uno,
  che nel mio seme se' tanto cortese!"'.

E segui`: '"Grato e lontano digiuno,
  tratto leggendo del magno volume
  du' non si muta mai bianco ne' bruno,

solvuto hai, figlio, dentro a questo lume
  in ch'io ti parlo, merce` di colei
  ch'a l'alto volo ti vesti` le piume.

Tu credi che a me tuo pensier mei
  da quel ch'e` primo, cosi` come raia
  da l'un, se si conosce, il cinque e 'l sei;

e pero` ch'io mi sia e perch'io paia
  piu` gaudioso a te, non mi domandi,
  che alcun altro in questa turba gaia.

Tu credi 'l vero; che' i minori e ' grandi
  di questa vita miran ne lo speglio
  in che, prima che pensi, il pensier pandi;

"O sanguis meus, O superinfusa
  Gratia Dei, sicut tibi, cui
  Bis unquam Coeli janua reclusa?"

Thus that effulgence; whence I gave it heed;
  Then round unto my Lady turned my sight,
  And on this side and that was stupefied;

For in her eyes was burning such a smile
  That with mine own methought I touched the bot-
    tom
  Both of my grace and of my Paradise!

Then, pleasant to the hearing and the sight,
  The spirit joined to its beginning things
  I understood not, so profound it spake;

Nor did it hide itself from me by choice,
  But by necessity; for its conception
  Above the mark of mortals set itself.

And when the bow of burning sympathy
  Was so far slackened, that its speech descended
  Towards the mark of our intelligence,

The first thing that was understood by me
  Was "Benedight be Thou, O Trine and One,
  Who hast unto my seed so courteous been!"

And it continued: "Hunger long and grateful,
  Drawn from the reading of the mighty volume
  Wherein is never changed the white nor dark,

Thou hast appeased, my son, within this light
  In which I speak to thee, by grace of her
  Who to this lofty flight with plumage clothed thee.

Thou thinkest that to me thy thought doth pass
  From Him who is the first, as from the unit,
  If that be known, ray out the five and six;

And therefore who I am thou askest not,
  And why I seem more joyous unto thee
  Than any other of this gladsome crowd.

Thou think'st the truth; because the small and great
  Of this existence look into the mirror
  Wherein, before thou think'st, thy thought thou
    showest.

380

ma perche' 'l sacro amore in che io veglio
  con perpetua vista e che m'asseta
  di dolce disiar, s'adempia meglio,
	But that the sacred love, in which I watch
	  With sight perpetual, and which makes me thirst
	  With sweet desire, may better be fulfilled,

la voce tua sicura, balda e lieta suoni la volonta`, suoni 'l disio,   a che la mia risposta e` gia` decreta!"".	Now let thy voice secure and frank and glad Proclaim the wishes, the desire proclaim, To which my answer is decreed already."

Io mi volsi a Beatrice, e quella udio
  pria ch'io parlassi, e arrisemi un cenno
  che fece crescer l'ali al voler mio.
	To Beatrice I turned me, and she heard
	  Before I spake, and smiled to me a sign,
	  That made the wings of my desire increase;

Poi cominciai cosi`: ""L'affetto e 'l senno,   come la prima equalita` v'apparse, d'un peso per ciascun di voi si fenno,	Then in this wise began I: "Love and knowledge, When on you dawned the first Equality, Of the same weight for each of you became;

pero` che 'l sol che v'allumo` e arse,
  col caldo e con la luce e` si` iguali,
  che tutte simiglianze sono scarse.
	For in the Sun, which lighted you and burned
	  With heat and radiance, they so equal are,
	  That all similitudes are insufficient.

Ma voglia e argomento ne' mortali,
  per la cagion ch'a voi e` manifesta,
  diversamente son pennuti in ali;
	But among mortals will and argument,
	  For reason that to you is manifest,
	  Diversely feathered in their pinions are.

ond'io, che son mortal, mi sento in questa
  disagguaglianza, e pero` non ringrazio
  se non col core a la paterna festa.
	Whence I, who mortal am, feel in myself
	  This inequality; so give not thanks,
	  Save in my heart, for this paternal welcome.

Ben supplico io a te, vivo topazio
  che questa gioia preziosa ingemmi,
  perche' mi facci del tuo nome sazio"".
	Truly do I entreat thee, living topaz!
	  Set in this precious jewel as a gem,
	  That thou wilt satisfy me with thy name."

""O fronda mia in che io compiacemmi
  pur aspettando, io fui la tua radice"":
  cotal principio, rispondendo, femmi.
	"O leaf of mine, in whom I pleasure took
	  E'en while awaiting, I was thine own root!"
	  Such a beginning he in answer made me.

Poscia mi disse: ""Quel da cui si dice
  tua cognazione e che cent'anni e piue
  girato ha 'l monte in la prima cornice,
	Then said to me: "That one from whom is named
	  Thy race, and who a hundred years and more
	  Has circled round the mount on the first cornice,

mio figlio fu e tuo bisavol fue:
  ben si convien che la lunga fatica
  tu li raccorci con l'opere tue.
	A son of mine and thy great-grandsire was;
	  Well it behoves thee that the long fatigue
	  Thou shouldst for him make shorter with thy works.

Fiorenza dentro da la cerchia antica,
  ond'ella toglie ancora e terza e nona,
  si stava in pace, sobria e pudica.
	Florence, within the ancient boundary
	  From which she taketh still her tierce and nones,
	  Abode in quiet, temperate and chaste.

Non avea catenella, non corona,
  non gonne contigiate, non cintura
  che fosse a veder piu` che la persona.
	No golden chain she had, nor coronal,
	  Nor ladies shod with sandal shoon, nor girdle
	  That caught the eye more than the person did.

Non faceva, nascendo, ancor paura
  la figlia al padre, che 'l tempo e la dote
  non fuggien quinci e quindi la misura.

Non avea case di famiglia vote;
  non v'era giunto ancor Sardanapalo
  a mostrar cio` che 'n camera si puote.

Non era vinto ancora Montemalo
  dal vostro Uccellatoio, che, com'e` vinto
  nel montar su`, cosi` sara` nel calo.

Bellincion Berti vid'io andar cinto
  di cuoio e d'osso, e venir da lo specchio
  la donna sua sanza 'l viso dipinto;

e vidi quel d'i Nerli e quel del Vecchio
  esser contenti a la pelle scoperta,
  e le sue donne al fuso e al pennecchio.

Oh fortunate! ciascuna era certa
  de la sua sepultura, e ancor nulla
  era per Francia nel letto diserta.

L'una vegghiava a studio de la culla,
  e, consolando, usava l'idioma
  che prima i padri e le madri trastulla;

l'altra, traendo a la rocca la chioma,
  favoleggiava con la sua famiglia
  d'i Troiani, di Fiesole e di Roma.

Saria tenuta allor tal maraviglia
  una Cianghella, un Lapo Salterello,
  qual or saria Cincinnato e Corniglia.

A cosi` riposato, a cosi` bello
  viver di cittadini, a cosi` fida
  cittadinanza, a cosi` dolce ostello,

Maria mi die`, chiamata in alte grida;
  e ne l'antico vostro Batisteo
  insieme fui cristiano e Cacciaguida.

Moronto fu mio frate ed Eliseo;
  mia donna venne a me di val di Pado,
  e quindi il sopranome tuo si feo.

Poi seguitai lo 'mperador Currado;
  ed el mi cinse de la sua milizia,
  tanto per bene ovrar li venni in grado.

Not yet the daughter at her birth struck fear
  Into the father, for the time and dower
  Did not o'errun this side or that the measure.

No houses had she void of families,
  Not yet had thither come Sardanapalus
  To show what in a chamber can be done;

Not yet surpassed had Montemalo been
  By your Uccellatojo, which surpassed
  Shall in its downfall be as in its rise.

Bellincion Berti saw I go begirt
  With leather and with bone, and from the mirror
  His dame depart without a painted face;

And him of Nerli saw, and him of Vecchio,
  Contented with their simple suits of buff
  And with the spindle and the flax their dames.

O fortunate women! and each one was certain
  Of her own burial-place, and none as yet
  For sake of France was in her bed deserted.

One o'er the cradle kept her studious watch,
  And in her lullaby the language used
  That first delights the fathers and the mothers;

Another, drawing tresses from her distaff,
  Told o'er among her family the tales
  Of Trojans and of Fesole and Rome.

As great a marvel then would have been held
  A Lapo Salterello, a Cianghella,
  As Cincinnatus or Cornelia now.

To such a quiet, such a beautiful
  Life of the citizen, to such a safe
  Community, and to so sweet an inn,

Did Mary give me, with loud cries invoked,
  And in your ancient Baptistery at once
  Christian and Cacciaguida I became.

Moronto was my brother, and Eliseo;
  From Val di Pado came to me my wife,
  And from that place thy surname was derived.

I followed afterward the Emperor Conrad,
  And he begirt me of his chivalry,
  So much I pleased him with my noble deeds.

Dietro li andai incontro a la nequizia
  di quella legge il cui popolo usurpa,
  per colpa d'i pastor, vostra giustizia.

Quivi fu' io da quella gente turpa
  disviluppato dal mondo fallace,
  lo cui amor molt'anime deturpa;

e venni dal martiro a questa pace"".

I followed in his train against that law's
  Iniquity, whose people doth usurp
  Your just possession, through your Pastor's fault.

There by that execrable race was I
  Released from bonds of the fallacious world,
  The love of which defileth many souls,

And came from martyrdom unto this peace."

Paradiso: Canto XVI

Dante's Noble Ancestry. Cacciaguida's Discourse of the Great Florentines.

O poca nostra nobilta` di sangue,
  se gloriar di te la gente fai
  qua giu` dove l'affetto nostro langue,

mirabil cosa non mi sara` mai:
  che' la` dove appetito non si torce,
  dico nel cielo, io me ne gloriai.

Ben se' tu manto che tosto raccorce:
  si` che, se non s'appon di di` in die,
  lo tempo va dintorno con le force.

Dal 'voi' che prima a Roma s'offerie,
  in che la sua famiglia men persevra,
  ricominciaron le parole mie;

onde Beatrice, ch'era un poco scevra,
  ridendo, parve quella che tossio
  al primo fallo scritto di Ginevra.

Io cominciai: ""Voi siete il padre mio;
  voi mi date a parlar tutta baldezza;
  voi mi levate si`, ch'i' son piu` ch'io.

Per tanti rivi s'empie d'allegrezza
  la mente mia, che di se' fa letizia
  perche' puo` sostener che non si spezza.

Ditemi dunque, cara mia primizia,
  quai fuor li vostri antichi e quai fuor li anni
  che si segnaro in vostra puerizia;

ditemi de l'ovil di San Giovanni
  quanto era allora, e chi eran le genti
  tra esso degne di piu` alti scanni"".

O thou our poor nobility of blood,
  If thou dost make the people glory in thee
  Down here where our affection languishes,

A marvellous thing it ne'er will be to me;
  For there where appetite is not perverted,
  I say in Heaven, of thee I made a boast!

Truly thou art a cloak that quickly shortens,
  So that unless we piece thee day by day
  Time goeth round about thee with his shears!

With 'You,' which Rome was first to tolerate,
  (Wherein her family less perseveres,)
  Yet once again my words beginning made;

Whence Beatrice, who stood somewhat apart,
  Smiling, appeared like unto her who coughed
  At the first failing writ of Guenever.

And I began: "You are my ancestor,
  You give to me all hardihood to speak,
  You lift me so that I am more than I.

So many rivulets with gladness fill
  My mind, that of itself it makes a joy
  Because it can endure this and not burst.

Then tell me, my beloved root ancestral,
  Who were your ancestors, and what the years
  That in your boyhood chronicled themselves?

Tell me about the sheepfold of Saint John,
  How large it was, and who the people were
  Within it worthy of the highest seats."

Come s'avviva a lo spirar d'i venti
  carbone in fiamma, cosi` vid'io quella
  luce risplendere a' miei blandimenti;
	As at the blowing of the winds a coal
	  Quickens to flame, so I beheld that light
	  Become resplendent at my blandishments.

e come a li occhi miei si fe' piu` bella,   cosi` con voce piu` dolce e soave, ma non con questa moderna favella,	And as unto mine eyes it grew more fair, With voice more sweet and tender, but not in This modern dialect, it said to me:
dissemi: ""Da quel di` che fu detto 'Ave'   al parto in che mia madre, ch'e` or santa, s'allevio` di me ond'era grave,	"From uttering of the 'Ave,' till the birth In which my mother, who is now a saint, Of me was lightened who had been her burden,

al suo Leon cinquecento cinquanta
  e trenta fiate venne questo foco
  a rinfiammarsi sotto la sua pianta.
	Unto its Lion had this fire returned
	  Five hundred fifty times and thirty more,
	  To reinflame itself beneath his paw.

Li antichi miei e io nacqui nel loco
  dove si truova pria l'ultimo sesto
  da quei che corre il vostro annual gioco.
	My ancestors and I our birthplace had
	  Where first is found the last ward of the city
	  By him who runneth in your annual game.

Basti d'i miei maggiori udirne questo:
  chi ei si fosser e onde venner quivi,
  piu` e` tacer che ragionare onesto.
	Suffice it of my elders to hear this;
	  But who they were, and whence they thither came,
	  Silence is more considerate than speech.

Tutti color ch'a quel tempo eran ivi
  da poter arme tra Marte e 'l Batista,
  eran il quinto di quei ch'or son vivi.
	All those who at that time were there between
	  Mars and the Baptist, fit for bearing arms,
	  Were a fifth part of those who now are living;

Ma la cittadinanza, ch'e` or mista
  di Campi, di Certaldo e di Fegghine,
  pura vediesi ne l'ultimo artista.
	But the community, that now is mixed
	  With Campi and Certaldo and Figghine,
	  Pure in the lowest artisan was seen.

Oh quanto fora meglio esser vicine
  quelle genti ch'io dico, e al Galluzzo
  e a Trespiano aver vostro confine,
	O how much better 'twere to have as neighbours
	  The folk of whom I speak, and at Galluzzo
	  And at Trespiano have your boundary,

che averle dentro e sostener lo puzzo
  del villan d'Aguglion, di quel da Signa,
  che gia` per barattare ha l'occhio aguzzo!
	Than have them in the town, and bear the stench
	  Of Aguglione's churl, and him of Signa
	  Who has sharp eyes for trickery already.

Se la gente ch'al mondo piu` traligna
  non fosse stata a Cesare noverca,
  ma come madre a suo figlio benigna,
	Had not the folk, which most of all the world
	  Degenerates, been a step-dame unto Caesar,
	  But as a mother to her son benignant,

tal fatto e` fiorentino e cambia e merca,   che si sarebbe volto a Simifonti,   la` dove andava l'avolo a la cerca;	Some who turn Florentines, and trade and discount, Would have gone back again to Simifonte There where their grandsires went about as beggars.

sariesi Montemurlo ancor de' Conti;
  sarieno i Cerchi nel piovier d'Acone,
  e forse in Valdigrieve i Buondelmonti.
	At Montemurlo still would be the Counts,
	  The Cerchi in the parish of Acone,
	  Perhaps in Valdigrieve the Buondelmonti.

Sempre la confusion de le persone
  principio fu del mal de la cittade,
  come del vostro il cibo che s'appone;

e cieco toro piu` avaccio cade
  che cieco agnello; e molte volte taglia
  piu` e meglio una che le cinque spade.

Se tu riguardi Luni e Orbisaglia
  come sono ite, e come se ne vanno
  di retro ad esse Chiusi e Sinigaglia,

udir come le schiatte si disfanno
  non ti parra` nova cosa ne' forte,
  poscia che le cittadi termine hanno.

Le vostre cose tutte hanno lor morte,
  si` come voi; ma celasi in alcuna
  che dura molto, e le vite son corte.

E come 'l volger del ciel de la luna
  cuopre e discuopre i liti sanza posa,
  cosi` fa di Fiorenza la Fortuna:

per che non dee parer mirabil cosa
  cio` ch'io diro` de li alti Fiorentini
  onde e` la fama nel tempo nascosa.

Io vidi li Ughi e vidi i Catellini,
  Filippi, Greci, Ormanni e Alberichi,
  gia` nel calare, illustri cittadini;

e vidi cosi` grandi come antichi,
  con quel de la Sannella, quel de l'Arca,
  e Soldanieri e Ardinghi e Bostichi.

Sovra la porta ch'al presente e` carca
  di nova fellonia di tanto peso
  che tosto fia iattura de la barca,

erano i Ravignani, ond'e` disceso
  il conte Guido e qualunque del nome
  de l'alto Bellincione ha poscia preso.

Quel de la Pressa sapeva gia` come
  regger si vuole, e avea Galigaio
  dorata in casa sua gia` l'elsa e 'l pome.

Grand'era gia` la colonna del Vaio,
  Sacchetti, Giuochi, Fifanti e Barucci
  e Galli e quei ch'arrossan per lo staio.

Ever the intermingling of the people
  Has been the source of malady in cities,
  As in the body food it surfeits on;

And a blind bull more headlong plunges down
  Than a blind lamb; and very often cuts
  Better and more a single sword than five.

If Luni thou regard, and Urbisaglia,
  How they have passed away, and how are passing
  Chiusi and Sinigaglia after them,

To hear how races waste themselves away,
  Will seem to thee no novel thing nor hard,
  Seeing that even cities have an end.

All things of yours have their mortality,
  Even as yourselves; but it is hidden in some
  That a long while endure, and lives are short;

And as the turning of the lunar heaven
  Covers and bares the shores without a pause,
  In the like manner fortune does with Florence.

Therefore should not appear a marvellous thing
  What I shall say of the great Florentines
  Of whom the fame is hidden in the Past.

I saw the Ughi, saw the Catellini,
  Filippi, Greci, Ormanni, and Alberichi,
  Even in their fall illustrious citizens;

And saw, as mighty as they ancient were,
  With him of La Sannella him of Arca,
  And Soldanier, Ardinghi, and Bostichi.

Near to the gate that is at present laden
  With a new felony of so much weight
  That soon it shall be jetsam from the bark,

The Ravignani were, from whom descended
  The County Guido, and whoe'er the name
  Of the great Bellincione since hath taken.

He of La Pressa knew the art of ruling
  Already, and already Galigajo
  Had hilt and pommel gilded in his house.

Mighty already was the Column Vair,
  Sacchetti, Giuochi, Fifant, and Barucci,
  And Galli, and they who for the bushel blush.

Lo ceppo di che nacquero i Calfucci
  era gia` grande, e gia` eran tratti
  a le curule Sizii e Arrigucci.

Oh quali io vidi quei che son disfatti
  per lor superbia! e le palle de l'oro
  fiorian Fiorenza in tutt'i suoi gran fatti.

Cosi` facieno i padri di coloro
  che, sempre che la vostra chiesa vaca,
  si fanno grassi stando a consistoro.

L'oltracotata schiatta che s'indraca
  dietro a chi fugge, e a chi mostra 'l dente
  o ver la borsa, com'agnel si placa,

gia` venia su`, ma di picciola gente;
  si` che non piacque ad Ubertin Donato
  che poi il suocero il fe' lor parente.

Gia` era 'l Caponsacco nel mercato
  disceso giu` da Fiesole, e gia` era
  buon cittadino Giuda e Infangato.

Io diro` cosa incredibile e vera:
  nel picciol cerchio s'entrava per porta
  che si nomava da quei de la Pera.

Ciascun che de la bella insegna porta
  del gran barone il cui nome e 'l cui pregio
  la festa di Tommaso riconforta,

da esso ebbe milizia e privilegio;
  avvegna che con popol si rauni
  oggi colui che la fascia col fregio.

Gia` eran Gualterotti e Importuni;
  e ancor saria Borgo piu` quieto,
  se di novi vicin fosser digiuni.

La casa di che nacque il vostro fleto,
  per lo giusto disdegno che v'ha morti,
  e puose fine al vostro viver lieto,

era onorata, essa e suoi consorti:
  o Buondelmonte, quanto mal fuggisti
  le nozze sue per li altrui conforti!

Molti sarebber lieti, che son tristi,
  se Dio t'avesse conceduto ad Ema
  la prima volta ch'a citta` venisti.

The stock from which were the Calfucci born
  Was great already, and already chosen
  To curule chairs the Sizii and Arrigucci.

O how beheld I those who are undone
  By their own pride! and how the Balls of Gold
  Florence enflowered in all their mighty deeds!

So likewise did the ancestors of those
  Who evermore, when vacant is your church,
  Fatten by staying in consistory.

The insolent race, that like a dragon follows
  Whoever flees, and unto him that shows
  His teeth or purse is gentle as a lamb,

Already rising was, but from low people;
  So that it pleased not Ubertin Donato
  That his wife's father should make him their kin.

Already had Caponsacco to the Market
  From Fesole descended, and already
  Giuda and Infangato were good burghers.

I'll tell a thing incredible, but true;
  One entered the small circuit by a gate
  Which from the Della Pera took its name!

Each one that bears the beautiful escutcheon
  Of the great baron whose renown and name
  The festival of Thomas keepeth fresh,

Knighthood and privilege from him received;
  Though with the populace unites himself
  To-day the man who binds it with a border.

Already were Gualterotti and Importuni;
  And still more quiet would the Borgo be
  If with new neighbours it remained unfed.

The house from which is born your lamentation,
  Through just disdain that death among you brought
  And put an end unto your joyous life,

Was honoured in itself and its companions.
  O Buondelmonte, how in evil hour
  Thou fled'st the bridal at another's promptings!

Many would be rejoicing who are sad,
  If God had thee surrendered to the Ema
  The first time that thou camest to the city.

Ma conveniesi a quella pietra scema
  che guarda 'l ponte, che Fiorenza fesse
  vittima ne la sua pace postrema.

Con queste genti, e con altre con esse,
  vid'io Fiorenza in si` fatto riposo,
  che non avea cagione onde piangesse:

con queste genti vid'io glorioso
  e giusto il popol suo, tanto che 'l giglio
  non era ad asta mai posto a ritroso,

ne' per division fatto vermiglio"".

But it behoved the mutilated stone
  Which guards the bridge, that Florence should pro-
    vide
  A victim in her latest hour of peace.

With all these families, and others with them,
  Florence beheld I in so great repose,
  That no occasion had she whence to weep;

With all these families beheld so just
  And glorious her people, that the lily
  Never upon the spear was placed reversed,

Nor by division was vermilion made."

Paradiso: Canto XVII

Cacciaguida's Prophecy of Dante's Banishment.

Qual venne a Climene', per accertarsi
  di cio` ch'avea incontro a se' udito,
  quei ch'ancor fa li padri ai figli scarsi;
	As came to Clymene, to be made certain
	  Of that which he had heard against himself,
	  He who makes fathers chary still to children,

tal era io, e tal era sentito
  e da Beatrice e da la santa lampa
  che pria per me avea mutato sito.
	Even such was I, and such was I perceived
	  By Beatrice and by the holy light
	  That first on my account had changed its place.

Per che mia donna ""Manda fuor la vampa
  del tuo disio"", mi disse, ""si` ch'ella esca
  segnata bene de la interna stampa;
	Therefore my Lady said to me: "Send forth
	  The flame of thy desire, so that it issue
	  Imprinted well with the internal stamp;

non perche' nostra conoscenza cresca
  per tuo parlare, ma perche' t'ausi
  a dir la sete, si` che l'uom ti mesca"".
	Not that our knowledge may be greater made
	  By speech of thine, but to accustom thee
	  To tell thy thirst, that we may give thee drink."

""O cara piota mia che si` t'insusi,
  che, come veggion le terrene menti
  non capere in triangol due ottusi,
	"O my beloved tree, (that so dost lift thee,
	  That even as minds terrestrial perceive
	  No triangle containeth two obtuse,

cosi` vedi le cose contingenti
  anzi che sieno in se', mirando il punto
  a cui tutti li tempi son presenti;
	So thou beholdest the contingent things
	  Ere in themselves they are, fixing thine eyes
	  Upon the point in which all times are present,)

mentre ch'io era a Virgilio congiunto
  su per lo monte che l'anime cura
  e discendendo nel mondo defunto,
	While I was with Virgilius conjoined
	  Upon the mountain that the souls doth heal,
	  And when descending into the dead world,

dette mi fuor di mia vita futura
  parole gravi, avvegna ch'io mi senta
  ben tetragono ai colpi di ventura;
	Were spoken to me of my future life
	  Some grievous words; although I feel myself
	  In sooth foursquare against the blows of chance.

per che la voglia mia saria contenta
  d'intender qual fortuna mi s'appressa;
  che' saetta previsa vien piu` lenta"".
	On this account my wish would be content
	  To hear what fortune is approaching me,
	  Because foreseen an arrow comes more slowly."

Cosi` diss'io a quella luce stessa
  che pria m'avea parlato; e come volle
  Beatrice, fu la mia voglia confessa.

Ne' per ambage, in che la gente folle
  gia` s'inviscava pria che fosse anciso
  l'Agnel di Dio che le peccata tolle,

ma per chiare parole e con preciso
  latin rispuose quello amor paterno,
  chiuso e parvente del suo proprio riso:

““La contingenza, che fuor del quaderno
  de la vostra matera non si stende,
  tutta e` dipinta nel cospetto etterno:

necessita` pero` quindi non prende
  se non come dal viso in che si specchia
  nave che per torrente giu` discende.

Da indi, si` come viene ad orecchia
  dolce armonia da organo, mi viene
  a vista il tempo che ti s'apparecchia.

Qual si partio Ipolito d'Atene
  per la spietata e perfida noverca,
  tal di Fiorenza partir ti convene.

Questo si vuole e questo gia` si cerca,
  e tosto verra` fatto a chi cio` pensa
  la` dove Cristo tutto di` si merca.

La colpa seguira` la parte offensa
  in grido, come suol; ma la vendetta
  fia testimonio al ver che la dispensa.

Tu lascerai ogne cosa diletta
  piu` caramente; e questo e` quello strale
  che l'arco de lo essilio pria saetta.

Tu proverai si` come sa di sale
  lo pane altrui, e come e` duro calle
  lo scendere e 'l salir per l'altrui scale.

E quel che piu` ti gravera` le spalle,
  sara` la compagnia malvagia e scempia
  con la qual tu cadrai in questa valle;

che tutta ingrata, tutta matta ed empia
  si fara` contr'a te; ma, poco appresso,
  ella, non tu, n'avra` rossa la tempia.

Thus did I say unto that selfsame light
  That unto me had spoken before; and even
  As Beatrice willed was my own will confessed.

Not in vague phrase, in which the foolish folk
  Ensnared themselves of old, ere yet was slain
  The Lamb of God who taketh sins away,

But with clear words and unambiguous
  Language responded that paternal love,
  Hid and revealed by its own proper smile:

"Contingency, that outside of the volume
  Of your materiality extends not,
  Is all depicted in the eternal aspect.

Necessity however thence it takes not,
  Except as from the eye, in which 'tis mirrored,
  A ship that with the current down descends.

From thence, e'en as there cometh to the ear
  Sweet harmony from an organ, comes in sight
  To me the time that is preparing for thee.

As forth from Athens went Hippolytus,
  By reason of his step-dame false and cruel,
  So thou from Florence must perforce depart.

Already this is willed, and this is sought for;
  And soon it shall be done by him who thinks it,
  Where every day the Christ is bought and sold.

The blame shall follow the offended party
  In outcry as is usual; but the vengeance
  Shall witness to the truth that doth dispense it.

Thou shalt abandon everything beloved
  Most tenderly, and this the arrow is
  Which first the bow of banishment shoots forth.

Thou shalt have proof how savoureth of salt
  The bread of others, and how hard a road
  The going down and up another's stairs.

And that which most shall weigh upon thy shoulders
  Will be the bad and foolish company
  With which into this valley thou shalt fall;

For all ingrate, all mad and impious
  Will they become against thee; but soon after
  They, and not thou, shall have the forehead scarlet.

Di sua bestialitate il suo processo
  fara` la prova; si` ch'a te fia bello
  averti fatta parte per te stesso.

Lo primo tuo refugio e 'l primo ostello
  sara` la cortesia del gran Lombardo
  che 'n su la scala porta il santo uccello;

ch'in te avra` si` benigno riguardo,
  che del fare e del chieder, tra voi due,
  fia primo quel che tra li altri e` piu` tardo.

Con lui vedrai colui che 'mpresso fue,
  nascendo, si` da questa stella forte,
  che notabili fier l'opere sue.

Non se ne son le genti ancora accorte
  per la novella eta`, che' pur nove anni
  son queste rote intorno di lui torte;

ma pria che 'l Guasco l'alto Arrigo inganni,
  parran faville de la sua virtute
  in non curar d'argento ne' d'affanni.

Le sue magnificenze conosciute
  saranno ancora, si` che ' suoi nemici
  non ne potran tener le lingue mute.

A lui t'aspetta e a' suoi benefici;
  per lui fia trasmutata molta gente,
  cambiando condizion ricchi e mendici;

e portera'ne scritto ne la mente
  di lui, e nol dirai""; e disse cose
  incredibili a quei che fier presente.

Poi giunse: ""Figlio, queste son le chiose
  di quel che ti fu detto; ecco le 'nsidie
  che dietro a pochi giri son nascose.

Non vo' pero` ch'a' tuoi vicini invidie,
  poscia che s'infutura la tua vita
  vie piu` la` che 'l punir di lor perfidie"".

Poi che, tacendo, si mostro` spedita
  l'anima santa di metter la trama
  in quella tela ch'io le porsi ordita,

io cominciai, come colui che brama,
  dubitando, consiglio da persona
  che vede e vuol dirittamente e ama:

Of their bestiality their own proceedings
  Shall furnish proof; so 'twill be well for thee
  A party to have made thee by thyself.

Thine earliest refuge and thine earliest inn
  Shall be the mighty Lombard's courtesy,
  Who on the Ladder bears the holy bird,

Who such benign regard shall have for thee
  That 'twixt you twain, in doing and in asking,
  That shall be first which is with others last.

With him shalt thou see one who at his birth
  Has by this star of strength been so impressed,
  That notable shall his achievements be.

Not yet the people are aware of him
  Through his young age, since only nine years yet
  Around about him have these wheels revolved.

But ere the Gascon cheat the noble Henry,
  Some sparkles of his virtue shall appear
  In caring not for silver nor for toil.

So recognized shall his magnificence
  Become hereafter, that his enemies
  Will not have power to keep mute tongues about it.

On him rely, and on his benefits;
  By him shall many people be transformed,
  Changing condition rich and mendicant;

And written in thy mind thou hence shalt bear
  Of him, but shalt not say it"—and things said he
  Incredible to those who shall be present.

Then added: "Son, these are the commentaries
  On what was said to thee; behold the snares
  That are concealed behind few revolutions;

Yet would I not thy neighbours thou shouldst envy,
  Because thy life into the future reaches
  Beyond the punishment of their perfidies."

When by its silence showed that sainted soul
  That it had finished putting in the woof
  Into that web which I had given it warped,

Began I, even as he who yearneth after,
  Being in doubt, some counsel from a person
  Who seeth, and uprightly wills, and loves:

""Ben veggio, padre mio, sì come sprona
  lo tempo verso me, per colpo darmi
  tal, ch'e' più grave a chi più s'abbandona;

per che di provedenza e' buon ch'io m'armi,
  sì che, se loco m'e' tolto più caro,
  io non perdessi li altri per miei carmi.

Giù per lo mondo sanza fine amaro,
  e per lo monte del cui bel cacume
  li occhi de la mia donna mi levaro,

e poscia per lo ciel, di lume in lume,
  ho io appreso quel che s'io ridico,
  a molti fia sapor di forte agrume;

e s'io al vero son timido amico,
  temo di perder viver tra coloro
  che questo tempo chiameranno antico"".

La luce in che rideva il mio tesoro
  ch'io trovai lì, si fe' prima corusca,
  quale a raggio di sole specchio d'oro;

indi rispuose: ""Coscienza fusca
  o de la propria o de l'altrui vergogna
  pur sentirà la tua parola brusca.

Ma nondimen, rimossa ogne menzogna,
  tutta tua vision fa manifesta;
  e lascia pur grattar dov'e' la rogna.

Che' se la voce tua sarà molesta
  nel primo gusto, vital nodrimento
  lascerà poi, quando sarà digesta.

Questo tuo grido farà come vento,
  che le più alte cime più percuote;
  e ciò non fa d'onor poco argomento.

Però ti son mostrate in queste rote,
  nel monte e ne la valle dolorosa
  pur l'anime che son di fama note,

che l'animo di quel ch'ode, non posa
  ne' ferma fede per essempro ch'aia
  la sua radice incognita e ascosa,

ne' per altro argomento che non paia"".

"Well see I, father mine, how spurreth on
  The time towards me such a blow to deal me
  As heaviest is to him who most gives way.

Therefore with foresight it is well I arm me,
  That, if the dearest place be taken from me,
  I may not lose the others by my songs.

Down through the world of infinite bitterness,
  And o'er the mountain, from whose beauteous summit
  The eyes of my own Lady lifted me,

And afterward through heaven from light to light,
  I have learned that which, if I tell again,
  Will be a savour of strong herbs to many.

And if I am a timid friend to truth,
  I fear lest I may lose my life with those
  Who will hereafter call this time the olden."

The light in which was smiling my own treasure
  Which there I had discovered, flashed at first
  As in the sunshine doth a golden mirror;

Then made reply: "A conscience overcast
  Or with its own or with another's shame,
  Will taste forsooth the tartness of thy word;

But ne'ertheless, all falsehood laid aside,
  Make manifest thy vision utterly,
  And let them scratch wherever is the itch;

For if thine utterance shall offensive be
  At the first taste, a vital nutriment
  'Twill leave thereafter, when it is digested.

This cry of thine shall do as doth the wind,
  Which smiteth most the most exalted summits,
  And that is no slight argument of honour.

Therefore are shown to thee within these wheels,
  Upon the mount and in the dolorous valley,
  Only the souls that unto fame are known;

Because the spirit of the hearer rests not,
  Nor doth confirm its faith by an example
  Which has the root of it unknown and hidden,

Or other reason that is not apparent."

Paradiso: Canto XVIII

The Sixth Heaven, Jupiter: Righteous Kings and Rulers. The Celestial Eagle. Dante's Invectives against ecclesiastical Avarice.

Gia` si godeva solo del suo verbo
  quello specchio beato, e io gustava
  lo mio, temprando col dolce l'acerbo;
	Now was alone rejoicing in its word
	  That soul beatified, and I was tasting
	  My own, the bitter tempering with the sweet,

e quella donna ch'a Dio mi menava
  disse: ““Muta pensier; pensa ch'i' sono
  presso a colui ch'ogne torto disgrava”“.
	And the Lady who to God was leading me
	  Said: "Change thy thought; consider that I am
	  Near unto Him who every wrong disburdens."

Io mi rivolsi a l'amoroso suono
  del mio conforto; e qual io allor vidi
  ne li occhi santi amor, qui l'abbandono:
	Unto the loving accents of my comfort
	  I turned me round, and then what love I saw
	  Within those holy eyes I here relinquish;

non perch'io pur del mio parlar diffidi,
  ma per la mente che non puo` redire
  sovra se' tanto, s'altri non la guidi.
	Not only that my language I distrust,
	  But that my mind cannot return so far
	  Above itself, unless another guide it.

Tanto poss'io di quel punto ridire,
  che, rimirando lei, lo mio affetto
  libero fu da ogne altro disire,
	Thus much upon that point can I repeat,
	  That, her again beholding, my affection
	  From every other longing was released.

fin che 'l piacere etterno, che diretto
  raggiava in Beatrice, dal bel viso
  mi contentava col secondo aspetto.
	While the eternal pleasure, which direct
	  Rayed upon Beatrice, from her fair face
	  Contented me with its reflected aspect,

Vincendo me col lume d'un sorriso,
  ella mi disse: ““Volgiti e ascolta;
  che' non pur ne' miei occhi e` paradiso”“.
	Conquering me with the radiance of a smile,
	  She said to me, "Turn thee about and listen;
	  Not in mine eyes alone is Paradise."

Come si vede qui alcuna volta
  l'affetto ne la vista, s'elli e` tanto,
  che da lui sia tutta l'anima tolta,
	Even as sometimes here do we behold
	  The affection in the look, if it be such
	  That all the soul is wrapt away by it,

cosi` nel fiammeggiar del folgor santo,
  a ch'io mi volsi, conobbi la voglia
  in lui di ragionarmi ancora alquanto.
	So, by the flaming of the effulgence holy
	  To which I turned, I recognized therein
	  The wish of speaking to me somewhat farther.

El comincio`: ““In questa quinta soglia
de l'albero che vive de la cima
e frutta sempre e mai non perde foglia,

spiriti son beati, che giu`, prima
che venissero al ciel, fuor di gran voce,
si` ch'ogne musa ne sarebbe opima.

Pero` mira ne' corni de la croce:
quello ch'io nomero`, li` fara` l'atto
che fa in nube il suo foco veloce”“.

Io vidi per la croce un lume tratto
dal nomar Iosue`, com'el si feo;
ne' mi fu noto il dir prima che 'l fatto.

E al nome de l'alto Macabeo
vidi moversi un altro roteando,
e letizia era ferza del paleo.

Cosi` per Carlo Magno e per Orlando
due ne segui` lo mio attento sguardo,
com'occhio segue suo falcon volando.

Poscia trasse Guiglielmo e Rinoardo
e 'l duca Gottifredi la mia vista
per quella croce, e Ruberto Guiscardo.

Indi, tra l'altre luci mota e mista,
mostrommi l'alma che m'avea parlato
qual era tra i cantor del cielo artista.

Io mi rivolsi dal mio destro lato
per vedere in Beatrice il mio dovere,
o per parlare o per atto, segnato;

e vidi le sue luci tanto mere,
tanto gioconde, che la sua sembianza
vinceva li altri e l'ultimo solere.

E come, per sentir piu` dilettanza
bene operando, l'uom di giorno in giorno
s'accorge che la sua virtute avanza,

si` m'accors'io che 'l mio girare intorno
col cielo insieme avea cresciuto l'arco,
veggendo quel miracol piu` addorno.

E qual e` 'l trasmutare in picciol varco
di tempo in bianca donna, quando 'l volto
suo si discarchi di vergogna il carco,

And it began: "In this fifth resting-place
Upon the tree that liveth by its summit,
And aye bears fruit, and never loses leaf,

Are blessed spirits that below, ere yet
They came to Heaven, were of such great renown
That every Muse therewith would affluent be.

Therefore look thou upon the cross's horns;
He whom I now shall name will there enact
What doth within a cloud its own swift fire."

I saw athwart the Cross a splendour drawn
By naming Joshua, (even as he did it,)
Nor noted I the word before the deed;

And at the name of the great Maccabee
I saw another move itself revolving,
And gladness was the whip unto that top.

Likewise for Charlemagne and for Orlando,
Two of them my regard attentive followed
As followeth the eye its falcon flying.

William thereafterward, and Renouard,
And the Duke Godfrey, did attract my sight
Along upon that Cross, and Robert Guiscard.

Then, moved and mingled with the other lights,
The soul that had addressed me showed how great
An artist 'twas among the heavenly singers.

To my right side I turned myself around,
My duty to behold in Beatrice
Either by words or gesture signified;

And so translucent I beheld her eyes,
So full of pleasure, that her countenance
Surpassed its other and its latest wont.

And as, by feeling greater delectation,
A man in doing good from day to day
Becomes aware his virtue is increasing,

So I became aware that my gyration
With heaven together had increased its arc,
That miracle beholding more adorned.

And such as is the change, in little lapse
Of time, in a pale woman, when her face
Is from the load of bashfulness unladen,

tal fu ne li occhi miei, quando fui volto,
  per lo candor de la temprata stella
  sesta, che dentro a se' m'avea ricolto.
	Such was it in mine eyes, when I had turned,
	  Caused by the whiteness of the temperate star,
	  The sixth, which to itself had gathered me.

Io vidi in quella giovial facella
  lo sfavillar de l'amor che li` era,
  segnare a li occhi miei nostra favella.
	Within that Jovial torch did I behold
	  The sparkling of the love which was therein
	  Delineate our language to mine eyes.

E come augelli surti di rivera,
  quasi congratulando a lor pasture,
  fanno di se' or tonda or altra schiera,
	And even as birds uprisen from the shore,
	  As in congratulation o'er their food,
	  Make squadrons of themselves, now round, now
	    long,

si` dentro ai lumi sante creature
  volitando cantavano, e faciensi
  or D, or I, or L in sue figure.
	So from within those lights the holy creatures
	  Sang flying to and fro, and in their figures
	  Made of themselves now D, now I, now L.

Prima, cantando, a sua nota moviensi;
  poi, diventando l'un di questi segni,
  un poco s'arrestavano e taciensi.
	First singing they to their own music moved;
	  Then one becoming of these characters,
	  A little while they rested and were silent.

O diva Pegasea che li 'ngegni
  fai gloriosi e rendili longevi,
  ed essi teco le cittadi e ' regni,
	O divine Pegasea, thou who genius
	  Dost glorious make, and render it long-lived,
	  And this through thee the cities and the kingdoms,

illustrami di te, si` ch'io rilevi
  le lor figure com'io l'ho concette:
  paia tua possa in questi versi brevi!
	Illume me with thyself, that I may bring
	  Their figures out as I have them conceived!
	  Apparent be thy power in these brief verses!

Mostrarsi dunque in cinque volte sette
  vocali e consonanti; e io notai
  le parti si`, come mi parver dette.
	Themselves then they displayed in five times seven
	  Vowels and consonants; and I observed
	  The parts as they seemed spoken unto me.

'DILIGITE IUSTITIAM', primai
  fur verbo e nome di tutto 'l dipinto;
  'QUI IUDICATIS TERRAM', fur sezzai.
	'Diligite justitiam,' these were
	  First verb and noun of all that was depicted;
	  'Qui judicatis terram' were the last.

Poscia ne l'emme del vocabol quinto rimasero ordinate; si` che Giove   pareva argento li` d'oro distinto.	Thereafter in the M of the fifth word Remained they so arranged, that Jupiter Seemed to be silver there with gold inlaid.

E vidi scendere altre luci dove
  era il colmo de l'emme, e li` quetarsi
  cantando, credo, il ben ch'a se' le move.
	And other lights I saw descend where was
	  The summit of the M, and pause there singing
	  The good, I think, that draws them to itself.

Poi, come nel percuoter d'i ciocchi arsi
  surgono innumerabili faville,
  onde li stolti sogliono agurarsi,
	Then, as in striking upon burning logs
	  Upward there fly innumerable sparks,
	  Whence fools are wont to look for auguries,

resurger parver quindi piu` di mille
  luci e salir, qual assai e qual poco,
  si` come 'l sol che l'accende sortille;

e quietata ciascuna in suo loco,
  la testa e 'l collo d'un'aguglia vidi
  rappresentare a quel distinto foco.

Quei che dipinge li`, non ha chi 'l guidi;
  ma esso guida, e da lui si rammenta
  quella virtu` ch'e` forma per li nidi.

L'altra beatitudo, che contenta
  pareva prima d'ingigliarsi a l'emme,
  con poco moto seguito` la 'mprenta.

O dolce stella, quali e quante gemme
  mi dimostraro che nostra giustizia
  effetto sia del ciel che tu ingemme!

Per ch'io prego la mente in che s'inizia
  tuo moto e tua virtute, che rimiri
  ond'esce il fummo che 'l tuo raggio vizia;

si` ch'un'altra fiata omai s'adiri
  del comperare e vender dentro al templo
  che si muro` di segni e di martiri.

O milizia del ciel cu' io contemplo,
  adora per color che sono in terra
  tutti sviati dietro al malo essemplo!

Gia` si solea con le spade far guerra;
  ma or si fa togliendo or qui or quivi
  lo pan che 'l pio Padre a nessun serra.

Ma tu che sol per cancellare scrivi,
  pensa che Pietro e Paulo, che moriro
  per la vigna che guasti, ancor son vivi.

Ben puoi tu dire: ""I' ho fermo 'l disiro
  si` a colui che volle viver solo
  e che per salti fu tratto al martiro,

ch'io non conosco il pescator ne' Polo"".

More than a thousand lights seemed thence to rise,
  And to ascend, some more, and others less,
  Even as the Sun that lights them had allotted;

And, each one being quiet in its place,
  The head and neck beheld I of an eagle
  Delineated by that inlaid fire.

He who there paints has none to be his guide;
  But Himself guides; and is from Him remembered
  That virtue which is form unto the nest.

The other beatitude, that contented seemed
  At first to bloom a lily on the M,
  By a slight motion followed out the imprint.

O gentle star! what and how many gems
  Did demonstrate to me, that all our justice
  Effect is of that heaven which thou ingemmest!

Wherefore I pray the Mind, in which begin
  Thy motion and thy virtue, to regard
  Whence comes the smoke that vitiates thy rays;

So that a second time it now be wroth
  With buying and with selling in the temple
  Whose walls were built with signs and martyrdoms!

O soldiery of heaven, whom I contemplate,
  Implore for those who are upon the earth
  All gone astray after the bad example!

Once 'twas the custom to make war with swords;
  But now 'tis made by taking here and there
  The bread the pitying Father shuts from none.

Yet thou, who writest but to cancel, think
  That Peter and that Paul, who for this vineyard
  Which thou art spoiling died, are still alive!

Well canst thou say: "So steadfast my desire
  Is unto him who willed to live alone,
  And for a dance was led to martyrdom,

That I know not the Fisherman nor Paul."

Paradiso: Canto XIX

The Eagle discourses of Salvation, Faith, and Virtue. Condemnation of the vile Kings of A.D. 1300.

Parea dinanzi a me con l'ali aperte
  la bella image che nel dolce frui
  liete facevan l'anime conserte;

parea ciascuna rubinetto in cui
  raggio di sole ardesse si` acceso,
  che ne' miei occhi rifrangesse lui.

E quel che mi convien ritrar testeso,
  non porto` voce mai, ne' scrisse incostro,
  ne' fu per fantasia gia` mai compreso;

ch'io vidi e anche udi' parlar lo rostro,
  e sonar ne la voce e ""io"" e ""mio"",
  quand'era nel concetto e 'noi' e 'nostro'.

E comincio`: ""Per esser giusto e pio
  son io qui essaltato a quella gloria
  che non si lascia vincere a disio;

e in terra lasciai la mia memoria
  si` fatta, che le genti li` malvage
  commendan lei, ma non seguon la storia"".

Cosi` un sol calor di molte brage
  si fa sentir, come di molti amori
  usciva solo un suon di quella image.

Ond'io appresso: ""O perpetui fiori
  de l'etterna letizia, che pur uno
  parer mi fate tutti vostri odori,

solvetemi, spirando, il gran digiuno
  che lungamente m'ha tenuto in fame,
  non trovandoli in terra cibo alcuno.

Appeared before me with its wings outspread
  The beautiful image that in sweet fruition
  Made jubilant the interwoven souls;

Appeared a little ruby each, wherein
  Ray of the sun was burning so enkindled
  That each into mine eyes refracted it.

And what it now behoves me to retrace
  Nor voice has e'er reported, nor ink written,
  Nor was by fantasy e'er comprehended;

For speak I saw, and likewise heard, the beak,
  And utter with its voice both 'I' and 'My,'
  When in conception it was 'We' and 'Our.'

And it began: "Being just and merciful
  Am I exalted here unto that glory
  Which cannot be exceeded by desire;

And upon earth I left my memory
  Such, that the evil-minded people there
  Commend it, but continue not the story."

So doth a single heat from many embers
  Make itself felt, even as from many loves
  Issued a single sound from out that image.

Whence I thereafter: "O perpetual flowers
  Of the eternal joy, that only one
  Make me perceive your odours manifold,

Exhaling, break within me the great fast
  Which a long season has in hunger held me,
  Not finding for it any food on earth.

Ben so io che, se 'n cielo altro reame
  la divina giustizia fa suo specchio,
  che 'l vostro non l'apprende con velame.

Sapete come attento io m'apparecchio
  ad ascoltar; sapete qual e` quello
  dubbio che m'e` digiun cotanto vecchio"".

Quasi falcone ch'esce del cappello,
  move la testa e con l'ali si plaude,
  voglia mostrando e faccendosi bello,

vid'io farsi quel segno, che di laude
  de la divina grazia era contesto,
  con canti quai si sa chi la` su` gaude.

Poi comincio`: ""Colui che volse il sesto
  a lo stremo del mondo, e dentro ad esso
  distinse tanto occulto e manifesto,

non pote' suo valor si` fare impresso
  in tutto l'universo, che 'l suo verbo
  non rimanesse in infinito eccesso.

E cio` fa certo che 'l primo superbo,
  che fu la somma d'ogne creatura,
  per non aspettar lume, cadde acerbo;

e quinci appar ch'ogne minor natura
  e` corto recettacolo a quel bene
  che non ha fine e se' con se' misura.

Dunque vostra veduta, che convene
  esser alcun de' raggi de la mente
  di che tutte le cose son ripiene,

non po` da sua natura esser possente
  tanto, che suo principio discerna
  molto di la` da quel che l'e` parvente.

Pero` ne la giustizia sempiterna
  la vista che riceve il vostro mondo,
  com'occhio per lo mare, entro s'interna;

che, ben che da la proda veggia il fondo,
  in pelago nol vede; e nondimeno
  eli, ma cela lui l'esser profondo.

Well do I know, that if in heaven its mirror
  Justice Divine another realm doth make,
  Yours apprehends it not through any veil.

You know how I attentively address me
  To listen; and you know what is the doubt
  That is in me so very old a fast."

Even as a falcon, issuing from his hood,
  Doth move his head, and with his wings applaud
    him,
  Showing desire, and making himself fine,

Saw I become that standard, which of lauds
  Was interwoven of the grace divine,
  With such songs as he knows who there rejoices.

Then it began: "He who a compass turned
  On the world's outer verge, and who within it
  Devised so much occult and manifest,

Could not the impress of his power so make
  On all the universe, as that his Word
  Should not remain in infinite excess.

And this makes certain that the first proud being,
  Who was the paragon of every creature,
  By not awaiting light fell immature.

And hence appears it, that each minor nature
  Is scant receptacle unto that good
  Which has no end, and by itself is measured.

In consequence our vision, which perforce
  Must be some ray of that intelligence
  With which all things whatever are replete,

Cannot in its own nature be so potent,
  That it shall not its origin discern
  Far beyond that which is apparent to it.

Therefore into the justice sempiternal
  The power of vision that your world receives,
  As eye into the ocean, penetrates;

Which, though it see the bottom near the shore,
  Upon the deep perceives it not, and yet
  'Tis there, but it is hidden by the depth.

Lume non e`, se non vien dal sereno
  che non si turba mai; anzi e` tenebra
  od ombra de la carne o suo veleno.

Assai t'e` mo aperta la latebra
  che t'ascondeva la giustizia viva,
  di che facei question cotanto crebra;

che' tu dicevi: "Un uom nasce a la riva
  de l'Indo, e quivi non e` chi ragioni
  di Cristo ne' chi legga ne' chi scriva;

e tutti suoi voleri e atti buoni
  sono, quanto ragione umana vede,
  sanza peccato in vita o in sermoni.

Muore non battezzato e sanza fede:
  ov'e` questa giustizia che 'l condanna?
  ov'e` la colpa sua, se ei non crede?"

Or tu chi se', che vuo' sedere a scranna,
  per giudicar di lungi mille miglia
  con la veduta corta d'una spanna?

Certo a colui che meco s'assottiglia,
  se la Scrittura sovra voi non fosse,
  da dubitar sarebbe a maraviglia.

Oh terreni animali! oh menti grosse!
  La prima volonta`, ch'e` da se' buona,
  da se', ch'e` sommo ben, mai non si mosse.

Cotanto e` giusto quanto a lei consuona:
  nullo creato bene a se' la tira,
  ma essa, radiando, lui cagiona"".

Quale sovresso il nido si rigira
  poi c'ha pasciuti la cicogna i figli,
  e come quel ch'e` pasto la rimira;

cotal si fece, e si` levai i cigli,
  la benedetta imagine, che l'ali
  movea sospinte da tanti consigli.

Roteando cantava, e dicea: ""Quali
  son le mie note a te, che non le 'ntendi,
  tal e` il giudicio etterno a voi mortali"".

Poi si quetaro quei lucenti incendi
  de lo Spirito Santo ancor nel segno
  che fe' i Romani al mondo reverendi,

There is no light but comes from the serene
  That never is o'ercast, nay, it is darkness
  Or shadow of the flesh, or else its poison.

Amply to thee is opened now the cavern
  Which has concealed from thee the living justice
  Of which thou mad'st such frequent questioning.

For saidst thou: 'Born a man is on the shore
  Of Indus, and is none who there can speak
  Of Christ, nor who can read, nor who can write;

And all his inclinations and his actions
  Are good, so far as human reason sees,
  Without a sin in life or in discourse:

He dieth unbaptised and without faith;
  Where is this justice that condemneth him?
  Where is his fault, if he do not believe?'

Now who art thou, that on the bench wouldst sit
  In judgment at a thousand miles away,
  With the short vision of a single span?

Truly to him who with me subtilizes,
  If so the Scripture were not over you,
  For doubting there were marvellous occasion.

O animals terrene, O stolid minds,
  The primal will, that in itself is good,
  Ne'er from itself, the Good Supreme, has moved.

So much is just as is accordant with it;
  No good created draws it to itself,
  But it, by raying forth, occasions that."

Even as above her nest goes circling round
  The stork when she has fed her little ones,
  And he who has been fed looks up at her,

So lifted I my brows, and even such
  Became the blessed image, which its wings
  Was moving, by so many counsels urged.

Circling around it sang, and said: "As are
  My notes to thee, who dost not comprehend them,
  Such is the eternal judgment to you mortals."

Those lucent splendours of the Holy Spirit
  Grew quiet then, but still within the standard
  That made the Romans reverend to the world.

esso ricomincio`: ““A questo regno
 non sali` mai chi non credette 'n Cristo,
 ne' pria ne' poi ch'el si chiavasse al legno.

Ma vedi: molti gridan "Cristo, Cristo!",
 che saranno in giudicio assai men prope
 a lui, che tal che non conosce Cristo;

e tai Cristian dannera` l'Etiope,
 quando si partiranno i due collegi,
 l'uno in etterno ricco e l'altro inope.

Che poran dir li Perse a' vostri regi,
 come vedranno quel volume aperto
 nel qual si scrivon tutti suoi dispregi?

Li` si vedra`, tra l'opere d'Alberto,
 quella che tosto movera` la penna,
 per che 'l regno di Praga fia diserto.

Li` si vedra` il duol che sovra Senna
 induce, falseggiando la moneta,
 quel che morra` di colpo di cotenna.

Li` si vedra` la superbia ch'asseta,
 che fa lo Scotto e l'Inghilese folle,
 si` che non puo` soffrir dentro a sua meta.

Vedrassi la lussuria e 'l viver molle
 di quel di Spagna e di quel di Boemme,
 che mai valor non conobbe ne' volle.

Vedrassi al Ciotto di Ierusalemme
 segnata con un i la sua bontate,
 quando 'l contrario segnera` un emme.

Vedrassi l'avarizia e la viltate
 di quei che guarda l'isola del foco,
 ove Anchise fini` la lunga etate;

e a dare ad intender quanto e` poco,
 la sua scrittura fian lettere mozze,
 che noteranno molto in parvo loco.

E parranno a ciascun l'opere sozze
 del barba e del fratel, che tanto egregia
 nazione e due corone han fatte bozze.

E quel di Portogallo e di Norvegia
 li` si conosceranno, e quel di Rascia
 che male ha visto il conio di Vinegia.

It recommenced: "Unto this kingdom never
 Ascended one who had not faith in Christ,
 Before or since he to the tree was nailed.

But look thou, many crying are, 'Christ, Christ!'
 Who at the judgment shall be far less near
 To him than some shall be who knew not Christ.

Such Christians shall the Ethiop condemn,
 When the two companies shall be divided,
 The one for ever rich, the other poor.

What to your kings may not the Persians say,
 When they that volume opened shall behold
 In which are written down all their dispraises?

There shall be seen, among the deeds of Albert,
 That which ere long shall set the pen in motion,
 For which the realm of Prague shall be deserted.

There shall be seen the woe that on the Seine
 He brings by falsifying of the coin,
 Who by the blow of a wild boar shall die.

There shall be seen the pride that causes thirst,
 Which makes the Scot and Englishman so mad
 That they within their boundaries cannot rest;

Be seen the luxury and effeminate life
 Of him of Spain, and the Bohemian,
 Who valour never knew and never wished;

Be seen the Cripple of Jerusalem,
 His goodness represented by an I,
 While the reverse an M shall represent;

Be seen the avarice and poltroonery
 Of him who guards the Island of the Fire,
 Wherein Anchises finished his long life;

And to declare how pitiful he is
 Shall be his record in contracted letters
 Which shall make note of much in little space.

And shall appear to each one the foul deeds
 Of uncle and of brother who a nation
 So famous have dishonoured, and two crowns.

And he of Portugal and he of Norway
 Shall there be known, and he of Rascia too,
 Who saw in evil hour the coin of Venice.

Oh beata Ungheria, se non si lascia
  piu` malmenare! e beata Navarra,
  se s'armasse del monte che la fascia!

E creder de' ciascun che gia`, per arra
  di questo, Niccosia e Famagosta
  per la lor bestia si lamenti e garra,

che dal fianco de l'altre non si scosta'"".

O happy Hungary, if she let herself
  Be wronged no farther! and Navarre the happy,
  If with the hills that gird her she be armed!

And each one may believe that now, as hansel
  Thereof, do Nicosia and Famagosta
  Lament and rage because of their own beast,

Who from the others' flank departeth not."

The Eagle praises the Righteous Kings of old. Benevolence of the Divine Will.

Quando colui che tutto 'l mondo alluma
  de l'emisperio nostro si` discende,
  che 'l giorno d'ogne parte si consuma,
	When he who all the world illuminates
	  Out of our hemisphere so far descends
	  That on all sides the daylight is consumed,

lo ciel, che sol di lui prima s'accende,
  subitamente si rifa` parvente
  per molte luci, in che una risplende;
	The heaven, that erst by him alone was kindled,
	  Doth suddenly reveal itself again
	  By many lights, wherein is one resplendent.

e questo atto del ciel mi venne a mente,
  come 'l segno del mondo e de' suoi duci
  nel benedetto rostro fu tacente;
	And came into my mind this act of heaven,
	  When the ensign of the world and of its leaders
	  Had silent in the blessed beak become;

pero` che tutte quelle vive luci,   vie piu` lucendo, cominciaron canti da mia memoria labili e caduci.	Because those living luminaries all, By far more luminous, did songs begin Lapsing and falling from my memory.

O dolce amor che di riso t'ammanti,
  quanto parevi ardente in que' flailli,
  ch'avieno spirto sol di pensier santi!
	O gentle Love, that with a smile dost cloak thee,
	  How ardent in those sparks didst thou appear,
	  That had the breath alone of holy thoughts!

Poscia che i cari e lucidi lapilli
  ond'io vidi ingemmato il sesto lume
  puoser silenzio a li angelici squilli,
	After the precious and pellucid crystals,
	  With which begemmed the sixth light I beheld,
	  Silence imposed on the angelic bells,

udir mi parve un mormorar di fiume che scende chiaro giu` di pietra in pietra,   mostrando l'uberta` del suo cacume.	I seemed to hear the murmuring of a river That clear descendeth down from rock to rock, Showing the affluence of its mountain-top.

E come suono al collo de la cetra
  prende sua forma, e si` com'al pertugio
  de la sampogna vento che penetra,
	And as the sound upon the cithern's neck
	  Taketh its form, and as upon the vent
	  Of rustic pipe the wind that enters it,

cosi`, rimosso d'aspettare indugio,
  quel mormorar de l'aguglia salissi
  su per lo collo, come fosse bugio.
	Even thus, relieved from the delay of waiting,
	  That murmuring of the eagle mounted up
	  Along its neck, as if it had been hollow.

Fecesi voce quivi, e quindi uscissi
  per lo suo becco in forma di parole,
  quali aspettava il core ov'io le scrissi.
	There it became a voice, and issued thence
	  From out its beak, in such a form of words
	  As the heart waited for wherein I wrote them.

""La parte in me che vede e pate il sole
  ne l'aguglie mortali"", incominciommi,
  ""or fisamente riguardar si vole,
	"The part in me which sees and bears the sun
	  In mortal eagles," it began to me,
	  "Now fixedly must needs be looked upon;

perche' d'i fuochi ond'io figura fommi,
  quelli onde l'occhio in testa mi scintilla,
  e' di tutti lor gradi son li sommi.
	For of the fires of which I make my figure,
	  Those whence the eye doth sparkle in my head
	  Of all their orders the supremest are.

Colui che luce in mezzo per pupilla,
  fu il cantor de lo Spirito Santo,
  che l'arca traslato` di villa in villa:
	He who is shining in the midst as pupil
	  Was once the singer of the Holy Spirit,
	  Who bore the ark from city unto city;

ora conosce il merto del suo canto,
  in quanto effetto fu del suo consiglio,
  per lo remunerar ch'e` altrettanto.
	Now knoweth he the merit of his song,
	  In so far as effect of his own counsel,
	  By the reward which is commensurate.

Dei cinque che mi fan cerchio per ciglio, colui che piu` al becco mi s'accosta,   la vedovella consolo` del figlio:	Of five, that make a circle for my brow, He that approacheth nearest to my beak Did the poor widow for her son console;

ora conosce quanto caro costa
  non seguir Cristo, per l'esperienza
  di questa dolce vita e de l'opposta.
	Now knoweth he how dearly it doth cost
	  Not following Christ, by the experience
	  Of this sweet life and of its opposite.

E quel che segue in la circunferenza
  di che ragiono, per l'arco superno,
  morte indugio` per vera penitenza:
	He who comes next in the circumference
	  Of which I speak, upon its highest arc,
	  Did death postpone by penitence sincere;

ora conosce che 'l giudicio etterno
  non si trasmuta, quando degno preco
  fa crastino la` giu` de l'odierno.
	Now knoweth he that the eternal judgment
	  Suffers no change, albeit worthy prayer
	  Maketh below to-morrow of to-day.

L'altro che segue, con le leggi e meco,
  sotto buona intenzion che fe' mal frutto,
  per cedere al pastor si fece greco:
	The next who follows, with the laws and me,
	  Under the good intent that bore bad fruit
	  Became a Greek by ceding to the pastor;

ora conosce come il mal dedutto
  dal suo bene operar non li e` nocivo,
  avvegna che sia 'l mondo indi distrutto.
	Now knoweth he how all the ill deduced
	  From his good action is not harmful to him,
	  Although the world thereby may be destroyed.

E quel che vedi ne l'arco declivo,
  Guiglielmo fu, cui quella terra plora
  che piagne Carlo e Federigo vivo:
	And he, whom in the downward arc thou seest,
	  Guglielmo was, whom the same land deplores
	  That weepeth Charles and Frederick yet alive;

ora conosce come s'innamora
  lo ciel del giusto rege, e al sembiante
  del suo fulgore il fa vedere ancora.
	Now knoweth he how heaven enamoured is
	  With a just king; and in the outward show
	  Of his effulgence he reveals it still.

Chi crederebbe giu` nel mondo errante,
  che Rifeo Troiano in questo tondo
  fosse la quinta de le luci sante?

Ora conosce assai di quel che 'l mondo
  veder non puo` de la divina grazia,
  ben che sua vista non discerna il fondo"".

Quale allodetta che 'n aere si spazia
  prima cantando, e poi tace contenta
  de l'ultima dolcezza che la sazia,

tal mi sembio` l'imago de la 'mprenta
  de l'etterno piacere, al cui disio
  ciascuna cosa qual ell'e` diventa.

E avvegna ch'io fossi al dubbiar mio
  li` quasi vetro a lo color ch'el veste,
  tempo aspettar tacendo non patio,

ma de la bocca, ""Che cose son queste?"",
  mi pinse con la forza del suo peso:
  per ch'io di coruscar vidi gran feste.

Poi appresso, con l'occhio piu` acceso,
  lo benedetto segno mi rispuose
  per non tenermi in ammirar sospeso:

""Io veggio che tu credi queste cose
  perch'io le dico, ma non vedi come;
  si` che, se son credute, sono ascose.

Fai come quei che la cosa per nome
  apprende ben, ma la sua quiditate
  veder non puo` se altri non la prome.

Regnum celorum violenza pate
  da caldo amore e da viva speranza,
  che vince la divina volontate:

non a guisa che l'omo a l'om sobranza,
  ma vince lei perche' vuole esser vinta,
  e, vinta, vince con sua beninanza.

La prima vita del ciglio e la quinta
  ti fa maravigliar, perche' ne vedi
  la region de li angeli dipinta.

Who would believe, down in the errant world,
  That e'er the Trojan Ripheus in this round
  Could be the fifth one of the holy lights?

Now knoweth he enough of what the world
  Has not the power to see of grace divine,
  Although his sight may not discern the bottom."

Like as a lark that in the air expatiates,
  First singing and then silent with content
  Of the last sweetness that doth satisfy her,

Such seemed to me the image of the imprint
  Of the eternal pleasure, by whose will
  Doth everything become the thing it is.

And notwithstanding to my doubt I was
  As glass is to the colour that invests it,
  To wait the time in silence it endured not,

But forth from out my mouth, "What things are these?"
  Extorted with the force of its own weight;
  Whereat I saw great joy of coruscation.

Thereafterward with eye still more enkindled
  The blessed standard made to me reply,
  To keep me not in wonderment suspended:

"I see that thou believest in these things
  Because I say them, but thou seest not how;
  So that, although believed in, they are hidden.

Thou doest as he doth who a thing by name
  Well apprehendeth, but its quiddity
  Cannot perceive, unless another show it.

'Regnum coelorum' suffereth violence
  From fervent love, and from that living hope
  That overcometh the Divine volition;

Not in the guise that man o'ercometh man,
  But conquers it because it will be conquered,
  And conquered conquers by benignity.

The first life of the eyebrow and the fifth
  Cause thee astonishment, because with them
  Thou seest the region of the angels painted.

D'i corpi suoi non uscir, come credi,
  Gentili, ma Cristiani, in ferma fede
  quel d'i passuri e quel d'i passi piedi.

Che' l'una de lo 'nferno, u' non si riede
  gia` mai a buon voler, torno` a l'ossa;
  e cio` di viva spene fu mercede:

di viva spene, che mise la possa
  ne' prieghi fatti a Dio per suscitarla,
  si` che potesse sua voglia esser mossa.

L'anima gloriosa onde si parla,
  tornata ne la carne, in che fu poco,
  credette in lui che potea aiutarla;

e credendo s'accese in tanto foco
  di vero amor, ch'a la morte seconda
  fu degna di venire a questo gioco.

L'altra, per grazia che da si` profonda
  fontana stilla, che mai creatura
  non pinse l'occhio infino a la prima onda,

tutto suo amor la` giu` pose a drittura:
  per che, di grazia in grazia, Dio li aperse
  l'occhio a la nostra redenzion futura;

ond'ei credette in quella, e non sofferse
  da indi il puzzo piu` del paganesmo;
  e riprendiene le genti perverse.

Quelle tre donne li fur per battesmo
  che tu vedesti da la destra rota,
  dinanzi al battezzar piu` d'un millesmo.

O predestinazion, quanto remota
  e` la radice tua da quelli aspetti
  che la prima cagion non veggion tota!

E voi, mortali, tenetevi stretti
  a giudicar; che' noi, che Dio vedemo,
  non conosciamo ancor tutti li eletti;

ed enne dolce cosi` fatto scemo,
  perche' il ben nostro in questo ben s'affina,
  che quel che vole Iddio, e noi volemo"".

Cosi` da quella imagine divina,
  per farmi chiara la mia corta vista,
  data mi fu soave medicina.

They passed not from their bodies, as thou thinkest,
  Gentiles, but Christians in the steadfast faith
  Of feet that were to suffer and had suffered.

For one from Hell, where no one e'er turns back
  Unto good will, returned unto his bones,
  And that of living hope was the reward,—

Of living hope, that placed its efficacy
  In prayers to God made to resuscitate him,
  So that 'twere possible to move his will.

The glorious soul concerning which I speak,
  Returning to the flesh, where brief its stay,
  Believed in Him who had the power to aid it;

And, in believing, kindled to such fire
  Of genuine love, that at the second death
  Worthy it was to come unto this joy.

The other one, through grace, that from so deep
  A fountain wells that never hath the eye
  Of any creature reached its primal wave,

Set all his love below on righteousness;
  Wherefore from grace to grace did God unclose
  His eye to our redemption yet to be,

Whence he believed therein, and suffered not
  From that day forth the stench of paganism,
  And he reproved therefor the folk perverse.

Those Maidens three, whom at the right-hand wheel
  Thou didst behold, were unto him for baptism
  More than a thousand years before baptizing.

O thou predestination, how remote
  Thy root is from the aspect of all those
  Who the First Cause do not behold entire!

And you, O mortals! hold yourselves restrained
  In judging; for ourselves, who look on God,
  We do not know as yet all the elect;

And sweet to us is such a deprivation,
  Because our good in this good is made perfect,
  That whatsoe'er God wills, we also will."

After this manner by that shape divine,
  To make clear in me my short-sightedness,
  Was given to me a pleasant medicine;

E come a buon cantor buon citarista
  fa seguitar lo guizzo de la corda,
  in che piu` di piacer lo canto acquista,

si`, mentre ch'e' parlo`, si` mi ricorda
  ch'io vidi le due luci benedette,
  pur come batter d'occhi si concorda,

con le parole mover le fiammette.

And as good singer a good lutanist
  Accompanies with vibrations of the chords,
  Whereby more pleasantness the song acquires,

So, while it spake, do I remember me
  That I beheld both of those blessed lights,
  Even as the winking of the eyes concords,

Moving unto the words their little flames.

Paradiso: Canto XXI

The Seventh Heaven, Saturn: The Contemplative. The Celestial Stairway. St. Peter Damiano. His Invectives against the Luxury of the Prelates.

Gia` eran li occhi miei rifissi al volto
  de la mia donna, e l'animo con essi,
  e da ogne altro intento s'era tolto.

E quella non ridea; ma ""S'io ridessi"",
  mi comincio`, ""tu ti faresti quale
  fu Semele` quando di cener fessi;

che' la bellezza mia, che per le scale
  de l'etterno palazzo piu` s'accende,
  com'hai veduto, quanto piu` si sale,

se non si temperasse, tanto splende,
  che 'l tuo mortal podere, al suo fulgore,
  sarebbe fronda che trono scoscende.

Noi sem levati al settimo splendore,
  che sotto 'l petto del Leone ardente
  raggia mo misto giu` del suo valore.

Ficca di retro a li occhi tuoi la mente,
  e fa di quelli specchi a la figura
  che 'n questo specchio ti sara` parvente"".

Qual savesse qual era la pastura
  del viso mio ne l'aspetto beato
  quand'io mi trasmutai ad altra cura,

conoscerebbe quanto m'era a grato
  ubidire a la mia celeste scorta,
  contrapesando l'un con l'altro lato.

Already on my Lady's face mine eyes
  Again were fastened, and with these my mind,
  And from all other purpose was withdrawn;

And she smiled not; but "If I were to smile,"
  She unto me began, "thou wouldst become
  Like Semele, when she was turned to ashes.

Because my beauty, that along the stairs
  Of the eternal palace more enkindles,
  As thou hast seen, the farther we ascend,

If it were tempered not, is so resplendent
  That all thy mortal power in its effulgence
  Would seem a leaflet that the thunder crushes.

We are uplifted to the seventh splendour,
  That underneath the burning Lion's breast
  Now radiates downward mingled with his power.

Fix in direction of thine eyes the mind,
  And make of them a mirror for the figure
  That in this mirror shall appear to thee."

He who could know what was the pasturage
  My sight had in that blessed countenance,
  When I transferred me to another care,

Would recognize how grateful was to me
  Obedience unto my celestial escort,
  By counterpoising one side with the other.

Dentro al cristallo che 'l vocabol porta,	Within the crystal which, around the world
cerchiando il mondo, del suo caro duce	Revolving, bears the name of its dear leader,
sotto cui giacque ogne malizia morta,	Under whom every wickedness lay dead,
di color d'oro in che raggio traluce	Coloured like gold, on which the sunshine gleams,
vid'io uno scaleo eretto in suso	A stairway I beheld to such a height
tanto, che nol seguiva la mia luce.	Uplifted, that mine eye pursued it not.
Vidi anche per li gradi scender giuso	Likewise beheld I down the steps descending
tanti splendor, ch'io pensai ch'ogne lume	So many splendours, that I thought each light
che par nel ciel, quindi fosse diffuso.	That in the heaven appears was there diffused.
E come, per lo natural costume,	And as accordant with their natural custom
le pole insieme, al cominciar del giorno,	The rooks together at the break of day
si movono a scaldar le fredde piume;	Bestir themselves to warm their feathers cold;
poi altre vanno via sanza ritorno,	Then some of them fly off without return,
altre rivolgon se' onde son mosse,	Others come back to where they started from,
e altre roteando fan soggiorno;	And others, wheeling round, still keep at home;
tal modo parve me che quivi fosse	Such fashion it appeared to me was there
in quello sfavillar che 'nsieme venne,	Within the sparkling that together came,
si` come in certo grado si percosse.	As soon as on a certain step it struck,
E quel che presso piu` ci si ritenne,	And that which nearest unto us remained
si fe' si` chiaro, ch'io dicea pensando:	Became so clear, that in my thought I said,
'Io veggio ben l'amor che tu m'accenne.	"Well I perceive the love thou showest me;
Ma quella ond'io aspetto il come e 'l quando	But she, from whom I wait the how and when
del dire e del tacer, si sta; ond'io,	Of speech and silence, standeth still; whence I
contra 'l disio, fo ben ch'io non dimando'.	Against desire do well if I ask not."
Per ch'ella, che vedea il tacer mio	She thereupon, who saw my silentness
nel veder di colui che tutto vede,	In the sight of Him who seeth everything,
mi disse: ""Solvi il tuo caldo disio"".	Said unto me, "Let loose thy warm desire."
E io incominciai: ""La mia mercede	And I began: "No merit of my own
non mi fa degno de la tua risposta;	Renders me worthy of response from thee;
ma per colei che 'l chieder mi concede,	But for her sake who granteth me the asking,
vita beata che ti stai nascosta	Thou blessed life that dost remain concealed
dentro a la tua letizia, fammi nota	In thy beatitude, make known to me
la cagion che si` presso mi t'ha posta;	The cause which draweth thee so near my side;
e di' perche' si tace in questa rota	And tell me why is silent in this wheel
la dolce sinfonia di paradiso,	The dulcet symphony of Paradise,
che giu` per l'altre suona si` divota"".	That through the rest below sounds so devoutly."
""Tu hai l'udir mortal si` come il viso"",	"Thou hast thy hearing mortal as thy sight,"
rispuose a me; ""onde qui non si canta	It answer made to me; "they sing not here,
per quel che Beatrice non ha riso.	For the same cause that Beatrice has not smiled.

Giu` per li gradi de la scala santa
  discesi tanto sol per farti festa
  col dire e con la luce che mi ammanta;

ne' piu` amor mi fece esser piu` presta;
  che' piu` e tanto amor quinci su` ferve,
  si` come il fiammeggiar ti manifesta.

Ma l'alta carita`, che ci fa serve
  pronte al consiglio che 'l mondo governa,
  sorteggia qui si` come tu osserve”“.

““Io veggio ben”“, diss'io, ““sacra lucerna,
  come libero amore in questa corte
  basta a seguir la provedenza etterna;

ma questo e` quel ch'a cerner mi par forte,
  perche' predestinata fosti sola
  a questo officio tra le tue consorte”“.

Ne' venni prima a l'ultima parola,
  che del suo mezzo fece il lume centro,
  girando se' come veloce mola;

poi rispuose l'amor che v'era dentro:
  ”“Luce divina sopra me s'appunta,
  penetrando per questa in ch'io m'inventro,

la cui virtu`, col mio veder congiunta,
  mi leva sopra me tanto, ch'i' veggio
  la somma essenza de la quale e` munta.

Quinci vien l'allegrezza ond'io fiammeggio;
  per ch'a la vista mia, quant'ella e` chiara,
  la chiarita` de la fiamma pareggio.

Ma quell'alma nel ciel che piu` si schiara,
  quel serafin che 'n Dio piu` l'occhio ha fisso,
  a la dimanda tua non satisfara,

pero` che si` s'innoltra ne lo abisso
  de l'etterno statuto quel che chiedi,
  che da ogne creata vista e` scisso.

E al mondo mortal, quando tu riedi,
  questo rapporta, si` che non presumma
  a tanto segno piu` mover li piedi.

La mente, che qui luce, in terra fumma;
  onde riguarda come puo` la` giue
  quel che non pote perche' 'l ciel l'assumma”“.

Thus far adown the holy stairway's steps
  Have I descended but to give thee welcome
  With words, and with the light that mantles me;

Nor did more love cause me to be more ready,
  For love as much and more up there is burning,
  As doth the flaming manifest to thee.

But the high charity, that makes us servants
  Prompt to the counsel which controls the world,
  Allotteth here, even as thou dost observe."

"I see full well," said I, "O sacred lamp!
  How love unfettered in this court sufficeth
  To follow the eternal Providence;

But this is what seems hard for me to see,
  Wherefore predestinate wast thou alone
  Unto this office from among thy consorts."

No sooner had I come to the last word,
  Than of its middle made the light a centre,
  Whirling itself about like a swift millstone.

When answer made the love that was therein:
  "On me directed is a light divine,
  Piercing through this in which I am embosomed,

Of which the virtue with my sight conjoined
  Lifts me above myself so far, I see
  The supreme essence from which this is drawn.

Hence comes the joyfulness with which I flame,
  For to my sight, as far as it is clear,
  The clearness of the flame I equal make.

But that soul in the heaven which is most pure,
  That seraph which his eye on God most fixes,
  Could this demand of thine not satisfy;

Because so deeply sinks in the abyss
  Of the eternal statute what thou askest,
  From all created sight it is cut off.

And to the mortal world, when thou returnest,
  This carry back, that it may not presume
  Longer tow'rd such a goal to move its feet.

The mind, that shineth here, on earth doth smoke;
  From this observe how can it do below
  That which it cannot though the heaven assume it?"

Si` mi prescrisser le parole sue,
  ch'io lasciai la quistione e mi ritrassi
  a dimandarla umilmente chi fue.
	Such limit did its words prescribe to me,
	  The question I relinquished, and restricted
	  Myself to ask it humbly who it was.

""Tra ' due liti d'Italia surgon sassi,
  e non molto distanti a la tua patria,
  tanto che ' troni assai suonan piu` bassi,
	"Between two shores of Italy rise cliffs,
	  And not far distant from thy native place,
	  So high, the thunders far below them sound,

e fanno un gibbo che si chiama Catria,
  di sotto al quale e` consecrato un ermo,
  che suole esser disposto a sola latria"".
	And form a ridge that Catria is called,
	  'Neath which is consecrate a hermitage
	  Wont to be dedicate to worship only."

Cosi` ricominciommi il terzo sermo;   e poi, continuando, disse: ""Quivi   al servigio di Dio mi fe' si` fermo,	Thus unto me the third speech recommenced, And then, continuing, it said: "Therein Unto God's service I became so steadfast,

che pur con cibi di liquor d'ulivi
  lievemente passava caldi e geli,
  contento ne' pensier contemplativi.
	That feeding only on the juice of olives
	  Lightly I passed away the heats and frosts,
	  Contented in my thoughts contemplative.

Render solea quel chiostro a questi cieli fertilemente; e ora e` fatto vano,   si` che tosto convien che si riveli.	That cloister used to render to these heavens Abundantly, and now is empty grown, So that perforce it soon must be revealed.

In quel loco fu' io Pietro Damiano,
  e Pietro Peccator fu' ne la casa
  di Nostra Donna in sul lito adriano.
	I in that place was Peter Damiano;
	  And Peter the Sinner was I in the house
	  Of Our Lady on the Adriatic shore.

Poca vita mortal m'era rimasa,
  quando fui chiesto e tratto a quel cappello,
  che pur di male in peggio si travasa.
	Little of mortal life remained to me,
	  When I was called and dragged forth to the hat
	  Which shifteth evermore from bad to worse.

Venne Cefas e venne il gran vasello
  de lo Spirito Santo, magri e scalzi,
  prendendo il cibo da qualunque ostello.
	Came Cephas, and the mighty Vessel came
	  Of the Holy Spirit, meagre and barefooted,
	  Taking the food of any hostelry.

Or voglion quinci e quindi chi rincalzi
  li moderni pastori e chi li meni,
  tanto son gravi, e chi di rietro li alzi.
	Now some one to support them on each side
	  The modern shepherds need, and some to lead
	    them,
	  So heavy are they, and to hold their trains.

Cuopron d'i manti loro i palafreni,
  si` che due bestie van sott'una pelle:
  oh pazienza che tanto sostieni!"".
	They cover up their palfreys with their cloaks,
	  So that two beasts go underneath one skin;
	  O Patience, that dost tolerate so much!"

A questa voce vid'io piu` fiammelle   di grado in grado scendere e girarsi,   e ogne giro le facea piu` belle.	At this voice saw I many little flames From step to step descending and revolving, And every revolution made them fairer.

Dintorno a questa vennero e fermarsi,
  e fero un grido di si` alto suono,
  che non potrebbe qui assomigliarsi;
	Round about this one came they and stood still,
	  And a cry uttered of so loud a sound,
	  It here could find no parallel, nor I

ne' io lo 'ntesi, si` mi vinse il tuono.	Distinguished it, the thunder so o'ercame me.

Paradiso: Canto XXII

St. Benedict. His Lamentation over the Corruption of Monks. The Eighth Heaven, the Fixed Stars.

Oppresso di stupore, a la mia guida
  mi volsi, come parvol che ricorre
  sempre cola` dove piu` si confida;

e quella, come madre che soccorre
  subito al figlio palido e anelo
  con la sua voce, che 'l suol ben disporre,

mi disse: ""Non sai tu che tu se' in cielo?
  e non sai tu che 'l cielo e` tutto santo,
  e cio` che ci si fa vien da buon zelo?

Come t'avrebbe trasmutato il canto,
  e io ridendo, mo pensar lo puoi,
  poscia che 'l grido t'ha mosso cotanto;

nel qual, se 'nteso avessi i prieghi suoi,
  gia` ti sarebbe nota la vendetta
  che tu vedrai innanzi che tu muoi.

La spada di qua su` non taglia in fretta
  ne' tardo, ma' ch'al parer di colui
  che disiando o temendo l'aspetta.

Ma rivolgiti omai inverso altrui;
  ch'assai illustri spiriti vedrai,
  se com'io dico l'aspetto redui"".

Come a lei piacque, li occhi ritornai,
  e vidi cento sperule che 'nsieme
  piu` s'abbellivan con mutui rai.

Io stava come quei che 'n se' represe
  la punta del disio, e non s'attenta
  di domandar, si` del troppo si teme;

Oppressed with stupor, I unto my guide
  Turned like a little child who always runs
  For refuge there where he confideth most;

And she, even as a mother who straightway
  Gives comfort to her pale and breathless boy
  With voice whose wont it is to reassure him,

Said to me: "Knowest thou not thou art in heaven,
  And knowest thou not that heaven is holy all
  And what is done here cometh from good zeal?

After what wise the singing would have changed thee
  And I by smiling, thou canst now imagine,
  Since that the cry has startled thee so much,

In which if thou hadst understood its prayers
  Already would be known to thee the vengeance
  Which thou shalt look upon before thou diest.

The sword above here smiteth not in haste
  Nor tardily, howe'er it seem to him
  Who fearing or desiring waits for it.

But turn thee round towards the others now,
  For very illustrious spirits shalt thou see,
  If thou thy sight directest as I say."

As it seemed good to her mine eyes I turned,
  And saw a hundred spherules that together
  With mutual rays each other more embellished.

I stood as one who in himself represses
  The point of his desire, and ventures not
  To question, he so feareth the too much.

e la maggiore e la piu` luculenta
  di quelle margherite innanzi fessi,
  per far di se' la mia voglia contenta.
	And now the largest and most luculent
	  Among those pearls came forward, that it might
	  Make my desire concerning it content.

Poi dentro a lei udi': ""Se tu vedessi
  com'io la carita` che tra noi arde,
  li tuoi concetti sarebbero espressi.
	Within it then I heard: "If thou couldst see
	  Even as myself the charity that burns
	  Among us, thy conceits would be expressed;

Ma perche' tu, aspettando, non tarde a l'alto fine, io ti faro` risposta   pur al pensier, da che si` ti riguarde.	But, that by waiting thou mayst not come late To the high end, I will make answer even Unto the thought of which thou art so chary.
Quel monte a cui Cassino e` ne la costa   fu frequentato gia` in su la cima da la gente ingannata e mal disposta;	That mountain on whose slope Cassino stands Was frequented of old upon its summit By a deluded folk and ill-disposed;
e quel son io che su` vi portai prima   lo nome di colui che 'n terra addusse   la verita` che tanto ci soblima;	And I am he who first up thither bore The name of Him who brought upon the earth The truth that so much sublimateth us.

e tanta grazia sopra me relusse,
  ch'io ritrassi le ville circunstanti
  da l'empio colto che 'l mondo sedusse.
	And such abundant grace upon me shone
	  That all the neighbouring towns I drew away
	  From the impious worship that seduced the world.

Questi altri fuochi tutti contemplanti
  uomini fuoro, accesi di quel caldo
  che fa nascere i fiori e ' frutti santi.
	These other fires, each one of them, were men
	  Contemplative, enkindled by that heat
	  Which maketh holy flowers and fruits spring up.

Qui e` Maccario, qui e` Romoaldo,
  qui son li frati miei che dentro ai chiostri
  fermar li piedi e tennero il cor saldo"".
	Here is Macarius, here is Romualdus,
	  Here are my brethren, who within the cloisters
	  Their footsteps stayed and kept a steadfast heart."

E io a lui: ""L'affetto che dimostri
  meco parlando, e la buona sembianza
  ch'io veggio e noto in tutti li ardor vostri,
	And I to him: "The affection which thou showest
	  Speaking with me, and the good countenance
	  Which I behold and note in all your ardours,

cosi` m'ha dilatata mia fidanza,
  come 'l sol fa la rosa quando aperta
  tanto divien quant'ell'ha di possanza.
	In me have so my confidence dilated
	  As the sun doth the rose, when it becomes
	  As far unfolded as it hath the power.

Pero` ti priego, e tu, padre, m'accerta
  s'io posso prender tanta grazia, ch'io
  ti veggia con imagine scoverta"".
	Therefore I pray, and thou assure me, father,
	  If I may so much grace receive, that I
	  May thee behold with countenance unveiled."

Ond'elli: ""Frate, il tuo alto disio
  s'adempiera` in su l'ultima spera,
  ove s'adempion tutti li altri e 'l mio.
	He thereupon: "Brother, thy high desire
	  In the remotest sphere shall be fulfilled,
	  Where are fulfilled all others and my own.

Ivi e` perfetta, matura e intera   ciascuna disianza; in quella sola   e` ogne parte la` ove sempr'era,	There perfect is, and ripened, and complete, Every desire; within that one alone Is every part where it has always been;

perche' non e` in loco e non s'impola;	For it is not in space, nor turns on poles,
e nostra scala infino ad essa varca,	And unto it our stairway reaches up,
onde cosi` dal viso ti s'invola.	Whence thus from out thy sight it steals away.
Infin la` su` la vide il patriarca	Up to that height the Patriarch Jacob saw it
Iacobbe porger la superna parte,	Extending its supernal part, what time
quando li apparve d'angeli si` carca.	So thronged with angels it appeared to him.
Ma, per salirla, mo nessun diparte	But to ascend it now no one uplifts
da terra i piedi, e la regola mia	His feet from off the earth, and now my Rule
rimasa e` per danno de le carte.	Below remaineth for mere waste of paper.
Le mura che solieno esser badia	The walls that used of old to be an Abbey
fatte sono spelonche, e le cocolle	Are changed to dens of robbers, and the cowls
sacca son piene di farina ria.	Are sacks filled full of miserable flour.
Ma grave usura tanto non si tolle	But heavy usury is not taken up
contra 'l piacer di Dio, quanto quel frutto	So much against God's pleasure as that fruit
che fa il cor de' monaci si` folle;	Which maketh so insane the heart of monks;
che' quantunque la Chiesa guarda, tutto	For whatsoever hath the Church in keeping
e` de la gente che per Dio dimanda;	Is for the folk that ask it in God's name,
non di parenti ne' d'altro piu` brutto.	Not for one's kindred or for something worse.
La carne d'i mortali e` tanto blanda,	The flesh of mortals is so very soft,
che giu` non basta buon cominciamento	That good beginnings down below suffice not
dal nascer de la quercia al far la ghianda.	From springing of the oak to bearing acorns.
Pier comincio` sanz'oro e sanz'argento,	Peter began with neither gold nor silver,
e io con orazione e con digiuno,	And I with orison and abstinence,
e Francesco umilmente il suo convento;	And Francis with humility his convent.
e se guardi 'l principio di ciascuno,	And if thou lookest at each one's beginning,
poscia riguardi la` dov'e` trascorso,	And then regardest whither he has run,
tu vederai del bianco fatto bruno.	Thou shalt behold the white changed into brown.
Veramente Iordan volto retrorso	In verity the Jordan backward turned,
piu` fu, e 'l mar fuggir, quando Dio volse,	And the sea's fleeing, when God willed were more
mirabile a veder che qui 'l soccorso'"".	A wonder to behold, than succour here."
Cosi` mi disse, e indi si raccolse	Thus unto me he said; and then withdrew
al suo collegio, e 'l collegio si strinse;	To his own band, and the band closed together;
poi, come turbo, in su` tutto s'avvolse.	Then like a whirlwind all was upward rapt.
La dolce donna dietro a lor mi pinse	The gentle Lady urged me on behind them
con un sol cenno su per quella scala,	Up o'er that stairway by a single sign,
si` sua virtu` la mia natura vinse;	So did her virtue overcome my nature;
ne' mai qua giu` dove si monta e cala	Nor here below, where one goes up and down
naturalmente, fu si` ratto moto	By natural law, was motion e'er so swift
ch'agguagliar si potesse a la mia ala.	That it could be compared unto my wing.

S'io torni mai, lettore, a quel divoto
  triunfo per lo quale io piango spesso
  le mie peccata e 'l petto mi percuoto,

tu non avresti in tanto tratto e messo
  nel foco il dito, in quant'io vidi 'l segno
  che segue il Tauro e fui dentro da esso.

O gloriose stelle, o lume pregno
  di gran virtu`, dal quale io riconosco
  tutto, qual che si sia, il mio ingegno,

con voi nasceva e s'ascondeva vosco
  quelli ch'e` padre d'ogne mortal vita,
  quand'io senti' di prima l'aere tosco;

e poi, quando mi fu grazia largita
  d'entrar ne l'alta rota che vi gira,
  la vostra region mi fu sortita.

A voi divotamente ora sospira
  l'anima mia, per acquistar virtute
  al passo forte che a se' la tira.

““Tu se' si` presso a l'ultima salute”“,
  comincio` Beatrice, ““che tu dei
  aver le luci tue chiare e acute;

e pero`, prima che tu piu` t'inlei,
  rimira in giu`, e vedi quanto mondo
  sotto li piedi gia` esser ti fei;

si` che 'l tuo cor, quantunque puo`, giocondo
  s'appresenti a la turba triunfante
  che lieta vien per questo etera tondo”“.

Col viso ritornai per tutte quante
  le sette spere, e vidi questo globo
  tal, ch'io sorrisi del suo vil sembiante;

e quel consiglio per migliore approbo
  che l'ha per meno; e chi ad altro pensa
  chiamar si puote veramente probo.

Vidi la figlia di Latona incensa
  sanza quell'ombra che mi fu cagione
  per che gia` la credetti rara e densa.

L'aspetto del tuo nato, Iperione,
  quivi sostenni, e vidi com'si move
  circa e vicino a lui Maia e Dione.

Reader, as I may unto that devout
  Triumph return, on whose account I often
  For my transgressions weep and beat my breast,—

Thou hadst not thrust thy finger in the fire
  And drawn it out again, before I saw
  The sign that follows Taurus, and was in it.

O glorious stars, O light impregnated
  With mighty virtue, from which I acknowledge
  All of my genius, whatsoe'er it be,

With you was born, and hid himself with you,
  He who is father of all mortal life,
  When first I tasted of the Tuscan air;

And then when grace was freely given to me
  To enter the high wheel which turns you round,
  Your region was allotted unto me.

To you devoutly at this hour my soul
  Is sighing, that it virtue may acquire
  For the stern pass that draws it to itself.

"Thou art so near unto the last salvation,"
  Thus Beatrice began, "thou oughtest now
  To have thine eves unclouded and acute;

And therefore, ere thou enter farther in,
  Look down once more, and see how vast a world
  Thou hast already put beneath thy feet;

So that thy heart, as jocund as it may,
  Present itself to the triumphant throng
  That comes rejoicing through this rounded ether."

I with my sight returned through one and all
  The sevenfold spheres, and I beheld this globe
  Such that I smiled at its ignoble semblance;

And that opinion I approve as best
  Which doth account it least; and he who thinks
  Of something else may truly be called just.

I saw the daughter of Latona shining
  Without that shadow, which to me was cause
  That once I had believed her rare and dense.

The aspect of thy son, Hyperion,
  Here I sustained, and saw how move themselves
  Around and near him Maia and Dione.

La Divina Commedia - The Divine Comedy

Quindi m'apparve il temperar di Giove
  tra 'l padre e 'l figlio: e quindi mi fu chiaro
  il variar che fanno di lor dove;

e tutti e sette mi si dimostraro
  quanto son grandi e quanto son veloci
  e come sono in distante riparo.

L'aiuola che ci fa tanto feroci,
  volgendom'io con li etterni Gemelli,
  tutta m'apparve da' colli a le foci;

poscia rivolsi li occhi a li occhi belli.

Thence there appeared the temperateness of Jove
  'Twixt son and father, and to me was clear
  The change that of their whereabout they make;

And all the seven made manifest to me
  How great they are, and eke how swift they are,
  And how they are in distant habitations.

The threshing-floor that maketh us so proud,
  To me revolving with the eternal Twins,
  Was all apparent made from hill to harbour!

Then to the beauteous eyes mine eyes I turned.

Paradiso: Canto XXIII

The Triumph of Christ. The Virgin Mary. The Apostles. Gabriel.

Come l'augello, intra l'amate fronde, posato al nido de' suoi dolci nati la notte che le cose ci nasconde,	Even as a bird, 'mid the beloved leaves, Quiet upon the nest of her sweet brood Throughout the night, that hideth all things from us,
che, per veder li aspetti disiati e per trovar lo cibo onde li pasca, in che gravi labor li sono aggrati,	Who, that she may behold their longed-for looks And find the food wherewith to nourish them, In which, to her, grave labours grateful are,
previene il tempo in su aperta frasca, e con ardente affetto il sole aspetta, fiso guardando pur che l'alba nasca;	Anticipates the time on open spray And with an ardent longing waits the sun, Gazing intent as soon as breaks the dawn:
cosi` la donna mia stava eretta e attenta, rivolta inver' la plaga sotto la quale il sol mostra men fretta:	Even thus my Lady standing was, erect And vigilant, turned round towards the zone Underneath which the sun displays less haste;
si` che, veggendola io sospesa e vaga, fecimi qual e` quei che disiando altro vorria, e sperando s'appaga.	So that beholding her distraught and wistful, Such I became as he is who desiring For something yearns, and hoping is appeased.
Ma poco fu tra uno e altro quando, del mio attender, dico, e del vedere lo ciel venir piu` e piu` rischiarando;	But brief the space from one When to the other; Of my awaiting, say I, and the seeing The welkin grow resplendent more and more.
e Beatrice disse: ""Ecco le schiere del triunfo di Cristo e tutto 'l frutto ricolto del girar di queste spere!"".	And Beatrice exclaimed: "Behold the hosts Of Christ's triumphal march, and all the fruit Harvested by the rolling of these spheres!"
Pariemi che 'l suo viso ardesse tutto, e li occhi avea di letizia si` pieni, che passarmen convien sanza costrutto.	It seemed to me her face was all aflame; And eyes she had so full of ecstasy That I must needs pass on without describing.
Quale ne' plenilunii sereni Trivia ride tra le ninfe etterne che dipingon lo ciel per tutti i seni,	As when in nights serene of the full moon Smiles Trivia among the nymphs eternal Who paint the firmament through all its gulfs,

vid'i' sopra migliaia di lucerne
  un sol che tutte quante l'accendea,
  come fa 'l nostro le viste superne;

e per la viva luce trasparea
  la lucente sustanza tanto chiara
  nel viso mio, che non la sostenea.

Oh Beatrice, dolce guida e cara!
  Ella mi disse: ""Quel che ti sobranza
  e` virtu` da cui nulla si ripara.

Quivi e` la sapienza e la possanza
  ch'apri` le strade tra 'l cielo e la terra,
  onde fu gia` si` lunga disianza""".

Come foco di nube si diserra
  per dilatarsi si` che non vi cape,
  e fuor di sua natura in giu` s'atterra,

la mente mia cosi`, tra quelle dape
  fatta piu` grande, di se' stessa uscio,
  e che si fesse rimembrar non sape.

""Apri li occhi e riguarda qual son io;
  tu hai vedute cose, che possente
  se' fatto a sostener lo riso mio""".

Io era come quei che si risente
  di visione oblita e che s'ingegna
  indarno di ridurlasi a la mente,

quand'io udi' questa proferta, degna
  di tanto grato, che mai non si stingue
  del libro che 'l preterito rassegna.

Se mo sonasser tutte quelle lingue
  che Polimnia con le suore fero
  del latte lor dolcissimo piu` pingue,

per aiutarmi, al millesmo del vero
  non si verria, cantando il santo riso
  e quanto il santo aspetto facea mero;

e cosi`, figurando il paradiso,
  convien saltar lo sacrato poema,
  come chi trova suo cammin riciso.

Saw I, above the myriads of lamps,
  A Sun that one and all of them enkindled,
  E'en as our own doth the supernal sights,

And through the living light transparent shone
  The lucent substance so intensely clear
  Into my sight, that I sustained it not.

O Beatrice, thou gentle guide and dear!
  To me she said: "What overmasters thee
  A virtue is from which naught shields itself.

There are the wisdom and the omnipotence
  That oped the thoroughfares 'twixt heaven and
    earth,
  For which there erst had been so long a yearning."

As fire from out a cloud unlocks itself,
  Dilating so it finds not room therein,
  And down, against its nature, falls to earth,

So did my mind, among those aliments
  Becoming larger, issue from itself,
  And that which it became cannot remember.

"Open thine eyes, and look at what I am:
  Thou hast beheld such things, that strong enough
  Hast thou become to tolerate my smile."

I was as one who still retains the feeling
  Of a forgotten vision, and endeavours
  In vain to bring it back into his mind,

When I this invitation heard, deserving
  Of so much gratitude, it never fades
  Out of the book that chronicles the past.

If at this moment sounded all the tongues
  That Polyhymnia and her sisters made
  Most lubrical with their delicious milk,

To aid me, to a thousandth of the truth
  It would not reach, singing the holy smile
  And how the holy aspect it illumed.

And therefore, representing Paradise,
  The sacred poem must perforce leap over,
  Even as a man who finds his way cut off;

Ma chi pensasse il ponderoso tema
  e l'omero mortal che se ne carca,
  nol biasmerebbe se sott'esso trema:

non e` pareggio da picciola barca
  quel che fendendo va l'ardita prora,
  ne' da nocchier ch'a se' medesmo parca.

""Perche' la faccia mia si` t'innamora,
  che tu non ti rivolgi al bel giardino
  che sotto i raggi di Cristo s'infiora?

Quivi e` la rosa in che 'l verbo divino
  carne si fece; quivi son li gigli
  al cui odor si prese il buon cammino"".

Cosi` Beatrice; e io, che a' suoi consigli
  tutto era pronto, ancora mi rendei
  a la battaglia de' debili cigli.

Come a raggio di sol che puro mei
  per fratta nube, gia` prato di fiori
  vider, coverti d'ombra, li occhi miei;

vid'io cosi` piu` turbe di splendori,
  folgorate di su` da raggi ardenti,
  sanza veder principio di folgori.

O benigna vertu` che si` li 'mprenti,
  su` t'essaltasti, per largirmi loco
  a li occhi li` che non t'eran possenti.

Il nome del bel fior ch'io sempre invoco
  e mane e sera, tutto mi ristrinse
  l'animo ad avvisar lo maggior foco;

e come ambo le luci mi dipinse
  il quale e il quanto de la viva stella
  che la` su` vince come qua giu` vinse,

per entro il cielo scese una facella,
  formata in cerchio a guisa di corona,
  e cinsela e girossi intorno ad ella.

Qualunque melodia piu` dolce suona
  qua giu` e piu` a se' l'anima tira,
  parrebbe nube che squarciata tona,

But whoso thinketh of the ponderous theme,
  And of the mortal shoulder laden with it,
  Should blame it not, if under this it tremble.

It is no passage for a little boat
  This which goes cleaving the audacious prow,
  Nor for a pilot who would spare himself.

"Why doth my face so much enamour thee,
  That to the garden fair thou turnest not,
  Which under the rays of Christ is blossoming?

There is the Rose in which the Word Divine
  Became incarnate; there the lilies are
  By whose perfume the good way was discovered."

Thus Beatrice; and I, who to her counsels
  Was wholly ready, once again betook me
  Unto the battle of the feeble brows.

As in the sunshine, that unsullied streams
  Through fractured cloud, ere now a meadow of
      flowers
  Mine eyes with shadow covered o'er have seen,

So troops of splendours manifold I saw
  Illumined from above with burning rays,
  Beholding not the source of the effulgence.

O power benignant that dost so imprint them!
  Thou didst exalt thyself to give more scope
  There to mine eyes, that were not strong enough.

The name of that fair flower I e'er invoke
  Morning and evening utterly enthralled
  My soul to gaze upon the greater fire.

And when in both mine eyes depicted were
  The glory and greatness of the living star
  Which there excelleth, as it here excelled,

Athwart the heavens a little torch descended
  Formed in a circle like a coronal,
  And cinctured it, and whirled itself about it.

Whatever melody most sweetly soundeth
  On earth, and to itself most draws the soul,
  Would seem a cloud that, rent asunder, thunders,

comparata al sonar di quella lira	Compared unto the sounding of that lyre
onde si coronava il bel zaffiro	Wherewith was crowned the sapphire beautiful,
del quale il ciel piu` chiaro s'inzaffira.	Which gives the clearest heaven its sapphire hue.
""Io sono amore angelico, che giro	"I am Angelic Love, that circle round
l'alta letizia che spira del ventre	The joy sublime which breathes from out the womb
che fu albergo del nostro disiro;	That was the hostelry of our Desire;
e girerommi, donna del ciel, mentre	And I shall circle, Lady of Heaven, while
che seguirai tuo figlio, e farai dia	Thou followest thy Son, and mak'st diviner
piu` la spera suprema perche' li` entre""`.	The sphere supreme, because thou enterest there."
Cosi` la circulata melodia	Thus did the circulated melody
si sigillava, e tutti li altri lumi	Seal itself up; and all the other lights
facean sonare il nome di Maria.	Were making to resound the name of Mary.
Lo real manto di tutti i volumi	The regal mantle of the volumes all
del mondo, che piu` ferve e piu` s'avviva	Of that world, which most fervid is and living
ne l'alito di Dio e nei costumi,	With breath of God and with his works and ways,
avea sopra di noi l'interna riva	Extended over us its inner border,
tanto distante, che la sua parvenza,	So very distant, that the semblance of it
la` dov'io era, ancor non appariva:	There where I was not yet appeared to me.
pero` non ebber li occhi miei potenza	Therefore mine eyes did not possess the power
di seguitar la coronata fiamma	Of following the incoronated flame,
che si levo` appresso sua semenza.	Which mounted upward near to its own seed.
E come fantolin che 'nver' la mamma	And as a little child, that towards its mother
tende le braccia, poi che 'l latte prese,	Stretches its arms, when it the milk has taken,
per l'animo che 'nfin di fuor s'infiamma;	Through impulse kindled into outward flame,
ciascun di quei candori in su` si stese	Each of those gleams of whiteness upward reached
con la sua cima, si` che l'alto affetto	So with its summit, that the deep affection
ch'elli avieno a Maria mi fu palese.	They had for Mary was revealed to me.
Indi rimaser li` nel mio cospetto,	Thereafter they remained there in my sight,
'Regina celi' cantando si` dolce,	'Regina coeli' singing with such sweetness,
che mai da me non si parti` 'l diletto.	That ne'er from me has the delight departed.
Oh quanta e` l'uberta` che si soffolce	O, what exuberance is garnered up
in quelle arche ricchissime che fuoro	Within those richest coffers, which had been
a seminar qua giu` buone bobolce!	Good husbandmen for sowing here below!
Quivi si vive e gode del tesoro	There they enjoy and live upon the treasure
che s'acquisto` piangendo ne lo essilio	Which was acquired while weeping in the exile
di Babillon, ove si lascio` l'oro.	Of Babylon, wherein the gold was left.
Quivi triunfa, sotto l'alto Filio	There triumpheth, beneath the exalted Son
di Dio e di Maria, di sua vittoria,	Of God and Mary, in his victory,
e con l'antico e col novo concilio,	Both with the ancient council and the new,

colui che tien le chiavi di tal gloria.

He who doth keep the keys of such a glory.

Paradiso: Canto XXIV

The Radiant Wheel. St. Peter examines Dante on Faith.

"O sodalizio eletto a la gran cena
  del benedetto Agnello, il qual vi ciba
  si`, che la vostra voglia e` sempre piena,

se per grazia di Dio questi preliba
  di quel che cade de la vostra mensa,
  prima che morte tempo li prescriba,

ponete mente a l'affezione immensa
  e roratelo alquanto: voi bevete
  sempre del fonte onde vien quel ch'ei pensa"".

Cosi` Beatrice; e quelle anime liete
  si fero spere sopra fissi poli,
  fiammando, a volte, a guisa di comete.

E come cerchi in tempra d'oriuoli
  si giran si`, che 'l primo a chi pon mente
  quieto pare, e l'ultimo che voli;

cosi` quelle carole, differente-
  mente danzando, de la sua ricchezza
  mi facieno stimar, veloci e lente.

Di quella ch'io notai di piu` carezza
  vid'io uscire un foco si` felice,
  che nullo vi lascio` di piu` chiarezza;

e tre fiate intorno di Beatrice
  si volse con un canto tanto divo,
  che la mia fantasia nol mi ridice.

Pero` salta la penna e non lo scrivo:
  che' l'imagine nostra a cotai pieghe,
  non che 'l parlare, e` troppo color vivo.

"O company elect to the great supper
  Of the Lamb benedight, who feedeth you
  So that for ever full is your desire,

If by the grace of God this man foretaste
  Something of that which falleth from your table,
  Or ever death prescribe to him the time,

Direct your mind to his immense desire,
  And him somewhat bedew; ye drinking are
  For ever at the fount whence comes his thought."

Thus Beatrice; and those souls beatified
  Transformed themselves to spheres on steadfast
    poles,
  Flaming intensely in the guise of comets.

And as the wheels in works of horologes
  Revolve so that the first to the beholder
  Motionless seems, and the last one to fly,

So in like manner did those carols, dancing
  In different measure, of their affluence
  Give me the gauge, as they were swift or slow.

From that one which I noted of most beauty
  Beheld I issue forth a fire so happy
  That none it left there of a greater brightness;

And around Beatrice three several times
  It whirled itself with so divine a song,
  My fantasy repeats it not to me;

Therefore the pen skips, and I write it not,
  Since our imagination for such folds,
  Much more our speech, is of a tint too glaring.

""O santa suora mia che si` ne prieghe
  divota, per lo tuo ardente affetto
  da quella bella spera mi disleghe""`.

Poscia fermato, il foco benedetto
  a la mia donna dirizzo` lo spiro,
  che favello` cosi` com'i' ho detto.

Ed ella: ""O luce etterna del gran viro
  a cui Nostro Segnor lascio` le chiavi,
  ch'ei porto` giu`, di questo gaudio miro,

tenta costui di punti lievi e gravi,
  come ti piace, intorno de la fede,
  per la qual tu su per lo mare andavi.

S'elli ama bene e bene spera e crede,
  non t'e` occulto, perche' 'l viso hai quivi
  dov'ogne cosa dipinta si vede;

ma perche' questo regno ha fatto civi
  per la verace fede, a gloriarla,
  di lei parlare e` ben ch'a lui arrivi""`.

Si` come il baccialier s'arma e non parla
  fin che 'l maestro la question propone,
  per approvarla, non per terminarla,

cosi` m'armava io d'ogne ragione
  mentre ch'ella dicea, per esser presto
  a tal querente e a tal professione.

""Di', buon Cristiano, fatti manifesto:
  fede che e`?""`. Ond'io levai la fronte
  in quella luce onde spirava questo;

poi mi volsi a Beatrice, ed essa pronte
  sembianze femmi perch'io spandessi
  l'acqua di fuor del mio interno fonte.

""La Grazia che mi da` ch'io mi confessi""`,
  comincia' io, ""da l'alto primipilo,
  faccia li miei concetti bene espressi""`.

E seguitai: ""Come 'l verace stilo
  ne scrisse, padre, del tuo caro frate
  che mise teco Roma nel buon filo,

fede e` sustanza di cose sperate
  e argomento de le non parventi;
  e questa pare a me sua quiditate""`.

"O holy sister mine, who us implorest
  With such devotion, by thine ardent love
  Thou dost unbind me from that beautiful sphere!"

Thereafter, having stopped, the blessed fire
  Unto my Lady did direct its breath,
  Which spake in fashion as I here have said.

And she: "O light eterne of the great man
  To whom our Lord delivered up the keys
  He carried down of this miraculous joy,

This one examine on points light and grave,
  As good beseemeth thee, about the Faith
  By means of which thou on the sea didst walk.

If he love well, and hope well, and believe,
  From thee 'tis hid not; for thou hast thy sight
  There where depicted everything is seen.

But since this kingdom has made citizens
  By means of the true Faith, to glorify it
  'Tis well he have the chance to speak thereof."

As baccalaureate arms himself, and speaks not
  Until the master doth propose the question,
  To argue it, and not to terminate it,

So did I arm myself with every reason,
  While she was speaking, that I might be ready
  For such a questioner and such profession.

"Say, thou good Christian; manifest thyself;
  What is the Faith?" Whereat I raised my brow
  Unto that light wherefrom was this breathed forth.

Then turned I round to Beatrice, and she
  Prompt signals made to me that I should pour
  The water forth from my internal fountain.

"May grace, that suffers me to make confession,"
  Began I, "to the great centurion,
  Cause my conceptions all to be explicit!"

And I continued: "As the truthful pen,
  Father, of thy dear brother wrote of it,
  Who put with thee Rome into the good way,

Faith is the substance of the things we hope for,
  And evidence of those that are not seen;
  And this appears to me its quiddity."

Allora udi': ""Dirittamente senti,
  se bene intendi perche' la ripuose
  tra le sustanze, e poi tra li argomenti"".

Then heard I: "Very rightly thou perceivest,
  If well thou understandest why he placed it
  With substances and then with evidences."

E io appresso: ""Le profonde cose
  che mi largiscon qui la lor parvenza,
  a li occhi di la` giu` son si` ascose,

And I thereafterward: "The things profound,
  That here vouchsafe to me their apparition,
  Unto all eyes below are so concealed,

che l'esser loro v'e` in sola credenza,
  sopra la qual si fonda l'alta spene;
  e pero` di sustanza prende intenza.

That they exist there only in belief,
  Upon the which is founded the high hope,
  And hence it takes the nature of a substance.

E da questa credenza ci convene
  silogizzar, sanz'avere altra vista:
  pero` intenza d'argomento tene"".

And it behoveth us from this belief
  To reason without having other sight,
  And hence it has the nature of evidence."

Allora udi': ""Se quantunque s'acquista
  giu` per dottrina, fosse cosi` 'nteso,
  non li` avria loco ingegno di sofista"".

Then heard I: "If whatever is acquired
  Below by doctrine were thus understood,
  No sophist's subtlety would there find place."

Cosi` spiro` di quello amore acceso;
  indi soggiunse: ""Assai bene e` trascorsa
  d'esta moneta gia` la lega e 'l peso;

Thus was breathed forth from that enkindled love;
  Then added: "Very well has been gone over
  Already of this coin the alloy and weight;

ma dimmi se tu l'hai ne la tua borsa"".
  Ond'io: ""Si` ho, si` lucida e si` tonda,
  che nel suo conio nulla mi s'inforsa"".

But tell me if thou hast it in thy purse?"
  And I: "Yes, both so shining and so round
  That in its stamp there is no peradventure."

Appresso usci` de la luce profonda
  che li` splendeva: ""Questa cara gioia
  sopra la quale ogne virtu` si fonda,

Thereafter issued from the light profound
  That there resplendent was: "This precious jewel,
  Upon the which is every virtue founded,

onde ti venne?"". E io: ""La larga ploia
  de lo Spirito Santo, ch'e` diffusa
  in su le vecchie e 'n su le nuove cuoia,

Whence hadst thou it?" And I: "The large outpour-
        ing
  Of Holy Spirit, which has been diffused
  Upon the ancient parchments and the new,

e` silogismo che la m'ha conchiusa
  acutamente si`, che 'nverso d'ella
  ogne dimostrazion mi pare ottusa"".

A syllogism is, which proved it to me
  With such acuteness, that, compared therewith,
  All demonstration seems to me obtuse."

Io udi' poi: ""L'antica e la novella
  proposizion che cosi` ti conchiude,
  perche' l'hai tu per divina favella?"".

And then I heard: "The ancient and the new
  Postulates, that to thee are so conclusive,
  Why dost thou take them for the word divine?"

E io: ""La prova che 'l ver mi dischiude,
  son l'opere seguite, a che natura
  non scalda ferro mai ne' batte incude"".

And I: "The proofs, which show the truth to me,
  Are the works subsequent, whereunto Nature
  Ne'er heated iron yet, nor anvil beat."

Risposto fummi: ""Di', chi t'assicura
  che quell'opere fosser? Quel medesmo
  che vuol provarsi, non altri, il ti giura"".

""Se 'l mondo si rivolse al cristianesmo"",
  diss'io, ""sanza miracoli, quest'uno
  e` tal, che li altri non sono il centesmo:

che' tu intrasti povero e digiuno
  in campo, a seminar la buona pianta
  che fu gia` vite e ora e` fatta pruno"".

Finito questo, l'alta corte santa
  risono` per le spere un 'Dio laudamo'
  ne la melode che la` su` si canta.

E quel baron che si` di ramo in ramo,
  essaminando, gia` tratto m'avea,
  che a l'ultime fronde appressavamo,

ricomincio`: ""La Grazia, che donnea
  con la tua mente, la bocca t'aperse
  infino a qui come aprir si dovea,

si` ch'io approvo cio` che fuori emerse;
  ma or conviene espremer quel che credi,
  e onde a la credenza tua s'offerse"".

""O santo padre, e spirito che vedi
  cio` che credesti si`, che tu vincesti
  ver' lo sepulcro piu` giovani piedi"",

comincia' io, ""tu vuo' ch'io manifesti
  la forma qui del pronto creder mio,
  e anche la cagion di lui chiedesti.

E io rispondo: Io credo in uno Dio
  solo ed etterno, che tutto 'l ciel move,
  non moto, con amore e con disio;

e a tal creder non ho io pur prove
  fisice e metafisice, ma dalmi
  anche la verita` che quinci piove

per Moise`, per profeti e per salmi,
  per l'Evangelio e per voi che scriveste
  poi che l'ardente Spirto vi fe' almi;

'Twas answered me: "Say, who assureth thee
  That those works ever were? the thing itself
  That must be proved, nought else to thee affirms
    it."

"Were the world to Christianity converted,"
  I said, "withouten miracles, this one
  Is such, the rest are not its hundredth part;

Because that poor and fasting thou didst enter
  Into the field to sow there the good plant,
  Which was a vine and has become a thorn!"

This being finished, the high, holy Court
  Resounded through the spheres, "One God we
    praise!"
  In melody that there above is chanted.

And then that Baron, who from branch to branch,
  Examining, had thus conducted me,
  Till the extremest leaves we were approaching,

Again began: "The Grace that dallying
  Plays with thine intellect thy mouth has opened,
  Up to this point, as it should opened be,

So that I do approve what forth emerged;
  But now thou must express what thou believest,
  And whence to thy belief it was presented."

"O holy father, spirit who beholdest
  What thou believedst so that thou o'ercamest,
  Towards the sepulchre, more youthful feet,"

Began I, "thou dost wish me in this place
  The form to manifest of my prompt belief,
  And likewise thou the cause thereof demandest.

And I respond: In one God I believe,
  Sole and eterne, who moveth all the heavens
  With love and with desire, himself unmoved;

And of such faith not only have I proofs
  Physical and metaphysical, but gives them
  Likewise the truth that from this place rains down

Through Moses, through the Prophets and the
    Psalms,
  Through the Evangel, and through you, who wrote
  After the fiery Spirit sanctified you;

e credo in tre persone etterne, e queste
  credo una essenza si` una e si` trina,
  che soffera congiunto 'sono' ed 'este'.

De la profonda condizion divina
  ch'io tocco mo, la mente mi sigilla
  piu` volte l'evangelica dottrina.

Quest'e` 'l principio, quest'e` la favilla
  che si dilata in fiamma poi vivace,
  e come stella in cielo in me scintilla"".

Come 'l segnor ch'ascolta quel che i piace,
  da indi abbraccia il servo, gratulando
  per la novella, tosto ch'el si tace;

cosi`, benedicendomi cantando,
  tre volte cinse me, si` com'io tacqui,
  l'appostolico lume al cui comando

io avea detto: si` nel dir li piacqui!

In Persons three eterne believe, and these
  One essence I believe, so one and trine
  They bear conjunction both with 'sunt' and 'est.'

With the profound condition and divine
  Which now I touch upon, doth stamp my mind
  Ofttimes the doctrine evangelical.

This the beginning is, this is the spark
  Which afterwards dilates to vivid flame,
  And, like a star in heaven, is sparkling in me."

Even as a lord who hears what pleaseth him
  His servant straight embraces, gratulating
  For the good news as soon as he is silent;

So, giving me its benediction, singing,
  Three times encircled me, when I was silent,
  The apostolic light, at whose command

I spoken had, in speaking I so pleased him.

Paradiso: Canto XXV

The Laurel Crown. St. James examines Dante on Hope. Dante's Blindness.

Se mai continga che 'l poema sacro
  al quale ha posto mano e cielo e terra,
  si` che m'ha fatto per molti anni macro,

vinca la crudelta` che fuor mi serra
  del bello ovile ov'io dormi' agnello,
  nimico ai lupi che li danno guerra;

con altra voce omai, con altro vello
  ritornero` poeta, e in sul fonte
  del mio battesmo prendero` 'l cappello;

pero` che ne la fede, che fa conte
  l'anime a Dio, quivi intra' io, e poi
  Pietro per lei si` mi giro` la fronte.

Indi si mosse un lume verso noi
  di quella spera ond'usci` la primizia
  che lascio` Cristo d'i vicari suoi;

e la mia donna, piena di letizia,
  mi disse: ""Mira, mira: ecco il barone
  per cui la` giu` si vicita Galizia"".

Si` come quando il colombo si pone
  presso al compagno, l'uno a l'altro pande,
  girando e mormorando, l'affezione;

cosi` vid'io l'un da l'altro grande
  principe glorioso essere accolto,
  laudando il cibo che la` su` li prande.

Ma poi che 'l gratular si fu assolto,
  tacito coram me ciascun s'affisse,
  ignito si` che vincea 'l mio volto.

If e'er it happen that the Poem Sacred,
  To which both heaven and earth have set their
    hand,
  So that it many a year hath made me lean,

O'ercome the cruelty that bars me out
  From the fair sheepfold, where a lamb I slumbered,
  An enemy to the wolves that war upon it,

With other voice forthwith, with other fleece
  Poet will I return, and at my font
  Baptismal will I take the laurel crown;

Because into the Faith that maketh known
  All souls to God there entered I, and then
  Peter for her sake thus my brow encircled.

Thereafterward towards us moved a light
  Out of that band whence issued the first-fruits
  Which of his vicars Christ behind him left,

And then my Lady, full of ecstasy,
  Said unto me: "Look, look! behold the Baron
  For whom below Galicia is frequented."

In the same way as, when a dove alights
  Near his companion, both of them pour forth,
  Circling about and murmuring, their affection,

So one beheld I by the other grand
  Prince glorified to be with welcome greeted,
  Lauding the food that there above is eaten.

But when their gratulations were complete,
  Silently 'coram me' each one stood still,
  So incandescent it o'ercame my sight.

Ridendo allora Beatrice disse:
 ""Inclita vita per cui la larghezza
 de la nostra basilica si scrisse,

fa risonar la spene in questa altezza:
 tu sai, che tante fiate la figuri,
 quante Iesu` ai tre fe' piu` carezza""".

""Leva la testa e fa che t'assicuri:
 che cio` che vien qua su` del mortal mondo,
 convien ch'ai nostri raggi si maturi"".

Questo conforto del foco secondo
 mi venne; ond'io levai li occhi a' monti
 che li 'ncurvaron pria col troppo pondo.

""Poi che per grazia vuol che tu t'affronti
 lo nostro Imperadore, anzi la morte,
 ne l'aula piu` secreta co' suoi conti,

si` che, veduto il ver di questa corte,
 la spene, che la` giu` bene innamora,
 in te e in altrui di cio` conforte,

di' quel ch'ell'e`, di' come se ne 'nfiora
 la mente tua, e di` onde a te venne"".
 Cosi` segui` 'l secondo lume ancora.

E quella pia che guido` le penne
 de le mie ali a cosi` alto volo,
 a la risposta cosi` mi prevenne:

""La Chiesa militante alcun figliuolo
 non ha con piu` speranza, com'e` scritto
 nel Sol che raggia tutto nostro stuolo:

pero` li e` conceduto che d'Egitto
 vegna in Ierusalemme per vedere,
 anzi che 'l militar li sia prescritto.

Li altri due punti, che non per sapere
 son dimandati, ma perch'ei rapporti
 quanto questa virtu` t'e` in piacere,

a lui lasc'io, che' non li saran forti
 ne' di iattanza; ed elli a cio` risponda,
 e la grazia di Dio cio` li comporti"".

Smiling thereafterwards, said Beatrice:
 "Illustrious life, by whom the benefactions
 Of our Basilica have been described,

Make Hope resound within this altitude;
 Thou knowest as oft thou dost personify it
 As Jesus to the three gave greater clearness."—

"Lift up thy head, and make thyself assured;
 For what comes hither from the mortal world
 Must needs be ripened in our radiance."

This comfort came to me from the second fire;
 Wherefore mine eyes I lifted to the hills,
 Which bent them down before with too great
  weight.

"Since, through his grace, our Emperor wills that
  thou
 Shouldst find thee face to face, before thy death,
 In the most secret chamber, with his Counts,

So that, the truth beholden of this court,
 Hope, which below there rightfully enamours,
 Thereby thou strengthen in thyself and others,

Say what it is, and how is flowering with it
 Thy mind, and say from whence it came to thee."
 Thus did the second light again continue.

And the Compassionate, who piloted
 The plumage of my wings in such high flight,
 Did in reply anticipate me thus:

"No child whatever the Church Militant
 Of greater hope possesses, as is written
 In that Sun which irradiates all our band;

Therefore it is conceded him from Egypt
 To come into Jerusalem to see,
 Or ever yet his warfare be completed.

The two remaining points, that not for knowledge
 Have been demanded, but that he report
 How much this virtue unto thee is pleasing,

To him I leave; for hard he will not find them,
 Nor of self-praise; and let him answer them;
 And may the grace of God in this assist him!"

Paradiso: Canto XXV

Come discente ch'a dottor seconda pronto e libente in quel ch'elli e` esperto,   perche' la sua bonta` si disasconda,	As a disciple, who his teacher follows, Ready and willing, where he is expert, That his proficiency may be displayed,

""Spene"", diss'io, ""e` uno attender certo
  de la gloria futura, il qual produce
  grazia divina e precedente merto.
	"Hope," said I, "is the certain expectation
	  Of future glory, which is the effect
	  Of grace divine and merit precedent.

Da molte stelle mi vien questa luce;
  ma quei la distillo` nel mio cor pria
  che fu sommo cantor del sommo duce.
	From many stars this light comes unto me;
	  But he instilled it first into my heart
	  Who was chief singer unto the chief captain.

'Sperino in te', ne la sua teodia
  dice, 'color che sanno il nome tuo':
  e chi nol sa, s'elli ha la fede mia?
	'Sperent in te,' in the high Theody
	  He sayeth, 'those who know thy name;' and who
	  Knoweth it not, if he my faith possess?

Tu mi stillasti, con lo stillar suo,
  ne la pistola poi; si` ch'io son pieno,
  e in altrui vostra pioggia repluo"".
	Thou didst instil me, then, with his instilling
	  In the Epistle, so that I am full,
	  And upon others rain again your rain."

Mentr' io diceva, dentro al vivo seno
  di quello incendio tremolava un lampo
  subito e spesso a guisa di baleno.
	While I was speaking, in the living bosom
	  Of that combustion quivered an effulgence,
	  Sudden and frequent, in the guise of lightning;

Indi spiro`: ""L'amore ond'io avvampo   ancor ver' la virtu` che mi seguette infin la palma e a l'uscir del campo,	Then breathed: "The love wherewith I am inflamed Towards the virtue still which followed me Unto the palm and issue of the field,

vuol ch'io respiri a te che ti dilette
  di lei; ed emmi a grato che tu diche
  quello che la speranza ti 'mpromette"".
	Wills that I breathe to thee that thou delight
	  In her; and grateful to me is thy telling
	  Whatever things Hope promises to thee."

E io: ""Le nove e le scritture antiche
  pongon lo segno, ed esso lo mi addita,
  de l'anime che Dio s'ha fatte amiche.
	And I: "The ancient Scriptures and the new
	  The mark establish, and this shows it me,
	  Of all the souls whom God hath made his friends.

Dice Isaia che ciascuna vestita
  ne la sua terra fia di doppia vesta:
  e la sua terra e` questa dolce vita;
	Isaiah saith, that each one garmented
	  In his own land shall be with twofold garments,
	  And his own land is this delightful life.

e 'l tuo fratello assai vie piu` digesta,   la` dove tratta de le bianche stole, questa revelazion ci manifesta"".	Thy brother, too, far more explicitly, There where he treateth of the robes of white, This revelation manifests to us."

E prima, appresso al fin d'este parole,
  'Sperent in te' di sopr'a noi s'udi`;
  a che rispuoser tutte le carole.
	And first, and near the ending of these words,
	  "Sperent in te" from over us was heard,
	  To which responsive answered all the carols.

Poscia tra esse un lume si schiari`   si` che, se 'l Cancro avesse un tal cristallo, l'inverno avrebbe un mese d'un sol di`.	Thereafterward a light among them brightened, So that, if Cancer one such crystal had, Winter would have a month of one sole day.

429

E come surge e va ed entra in ballo vergine lieta, sol per fare onore a la novizia, non per alcun fallo,	And as uprises, goes, and enters the dance A winsome maiden, only to do honour To the new bride, and not from any failing,
cosi` vid'io lo schiarato splendore venire a' due che si volgieno a nota qual conveniesi al loro ardente amore.	Even thus did I behold the brightened splendour Approach the two, who in a wheel revolved As was beseeming to their ardent love.
Misesi li` nel canto e ne la rota; e la mia donna in lor tenea l'aspetto, pur come sposa tacita e immota.	Into the song and music there it entered; And fixed on them my Lady kept her look, Even as a bride silent and motionless.
""Questi e` colui che giacque sopra 'l petto del nostro pellicano, e questi fue di su la croce al grande officio eletto"".	"This is the one who lay upon the breast Of him our Pelican; and this is he To the great office from the cross elected."
La donna mia cosi`; ne' pero` piue mosser la vista sua di stare attenta poscia che prima le parole sue.	My Lady thus; but therefore none the more Did move her sight from its attentive gaze Before or afterward these words of hers.
Qual e` colui ch'adocchia e s'argomenta di vedere eclissar lo sole un poco, che, per veder, non vedente diventa;	Even as a man who gazes, and endeavours To see the eclipsing of the sun a little, And who, by seeing, sightless doth become,
tal mi fec'io a quell'ultimo foco mentre che detto fu: ""Perche' t'abbagli per veder cosa che qui non ha loco?	So I became before that latest fire, While it was said, "Why dost thou daze thyself To see a thing which here hath no existence?
In terra e` terra il mio corpo, e saragli tanto con li altri, che 'l numero nostro con l'etterno proposito s'agguagli.	Earth in the earth my body is, and shall be With all the others there, until our number With the eternal proposition tallies.
Con le due stole nel beato chiostro son le due luci sole che saliro; e questo apporterai nel mondo vostro"".	With the two garments in the blessed cloister Are the two lights alone that have ascended: And this shalt thou take back into your world."
A questa voce l'infiammato giro si quieto` con esso il dolce mischio che si facea nel suon del trino spiro,	And at this utterance the flaming circle Grew quiet, with the dulcet intermingling Of sound that by the trinal breath was made,
si` come, per cessar fatica o rischio, li remi, pria ne l'acqua ripercossi, tutti si posano al sonar d'un fischio.	As to escape from danger or fatigue The oars that erst were in the water beaten Are all suspended at a whistle's sound.
Ahi quanto ne la mente mi commossi, quando mi volsi per veder Beatrice, per non poter veder, benche' io fossi	Ah, how much in my mind was I disturbed, When I turned round to look on Beatrice, That her I could not see, although I was
presso di lei, e nel mondo felice!	Close at her side and in the Happy World!

Paradiso: Canto XXVI

St. John examines Dante on Charity. Dante's Sight. Adam.

Mentr'io dubbiava per lo viso spento,
  de la fulgida fiamma che lo spense
  usci` un spiro che mi fece attento,

dicendo: ""Intanto che tu ti risense
  de la vista che hai in me consunta,
  ben e` che ragionando la compense.

Comincia dunque; e di' ove s'appunta
  l'anima tua, e fa' ragion che sia
  la vista in te smarrita e non defunta:

perche' la donna che per questa dia
  region ti conduce, ha ne lo sguardo
  la virtu` ch'ebbe la man d'Anania"".

Io dissi: ""Al suo piacere e tosto e tardo
  vegna remedio a li occhi, che fuor porte
  quand'ella entro` col foco ond'io sempr'ardo.

Lo ben che fa contenta questa corte,
  Alfa e O e` di quanta scrittura
  mi legge Amore o lievemente o forte"".

Quella medesma voce che paura
  tolta m'avea del subito abbarbaglio,
  di ragionare ancor mi mise in cura;

e disse: ""Certo a piu` angusto vaglio
  ti conviene schiarar: dicer convienti
  chi drizzo` l'arco tuo a tal berzaglio"".

E io: ""Per filosofici argomenti
  e per autorita` che quinci scende
  cotale amor convien che in me si 'mprenti:

While I was doubting for my vision quenched,
  Out of the flame refulgent that had quenched it
  Issued a breathing, that attentive made me,

Saying: "While thou recoverest the sense
  Of seeing which in me thou hast consumed,
  'Tis well that speaking thou shouldst compensate it.

Begin then, and declare to what thy soul
  Is aimed, and count it for a certainty,
  Sight is in thee bewildered and not dead;

Because the Lady, who through this divine
  Region conducteth thee, has in her look
  The power the hand of Ananias had."

I said: "As pleaseth her, or soon or late
  Let the cure come to eyes that portals were
  When she with fire I ever burn with entered.

The Good, that gives contentment to this Court,
  The Alpha and Omega is of all
  The writing that love reads me low or loud."

The selfsame voice, that taken had from me
  The terror of the sudden dazzlement,
  To speak still farther put it in my thought;

And said: "In verity with finer sieve
  Behoveth thee to sift; thee it behoveth
  To say who aimed thy bow at such a target."

And I: "By philosophic arguments,
  And by authority that hence descends,
  Such love must needs imprint itself in me;

La Divina Commedia - The Divine Comedy

che' 'l bene, in quanto ben, come s'intende,
  cosi` accende amore, e tanto maggio
  quanto piu` di bontate in se' comprende.

Dunque a l'essenza ov'e` tanto avvantaggio,
  che ciascun ben che fuor di lei si trova
  altro non e` ch'un lume di suo raggio,

piu` che in altra convien che si mova
  la mente, amando, di ciascun che cerne
  il vero in che si fonda questa prova.

Tal vero a l'intelletto mio sterne
  colui che mi dimostra il primo amore
  di tutte le sustanze sempiterne.

Sternel la voce del verace autore,
  che dice a Moise`, di se' parlando:
  'Io ti faro` vedere ogne valore'.

Sternilmi tu ancora, incominciando
  l'alto preconio che grida l'arcano
  di qui la` giu` sovra ogne altro bando"".

E io udi': ""Per intelletto umano
  e per autoritadi a lui concorde
  d'i tuoi amori a Dio guarda il sovrano.

Ma di' ancor se tu senti altre corde
  tirarti verso lui, si` che tu suone
  con quanti denti questo amor ti morde"".

Non fu latente la santa intenzione
  de l'aguglia di Cristo, anzi m'accorsi
  dove volea menar mia professione.

Pero` ricominciai: ""Tutti quei morsi
  che posson far lo cor volgere a Dio,
  a la mia caritate son concorsi:

che' l'essere del mondo e l'esser mio,
  la morte ch'el sostenne perch'io viva,
  e quel che spera ogne fedel com'io,

con la predetta conoscenza viva,
  tratto m'hanno del mar de l'amor torto,
  e del diritto m'han posto a la riva.

Le fronde onde s'infronda tutto l'orto
  de l'ortolano etterno, am'io cotanto
  quanto da lui a lor di bene e` porto"".

For Good, so far as good, when comprehended
  Doth straight enkindle love, and so much greater
  As more of goodness in itself it holds;

Then to that Essence (whose is such advantage
  That every good which out of it is found
  Is nothing but a ray of its own light)

More than elsewhither must the mind be moved
  Of every one, in loving, who discerns
  The truth in which this evidence is founded.

Such truth he to my intellect reveals
  Who demonstrates to me the primal love
  Of all the sempiternal substances.

The voice reveals it of the truthful Author,
  Who says to Moses, speaking of Himself,
  'I will make all my goodness pass before thee.'

Thou too revealest it to me, beginning
  The loud Evangel, that proclaims the secret
  Of heaven to earth above all other edict."

And I heard say: "By human intellect
  And by authority concordant with it,
  Of all thy loves reserve for God the highest.

But say again if other cords thou feelest,
  Draw thee towards Him, that thou mayst proclaim
  With how many teeth this love is biting thee."

The holy purpose of the Eagle of Christ
  Not latent was, nay, rather I perceived
  Whither he fain would my profession lead.

Therefore I recommenced: "All of those bites
  Which have the power to turn the heart to God
  Unto my charity have been concurrent.

The being of the world, and my own being,
  The death which He endured that I may live,
  And that which all the faithful hope, as I do,

With the forementioned vivid consciousness
  Have drawn me from the sea of love perverse,
  And of the right have placed me on the shore.

The leaves, wherewith embowered is all the garden
  Of the Eternal Gardener, do I love
  As much as he has granted them of good."

432

Si` com'io tacqui, un dolcissimo canto
  risono` per lo cielo, e la mia donna
  dicea con li altri: ""Santo, santo, santo!"".

E come a lume acuto si disonna
  per lo spirto visivo che ricorre
  a lo splendor che va di gonna in gonna,

e lo svegliato cio` che vede aborre,
  si` nescia e` la subita vigilia
  fin che la stimativa non soccorre;

cosi` de li occhi miei ogni quisquilia
  fugo` Beatrice col raggio d'i suoi,
  che rifulgea da piu` di mille milia:

onde mei che dinanzi vidi poi;
  e quasi stupefatto domandai
  d'un quarto lume ch'io vidi tra noi.

E la mia donna: ""Dentro da quei rai
  vagheggia il suo fattor l'anima prima
  che la prima virtu` creasse mai"".

Come la fronda che flette la cima
  nel transito del vento, e poi si leva
  per la propria virtu` che la soblima,

fec'io in tanto in quant'ella diceva,
  stupendo, e poi mi rifece sicuro
  un disio di parlare ond'io ardeva.

E cominciai: ""O pomo che maturo
  solo prodotto fosti, o padre antico
  a cui ciascuna sposa e` figlia e nuro,

divoto quanto posso a te supplico
  perche' mi parli: tu vedi mia voglia,
  e per udirti tosto non la dico"".

Talvolta un animal coverto broglia,
  si` che l'affetto convien che si paia
  per lo seguir che face a lui la 'nvoglia;

e similmente l'anima primaia
  mi facea trasparer per la coverta
  quant'ella a compiacermi venia gaia.

As soon as I had ceased, a song most sweet
  Throughout the heaven resounded, and my Lady
  Said with the others, "Holy, holy, holy!"

And as at some keen light one wakes from sleep
  By reason of the visual spirit that runs
  Unto the splendour passed from coat to coat,

And he who wakes abhorreth what he sees,
  So all unconscious is his sudden waking,
  Until the judgment cometh to his aid,

So from before mine eyes did Beatrice
  Chase every mote with radiance of her own,
  That cast its light a thousand miles and more.

Whence better after than before I saw,
  And in a kind of wonderment I asked
  About a fourth light that I saw with us.

And said my Lady: "There within those rays
  Gazes upon its Maker the first soul
  That ever the first virtue did create."

Even as the bough that downward bends its top
  At transit of the wind, and then is lifted
  By its own virtue, which inclines it upward,

Likewise did I, the while that she was speaking,
  Being amazed, and then I was made bold
  By a desire to speak wherewith I burned.

And I began: "O apple, that mature
  Alone hast been produced, O ancient father,
  To whom each wife is daughter and daughter-in-
    law,

Devoutly as I can I supplicate thee
  That thou wouldst speak to me; thou seest my wish;
  And I, to hear thee quickly, speak it not."

Sometimes an animal, when covered, struggles
  So that his impulse needs must be apparent,
  By reason of the wrappage following it;

And in like manner the primeval soul
  Made clear to me athwart its covering
  How jubilant it was to give me pleasure.

Indi spiro`: ““Sanz'essermi proferta
da te, la voglia tua discerno meglio
che tu qualunque cosa t'e` piu` certa;

perch'io la veggio nel verace speglio
che fa di se' pareglio a l'altre cose,
e nulla face lui di se' pareglio.

Tu vuogli udir quant'e` che Dio mi puose
ne l'eccelso giardino, ove costei
a cosi` lunga scala ti dispuose,

e quanto fu diletto a li occhi miei,
e la propria cagion del gran disdegno,
e l'idioma ch'usai e che fei.

Or, figluol mio, non il gustar del legno
fu per se' la cagion di tanto essilio,
ma solamente il trapassar del segno.

Quindi onde mosse tua donna Virgilio,
quattromilia trecento e due volumi
di sol desiderai questo concilio;

e vidi lui tornare a tutt'i lumi
de la sua strada novecento trenta
fiate, mentre ch'io in terra fu' mi.

La lingua ch'io parlai fu tutta spenta
innanzi che a l'ovra inconsummabile
fosse la gente di Nembrot attenta:

che' nullo effetto mai razionabile,
per lo piacere uman che rinovella
seguendo il cielo, sempre fu durabile.

Opera naturale e` ch'uom favella;
ma cosi` o cosi`, natura lascia
poi fare a voi secondo che v'abbella.

Pria ch'i' scendessi a l'infernale ambascia,
I s'appellava in terra il sommo bene
onde vien la letizia che mi fascia;

e El si chiamo` poi: e cio` convene,
che' l'uso d'i mortali e` come fronda
in ramo, che sen va e altra vene.

Nel monte che si leva piu` da l'onda,
fu' io, con vita pura e disonesta,
da la prim'ora a quella che seconda,

Then breathed: "Without thy uttering it to me,
Thine inclination better I discern
Than thou whatever thing is surest to thee;

For I behold it in the truthful mirror,
That of Himself all things parhelion makes,
And none makes Him parhelion of itself.

Thou fain wouldst hear how long ago God placed me
Within the lofty garden, where this Lady
Unto so long a stairway thee disposed.

And how long to mine eyes it was a pleasure,
And of the great disdain the proper cause,
And the language that I used and that I made.

Now, son of mine, the tasting of the tree
Not in itself was cause of so great exile,
But solely the o'erstepping of the bounds.

There, whence thy Lady moved Virgilius,
Four thousand and three hundred and two circuits
Made by the sun, this Council I desired;

And him I saw return to all the lights
Of his highway nine hundred times and thirty,
Whilst I upon the earth was tarrying.

The language that I spake was quite extinct
Before that in the work interminable
The people under Nimrod were employed;

For nevermore result of reasoning
(Because of human pleasure that doth change,
Obedient to the heavens) was durable.

A natural action is it that man speaks;
But whether thus or thus, doth nature leave
To your own art, as seemeth best to you.

Ere I descended to the infernal anguish,
'El' was on earth the name of the Chief Good,
From whom comes all the joy that wraps me round

'Eli' he then was called, and that is proper,
Because the use of men is like a leaf
On bough, which goeth and another cometh.

Upon the mount that highest o'er the wave
Rises was I, in life or pure or sinful,
From the first hour to that which is the second,

come 'l sol muta quadra, l'ora sesta"".   As the sun changes quadrant, to the sixth."

Paradiso: Canto XXVII

St. Peter's reproof of bad Popes. The Ascent to the Ninth Heaven, the 'Primum Mobile.'

'Al Padre, al Figlio, a lo Spirito Santo',
  comincio`, 'gloria!', tutto 'l paradiso,
  si` che m'inebriava il dolce canto.

Cio` ch'io vedeva mi sembiava un riso
  de l'universo; per che mia ebbrezza
  intrava per l'udire e per lo viso.

Oh gioia! oh ineffabile allegrezza!
  oh vita integra d'amore e di pace!
  oh sanza brama sicura ricchezza!

Dinanzi a li occhi miei le quattro face
  stavano accese, e quella che pria venne
  incomincio` a farsi piu` vivace,

e tal ne la sembianza sua divenne,
  qual diverrebbe Iove, s'elli e Marte
  fossero augelli e cambiassersi penne.

La provedenza, che quivi comparte
  vice e officio, nel beato coro
  silenzio posto avea da ogne parte,

quand'io udi': ""Se io mi trascoloro,
  non ti maravigliar, che', dicend'io,
  vedrai trascolorar tutti costoro.

Quelli ch'usurpa in terra il luogo mio,
  il luogo mio, il luogo mio, che vaca
  ne la presenza del Figliuol di Dio,

fatt'ha del cimitero mio cloaca
  del sangue e de la puzza; onde 'l perverso
  che cadde di qua su`, la` giu` si placa"".

"Glory be to the Father, to the Son,
  And Holy Ghost!" all Paradise began,
  So that the melody inebriate made me.

What I beheld seemed unto me a smile
  Of the universe; for my inebriation
  Found entrance through the hearing and the sight.

O joy! O gladness inexpressible!
  O perfect life of love and peacefulness!
  O riches without hankering secure!

Before mine eyes were standing the four torches
  Enkindled, and the one that first had come
  Began to make itself more luminous;

And even such in semblance it became
  As Jupiter would become, if he and Mars
  Were birds, and they should interchange their
        feathers.

That Providence, which here distributeth
  Season and service, in the blessed choir
  Had silence upon every side imposed.

When I heard say: "If I my colour change,
  Marvel not at it; for while I am speaking
  Thou shalt behold all these their colour change.

He who usurps upon the earth my place,
  My place, my place, which vacant has become
  Before the presence of the Son of God,

Has of my cemetery made a sewer
  Of blood and stench, whereby the Perverse One,
  Who fell from here, below there is appeased!"

Di quel color che per lo sole avverso
  nube dipigne da sera e da mane,
  vid'io allora tutto 'l ciel cosperso.

E come donna onesta che permane
  di se' sicura, e per l'altrui fallanza,
  pur ascoltando, timida si fane,

cosi` Beatrice trasmuto` sembianza;
  e tale eclissi credo che 'n ciel fue,
  quando pati` la supprema possanza.

Poi procedetter le parole sue
  con voce tanto da se' trasmutata,
  che la sembianza non si muto` piue:

““Non fu la sposa di Cristo allevata
  del sangue mio, di Lin, di quel di Cleto,
  per essere ad acquisto d'oro usata;

ma per acquisto d'esto viver lieto
  e Sisto e Pio e Calisto e Urbano
  sparser lo sangue dopo molto fleto.

Non fu nostra intenzion ch'a destra mano
  d'i nostri successor parte sedesse,
  parte da l'altra del popol cristiano;

ne' che le chiavi che mi fuor concesse,
  divenisser signaculo in vessillo
  che contra battezzati combattesse;

ne' ch'io fossi figura di sigillo
  a privilegi venduti e mendaci,
  ond'io sovente arrosso e disfavillo.

In vesta di pastor lupi rapaci
  si veggion di qua su` per tutti i paschi:
  o difesa di Dio, perche' pur giaci?

Del sangue nostro Caorsini e Guaschi
  s'apparecchian di bere: o buon principio,
  a che vil fine convien che tu caschi!

Ma l'alta provedenza, che con Scipio
  difese a Roma la gloria del mondo,
  soccorra` tosto, si` com'io concipio;

e tu, figliuol, che per lo mortal pondo
  ancor giu` tornerai, apri la bocca,
  e non asconder quel ch'io non ascondo”“.

With the same colour which, through sun adverse,
  Painteth the clouds at evening or at morn,
  Beheld I then the whole of heaven suffused.

And as a modest woman, who abides
  Sure of herself, and at another's failing,
  From listening only, timorous becomes,

Even thus did Beatrice change countenance;
  And I believe in heaven was such eclipse,
  When suffered the supreme Omnipotence;

Thereafterward proceeded forth his words
  With voice so much transmuted from itself,
  The very countenance was not more changed.

"The spouse of Christ has never nurtured been
  On blood of mine, of Linus and of Cletus,
  To be made use of in acquest of gold;

But in acquest of this delightful life
  Sixtus and Pius, Urban and Calixtus,
  After much lamentation, shed their blood.

Our purpose was not, that on the right hand
  Of our successors should in part be seated
  The Christian folk, in part upon the other;

Nor that the keys which were to me confided
  Should e'er become the escutcheon on a banner,
  That should wage war on those who are baptized;

Nor I be made the figure of a seal
  To privileges venal and mendacious,
  Whereat I often redden and flash with fire.

In garb of shepherds the rapacious wolves
  Are seen from here above o'er all the pastures!
  O wrath of God, why dost thou slumber still?

To drink our blood the Caorsines and Gascons
  Are making ready. O thou good beginning,
  Unto how vile an end must thou needs fall!

But the high Providence, that with Scipio
  At Rome the glory of the world defended,
  Will speedily bring aid, as I conceive;

And thou, my son, who by thy mortal weight
  Shalt down return again, open thy mouth;
  What I conceal not, do not thou conceal."

Si` come di vapor gelati fiocca
  in giuso l'aere nostro, quando 'l corno
  de la capra del ciel col sol si tocca,

in su` vid'io cosi` l'etera addorno
  farsi e fioccar di vapor triunfanti
  che fatto avien con noi quivi soggiorno.

Lo viso mio seguiva i suoi sembianti,
  e segui` fin che 'l mezzo, per lo molto,
  li tolse il trapassar del piu` avanti.

Onde la donna, che mi vide assolto
  de l'attendere in su`, mi disse: ""Adima
  il viso e guarda come tu se' volto"".

Da l'ora ch'io avea guardato prima
  i' vidi mosso me per tutto l'arco
  che fa dal mezzo al fine il primo clima;

si` ch'io vedea di la` da Gade il varco
  folle d'Ulisse, e di qua presso il lito
  nel qual si fece Europa dolce carco.

E piu` mi fora discoverto il sito
  di questa aiuola; ma 'l sol procedea
  sotto i mie' piedi un segno e piu` partito.

La mente innamorata, che donnea
  con la mia donna sempre, di ridure
  ad essa li occhi piu` che mai ardea;

e se natura o arte fe' pasture
  da pigliare occhi, per aver la mente,
  in carne umana o ne le sue pitture,

tutte adunate, parrebber niente
  ver' lo piacer divin che mi refulse,
  quando mi volsi al suo viso ridente.

E la virtu` che lo sguardo m'indulse,
  del bel nido di Leda mi divelse,
  e nel ciel velocissimo m'impulse.

Le parti sue vivissime ed eccelse
  si` uniforme son, ch'i' non so dire
  qual Beatrice per loco mi scelse.

Ma ella, che vedea 'l mio disire,
  incomincio`, ridendo tanto lieta,
  che Dio parea nel suo volto gioire:

As with its frozen vapours downward falls
  In flakes our atmosphere, what time the horn
  Of the celestial Goat doth touch the sun,

Upward in such array saw I the ether
  Become, and flaked with the triumphant vapours,
  Which there together with us had remained.

My sight was following up their semblances,
  And followed till the medium, by excess,
  The passing farther onward took from it;

Whereat the Lady, who beheld me freed
  From gazing upward, said to me: "Cast down
  Thy sight, and see how far thou art turned round."

Since the first time that I had downward looked,
  I saw that I had moved through the whole arc
  Which the first climate makes from midst to end;

So that I saw the mad track of Ulysses
  Past Gades, and this side, well nigh the shore
  Whereon became Europa a sweet burden.

And of this threshing-floor the site to me
  Were more unveiled, but the sun was proceeding
  Under my feet, a sign and more removed.

My mind enamoured, which is dallying
  At all times with my Lady, to bring back
  To her mine eyes was more than ever ardent.

And if or Art or Nature has made bait
  To catch the eyes and so possess the mind,
  In human flesh or in its portraiture,

All joined together would appear as nought
  To the divine delight which shone upon me
  When to her smiling face I turned me round.

The virtue that her look endowed me with
  From the fair nest of Leda tore me forth,
  And up into the swiftest heaven impelled me.

Its parts exceeding full of life and lofty
  Are all so uniform, I cannot say
  Which Beatrice selected for my place.

But she, who was aware of my desire,
  Began, the while she smiled so joyously
  That God seemed in her countenance to rejoice:

““La natura del mondo, che quieta
  il mezzo e tutto l'altro intorno move,
  quinci comincia come da sua meta;

e questo cielo non ha altro dove
  che la mente divina, in che s'accende
  l'amor che 'l volge e la virtu` ch'ei piove.

Luce e amor d'un cerchio lui comprende,
  si` come questo li altri; e quel precinto
  colui che 'l cinge solamente intende.

Non e` suo moto per altro distinto,
  ma li altri son mensurati da questo,
  si` come diece da mezzo e da quinto;

e come il tempo tegna in cotal testo
  le sue radici e ne li altri le fronde,
  omai a te puo` esser manifesto.

Oh cupidigia che i mortali affonde
  si` sotto te, che nessuno ha podere
  di trarre li occhi fuor de le tue onde!

Ben fiorisce ne li uomini il volere;
  ma la pioggia continua converte
  in bozzacchioni le sosine vere.

Fede e innocenza son reperte
  solo ne' parvoletti; poi ciascuna
  pria fugge che le guance sian coperte.

Tale, balbuziendo ancor, digiuna,
  che poi divora, con la lingua sciolta,
  qualunque cibo per qualunque luna;

e tal, balbuziendo, ama e ascolta
  la madre sua, che, con loquela intera,
  disia poi di vederla sepolta.

Cosi` si fa la pelle bianca nera
  nel primo aspetto de la bella figlia
  di quel ch'apporta mane e lascia sera.

Tu, perche' non ti facci maraviglia,
  pensa che 'n terra non e` chi governi;
  onde si` svia l'umana famiglia.

"The nature of that motion, which keeps quiet
  The centre and all the rest about it moves,
  From hence begins as from its starting point.

And in this heaven there is no other Where
  Than in the Mind Divine, wherein is kindled
  The love that turns it, and the power it rains.

Within a circle light and love embrace it,
  Even as this doth the others, and that precinct
  He who encircles it alone controls.

Its motion is not by another meted,
  But all the others measured are by this,
  As ten is by the half and by the fifth.

And in what manner time in such a pot
  May have its roots, and in the rest its leaves,
  Now unto thee can manifest be made.

O Covetousness, that mortals dost ingulf
  Beneath thee so, that no one hath the power
  Of drawing back his eyes from out thy waves!

Full fairly blossoms in mankind the will;
  But the uninterrupted rain converts
  Into abortive wildings the true plums.

Fidelity and innocence are found
  Only in children; afterwards they both
  Take flight or e'er the cheeks with down are covered.

One, while he prattles still, observes the fasts,
  Who, when his tongue is loosed, forthwith devours
  Whatever food under whatever moon;

Another, while he prattles, loves and listens
  Unto his mother, who when speech is perfect
  Forthwith desires to see her in her grave.

Even thus is swarthy made the skin so white
  In its first aspect of the daughter fair
  Of him who brings the morn, and leaves the night.

Thou, that it may not be a marvel to thee,
  Think that on earth there is no one who governs;
  Whence goes astray the human family.

Ma prima che gennaio tutto si sverni
  per la centesma ch'e` la` giu` negletta,
  raggeran si` questi cerchi superni,

che la fortuna che tanto s'aspetta,
  le poppe volgera` u' son le prore,
  si` che la classe correra` diretta;

e vero frutto verra` dopo 'l fiore"".

Ere January be unwintered wholly
  By the centesimal on earth neglected,
  Shall these supernal circles roar so loud

The tempest that has been so long awaited
  Shall whirl the poops about where are the prows;
  So that the fleet shall run its course direct,

And the true fruit shall follow on the flower."

Paradiso: Canto XXVIII

God and the Angelic Hierarchies.

Poscia che 'ncontro a la vita presente
  d'i miseri mortali aperse 'l vero
  quella che 'mparadisa la mia mente,
	After the truth against the present life
	  Of miserable mortals was unfolded
	  By her who doth imparadise my mind,

come in lo specchio fiamma di doppiero
  vede colui che se n'alluma retro,
  prima che l'abbia in vista o in pensiero,
	As in a looking-glass a taper's flame
	  He sees who from behind is lighted by it,
	  Before he has it in his sight or thought,

e se' rivolge per veder se 'l vetro
  li dice il vero, e vede ch'el s'accorda
  con esso come nota con suo metro;
	And turns him round to see if so the glass
	  Tell him the truth, and sees that it accords
	  Therewith as doth a music with its metre,

cosi` la mia memoria si ricorda
  ch'io feci riguardando ne' belli occhi
  onde a pigliarmi fece Amor la corda.
	In similar wise my memory recollecteth
	  That I did, looking into those fair eyes,
	  Of which Love made the springes to ensnare me.

E com'io mi rivolsi e furon tocchi
  li miei da cio` che pare in quel volume,
  quandunque nel suo giro ben s'adocchi,
	And as I turned me round, and mine were touched
	  By that which is apparent in that volume,
	  Whenever on its gyre we gaze intent,

un punto vidi che raggiava lume
  acuto si`, che 'l viso ch'elli affoca
  chiuder conviensi per lo forte acume;
	A point beheld I, that was raying out
	  Light so acute, the sight which it enkindles
	  Must close perforce before such great acuteness.

e quale stella par quinci piu` poca,
  parrebbe luna, locata con esso
  come stella con stella si colloca.
	And whatsoever star seems smallest here
	  Would seem to be a moon, if placed beside it.
	  As one star with another star is placed.

Forse cotanto quanto pare appresso
  alo cigner la luce che 'l dipigne
  quando 'l vapor che 'l porta piu` e` spesso,
	Perhaps at such a distance as appears
	  A halo cincturing the light that paints it,
	  When densest is the vapour that sustains it,

distante intorno al punto un cerchio d'igne si girava si` ratto, ch'avria vinto   quel moto che piu` tosto il mondo cigne;	Thus distant round the point a circle of fire So swiftly whirled, that it would have surpassed Whatever motion soonest girds the world;

e questo era d'un altro circumcinto,
  e quel dal terzo, e 'l terzo poi dal quarto,
  dal quinto il quarto, e poi dal sesto il quinto.
	And this was by another circumcinct,
	  That by a third, the third then by a fourth,
	  By a fifth the fourth, and then by a sixth the fifth;

Sopra seguiva il settimo si` sparto   gia` di larghezza, che 'l messo di Iuno intero a contenerlo sarebbe arto.	The seventh followed thereupon in width So ample now, that Juno's messenger Entire would be too narrow to contain it.
Cosi` l'ottavo e 'l nono; e chiascheduno   piu` tardo si movea, secondo ch'era in numero distante piu` da l'uno;	Even so the eighth and ninth; and every one More slowly moved, according as it was In number distant farther from the first.
e quello avea la fiamma piu` sincera   cui men distava la favilla pura,   credo, pero` che piu` di lei s'invera.	And that one had its flame most crystalline From which less distant was the stainless spark, I think because more with its truth imbued.

La donna mia, che mi vedea in cura
  forte sospeso, disse: ""Da quel punto
  depende il cielo e tutta la natura.
	My Lady, who in my anxiety
	  Beheld me much perplexed, said: "From that point
	  Dependent is the heaven and nature all.

Mira quel cerchio che piu` li e` congiunto;
  e sappi che 'l suo muovere e` si` tosto
  per l'affocato amore ond'elli e` punto"".
	Behold that circle most conjoined to it,
	  And know thou, that its motion is so swift
	  Through burning love whereby it is spurred on."

E io a lei: ""Se 'l mondo fosse posto
  con l'ordine ch'io veggio in quelle rote,
  sazio m'avrebbe cio` che m'e` proposto;
	And I to her: "If the world were arranged
	  In the order which I see in yonder wheels,
	  What's set before me would have satisfied me;

ma nel mondo sensibile si puote veder le volte tanto piu` divine,   quant'elle son dal centro piu` remote.	But in the world of sense we can perceive That evermore the circles are diviner As they are from the centre more remote

Onde, se 'l mio disir dee aver fine
  in questo miro e angelico templo
  che solo amore e luce ha per confine,
	Wherefore if my desire is to be ended
	  In this miraculous and angelic temple,
	  That has for confines only love and light,

udir convienmi ancor come l'essemplo
  e l'essemplare non vanno d'un modo,
  che' io per me indarno a cio` contemplo"".
	To hear behoves me still how the example
	  And the exemplar go not in one fashion,
	  Since for myself in vain I contemplate it."

""Se li tuoi diti non sono a tal nodo sufficienti, non e` maraviglia:   tanto, per non tentare, e` fatto sodo!"".	"If thine own fingers unto such a knot Be insufficient, it is no great wonder, So hard hath it become for want of trying."
Cosi` la donna mia; poi disse: ""Piglia   quel ch'io ti dicero`, se vuo' saziarti; e intorno da esso t'assottiglia.	My Lady thus; then said she: "Do thou take What I shall tell thee, if thou wouldst be sated, And exercise on that thy subtlety.

Li cerchi corporai sono ampi e arti
  secondo il piu` e 'l men de la virtute
  che si distende per tutte lor parti.
	The circles corporal are wide and narrow
	  According to the more or less of virtue
	  Which is distributed through all their parts.

Maggior bonta` vuol far maggior salute;
  maggior salute maggior corpo cape,
  s'elli ha le parti igualmente compiute.

Dunque costui che tutto quanto rape
  l'altro universo seco, corrisponde
  al cerchio che piu` ama e che piu` sape:

per che, se tu a la virtu` circonde
  la tua misura, non a la parvenza
  de le sustanze che t'appaion tonde,

tu vederai mirabil consequenza
  di maggio a piu` e di minore a meno,
  in ciascun cielo, a sua intelligenza"".

Come rimane splendido e screno
  l'emisperio de l'aere, quando soffia
  Borea da quella guancia ond'e` piu` leno,

per che si purga e risolve la roffia
  che pria turbava, si` che 'l ciel ne ride
  con le bellezze d'ogne sua paroffia;

cosi` fec'io, poi che mi provide
  la donna mia del suo risponder chiaro,
  e come stella in cielo il ver si vide.

E poi che le parole sue restaro,
  non altrimenti ferro disfavilla
  che bolle, come i cerchi sfavillaro.

L'incendio suo seguiva ogne scintilla;
  ed eran tante, che 'l numero loro
  piu` che 'l doppiar de li scacchi s'inmilla.

Io sentiva osannar di coro in coro
  al punto fisso che li tiene a li ubi,
  e terra` sempre, ne' quai sempre fuoro.

E quella che vedea i pensier dubi
  ne la mia mente, disse: ""I cerchi primi
  t'hanno mostrato Serafi e Cherubi.

Cosi` veloci seguono i suoi vimi,
  per somigliarsi al punto quanto ponno;
  e posson quanto a veder son soblimi.

Quelli altri amori che 'ntorno li vonno,
  si chiaman Troni del divino aspetto,
  per che 'l primo ternaro terminonno;

The greater goodness works the greater weal,
  The greater weal the greater body holds,
  If perfect equally are all its parts.

Therefore this one which sweeps along with it
  The universe sublime, doth correspond
  Unto the circle which most loves and knows.

On which account, if thou unto the virtue
  Apply thy measure, not to the appearance
  Of substances that unto thee seem round,

Thou wilt behold a marvellous agreement,
  Of more to greater, and of less to smaller,
  In every heaven, with its Intelligence."

Even as remaineth splendid and serene
  The hemisphere of air, when Boreas
  Is blowing from that cheek where he is mildest,

Because is purified and resolved the rack
  That erst disturbed it, till the welkin laughs
  With all the beauties of its pageantry;

Thus did I likewise, after that my Lady
  Had me provided with her clear response,
  And like a star in heaven the truth was seen.

And soon as to a stop her words had come,
  Not otherwise does iron scintillate
  When molten, than those circles scintillated.

Their coruscation all the sparks repeated,
  And they so many were, their number makes
  More millions than the doubling of the chess.

I heard them sing hosanna choir by choir
  To the fixed point which holds them at the 'Ubi,'
  And ever will, where they have ever been.

And she, who saw the dubious meditations
  Within my mind, "The primal circles," said,
  "Have shown thee Seraphim and Cherubim.

Thus rapidly they follow their own bonds,
  To be as like the point as most they can,
  And can as far as they are high in vision.

Those other Loves, that round about them go,
  Thrones of the countenance divine are called,
  Because they terminate the primal Triad.

e dei saper che tutti hanno diletto
  quanto la sua veduta si profonda
  nel vero in che si queta ogne intelletto.

Quinci si puo` veder come si fonda
  l'essere beato ne l'atto che vede,
  non in quel ch'ama, che poscia seconda;

e del vedere e` misura mercede,
  che grazia partorisce e buona voglia:
  cosi` di grado in grado si procede.

L'altro ternaro, che cosi` germoglia
  in questa primavera sempiterna
  che notturno Ariete non dispoglia,

perpetualemente 'Osanna' sberna
  con tre melode, che suonano in tree
  ordini di letizia onde s'interna.

In essa gerarcia son l'altre dee:
  prima Dominazioni, e poi Virtudi;
  l'ordine terzo di Podestadi ee.

Poscia ne' due penultimi tripudi
  Principati e Arcangeli si girano;
  l'ultimo e` tutto d'Angelici ludi.

Questi ordini di su` tutti s'ammirano,
  e di giu` vincon si`, che verso Dio
  tutti tirati sono e tutti tirano.

E Dionisio con tanto disio
  a contemplar questi ordini si mise,
  che li nomo` e distinse com'io.

Ma Gregorio da lui poi si divise;
  onde, si` tosto come li occhi aperse
  in questo ciel, di se' medesmo rise.

E se tanto secreto ver proferse
  mortale in terra, non voglio ch'ammiri;
  che' chi 'l vide qua su` gliel discoperse

con altro assai del ver di questi giri'"'.

And thou shouldst know that they all have delight
  As much as their own vision penetrates
  The Truth, in which all intellect finds rest.

From this it may be seen how blessedness
  Is founded in the faculty which sees,
  And not in that which loves, and follows next;

And of this seeing merit is the measure,
  Which is brought forth by grace, and by good will;
  Thus on from grade to grade doth it proceed.

The second Triad, which is germinating
  In such wise in this sempiternal spring,
  That no nocturnal Aries despoils,

Perpetually hosanna warbles forth
  With threefold melody, that sounds in three
  Orders of joy, with which it is intrined.

The three Divine are in this hierarchy,
  First the Dominions, and the Virtues next;
  And the third order is that of the Powers.

Then in the dances twain penultimate
  The Principalities and Archangels wheel;
  The last is wholly of angelic sports.

These orders upward all of them are gazing,
  And downward so prevail, that unto God
  They all attracted are and all attract.

And Dionysius with so great desire
  To contemplate these Orders set himself,
  He named them and distinguished them as I do.

But Gregory afterwards dissented from him;
  Wherefore, as soon as he unclosed his eyes
  Within this heaven, he at himself did smile.

And if so much of secret truth a mortal
  Proffered on earth, I would not have thee marvel,
  For he who saw it here revealed it to him,

With much more of the truth about these circles."

Paradiso: Canto XXIX

Beatrice's Discourse of the Creation of the Angels, and of the Fall of Lucifer. Her Reproof of Foolish and Avaricious Preachers.

Quando ambedue li figli di Latona,
  coperti del Montone e de la Libra,
  fanno de l'orizzonte insieme zona,

quant'e` dal punto che 'l cenit inlibra
  infin che l'uno e l'altro da quel cinto,
  cambiando l'emisperio, si dilibra,

tanto, col volto di riso dipinto,
  si tacque Beatrice, riguardando
  fiso nel punto che m'avea vinto.

Poi comincio`: ""Io dico, e non dimando,
  quel che tu vuoli udir, perch'io l'ho visto
  la` 've s'appunta ogne ubi e ogne quando.

Non per aver a se' di bene acquisto,
  ch'esser non puo`, ma perche' suo splendore
  potesse, risplendendo, dir "Subsisto",

in sua etternita` di tempo fore,
  fuor d'ogne altro comprender, come i piacque,
  s'aperse in nuovi amor l'etterno amore.

Ne' prima quasi torpente si giacque;
  che' ne' prima ne' poscia procedette
  lo discorrer di Dio sovra quest'acque.

Forma e materia, congiunte e purette,
  usciro ad esser che non avia fallo,
  come d'arco tricordo tre saette.

E come in vetro, in ambra o in cristallo
  raggio resplende si`, che dal venire
  a l'esser tutto non e` intervallo,

At what time both the children of Latona,
  Surmounted by the Ram and by the Scales,
  Together make a zone of the horizon,

As long as from the time the zenith holds them
  In equipoise, till from that girdle both
  Changing their hemisphere disturb the balance,

So long, her face depicted with a smile,
  Did Beatrice keep silence while she gazed
  Fixedly at the point which had o'ercome me.

Then she began: "I say, and I ask not
  What thou dost wish to hear, for I have seen it
  Where centres every When and every 'Ubi.'

Not to acquire some good unto himself,
  Which is impossible, but that his splendour
  In its resplendency may say, 'Subsisto,'

In his eternity outside of time,
  Outside all other limits, as it pleased him,
  Into new Loves the Eternal Love unfolded.

Nor as if torpid did he lie before;
  For neither after nor before proceeded
  The going forth of God upon these waters.

Matter and Form unmingled and conjoined
  Came into being that had no defect,
  E'en as three arrows from a three-stringed bow.

And as in glass, in amber, or in crystal
  A sunbeam flashes so, that from its coming
  To its full being is no interval,

cosi` 'l triforme effetto del suo sire ne l'esser suo raggio` insieme tutto sanza distinzione in essordire.	So from its Lord did the triform effect Ray forth into its being all together, Without discrimination of beginning.
Concreato fu ordine e costrutto a le sustanze; e quelle furon cima nel mondo in che puro atto fu produtto;	Order was con-created and constructed In substances, and summit of the world Were those wherein the pure act was produced.
pura potenza tenne la parte ima; nel mezzo strinse potenza con atto tal vime, che gia` mai non si divima.	Pure potentiality held the lowest part; Midway bound potentiality with act Such bond that it shall never be unbound.
Ieronimo vi scrisse lungo tratto di secoli de li angeli creati anzi che l'altro mondo fosse fatto;	Jerome has written unto you of angels Created a long lapse of centuries Or ever yet the other world was made;
ma questo vero e` scritto in molti lati da li scrittor de lo Spirito Santo, e tu te n'avvedrai se bene agguati;	But written is this truth in many places By writers of the Holy Ghost, and thou Shalt see it, if thou lookest well thereat.
e anche la ragione il vede alquanto, che non concederebbe che ' motori sanza sua perfezion fosser cotanto.	And even reason seeth it somewhat, For it would not concede that for so long Could be the motors without their perfection.
Or sai tu dove e quando questi amori furon creati e come: si` che spenti nel tuo disio gia` son tre ardori.	Now dost thou know both where and when these Loves Created were, and how; so that extinct In thy desire already are three fires.
Ne' giugneriesi, numerando, al venti si` tosto, come de li angeli parte turbo` il suggetto d'i vostri alementi.	Nor could one reach, in counting, unto twenty So swiftly, as a portion of these angels Disturbed the subject of your elements.
L'altra rimase, e comincio` quest'arte che tu discerni, con tanto diletto, che mai da circuir non si diparte.	The rest remained, and they began this art Which thou discernest, with so great delight That never from their circling do they cease.
Principio del cader fu il maladetto superbir di colui che tu vedesti da tutti i pesi del mondo costretto.	The occasion of the fall was the accursed Presumption of that One, whom thou hast seen By all the burden of the world constrained.
Quelli che vedi qui furon modesti a riconoscer se' da la bontate che li avea fatti a tanto intender presti:	Those whom thou here beholdest modest were To recognise themselves as of that goodness Which made them apt for so much understanding;
per che le viste lor furo essaltate con grazia illuminante e con lor merto, si c'hanno ferma e piena volontate;	On which account their vision was exalted By the enlightening grace and their own merit, So that they have a full and steadfast will.

Paradiso: Canto XXIX

e non voglio che dubbi, ma sia certo,
 che ricever la grazia e` meritorio
 secondo che l'affetto l'e` aperto.

Omai dintorno a questo consistorio
 puoi contemplare assai, se le parole
 mie son ricolte, sanz'altro aiutorio.

Ma perche' 'n terra per le vostre scole
 si legge che l'angelica natura
 e` tal, che 'ntende e si ricorda e vole,

ancor diro`, perche' tu veggi pura
 la verita` che la` giu` si confonde,
 equivocando in si` fatta lettura.

Queste sustanze, poi che fur gioconde
 de la faccia di Dio, non volser viso
 da essa, da cui nulla si nasconde:

pero` non hanno vedere interciso
 da novo obietto, e pero` non bisogna
 rememorar per concetto diviso;

si` che la` giu`, non dormendo, si sogna,
 credendo e non credendo dicer vero;
 ma ne l'uno e` piu` colpa e piu` vergogna.

Voi non andate giu` per un sentiero
 filosofando: tanto vi trasporta
 l'amor de l'apparenza e 'l suo pensiero!

E ancor questo qua su` si comporta
 con men disdegno che quando e` posposta
 la divina Scrittura o quando e` torta.

Non vi si pensa quanto sangue costa
 seminarla nel mondo e quanto piace
 chi umilmente con essa s'accosta.

Per apparer ciascun s'ingegna e face
 sue invenzioni; e quelle son trascorse
 da' predicanti e 'l Vangelio si tace.

Un dice che la luna si ritorse
 ne la passion di Cristo e s'interpuose,
 per che 'l lume del sol giu` non si porse;

e mente, che' la luce si nascose
 da se': pero` a li Spani e a l'Indi
 come a' Giudei tale eclissi rispuose.

I would not have thee doubt, but certain be,
 'Tis meritorious to receive this grace,
 According as the affection opens to it.

Now round about in this consistory
 Much mayst thou contemplate, if these my words
 Be gathered up, without all further aid.

But since upon the earth, throughout your schools,
 They teach that such is the angelic nature
 That it doth hear, and recollect, and will,

More will I say, that thou mayst see unmixed
 The truth that is confounded there below,
 Equivocating in such like prelections.

These substances, since in God's countenance
 They jocund were, turned not away their sight
 From that wherefrom not anything is hidden;

Hence they have not their vision intercepted
 By object new, and hence they do not need
 To recollect, through interrupted thought.

So that below, not sleeping, people dream,
 Believing they speak truth, and not believing;
 And in the last is greater sin and shame.

Below you do not journey by one path
 Philosophising; so transporteth you
 Love of appearance and the thought thereof.

And even this above here is endured
 With less disdain, than when is set aside
 The Holy Writ, or when it is distorted.

They think not there how much of blood it costs
 To sow it in the world, and how he pleases
 Who in humility keeps close to it.

Each striveth for appearance, and doth make
 His own inventions; and these treated are
 By preachers, and the Evangel holds its peace.

One sayeth that the moon did backward turn,
 In the Passion of Christ, and interpose herself
 So that the sunlight reached not down below;

And lies; for of its own accord the light
 Hid itself; whence to Spaniards and to Indians,
 As to the Jews, did such eclipse respond.

447

Non ha Fiorenza tanti Lapi e Bindi
  quante si` fatte favole per anno
  in pergamo si gridan quinci e quindi;

si` che le pecorelle, che non sanno,
  tornan del pasco pasciute di vento,
  e non le scusa non veder lo danno.

Non disse Cristo al suo primo convento:
  'Andate, e predicate al mondo ciance';
  ma diede lor verace fondamento;

e quel tanto sono` ne le sue guance,
  si` ch'a pugnar per accender la fede
  de l'Evangelio fero scudo e lance.

Ora si va con motti e con iscede
  a predicare, e pur che ben si rida,
  gonfia il cappuccio e piu` non si richiede.

Ma tale uccel nel becchetto s'annida,
  che se 'l vulgo il vedesse, vederebbe
  la perdonanza di ch'el si confida;

per cui tanta stoltezza in terra crebbe,
  che, sanza prova d'alcun testimonio,
  ad ogne promession si correrebbe.

Di questo ingrassa il porco sant'Antonio,
  e altri assai che sono ancor piu` porci,
  pagando di moneta sanza conio.

Ma perche' siam digressi assai, ritorci
  li occhi oramai verso la dritta strada,
  si` che la via col tempo si raccorci.

Questa natura si` oltre s'ingrada
  in numero, che mai non fu loquela
  ne' concetto mortal che tanto vada;

e se tu guardi quel che si revela
  per Daniel, vedrai che 'n sue migliaia
  determinato numero si cela.

La prima luce, che tutta la raia,
  per tanti modi in essa si recepe,
  quanti son li splendori a chi s'appaia.

Onde, pero` che a l'atto che concepe
  segue l'affetto, d'amar la dolcezza
  diversamente in essa ferve e tepe.

Florence has not so many Lapi and Bindi
  As fables such as these, that every year
  Are shouted from the pulpit back and forth,

In such wise that the lambs, who do not know,
  Come back from pasture fed upon the wind,
  And not to see the harm doth not excuse them.

Christ did not to his first disciples say,
  'Go forth, and to the world preach idle tales,'
  But unto them a true foundation gave;

And this so loudly sounded from their lips,
  That, in the warfare to enkindle Faith,
  They made of the Evangel shields and lances.

Now men go forth with jests and drolleries
  To preach, and if but well the people laugh,
  The hood puffs out, and nothing more is asked.

But in the cowl there nestles such a bird,
  That, if the common people were to see it,
  They would perceive what pardons they confide in,

For which so great on earth has grown the folly,
  That, without proof of any testimony,
  To each indulgence they would flock together.

By this Saint Anthony his pig doth fatten,
  And many others, who are worse than pigs,
  Paying in money without mark of coinage.

But since we have digressed abundantly,
  Turn back thine eyes forthwith to the right path,
  So that the way be shortened with the time.

This nature doth so multiply itself
  In numbers, that there never yet was speech
  Nor mortal fancy that can go so far.

And if thou notest that which is revealed
  By Daniel, thou wilt see that in his thousands
  Number determinate is kept concealed.

The primal light, that all irradiates it,
  By modes as many is received therein,
  As are the splendours wherewith it is mated.

Hence, inasmuch as on the act conceptive
  The affection followeth, of love the sweetness
  Therein diversely fervid is or tepid.

Vedi l'eccelso omai e la larghezza
  de l'etterno valor, poscia che tanti
  speculi fatti s'ha in che si spezza,

uno manendo in se' come davanti"".

The height behold now and the amplitude
  Of the eternal power, since it hath made
  Itself so many mirrors, where 'tis broken,

One in itself remaining as before."

Paradiso: Canto XXX

The Tenth Heaven, or Empyrean. The River of Light. The Two Courts of Heaven. The White Rose of Paradise. The great Throne.

Forse semilia miglia di lontano
  ci ferve l'ora sesta, e questo mondo
  china gia` l'ombra quasi al letto piano,

quando 'l mezzo del cielo, a noi profondo,
  comincia a farsi tal, ch'alcuna stella
  perde il parere infino a questo fondo;

e come vien la chiarissima ancella
  del sol piu` oltre, cosi` 'l ciel si chiude
  di vista in vista infino a la piu` bella.

Non altrimenti il triunfo che lude
  sempre dintorno al punto che mi vinse,
  parendo inchiuso da quel ch'elli 'nchiude,

a poco a poco al mio veder si stinse:
  per che tornar con li occhi a Beatrice
  nulla vedere e amor mi costrinse.

Se quanto infino a qui di lei si dice
  fosse conchiuso tutto in una loda,
  poca sarebbe a fornir questa vice.

La bellezza ch'io vidi si trasmoda
  non pur di la` da noi, ma certo io credo
  che solo il suo fattor tutta la goda.

Da questo passo vinto mi concedo
  piu` che gia` mai da punto di suo tema
  soprato fosse comico o tragedo:

che', come sole in viso che piu` trema,
  cosi` lo rimembrar del dolce riso
  la mente mia da me medesmo scema.

Perchance six thousand miles remote from us
  Is glowing the sixth hour, and now this world
  Inclines its shadow almost to a level,

When the mid-heaven begins to make itself
  So deep to us, that here and there a star
  Ceases to shine so far down as this depth,

And as advances bright exceedingly
  The handmaid of the sun, the heaven is closed
  Light after light to the most beautiful;

Not otherwise the Triumph, which for ever
  Plays round about the point that vanquished me,
  Seeming enclosed by what itself encloses,

Little by little from my vision faded;
  Whereat to turn mine eyes on Beatrice
  My seeing nothing and my love constrained me.

If what has hitherto been said of her
  Were all concluded in a single praise,
  Scant would it be to serve the present turn.

Not only does the beauty I beheld
  Transcend ourselves, but truly I believe
  Its Maker only may enjoy it all.

Vanquished do I confess me by this passage
  More than by problem of his theme was ever
  O'ercome the comic or the tragic poet;

For as the sun the sight that trembles most,
  Even so the memory of that sweet smile
  My mind depriveth of its very self.

Dal primo giorno ch'i' vidi il suo viso
  in questa vita, infino a questa vista,
  non m'e` il seguire al mio cantar preciso;
	From the first day that I beheld her face
	  In this life, to the moment of this look,
	  The sequence of my song has ne'er been severed;

ma or convien che mio seguir desista
  piu` dietro a sua bellezza, poetando,
  come a l'ultimo suo ciascuno artista.
	But now perforce this sequence must desist
	  From following her beauty with my verse,
	  As every artist at his uttermost.

Cotal qual io lascio a maggior bando
  che quel de la mia tuba, che deduce
  l'ardua sua matera terminando,
	Such as I leave her to a greater fame
	  Than any of my trumpet, which is bringing
	  Its arduous matter to a final close,

con atto e voce di spedito duce ricomincio`: ""Noi siamo usciti fore   del maggior corpo al ciel ch'e` pura luce:	With voice and gesture of a perfect leader She recommenced: "We from the greatest body Have issued to the heaven that is pure light;

luce intellettual, piena d'amore;
  amor di vero ben, pien di letizia;
  letizia che trascende ogne dolzore.
	Light intellectual replete with love,
	  Love of true good replete with ecstasy,
	  Ecstasy that transcendeth every sweetness.

Qui vederai l'una e l'altra milizia
  di paradiso, e l'una in quelli aspetti
  che tu vedrai a l'ultima giustizia"".
	Here shalt thou see the one host and the other
	  Of Paradise, and one in the same aspects
	  Which at the final judgment thou shalt see."

Come subito lampo che discetti li spiriti visivi, si` che priva   da l'atto l'occhio di piu` forti obietti,	Even as a sudden lightning that disperses The visual spirits, so that it deprives The eye of impress from the strongest objects,

cosi` mi circunfulse luce viva,
  e lasciommi fasciato di tal velo
  del suo fulgor, che nulla m'appariva.
	Thus round about me flashed a living light,
	  And left me swathed around with such a veil
	  Of its effulgence, that I nothing saw.

""Sempre l'amor che queta questo cielo
  accoglie in se' con si` fatta salute,
  per far disposto a sua fiamma il candelo"".
	"Ever the Love which quieteth this heaven
	  Welcomes into itself with such salute,
	  To make the candle ready for its flame."

Non fur piu` tosto dentro a me venute
  queste parole brievi, ch'io compresi
  me sormontar di sopr'a mia virtute;
	No sooner had within me these brief words
	  An entrance found, than I perceived myself
	  To be uplifted over my own power,

e di novella vista mi raccesi
  tale, che nulla luce e` tanto mera,
  che li occhi miei non si fosser difesi;
	And I with vision new rekindled me,
	  Such that no light whatever is so pure
	  But that mine eyes were fortified against it.

e vidi lume in forma di rivera
  fulvido di fulgore, intra due rive
  dipinte di mirabil primavera.
	And light I saw in fashion of a river
	  Fulvid with its effulgence, 'twixt two banks
	  Depicted with an admirable Spring.

Di tal fiumana uscian faville vive,
  e d'ogne parte si mettien ne' fiori,
  quasi rubin che oro circunscrive;
	Out of this river issued living sparks,
	  And on all sides sank down into the flowers,
	  Like unto rubies that are set in gold;

poi, come inebriate da li odori,
  riprofondavan se' nel miro gurge;
  e s'una intrava, un'altra n'uscia fori.

And then, as if inebriate with the odours,
  They plunged again into the wondrous torrent,
  And as one entered issued forth another.

""L'alto disio che mo t'infiamma e urge,
  d'aver notizia di cio` che tu vei,
  tanto mi piace piu` quanto piu` turge;

"The high desire, that now inflames and moves thee
  To have intelligence of what thou seest,
  Pleaseth me all the more, the more it swells.

ma di quest'acqua convien che tu bei
  prima che tanta sete in te si sazi"":
  cosi` mi disse il sol de li occhi miei.

But of this water it behoves thee drink
  Before so great a thirst in thee be slaked."
  Thus said to me the sunshine of mine eyes;

Anche soggiunse: ""Il fiume e li topazi
  ch'entrano ed escono e 'l rider de l'erbe
  son di lor vero umbriferi prefazi.

And added: "The river and the topazes
  Going in and out, and the laughing of the herbage,
  Are of their truth foreshadowing prefaces;

Non che da se' sian queste cose acerbe;
  ma e` difetto da la parte tua,
  che non hai viste ancor tanto superbe"".

Not that these things are difficult in themselves,
  But the deficiency is on thy side,
  For yet thou hast not vision so exalted."

Non e` fantin che si` subito rua
  col volto verso il latte, se si svegli
  molto tardato da l'usanza sua,

There is no babe that leaps so suddenly
  With face towards the milk, if he awake
  Much later than his usual custom is,

come fec'io, per far migliori spegli
  ancor de li occhi, chinandomi a l'onda
  che si deriva perche' vi s'immegli;

As I did, that I might make better mirrors
  Still of mine eyes, down stooping to the wave
  Which flows that we therein be better made.

e si` come di lei bevve la gronda
  de le palpebre mie, cosi` mi parve
  di sua lunghezza divenuta tonda.

And even as the penthouse of mine eyelids
  Drank of it, it forthwith appeared to me
  Out of its length to be transformed to round.

Poi, come gente stata sotto larve,
  che pare altro che prima, se si sveste
  la sembianza non sua in che disparve,

Then as a folk who have been under masks
  Seem other than before, if they divest
  The semblance not their own they disappeared in,

cosi` mi si cambiaro in maggior feste
  li fiori e le faville, si` ch'io vidi
  ambo le corti del ciel manifeste.

Thus into greater pomp were changed for me
  The flowerets and the sparks, so that I saw
  Both of the Courts of Heaven made manifest.

O isplendor di Dio, per cu' io vidi
  l'alto triunfo del regno verace,
  dammi virtu` a dir com'io il vidi!

O splendour of God! by means of which I saw
  The lofty triumph of the realm veracious,
  Give me the power to say how it I saw!

Lume e` la` su` che visibile face
  lo creatore a quella creatura
  che solo in lui vedere ha la sua pace.

There is a light above, which visible
  Makes the Creator unto every creature,
  Who only in beholding Him has peace,

E' si distende in circular figura,
  in tanto che la sua circunferenza
  sarebbe al sol troppo larga cintura.

And it expands itself in circular form
  To such extent, that its circumference
  Would be too large a girdle for the sun.

Fassi di raggio tutta sua parvenza
  reflesso al sommo del mobile primo,
  che prende quindi vivere e potenza.

E come clivo in acqua di suo imo
  si specchia, quasi per vedersi addorno,
  quando e` nel verde e ne' fioretti opimo,

si`, soprastando al lume intorno intorno,
  vidi specchiarsi in piu` di mille soglie
  quanto di noi la` su` fatto ha ritorno.

E se l'infimo grado in se' raccoglie
  si` grande lume, quanta e` la larghezza
  di questa rosa ne l'estreme foglie!

La vista mia ne l'ampio e ne l'altezza
  non si smarriva, ma tutto prendeva
  il quanto e 'l quale di quella allegrezza.

Presso e lontano, li`, ne' pon ne' leva:
  che' dove Dio sanza mezzo governa,
  la legge natural nulla rileva.

Nel giallo de la rosa sempiterna,
  che si digrada e dilata e redole
  odor di lode al sol che sempre verna,

qual e` colui che tace e dicer vole,
  mi trasse Beatrice, e disse: ""Mira
  quanto e` 'l convento de le bianche stole!

Vedi nostra citta` quant'ella gira;
  vedi li nostri scanni si` ripieni,
  che poca gente piu` ci si disira.

E 'n quel gran seggio a che tu li occhi tieni
  per la corona che gia` v'e` su` posta,
  prima che tu a queste nozze ceni,

sedera` l'alma, che fia giu` agosta,
  de l'alto Arrigo, ch'a drizzare Italia
  verra` in prima ch'ella sia disposta.

La cieca cupidigia che v'ammalia
  simili fatti v'ha al fantolino
  che muor per fame e caccia via la balia.

E fia prefetto nel foro divino
  allora tal, che palese e coverto
  non andera` con lui per un cammino.

The semblance of it is all made of rays
  Reflected from the top of Primal Motion,
  Which takes therefrom vitality and power.

And as a hill in water at its base
  Mirrors itself, as if to see its beauty
  When affluent most in verdure and in flowers,

So, ranged aloft all round about the light,
  Mirrored I saw in more ranks than a thousand
  All who above there have from us returned.

And if the lowest row collect within it
  So great a light, how vast the amplitude
  Is of this Rose in its extremest leaves!

My vision in the vastness and the height
  Lost not itself, but comprehended all
  The quantity and quality of that gladness.

There near and far nor add nor take away;
  For there where God immediately doth govern,
  The natural law in naught is relevant.

Into the yellow of the Rose Eternal
  That spreads, and multiplies, and breathes an odour
  Of praise unto the ever-vernal Sun,

As one who silent is and fain would speak,
  Me Beatrice drew on, and said: "Behold
  Of the white stoles how vast the convent is!

Behold how vast the circuit of our city!
  Behold our seats so filled to overflowing,
  That here henceforward are few people wanting!

On that great throne whereon thine eyes are fixed
  For the crown's sake already placed upon it,
  Before thou suppest at this wedding feast

Shall sit the soul (that is to be Augustus
  On earth) of noble Henry, who shall come
  To redress Italy ere she be ready.

Blind covetousness, that casts its spell upon you,
  Has made you like unto the little child,
  Who dies of hunger and drives off the nurse.

And in the sacred forum then shall be
  A Prefect such, that openly or covert
  On the same road he will not walk with him.

Ma poco poi sara` da Dio sofferto
  nel santo officio; ch'el sara` detruso
  la` dove Simon mago e` per suo merto,

e fara` quel d'Alagna intrar piu` giuso"".

But long of God he will not be endured
  In holy office; he shall be thrust down
  Where Simon Magus is for his deserts,

And make him of Alagna lower go!"

Paradiso: Canto XXXI

The Glory of Paradise. Departure of Beatrice. St. Bernard.

In forma dunque di candida rosa
 mi si mostrava la milizia santa
 che nel suo sangue Cristo fece sposa;

ma l'altra, che volando vede e canta
 la gloria di colui che la 'nnamora
 e la bonta` che la fece cotanta,

si` come schiera d'ape, che s'infiora
 una fiata e una si ritorna
 la` dove suo laboro s'insapora,

nel gran fior discendeva che s'addorna
 di tante foglie, e quindi risaliva
 la` dove 'l suo amor sempre soggiorna.

Le facce tutte avean di fiamma viva,
 e l'ali d'oro, e l'altro tanto bianco,
 che nulla neve a quel termine arriva.

Quando scendean nel fior, di banco in banco
 porgevan de la pace e de l'ardore
 ch'elli acquistavan ventilando il fianco.

Ne' l'interporsi tra 'l disopra e 'l fiore
 di tanta moltitudine volante
 impediva la vista e lo splendore:

che' la luce divina e` penetrante
 per l'universo secondo ch'e` degno,
 si` che nulla le puote essere ostante.

Questo sicuro e gaudioso regno,
 frequente in gente antica e in novella,
 viso e amore avea tutto ad un segno.

In fashion then as of a snow-white rose
 Displayed itself to me the saintly host,
 Whom Christ in his own blood had made his bride,

But the other host, that flying sees and sings
 The glory of Him who doth enamour it,
 And the goodness that created it so noble,

Even as a swarm of bees, that sinks in flowers
 One moment, and the next returns again
 To where its labour is to sweetness turned,

Sank into the great flower, that is adorned
 With leaves so many, and thence reascended
 To where its love abideth evermore.

Their faces had they all of living flame,
 And wings of gold, and all the rest so white
 No snow unto that limit doth attain.

From bench to bench, into the flower descending,
 They carried something of the peace and ardour
 Which by the fanning of their flanks they won.

Nor did the interposing 'twixt the flower
 And what was o'er it of such plenitude
 Of flying shapes impede the sight and splendour;

Because the light divine so penetrates
 The universe, according to its merit,
 That naught can be an obstacle against it.

This realm secure and full of gladsomeness,
 Crowded with ancient people and with modern,
 Unto one mark had all its look and love.

O trina luce, che 'n unica stella
  scintillando a lor vista, si` li appaga!
  guarda qua giuso a la nostra procella!

Se i barbari, venendo da tal plaga
  che ciascun giorno d'Elice si cuopra,
  rotante col suo figlio ond'ella e` vaga,

veggendo Roma e l'ardua sua opra,
  stupefaciensi, quando Laterano
  a le cose mortali ando` di sopra;

io, che al divino da l'umano,
  a l'etterno dal tempo era venuto,
  e di Fiorenza in popol giusto e sano

di che stupor dovea esser compiuto!
  Certo tra esso e 'l gaudio mi facea
  libito non udire e starmi muto.

E quasi peregrin che si ricrea
  nel tempio del suo voto riguardando,
  e spera gia` ridir com'ello stea,

su per la viva luce passeggiando,
  menava io li occhi per li gradi,
  mo su`, mo giu` e mo recirculando.

Vedea visi a carita` suadi,
  d'altrui lume fregiati e di suo riso,
  e atti ornati di tutte onestadi.

La forma general di paradiso
  gia` tutta mio sguardo avea compresa,
  in nulla parte ancor fermato fiso;

e volgeami con voglia riaccesa
  per domandar la mia donna di cose
  di che la mente mia era sospesa.

Uno intendea, e altro mi rispuose:
  credea veder Beatrice e vidi un sene
  vestito con le genti gloriose.

Diffuso era per li occhi e per le gene
  di benigna letizia, in atto pio
  quale a tenero padre si convene.

E ""Ov'e` ella?"", subito diss'io.
  Ond'elli: ""A terminar lo tuo disiro
  mosse Beatrice me del loco mio;

O Trinal Light, that in a single star
  Sparkling upon their sight so satisfies them,
  Look down upon our tempest here below!

If the barbarians, coming from some region
  That every day by Helice is covered,
  Revolving with her son whom she delights in,

Beholding Rome and all her noble works,
  Were wonder-struck, what time the Lateran
  Above all mortal things was eminent,—

I who to the divine had from the human,
  From time unto eternity, had come,
  From Florence to a people just and sane,

With what amazement must I have been filled!
  Truly between this and the joy, it was
  My pleasure not to hear, and to be mute.

And as a pilgrim who delighteth him
  In gazing round the temple of his vow,
  And hopes some day to retell how it was,

So through the living light my way pursuing
  Directed I mine eyes o'er all the ranks,
  Now up, now down, and now all round about.

Faces I saw of charity persuasive,
  Embellished by His light and their own smile,
  And attitudes adorned with every grace.

The general form of Paradise already
  My glance had comprehended as a whole,
  In no part hitherto remaining fixed,

And round I turned me with rekindled wish
  My Lady to interrogate of things
  Concerning which my mind was in suspense.

One thing I meant, another answered me;
  I thought I should see Beatrice, and saw
  An Old Man habited like the glorious people.

O'erflowing was he in his eyes and cheeks
  With joy benign, in attitude of pity
  As to a tender father is becoming.

And "She, where is she?" instantly I said;
  Whence he: "To put an end to thy desire,
  Me Beatrice hath sent from mine own place.

e se riguardi su` nel terzo giro
  dal sommo grado, tu la rivedrai
  nel trono che suoi merti le sortiro"".

Sanza risponder, li occhi su` levai,
  e vidi lei che si facea corona
  reflettendo da se' li etterni rai.

Da quella region che piu` su` tona
  occhio mortale alcun tanto non dista,
  qualunque in mare piu` giu` s'abbandona,

quanto li` da Beatrice la mia vista;
  ma nulla mi facea, che' sua effige
  non discendea a me per mezzo mista.

""O donna in cui la mia speranza vige,
  e che soffristi per la mia salute
  in inferno lasciar le tue vestige,

di tante cose quant'i' ho vedute,
  dal tuo podere e da la tua bontate
  riconosco la grazia e la virtute.

Tu m'hai di servo tratto a libertate
  per tutte quelle vie, per tutt'i modi
  che di cio` fare avei la potestate.

La tua magnificenza in me custodi,
  si` che l'anima mia, che fatt'hai sana,
  piacente a te dal corpo si disnodi"".

Cosi` orai; e quella, si` lontana
  come parea, sorrise e riguardommi;
  poi si torno` a l'etterna fontana.

E 'l santo sene: ""Accio` che tu assommi
  perfettamente"", disse, ""il tuo cammino,
  a che priego e amor santo mandommi,

vola con li occhi per questo giardino;
  che' veder lui t'acconcera` lo sguardo
  piu` al montar per lo raggio divino.

E la regina del cielo, ond'io ardo
  tutto d'amor, ne fara` ogne grazia,
  pero` ch'i' sono il suo fedel Bernardo"".

Qual e` colui che forse di Croazia
  viene a veder la Veronica nostra,
  che per l'antica fame non sen sazia,

And if thou lookest up to the third round
  Of the first rank, again shalt thou behold her
  Upon the throne her merits have assigned her."

Without reply I lifted up mine eyes,
  And saw her, as she made herself a crown
  Reflecting from herself the eternal rays.

Not from that region which the highest thunders
  Is any mortal eye so far removed,
  In whatsoever sea it deepest sinks,

As there from Beatrice my sight; but this
  Was nothing unto me; because her image
  Descended not to me by medium blurred.

"O Lady, thou in whom my hope is strong,
  And who for my salvation didst endure
  In Hell to leave the imprint of thy feet,

Of whatsoever things I have beheld,
  As coming from thy power and from thy goodness
  I recognise the virtue and the grace.

Thou from a slave hast brought me unto freedom,
  By all those ways, by all the expedients,
  Whereby thou hadst the power of doing it.

Preserve towards me thy magnificence,
  So that this soul of mine, which thou hast healed,
  Pleasing to thee be loosened from the body."

Thus I implored; and she, so far away,
  Smiled, as it seemed, and looked once more at me;
  Then unto the eternal fountain turned.

And said the Old Man holy: "That thou mayst
  Accomplish perfectly thy journeying,
  Whereunto prayer and holy love have sent me,

Fly with thine eyes all round about this garden;
  For seeing it will discipline thy sight
  Farther to mount along the ray divine.

And she, the Queen of Heaven, for whom I burn
  Wholly with love, will grant us every grace,
  Because that I her faithful Bernard am."

As he who peradventure from Croatia
  Cometh to gaze at our Veronica,
  Who through its ancient fame is never sated,

ma dice nel pensier, fin che si mostra:
  'Segnor mio Iesu` Cristo, Dio verace,
  or fu si` fatta la sembianza vostra?';

tal era io mirando la vivace
  carita` di colui che 'n questo mondo,
  contemplando, gusto` di quella pace.

""Figliuol di grazia, quest'esser giocondo""",
  comincio` elli, ""non ti sara` noto,
  tenendo li occhi pur qua giu` al fondo;

ma guarda i cerchi infino al piu` remoto,
  tanto che veggi seder la regina
  cui questo regno e` suddito e devoto""".

Io levai li occhi; e come da mattina
  la parte oriental de l'orizzonte
  soverchia quella dove 'l sol declina,

cosi`, quasi di valle andando a monte
  con li occhi, vidi parte ne lo stremo
  vincer di lume tutta l'altra fronte.

E come quivi ove s'aspetta il temo
  che mal guido` Fetonte, piu` s'infiamma,
  e quinci e quindi il lume si fa scemo,

cosi` quella pacifica oriafiamma
  nel mezzo s'avvivava, e d'ogne parte
  per igual modo allentava la fiamma;

e a quel mezzo, con le penne sparte,
  vid'io piu` di mille angeli festanti,
  ciascun distinto di fulgore e d'arte.

Vidi a lor giochi quivi e a lor canti
  ridere una bellezza, che letizia
  era ne li occhi a tutti li altri santi;

e s'io avessi in dir tanta divizia
  quanta ad imaginar, non ardirei
  lo minimo tentar di sua delizia.

Bernardo, come vide li occhi miei
  nel caldo suo caler fissi e attenti,
  li suoi con tanto affetto volse a lei,

che ' miei di rimirar fe' piu` ardenti.

But says in thought, the while it is displayed,
  "My Lord, Christ Jesus, God of very God,
  Now was your semblance made like unto this?"

Even such was I while gazing at the living
  Charity of the man, who in this world
  By contemplation tasted of that peace.

"Thou son of grace, this jocund life," began he,
  "Will not be known to thee by keeping ever
  Thine eyes below here on the lowest place;

But mark the circles to the most remote,
  Until thou shalt behold enthroned the Queen
  To whom this realm is subject and devoted."

I lifted up mine eyes, and as at morn
  The oriental part of the horizon
  Surpasses that wherein the sun goes down,

Thus, as if going with mine eyes from vale
  To mount, I saw a part in the remoteness
  Surpass in splendour all the other front.

And even as there where we await the pole
  That Phaeton drove badly, blazes more
  The light, and is on either side diminished,

So likewise that pacific oriflamme
  Gleamed brightest in the centre, and each side
  In equal measure did the flame abate.

And at that centre, with their wings expanded,
  More than a thousand jubilant Angels saw I,
  Each differing in effulgence and in kind.

I saw there at their sports and at their songs
  A beauty smiling, which the gladness was
  Within the eyes of all the other saints;

And if I had in speaking as much wealth
  As in imagining, I should not dare
  To attempt the smallest part of its delight.

Bernard, as soon as he beheld mine eyes
  Fixed and intent upon its fervid fervour,
  His own with such affection turned to her

That it made mine more ardent to behold.

Paradiso: Canto XXXII

St. Bernard points out the Saints in the White Rose.

Affetto al suo piacer, quel contemplante
  libero officio di dottore assunse,
  e comincio` queste parole sante:
	Absorbed in his delight, that contemplator
	  Assumed the willing office of a teacher,
	  And gave beginning to these holy words:

""La piaga che Maria richiuse e unse, quella ch'e` tanto bella da' suoi piedi   e` colei che l'aperse e che la punse.	"The wound that Mary closed up and anointed, She at her feet who is so beautiful, She is the one who opened it and pierced it.

Ne l'ordine che fanno i terzi sedi,
  siede Rachel di sotto da costei
  con Beatrice, si` come tu vedi.
	Within that order which the third seats make
	  Is seated Rachel, lower than the other,
	  With Beatrice, in manner as thou seest.

Sarra e Rebecca, Iudit e colei
  che fu bisava al cantor che per doglia
  del fallo disse 'Miserere mei',
	Sarah, Rebecca, Judith, and her who was
	  Ancestress of the Singer, who for dole
	  Of the misdeed said, 'Miserere mei,'

puoi tu veder cosi` di soglia in soglia   giu` digradar, com'io ch'a proprio nome vo per la rosa giu` di foglia in foglia.	Canst thou behold from seat to seat descending Down in gradation, as with each one's name I through the Rose go down from leaf to leaf.

E dal settimo grado in giu`, si` come
  infino ad esso, succedono Ebree,
  dirimendo del fior tutte le chiome;
	And downward from the seventh row, even as
	  Above the same, succeed the Hebrew women,
	  Dividing all the tresses of the flower;

perche', secondo lo sguardo che fee
  la fede in Cristo, queste sono il muro
  a che si parton le sacre scalee.
	Because, according to the view which Faith
	  In Christ had taken, these are the partition
	  By which the sacred stairways are divided.

Da questa parte onde 'l fiore e` maturo
  di tutte le sue foglie, sono assisi
  quei che credettero in Cristo venturo;
	Upon this side, where perfect is the flower
	  With each one of its petals, seated are
	  Those who believed in Christ who was to come.

da l'altra parte onde sono intercisi
  di voti i semicirculi, si stanno
  quei ch'a Cristo venuto ebber li visi.
	Upon the other side, where intersected
	  With vacant spaces are the semicircles,
	  Are those who looked to Christ already come.

E come quinci il glorioso scanno
  de la donna del cielo e li altri scanni
  di sotto lui cotanta cerna fanno,

cosi` di contra quel del gran Giovanni,
  che sempre santo 'l diserto e 'l martiro
  sofferse, e poi l'inferno da due anni;

e sotto lui cosi` cerner sortiro
  Francesco, Benedetto e Augustino
  e altri fin qua giu` di giro in giro.

Or mira l'alto proveder divino:
  che' l'uno e l'altro aspetto de la fede
  igualmente empiera` questo giardino.

E sappi che dal grado in giu` che fiede
  a mezzo il tratto le due discrezioni,
  per nullo proprio merito si siede,

ma per l'altrui, con certe condizioni:
  che' tutti questi son spiriti ascolti
  prima ch'avesser vere elezioni.

Ben te ne puoi accorger per li volti
  e anche per le voci puerili,
  se tu li guardi bene e se li ascolti.

Or dubbi tu e dubitando sili;
  ma io disciogliero` 'l forte legame
  in che ti stringon li pensier sottili.

Dentro a l'ampiezza di questo reame
  casual punto non puote aver sito,
  se non come tristizia o sete o fame:

che' per etterna legge e` stabilito
  quantunque vedi, si` che giustamente
  ci si risponde da l'anello al dito;

e pero` questa festinata gente
  a vera vita non e` sine causa
  intra se' qui piu` e meno eccellente.

Lo rege per cui questo regno pausa
  in tanto amore e in tanto diletto,
  che nulla volonta` e` di piu` ausa,

And as, upon this side, the glorious seat
  Of the Lady of Heaven, and the other seats
  Below it, such a great division make,

So opposite doth that of the great John,
  Who, ever holy, desert and martyrdom
  Endured, and afterwards two years in Hell.

And under him thus to divide were chosen
  Francis, and Benedict, and Augustine,
  And down to us the rest from round to round.

Behold now the high providence divine;
  For one and other aspect of the Faith
  In equal measure shall this garden fill.

And know that downward from that rank which
    cleaves
  Midway the sequence of the two divisions,
  Not by their proper merit are they seated;

But by another's under fixed conditions;
  For these are spirits one and all assoiled
  Before they any true election had.

Well canst thou recognise it in their faces,
  And also in their voices puerile,
  If thou regard them well and hearken to them.

Now doubtest thou, and doubting thou art silent;
  But I will loosen for thee the strong bond
  In which thy subtile fancies hold thee fast.

Within the amplitude of this domain
  No casual point can possibly find place,
  No more than sadness can, or thirst, or hunger;

For by eternal law has been established
  Whatever thou beholdest, so that closely
  The ring is fitted to the finger here.

And therefore are these people, festinate
  Unto true life, not 'sine causa' here
  More and less excellent among themselves.

The King, by means of whom this realm reposes
  In so great love and in so great delight
  That no will ventureth to ask for more,

le menti tutte nel suo lieto aspetto
  creando, a suo piacer di grazia dota
  diversamente; e qui basti l'effetto.

E cio` espresso e chiaro vi si nota
  ne la Scrittura santa in quei gemelli
  che ne la madre ebber l'ira commota.

Pero`, secondo il color d'i capelli,
  di cotal grazia l'altissimo lume
  degnamente convien che s'incappelli.

Dunque, sanza merce' di lor costume,
  locati son per gradi differenti,
  sol differendo nel primiero acume.

Bastavasi ne' secoli recenti
  con l'innocenza, per aver salute,
  solamente la fede d'i parenti;

poi che le prime etadi fuor compiute,
  convenne ai maschi a l'innocenti penne
  per circuncidere acquistar virtute;

ma poi che 'l tempo de la grazia venne,
  sanza battesmo perfetto di Cristo
  tale innocenza la` giu` si ritenne.

Riguarda omai ne la faccia che a Cristo
  piu` si somiglia, che' la sua chiarezza
  sola ti puo` disporre a veder Cristo"".

Io vidi sopra lei tanta allegrezza
  piover, portata ne le menti sante
  create a trasvolar per quella altezza,

che quantunque io avea visto davante,
  di tanta ammirazion non mi sospese,
  ne' mi mostro` di Dio tanto sembiante;

e quello amor che primo li` discese,
  cantando 'Ave, Maria, gratia plena',
  dinanzi a lei le sue ali distese.

Rispuose a la divina cantilena
  da tutte parti la beata corte,
  si` ch'ogne vista sen fe' piu` serena.

""O santo padre, che per me comporte
  l'esser qua giu`, lasciando il dolce loco
  nel qual tu siedi per etterna sorte,

In his own joyous aspect every mind
  Creating, at his pleasure dowers with grace
  Diversely; and let here the effect suffice.

And this is clearly and expressly noted
  For you in Holy Scripture, in those twins
  Who in their mother had their anger roused.

According to the colour of the hair,
  Therefore, with such a grace the light supreme
  Consenteth that they worthily be crowned.

Without, then, any merit of their deeds,
  Stationed are they in different gradations,
  Differing only in their first acuteness.

'Tis true that in the early centuries,
  With innocence, to work out their salvation
  Sufficient was the faith of parents only.

After the earlier ages were completed,
  Behoved it that the males by circumcision
  Unto their innocent wings should virtue add;

But after that the time of grace had come
  Without the baptism absolute of Christ,
  Such innocence below there was retained.

Look now into the face that unto Christ
  Hath most resemblance; for its brightness only
  Is able to prepare thee to see Christ."

On her did I behold so great a gladness
  Rain down, borne onward in the holy minds
  Created through that altitude to fly,

That whatsoever I had seen before
  Did not suspend me in such admiration,
  Nor show me such similitude of God.

And the same Love that first descended there,
  "Ave Maria, gratia plena," singing,
  In front of her his wings expanded wide.

Unto the canticle divine responded
  From every part the court beatified,
  So that each sight became serener for it.

"O holy father, who for me endurest
  To be below here, leaving the sweet place
  In which thou sittest by eternal lot,

qual e` quell'angel che con tanto gioco   guarda ne li occhi la nostra regina,   innamorato si` che par di foco?"".	Who is the Angel that with so much joy Into the eyes is looking of our Queen, Enamoured so that he seems made of fire?"

Cosi` ricorsi ancora a la dottrina
  di colui ch'abbelliva di Maria,
  come del sole stella mattutina.
	Thus I again recourse had to the teaching
	  Of that one who delighted him in Mary
	  As doth the star of morning in the sun.

Ed elli a me: ""Baldezza e leggiadria
  quant'esser puote in angelo e in alma,
  tutta e` in lui; e si` volem che sia,
	And he to me: "Such gallantry and grace
	  As there can be in Angel and in soul,
	  All is in him; and thus we fain would have it;

perch'elli e` quelli che porto` la palma
  giuso a Maria, quando 'l Figliuol di Dio
  carcar si volse de la nostra salma.
	Because he is the one who bore the palm
	  Down unto Mary, when the Son of God
	  To take our burden on himself decreed.

Ma vieni omai con li occhi si` com'io   andro` parlando, e nota i gran patrici di questo imperio giustissimo e pio.	But now come onward with thine eyes, as I Speaking shall go, and note the great patricians Of this most just and merciful of empires.

Quei due che seggon la` su` piu` felici
  per esser propinquissimi ad Augusta,
  son d'esta rosa quasi due radici:
	Those two that sit above there most enrapture
	  As being very near unto Augusta,
	  Are as it were the two roots of this Rose.

colui che da sinistra le s'aggiusta
  e` il padre per lo cui ardito gusto
  l'umana specie tanto amaro gusta;
	He who upon the left is near her placed
	  The father is, by whose audacious taste
	  The human species so much bitter tastes.

dal destro vedi quel padre vetusto
  di Santa Chiesa a cui Cristo le clavi
  raccomando` di questo fior venusto.
	Upon the right thou seest that ancient father
	  Of Holy Church, into whose keeping Christ
	  The keys committed of this lovely flower.

E quei che vide tutti i tempi gravi,
  pria che morisse, de la bella sposa
  che s'acquisto` con la lancia e coi clavi,
	And he who all the evil days beheld,
	  Before his death, of her the beauteous bride
	  Who with the spear and with the nails was won,

siede lungh'esso, e lungo l'altro posa
  quel duca sotto cui visse di manna
  la gente ingrata, mobile e retrosa.
	Beside him sits, and by the other rests
	  That leader under whom on manna lived
	  The people ingrate, fickle, and stiff-necked.

Di contr'a Pietro vedi sedere Anna,
  tanto contenta di mirar sua figlia,
  che non move occhio per cantare osanna;
	Opposite Peter seest thou Anna seated,
	  So well content to look upon her daughter,
	  Her eyes she moves not while she sings Hosanna.

e contro al maggior padre di famiglia
  siede Lucia, che mosse la tua donna,
  quando chinavi, a rovinar, le ciglia.
	And opposite the eldest household father
	  Lucia sits, she who thy Lady moved
	  When to rush downward thou didst bend thy brows.

Ma perche' 'l tempo fugge che t'assonna,
  qui farem punto, come buon sartore
  che com'elli ha del panno fa la gonna;
	But since the moments of thy vision fly,
	  Here will we make full stop, as a good tailor
	  Who makes the gown according to his cloth,

462

e drizzeremo li occhi al primo amore,
  si` che, guardando verso lui, penetri
  quant'e` possibil per lo suo fulgore.

Veramente, ne forse tu t'arretri
  movendo l'ali tue, credendo oltrarti,
  orando grazia conven che s'impetri

grazia da quella che puote aiutarti;
  e tu mi seguirai con l'affezione,
  si` che dal dicer mio lo cor non parti"".

E comincio` questa santa orazione:

And unto the first Love will turn our eyes,
  That looking upon Him thou penetrate
  As far as possible through his effulgence.

Truly, lest peradventure thou recede,
  Moving thy wings believing to advance,
  By prayer behoves it that grace be obtained;

Grace from that one who has the power to aid thee;
  And thou shalt follow me with thy affection
  That from my words thy heart turn not aside."

And he began this holy orison.

Paradiso: Canto XXXIII

Prayer to the Virgin. The Threefold Circle of the Trinity. Mystery of the Divine and Human Nature.

""Vergine Madre, figlia del tuo figlio, umile e alta piu` che creatura, termine fisso d'etterno consiglio,	"Thou Virgin Mother, daughter of thy Son, Humble and high beyond all other creature, The limit fixed of the eternal counsel,
tu se' colei che l'umana natura nobilitasti si`, che 'l suo fattore   non disdegno` di farsi sua fattura.	Thou art the one who such nobility To human nature gave, that its Creator Did not disdain to make himself its creature.
Nel ventre tuo si raccese l'amore, per lo cui caldo ne l'etterna pace cosi` e` germinato questo fiore.	Within thy womb rekindled was the love, By heat of which in the eternal peace After such wise this flower has germinated.
Qui se' a noi meridiana face di caritate, e giuso, intra ' mortali, se' di speranza fontana vivace.	Here unto us thou art a noonday torch Of charity, and below there among mortals Thou art the living fountain-head of hope.
Donna, se' tanto grande e tanto vali, che qual vuol grazia e a te non ricorre sua disianza vuol volar sanz'ali.	Lady, thou art so great, and so prevailing, That he who wishes grace, nor runs to thee, His aspirations without wings would fly.
La tua benignita` non pur soccorre a chi domanda, ma molte fiate liberamente al dimandar precorre.	Not only thy benignity gives succour To him who asketh it, but oftentimes Forerunneth of its own accord the asking.
In te misericordia, in te pietate, in te magnificenza, in te s'aduna quantunque in creatura e` di bontate.	In thee compassion is, in thee is pity, In thee magnificence; in thee unites Whate'er of goodness is in any creature.
Or questi, che da l'infima lacuna de l'universo infin qui ha vedute le vite spiritali ad una ad una,	Now doth this man, who from the lowest depth Of the universe as far as here has seen One after one the spiritual lives,
supplica a te, per grazia, di virtute tanto, che possa con li occhi levarsi piu` alto verso l'ultima salute.	Supplicate thee through grace for so much power That with his eyes he may uplift himself Higher towards the uttermost salvation.

E io, che mai per mio veder non arsi
  piu` ch'i' fo per lo suo, tutti miei prieghi
  ti porgo, e priego che non sieno scarsi,

perche' tu ogne nube li disleghi
  di sua mortalita` co' prieghi tuoi,
  si` che 'l sommo piacer li si dispieghi.

Ancor ti priego, regina, che puoi
  cio` che tu vuoli, che conservi sani,
  dopo tanto veder, li affetti suoi.

Vinca tua guardia i movimenti umani:
  vedi Beatrice con quanti beati
  per li miei prieghi ti chiudon le mani!"".

Li occhi da Dio diletti e venerati,
  fissi ne l'orator, ne dimostraro
  quanto i devoti prieghi le son grati;

indi a l'etterno lume s'addrizzaro,
  nel qual non si dee creder che s'invii
  per creatura l'occhio tanto chiaro.

E io ch'al fine di tutt'i disii
  appropinquava, si` com'io dovea,
  l'ardor del desiderio in me finii.

Bernardo m'accennava, e sorridea,
  perch'io guardassi suso; ma io era
  gia` per me stesso tal qual ei volea:

che' la mia vista, venendo sincera,
  e piu` e piu` intrava per lo raggio
  de l'alta luce che da se' e` vera.

Da quinci innanzi il mio veder fu maggio
  che 'l parlar mostra, ch'a tal vista cede,
  e cede la memoria a tanto oltraggio.

Qual e` colui che sognando vede,
  che dopo 'l sogno la passione impressa
  rimane, e l'altro a la mente non riede,

cotal son io, che' quasi tutta cessa
  mia visione, e ancor mi distilla
  nel core il dolce che nacque da essa.

Cosi` la neve al sol si disigilla;
  cosi` al vento ne le foglie levi
  si perdea la sentenza di Sibilla.

And I, who never burned for my own seeing
  More than I do for his, all of my prayers
  Proffer to thee, and pray they come not short,

That thou wouldst scatter from him every cloud
  Of his mortality so with thy prayers,
  That the Chief Pleasure be to him displayed.

Still farther do I pray thee, Queen, who canst
  Whate'er thou wilt, that sound thou mayst preserve
  After so great a vision his affections.

Let thy protection conquer human movements;
  See Beatrice and all the blessed ones
  My prayers to second clasp their hands to thee!"

The eyes beloved and revered of God,
  Fastened upon the speaker, showed to us
  How grateful unto her are prayers devout;

Then unto the Eternal Light they turned,
  On which it is not credible could be
  By any creature bent an eye so clear.

And I, who to the end of all desires
  Was now approaching, even as I ought
  The ardour of desire within me ended.

Bernard was beckoning unto me, and smiling,
  That I should upward look; but I already
  Was of my own accord such as he wished;

Because my sight, becoming purified,
  Was entering more and more into the ray
  Of the High Light which of itself is true.

From that time forward what I saw was greater
  Than our discourse, that to such vision yields,
  And yields the memory unto such excess.

Even as he is who seeth in a dream,
  And after dreaming the imprinted passion
  Remains, and to his mind the rest returns not,

Even such am I, for almost utterly
  Ceases my vision, and distilleth yet
  Within my heart the sweetness born of it;

Even thus the snow is in the sun unsealed,
  Even thus upon the wind in the light leaves
  Were the soothsayings of the Sibyl lost.

O somma luce che tanto ti levi
  da' concetti mortali, a la mia mente
  ripresta un poco di quel che parevi,
	O Light Supreme, that dost so far uplift thee
	  From the conceits of mortals, to my mind
	  Of what thou didst appear re-lend a little,

e fa la lingua mia tanto possente,
  ch'una favilla sol de la tua gloria
  possa lasciare a la futura gente;
	And make my tongue of so great puissance,
	  That but a single sparkle of thy glory
	  It may bequeath unto the future people;

che', per tornare alquanto a mia memoria
  e per sonare un poco in questi versi,
  piu` si concepera` di tua vittoria.
	For by returning to my memory somewhat,
	  And by a little sounding in these verses,
	  More of thy victory shall be conceived!

Io credo, per l'acume ch'io soffersi
  del vivo raggio, ch'i' sarei smarrito,
  se li occhi miei da lui fossero aversi.
	I think the keenness of the living ray
	  Which I endured would have bewildered me,
	  If but mine eyes had been averted from it;

E' mi ricorda ch'io fui piu` ardito
  per questo a sostener, tanto ch'i' giunsi
  l'aspetto mio col valore infinito.
	And I remember that I was more bold
	  On this account to bear, so that I joined
	  My aspect with the Glory Infinite.

Oh abbondante grazia ond'io presunsi
  ficcar lo viso per la luce etterna,
  tanto che la veduta vi consunsi!
	O grace abundant, by which I presumed
	  To fix my sight upon the Light Eternal,
	  So that the seeing I consumed therein!

Nel suo profondo vidi che s'interna
  legato con amore in un volume,
  cio` che per l'universo si squaderna:
	I saw that in its depth far down is lying
	  Bound up with love together in one volume,
	  What through the universe in leaves is scattered;

sustanze e accidenti e lor costume,
  quasi conflati insieme, per tal modo
  che cio` ch'i' dico e` un semplice lume.
	Substance, and accident, and their operations,
	  All interfused together in such wise
	  That what I speak of is one simple light.

La forma universal di questo nodo
  credo ch'i' vidi, perche' piu` di largo,
  dicendo questo, mi sento ch'i' godo.
	The universal fashion of this knot
	  Methinks I saw, since more abundantly
	  In saying this I feel that I rejoice.

Un punto solo m'e` maggior letargo
  che venticinque secoli a la 'mpresa,
  che fe' Nettuno ammirar l'ombra d'Argo.
	One moment is more lethargy to me,
	  Than five and twenty centuries to the emprise
	  That startled Neptune with the shade of Argo!

Cosi` la mente mia, tutta sospesa,
  mirava fissa, immobile e attenta,
  e sempre di mirar faceasi accesa.
	My mind in this wise wholly in suspense,
	  Steadfast, immovable, attentive gazed,
	  And evermore with gazing grew enkindled.

A quella luce cotal si diventa,
  che volgersi da lei per altro aspetto
  e` impossibil che mai si consenta;
	In presence of that light one such becomes,
	  That to withdraw therefrom for other prospect
	  It is impossible he e'er consent;

pero` che 'l ben, ch'e` del volere obietto,
  tutto s'accoglie in lei, e fuor di quella
  e` defettivo cio` ch'e` li` perfetto.
	Because the good, which object is of will,
	  Is gathered all in this, and out of it
	  That is defective which is perfect there.

Omai sara` piu` corta mia favella,	Shorter henceforward will my language fall
pur a quel ch'io ricordo, che d'un fante	Of what I yet remember, than an infant's
che bagni ancor la lingua a la mammella.	Who still his tongue doth moisten at the breast.
Non perche' piu` ch'un semplice sembiante	Not because more than one unmingled semblance
fosse nel vivo lume ch'io mirava,	Was in the living light on which I looked,
che tal e` sempre qual s'era davante;	For it is always what it was before;
ma per la vista che s'avvalorava	But through the sight, that fortified itself
in me guardando, una sola parvenza,	In me by looking, one appearance only
mutandom'io, a me si travagliava.	To me was ever changing as I changed.
Ne la profonda e chiara sussistenza	Within the deep and luminous subsistence
de l'alto lume parvermi tre giri	Of the High Light appeared to me three circles,
di tre colori e d'una contenenza;	Of threefold colour and of one dimension,
e l'un da l'altro come iri da iri	And by the second seemed the first reflected
parea reflesso, e 'l terzo parea foco	As Iris is by Iris, and the third
che quinci e quindi igualmente si spiri.	Seemed fire that equally from both is breathed.
Oh quanto e` corto il dire e come fioco	O how all speech is feeble and falls short
al mio concetto! e questo, a quel ch'i' vidi,	Of my conceit, and this to what I saw
e` tanto, che non basta a dicer 'poco'.	Is such, 'tis not enough to call it little!
O luce etterna che sola in te sidi,	O Light Eterne, sole in thyself that dwellest,
sola t'intendi, e da te intelletta	Sole knowest thyself, and, known unto thyself
e intendente te ami e arridi!	And knowing, lovest and smilest on thyself!
Quella circulazion che si` concetta	That circulation, which being thus conceived
pareva in te come lume reflesso,	Appeared in thee as a reflected light,
da li occhi miei alquanto circunspetta,	When somewhat contemplated by mine eyes,
dentro da se', del suo colore stesso,	Within itself, of its own very colour
mi parve pinta de la nostra effige:	Seemed to me painted with our effigy,
per che 'l mio viso in lei tutto era messo.	Wherefore my sight was all absorbed therein.
Qual e` 'l geometra che tutto s'affige	As the geometrician, who endeavours
per misurar lo cerchio, e non ritrova,	To square the circle, and discovers not,
pensando, quel principio ond'elli indige,	By taking thought, the principle he wants,
tal era io a quella vista nova:	Even such was I at that new apparition;
veder voleva come si convenne	I wished to see how the image to the circle
l'imago al cerchio e come vi s'indova;	Conformed itself, and how it there finds place;
ma non eran da cio` le proprie penne:	But my own wings were not enough for this,
se non che la mia mente fu percossa	Had it not been that then my mind there smote
da un fulgore in che sua voglia venne.	A flash of lightning, wherein came its wish.
A l'alta fantasia qui manco` possa;	Here vigour failed the lofty fantasy:
ma gia` volgeva il mio disio e 'l velle,	But now was turning my desire and will,
si` come rota ch'igualmente e` mossa,	Even as a wheel that equally is moved,

l'amor che move il sole e l'altre stelle.   The Love which moves the sun and the other stars.

The Song of Hiawatha - An Epic Poem; also with: The Skeleton in Armor, The Wreck of the Hesperus, The Luck of Edenhall, The Elected Knight, and The Children of the Lord's Supper
Henry Wadsworth Longfellow
Benediction Classics, 2011
220 pages
ISBN: 978-1-84902-340-5

Available from www.amazon.com, www.amazon.co.uk

The Song of Hiawatha is an epic poem, written in 1855 by Henry Wadsworth Longfellow. This version comes with copious illustrations and with line numbers, it also comprises five other poems: The Skeleton in Armor, The Wreck of the Hesperus, The Luck of Edenhall, The Elected Knight, and The Children of the Lord's Supper. The Song of Hiawatha is about an Indian hero who is based on the legends of the Ojibwe and other Native American peoples. Longfellow's work is a saga in the genre of American Romantic literature, and is not representative of Native American oral tradition. Longfellow had originally planned to call his hero Manabozho, which was the name of a Ojibwe folklore trickster-transformer . However, in his journal entry on June 28th, 1854, he wrote, "Work at 'Manabozho;' or, as I think I shall call it, 'Hiawatha'-that being another name for the same personage." Longfellow was mistaken about this, Hiawatha was probably an Iroquois hero. But as a result of the popularity of the poem, "Hiawatha" was used as a common name for everything, from towns to a telephone company, in the region of the western Great Lakes, where no Iroquois live.

Les Fleurs du Mal and The Flowers of Evil - French Edition and English Translation Edition with The Generous Gambler in English
Charles Pierre Baudelaire
Benediction Classics, 2012
276 pages
ISBN: 978-1-78139-206-5

Available from www.amazon.com, www.amazon.co.uk

Charles Pierre Baudelaire (1821-67) was a French poet. His most famous work Les Fleurs du mal (The Flowers of Evil) is included in this volume in both French and English. It describes the changing nature of beauty in modern industrialising Paris. Baudelaire's style of prose-poetry was highly original and influenced many poets who drew on his work.

Borrow's Ballads
George Borrow
Benediction Classics, 2012
702 pages
ISBN: 978-1-78139-142-6

Available from www.amazon.com, www.amazon.co.uk

Over 150 Ballads from George Borrow are contained within this book. It is compiled from 38 limited edition booklets of ballads that were produced at the beginning of the 20th Century. George Borrow was a lover of travel and was fluent in several languages including Romany. He was particularly taken with the poetry of the Northern Races and many of his ballads are translated from the Danish. These pamphlets contained his later poetic works and they considered to be much superior to his earlier book "Romantic Ballads".

The Poetical Works of Elizabeth Barrett Browning - Volume IV
Elizabeth Barrett Browning
Benediction Classics, 2011
212 pages
ISBN: 978-1-78139-027-6

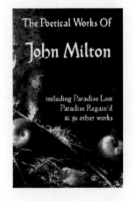

Available from www.amazon.com, www.amazon.co.uk

Elizabeth Barrett Browning (6 March 1806 - 29 June 1861) was an English poet and one of the most prominent poets of her time. During her lifetime her poetry gained great applaud both in England and in the United States.. This Volume contains the following poems, including "How do I love thee? Let me count the ways": Poems A Child's Grave At Florence. Catarina To Camoens Life And Love. A Denial. Proof And Disproof. Question And Answer. Inclusions. Insufficiency. Sonnets From The Portuguese Casa Guidi Windows. Poems Before Congress Napoleon Iii. In Italy. The Dance. A Tale Of Villafranca. Told In Tuscany. A Court Lady. An August Voice. Christmas Gifts. Italy And The World. A Curse For A Nation. Prologue. The Curse. Last Poems Little Mattie. A False Step. Void In Law. Lord Walter's Wife. Bianca Among The Nightingales. My Kate. A Song For The Ragged School Of London. Written In Rome. May's Love. Amy's Cruelty. My Heart And I. The Best Thing In The World. Where's Agnes?

Paradise Lost, Paradise Regained, and other poems. The Poetical Works Of John Milton
John Milton
Benediction Classics, 2012
576 pages
ISBN: 978-1-78139-173-0

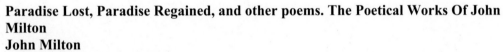

Available from www.amazon.com, www.amazon.co.uk

This book contains John Milton's poetical works, with line numbers and footnotes. This includes Paradise lost, Paradise Regain'd and Sampson Agonistes as well as forty-nine other works.

Enamels and Cameos and other Poems
Théophile Gautier
Benediction Classics, 2012
122 pages
ISBN: 978-1-78139-135-8

Available from www.amazon.com, www.amazon.co.uk

Pierre Jules Théophile Gautier (1811 - 1872) was a French writer and critic. This book of poems - Enamels and Cameos - is his last and some consider his most important work. It focusses on the beauty of everyday life, his poetry becoming compact and Gautier's poetry changes profoundly, becoming compact and stark, as Gautier explained, "treating tiny subjects in a severely formal way." He was widely esteemed by writers as diverse as Balzac, Baudelaire, the Goncourt brothers, Flaubert, Proust and Oscar Wilde.

Also from Benediction Books …
Wandering Between Two Worlds: Essays on Faith and Art
Anita Mathias
Benediction Books, 2007
152 pages
ISBN: 0955373700

Available from www.amazon.com, www.amazon.co.uk

In these wide-ranging lyrical essays, Anita Mathias writes, in lush, lovely prose, of her naughty Catholic childhood in Jamshedpur, India; her large, eccentric family in Mangalore, a sea-coast town converted by the Portuguese in the sixteenth century; her rebellion and atheism as a teenager in her Himalayan boarding school, run by German missionary nuns, St. Mary's Convent, Nainital; and her abrupt religious conversion after which she entered Mother Teresa's convent in Calcutta as a novice. Later rich, elegant essays explore the dualities of her life as a writer, mother, and Christian in the United States-- Domesticity and Art, Writing and Prayer, and the experience of being "an alien and stranger" as an immigrant in America, sensing the need for roots.

About the Author

Anita Mathias is the author of *Wandering Between Two Worlds: Essays on Faith and Art*. She has a B.A. and M.A. in English from Somerville College, Oxford University, and an M.A. in Creative Writing from the Ohio State University, USA. Anita won a National Endowment of the Arts fellowship in Creative Nonfiction in 1997. She lives in Oxford, England with her husband, Roy, and her daughters, Zoe and Irene.

Anita's website:
    http://www.anitamathias.com, and
Anita's blog Dreaming Beneath the Spires:
    http://dreamingbeneaththespires.blogspot.com

The Church That Had Too Much
Anita Mathias
Benediction Books, 2010
52 pages
ISBN: 9781849026567

Available from www.amazon.com, www.amazon.co.uk

The Church That Had Too Much was very well-intentioned. She wanted to love God, she wanted to love people, but she was both hampered by her muchness and the abundance of her possessions, and beset by ambition, power struggles and snobbery. Read about the surprising way The Church That Had Too Much began to resolve her problems in this deceptively simple and enchanting fable.

About the Author

Anita Mathias is the author of *Wandering Between Two Worlds: Essays on Faith and Art*. She has a B.A. and M.A. in English from Somerville College, Oxford University, and an M.A. in Creative Writing from the Ohio State University, USA. Anita won a National Endowment of the Arts fellowship in Creative Nonfiction in 1997. She lives in Oxford, England with her husband, Roy, and her daughters, Zoe and Irene.

Anita's website:
    http://www.anitamathias.com, and
Anita's blog Dreaming Beneath the Spires:
    http://dreamingbeneaththespires.blogspot.com

Printed by BoD"in Norderstedt, Germany

9 781781 395493